ANTHROPOLOGY AND

177-199

ANTHROPOLOGY AND POLITICS

Visions, Traditions, and Trends

JOAN VINCENT

THE UNIVERSITY OF ARIZONA PRESS   TUCSON & LONDON

The University of Arizona Press

Copyright © 1990
The Arizona Board of Regents
All Rights Reserved

This book was set in 10/13 Linotype CRT Trump.
Manufactured in the United States of America
⊚ This book is printed on acid-free, archival-quality paper.

98 97 96 95   5 4 3 2

Library of Congress Cataloging-in-Publication Data

Vincent, Joan.
    Anthropology and politics : visions, traditions, and trends / Joan
Vincent.
        p.   cm.
    Includes bibliographical references.
    ISBN 0-8165-1137-3 (alk. paper)
    ISBN 0-8165-1510-7 (pbk.; alk. paper)
    1. Political anthropology — History.   2. Political customs and
rites — United States.   3. Political customs and rites — Great
Britain.   I. Title.
GN492.V55   1990
306.2–dc20   89-20644
                                                                        CIP

British Cataloguing-in-Publication Data
A catalogue record for this book is available from the British Library.

Contents

Figures and Tables

Acknowledgments

I wish to acknowledge the assistance of several institutions in the making of this book: the libraries of Columbia University (particularly the interlibrary loan division); the University of Cape Town; the Institute for Advanced Study at Princeton and Princeton University; the National Humanities Center and the University of North Carolina; the University of Sussex; and the New York Public Library. Research in my own specialization within intellectual history, the Edwardian and Progressive eras (discussed in Chapter 2) was conducted with the help of archivists and librarians at Bodleian Library, Oxford; the Public Record Office, Kew Gardens; the Royal Anthropological Institute; the School of Oriental and African Studies, London; the Museum of Archaeology and Ethnology, Cambridge; the Regenstein Library of the University of Chicago; the Library at Yale University; the National Archives; and the Smithsonian Institution.

I am grateful to those who have typed drafts of chapters in various places over the years: Peggy Clark and her staff at the Institute for Advanced Study, Princeton; Karla Chaucer in Durham, North Carolina; and Mary Missirian at Barnard College, Columbia University. For assistance in the final stages of book preparation, I owe a not inconsiderable debt to Diane Ciecawy, Alice Peinado, and Monica Von Thun Calderon, of the Anthropology Department and the Anthropology and Education Program at Teachers College, Columbia University, and to Sharifa M. Zawawi for material and moral support. Gregory Ruf drew the figures. For permission to adapt and use figures I acknowledge the permission of Cambridge University Press (Fig. 5.1), the University of Chicago Press (Fig. 4.1), and Routledge and Kegan Paul (Table 2.2., Figs. 2.1, 2.2).

The generous and understanding faculty leave policy of Barnard College permitted me time to undertake this work, and I acknowledge with gratitude the support of President Ellen Futter and Vice-President and Dean of Faculty Robert McCaughey. My colleagues in the anthropology departments and programs in Milbank, Thompson, and Schermerhorn halls have been tolerant of my absences, and I thank them for the forbearance they have shown.

I have been fortunate in my teachers in the anthropology of politics at the London School of Economics (particularly Lucy Mair), the University of Chicago (F. G. Bailey, David Easton, Colin Leys, and Aristide Zolberg), and at Columbia University (Conrad Arensberg and Morton Fried). It would be invidious to thank other colleagues from whom I have learned a great deal; let the text speak for itself. I may, perhaps, single out those who read various chapters in the making: George C. Bond, David Nugent, Nan Rothschild, and Ida S. Susser. Shirley Charles was responsible for seeing that I wrote English rather than jargon.

Materials from the book have been used in classes both in the United States and Africa. I first taught political sociology at Makerere University in Kampala, Uganda, in 1967 during a state of emergency and returned briefly in the summer of 1988. Students at the University of Cape Town and the University of the Western Cape in 1977 added particular challenges to my perception of the tasks of an anthropology of politics. My greatest debt over the years from 1978 to 1989 has been to my students on Morningside Heights, not least those who have shared with me my course, Political Anthropology. This book is dedicated to them and to my colleagues throughout Columbia, as well as to my friends in the New York anthropological community. It would have been a very different book without them. Finally I would like to thank the two anonymous anthropologists who were prepared to read—let alone recommend publication of—such an elephant of a book.

New York, June 1989

ANTHROPOLOGY AND POLITICS

Introduction

When memory goes out to pick up dead wood, it brings back the faggot that it likes.

—MOSSI PROVERB

This study deals with the way anthropologists have chosen to look at and write about politics. Its main contention is that the anthropological study of politics is itself an historical process. The pages that follow contain a great deal about the knowledge that came to be known as political anthropology. Several questions are raised, including why certain topics have entered the discourse of anthropologists interested in politics while others have not. The study begins to be concerned with causation, and for that reason, it takes the form of a narrative. Since the book is largely about the content of political anthropology, the purpose of this introduction is to lay bare some of the thinking that has gone into its mode of presentation. The chapters themselves are written both above and below the line: references to the cognate disciplines whose ideas and findings have shaped my "contextualization" of the content of political anthropology appear almost entirely in notes.[1] So, too, are the Whiggish observations that, I argue, it is useful to perpetrate in a work of this nature, a subterranean commentary on the text.

The question of how anthropologists have studied politics, along with some of the political ethnography they have created and some of the conclusions they have reached, requires critical inquiry. This is a body of knowledge that has become hegemonic within the discipline, reflecting as knowledge the realities of action in a global arena at a specific moment in world history. As a selective work, therefore, the subject matter of this book is limited for the most part to the anthropology of the English-speaking world and particularly to that of Britain and the United States of America in the late nineteenth and twentieth centuries. This coverage is not as partial as might be supposed, since any dominant ideology or body of knowledge is shaped in part by that which it excludes or suppresses. The people anthropologists study are themselves active participants in the ethnographic enterprise (Murphy 1971).[2] This was particularly the case in late Victorian and Edwardian times, when non-Western anthropologists and academics prospered (see Chapter 2). With the crystallization of the subfield in 1940, their voices tended to be muted (Chapter 4). The irony of the situation is today a subject of political comment for third world scholars—striking back, as it were (Chapter 6).

Whether today's perception of anthropology as a "colonial encounter" is well conceived is questioned in this study. Political anthropologists might, indeed, be somewhat flattered by the aggrandizement of their practice by historians of science. Lewis Pyenson, for example, noted that imperialist expansion involved scientists and technicians traveling from a metropolitan center to colonial outposts. His inventory included geographers, geologists, meteorologists, agronomists, and anthropologists, "who arrive to identify the local power structure" (1982:1). Were it ever that simple. Although anthropology as a profession was stimulated by the possession of an empire, it is historically inaccurate to regard the discipline simply as a form of colonial ideology. Both the American and British experiences are proof of that, and a prior and more complex set of historical processes has to be taken into account.

Throughout its comparatively short history, much of the "relevance of anthropology lay in the fact that it studied groups and institutions on which social and moral as well as scientific problems centered" (Weber 1974:275). These groups included the disadvantaged of the metropolitan countries themselves. Anthropology's first ethnographic surveys, in fact, were conducted not among colonial peoples but in the English and Irish countryside (Chapter 1). Nor was the profession's struggle to be useful to imperialism easy, since few in power recognized it as a science whose data and predictions might usefully be harnessed to colonial policy or practice. For many of the anthropologists involved, the "natives" rather than officialdom were seen to be the beneficiaries of ethnographic research. The ambiguities that arose for the "European" anthropologist in the explicitly colonial situation were epitomized in the career of Lucy Mair, an eminent and exceptional political anthropologist whose academic practice was variously conducted under the rubrics of colonial administration, applied anthropology, and political anthropology.[3] Never one to primitivize colonial subject peoples, her long career at the London School of Economics captured all the contradictions of the Malinowskian vision (Chapters 3 and 4) and carried political anthropology, flags flying, into the comparative study of new nations (Chapter 5).

Historians of science deplore what they call Whig interpretations of history and generally struggle against them.[4] Some are most entertaining in their diatribes against the genre, thus:

> there is an unfortunately familiar way of simplifying the complexity of the intellectual life of the past into a conveniently unified story, one that is particularly favored when supposedly tracing the history of a modern academic discipline, especially, perhaps, a discipline drawn from what are now regarded as the social sciences. In essence it consists in writing history backwards. The present theoretical consensus of the discipline, or possibly some polemical version of what that consensus should be, is in effect taken as definitive, and the past is then reconstituted as a teleology leading up to and fully manifested in it. Past authors are inducted into the canon of the discipline as precursors or forebears, and passed in review as though by a general distributing medals—and sometimes reprimands—at the end of a successful campaign, with the useful, implied corollary that if medals can be distributed the campaign must have been brought to a satisfactory conclusion and the discipline duly established. The list of canonical precursors, arrayed in chronological order, each wearing a label conveniently summarizing his "contribution," then becomes the history of the discipline in question. . . . [R]ival teams of great predecessors may be assembled in this way, ostensibly to proclaim and honor a tradition of surprising antiquity, but in fact to legitimate the claims of the current protagonists in the struggle for power. (Collini, Winch and Burrow 1984:4)

An anthropology of politics must, of course, question any commitment to a canonical idea of tradition. This study precludes any essentialist suggestion of defining, by inclusion and exclusion, any actual canon. Rather, it is directed toward the dynamic and dialectical process of canon formation, as Paul de Man calls it (1982:xi). Although we will certainly be concerned with power struggles among teams of anthropologists, we will be concerned with other forms of genealogical manipulation and Whiggish tendencies as well.

Anthropologists may be more prepared than historians to recognize that it is impossible to take any stance except one informed by a present state of knowledge: "The past will only answer the questions we put to it, and . . . in framing these questions we are inescapably under the sway of our present interests" (Collini 1978:48). What is required is that our questioning itself be placed in a context broader than that of intellectual history alone. This is why, at the end of this study, it is possible to scrutinize again the past, discussing it not only in its own terms, as is attempted in the preceding chapters, but also in relation to what have emerged over time as dominant and subterranean traditions. In this sense, contemporary medals can be bestowed not simply on victors but also on gallant losers, particularly those in the lower ranks.

The ceremony can then be viewed as marking merely the end of a campaign, not the war.

CONTENT

The representation of the views of anthropologists about what political anthropology is and what they have unearthed in the field is provided here by an analysis of their writings from 1879 to the present. This entails drawing on the work of some who never write about specifically political anthropology and who may, indeed, even frown on its development as a subfield. The implications of specialization are addressed explicitly in Chapter 5.

This work also contains the names and a discussion of the work of some men and women who rarely enter into the annals of more general histories of anthropology. Because anthropologists at first studied politics almost incidentally to their other interests, it has been necessary to mine the work of earlier periods diligently to extract the ideas and ethnography related to political matters. A better metaphor would be that of Jack Hexter (1972), who writes of "The Sown and the Waste" in the village community of the Middle Ages. The common land, or commons, that lay "waste" around the medieval village was not really waste at all. Commons were the grazing areas worked, unlike the well-cultivated plots, by labor-extensive methods. The welfare of the village community depended on the very existence of the waste and the balance between the waste and the sown. The anthropology of politics (Chapters 1–3) and political anthropology (Chapters 4–5) bear just such a relationship. There coexist "cultivated patches of systematically structured knowledge" (political anthropology) and beyond the sown, "not desert, not mere ignorance and confusion, but 'waste'" (the anthropology of politics). The "waste" is "rich in knowledge, yet knowledge in a sense qualitatively different from the knowledge in the cultivated patches." It is therefore to be "exploited in a somewhat different way" (Hexter 1972:18).

Sometime around 1973 the soil became exhausted and overworked in the sown land and a move was made to reclaim and colonize deep into the waste. Political anthropology began to spill over its boundaries as a dramatic consequence of both global and paradigmatic crises. Its "systematically structured knowledge" came under assault, and an alternative anthropology of politics emerged, cultivating knowledge of a qualitatively different kind: diffusionist, humanist, historical, nondisciplinary, and above all, cosmopolitan (Chapter 6).

What brings together the men and women considered in this study is their relation, sometimes conscious and sometimes not, to an interest in pursuing "things political" (to adopt a usefully vague term common in the eighteenth century before Macaulay's "noble science of politics" became the order of the day). The phrase "things political" allows us in the early chapters to mine the work of practitioners in a field that in Victorian England was called simply "Mr. Tylor's science," and in Europe a few years later "Mr. Westermarck's science." The moment arrives at which Anna Gayton expresses an interest—almost apologetically, as we shall see—in the "particularly political" in the United States in the 1930s. The field of political anthropology is enclosed, of course, only by the boundary agreements of the social sciences. By 1940 it is clear that the labor-intensive methods of anthropologists have wrested cultivated plots from the political terrain. Political anthropology as a bounded domain becomes distinctive; after that time the sown and the waste are worked side by side. This is one of the reasons why ethnography is so important to the anthropological study of politics: it provides a large part of "the Second Record"—a record that is individual, unique to each anthropologist, and partly private and personal (Hexter 1972). But a metaphor, even an extended metaphor, can hardly provide periodization for this shift from the anthropology of politics to political anthropology and back again, so a more explicit methodological statement follows.

PERIODIZATION

This book is divided into six parts, with each span of years representing the work of approximately a generation—or more accurately, a cohort—of intellectuals. Each period generated its own configuration of topics. I initially arrived at these by simply counting and clustering bibliographic entries. The arrangement of the topics in Part 1 appears somewhat ad hoc—the product of applying the new "cinderella complex" of ethnography to the old questions of nineteenth-century ethnology. The arrangement of Part 2 reflects to a greater extent systemic interrelationships among a simpler range of topics. Some topics were enduring; others reflected the dominant interests of particular eras. With the emergence of area studies and regional specializations, topics began to be generated by clusters of interests from particularized field data.

Dominant themes become clearly visible, the well-documented subjects of group endeavor. Subterranean traditions had to be rescued from relative obscurity but were nevertheless always in evidence. Themes not self-consciously addressed by practitioners also emerged in the course of this study. Present only in skeletal form, some were quite unexpected. Conjointly they form a body of problems not addressed in political anthropology, although generated by it. The concluding chapter attempts to bring them together.

In spite of the apparent refinements of periodization reflected in this trajectory, which spans little more than a century, the broader context within which anthropology is embedded was the rise of capitalism in western Europe. For this reason, many of the concept-metaphors within the hegemonic anthropology of Britain and the United States originated with scholars working on the frontiers of early modern capitalism. These included, in the eighteenth century, the Scots political economists on the periphery of England's expansion and, in the nineteenth century, Sir Henry Maine, who crystalized in his writing on law the essentially individualistic and contractual nature of emergent capitalist society. Small wonder, then, that some of the earliest discourse in professional anthropology dealt with private and communal property rights, the freedom of the individual, and the authority of the group— large moral themes that for much of the history of political anthropology were, to use Mary Douglas's term, backgrounded, relegated to a "clutter of suppressed information . . . actively thrust out of the way because of difficulties in making it fit" (1975:3). Only recently have these larger issues reentered the anthropological study of politics, forced upon it, perhaps, by a recognition of knowledge and power structures that preceded colonialism, coexisted with it, and outlived its brief existence.

Professionalization coincided with the culmination of industrial capitalism and the rise and spread of its successor: monopoly, or finance, capitalism. These today have been superceded by what political anthropologists in 1983 began to call monetarism.[5] Throughout this period, first Britain and then the United States was at the center of a global capitalist economy. Capitalism itself has proved to be, as Richard Hofstadter put it, "a flourishing success" (Elkins and McKitrick 1974). Several characteristics of monopoly capitalism, which we may provisionally date as lasting from 1898 until 1974, are of particular significance for the anthropology of politics. First, the increased penetration of state power into the "internal" life of the peoples; second, militarism; and, third, imperialism. Their interrelationships have been the subject matter of the study of man in Britain and America since the eighteenth century.

When in capitalist societies ideas emerge that are hostile to the society's working arrangements, they are "slowly and persistently insulated, as an oyster deposits nacre around an irritant" (Hofstadter 1948:viii–ix). A distinction might be derived from the "binary fission" in Western social thought between Comte's positivist social science and Marx's dialectical materialism (Gouldner 1970; Burawoy 1977), between the orthodox or mainstream school of thought and the challenging idea. Such a dichotomy is too gross for the purposes of this study. It would be a disservice to see conflict between orthodox and radical streams of thought as an explanatory mechanism. Not only would this hide the complexity that exists, a complexity arising challengingly out of the supposedly simple societies within which anthropologists worked, it would also conceal as much as it revealed. Marked differences between the two philosophies certainly exist, but commonalities also exist, and anthropology as a discipline often seems to take a middle ground. Nevertheless, since political anthropology as a specialized field of study developed within capitalist societies, orthodox themes predominate, and radical alternatives tend to appear as subterranean discourse. This is not simply a matter of coexistence, because the relationship between them is antagonistic. As Talal Asad noted, the mainstream presents itself as authoritative and "seeks continually to preempt the space of radically opposed utterances and so to prevent them from being uttered" (1979:621). There is a particular irony in the fact that Asad voiced his observation in his Malinowski Lecture at the London School of Economics, for, as we shall see, Malinowski was a grand master at establishing authoritative discourse, securing its material foundation, and preempting space.

The application of a "conflict formula" to political anthropology appears eminently appealing: functionalists versus evolutionists, British social anthropology versus American cultural anthropology, Columbia versus Chicago, Gluckman versus Leach, all appear in advancing concreteness in the pages that follow. Yet there is also a continuity of community and resources regardless of conflict and common elements that may outlast what appear to be philosophical or institutional oppositions. These, too, have to be accounted for, and this study attempts to address both continuity and change.

To a striking extent, wars between European powers and between Britain and America and their dependencies (as well as intervening troughs of world depression and domestic social unrest) gave shape to the anthropology of politics. As Sheldon Wolin observed, "Many of the great theories of the past arose in response to a crisis in the world, not in the community of theorists" (Wolin 1960:147). America's Indian wars marked its professional formulation. The Boer War in South Africa (1898–1902), the Spanish-American War (1898), the Russian Revolution (1917), and the two so-called world wars (1914–1918; 1939–1945) affected its direction. After 1946, the breakup of the British Empire, with its potential for adding to the number of warring nations, and the United States' increasing involvement in global military adventures advanced it further.

This tends to nullify the ahistoricity of anthropological theory and practice as it is frequently presented. When universalism and structuralism provided dominant paradigms for the discipline, such a view of theory was understandable: the systematics of theory prevailed. Since the Social Science Research Council's conference on the history of anthropology in 1962, anthropology has had history and reflexivity forced upon it. For this reason, the introductory section to each chapter in this book attempts to portray something of the material and intellectual milieu in which the anthropology of politics existed. In this respect, periodization is a poor heuristic device and must not be taken too seriously. The academy and the field are manifolds whose totalities extend beyond any compartmentalization. Thus a surge of writings on any topic may or may not reflect worldly realities; "it is naive to assume that theoretical developments and methodological choices always follow the empirical incidence of phenomena" (Fabian 1979:12).

George Stocking has suggested that "there are clearly points at which the organizational history of the discipline becomes the focus for significant historical change—the place where the divergent threads of intellectual and institutional development, embodied in the interaction of particular individuals, responding to the impact of broader forces from 'outside' the discipline, can all be grasped at once" (1976:1). Several of the dynamic tensions that shaped political anthropology lay in the enduring coexistence of a divided hegemony: two intellectual traditions overlapping two national bodies of organization. In the organizational history of American anthropology, two such moments were the Boas censure of 1919, which Stocking analyzed, and the reorganization of the American Anthropological Association in 1946. A third would be the reorganization of the same association in 1983. In Britain, Malinowski's privileged access to the African Institute, Radcliffe-Brown's return to take up the chair at Oxford, the formation of the Association of Social Anthropologists of Great Britain and the Commonwealth (ASA) in 1946, and its 1983 recognition of a development crisis might provide rough equivalents.

A dialectic of a sort can be seen to work itself out through the periodization used in this study. Each period roughly corresponds to the publications of a cohort, using that term in its most technical sense to mean a group of men and women with shared life experiences. But each period is visibly humpbacked, with landmark texts and historical turning points somewhere near the middle. Edmund Leach's *Political Systems of Highland Burma*, published in 1954, is discussed explicitly in these terms in Chapter 5. This dialectic emerged in the process of my inquiry, which started simply as an effort to accumulate a comprehensive bibliography of political anthropology, treating it as an intellectual pursuit and following up references, clues, and hidden agendas. My goal was to look at political anthropology not as anthropologists say it is, nor as it might be, but as a body of work actually produced. Georges Balandier's 1967 perception of its multifarious discourse provided a stimulus that itself had to be placed in context.

Viewing the content of this bibliography as a landscape, I then sought landmarks by which to chart a passage across it. These landmarks serve to periodize the narrative of the expedition, providing the starting places or destinations of the chapters that follow. Hermann J. Nieboer's *Slavery as an Industrial System* (1900), Robert Lowie's *The Origin of the State* (1927b), Meyer Fortes and E. E. Evans-Pritchard's edited volume *African Political Systems* (1940), Edmund Leach's *Political Systems of Highland Burma* (1954), Marc Swartz, Victor Turner, and Arthur Tuden's *Political Anthropology* (1966), and Immanuel Wallerstein's *The Modern World-System* (1974b) were publications that appeared to be such landmarks. But I found them to be not the monographic peaks that I had anticipated but rather (and logically, in light of the argument that is developed here) rounded hillocks, with their bases resting in what lay in their immediate past and future. Still, by focusing on these landmarks it was possible to map the terrain around them.

To conceptualize these texts as landmarks extends my agrarian metaphor from the anthropologists' study of "things political" as the waste and the sown to subterranean activities and even to tunnel vision. It would therefore be salutary to recall what "classic" texts are. The conventional notion is that the greatness of a classic lies in its power to transcend historical circumstances. Samuel Johnson, that great student of patronage and favor, provided the seminal definition: "Where productions of genius are concerned," he wrote, "of which the excellence is not absolute and definite, but gradual and comparative ... no other test can be applied than length of duration and continuance of esteem." Once a great author has outlived his century, he observed, "whatever advantages he might once derive from personal allusions, local customs, or temporary opinions, have for many years been lost. ... The effects of favour and competition are at an end; his works, ... thus unassisted by interest or passion, ... have passed through variations of taste and changes of manners, and, as they devolved from one generation to another, have received new honors at every transmission" (quoted in Tompkins 1985:3).

There are as yet few political anthropologists who have "outlived" their centuries, although a considerable number have produced classic works that have outlived their generation even if, in some cases, this entailed a "laundering" of their texts. Johnson's observation does, however, direct our attention away from the classics themselves and toward the circumstances in which they are read; in the case of political anthropology, this is to the institutionalization of a readership. Tompkins (1985) argues that a literary reputation can never be anything but a political matter. Works that are esteemed as classics because they are believed to embody universal values in fact embody only the interests of whatever parties or factions are responsible for maintaining them in their preeminent position. This means that claims to esteem are open to challenge by other groups, which represent equally partisan interests. "The use of classics as badges of affiliation then tends to produce sects rather than open intellectual communities. What endures is the tradition not the text." And traditions, as we all know, may be invented (Hobsbawm and Ranger 1983, but see also Butler 1985).

In essence, the argument is that political anthropology is both manmade and woman-made and historically produced. Further, the written forms that make up political anthropology are read in a context of activity that is not performed outside of institutional structures and political struggles but that arises from them (Vincent 1986a). Much that political anthropology takes for granted is problematic in the extreme, and this study attempts to explore its canon critically and in many instances to convert absences into presences.

In these terms we may begin to understand why, in political anthropology, bibliographies that might once have been colored by the writings of British social anthropologists and Africanists, and to have contained little else, might now take on a different hue. Those who read that "Radcliffe-Brown naturally was elected as President" of the ASA

(Firth 1986:5) might today ask, Why "naturally"? Today it may appear that the Boasian interest at Columbia University outlived its usefulness, particularly within Columbia, long before Papa Franz retired in 1936. The rehabilitation of evolutionary paradigms in the years following World War II, in spite of their trivialization of the ethnographic lifeblood of the discipline (Moore 1985a), cries out for explanation. When and where academic anthropology was in dialogue with Marxist scholarship are questions that have frequently been raised but inadequately answered. Why do some anthropologists believe that there is a crisis in anthropology? What contending interests, practical and theoretical, suggest such a perception? Periodization permits at least a cursory delineation of political anthropology as a changing field of force.

GENEALOGIES

Genealogies are both the laziest form of history and the most succinct form of political construction, providing charters or constitutions that bound territorial rights and constrain those who claim them. In tracing the history of anthropological thought, scholars often adopt the genealogical method, although usually without the self-consciousness and sophistication that W.H.R. Rivers himself applied (Chapter 2). Because pedigrees and genealogical amnesia have political significance, they must be touched upon here.

The tracing of genealogies may be seen as an exercise in political ideology,[6] one of the several practices accompanying the institutionalization of political anthropology as a specialized subfield after 1940. Genealogies are manipulated and past connections are made to serve present needs. Some links are stressed while others are forgotten or overlooked until the time comes when their resurrection is advantageous. New legitimacies emerge to challenge the old. Genealogies may thus be used to broaden or narrow a field of study, but the endeavor always rests upon the legitimacy of a chosen past. Frederick Bailey, a distinguished anthropologist who, as a student of politics, has been compared with Niccolò Machiavelli (King 1969), was fully aware of the niceties of genealogical manipulation when he wrote:

> When, as happens, anthropologists are taunted by their colleagues in older, more respectable moribund disciplines like the classics or history—being told that anthropology is so new that it can hardly be recognized as a branch of learning—they sometimes make the mistake of claiming for themselves a long pedigree. The first anthropologist, they say, was Herodotus; or they will name some antique Chinese or Arabian traveller who has left to us a

story of his journeys to strange peoples in foreign parts. To be descended
from Herodotus would be incontrovertible evidence of senior status; yet,
like the claim to be descended from Adam, it is hardly a mark of distinction.
(Bailey 1966:55)

Bailey then goes on to claim descent from the scholars of the French
Enlightenment, an ancestry shared, perhaps not surprisingly, with
Georges Balandier, whose *Political Anthropology*, published in French
in 1967, was the first textbook on the subject.

The Edwardians, on the other hand, chose to draw attention to the
newness of their science. For R. R. Marett, Edward Tylor was the
"Adam of Anthropology" (1912), and John Linton Myres, speaking of
the influence of anthropology on the course of political science, called
it a young science "in the unfolding of that full bloom of rational culture, which sprang from the seeds of the Renaissance, and of which we
are the heirs and trustees, [which] found its place in the sunlight later
than most; and almost alone among the sciences can reckon any of its
founders among the living. This was, of course, partly an accident of
birth and circumstance; for in the House of Wisdom there are many
mansions; a Virchow, a Bastian, or a Tylor might easily have strayed
through the gate of knowledge into other fields of work; just as Locke
and Montesquieu only narrowly missed the trail into anthropology"
(1916:2).

To each his own. More recently, Max Gluckman opted for Aristotle
as a founder, and Sir Edmund Leach gave a nod to Pareto. Sir Edward
Euan Evans-Pritchard traced his own roots back to the Scottish political economists, whom he chose to call moral philosophers. Karl Marx
haunts many who do not openly acknowledge his legacy, particularly
in the United States, where huge flowcharts of isms, amorphous and
disembodied, may stand in place of family trees (Herskovits 1965).

A genealogy is represented as a family tree, showing roots, trunk,
branches, and twigs, in Lewellen's "Political Anthropology Family
Tree" (1983:3), and indeed the image of the family tree is not simply
beguiling but revealing. "The trees always [seem] to be Northern European ones, like oaks and maples, and . . . never . . . [a] typical South
Asian tree, the banyan, which grows up, out and down at the same
time" (Cohn 1985:327). Indeed, as in so much else in Western society,
patrilineal descent and the inheritance of property provide a charter
for the intellectual transmission of knowledge in the anthropology of
politics. There is a difference, however, between the United States and
the United Kingdom in this regard. In Britain each budding anthropologist knows his place, his lineage, his corporate responsibilities within

an insular society. In the United States, jargon-loving fellowship provides a locus of identification in an open, chaotically broad society. Yet, looking beyond the pedigrees and the social movements, it is possible to discern both cast-off kinsmen of the British and unacknowledged ancestors of the Americans.

Colonial cousins, neighbors, and dependents appear at the edges of this genealogy. Canadian anthropologists uneasily reflect the tensions that exist between the British and American anthropologies of politics. The living vitality, even the very existence, of those South African scholars who did not choose to leave the semiperiphery is strangely at odds with their pariah status within the profession. Yet, within the anthropology of politics, their early protests against the practices of their own governments, their refusal to accept the ethnological ideologies of mainstream Afrikaner Volkekunde, and their scientific activism in the apartheid republic represent a dimension of anthropology that critics of the colonial period find lacking. Social distancing has led to the segregation of South African urban industrial ethnography from what is generally conceived to be sub-Saharan anthropology, as if it were an anomaly rather than an extreme form of political organization. This has served to deflect attention from the capitalist framework of European conquest and domination in the continent. The means by which the republic attains its ends in the control and management of its African population, and the exclusion its powerholders are able to maintain, represent in an overt form the attainment of similar ends within the colonial states in which most political anthropologists have worked and the more subtle means of attaining those ends within democratic republics elsewhere.

If the Canadian voice appears muted and the South African unheard, that of the Australian issues the contemporary challenge to the establishment. It calls, among other things, for a rewriting of genealogies. Historically, Australian scholarship frequently bridged the gap between British and American anthropology. With the lessening of structuralist hegemony in Europe, new dates are beginning to be recognized as significant in the foundation of anthropology. These place the West's encounter with the cultural complexity of the rest of the world squarely in Australia's backyard. Thus the philosopher Stephen Toulmin (1972: 42) traces the conflict between "the traditional [western] assumptions of philosophy and theology and the facts of historical and cultural variety" that confuse it, to April 13, 1769—the occasion of Captain James Cook's arrival at Tahiti on his voyage round the world. Fred W. Voget in his *History of Ethnology* (1975) devotes a section to imperialism and scientific expeditions, beginning with Captain Nicholas Baudin's scientific exploration and survey of New Holland (Australia) between 1800 and 1804. It is well accepted within the history of the discipline in Britain that the Torres Straits Expeditions of Haddon and his colleagues established the scientific foundations of anthropology at the end of the nineteenth century.

What is less well appreciated is the extent to which a concern with flux, historical movement, conquest (colonial, in this case), and the cultural development of complex societies that developed within the Australasian context lost the battle for mainstream status in political anthropology during the greater part of the period with which this study is concerned. The passing of functional and structural modes of thinking has revived an interest in the subject matter of long-denigrated "diffusionist" scholars such as W.H.R. Rivers, Arthur Hocart, and Grafton Elliot Smith. New biographical studies and inaugural lectures have reinstated the legitimate claims of many of the late Victorian and Edwardian scholars with whom this study opens. Those of Kennelm Burridge (1973) and Peter Lawrence (1975) are particularly significant in this regard; as they are on the periphery of the English establishment, they do not appear to feel the compulsion to regard any deviation from the orthodoxy of Oxbridge as maverick behavior. Lawrence's 1967 critique of the ahistoricism of much of anthropology actually takes the form of a narrative poem.

Genealogy, then, is not a solution to the problem of identifying those anthropologists who have contributed to the study of politics; it is part of the problem.[7]

INSTITUTIONALIZATION

One of the main purposes of field research is to uncover "invisible realities," as Malinowski (1935) called them, to lay bare the organizational underpinnings of the subject under scrutiny. An academic discipline is both a method of investigation and a group of scholars in persisting social relations (Redfield 1953). Anthropology is marked both by a body of distinctive knowledge and, because it is a living activity in a changing world, by the manner in which its practitioners are set apart from others. "Often uncharitably referred to as 'politics,' the informal, often nondirective communications between persons involved in the matters and operation of the discipline give rise to at least the temporary form that the discipline will have; the stability of that form will depend upon the particular characteristics—influence, power, etc.—of its adherents" (Gruber 1966:19–20).

A Great Man approach to anthropology provides its folklore. "An historian friend of mine," recalled Raymond Firth, "once jokingly remarked that British social anthropologists are like comets—they blaze for a while across the sky with a brilliant light and then fade out, leaving a trail of gas behind" (1960:37). The same could be said of American anthropology, of course—and the statement would be equally false. The longevity of anthropologists, even political anthropologists, emerged strikingly from this study, with all the attributes of age in gerontocracies: a dominant institutionalized figure, wielding academic power long after the creative years had passed. Indeed, the most apt part of the metaphor relates not to the comets' brilliance but to their "tails," for anthropology is, indeed, prone to academic followings.

Max Gluckman viewed "the production of knowledge as a social process mediated by and through individuals." He recognized that "the data on which 'science' is based is itself a social product of the society which it describes and analyses, of the social groupings to which the scientists belong, and of a productive process which involves interaction between society and analyst" (Frankenberg 1982:3). The notion of the production of knowledge directs the reader to action, or to use Giddens's term, *agency*, which he defines as "a stream of actual or contemplated causal interventions of corporeal human beings in the ongoing process of events-in-the-world" (1979:55). The political anthropologist is a producer in the factory of scholarship. This idea underpins the work in political anthropology of the Mancunians, Gluckman's Manchester colleagues, discussed in Chapter 5. Such concepts as unified groups of workers, correspondence networks, social circles, scientific communities, invisible colleges, and informal interpersonal relations are to be found throughout the cognate disciplines (e.g., Price 1963, 1965; Crane 1972; Mullins 1973; Dolby 1977) and underlie the chapters that follow. Not surprisingly, however, they are drawn as much from the processual approach within political anthropology as from the sociology of knowledge and the history of science.

Scientific behavior may be viewed as an exchange of information for recognition (Hagstrom 1965), and a most important element in this is clearly the reproduction of ideas through the academy. Academic professionalization underpinned the development of political anthropology as a discipline and indeed accounted in part for the focus of its interests through successive phases. The starting point of this study is therefore the establishment in 1879 of the Bureau of Ethnology at the Smithsonian Institution, which provided political anthropology with its first professionals.

Yet the trajectory of political anthropology can also be interpreted more politically as "serving power" (Silva and Slaughter 1984). In this reading of events, academic disciplines are also shaped by service outside the university. As experts, academics link the state and the economy, and in return for serving power, they receive resources to invest in part in the reproduction of their discipline within the academy. Some also achieve responsible positions of power for "binding knowledge to power" within the existing political system (Silva and Slaughter 1984:4–5). Resource exchange theory therefore has to be added to sociological models of professionalism to provide a more complete history of political anthropology.

Both the formal sociology of knowledge and interpretive approaches within anthropology tend to lack an analytical appreciation of historicity. Critically important *at certain times* for the development of political anthropology as a subfield have been various forms of governmental and institutional support and funding such as that provided by the Colonial Office in Britain (Richards 1977) or the federal government in the United States (Dupree 1957). This is a theme addressed directly in the chapters that follow. The failure of earlier anthropologists to attract such support in part accounted for the adventurous and unroutinized form that the anthropology of politics took in its "middle phase" (Chapter 2). Similarly, the funding of a cohort of army veterans in major universities in 1946 (Ardener and Ardener 1965; Murphy 1971; Mead 1973) led to dramatic paradigmatic shifts in political anthropology (Chapter 5).

One of the main questions asked here is, What produces political anthropology's orthodox body of writing, its mainstream? In establishing what does, what does not becomes more visible, and inasmuch as what becomes dominant tends toward homogeneity and exclusivity and what remains subordinate is multiplex and fractured, revealing the dimensions of the latter is the more difficult task. Several modes of explanation are available, and here, in a text on politics, the political is favored.

Explanations of dominance are to be found, as George Stocking has demonstrated, not in the valency of ideas but in academic power, control, and institutionalization (1968). These operate in international, imperial, national, and local domains. This study's parameters are set by the historical emergence of anthropology as a profession in 1879 (Chapter 1), by the historical "nationalization" of colonial knowledge by Third World countries after they attained their independence (Chapter 5), and by the subsequent transnationalization of that knowledge in the 1970s and 1980s (Chapter 6). Of course, academic power, control, and institutionalization reflected wider political realities of knowledge and power.

Models of the "growth of knowledge" encountered in the cognate disciplines do not closely reflect what has happened in the anthropology of politics since 1879. Anthropologists have, perhaps, a more individualistic orientation than scholars in the pure and social sciences, and in this their scholarship approaches an aesthetic rather than a science. They coauthor few articles and exhibit a widespread reluctance to conduct team research. Anthropology's comparatively poor access to government and private funding and its lack of "pure" anthropological research centers tend to operate against the growth and transmission of incremental knowledge. Or perhaps the very centrifugal tendencies of its subject matter and the hermeneutic elements in field research render anthropology an anomalous discipline. Yet barriers do exist to the consolidation, diffusion, and transmission of knowledge. In some cases, scientists themselves resist certain discoveries (Barber 1961). Dolby has described the nature of both active and passive resistance. His central tenet—that "the processes by which science is transmitted also select and transform its content" (1977:32)—informs this whole study.

Even so, one cannot deny anthropology some degree of accumulation of knowledge. The most general, and perhaps the most mechanistic, analysis of theories and theory groups in social science suggests that the cumulative production of knowledge may be traced through four stages: normal science, a network stage, clusters, and specialties (Mullins 1973). Although never approaching the distinction of theory, or even systematic conceptualization, many notions such as these are current in the formal sociology of knowledge and also in 1950s anthropology (Redfield 1953; Kroeber 1957, 1959). Yet when applied today they tend to be scorned as navel watching. The professional's lack of sensitivity to the political implications of how anthropological knowledge is produced and transmitted has been illuminated by Graham Watson (1984) in his writing on the construction of boundaries between social and cultural anthropology in Britain and North America.

This is not the place to review his argument or to consider what such division within the hegemonic culture signifies but simply to draw attention to the unreflexive manner in which establishment figures defined their practice and its distinctive attributes, and asserted intellectual genealogies, while they ignored the analytical tools their own discipline provided for the study of such behavior. Domination, hegemony, and vested interests shriek through the quotations Watson used to make his case. The political results of such boundary activity came to a head just after World War II, and its implications for political anthropology are explored in Chapter 5.

Academic anthropology has not yet been analyzed through its structure, although preliminary studies are underway. For the most part, anthropologists focus on "the leaders of the discipline" and the valency of their ideas; even the most materialist among them has not moved far along the path from "thinker" to "leader," and from "institution" to "interaction." Anthropologists have paid even less attention to processes of departmental decline.

In some disciplines, professors wield considerable power in the evaluation of both scientific research and its practitioners. Anthropology is somewhat fortunate inasmuch as peer review in professional journals and recently (and perhaps only in some departments) the growing strength of students and nontenured academics provides for some dilution of this power. Review articles are critical for the realization of visions, the instigation of trends, and in the long run, the establishment of the traditions with which this study deals.

As the training of students has increased (particularly after 1946), so too has the students' importance, not simply for furthering research and transmitting the knowledge that is political anthropology but ultimately also for its questioning (Gouldner 1970). It is so often they who are responsible for the series of reevaluations that appear in this book and that frequently signify alternative political anthropologies from that currently dominant. Some even reflect turning points in the trajectory of the discipline (e.g., Smith 1956; Worsley 1956; Gough 1971). In political terms, the relation of professor to student is akin to that of patron to client. Political anthropological theory can be brought into play to explain why patron-client relations rarely develop into a cluster, to use Mullins's term (1973). Clusters require a minimum stable size (I don't think he intends a pun) of from seven to twenty five persons, including three collaborative faculty members (compare Geison's "research schools," made up of mature scholars and students [1981]). The nature of all known anthropology departments suggests why not only political anthropology but anthropology at large lacks unity as a profession and suffers from constant fragmentation. Indeed Mullins's model of the growth of knowledge serves best (as he himself demonstrates) to account for "the light that failed" at Harvard, to the detriment of political anthropology (Chapter 4).

An institution found to be critically important in this study, partly because it may cut across patron-client relations, is the seminar. Introduced from Germany at the end of the nineteenth century as a pedagogical device, the graduate seminar operated to shape the minds not only of the students but of the grand masters themselves at Columbia among the Boasians, in Malinowski's London School of Economics and Political Science, and to a lesser extent at Harvard, Berkeley, and Manchester.

Other features of the academy that are clearly important in the nurturing and fostering of visions and traditions in political anthropology are the "lady professor" as teacher (particularly of "voluntary" tutorials) in large research-oriented departments, and the professor (of either sex) who may not publish a great deal but who teaches well. The informal oral communication of knowlege is one of those intangibles that may be particularly significant in the transmission of political insights, visions, traditions, and ideas. The sociology of knowledge relies almost entirely on the analysis of published materials, yet 50 percent of all social science scholars with a doctorate apparently publish nothing other than their dissertations (Price 1965). As yet there has been little or no research into classrooms, readerships, and the transmission of knowlege in political anthropology.

In many ways, more important than university departments and academic settings are the "invisible colleges" of which Diana Crane wrote (1972). These take many forms, and their exposure often requires the reading of some rather off-putting autobiographies and biographies, because limning the "invisible colleges" often exposes a network. What emerges is the finding that normative control exercised informally by the scientific community through certain elite organizations and the institutionalization of a discipline within society—both British and American—become ends in themselves. Careers and the control of knowledge inevitably collide.

Beginning to emerge within this history of the profession are the lonely figures of mavericks. Arthur Hocart has been characterized as such, and in the study that follows, such contributors to the study of politics as William Christie MacLeod and perhaps Alexander Lesser appear to fall within this category. For much of their working lives unattached to major universities and unconstrained by academic careers, such men—marginal as they were—were well placed to be the frontiersmen of political anthropology.

By most of the usual criteria, political anthropology is not a viable subfield of anthropology. It lacks distinctive boundaries and recognized elite practitioners. No common paradigm has arisen and been consolidated within it; no common theoretical orientation has ever prevailed. Instead, contesting interests and parties make up any trends that may be acknowledged. When this contesting is absent, political anthropology barely exists; when it comes to the fore—whether among Marxists, idealists, materialists, conservatives, or interpretivists—the anthropology of politics thrives. Political anthropology resembles guerrilla warfare, frequently shifting its ground and constantly dividing its ranks, a running intellectual battleground.

Nevertheless, there have been times in its history when, for brief moments and among certain groups, some of the goals of institutionalized specialization have appeared. Leaders, or more frequently middle-tier practitioners, have sought to organize fellow anthropologists interested in politics, or more viably, law and politics. Yet no research centers for the study of political anthropology have been set up, and one wonders how long such institutions would, indeed, survive. Scholars interested in politics in the service of the state, like those on the left, tend to come together only in informal or occasional environments, such as conferences and periodic meetings of professional associations. Certain universities, or certain departments within universities, produce specific orientations that, through hierarchy, recruitment, and all the operations of academic reproduction, may perpetuate certain traditions at certain times, but usually only for short periods, since there is a built-in centrifugality to such "theory group" building. The means by which such centers transmit their values to the periphery have been studied in "traditional" societies (Geertz 1977) but not within anthropology itself.

Even in more ephemeral, less well funded enterprises of specialization, such as newsletters, journals, and conferences, political anthropology has found it extremely difficult to establish itself. As the concluding chapter of this study shows, this is because the anthropology of politics tends not to be specialized but pervasive, with the only lasting specializations reflecting regional or areal interests. These have a material base: most funding for scholarly research is distributed by region. Ultimately, therefore, the nature of the discipline depends on the culture of those "objectified" rather than that of the academic. In 1988, a total of 96 of the 540 members of the leading professional association of anthropologists in Britain expressed a theoretical interest in political anthropology; in the United States, only 265 out of 3,078 evinced a similar interest.[8]

CONTEXT

Concern with context takes several forms in this book. Taking political anthropology to be the text, the immediate context of any production is the body of contemporary research publications of scholars in other disciplines and other branches of anthropology—Nettl's "catchment area" (1967). Context also has a temporal dimension in that these producers in the present draw upon writings of "classical" nondisciplinary scholars from the past—sometimes captured in the phrase "intellectual heritage." Within the field of political anthropology, the notion of context draws attention, as we have seen, to placing mainstream, dominant products within a residual "clutter of suppressed information" (Douglas 1975:3). Yet it is the neglected residue that gives the classic texts their contemporary point and makes their underlying assumptions intelligible (Collini, Winch, and Burrow 1984). This introduction is intended to alert the reader to this limitation, which, regrettably, the study itself can do little to redress. This is a particularly severe limitation in respect to political ethnography, where the institutionalization of more specialized readerships, as in "area studies" or what I begin to define in Chapter 6 as "subaltern studies," has made the perception and analysis of such residues much more difficult.

Inadequate and simplistic as it is, and in danger of suggesting causal and teleological relations that are not intended, the contextualization that opens each chapter should be viewed not as a background or framework for what follows but as an integral part of it. Understanding the texts of political anthropologists requires knowing not merely what arguments they were presenting but also what questions they were trying to answer and how far they were accepting and endorsing, questioning and repudiating, or perhaps even polemically ignoring, the prevailing assumptions and conventions of political debate. We cannot expect to attain this level of understanding if we study only the texts themselves. In order to see the texts as answers to specific questions, we need to know something about the society in which they were written (Skinner 1969).

In a general work such as this, the goal of contextualization can only be suggested, not reached. Considerably more questions about connections and interrelatedness are raised here than are answered, indicating the vast amount of research yet to be done. Very little has been carried out in one area to which this approach most certainly leads: connections between political anthropological theory and political practice. Where such connections have been posited—as with religious dissent and political party candidacy (Chapter 2), government service (Chapter 3), or participation in the Spanish Civil War (Chapter 4) or the Communist party (Chapter 5)—spadework of a caliber to satisfy historians of science has simply not been done.

In this book the spatial and temporal notions of context are integrated through the concept of the *social field*. If social fields are viewed as "components arranged in a specific fashion to meet the interests of men at a particular time, it then becomes possible to see how a shift in their positions, the addition of new components, or the elimination of others produce this or that effect" (Peters 1967:281). A social fields approach renders manageable a wide universe of discourse. Since this study opens in 1879, the earlier contributions of major thinkers—Ferguson, Morgan, Maine, and Marx, for example—are discussed as they were brought into play, as it were, within the institutionalizing arenas of anthropology. They are components introduced to "meet the interests of men at a particular time." The intellectual contributions of non-Anglophone scholars—Durkheim, Weber, Gramsci, and Norbert Elias, for example—are similarly introduced when (often only after translation) they become part of the currency of political anthropology in Britain and the United States. Clearly it has also been advantageous at times for such intellectual content to be divorced from its original political contextualization within "worldly affairs," and the notes attempt to draw attention to when and where this occurs, and even at times to hazard a why.

Social fields analysis makes sense of the emerging evidence of both conflating and conflicting approaches within political anthropology, the recognition of very different problems, and even the use of alternative repertoires of concepts. It thus makes sense, too, of the patterning of theoretical change. Relying mainly on published materials, this study is, however, obliged to approach such matters less through the internal politics of academe than through the use of concepts and their histories. This is less of a handicap than might be supposed, since "concepts play their parts in the lives of individuals, and scarcely have any actuality apart from these roles. At the same time, individual concept-users acquire the concepts they do within a social context, and the sets of concepts they employ play identifiable parts also in the lives of human communities—whether societies, congregations, or professions" (Toulmin 1972:36).

The introduction of new concepts and the passing of the old chart the course of political anthropology as a set of ideas, as an ideology. Yet all enter the social field as contested elements. Thus the more keenly one is aware of the interdependence of concepts and their contexts, the more indispensable certain distinctions become: that between the intrinsic authority of ideas and the magisterial authority of books, between men and institutions, and between the pragmatic acceptance of concepts whose merits have been demonstrated and the dogmatic acceptance of concepts whose merits are unproved (Toulmin 1972). The fate of the municipio in Mesoamerican ethnology (Chapter 4) and of the segmentary lineage system in the political ethnology of sub-Saharan Africa (Chapter 5) provide instances of this. Intellectually, then, political anthropology may be regarded as "an 'historical population' of logically independent concepts and theories, each with its own separate history, structure, and implications" (Toulmin 1972:130).

Included in this study, inevitably, are many concepts that fail to survive, as well as false starts, archaic doctrines, and fruitless errors. An impressive number of subterranean channels exist beneath the visible mainstream. Each stream and channel makes selective use of certain concepts, an in-group language, genealogies, and charter myths. Although this is desirable for the advancement of particular knowledge, it increases the possibility of tunnel vision within the larger landscape of political anthropology.

As Thomas Kuhn has pointed out (1977), although the insulation of a mature scientific discipline is an insulation primarily with respect to concepts and secondarily with respect to *problem structures*, the timing of what he calls scientific advance depends not on immanent factors but on events in the world outside the discipline itself. For anthropologists this abstraction tends to have global dimensions. Anthropology is a product of social processes that have changed its material and developed its methods as world relationships have changed and developed. Raymond Firth (1944) accounted for anthropology's shift from the study of "primitive societies" to the study of "peasant societies" in these terms (Chapter 4). Postwar efforts to reevaluate the historical construction of colonial knowledge and the colonial state reflect Europe's loss of global hegemony while deconstructing anthropology as history (Chapter 5). Some scholars (who assume a world order of knowledge paralleling a world economy) have made the imperial construction of global knowledge the subject of inquiry (Chapter 6). And so, for political anthropology, there has been a self-conscious return to Eric Hobsbawm's observations on the global character of subaltern classes (Chapter 6).

ETHNOGRAPHY

For much of its history, the work of earlier scholars and the contributions of alien intellectuals provided the theoretical content of political anthropology. Not until the 1950s, in the face of challenges from other disciplines on the eve of their massive intervention in the anthropological domain, did anthropologists make manifest that "anthropology is characterized by a set of methods rather than bound by a subject matter" (Bohannan 1967:xiv). Today we might question Bohannan's use of the singular, but the main point stands. This book mines the contributions of James Mooney, W.H.R. Rivers, Bronislaw Malinowski, Robert Redfield, F. G. Bailey, and Clifford Geertz (among others) to suggest the extent to which in the anthropological study of politics, theory does not precede but rather follows innovative field research. Distinctive of political anthropology is a critical component that other disciplines, such as political science and political sociology, do not possess, a body of substantive material derived from professional research in the field. In essence, the contribution of anthropology to the study of politics is political ethnography: anthropology is the ideographic science par excellence (Pletsch 1981).

In their struggle for professional status, anthropologists found it useful to distinguish between ethnology (an historical and comparative study of societies and cultures) and ethnography (a graphic description of "how things really were"). Today we are more aware of the extent to which theoretical perceptions shape field observations. These perceptions determine more what is included and what is left out of the published monograph than what is recorded in the field notebook. In political monographs, vast areas of practical sensitivity cannot be exposed. Some anthropologists are moving in the direction of political ethnohistory or historical anthropology for this very reason. This has implications both for the analysis of the production of knowlege in political anthropology and for the writing of its history. Ethnohistory has played a distinctive part in the anthropology of politics from Mooney and Swanton to Leacock and Lurie and beyond, and I attempt here to recover at least part of its tradition and the alternative it offered.

Within this genre, anthropologists interested in politics are turning more and more to colonial ethnography to reveal the underpinnings of power and knowledge (Chapter 6). For them, political ethnography records the activities and ideal structures of specific persons, colonizers as well as colonized, in a certain place at a particular time; it is social history. The "ethnographic present" is extended by the use of oral history, archives, documents, and government records. As yet, however, most political ethnographers still observe, describe, categorize, and analyze "societies" and "cultures" at egocentered moments of historical time.

Political anthropology renews itself through ethnography. Particularly valuable, then, are the reevaluations of earlier ethnographies that appear periodically. Besides telling us something about societies at different times, they tell us a great deal about changing perceptions of problems within political anthropology, as in the classic cases of Redfield and Lewis (Chapter 4) and Fortes and Worsley (Chapter 5). Evaluations and reevaluations of ethnography provide both the bedrock and the shifting sands of political anthropology.[9]

Too little political ethnography is included here in light of its strategic importance. This study undertakes no specific inquiry into why political anthropology seems more preoccupied with some societies or cultures than others, although this is clearly a critical question. Kwakiutl haunt the pages that follow; Natchez appear fleetingly. Ifugao and Todas, so important in the literary training of the first professionals, are virtually forgotten today. Nuer and Swat Pathan march on. The explanation for this lies partly in the production process of ethnographic scholarship, as when the coherence of departments such as Berkeley in the 1920s or Oxford in the 1950s generated clusters of close-knit regional studies. But it lies even more in the reception process and the threshold of reproduction, as in the case of Barton's Ifugao studies and Barth's writings on the Swat Pathan (Chapter 5).

Conjunctions of funding, field research, and local manifestations of global history construct the "texts" of political anthropology. The particular locale of field research is frequently a result of nondisciplinary interests. The needs of a government, a colonial establishment, a commercial enterprise, a mission effort—and often their resources—may determine which societies and cultures become part of the repertoire of the political anthropologist. It is often possible to discern reasons for the production of a first ethnography entering the mainstream, but the constant return to old chestnuts (such as political inequality among the Kwakiutl or the importance of lineage ideology among African pastoralists) requires a different explanation. In some cases, successive ethnographies reveal the unquestioning pursuit of the problematically defined. In others, academic struggles over turf may be at stake. The ethnographic course of politics is littered with private and public concerns that lost out in the struggle to define the discipline in one way rather than another.

The primitivization of anthropology, for example, involved setting aside historical realities: the recognition of where sovereignty lay, regional and global interdependencies, ruling classes, and for a long time the urban, industrial, nontropical world. This is most blatantly seen in anthropology's selective application of Marxist theory (Vincent 1985), but it has been a constant though invisible reality within the discipline in its process of self-definition throughout its hundred-year history. Having so-called acculturation studies recognized as anthropology was, indeed, a victory; their recognition as political anthropology is yet to be achieved (Chapter 3). The failure, as yet, to place communal violence and legal discrimination in Britain and the United States on the agenda of political anthropology reflects the inclusion and exclusion processes this study attempts to address. Most critical, perhaps, in the sidelining of certain problem areas is the neglect of education as a political process of social control and social reproduction. This is particularly ironic in an academy in which anthropology as a discipline singles itself out for its self-reflexivity. It might even be said to smack of "mystification."[10]

This is not the place to evaluate either Alfred Kroeber's seminal contribution to the new history of anthropology, intellectual history, and critical science, or the questions raised by cognate disciplines. But something of a compromise may be achieved by introducing Clifford Geertz's view of anthropology as an interpretive science, extrapolating the way he sees ethnography contributing to the growth of knowledge within the discipline. Geertz is the intellectual heir of both Kroeber and Talcott Parsons, whose work has been so influential in this field. Geertz observes that

> empirical fact, our knowledge of culture . . . cultures . . . a culture . . . grows in spurts. Rather than following a rising curve of cumulative findings, cultural analysis breaks into a disconnected yet coherent sequence of bolder and bolder sorties. Studies do build on other studies not in the sense that they take up where the others leave off, but in the sense that, better informed and better conceptualized, they plunge more deeply into the same things. Every serious cultural analysis starts from a sheer beginning and ends where it manages to get before exhausting its intellectual impulse. Previously discovered facts are mobilized, previously developed concepts used, previously formulated hypotheses tried out; but the movement is not from already proven theorems to newly proven ones, it is from an awkward fumbling for the most elementary understanding to a support claim that one has achieved that and surpassed it. A study is an advance if it is more incisive—whatever that may mean—than those that preceded it; but it less stands on their shoulders than, challenged and challenging, runs by their side. . . . Old theories tend less to die than to go into second editions.
> (Geertz 1973:25, 27n.5)

Earlier in the same text, Geertz suggested: "If you want to understand what a science is, you should look in the first instance not at its theories or its findings, and certainly not at what its apologists say about it; you should look at what the practitioners of it do. In anthropology, or anyway social anthropology, what the practitioners do is ethnography. And it is in understanding what ethnography is, or more exactly *what doing ethnography is*, that a start can be made toward grasping what anthropological analysis amounts to as a form of knowledge" (Geertz 1973:5–6).

Geertz's view of what he is doing when he is doing ethnography differs from what most of his predecessors have thought they were doing when they were doing ethnography. Some of his colleagues think him to be simply wrong, and others, since his words are addressed as much to practitioners in other disciplines as to anthropologists, consider them harmful and unrepresentative. Nevertheless, his perception that ethnography lies at the heart of the growth of knowledge in anthropology is shared by most. Further, his emphasis on the writing of ethnography and on anthropology as text encourages the critical analysis of a monograph or treatise as a production, as an art form or artifact, raising questions of a political nature about its reception and reproduction.

Colson (1974) suggested that Geertz lacks sensitivity to political issues, a charge he has denied (Geertz 1983). More to the point, perhaps, is the fact that his emulators have carried his weakness to excess. An apolitical stance is most certainly not a necessary feature of literary criticism, as attested by the work of Benjamin, Jameson, La Capra, McGann, Tompkins, Thorburn, and Weimann, among others. An interpretive political anthropology is, indeed, in the making. So, too, is a broader critique of Geertz's work that leads one to date the end of his intellectual dominance—in contradistinction to his institutional and political dominance—to the early 1980s (Chapter 6).

Critical textual analysis draws attention not simply to the "body" of the text but also to marginalized types of discourse such as legal languages, the fragment, the anecdote, the autobiography, the preface, the note, the quotation, the acknowledgments, and the dedication as so many "distinct generic modes" (Jameson 1981). It sensitizes us, too, to recognize when an author is addressing two distinct publics at once; when, perhaps, a coding system is used whereby an ostensibly abstract statement may include a specific polemical position on issues within a more closed or submerged tradition, a matter discussed in the context of political anthropology during the McCarthy era in the United States (Chapter 4). No view of political anthropology can be unprejudiced.

"The reader does not exist . . . who, when he has his text before him, simply reads what is there. Rather, all reading involves application, so that a person reading a text is himself part of the meaning he apprehends" (Gadamer 1976:304).

Add then, to Geertz's anthropology as text, the idea that the text be considered not an inscription but a palimpsest and that the reader is part of the text in the broadest sense. This study places emphasis on the anthropologist as reader as well as writer of the product—political ethnography—and views the continued existence of texts as both scholarly artifices and political acts as itself requiring explanation. Textual analysis must be accompanied by the recovery of archival materials and social historical knowledge. To follow Geertz too closely into believing that "the building of general theory proceeds by refinements in the way that field material is handled textually by successive ethnographic writers rather than by collecting more data for covering theory built on comparisons" (Marcus and Cushman 1982:59) is to be partially misled. Mainstream anthropology has, indeed, advanced its theorizing in this manner to some extent, and certainly this is the most visible way in which its production of knowledge has expanded. But this is not the whole story; anthropology has also advanced through the exposure of its contradictions and the rejection of refinements in favor of alternative agendas. Political ethnography is particularly prominent in these pages when it is conducive to, or supportive of, shifts in conceptual orientation and the opening up of new problem areas.

Placing classic political ethnography alongside works that may be less well known raises questions about "images," "visibility," and "modes of discourse." Images of "the primitive" and "the peasant" arise to be put in their place. Anthropology's pragmatic orientation, grounded in our own personal field laboratories, ensures that, unless we make an exceptional effort, our knowledge of political anthropology is based on received opinion and rarely subjected to skepticism. There is little weighting of the literary tradition in anthropology, only a selective practical application of received ideas to ever recurring field-engendered intellectual problems. Such critical analysis as there is tends to be piecemeal, appearing in reviews and the opening paragraphs of articles preceding field data. Here more has been made of book reviews and critical essays than is perhaps usual. This is due to criticism's innate resistance to tendencies toward systematization and closure. Scavenging in these two genres serves to remind us that in the anthropology of politics, "the context of knowledge and perception has yet to be breached" (Dolby 1977:2).

PROCEDURE

This is a study with innumerable asides. In the text, I strive to maintain the historical integrity of the subject matter—contemporaries debate one another; contributions are recognized within a life span. In the endnotes, since this study purports to be not only a history but also a commentary with implications for the present, I provide context and criticism. Occasionally some of the discussion from below boils up into the text.

Somewhat more extensive quotation than usual accompanies a review of the published work. The intention is to allow earlier scholars to speak in their own voices because, with the professionalization of anthropology and the development of political anthropology, a tendency grew either to bury the past or to rewrite it. Aidan Southall referred to political anthropologists' "Madison Avenue approach" in the 1960s as "a prevalence among colleagues, each addicted to new and unique ethnographic experiences, for setting up straw men, heralding the new approach, crying in the wilderness" (1968:43). Full and close quotation is necessary to document such continuity as exists and to demonstrate that some ideas and concepts that in a later time were thought to be radical or innovative came first from the lips and pens of earlier scholars. The most striking example of this is found in the work of John Wesley Powell and his colleagues (Chapter 1), and one wonders whether many social anthropologists, particularly the Africanists who attributed so much to Durkheim and Radcliffe-Brown, actually read Bureau of Ethnology publications. A focus on continuity reveals what at times is forgotten and puts on the agenda once again timeless questions and submerged issues. Even more critical, a pursuit of continuity carries one into the corridors of power.

To conclude, this study is intended not only as a representation but also, to some extent, as a reinterpretation. It arises from questioning accepted views and unexamined assumptions. It suggests that a more rigorous exercise in historical revisionism is required by those more specialized in the fields covered. My effort here has drawn little from unpublished materials and not at all from the rich harvest to be gleaned from interviews with practitioners. Above all, it points up the extent to which the anthropological academy has manufactured ignorance at the same time as it has shaped knowledge. Much that has been pushed into the background in the history of the profession has been brought forward, and voices silenced by professionalization have been listened to anew. Time alone has permitted this, and the chapters that follow reflect three phases in the production and reproduction of anthropology—and political vision within it. Chapters 1 and 2 (1879–1918) find the anthropology of politics struggling to define itself, and they draw attention to the lost endeavors of American ethnohistory and British diffusionism. Chapters 3 and 4 (1919–1953) explore the dominance of the functional and structural approaches and describe the type of political anthropology that emerged as a specialization. Finally, Chapters 5 and 6 (1954 to the present) present the alternatives and ultimately the counterpressure that enriched the complex relation—academic and nonacademic—between anthropology and politics.

Part 1

The Anthropology of Politics

1 The Moving Frontier, 1879–1897

*Anthropology, as a discipline, was formed by and battened on the frontier—
but, from a relatively early stage, anthropologists were interested in the
"great beyond."*

—PAUL BOHANNAN

*Facts are the raw material of science. They are to philosophy and history what
cotton and iron are to cloth and steam-engines. Like the raw material of the
manufacturer, they form the bases of innumerable fabrics, are woven into many
theories finely spun or coarsely spun, which wear out with time, become
unfashionable, or else prove to be indeed true and fit, and as such remain. This
raw material of the scholar, like that of the manufacturer, is always a staple
article; its substance never changes, its value never diminishes; whatever may
be the condition of society, or howsoever advanced the mind, it is indispensable.
Theories may be only for the day, but facts are for all times and for all science.*

—HUBERT HOWE BANCROFT

It is a truism among historians of science that "a reach into otherness"
is a distinctive part of the European heritage.[1] From the sixteenth century on, European governments have adopted schedules and questionnaires to inquire into the ways of life of subject peoples. The Spanish
crown issued them to their colonial officials in the New World and the
Philippines in the sixteenth century. The Royal Society at Oxford published "programmes of research" for travelers and navigators in the
1660s. Sir William Petty's schedule for inquiry into the customs and
manners of Pennsylvania's Native Americans was published in 1686.
Anatole Baudin's expedition to Australia in 1880 carried with it long
questionnaires (Hodgen 1964). Imperial adventures required foreign intelligence. The first edition of *Notes and Queries on Anthropology: For
the Use of Travellers and Residents in Uncivilized Lands* was issued
by the British Association for the Advancement of Science in 1874.
Scholars engaged in making the science of man into a modern profession argued that knowledge of non-European civilizations justified the
place of their discipline in the academic marketplace.

This is all very well, but professional ethnology was not, in fact, initially concerned only with noncivilized lands. Some of its first ethnographic surveys were carried out at home. When we speak of the moving frontier during the second half of the nineteenth century, we use
the metaphor in three senses. First, certainly, anthropology advanced
on the expansive frontier of industrial capitalism both within the
American continent and, for the British, overseas. But we also recognize

the penetration of a second internal frontier as first electoral representation and then public education were introduced into British and
American society. Finally, of course, the metaphor was commonly used
in late Victorian times to refer to the frontiers of science. The Victorian
era was one of uncertainty, and at times social disorder threatened public security; the uncouth were knocking at the doors. Developing industrial capitalism extracted people from their rural economies and kept
them on the move. As the nineteenth century progressed, massive
numbers of laboring people crossed the Atlantic, severing ties of community to reshape the national economies of both Europe and the
Americas. Knowledge was the agency of progress.

The scientific framework that scholars erected did more than just
explain how things had come to be in the world the Victorians knew.
Evolutionary theory also provided a growing literate public with a justification for emigration, expansion, and empire. Earlier travelers and
explorers had crossed oceans and visited alien shores only for comparatively brief periods, but by the mid nineteenth century they were settling and staying. Ethnology was no longer marginal to political thought.

The American Civil War had repercussions for the world at large. The
United States that emerged from the civil strife began to embark so
successfully on global business ventures that older imperial powers
were forced to reorganize their colonial governments to meet the challenges of a transformed global economy. Some began to embark on new
overseas conquest, and toward the end of the century, the United
States, having settled its continental territory as far as the Pacific
Coast, followed suit. On the frontiers of Euro-American colonization,
indigenous primitive capitalists arose. In the pages that follow, we meet
the Ute political entrepreneur Kanosh, for by 1868 the ethnographer
was there to record his presence. It was a long time, however, before the
discipline was able to reconcile the contradiction apparent in his existence. In one respect, Kanosh was a survivor on the universal human
stage presaged in the theoretical writings of Herbert Spencer and
Charles Darwin. Yet he was also an interstitial figure, an entrepreneur,
a middleman, a broker on the moving frontier of capitalism.

Superficially, evolutionary theory rationalized the moving frontiers
of empire, but its underpinnings lay in that form of capitalism of which
colonialism was itself a late expression. Whether that expansion took
place across continents or across oceans was immaterial, as William
Christie MacLeod was subsequently to show (Chapter 3). To view the
extension of empire as involving only overseas conquest and domina-

tion—the saltwater fallacy—was itself a product of a particular historical political culture.

Expansive industrial capitalism underwent critical change during the nineteenth century, and the adoption of cultural evolutionism as a dominant mode of inquiry in the middle of the century reflected in both England and the United States a shift of power away from the landowning aristocrat to the business tycoon: "from a stable elitism to a competitive elitism," as Burridge puts it (1973:27). The passage of mankind from savagery through barbarism to civilization provided a chart upon which traveler and explorer, missionary and administrator, businessman and lawyer, student of comparative religion and student of jurisprudence, gentleman archaeologist and amateur ethnologist alike could locate the *material huberei*, the accumulating data on the varieties of mankind (Burridge 1973; Kuhn 1977). But evolutionary theory also served other ends, rationalizing the destruction of savage societies and suggesting that it was inevitable. Charles Darwin attributed the extinction of savages to competition with the civilized races (1871:228-331), even as earlier a parliamentary commision had attributed massive depopulation among aboriginal peoples to European expansion. The use of evolutionary theory by American and British ethnologists during the last two decades of the nineteenth century forms the substance of this chapter, along with an account of how the practice gradually came to be challenged as the century drew to a close.

Lewis Henry Morgan's *The League of the Iroquois* and *Ancient Society* framed between 1851 and 1877 the preprofessional phase of American ethnology. Morgan's first book appeared when Darwinian evolutionary theory was still in the mind of its creator in his study in Cambridgeshire; the proliferation of evolutionary theorizing that then existed, including that of young Herbert Spencer, was highly speculative. It ran counter to those forms of evolutionary theory that viewed Victorian society as the pinnacle of progressive civilization. Morgan valued the communalism of Native American society above the competitive individualism of the New England Yankee and, as his passionate conclusion to *Ancient Society* (1877) shows, he deplored the way in which many of his contemporaries viewed the ownership of private property as the primary agent of progress. A New York corporation lawyer, he was honored in due course by election to the American Academy of Science; a bourgeois Engels of Native American ethnography, he might otherwise have been judged to be socialistic like his English contemporaries William Morris and John Ruskin.[2]

Morgan reacted to industrializing capitalism as a man born on its periphery. The paradigm of *Ancient Society* reflected not the sociology and biology of Spencer and Darwin but the ideas of that earlier age of British capitalist expansion when, on an eighteenth-century periphery, a body of Scottish savants reflected upon the stages of mankind's progress from civil to ranked political society.[3] Led by Adam Ferguson, John Millar, William Robertson, and Adam Smith, the Scots derived much of their understanding of the development of human society from newly acquired knowledge of the way of life of the aboriginal peoples of the American continent. Their developmental theory provided the origin myth of Western capitalism. Adam Smith first set out the four-stage theory of the development of human societies in 1750, but the Scots as a body sought to relate modes of subsistence to "different sets of ideas and institutions relating to law, property, and government, and also different sets of customs, manners and morals" (Meek 1976:2). Morgan's vision, like theirs, was timely:

> Since the advent of civilization, the outgrowth of property has been so immense, its forms so diversified, its uses so expanding and its management so intelligent in the interests of its owners, that it has become, on the part of the people, an unmanageable power. The human mind stands bewildered in the presence of its own creation. The time will come, nevertheless, when human intelligence will rise to the mastery over property, and define the relations of the state to the property it protects, as well as the obligations and the limits of the rights of its owners. The interests of society are paramount to individual interests, and the two must be brought into just and harmonious relations. A mere property career is not the final destiny of mankind, if progress is to be the law of the future as it has been of the past. The time which has passed away since civilization began is but a fragment of the ages yet to come. The dissolution of society bids fair to become the termination of a career of which property is the end and aim; because such a career contains the elements of self-destruction. Democracy in government, brotherhood in society, equality in rights and privileges, and universal education, foreshadow the next higher plane of society to which experience, intelligence and knowledge are steadily tending. It will be a revival, in a higher form, of the liberty, equality and fraternity of the ancient gentes. (Morgan 1877:560–561)

The issues of property, the individual, communality, and territory thereafter repeatedly provided point and counterpoint in the professionalizing of anthropology. In an age moving toward industrial organization at home and empire building overseas, the socialist philosophers' near beatification of Morgan now appears almost inevitable.

Introductory textbooks teach that much of Morgan's thinking "has been absorbed into modern anthropology . . . especially . . . in relation to politics," including his emphasis on kinship "as a primary medium of political articulation at the subsistence levels of hunting/gathering and horticulture," his discovery of the gens as a corporate lineage, and his "recognition of the egalitarianism of primitive society and the lack of a concept of property" (Lewellen 1983:4). Yet many anthropologists who "look at the ethnographic record find no such compelling fit between modes of subsistence and political order, nor do [they] find that the human ability to invent political relationships conforms easily to the provision of a small number of pigeonholes" (Colson 1985c:16). The complexity and contradictions in Morgan's vision and the traditions it has engendered initiate a distinction to which we shall return later in this chapter: the alternative construction of political data that derives from historical as opposed to evolutionary thinking.[4]

Although Morgan (like Powell later) saw himself as a practitioner of a peculiarly nativist American scholarship, European scholars turned his work into a treatise against capitalism. We do not know what Marx would have made of Morgan's work. We may conjecture, however, that it might well have been something different from what became Engels's *The Origin of the Family, Private Property and the State*, first published in German in 1884 and with four editions appearing by 1892. *Ancient Society*, with its clarion conclusions, had first been published in 1877 and was reprinted almost immediately. It was not reprinted again, shorn of its Greek and Latin texts, until 1907. From correspondence between Morgan and Maine, it appears that the work was not readily available in England; Marx apparently borrowed a copy brought from the United States. Engels thought there was "a conspiracy of its suppression by silence" within the established intellectual circles (Vinnikov 1935). Scientific anthropology, as it emerged in Britain, found evolutionary Comteism and reform-minded Fabianism relevant and compatible, evolution and reform, but not historical, revolutionary socialism. Historical materialism lingered on in anthropology nevertheless; what reads today as monologue and discourse was once resonant of dialogic dispute.

At the heart of the debate lay three contrasting visions of human society: the biological or racial, the historical, and the evolutionary (Balandier 1970). Throughout his career, Morgan rejected the first while shifting away from the historical analysis of Iroquois society toward the evolutionary taxonomizing of known human societies in *Ancient Society*. The Morgan corpus embodies the dialectic of ethnography and ethnology that pervades the anthropological study of politics and that ultimately brought the Bureau of Ethnology to disarray and then to defeat at the hands of the academicians.

Morgan owed a great deal to the English jurist Sir Henry Maine. Maine discerned two revolutions in the development of Indo-European societies: first, a change from societies based on status to societies based on contract, and second, a change from organization based on kinship to "local contiguity" as "the basis of common political action" (Maine 1861). Morgan substitutes territory for local contiguity when he sets out two forms of government: "The first, in the order of time, is founded upon persons, and upon relations purely personal, and may be distinguished as a society (societas). . . . The second is founded upon territory and upon property, and may be distinguished as a state (civitas). . . . Political society is organized upon territorial areas, and deals with property as well as with persons through territorial relations" (1877:6–7). Later, political anthropologists would argue these matters, applying ethnography to test their validity again and again in the generations that followed.

Morgan had no connection with either universities or museums. He was, however, far more than an armchair scholar, collating and synthesizing the reports of missionaries, traders, and administrators in the manner of other "evolutionary schematists" in Britain and the United States. As an independent scholar, Morgan was particularly vulnerable to shifts in political fashion in the society in which he lived, and much of his change of vision between 1851 and 1877 must be attributed to the course that the development of professional anthropology was itself taking. One example may be given. Morgan never provided a definition of the political units he found among the Iroquois. He wrote of the Iroquois as "our predecessors in sovereignty," and his aim was not "to narrate their political events; but to inquire into the structure and spirit of their government, and the nature of institutions, under and through which these historical results were produced" (1851:56). Twenty-five years later he no longer viewed them as a sovereign nation; the groupings that he called "tribe" and "nation" in *The League* he classified as "clan" and "tribe" in *Ancient Society*. In 1851 he was using the terms that any nineteenth-century gentleman might have used to describe a foreign nation. By 1877 he was writing as an ethnologist; he introduced *clan* as a technical term, and his shift from *nation* to *tribe* reflected a process of primitivization already under way. This was a matter of considerable significance in the work of the professionals at the Bureau of Ethnology.

THE AMERICAN TRADITION

This section begins to explore why studies of Native American political organization have not been part and parcel of mainstream anthropology. The American tradition reflected a local interest in Native Americans, their origins and history, and their place in the human universe; in the work of the first professionals at the Bureau of American Ethnology, archaeological sites figured as prominently as native peoples. In Morgan's work, an appreciation of material culture was fused with historical process and perceptions of human progress. It was a tradition derailed by 1898.

Were a political anthropologist of today to peruse the publications of the Bureau of Ethnology between 1879 and 1897, five elements might engage his or her interest: (1) the overriding political existence of the frontier and all that entailed for political relations both of equality and interdependence, and of conquest and domination; (2) the related question of the political reality of violence and war in such contact situations; (3) concomitantly, law in both its internal and international aspects; (4) a clear conceptualization and definition of what bureau ethnologists called a *kinship polity*; and (5) at the same time, accounts of political movements that were *not* based on the kinship or territorial aspects that American tradition stressed. All five elements derived from the structuring of Native American political institutions within the political bounds of an expansive United States.

Politics on the American Frontier

From the beginning, the bureau was engaged in politics, both because of its position as an institution funded by the federal government and because of its prescribed objectives.[5] These included the collection of information about the languages and organization of Native American peoples, many of whom were about to be settled on reservations. Perspectives on their politics were shaped, and held in shape at first, by the bureau's founding director, Major John Wesley Powell, whose approach to politics reflected his early experience in the mountains of Colorado and his reading of, and personal admiration for, Lewis Henry Morgan. His directives imposed on the bureau the theoretical framework of Morgan's *Ancient Society*, but by the close of the century, as we shall see, the American government had become responsive to political initiatives among the Native American peoples, and a younger generation of ethnologists was able to redefine its own scholarly objectives. These, inevitably, were somewhat in contradiction to those of 1879.

Academic anthropology was able to sideline Native American ethnology by suggesting that most of its data consisted of the recollections of an ethnographer's oldest informants. This is just not true. The earliest accounts of Native American political organization were written under conditions of war on the frontier in the 1860s. John Wesley Powell carried out field research in Colorado among Native Americans at a time when a decade of resistance to Euro-American encroachment on their lands was drawing to an end. Thus, precisely at the moment in American history when Native Americans became an internal rather than an external problem, when they could no longer be shunted aside, as Curtiss Hinsley puts it, "deeper understanding became a matter of public welfare" (1979:19). The Native American, Powell told a congressional committee, "is among us, and we must either protect him or destroy him" (Fowler and Fowler 1971:119).

Powell's ethnographic work among the Native Americans of the Rocky Mountain region began when, as a geologist, he became increasingly interested in native peoples, dispensing with a military escort and traveling freely among them. The dominant fact of the Basin-Plateau environment was aridity, and by observing the people who already had extensive experience living there—both Native Americans and Mormons—he began to relate the region's geological and geographic base to those who settled upon it. In the context of new legal arrangements that would be required as the economic frontier advanced ever westward, Powell's science grew (Dupree 1957).

In the 1860s the Shoshoni roamed the extreme northwest of Colorado Territory, and the Ute occupied the entire central and western portions. Powell's account revealed the conditions under which they operated in the early dawn of their "capitalist" era.[6] To the settlers they were "Diggers" or "Pai-utes," both derogatory terms. The settlers also knew them as Sho-sho-nees, Bannocks, Utes, Mo-quis, Chem-a-hue-vas, and Comanhas. They were considered among the lowest forms of mankind, foragers who subsisted on roots and insects. Moving about in small bands, they hunted small animals on foot and slept in crude brush shelters. They were quite unlike the noble savages of the Plains familiar to Victorians from literature. Powell planned to write an ethnography, and to this end he recorded their subsistence and way of life in great detail. His appointment as director of the Bureau of Ethnology in 1879, and the changing fashions of the Washington academic circle in which he moved, inhibited the ethnography he was so uniquely qualified to undertake.

Between 1868 and 1879 much of Powell's public energy was directed to correcting the popular view of Native Americans as savages, a goal Morgan had sought a decade and a half earlier.[7] This he did in reports to Washington (which were published for public consumption) and on lecture tours in small frontier towns. On one occasion he described the Native American system of government. His idealized account, for all its humane purpose, was propaganda, a romantic reconstruction rendered doubly pathetic by his firsthand knowledge of the deprivation and misery of the Shoshoni and Utes.[8] Morgan's Iroquois provided the noblest ideal; this was how all Native Americans once had been. It was not that they had degenerated. As a good Republican, Powell firmly believed in technological progress and the advancement of knowledge—in short, in an evolutionary creed. In a more authentic account submitted to the Department of the Interior, however, he made it clear that the scattered bands that scavenged the Rocky Mountain region were, indeed, the outcome of Euro-American intrusion into their territories. "Their hunting grounds have been spoiled," he wrote, "their favorite valleys are occupied by white men, and they are compelled to scatter in small bands in order to obtain subsistence. Formerly they were organized into nations, or confederacies, under the influence of great chiefs, but such men have lost their power in the presence of white men, and it is no longer possible to treat with these people as nations, but each little tribe must be dealt with separately" (Fowler and Fowler 1971:99). To explain the condition of these contemporary foraging peoples, Powell thus introduced the relationship of ecological adaptation to historical change as a problematic.

Powell undertook his research and lecture tours in the Colorado region when the Native Americans were openly "at war" with the settlers in their midst. The area had been nominally under military government since 1832, but the army was no peacekeeping force. Settlers, as Powell put it, vented indignities on the Native Americans, who were "terrified"—today we would say terrorized. "A vicious Indian commits a depredation, and flies to the mountains. No effort is made to punish the real offender, but the first Indian met is shot at sight" (Fowler and Fowler 1971:118). The settlers seized the lands of those who fled. Powell's recommendation that the army be withdrawn from the region was not welcomed in Washington.

Powell found that the Shoshoni and Utes fully appreciated "the hopelessness of tending against the Government of the United States and the tide of civilization. They are broken into many small tribes, and their homes so interspersed among the settlements of white men, that their power is entirely broken and no fear should be entertained of a general war with them. The time has passed when it was necessary to buy peace" (Fowler and Fowler 1971:116). His report to the commissioner of Indian affairs urged the need for tribal reservations where they would be safe from harassment. His main concern was that every reservation should include good farmland. Only then, he assured the government, would their passage from savagery to civilization be assured. By 1873 his field inquiries led him to believe that reservations were also what the native peoples wanted.

Powell's Morganic view of cultural evolution challenged the interests of those who wanted to exploit the industrial and commercial opportunities of the Indian country. He could have adopted a purely Darwinian theory and charged the bureau to demonstrate that Native Americans were biologically inferior. Some Euro-Americans eagerly awaited just such scientific justification for their hardline racial policies. But Powell believed in the peaceful evolution of peoples rather than the survival of the fittest. Biological analogies to human cultural evolution were, he asserted, unscientific and in error (Hinsley 1981). Believing that man had evolved not by reason of his brutal nature but through the evolution of the humanities, Powell concluded that pacification could best be achieved by ensuring that the Indian reservations provided for settled agriculture. He rested his case on ethnographic fact, describing a band of Utes south of Salt Lake City as having a warlike reputation. "They are a well-mounted, daring people, and very skillful in border warfare. . . . For the last ten years they have subsisted chiefly on the spoils of war." But now, Powell reported, they had "of their own accord given up their marauding life and they signified their willingness to go on a reservation and adopt the habits of civilized men" (Fowler and Fowler 1971:103). One reason for this lay in their belief that their recent high mortality was attributable to either sorcery or divine retribution for their warmongering. The moral hegemony of missionary and agent was apparently already having its effect.

Emergent Leadership on the Economic Frontier

In his lectures and manuscripts, John Wesley Powell deliberately provided a formal account of Native American government that reconstructed its orderliness and efficiency. Yet, good ethnographer that he was, he also documented the existence of a particular type of political leadership that emerged and thrived on the new economic frontier. Such a leader will appear again on several occasions as the anthropology

of politics, grounded in observation and ethnography, outstrips the ethnological theory of its time.

Among a Ute band that had settled at Corn Creek near Fillmore in
central Utah was a leader known to the Euro-Americans as Kanosh.[9]
His indigenous name was Mo-a-agi-tup. He was a well-known "chief"
when Powell first met him in 1873. His band was said to number some
1,200, but Powell found only 57 men, 42 women, and 32 children, a
total of 131 souls. They subsisted by cultivating the soil; by gathering
seeds, fruit, and roots; and by hunting, as well as by begging from
settlers. Poor as they were, Powell considered them better off than any
other Indians not yet on reservations throughout Utah, Nevada, southern Idaho, northern Arizona, and southeastern California. He believed
this was because Kanosh, their chief, was doing all he could to persuade
his people to cultivate.

Powell found thirty acres of standing wheat when he visited the band
in 1873, although that year, he noted, the harvest was poor. Kanosh
himself grew not only enough grain for his family but a surplus to sell.
(Powell does not mention the source of his labor force.) From this,
Kanosh derived "a respectable revenue." He lived in a house built for
him by a former superintendent of Indian affairs for Utah. A photograph
taken sometime before 1869 shows him in a heavy Victorian vest and
jacket. His well-trimmed hair, pointed beard, and groomed mustache
suggest that he was truly on the road to "civilization." He also had
good connections with the Mormon church and considerable government support, the federal government having taken responsibility for
feeding nonreservation Indians. Kanosh's people received proportion-
ately three times as much from the government as any other tribe.
"That generous treatment on the part of the Government," Powell
wrote, "has added to the influence of Kanosh, for he has thus proved to
the surrounding tribes his ability to influence the Government officials
and he is their admiration and envy; and they have learned to consult
him, to a great extent, concerning all their dealings with the officers of
the Indian Department" (Fowler and Fowler 1971:111). His influence
extended, indeed, over most of central Utah. What is more, Kanosh
appears to have exercised autonomy: a table accompanying the 1873
report showed him to be the only man listed as not subordinated to a
"Chief of Alliance."

The Corn Creek Utes opposed Powell's recommendation that they
join a reservation. They wished to remain at Corn Creek. Powell
suggested to the government that in future, "goods" should be issued
to them only on a reservation. At the time of writing, Powell was not

sure what the outcome would be. On the one hand, Kanosh had agreed that if the president of the United States insisted on their moving and would assist them to become farmers, they would go. On the other hand, Powell feared that when the time came to move, "circumstances connected with his relation to the Mormon Church" (he is not more explicit) would make Kanosh reluctant to leave. Powell urged the government to make it more beneficial for them to move, but if Kanosh still refused, he concluded that it should use force.

Bureau of Ethnology Directives

The bureau's first annual report appeared in 1880. Given its government origins, it is not surprising that it included an account of Native American civil and military government. The synopsis Powell presented became, indeed, a model for future ethnographies, yet it was, in a sense, a betrayal of much that Powell's field researches had promised. It reflected, perhaps, the autodidact's sense of inferiority with respect to the acclaimed ethnologist, the amateur's inferiority to the scholar. Thus in a November 16, 1876, letter to Morgan, Powell told him that, while going ahead with his other projects, he planned to withold all materials relating to the organization of society and government among the Indians for further study until after he had received a copy of *Ancient Society*. He then proposed to "review the material on hand, and collections of new materials, in the light which will be thrown upon the subject by the publication of your researches" (Vinnikov 1935:72).

In the next two years the deskbound director provided his team, and the public at large, with a set of interrelated ideas and definitions constructed around the concepts of the *kinship polity* and the *tribe*. It was formulated after a visit from Chief Gray Eyes of the Wyandotte, the Huron whose confederacy had been destroyed by Morgan's famed Iroquois League. Questioning elicited from Chief Gray Eyes a sociological account of Wyandotte government that Powell described in 1881 as typical of Native American tribal structure. He knew better, of course, and in the next breath he observed that "among the several hundred distinct Indian governments there is great variety." In spite of his earlier field experience, Powell made no attempt to relate this variation to environment. Their "different degrees of organization," he stated, "were determined by the differentiation of the functions of the correlative specialization of organic elements" (1881:68). The practical frontiersman had discovered sociological jargon. Not only this but the deskbound organicist used the present tense throughout his account, thus rendering timeless the Wyandotte government of which Chief Gray Eyes spoke. This legitimation of what became known as "the ethnographic present" in ethnology robbed Native Americans of their history.

Native American society, in Powell's account, comprised four groups: the gens (or clan, an organized consanguineal body of kindred in the female line), the phratry, the tribe, and the family or household. The first three constituted a series of "organic units"; the family was a unit of a different type. Society was maintained by the establishment of government, since rights had to be recognized and duties performed. Civil government inhered in a hierarchical system of councils and chiefs. In each gens a council of four women was chosen by the heads of households, themselves women. The women council members then selected a chief of the gens from among its male members—that is, from their brothers and sons. Together the gentile councils made up the council of the tribe. One-fifth of the tribal council was therefore composed of men and four-fifths of women. The sachem or chief of the tribe was chosen by the heads of the gentes (clans). Military government was completely separated from civil government.

At this point the old Adam of an ethnographer in Powell reasserted itself, and his description shifted momentarily from the characteristic structure of government to its actuality at that moment among the Wyandotte. He noticed that, although customarily the sachemship inhered in the Bear clan, because death had carried away all their wise men, Gray Eyes had been chosen from the Deer clan. Powell then reverted to his formal account.

The tribal grand council was held regularly on the night of the full moon and whenever else the sachem thought necessary. Meetings of the gentile councils were very informal, but those of the tribal council were conducted with due ceremony. When all were assembled, the chief of the Wolf gens called for order, and the sachem, after passing round the pipe, explained why they were meeting. Each man and woman spoke in turn. If a majority were in agreement, the sachem did not express his opinion but simply announced the decision. If there was protracted debate or a tie, the sachem made the final judgment. Such, said Powell, were the organic elements of Wyandotte civil government. He then turned to its function.

The function of all government is to preserve rights and enforce the performance of duties. Rights imply duties, and duties imply rights. Powell distinguished eight classes of rights related to (1) marriage, (2) names, (3) personal adornments, (4) order in encampments and migrations, (5) property, (6) person, (7) community, and (8) religion. After a discussion of each in turn, he distinguished six violations of rights or crimes by the courts in which they were adjudicated. A woman's adultery (he does not write of men at all in this connection) is dealt with by the councilwomen of her gens. Theft, maiming, and murder are adjudicated by gens councils. If both murderer and victim belong to the same gens, the gentile council acts on the complaint of the head of household of the injured party, although there may be an appeal to the tribal council. If they are of different gens, the chief of the plaintiff's gens appears before the council of the offender's gens. If compensation cannot be agreed upon, it is the duty of the victim's nearest relative to avenge the wrong. Treason and witchcraft, the two remaining crimes Powell discussed, are investigated by the grand council of the tribe. Treason is punishable by death; witchcraft is ascertained by ordeal.

Powell did not find it problematic to use the categories and concepts of Euro-American law and government to structure his discourse. The sociological concepts he used were familiar to his readers from the writings of Herbert Spencer, and his mode of generalizing from a single case was standard sociological practice. Powell's explicit systemic analysis, with its focus on functional specialization, blended the contemporary sociology of Spencer with that of a colleague of his at the bureau, Lester Ward, and imposed both on the kinship primacy that Maine and Morgan had attributed to prepolitical *societas*.[10] "Tribal government in North America," he wrote, "is based on kinship in that the fundamental units of social organization are bodies of consanguineal kindred [gentes] either in the male or female line. These are organized into tribes by ties of relationship and affinity, and this organization is of such a character that the man's position in his tribe is fixed by his kinship. The fabric of Indian society is a complex tissue of kinship. The warp is made of streams of kinship blood, and the woof of marriage ties" (Powell 1881:68–69). The John Wesley Powell who wrote this was no longer in dialogue with Native Americans, nor even primarily with government policymakers, but with a growing international community of scientists. One cannot help but regret the transmogrification of the pioneer ethnographer of twenty years earlier; would the ethnology of the bureau he directed have been very different if the Morgan of those years rather than the Morgan of *Ancient Society* had been his guiding light?

Besides presenting an ideal type of Native American government in line with Morgan's brand of scientific evolutionism, Powell went to great pains to provide his bureau workers with strict definitions of interrelated concepts. The problem of the tribe, the political import of the clan, the nature of the feud, and segmentation, fusion, and fission were all on his agenda. Concern with such kinship-related matters was to bring political anthropology into the mainstream of the discipline in the 1940s.

Having provided the bureau with an analytical account of tribal government as a system, along with a set of precisely defined concepts, Powell in February 1882 stepped into a wider scientific arena when he delivered the Anthropology Society of Washington's first presidential address (Powell 1882). The society was made up of lawyers and doctors, museum and university scientists, amateur archaeologists, and bureaucrats. (No women were allowed, and they formed their own anthropological society, which Powell addressed later on a less auspicious occasion.) Most would have had the benefit of a college education, unlike Powell himself. The self-educated professional soldier, explorer, geologist, linguist, and ethnologist chose to provide the assembled body with his own personal outline of sociology. His composite of the evolutionary ideas of his time, standing on the shoulders of the giants—Spencer, Darwin, Maine, and Morgan—was essentially political.

The format that follows, with the text being included within the symbols "<<<" and ">>>," indicates that the purpose is to convey the gist of the contribution, the style of the author, and frequently the "modernity" of the ideas expressed. My procedure has been to string together and combine key sentences to make paragraphs. All the phrases and sentences in the inset text are those of the author and appear in the same sequence in the original document. Bracketed statements provide continuity, but no editorial comment or glossing of concepts appears in the inset passages. This heuristic device is also used later in this study.

The Body Politic

<<<By organized association men live together in bodies politic. That men may live in peace, render one another assistance, and act together as units for mutual protection, is the purpose subserved by organized association. In order that men may associate, their conduct must be regulated. For the regulation of conduct there must be organization, and the plan upon which a body politic is organized depends upon the nature of the regulation for which it is used—organ is adapted to function.

The organization of the body politic constitutes the State. Again, there must be: First, some method of determining the particulars of conduct that require regulation and the quality and quantity of regulation required. Second, there must be means of enforcing regulation. Third, there must be means of determining whether conduct conforms to rule. The machinery established by a society for accomplishing these purposes constitutes Government. There are [also] rules which the body politic determines to be necessary for peace, mutual assistance, protection, and the common welfare, and these constitute the Law.

The science of sociology, from the nature of the functions of social organization, may be fundamentally divided into three subjects: the constitution of the state; the form of the government; and the regulation embodied in the law.

The Evolution of the State, Government, and Law

The particulars of conduct may relate to the perpetuation of the species or it may relate to the welfare of the individual. . . . In the earlier and lower stages of society, [the former] is paramount; in the highest forms of social organization [the latter]. In both cases, however, the matter is one of primary and secondary degree, not of absolute difference.

In the perpetuation of the species, the functions of reproduction are dependent upon the biologic organization of mankind, dividing the human race into two classes—*male* and *female*—and the very earliest states yet discovered have their plans of organization based on sex, and composed of classified bodies of kindred. . . . This gives us kinship society and tribal government.

In the earliest stages of society small wealth is accumulated, and industries for the production of property and wealth are comparatively undeveloped. In the higher stages of society greatly accumulated wealth is found, and industries are differentiated and industrial organizations multiplied beyond all others. . . . [T]he plan of government in such a state must be based on property. Thus property, society, and national government are constituted.

In kinship states the fundamental classification of the people for purposes of government is by kindred; in property states [it] is by territory. . . . The history of the constitution of the state is the history of the evolution of kinship society into property society. . . .

[T]his evolution [is also characterized by] the progressing differentiation of the organs of the state, and by the progressing integration of states. [This is reflected in] first, the multiplication of organs of government; second, the multiplication of the orders of units and the specialization of the subordinate units; . . . and third, the multiplication of corporations for specific purposes. . . .

[Both Government and Law evolve. Government evolves when] an assembly composed of men from which are excluded all deemed too young or too old to exhibit due wisdom [gives way to a more definitely organized form of assembly, with a presiding officer, a differentiation of legislative, executive and judicial departments,] represented by the *assembly*, the *ruler*, and the *court*. The evolution of Law [has three features: change from Personal Law to Property Law; multiplication of the classes of Crimes recognized; and the development of "loopholes" to] "the fundamental and primary principle of primitive society that justice be done." >>>

At this point, as Powell began to introduce the evolution of ethi(his allotted time apparently ran out. He regretted that he would not be able to talk about the differentiation of industries and their integration through commerce. Nor could he discuss the evolution of corporate law. Clearly, in setting forth his vision of political organization and its evolution, Powell had no intention of restricting his professed sociology to the earliest states of society or kinship polities. Quite the contrary; he may have had in mind the arguments of the Scottish political econo-mists whereby the regulation of industry and commerce was related to the social division of labor and the development of ranks in civil society (Ferguson 1767). But it is also likely that he was concerned (as he once had been with the Shoshoni) with the realities of politics all around him in the expansive United States. That he did not incorporate the powerful forces of American corporate enterprise into his recognition of shifting boundaries between corporations and government within the state was (or, at least, so he conveyed) due only to a lack of time. He did not rule them out of bounds for his sociological ethnology.

Powell's address was published in various forms in several places, but it was not clothed in the scholarly regalia of reference and citation. The image that academic anthropology created for itself at the beginning of the following century obscured these political roots. No one reads Pow-ell anymore, just as no one reads Spencer or Lester Ward, although their evolutionary tradition lives on in some circles. But it should be noted that the bureau ethnologists presaged another tradition, too, inasmuch as they viewed societies as organic systems and described their work as sociology a generation before Radcliffe-Brown began to preempt space for a similar discourse about form and function.

The Kinship Polity

The first clear delineation of a kinship polity appeared in *Omaha Soci-ology*, by James Owen Dorsey, in 1883.[11] Dorsey, a Methodist minister, had already lived among the Omaha for almost two years when he was recruited by the bureau. He spoke the language fluently and knew inti-mately some 220 families living on the small Nebraska reservation. His terms of reference were those laid down by Powell in his presidential address. Dorsey defined the kinship state as "one in which governmen-tal functions are performed by men whose positions in the government are determined by kinship, and rules relating to kinship and reproduc-tion of the species constitute the larger body of the law" (1883:215).

Dorsey first reported on the three features of political organization that Powell considered definitive: the differentiation of legislative, executive, and judicial organs; propertied classes; and the existence of corporations. Among the Omaha, governmental organizations were *not* differentiated. Dorsey distinguished three classes of men (chiefs, policemen or braves, and young men or "the common people"), and there were also servants. Brotherhoods and feasting associations were the only corporations. Dorsey's chapters then described, in order, the Omaha gentile system, the kinship system and marriage laws, domestic life, industries, and the law. Warfare he considered a protective industry, whereas government and religion were regulative industries. (Later anthropologists would come to call these *institutions* rather than *industries* and in so doing would impart a normative and nomothetic character to them.)

Dorsey described the political organization of the Omaha as he watched it in operation on the reservation. When the tribe settled there in 1855, each man had acquired land on patent from the Bureau of Indian Affairs. As the Omaha warriors became farmers, the office of sachem fell into disuse, and in 1880 Dorsey witnessed the election of seven chiefs, all equal in rank. Each had several subordinates, who were obliged to resign upon his death or retirement. Two years earlier, three of these subordinate chiefs had been appointed by the federal government, but these were not considered "regular chiefs" by the Omaha. These three men worked closely with the Indian agent and "always appeared to stand together, forming a third party in the tribe, as opposed to the chiefs' party (to which the others belonged) and that of the young men or progressives" (Dorsey 1883:357–358).

The chiefs' authority was wide ranging. It included the power to order policemen to strike the disobedient, to order the crier to proclaim assembly decisions, to call on braves to provide food for feasts, to take the principal seats at the tribal assembly, and to place, and so promote, newly elected chiefs. Subordinate chiefs had what might seem to be even more critical rights. Besides sitting in the assembly, they regulated the buffalo hunt, approved or disapproved small war parties, acted as go-betweens or diplomats to other tribes; intervened in quarrels, and "in modern times" contracted for the sale of land to the United States government.

Dorsey's *Omaha Sociology* is in no sense an historical reconstruction. It is a straightforward account of the political arrangements of a Native American tribe in the limited domain in which they conducted their own affairs on a peaceful reservation between 1855 and 1883. Bureau researchers elsewhere drew attention to "medicine men" who actively contested the authority of the federal government and their recognized chiefs.[12] Not even the Ghost Dance, soon to be the subject of ethnological inquiry, stimulated political opposition among the Omaha.

Law, Crime, and Punishment

When Native Americans ceased being wards of the U.S. Army, their reservations were administered first by the Department of the Interior and then by the Bureau of Indian Affairs. They increasingly lost control over the management of their own affairs. Crime and violent politics among them were clearly of interest to the bureau's funders and were intermittently as open to observation as to reconstruction. Once again Powell's generalizing program must be distinguished from the ethnographic practice of his fieldworkers. Out of their differences they established a paradigm for the study of law and war that moved away from origins—the concern of evolutionists—toward historical process.

First, Powell proposed a definition of law that would hold good, he said, under all circumstances, "divested of the many theories of its origin, the source of its authority, and its ethical character." It was short and to the point: "A law is a rule of conduct which organized society endeavored to enforce" (Powell 1881–82:lvii). In what followed Powell was not simply schematic but dogmatic. "In civilization, law is theoretically founded on justice; but in savagery, principles of justice have little consideration" (Powell 1881–82:lvii). Two fundamentals underlay savage law: (1) controversy should be prevented; and (2) controversy should be terminated. A third principle was derivative from these: infractions of the law should be punished.

Powell then provided documentation. Following Morgan, he saw institutions that operated against the accumulation of property as maintaining a peaceful kinship state. Certain kinship practices muted controversy: the authority of elders and the use of kinship terms instead of personal names. Kinship also served to deter controversy between gens because marriage selection was by "legal appointment" rather than personal choice. If controversy could not be prevented, various methods were used to terminate it. First, disputes might be settled by destroying disputed property. Powell delighted in the observation that "purely personal property is inherited by the grave"—a phrase he used several times. Second, arbitration might take the form of an exchange of blows, providing that no one was maimed or killed. Third, a periodic festival might provide a day of amnesty.

Although Powell provided no citations or references for his discussion of Native American law, he was clearly drawing on materials collected by bureau ethnologists. The paradigm he was using remained that of Maine and Morgan, but even so, ethnography was beginning to shake the evolutionary edifice, albeit ever so gently. Powell's legal criteria placed Native Americans squarely in the upper stages of barbarism (where, indeed, Morgan had originally placed the Iroquois), but the paradigmatic *Ancient Society* had placed them in the lower stages, legislation originating with the ancient Greeks.

For the bureau ethnographer in the field, such issues were academic. Internal evidence suggests that Dorsey, for one, was working with some kind of checklist in his inquiry into Omaha law, but it was not provided by the bureau, as far as we know, and may have been derived simply from discussions with other fieldworkers or from reading their accounts. It may have been prompted by questions from Powell on his manuscript. Whatever the case, Dorsey recorded: No, there was no slavery among the Omaha; no, none had ever killed an affine; no, there was no set scale in the compensation to be paid to kin. Whatever their provenance, issues in comparative law were clearly on the agenda.

Dorsey had no problem in classifying law among the Omaha as personal, property, corporate, government, international, military, and religious law, following Powell in adopting the categories of contemporary American jurisprudence. After remarking that a large part of personal law was gentile or family law, he dismissed marriage and incest in three sentences before passing on to topics that were for him, as a missionary, more interesting: witchcraft, maiming, slander, adultery, prostitution, pederasty, and rape. He paid little attention to government law: two sentences on the buffalo hunt.

Wars of Resistance

Bureau descriptions of Native American warfare diverged both from the practical knowledge of frontiersmen—with their tales of torture, scalping, and counting coups—and from the visions of evolutionary theorists. Native Americans in their "natural state," unprovoked by Euro-Americans, were deemed pacific, law-abiding peoples. Not until the United States embarked on its overseas adventures and the pacification of colonial indigenes were Native Americans again viewed as "by nature" warlike and hostile. When this occurred, a whole new scientific taxonomy of the primitive was constructed to rationalize the brutal actions needed to impose law and order.

It would be misleading to suggest that the bureau ethnologists provided a theoretically coherent analysis of warfare. The institution and its members reflected the contradictions of a rapidly changing society, within which they comprised a somewhat tangled ideological strand. Their earlier training as geologists, soldiers, missionaries, or journalists engendered very different attitudes toward the Indian warrior. Yet, by and large, their portrayal of Native American warfare as a protective industry contributed to the favorable light in which most strove to have the subject peoples viewed. When some Native Americans, unreconciled to reservation life, took up arms in 1890, the credibility of the bureau's image of the law-abiding Indian was sorely tested. To an increasingly politicized dialogue James Mooney brought political realism, first by reporting the political views of the Native Americans themselves and then by producing a narrative and through it an explanation of what was occurring.

Like Powell and Dorsey, Mooney had been raised in the Midwest, acquiring his interest in Native Americans through occasional attendance at a Quaker college. Politically, he was active in Irish-American affairs, organizing and directing a branch of the Land League in Indiana. Mooney's interest in things Irish—and most of these were particularly political—ran in harness with his Native American research at the bureau, where he served an apprenticeship under Dorsey. Office conversations with John Swanton were more often than not about socialism or the Irish struggle for independence.[13]

Mooney was even more prone than most to question the utility of evolutionary theory and Powell's sociological paradigm. For three successive seasons beginning in 1885 he worked with the Cherokee in North Carolina. The Cherokee were famous for their resistance to a forced march along the Trail of Tears to the reservations of the 1830s, and Mooney reconstructed this experience from interviews. Ever the realist, he also interviewed the soldiers who had been involved in the action. He also reconstructed, through census data, the high mortality rate of the Cherokee once on the reservation, incidentally contributing to medical research on consumption. Mooney also collected folktales among isolated Carolina mountain folk, recognizing their affinity with the peasantry of the British Isles but explaining their social organization as "developed by the environment and isolation into something distinctively American" (1889:95). Both bodies of research bear testimony to Mooney's gift of genuine immersion in the conditions and problems of those among whom he lived and worked, whether Native Americans or rural people, or for that matter, government agents and military men. Each, for Mooney, had knowledge and beliefs and acted in specific ways. He was concerned to inquire into how the events of the past and present came about, and part of his answer lay in the understanding individuals had of the situations in which they found themselves.

Mooney followed the same field practice in what became a classic inquiry into the Ghost Dance and the Sioux uprising of 1890, which culminated in the massacre at Wounded Knee. He placed evidence collected from participants alongside that of Indian agents, army officers, law officers, and ranchers. He then analyzed all this along with the documents produced by commissions of inquiry, giving each of them equal weight as he recreated the sequence of events in an effort to arrive at both an explanation and an understanding of what had happened. "The Ghost Dance Religion and the Sioux Outbreak of 1890," published in the bureau's annual report for 1896, was the result.

Mooney began his inquiry in December 1890 with four months' fieldwork among the Arapaho, Cheyenne, Kiowa, Comanche, Apache, Caddo, and Wichita in western Indian Territory (Oklahoma). All were partially under the influence of the new movement. He then returned to Washington to examine documents in the Indian Office and the War Department, after which he set out for the Walker Lake Reservation in Nevada to interview Wovoka (Jack Wilson), said to be the instigator of the new prophetic religion. After a successful interview, he talked with neighboring ranchers and then carried an account of his meeting with Wovoka back to friends among the Arapaho and Cheyenne.

Mooney's sympathy for the prophet's cause is apparent. From the start he viewed it as a millenary movement, recognizing its universal features and placing it in a familiar world of poetry and romance:

> The wise men tell us that the world is growing happier—that we live longer than did our fathers, have more of comfort and less of toil, fewer wars and discords, and higher hopes and aspirations. So say the wise men; but deep in our hearts we know they are wrong. For were not we, too, born in Arcadia, and have we not—each one of us—in that May of life when the world was young, started out lightly and airily along the path that led through green meadows to the blue mountains on the distant horizon, beyond which lay the great world we were to conquer? And though others dropped behind, have we not gone on through morning brightness and noonday heat, with eyes always steadily forward, until the fresh grass began to be parched and withered, and the way grew hard and stony, and the blue mountains resolved into the grey rocks and thorny cliffs? And when at last we reached the toilsome summits, we found the glory that had lured us onward was only the sunset glow that fades into darkness while we look, and leaves us at the very goal to sink down, tired in body and sick at heart, with strength and courage gone, to close our eyes and dream again, not of the fame and fortune that were to be ours, but only of the old-time happiness that we have left so far behind.

As with men so it is with nations. . . . [W]hen the race lies crushed and
groaning beneath an alien yoke, how natural is the dream of a redeemer, an
Arthur, who shall return from exile or awake from some long sleep to drive
out the usurper and win back for his people what they have lost. The hope
becomes a faith and the faith becomes the creed of priests and prophets,
until the hero is god and the dream a religion, looking to some great miracle
of nature for its culmination and accomplishment. (Mooney 1896:1)

Mooney traced the origin of the Ghost Dance among the Sioux to
Wovoka, noting in passing the approval given him by nearby Mormons.
Men from neighboring tribes visited the prophet and returned home to
spread his doctrine. Like him, many were employed on ranches and
trading posts, and the message was one both of conservation of the old
and peaceful coexistence with the new.

Mooney did not attempt to explain why the movement spread among
some tribes but not others. Even among the Sioux (on whom the army
exacted vicious reprisals), only a minority embraced the new religion,
and Mooney attributed violence and resistance among them to a few
dissident chiefs. As he saw it, the causal factors in the chain of events
leading to the massacre of men, women, and children at Wounded Knee
were government action in withholding the meat ration from starving
Indians, the inexperience of certain Indian agents, the army's overreac-
tion, and in the final incident, the anger of a few Sioux braves and the
savage reprisals certain troopers exacted when their comrades were
killed. Ultimately, both "natives" and "whites" were found wanting.

Mooney's account of the Ghost Dance contributed to later theoretical analyses of resistance movements as "religions of the oppressed"
(Lanternari 1963).[14] Further research also disclosed errors of detail. Anthony Wallace (1965) chose to abridge Mooney's "classic" study by
omitting his discussion of similar religious movements elsewhere and
his theoretical remarks, tailoring the work to a narrower vision of
anthropology than Mooney's. It was of momentous significance that
Mooney interviewed those who had taken part in the movement and
the massacre, and shared with them a perception of the relevance and
meaning of each. On the frontier of professionalism, Mooney achieved
a cosmopolitical frame of reference that the academy would deny to the
anthropology of politics for several generations to come.

The uprising of 1890 interrupted Mooney's work among the Cherokee and threatened the scientific reputation of Powell's bureau.[15] While
the initiative had been Mooney's, Powell had been receptive to his suggestion that the Ghost Dance be studied, perhaps sensing that the uprising was a response to the same commercial threats to the environment

that earlier had provoked his own battle for irrigation rights in the arid lands. While Mooney rationalized resistance in Indian Territory, Powell fought expanding business interests in Washington. Shortly afterward, Powell was forced to resign. "Congressmen and many western mining, timber and land barons had never liked the politics the major promulgated" (Stegner 1954; Colby 1977:287).

This political context explains why the bureau's first commissioned work, used in manuscript by all who worked there, was not published until 1897. It was an account by Charles C. Royce of the treaties Native American tribes and nations had made with the federal government. A seminal study in land cessions and the politics of population movement, it became the first study of international law in ethnology. Such an inquiry into the legal relations of the federal government was not without its hazards. Powell had enumerated the benefits civilization had brought to Native Americans under the laws of acculturation; Royce documented a less benign set of circumstances. Of the Cherokee, for example, he wrote that their very existence as a people had for two hundred years been maintained against the unscrupulous rapacity of Anglo-Saxon civilization and that their removal to reservations had "turned the Cherokee back in the calendar of progress and civilization at least a quarter of a century" (1884:375). Powell's delay in publishing Royce's *Indian Land Cessions in the United States* (1889) and his prefatorial laundering of it accompanied his ultimate withdrawal, under political pressure, from public affairs (Hinsley 1981). Intended as a guide to policy, Royce's study was belatedly published as "strictly ethnologic" (Powell 1884).

Mooney lived on to fight another day. His career after Powell's resignation led him more and more into the political arena. He became even more active in Native American legal affairs and in the Irish Home Rule struggle. In his thinking he moved even farther away from evolutionism toward ethnohistory, toward a comparative ethnological framework that did not restrict itself to savages, and toward a scientific scholarship based on meticulous research in the field. This trajectory led Mooney, and the bureau as a whole, toward a confrontation with both the federal bureaucracy and the new academic anthropology of Franz Boas. Their respective approaches to North American political organization are the subject matter of the next chapter.

THE BRITISH TRADITION

By the last quarter of the nineteenth century, an intellectual maelstrom had developed in England as the evolutionary ideas of the Victorians gave way to a flourishing philosophical idealism. Several of its features contributed to social anthropology as it was fashioned in the twentieth century. Utilitarian and contract theories "won out," as it were. Among their prominent features were: (1) methodological collectivism or holism, (2) discernment of the origin of institutions in meaningful actions, (3) a concentration on the differences between the social and natural sciences, and (4) an intellectual concern with the relation of the individual to society (Collini 1978).[16]

The work of the leading idealists (D. G. Ritchie, F. H. Bradley, and Bernard Bosanquet) contributed a Hegelian notion of political unity, but their emphasis on the state generated an opposition that contributed more to political anthropology than did the ideas themselves. Intellectually and institutionally, their connections lay with historical jurisprudence, and the writings of Sir Henry Maine between 1861 and 1890 epitomized the philosophical and historical political anthropology that might have been. Community studies (Chapter 4) were an explicit expression of these connections.

As it was, the science of anthropology was created out of a compromise between a group of men with largely historical and antiquarian interests and a group of Darwinian natural scientists. The founding of the British Association for the Advancement of Science celebrated the dominance of the latter. The formation within the British Association of a special section for anthropology (Section H) encouraged the members of the conservatively inclined Anthropological Society of London to collaborate with the natural scientists of the London Ethnological Society, and in 1871 the Anthropological Institute of Great Britain and Ireland was founded.[17]

It was by no means certain at this time that a vision would prevail of anthropology as a comparative study of the savage races that were not sufficiently advanced in civilization to have histories. Yet it was the institutionalization of anthropology as a vehicle for this group of scholars, who drew their ideas and ideologies from the intellectual currents of the Victorian era, that began to shape the new anthropology. Throughout this era the new science of anthropology depended on the unprofessional interests of the amateur: the traveler, collector, trader, administrator, and missionary. The elite of amateur science strove to circumscribe a profession, but they were dependent on the patronage and privileged social ties of many who did not share their disciplined view of ethnology as a science. The former group's determined effort to domesticate the amateur ethnographer resulted only in an uneasy truce between them.

The publication in 1874 of *Notes and Queries*, a vade mecum for the enthusiastic amateur, was a self-proclaimed professional manifesto. Even as the era of Britain's Second Imperialism dawned, they hoped that the man-on-the-spot—"travellers and residents in uncivilized lands" (BAAS 1874:1)—would contribute to the new science. Their objectives were extractive, even exploitive: "to promote accurate anthropological observation on the part of travellers, and to enable those who are not anthropologists themselves to supply the information which is wanted for the scientific study of anthropology at home" (BAAS 1874:1). *Notes and Queries* reflected the span of the new science, ranging from Darwin on the "Constitution of Man" to Tylor on history and culture. Edward Brabrook wrote on government, law, and crime, and Augustus Lane-Fox Pitt-Rivers on war. Morals, property, and slavery were also addressed. A final section discussed methods. The volume expressed above all else a dissatisfaction with the existing anthropological record as the descriptive base of a science. Moreover, the "rapid extermination of savages at the present time, and the rapidity with which they are being reduced to the standard of European manners" rendered their study a matter of some urgency (BAAS 1874:1).

The first ethnographic surveys funded by the British Association were nevertheless conducted not in savage societies but in English and Irish rural communities. They were a response to the emergence of a rapidly industrializing, urbanizing, relocating population of industrial workers whose volatility threatened the social order. Intellectual resistance to surveys in 1893 resulted not from an objection to the study of peoples who were not savages but to the extensive use of the statistical method. "Men have to be weighed, not counted," the humanists contended.

The association had come into being to foster a recognition of the contribution the social sciences might make to government policy and practice (Thackray and Morrell 1981), but it was singularly unsuccessful as far as anthropology was concerned. Little government funding flowed in its direction, and the ethnological inquiries of the late Victorian era were financed by universities (the Torres Straits Expedition), by industrialists (the Jessup Expedition), by the overseas colonies,[18] or by the association itself. Tylor, doyen of Britain's academic establishment, was left with no illusions about the government's attitude to his "reformer's science." "If we talked of working a government institution in England for the progress of anthropology in the way in which it is being done [in Washington]," Tylor wrote, "we should be met with—silence, or a civil answer, but with no practical result; and anyone venturing to make the suggestion might run the risk of being classed with that large body described here as 'cranks'" (1884:92). Nevertheless, toward the end of the nineteenth century, two of Britain's oldest possessions, India and Canada, raised substantive problems that invited anthropological research. The case of India is the most illuminating because it involved categorizing the people of that vast civilization, already familiar to British civil servants and laymen through the historical studies of Sir Henry Maine. But the research that entered the mainstream, capturing the anthropological imagination, was that carried out in Canada by a German scholar, Franz Boas.

Harnessing the Amateur

Edward Brabrook wrote the guidelines for recording scientific data on government, law, and crime in the first edition of *Notes and Queries* (1874). Apart from the fact that he was a lawyer, it is not apparent why he was given the task. As a former member of the Cannibal Club (the inner clique around the Anthropological Society's founder, James Hunt), Brabrook led the antiquarian faction within the new Anthropological Institute (Van Keuren 1982). Authorship may have been a reward for his vote for amalgamation. As a member of the English gentry, his politics were conservative and magisterial. His entry on government appears somewhat untutored, indicating a scholarly awareness of neither evolutionary theory (and this, of course, may have been deliberate on his part) nor the comparative method of historical jurisprudence. His interest lay in civilizations, not savage societies, and he encouraged notetaking under only three headings: Head of Government, Inferior Offices, and Counselors or Ministers. His "government" was to be found only in the state, which he considered universal, and only in formal officeholding.

As might be expected, *crimen laesae majestatis* had a prominent place in his consideration of crime, although homicide, suicide, arson, abduction, and unnatural offenses also attracted his attention. Brabrook's preamble to his section on crime suggests a magistrate's predilection for a systemic view of justice: "Even the rudest communities have something approaching an unwritten criminal code. *The administration of justice readily conforms itself to system,* and unconsciously crime and punishment fall into relation with each other. Inquiry will be made under this head as to what acts are regarded as criminal (a) against person, (b) against property, (c) against the state, (d) against religion; and the reason why they are so regarded" (Brabrook 1874:46, emphasis added).

Under the subhead "Laws" Brabrook dealt with procedures in the administration of justice relating to land, game, inheritance, the administration of justice, and punishments. His English gentry affiliation could not have been clearer. Indeed, his social background and his interest in Indian civilization provided the only launching pad he had to offer the aspiring ethnographer. Although the announced goal of *Notes and Queries* was to liberate the observer from his own socially formed preconceptions, guidelines for the study of government, law, and crime were quintessentially gentrified English.

This remained true until the end of the century. Further editions of *Notes and Queries* were published in 1892 and 1899. Brabrook acquired a string of letters after his name and was elected president of the Anthropological Institute in 1895. By this time Britain was well embarked upon the colonization of "savage" Africa, and other handbook entries had changed quite dramatically. Not so those on government, law, and crime. A few small additions reflected new ethnography coming out of the Dark Continent, but by and large, Brabrook's Orientalist entries stood, and apparently no one sought to have them changed.

On War

While American ethnology was faced in the 1870s with a situation in which armed resistance was part of the observed life of the peoples studied, British anthropology remained committed to an evolutionary analysis of warfare based on material culture. The colonized were certainly fighting—this was an era of resistance to pacification throughout the British Empire—but neither the Foreign Office nor the Colonial Office was supportive of anthropological research into the phenomenon. Captain Lane-Fox, in his magisterial note on warfare in *Notes and Queries* (1874), did not encourage the amateurs to send in their observations, as was done elsewhere in the volume, but implicitly to send in specimens of armaments, as his interest lay in weaponry and in what this might reveal about the evolution of society. That British and American approaches to warfare were so far apart at this time was due not to contrasts in the political experiences of the two countries but to the fact that government funds had impelled American ethnology from the museum to the field, while in Britain progress rested on amateurs in the field responding to a scholar whose interests were antiquarian.

If Brabrook's ethnological credentials were somewhat dubious, those of Lane-Fox Pitt-Rivers were not.[19] He (like Tylor) had been a member of both the Anthropological Society of London and the London Ethnological Society. As conflict heightened between them, he (again like Tylor) chose to align with the professionalizing natural scientists. His interests lay in archaeology and material culture, and his thinking, unlike Brabrook's, was evolutionary. As a young captain in the Grenadier Guards he had begun a collection of weapons that by 1890 contained over 14,000 items. Its acquisition by Oxford University provided the grounds on which a lectureship in anthropology was established and given to Tylor.[20]

Pitt-Rivers not only demonstrated the processes by which cultural evolution occurred but also self-consciously and explicitly voiced the social implications of his discovery. His lifetime spanned the uncertainties that industrialism bequeathed on a member of the landed gentry, conscious of struggles between the classes so severe that its own prime minister described the queen's realm as "Two Nations." A Tory, Pitt-Rivers recognized the implications of an anthropology that advocated conservatism and gradualism not only for the abstract world of ideas but also for the real world of the working class. In 1888 he suggested to his fellow academicians: "Anything which tends to impress the mind with the slow growth and stability of human institutions and industries, and their dependence upon antiquity, must, I think, contribute to check revolutionary ideas, and the tendency which now exists, and which is encouraged by some who should know better, to break drastically with the past, and must help to inculcate conservative principles, which are urgently needed at the present time, if the civilisation that we enjoy is to be maintained and to be permitted to develop itself" (quoted in Van Keuren 1982:153). In the intervening years he had seen: the franchise extended to the workingman; Gladstone's promise of home rule to Ireland; the foundation of the Socialist Democratic Federation in London by Marx's translator, H. M. Hyndman; the beginnings of the Fabian Society; and the advocacy of state socialism by a group of British intellectuals.

Regardless of his personal and political dilemmas, or perhaps because of the edge they gave to his intellectual pursuits, Pitt-Rivers's contribution to *Notes and Queries* in 1874 (reprinted virtually without alteration in 1892 and 1899) was vastly superior to that of any other ethnologist. Tylor (indebted to Pitt-Rivers in so many ways) carried his message to the United States, addressing the Anthropological Society of Washington in the following manner:

> The principle of development in civilization which represents one side of the great problem I have been speaking of, is now beginning to receive especial cultivation in England. While most museums have been at work, simply collecting objects and implements, the museum of General Pitt-

Rivers, now about to be removed from London to Oxford, is entirely devoted to the working out of the development theory on a scale hardly attempted hitherto. In this museum are collected specimens of weapons and implements, so as to ascertain by what steps they may be considered to have arisen among mankind, and to arrange them in consecutive series. Development, however, is not always progress, but may work itself out into lines of degeneration. There are certain states of society in which the going-down of arts and sciences is as inevitable a state of things as progress is in the more fortunate regions in which we live. Anthropologists will watch with the greatest interest what effect this museum of development will have upon their science. Gen. Pitt-Rivers was led into the formation of the remarkable collection in question in an interesting manner. He did not begin life either as an evolutionist or as an anthropologist. He was a soldier. His business, at a particular time of his life, was to serve on a committee on small-arms, appointed to reform the armament of the British army, which at that time was to a great extent only provided with the most untrustworthy of percussion-muskets. He then found that a rifle was an instrument of gradual growth; for the new rifles which it was his duty to inspect had not come into existence at once and independently. When he came to look carefully into the history of his subject, it appeared that some one had improved the lock, then some one the rifling, and then others had made further improvements; and this process had gone on until at last there came into existence a gun, which, thus perfected, was able to hold its own in a permanent form. He collected the intermediate stages through which a good rifle arose out of a bad one; and the idea began to cross his mind that the course of change which happened to rifles was very much what ordinarily happens with other things. So he set about collecting, and filled his house from the cellar to the attic, hanging on his walls series of all kinds of weapons and other instruments which seemed to him to form links in a great chain of development. The principle that thus became visible to him in weapon-development is not less true through the whole range of civilization; and we shall soon be able to show to every anthropologist who visits Oxford the results of that attempt. And when the development theory is seen in that way, explaining the nature and origin of our actual arts and customs and ideas, and their gradual growth from ruder and earlier states of culture, then anthropology will come before the public mind as a new means of practical instruction in life. (Tylor 1884:90–91)

Tylor was speaking of a man's lifework, a man, moreover, who had devoted his life to the singleminded analysis of the evolution of weaponry in an age when most of his fellows were making their exploratory way from the physical to the social sciences, from the laboratory to the university lecture hall. Pitt-Rivers's materialist concerns, inherited from his evolutionary forebears, were shortly to be lost to the anthropological study of politics.

Pitt-Rivers first published his analysis of the gradual processes of cultural evolution in 1867. After inheriting the estate of his paternal grandmother's brother, the second Baron Rivers, in 1879, he began to consolidate his position within anthropological circles. Ultimate recognition came with his election to the presidency of the Anthropological Institute in 1876. Posthumous accord was given his work by John Linton Myres (a lecturer in classical archaeology at Oxford, where he was largely responsible for introducing anthropology), who set out to argue its utility in the service of the state. Myres edited Pitt-Rivers's lectures and posthumously published them as *The Evolution of Culture and Other Essays* in 1906.

In spite of his reception at the turn of the century, for recent and contemporary authorities on warfare such as Harry Holbert Turney-High (1949, 1981), Keith Otterbein (1973), and William Divale (1971), Augustus Lane-Fox Pitt-Rivers might never have lived.[21] Yet for those whose intellectual and revolutionary contributions to Victorian England Pitt-Rivers most feared, his very life and work vindicated a central principle of their philosophy. The history of ethnology in Britain bore out Marx's contention that advances in invention and technology have appeared first in the military arts and only later in society at large.

Partly because of its close association with archaeology and museum collections, partly because of its reliance for evidence on travelers' tales of the savage peoples through whose territory they passed, partly because of the search for theories attributing the origin of political society to conquest, and partly because of the increasing evidence all around that a passage from militarism to industrialism was open to question, the anthropological study of warfare at the turn of the century epitomized the transformation taking place both in the discipline and in the world at large. By 1898 ethnological museums were ceding pride of place to the universities. The global reporting of amateurs was being denigrated by professionals. A search for origins was being replaced by the recognition of contact and diffusion. Above all, the climax of the industrial revolution augured a new military fervor, which at the turn of the century was linked to the acquisition of dependent territories overseas. With this, the question of the applicability of the science of anthropology and its practicality in the service of government became the burning question of the new era.

Political Ethnology on the Imperial Frontier:
The Impress of India

One of the arguments of this study is that the objective world fashions the anthropology of politics as much as anthropology constructs and reconstructs the world in which its practitioners find themselves. This was particularly manifest in the sunset years of the Victorian era. The construction of autonomous disciplines was in its infancy, and the ethnographic revolution contributed to the redrawing of the "map of learning." But ethnography had deep roots, and the deeper the roots, the greater the unconscious assimilation of nonacademic constructions of knowledge. Nowhere was this more true than in the colonial ethnology of India, which has to be placed in the context both of British conservative and liberal traditions of laissez-faire economics and philosophies of progress, and of the immediate intense debate over the Land Question in Ireland. Anthropologists were to be found on both sides of the ideological divide, but at the end of the day, in practical terms, they found themselves practitioners of a discipline that had been deflected from the study of Indian civilization to the "simpler" societies of Africa. Here we are concerned with three features of Indian ethnology that entered the anthropological study of politics.

The Village Community. Britain first evinced her imperial interests in India through the East India Company in the eighteenth century, but the character of her rule changed markedly in the 1860s when in response to domestic industrial concerns India's economy was geared up to produce for the world market. This required greater penetration of the countryside by the colonial government and hence a programmatic understanding of the nature of the Indian agrarian structure. Long-standing classical delineations of "oriental despotism" were inadequate for this purpose; what was needed was a worldview that placed India and Europe within the same framework of explanation so that the possibility of patterning Indian progress on that achieved earlier in Europe might be exploited. This framework was supplied by comparative linguists who discerned an Indo-Aryan language community; by historians and jurisprudes (like Sir Henry Sumner Maine) who compared Indian village communities with those of Russia, Slavic Europe, and medieval England; and by anthropologists, like Tylor, who promoted the idea of "survivals."

Conservatism in Britain tended to idealize village communities as autonomous republics quite apart from the politics of the state in which they were enmeshed (Dewey 1972). Through the ages, conquest, including colonial conquest, had left them unscathed. In both English and Indian historiography, the village community became a romantic symbol, and "with new theories of linguistic race—the Indo-Aryan diaspora—and widespread acceptance of Sir Henry Maine's application of the comparative method—the European Past became the Indian Present: the Indian village became the early English village extant" (Dewey 1972:307).[22]

Maine quite explicitly elaborated an *historical* analysis of village communities in opposition to prevailing opinion: "I am aware that the popular impression [in England] is that Indian society is divided, so to speak, into a number of horizontal strata, each representing a caste. This is an entire mistake. . . . [C]aste is merely a name for trade and occupation, and the sole tangible effect of brahmanical theory is that it creates a religious sanction for what is really a primitive and natural distribution of classes" (1876:57).[23] Maine had served as a legal member of the Council of India for seven years before becoming a professor of jurisprudence at Oxford in 1869, and he rightly believed that he knew India at firsthand. Indeed, his field experience rendered his works on India (1871, 1875b, 1883, in particular) much richer in detail than the documentary sources on which his better-known *Ancient Law* (1861) rested.

In the 1870s the ethnology of India fell victim to British intellectual and political concern with the history of property, particularly its communal ownership. Maine, on the basis of the British imperial experience in India, specifically came down on the opposite side of the fence from Lewis Henry Morgan, whose views (1877) were quoted in a previous section. Whereas Morgan deplored the "unmanageable power of property" and "the property career" of mankind (1877:560–561), Maine considered the historical movement of property from collective to individual forms to be an undeniable advance. "No one is at liberty to attack several property," he wrote, "and to say at the same time he values civilization" (Feaver 1969:215). There are implications here for those who treasure Engels's advocacy of Morgan while failing to appreciate that Marx's position on the question was much closer to that of Maine. At the time, the utilitarian spirit in Tylor, when reviewing Maine's *Village-Communities in the East and West* from his Oxford armchair, condemned his romantic vision. Morgan, on the industrial frontier of New York State, in effect sustained it. Both Morgan and Maine advocated greater state (U.S. federal and British colonial) intervention in the countryside, the one to preserve, the other to transform their respective Indian agrarian cultures. Both were, in effect, ideologues on the frontiers of state expansion.

The adoption of an idealized vision of village communities by those who read Maine for the contemporary political implications of his findings or for its evolutionary message[24] created a precedent for the study not simply of political organization in India but of agrarian society worldwide. Hiding from view that which does not "fit" in the community (in India the Untouchables) proved to be a flaw with a future. Maine described Untouchables as forming "no part of the natural and organic aggregate to which the bulk of the villagers belong" (1876:127–128). In the tenor of his times, he believed this was because they represented a "population of alien blood ... too obstinately and obtrusively foreign to be completely absorbed" (1876:127–128). Underclasses are frequently overlooked by systems analysts.

Even while Maine was writing, an alternative vision existed. In India itself, B. H. Baden-Powell's 1892 critique of Maine's vision of village India and Baden-Powell's inversion of the historical movement of property from the collective to the individual (a much more politically acute observation, which struck at the heart of problems of aggrandizement and inheritance patterns) permitted a closer appreciation of political inequality and hierarchy within agrarian society and of the part played by landlords within it. Along with Frederic Maitland, a British economic historian working in a similar vein on the manorial system of Domesday England, Baden-Powell argued the dangers of applying British concepts of property to Indian society. Such a practice was, indeed, part of the trend that distanced other cultures from the evolutionary pinnacle attained by the colonial powers themselves and, in the long run, primitivized them.

It was also characteristic of the trend that saw anthropology professionalizing itself at the expense of its lay readership. "The man of education in those days knew more about India and Indian civilization then, than one does now: about the Aryans and about Sanskrit, about the Indian scriptures and about the code of Manu, about Indian villages and castes, about current controversies over Indian land law, taxation law and codification. India was part of English intellectual life, and perhaps had more influence on English thought than the strong continuing links with the United States, the weaker links with Canada and Australasia" (Mackenzie 1982:45). For this, Maine was largely responsible. His famous lecture on "The Effects of Observation of India on Modern European Thought" (1875b) did much to establish the place of comparative social science, politics, and anthropology in a late Victorian education. Ethnology's shift in focus toward physical anthropology and kinship (caste and tribe) deflected attention from the familiar, similar, and comparable to the exotic. Furthermore, the practical needs of the Indian Civil Service, in the form of a census of the population, helped solidify the categories used in Indian ethnology thereafter. Not until 1946 did India again become prominent in the anthropology of politics (Chapter 5).

History and Science. A word needs to be said about Maine's contribution to what has come to be called *the* comparative method. The word is revisionist—and a divided revisionism at that (Bock 1974; Collini, Winch, and Burrow 1984). This is no small matter for political anthropology, since a failure to distinguish between two modes of practicing the comparative method led to a misreading of some of its applications. The modes may be described as the linguistic-historical and the socio-logical-evolutionary. Maine's use of the comparative method falls into the first category (along with that of Robertson Smith, Frederic Maitland, Franz Boas, and Max Weber) and must today still be viewed as an alternative subterranean tradition.[25]

At Cambridge, Maine lectured on ancient law, village communities, and early institutions. A leading figure in comparative and historical jurisprudence, his talks drew on his firsthand knowledge of India, Sanskritic law, and litigation. He used his erudition in the tradition of a fellow Scot, Adam Ferguson, to compare classical Roman and newly discovered Irish (Brehon) institutions, laws, and customs with those of India. Custom united Maine and Tylor, but Tylor's expansive generalizing science was, by and large, addressed to a different audience.

What was critically different between Maine's study of institutions using the comparative method and anthropological practice under the same name was, first, his focus on similarity and continuity, theirs on contrasts and divergences; second, his closure of his field of inquiry to that which was historically related, their decontextualizing (historically and spatially) in their unbounded pursuit of the ethnographic instance; third, and most important, his recognition of complexity, theirs of simplicity. Finally, whereas he looked for process, they looked at form. In Maine's writings, "adherence to 'history' was deep, the language of 'science' usually perfunctory" (Collini, Winch, and Burrow 1984:213).

In the early 1880s another lawyer with an historical rather than an evolutionary bent was also addressing himself to the ethnology of Indian society.[26] His sources were the works of the very administrator-ethnologists whose writing briefly entered academic anthropology at the turn of the century. Sir John Budd Phear's *The Aryan Village in India and Ceylon* (1880) and Sir Henry Maine's *Lectures on the Early History of Institutions* (1875) were foremost among them. Sir John Lubbock's

The Origin of Civilization and the Primitive Condition of Man (1870) also helped shape his thinking, as did, of course, Morgan's *Ancient Society* (1877). Common to all was the acceptance of certain "motors" of change: war, the domestication of animals, and the private ownership of property.

What was most problematic for those who were reading Indian ethnology at the time was comparative kinship. Easy transitions from kin to territory as the basis of political community, from the simple to the complex in terms of technology and the economy, and from the supernatural to science in the growth of knowledge were dashed on the rocks of Indian civilization. Its monuments were colossal, its Sanskritic lore erudite, its caste system anomalous. Two alternatives existed. India could either be situated on an evolutionary path distinct from that followed by Europe (an Asiatic road) or it could be assimilated into a conquest theory of the origin of the state and civilization.

Karl Marx, the lawyer in question, adopted the first course. It is not clear exactly what Marx was about as he worked on his ethnological notebooks in the British Museum between 1880 and his death in 1884. It remains uncertain whether India provided the colonial ethnography he required for a critique of imperialism as an integral part of capitalism; whether he was moving toward a study of "the peripheries of capitalism"; whether he was delineating a precursor or alternative to western European capitalism; or whether he was seeking "facts" on which to model an analysis of a shift from industrial to finance capitalism (Vincent 1985). What is clear, however, is that he was a man at work in the spirit of his times, because India was in the forefront of late Victorian scholarly and practical interests.

Ethnology's view of India had been shaped by its relations with more dominant fields of study—philology and jurisprudence as the Victorian era opened and physical anthropology as it closed. Each reflected political shifts in the objective colonial world between successive phases in a changing capitalism. Knowledge couched in the language of race and ethnicity served Britain's imperialism at the beginning of the new century even as nationalism, internationalism, and its counterparts struggled to be born. For a short while, and then intermittently, Asiatic ethnology offered an alternative to anthropology's seemingly inevitable trend toward focusing on kinship and the primitive. By 1901, it too had passed.

Race and Caste. Conquest theory developed in Europe after 1880 (as it happens, the date of the Congress of Berlin). It provided a scientific rationale for associating progress with imperial conquest and required a certain rethinking of the "natural conditions" of pacific peoples, as with Native Americans. But nowhere was isolation from European contact viewed more often as an impediment to progress than in India, the jewel in Victoria's imperial crown. And nothing was seen to be more uniquely characteristic of India than the inequities of its caste system. A view of the Indian village community as a political society of egalitarian co-owners of land opened the era; a view of the subcontinent as ridden by stratified castes concluded it. Yet substantive data on the state, caste, and even slavery were ever present in the accounts of the Indian civil service officers on whom the scholars depended (Dumont 1966).

As anthropology became professional, it drew closer to the administrators of the imperial possession, the man-on-the-spot. By 1900, colonial civil servants made up 9 percent of the membership of the Anthropological Institute in London (Van Keuren 1982), and most had served in India. Sir Herbert Risley, a former member of the Bengal Civil Service, became its president. At Cambridge, A. H. Keane, a professor of Hindustani, instructed Indian Civil Service cadets and wrote an introductory textbook, *Ethnology*. Views on caste in India—whether they were held by philologists like Keane or colonial civil servants—were colored by assumptions of its origins in racial difference, particularly between Aryan peoples and those whom they had conquered.[27] They were also related to the way in which information about the caste system was collected.

Risley, using the first edition of *Notes and Queries* (1874), was explicit about the difficulty of distinguishing minutely between administrative utility and scientific interest in the Indian government's census procedures (1890–91). To him,

> a caste was a 'thing', an entity, which was concrete and measurable; above all it had definable characteristics—endogamy, commensality rules, fixed occupation, common ritual practices. These were things which supposedly one could find out by sending assistants into the field with a questionnaire and which could be quantified for reports and surveys; or one could learn about the castes of a particular district by sitting on one's horse or in the shade of a village banyan tree as the adjunct of one's official duty. What was recorded could be collated so that the Lohars, or the Ahirs, or the Mahishyas, or the Okkaligas could be pigeon-holed and one could then go on to the next group to be described. This way of thinking about a particular caste was useful to the administrator, because it gave the illusion of knowing the people; he did not have to differentiate too much among individual Indians—a man was a Brahman, and Brahmans had certain characteristics. . . . Not only could one know a 'people' by knowing their caste and what its customs and rules were; what one 'knew' could be reduced to hard facts. (Cohn 1968:15–16)

The results of this method of understanding Indian society can be seen most clearly in the first volume of Risley's *The Tribes and Castes of Bengal* (1892) and his book *The People of India* (1908). He provided a gazeteerlike account of each caste and a series of maps showing their distribution throughout the subcontinent. Using two hundred official and nonofficial correspondents scattered throughout Bengal, his object was to collect as many independent observations as possible so that others might later apply the comparative method. The urgency of the proceeding is suggested by a fellow administrator who worked on the census with him: "We in India have an inexhaustible store-house of facts at our very doors, and unequalled facilities for ascertaining and recording them. Every year sees some of the existing material disappear under the powerful solvent of contact with European thought and the appliances of civilization. We are probably too near our subject to generalize with success; but we, and we alone, can obtain the facts from which generalizations can be made" (Ibbetson 1892:188). The "we" referred to in Ibbetson's memorandum were the 188 census officials. Of these, 34 were named ex officio, 24 bore British names, and 130 appear to have been Indians.[28]

Risley's official, racial view of caste in India was to have long-term consequences for the study of political organization throughout the subcontinent. The extent to which the census procedures reflected an objective reality was questioned even at the time. In an appendix to Risley's 1892 study, Denzil Ibbetson observed that the product was a crystalization of a social and political situation very much in flux. This flux, he believed, represented not a progressive movement from an immediate, simple past to an ordered present but competition within the Indian population itself; differences among caste members were as important as similarities. Unfortunately, Ibbetson was in a position to view the matter only as a procedural problem, and he engendered no alternative vision of Indian society.

Boas in Canada

The coastal peoples of the Canadian Pacific had been engaged in commercial trapping and trading and had worked for wage labor on ships and in trading posts for some years before 1858, when major European settlement began.[29] By the 1870s a trade with museums and private collectors had developed in "traditional" ceremonial and utilitarian items. Sometime around the 1880s, lay ethnohistorians and ethnographers were at work among their own people, while at more or less the same time Northwest Coast teams gave public exhibitions of their native dances in Germany, Chicago, St. Louis, and New York, appearing at museums, expositions, and world's fairs (Knight 1978).

To this coast the British Association for the Advancement of Science dispatched the Jessup Expedition in 1884. It was jointly funded by the association, the Canadian government, and the Canadian industrialist after whom it was named. Its objective was to survey the entire coastal region, collecting information on the differences between groups, and it was conducted by a German ethnographer who had earlier worked in British Columbia for three months: Franz Boas. Boas's early work was shaped by the research directives of Horatio Hale, a philologist (Gruber 1967; Cole 1973), although all attempts at the reconstruction of indigenous Kwakiutl culture were constantly assaulted by the events going on all around, including those related to secret societies, social institutions, tribal government, land tenure, and the like (Gruber 1967).

Political organization among the coastal peoples, in Boas's view, may at first have been related to kinship. Tylor (a member of the expedition's committee) gave him an advance copy of his paper on statistical correlations among the institutions of a culture (Stocking 1974), with its suggestion that shifts from matriliny to patriliny "promoted extensive political networks" (Adams 1981:365). Whether Boas ever saw or used the 1874 edition of *Notes and Queries* is not known. Tylor, in his capacity as expedition director, may have drawn it to his attention. The fact of the matter is that the ranked kin groups Boas found along the coast in 1886—corporate descent groups that traced their genealogies through seven generations—existed in a milieu dominated by Christianity and commerce. It was their ranked relationship rather than their form or function that forced itself upon the ethnographer, a tendency accentuated, perhaps, by Boas's dependence on George Hunt's texts, which led him to place particular emphasis on names, ranks, and titles. Rank was acquired by means of a ceremonial giving away of property, so Boas's attention was drawn to the Kwakiutl potlatch—at the expense, perhaps, of other motors of political inequality within Kwakiutl society.[30] Although he refers to nobles and slaves and suggests differences of class within the population at large, Boas found his co-workers and informants mostly among Kwakiutl families known to Hunt, which were notable for their economic and political enterprise. Together they probably reconstructed a more homogeneous Kwakiutl "culture" than had ever existed on the Northwest Coast. Boas's focus on rank among the Kwakiutl may well have reflected, indeed, their concern for "rank" in the traditional world and "class" in the modern (Cannizzo 1983).

The Northwest Coast potlatch has become an ethnographic chestnut roasted in the embers of successive bursts of anthropological theorizing. Drucker and Heizer (1967) have suggested that only the derivation of the term *potlatch* from the Chinook verb that means *to give* unites all potlatch scholars. Above the fray, Boas never once changed his first interpretation of it. From the start, he placed the many potlatches Hunt and he attended both in Fort Rupert and elsewhere squarely in the realm of political economy. The potlatch was a method of acquiring rank. "This is done by . . . the distribution of property. This custom has been described often, but it has been thoroughly misunderstood by most observers. The underlying principle is that of the interest-bearing investment of property" (1895/1925:77).

A potlatch was organized in Fort Rupert in the winter of 1894–95 for the transmission of the highest value copper then existing among the Kwakiutl. It was valued at 7,500 blankets. Watching it, Boas conducted what appears to have been a hurriedly concluded interview with an informant about "the way to be walked by a true chief." He describes the career ladder of an aspiring Kwakiutl Indian in "The Order of a Chief's Potlatches." The potlatches Boas observed were also manifestations of rivalry between, as he put it, "chiefs and clans." This rivalry reached its "strongest expression" not in the giving but in the destruction of property.

In the course of his later publications, further details about potlatches emerged from Boas's transcripts of texts, speeches, and songs. Data on the potlatch is embedded in family histories and above all in a long document detailing the social and potlatching career of one distinguished Kwakiutl individual (Codere 1966). This material only saw the light of day between 1921 and 1925, toward the end of Boas's long career. For the first twenty years of the new century, he promulgated the creed that the task of anthropology as a new science was to study culture subjectively: his aim was to present Kwakiutl culture as it appeared to the Native Americans themselves. In an act itself reminiscent of an extreme form of potlatch in which property is destroyed in order to demonstrate paramount rank, Boas "did not consider that he had a sufficient amount of reliable data as a basis for clear conclusions and interpretations, [and so] literally condemned to oblivion the first decade of his Northwest Coast publications [over 60 in number] including those on the Kwakiutl. He regarded his early work, especially that he did for the British Association as too hurried" (Codere 1966:13).

In 1884, two years before Boas's first summer of fieldwork, the potlatch had been made illegal by the Canadian government on the grounds that it was demoralizing and heathenish. The law was virtually impossible to enforce, as Boas's rich body of material shows. Its chief impact on Boas was to make it necessary for him to prove that he was not a government agent. In 1889 a Kwakiutl chief was convicted and sentenced to prison for potlatching, but the sentence was overturned on appeal, the judge finding the offense inadequately defined (Fisher 1977). Boas was among those active in calling for the law's repeal, but it was revised in 1895 and kept on the statute books.

Viewed in its historical context, the illegal potlatch might be seen as a product of European commerce as it reached the Pacific Coast, bearing the seeds of its own destruction. Fortunately, Boas was as well trained an observer as he was a reluctant analyst. Extant in his unpublished notes, censuses, family histories, seating plans, and the like is the raw material for an analysis of potlatch occurrences as political events. A synthesis may yet be made of the Fort Rupert potlatch that would justify a description of it as a competitive system. Whether its anticolonial dimensions can ever be fully explored is a different matter.

AMATEURS AND ACADEMICS

At the end of the nineteenth century in Britain, unlike the United States, academic anthropologists were still largely dependent on the "man-on-the-spot," to adopt a colonial phrase. Advances in postal, rail, and steamer communication made the continuous exchange of correspondence a worldwide reality, and the man and woman in the field conducted inquiries, mostly into kinship or religion, almost as the research agent of an armchair scholar at home. Ethnography by mail, however, as a professional academic technique, was open to manifest abuse. As funds became available for intensive field research and as universities began to grant their professors research leaves, the imaginative work of the armchair scholar, tidying up the loose ends of on-the-ground reality, came to be subjected to severe professional criticism. In a field in which theory so often followed ethnography, this ordering of data by the ethnologist was viewed at the time as professionalism. Today we may recognize in it what in Chapter 3 is labeled the Daisy Bates syndrome.

In the domain of politics, amateur ethnography permitted the reconstruction of the contact situation of the past. From John Wesley Powell's eye-witness account of the Utes in 1859, as we have seen, it was possible to discern emergent entrepreneurial leadership on the American frontier. Kanosh becomes the prototypical Native American capitalist, a self-made chief. At no later time did the professionals of the bureau explicitly concern themselves with the ethnography of such men, or with such politically significant phenomena.

The accurate and detailed reporting of persons and events in such nonprofessional accounts provides the raw material of the colonial ethnography that actually underlies a great deal of the anthropological record. For there is little twentieth-century anthropology that has not been colonial ethnography. Amateur accounts of "primitive societies," along with notebooks and diaries, have taken on new value. Some—a few—add to our professional knowledge of the political domain.

The downgrading of the observations that accompanied the professionalization of anthropology as a science and reports of missionaries, administrators, and traders did not pass without comment at the time. Mary Kingsley, who was reported to have been called upon for advice by Joseph Chamberlain, Britain's secretary of state for the colonies, wrote quite explicitly on the subject, and she was uniquely well placed to do so. Her influence was extensive. Bernard Porter actually described her as one of the first social anthropologists, as well as an early propagator of the concept of "indirect rule" (1968:150). Her writings as a traveler and trader in West Africa thrived in a cultural relativist ideal at the high point of imperial jingoism in Victorian Britain. She was partly responsible for shifting anthropological attention away from India toward Africa and the study of black races. Her ideas led the Anthropological Institute "to start abandoning their rather esoteric interest in the relics of the African past and begin moving towards the study of change in contemporary African cultures as part of the study of colonial administration" (Rich 1986:33).

As an intermediary between the man-on-the-spot (particularly her fellow traders) and the scientist, Mary Kingsley deplored the professional ethnological sojourner.[31] Since the amateur ethnographers are soon to be silenced in these pages, let Mary Kingsley have the last word. "Regarding the difficulty of getting reliable information upon native customs," she suggested, "it is not necessary for me to speak at great length, because it is now [1898] fully recognized by scientific students of the subject. The best way of surmounting the difficulty is for the ethnologist to go and study the mind of the native personally" but, because of the climate and other drawbacks in West Africa—the scene of her own extensive travels—this could not be done. "Yet, even if the professional did undertake this method," she argued, "it is still greatly to the student's advantage to compare his own collected information with that of men who have for years been resident in West Africa, and who are well acquainted with the native language, and who have had

opportunities of observing the native conduct under all sorts of difficulties, dangers, joys and sorrows—who have, as the old saying puts it,
summered and wintered among them" (1898:3). Of such residents, in
her opinion, the trader was particularly well placed to instruct the
ethnologist during his sojourn in African surroundings, and she provided an anecdote to show how easy it would be to misinterpret certain
happenings. It serves as a reminder of how easily *law* and *war* were,
indeed, misread in this imperial age:

> To give you an instance of the ease with which native customs might be
> badly observed by a traveller, I will cite an experience of my own when I . . .
> nearly fell into error. Passing down a branch of the Karkola River in the
> Oroungou country, in a canoe with a choice band of natives for crew, we
> suddenly came upon a gentleman on the bank who equally suddenly gave
> several dismal howls and fired at us with the scatter gun prevalent in West
> Africa. Having a rooted antipathy to being fired at, and knowing that the
> best way to prevent a recurrence of the unpleasantness when dealing with a
> solitary native is to tackle him before he reloads, I jumped onto the bank.
> The man turned and fled, and I after him down a narrow bush-path followed
> at a discreet distance by a devoted member of the crew yelling for me to
> come back. I succeeded in getting hold of my flying friend by his powder-bag
> and asked him why he had behaved so extremely badly. Then, when the rest
> of the crew saw that the incident promised entertainment without danger,
> they joined us, and we found the poor man was merely suffering under
> domestic affliction. One of his wives had run away with a gentleman from
> a neighboring village, and so he had been driven to fire at and attempt to
> kill a member of any canoe-crew from yet another village that might pass
> his way; because, according to the custom of the country, the men of this
> village would thereby have to join him in attacking the village of the man
> who had stolen his wife. So you see, if I had not minded being fired at, but
> just put down in my notebook that the people of this region were hostile
> savages and passed on, I should not have come across this interesting piece
> of native law, nor any of the other interesting pieces of native law I gained
> knowledge of during the subsequent palavers. (Kingsley 1898:4)

Mary Kingsley took delight in describing herself as "not being a true
traveler but a wandering student of early law" (1898:iii). Her use of
"early" rather than "primitive" is noteworthy.[32] It would be invidious
to compare the influence of Mary Kingsley, the well-connected amateur, with that of the academic anthropologist at the end of the nineteenth century. Her main achievement, Flint suggests, was "to revolu-
tionize the attitude towards Africans of British Governments, British
officials, and even of that informed section of British public opinion
which deigned to consider African problems" (1964:xxv). Intellectually,
she confronted the rising tide of social Darwinism. Flint contended
that she, "more than any other writer of her time, changed the English-

man's concept of the African into that of a complex, likeable, rational and fully adult human being, who was above all a fit and proper subject for intelligent study" (1964:xxxix). Mary Kingsley, of all people, would have objected to that last dehumanizing phrase, although she would no doubt have accepted the intended compliment.[33] Paul Rich was even prepared to write of "The Kingsleyite School" and "Mary Kingsley and her acolytes" when he considered the impact of her ideas on her contemporaries. Both R. E. Dennett, a trader, and Edward Dene Morel, a severe critic of colonialism in Africa, owed a great deal to her patronage. One of the first major works to reflect her ideas was John A. Hobson's *Imperialism* (1902).

Mary Kingsley, Flint wrote, "helped to change in a profound way the attitudes of European colonial administrators towards their African subjects, to create a scientific basis for the anthropological study of Africans, and even to mold the ideas which educated Africans held about themselves in the early stages of the nationalist movement in West Africa" (1965:7). Not until the late 1950s was another English-woman again to be so well placed to capture the ear of the politicians and administrators who shaped the destiny of the Africans they ruled.[34]

CONCLUSION

This chapter has reviewed the ways in which professional anthropologists conducted research into political matters during the last two decades of the nineteenth century. To a striking extent, their interests and the very manner in which they conceptualized political forms and activities were a legacy of earlier scholars—chief among them, Spencer, Maine, Marx, and Morgan. But their subject matter was distinctively their own, born of their own rather troubled times.

American ethnologists—government servants funded by public moneys and led by John Wesley Powell—inquired into the political condition of Native Americans, both reconstructing their historical forms of political organization in order to place them within a strategic evolutionary schema and, at the same time, carrying out intensive field research that led them to record the contemporary suffering and tension that made wars of resistance appear almost inevitable. Contradictions between the concept of "the savage tribe" and the frontier of expanding industrial capitalism were encapsulated in the very different political activities of Kanosh of the Ute and Wovoka (Jack Wilson).

British ethnologists—academics led by Edward Tylor—envied the Americans their bureau and the richly detailed field ethnographies its researchers produced. British anthropology of politics at this time derived largely from surveys conducted both in the British Isles and in imperial possessions, and from ethnography by mail, the responses of amateurs in the field to the scientific inquiries of academics. Two imperial possessions in particular contributed to the advancement of knowledge: India, where long-established problems of caste inequality, racial categorization, and local community organization predominated; and Canada, where old institutions such as the potlatch were becoming politically problematic as commerce and missions expanded along the Pacific Coast.

Shaped by the historical researches of lawyers, Maine and Marx, Indian ethnology acquired new sociological dimensions with the Census of India in 1890. Yet the Indian experts so numerous in the ethnological societies of Victorian Britain and in the academy represented a dying breed as the professional replaced the amateur, "savage races" replaced civilizations, and concern with the present replaced inquiry into the past. If Sir Herbert Risley or Mary Kingsley represented nineteenth-century ethnology, Franz Boas, working in Canada among the Kwakiutl, heralded its future (Chapter 2).

Many of the concerns of the nineteenth century continued into the twentieth. Among those discussed in this chapter were what were then called "motors of change," including the development of private property, military conquest, and the contact of peoples ("acculturation"). The evolution of war and the operation of law were subjected to considerable speculation and categorization. Bureau ethnologists laid out the schema of "the kinship polity," the analysis of which later became the hallmark of political anthropology as a specialized field (Chapter 4). They also made inquiries into the relation of kinship and territory to political organization, another topic that was to loom large in political anthropology for many decades to come. They recorded and studied political movements such as the Ghost Dance, and their work was characterized by a marked lack of distancing as "other" the unfortunate participants. The same was true in the study of law; human rather than savage qualities were discerned.

In some cases, ethnologists—Mary Kingsley and James Mooney come to mind—were prepared to act as political brokers between government and the peoples among whom they were working. In both Britain and America, the profession shortly came to frown on this, and anthropology's paradoxical political stance—alternating between practical involvement and scientific disengagement—became a central issue for the emergent subfield in the twentieth century, as we will see in Chapter 2.

2 The Uneasy Years, 1898–1918

Take up the White Man's burden,
Send forth the best ye breed,
To wait in heavy harness,
On fluttered folk and wild—
Your new-caught, sullen peoples,
Half-devil and half-child.
Take up the White Man's burden,
The savage wars of peace—
Fill full the mouth of Famine
And bid the sickness cease;
Take up the White Man's burden—.

          —RUDYARD KIPLING

Political anthropology as a recognized subfield developed out of a series of academic struggles whose origins lay in Edwardian Britain between 1901 and 1914. To the victors, the self-proclaimed functionalists, went the immediate spoils. But in the long run, those who questioned the dominant paradigm, branded as diffusionists by their opponents, provided a subterranean discourse that carried the anthropology of politics into today's arena. Because the years between 1898 and 1919 were critically formative within the discipline at large, it is important to question how and why political anthropology moved in certain directions rather than in others. The question requires a global answer. A national context was sufficient to understand the role the Bureau of American Ethnology played in the framing of American ethnology in the nineteenth century, but an imperial setting is required for an understanding of how it developed in the twentieth.

The era opened with distant wars. The Spanish-American War was America's "coming out party" as she ousted old imperialist Spain from a string of possessions: following an invasion of Puerto Rico in 1898 the Caribbean was turned into "an American lake"; in the same year on the opposite side of the world, the United States annexed Hawaii on the grounds that its monarchy was "dissolute and corrupt" (Perkins 1962:64); finally, the Philippines—the gateway to China and the commerce of the Orient—were acquired in 1902. A latecomer to the imperial game, the United States began to ensure that it would not be excluded from "the competition for the wealth and markets of Asia as it had previously been excluded from the carving up of Africa" (Lopez 1966:9).

By 1902 the United States had acquired an overseas empire that included the Philippines, Guam, a portion of Samoa, Hawaii, Alaska, Puerto Rico, the Virgin Islands, the Canal Zone, Guantánamo Bay, the Corn Islands, and miscellaneous small islands in the Pacific. Continental America's imperial responsibilities embraced a population more than a tenth the size of its own. This population would add to the repertoire of political anthropology ethnographies of law, plantation economies, and divine kingship, among other topics. Moreover, unlike the old European capitalisms, that of the United States in the twentieth century was driven by what has been called monopoly capitalism. This led to certain political paradoxes within the territorial dependencies, which political ethnographies were not slow to document. Within the newly emergent profession, imperialism found both admirers and detractors. Their pioneer contributions to the study of *primitive* political organization were, in fact, colonial ethnography.

The years from 1898 to 1901 were also a turning point for Britain and its colonies. War against the Dutch settlers of southern Africa marked the end of one era and the beginning of another both at home and overseas. With the United States for the first time an overt competitor in the imperial marketplace, Edwardian England shifted from colonization to colonial development. The study of political anthropology developed for Americans as their frontiers expanded and as their overseas empire came into being; for British anthropologists, the imperial structure had been in place for centuries, and often what happened at home was more decisive than what happened overseas; the perception of politics in the home country colored the perception of politics abroad.[1]

Practical and academic concerns clashed in the arena of colonial politics. The rich panoply of new imperial ethnography left its practitioners confused and their theories confusing. Denying themselves the analytical framework of the imperial adventure itself, whether of Hobson or Lenin, their ethnographic "facts" about "primitives" were framed in a kaleidoscopic array of evolutionary, diffusionist, and functional "theory." The way ahead for an anthropology of politics remained uncharted in spite of advances in the scientific method of observation and inquiry. At the center of the paradigmatic struggle was W.H.R. Rivers, activist and victim.

As anthropology became more firmly established as a reputable academic discipline, it generated its own impetus, more and more defining its own problems of inquiry in accordance with its own lights. At the beginning of the Edwardian era, however, the milieu within which the anthropology of politics developed was critical to the path it eventually took. The era was characterized by "waves and eddies of violence" (Marwick 1965:10). English society faced a revolt of the conservative upper classes that expressed itself most forcefully in feminism and Ulster nationalism. At one point, the army itself was on the verge of mutiny, the House of Lords was under political attack, and the technological education of the working class was not proving as successful a weapon against a vibrant labor movement as had been hoped. A "deep self-questioning" was manifest at all levels of society (Thompson 1975:15). Joseph Chamberlain as secretary of state for the colonies in 1901 transformed British imperialism. The coercive force required for such an endeavor demanded a different kind of knowledge. Edwardian ethnologists claimed the right to become part of the process, drawing on the experiences of their American colleagues in government service and government-funded ethnological research. Their liberal goal was a better understanding of the native in the belief that humane rule would follow. They failed miserably. Not until American capital entered the British scene was anthropological research funded on any considerable scale. The interest of American capitalists in maintaining peaceful conditions of trade in overseas territories gave a marked impetus to the study of law, government, and the economy.

THE NEW UNIVERSITIES

In both Britain and the United States between 1898 and 1918, anthropology charted its way between foreign wars. The governments of both countries were highly responsive to the disorders that accompanied the global revolution in technology and communications. In response to domestic unrest, military ambitions, and production and market needs, both embarked on the increased deployment of personnel overseas, and both experienced greater government intervention within the domestic economy than ever before. Liberal reform in England and progressivism in the United States provided for the first time an environment for the professionalization and institutionalization of the social sciences, replacing momentarily in the public eye the privileged humanities and the young natural sciences of the nineteenth century. Colleges developed into universities with graduate programs, the curriculum broadened, and endowments accumulated. In the United States at the beginning of this era, as in Britain by the end, universities became "headquarters of fundamental research" (Dupree 1957:296–297). For anthropology, the new imperial landscape provided a generous spur to its development as a field science. Museums and theoretical evolutionism declined in importance. Teaching departments of anthropology were established in colleges and universities, and through the professorial seminar, the systematic reproduction of new specializations emerged. By the time anthropology was insisting on both language competence and fieldwork as its canons of research, university departments were beginning to line up their own colonial dependencies, as it were—Columbia with China, Chicago with the Philippines, and so on.

Here was the seedbed of patronage in the governmental, commercial, and academic spheres. Here, too, was the springboard of a meteoric rise to positions of influence and authority, power even, within the academic world. Here, too, marginally, were the nonconformists and mavericks. Several of the anthropologists who contributed most to the study of politics in this era do not today figure as apical ancestors in the genealogies of our teachers. Yet their intellectual contributions were as significant as many who do.

More important, however, than either the changing contours of imperialism or academic institutionalization was capitalism itself: the era saw the beginning of the funding of anthropological research that was neither connected with exhibits of material culture nor controlled by government. This was the era in which "the foundations of men wealthy enough to rival the government itself" emerged in the United States (Dupree 1957:297). Men like Andrew Carnegie and John D. Rockefeller founded research institutions and university departments, provided personal grants to individuals, and supported publication. They favored research both at home and overseas, particularly in China, Japan, Latin America, and Africa. Similar nouveau riche public benefactors and business interests operated on a smaller scale in Britain.

Not all those trained in anthropology were assured a professional career. The inculcation and reproduction of knowledge outpaced openings in the new profession. For scholars without private means, both those as eminent as Frederick Starr of Chicago and as obscure as Gerald Camden Wheeler of London, commissions had to be taken on the side for translating, editing, artifact collecting, movie making, and delivering popular lectures. For students from overseas (such as V. Gordon Childe) and for women (such as Barbara Freire-Marreco), circumstances were even more unfavorable.

There probably never was another time when anthropology was as international as in this era. The nineteenth century had engendered for British, German, French, and American anthropologists alike a body of evolutionary theory from which to launch new scientific endeavors. The body of ethnography underlying their work was international. For example, H. J. Nieboer's *Slavery as an Industrial System* (1900), Rudolph Holsti's *The Relation of War to the Origin of the State* (1914), and L. T. Hobhouse, G. C. Wheeler, and M. Ginsberg's *The Material Culture and Social Institutions of the Simpler Peoples* (1915) drew, on average, 59 percent from English ethnography, 20 percent from German, and 10 percent from French.[2] British anthropologists served as external readers for continental dissertations, apprentice anthropologists from England went to study in Berlin, those from Canada went to American universities, and those from America to Oxford. German scholars settled in the United States. National journals reviewed each other's books. Leading scholars began to embark on the circuit of international lecture exchanges, consultantships, and teaching appointments, which had been the prerogative of only the most eminent of Victorians. The revolution in communications—post office, telecommunications, steamship, and express train—brought all within one world of discourse just as their governments' imperial interests brought them into one global orbit.

World War I changed everything. "National anthropologies" developed, within which scholars did most of their reading in their native language, carried out research mostly in the metropole's overseas territories, and usually trained fellow nationals and colonials. Germany, once in the vanguard of ethnological inquiry, like much of the rest of war-torn Europe fell back on a nineteenth-century folk ethnology, lacking an imperial subject matter. After World War I (which for the United States was a short-lived affair, jerry-built on the rubble of three years of fighting that gutted the economies of Germany, France, and Britain) only Japan and America emerged as truly global powers.

Other social sciences—potential competitors in the search for recognition and funding—became more firmly established, and as governments and foundations extended their activities at home and overseas, twentieth-century enterprise provided careers not only for anthropologists but also for economists, statisticians, political scientists, and above all, for sociologists. Sociology developed particularly strongly in the United States under the leadership of Lester Ward, William Graham Sumner, Frank Giddings, and Edward Albion Ross, all of whom deflected in one way or another the course taken by American cultural anthropology. In England sociology developed less effectively, perhaps because many of the most able sociologists, among them Graham Wallas and Beatrice and Sidney Webb, chose to engage in practical reform politics. What came to distinguish anthropology as a profession was its concentration on the cultures that imperial expansion was uncovering in every quarter of the globe.

Two traditions carried over from the Victorian era into the twentieth century, but these were quickly and skillfully depicted as antiquarian by a third. The first, comparative sociology, was as concerned with "archaic" societies as with the "savage" societies of Victorian ethnography. Slavery, war, law, and morals provided its subject matter and London its heartland, a function surely of the many excellent libraries in the cosmopolitan capital city. The second tradition was ethnology, at home equally in Germany, Britain, and America until its mangling at the hands of opponents and its discrediting as "diffusionism." Ethnological theorizing about the movements of peoples and contacts among them was the social science counterpart of liberal reformers' concern over the coolie trade, forced labor, and the excessively high mortality rates to be found in the colonies and protectorates of the British Empire. By 1919 both comparative sociology and ethnology were on the way to being superseded by what became known as functional anthropology. Functionalism, in the form of Boasian historical particularism in the United States and the natural history model of Malinowski in Britain, was to provide the most productive mode of analysis for ethnography on both sides of the Atlantic for much of the rest of the century.

Professional anthropology had come of age in Britain by the end of the Edwardian era. It was characterized, as is often the case in formative periods, by advances in technique rather than new interests or ideas. Topics of political import that received attention included order and anarchy, intertribal relations, war, slavery, and the economic basis of government. Although no effort was made at the time to delineate the distinguishing aspects of political organization, domination and order were uppermost. "The sanguine expectation of progress gave way to the grim problem of order" (Gouldner 1970:127). For the most part, "government" continued to be viewed as a subfield of social organization, a domain in which the study of kinship per se dominated.

Fieldwork now became the hallmark of ethnographic and sociological anthropology. Bronislaw Malinowski adopted the research methods advocated by Robert Ranulph Marett and William Halse Rivers Rivers, and dominated the discipline in the following decade. Alfred Reginald Brown (later Radcliffe-Brown), adopting the deliberately restrictive theoretical emphases of Emile Durkheim, waited in the wings of a stage on which Malinowski strutted. Both were scholars of the Edwardian era. The folklore of anthropology attributes the academic success of functional theory to these two men, but it was in the *first* decade of the twentieth century that "the very real disjuncture of 1922 was being prepared" (Stocking 1984:182).[3]

In America, two intellectual traditions confronted each other, both of European origin. Until this time, practitioners of Native American ethnology had been native-born Americans of Scottish and English extraction, many of them born in the South or Midwest. They drew, for the most part, on the intellectual capital of Morgan and possibly shared, at a time of rising internationalism, his expressed desire to establish a nativist American anthropology. As academic anthropology established itself, however, particularly in New York, the frontiersmen who had earlier shaped professional American ethnology found themselves sidelined as civil servants or administrators. Immigrants and sons of immigrants began to transform the new discipline in the image of nineteenth-century German scholarship, which focused on the primitive and the exotic, the Indian of the Plains, and above all, a philological conception of culture.

Yet these were years in which the social landscape of the United States was changing drastically. A population of around 76 million in 1900 grew to 106 million by 1920, with only a little over half made up of what the census called "native whites, of native parentage." The rest were immigrants from Europe, African-Americans, and Native Americans. This melting pot became the academic testing ground of American sociology. The relict Native American population among whom anthropologists worked were not citizens, yet anthropology was not a residual science, because it operated beyond the shores of the continental United States on the cutting edge of American imperialism. Most departments had both their stateside Native Americans and their overseas interests; most leading practitioners began with the first and reached out toward the second, often on the grounds that new opportunities for overseas research would build up their departments and provide their students with new ethnography and the science of anthropology with new comparative data. It did not, however, become "one world" for them. Boas's work on the Northwest Coast remained separate intellectually from his engagements in Mexico; Kroeber's California data were unrelated to Berkeley's interest in the Philippines. The political anthropology of American practitioners at this time was quite unself-conscious; it was simply an aspect of the nation's global hegemony.

Then, in 1917, there occurred that event that shook the world, the Russian Revolution. The gradual expansion of Russia from 1891, when the Trans-Siberian Railroad was begun, through the occupation of Manchuria in 1900, the Russo-Japanese War, and the revolutions that followed in 1905 and 1917 augured global changes. European, American, and Canadian troops attempted to overthrow the Bolshevik government, invading its territory. At home in the United States, radicals—many of them labor organizers—were deported during the Red Scare of 1919. Nativism surrounded government policies and popular attitudes toward both Russians and Germans. Racism bred immigration quotas and the lynching of African-Americans. The Ku Klux Klan spread from its southern homeland to northern states. Anthropologists figured prominently in "the Red and the Black" intellectual coalition to fight racism.[4]

Conflict within the academy over the real-world politics of its members overshadowed much else. Sociologists Ross at Wisconsin and Boas at Columbia participated in the domestic political arena at the cost of the departments in which they worked. Political interests at home, piecemeal and reactive as they were, ensured anthropology a place in the mainstream of the social sciences in a way that work with Native Americans or overseas populations might never have done. Its most marked features were a scientific analysis of racism and an attack on social Darwinism. The move away from evolutionary theory and physical anthropology (anthropometry) occurred not overseas but in the domestic arena, the assault launched most vehemently by German immigrants vulnerable to charges of un-American activity. In an economy of effort, they disassociated themselves from both Morgan and international communism at the same time. Political anthropology thus entered into a dialogue with Morgan, Marx, and Engels in circumstances that led to disassociation rather than critical opposition. When the opposing imperialisms of the USSR and the United States became all-encompassing in the twentieth century, the ideas of Marx frequently had to be decontaminated before they entered into anthropological discourse.

First, however, the dominance of the evolutionary paradigm had to be challenged, and this was achieved not through an intellectual confrontation but as a result of changes in technique, a feature of a scientific revolution.

THE SCIENTIFIC REVOLUTION

The new science denounced the speculative, imaginative, conjectural thinking of the early Victorian era. In political anthropology it systematically put to the test statements about cultural evolution and human progress. It tended to set aside concern with morals, ethics, and knowledge in pursuit of phenomena that were more simply discerned, compared, and where possible, measured. Auguste Comte's first law of social statics, that there were relations of interdependence among the various features of social life which formed a *system* or *coherent whole*, went unquestioned by either British or American ethnologists. Their goal, as they saw it, was to weigh and measure these relationships. Edward Tylor's attempt in 1887 to prove statistical correlations among certain elements within the social system, "adhesions," was a modest first step. Its scientific feasibility was immediately questioned by Joseph Galton, who presided over the session of the British Association at which Tylor first presented his thesis. In spite of Galton's objections, the comparative method became the lodestone of the new science of anthropology. "In statistical investigation," Tylor claimed, "the future of anthropology lies" (1889:269).

At the end of the nineteenth century, the mass of raw information about non-European peoples that accumulated as European interests expanded overseas was still ordered by the classificatory schema of evolutionary theory. By the first decade of the twentieth century, library facilities had improved so that vast collections of cross-cultural data could be consulted rapidly. The scientific response to the masses of accumulating ethnographic data, the slip system, was recalled in wry detail by its practitioners faced with the problem of ordering the complex and apparently unrelated data from savage societies, "the intricate jungle of anthropological literature," as Marett called it (1941:117).

The slip system was put into effect under the great dome of the British Museum Reading Room or in the Royal Library of The Hague, as well as in the private study. It operated on the principle of isolating "the facts," the occurrence and nature of certain institutions, and then of "explaining" their occurrence within a framework of material culture. No domain of society was more accessible to this synthesizing activity than were social organization, economics, and politics. Scholars systematically combed French, German, English, and American ethnographic literature. The reliability of some of this data was later questioned, but the goal of comprehensiveness can only be admired.

All three aspects of the methodological revolution brought anthropology a "pay-off" for the study of politics: each, in turn, brought incremental gain. The Edwardians applied the statistical method to four political domains: (1) slavery, the critical form of property that, for evolutionists, epitomized the transition from a kinship polity to a territorial state; (2) the state, particularly the relation of warfare to its "origins"; (3) warfare among "simpler peoples" and its relation to other institutions; and (4) government and justice, and their economic correlations. Political ethnology thus progressed from the most specific

(Nieboer 1900; Holsti 1914) to the more general (Hobhouse, Wheeler, and Ginsberg 1915). Whether questioning the theses of Morgan, Engels, and Marx inspired these applications is not clear, but certainly their ideas were circulating at the time. The emergent discipline chose to draw attention to the new, not to claim continuity with the past.

The "scientific method" advanced the revolution from above aimed at expelling the trader, missionary, and colonial administrator from the field of comparative ethnology. While the amateurs might write, with more or less authority, about particular savages, the professional scholar alone was qualified to arrive at an appreciation of universals.

Scientific Method

Hermann Nieboer's study of slavery as an industrial system provided political anthropology with one of its clearest discussions of correct methodology.[5] Besides its use of the sociological-evolutionary comparative method, it was characterized by (1) a search for laws; (2) a recognition of universal institutions of mankind; (3) an ambivalence, therefore, about completely divorcing the study of savage from civilized societies; (4) explanations that focused on institutions rather than race; and (5) an ambivalence about historical explanation, particularly in the case of apparent exceptions to universals or laws. Nieboer's discussion of methods of analysis is both thorough and a model for the form of inquiry adopted by twentieth-century anthropologists studying politics. We may see in his careful exposition many of the issues later addressed by Radcliffe-Brown, Max Gluckman, and Edmund Leach in their exegesis and critique of the scientific method[6] but not until the 1970s, in a renaissance of studies of slavery, was Nieboer's contribution given its due recognition (Chapter 6).

The intellectual ancestry of the statistical method lay with Tylor, whose essay "On a Method of Investigating the Development of Institutions: Applied to Laws of Marriage and Descent" appeared in 1889. It was a prepublication copy of this article, remember, that Tylor gave Franz Boas as he embarked on the Jessup Expedition. Tylor argued that the frequency with which cultural traits or elements appeared in association, if it exceeded that which might be expected by chance combinations, indicated a *causal* relationship. Five years later S. R. Steinmetz applied the method to the evolution of punishment in a doctoral thesis for which Tylor was one of the examiners. Nieboer's work in turn influenced Hobhouse, Wheeler, and Ginsberg in their analysis of the material bases of government and justice, the family, war, and social structure (1915).

Nieboer was as frank in his discussion of the ethnography of this era as he was in discussing the goals of the comparative method and the shortcomings of Tylor's statistical analysis. The ethnologist, he observed, always had to rely on ethnographers, many of whom had no notion of ethnology and sometimes no notion of science at all. "It is true," he suggested, that "if the ethnographical literature were better, ethnology would greatly profit from it; but, on the other hand, even with the help of the existing literature, which, after all, is not so very bad, much more might be attained than is actually done. And as long as ethnology is still in an unsettled condition, it is perhaps better that an ethnographer should have no ideas at all on ethnological subjects, than premature, quasi-scientific, and probably erroneous ideas. . . . [I]t is better to have an ethnographer who only knows that every correct statement of his will interest the men of science, than one whose perceptive faculties are troubled by preconceived opinions" (Nieboer 1900:xvii–xviii).

The scholarly discipline that had relied in its formative stage on correspondence with missionaries, traders, and administrators in the field had become wholly transformed into an academic profession based on the pursuit of *scientific* knowledge. What then of the *content* of Nieboer's investigation? What of his scientific findings?

Slavery, as we saw in our discussion of the Northwest Coast, had long been viewed by political economists as a critical feature of the transformation of society. Nieboer, seeking the conditions under which civilization arose, deliberately isolated for analysis only a very small portion of the subject. He defined slavery as "the fact that one man is the *property or possession* of another" (1900:xix, emphasis in the original). Subordination and compulsory labor underwrote a slave's condition.[7] Nieboer thus declared himself heir to materialist thinking, placing the emphasis on property rather than person. He also drew attention to slaves as an underclass.

The proposition Nieboer sought to test was simple: "All the peoples of the earth," he suggested, "can be divided into peoples with *open* and *closed* resources" (1900:387); slavery as an industrial system would be found only where there were open resources. It would disappear as soon as all land had been appropriated. While his "leading idea" was derived from classical economy,[8] the bulk of Nieboer's data came from ethnography; his first task, as he saw it, was to test the theoretical formulations of classical economy against the hard ethnological data.[9] His statistical findings are summarized in Table 2.1.

Nieboer noted the prevalence of slavery among the native peoples of

Table 2.1. Nieboer's Statistical Findings on Slavery

Region	Reportings of Slavery Positive	Reportings of Slavery Negative	Location of Positive Reports
North America	15	42	Pacific Coast
Central and South America	9	18	scattered
Australia	0	23	
Oceania (Melanesia, Micronesia, Polynesia)	7	23	Tahiti, New Zealand, western New Guinea
Malay Archipelago	62	7	
India and the Indian-Chinese Archipelago	12	11	
Central Asia	0	4	
Siberia	1	7	
Caucasus	3	1	
Arabia	2	0	
Africa	65	28	Guinea coast, Congo

SOURCE: Compiled from Nieboer 1900.

the Pacific Coast and its absence elsewhere on the American continent. He also made a passing reference to the 1860 federal census, from which he learned that the Creek, Seminole, and Shawnee owned Negro slaves. Africa provided the greatest number of cases of slavery, even with North Africa being excluded from the reckoning because it was, as Nieboer put it, "inhabited by semi-civilized peoples" (1900:164). Most instances were reported from the Guinea coast and the Congo, where German ethnographers had reported "large agglomerations of slave-keeping tribes" (1900:165).

Most of Nieboer's text was devoted to extrapolating information on economies and relating this to the presence or absence of slavery. The existence of polygamy and a rich man's use of wives as plantation laborers led him into a discussion of the position of women. He did not address Engels's observation that in the course of history most slaves *were* women. His scientific interest lay in system and function, not in origins. Where wives were, as he saw it, "purchased," Nieboer was prepared to write of the "slavery of women" (1900:392). He argued that "the position held by a woman . . . determines to some extent whether or not slaves are wanted" (1900:391). He also discussed the use of slaves to perform domestic (female) labor and the extent to which the introduction of slaves into an economy liberated women.

Warfare and the Origin of the State

Nieboer accepted as given the idea that warfare played a large part in savage life, but since it was almost everywhere the "business of free-men," he was little concerned with it in his analysis of slavery as an industrial system. In some cases warfare prevented the adoption of slavery; in others it furthered it. In 1913 the slip system provided the basis for one of the most comprehensive analyses of warfare ever undertaken. Rudolph Holsti, a student of Edward Westermarck,[10] asked the simple question (1914:12): Is warfare the normal condition of savage society?

Holsti's magnum opus has been either overlooked or ignored by to-day's scholars who specialize in the anthropology of war. The manufacture of ignorance, as with Nieboer's work, itself demands inquiry. Here I merely put forward the proposition that in establishing itself as a discipline whose subject matter was primitive peoples and thus in protectively isolating itself from nineteenth-century political economy and early-twentieth-century historical sociology, scientific anthropology denied its mongrel origins.

Holsti first delineated the intellectual catchment area of theorizing on the state. He noted how philosophical and political theories were giving way to theories that were juristic and sociological. In a manner that was to become even more characteristic of the scientific practitioners of political anthropology, Holsti reviewed only the work of his own and his teachers' generation. The new scientific age had dawned: Aristotle and Machiavelli had had their day. Spencer, Westermarck, and Giddings, moderate English sociologists, confronted Gumplowicz, Ratzenhofer, and Oppenheimer, German militants. On the eve of World War 1 it is almost as if national predilections underlay the young Finn's dichotomy. Yet between the two schools of thought, the largely British and the largely German, lay a comparatively small bone of contention. The first group of partisans viewed the state as universal, originating in "very primitive forms of social integration" (1914:7); the second group saw the state as natural, developing in response to biological and psychological needs.

More significant, perhaps, than this squabble over natural origins was the assured manner in which Holsti ruled out of court, as it were, the arguments of Engels's *The Origin of the Family, Private Property and the State.* Nor do the publications of Marx and Engels appear in his otherwise comprehensive bibliography; these were considered political, not scholarly, tracts in the Edwardian era, with Marxist scholarship as yet unborn.

Like so many of his generation, Holsti felt the impact of the magnificent ethnography of Baldwin Spencer and his trader collaborator, Frank Gillen. But unlike most of his generation—Frazer, Freud, Durkheim, Radcliffe-Brown, and Malinowski—Holsti employed Australian ethnography to further the analysis not of religion or kinship but of warfare and the origin of the state.

The origin of the state, Holsti claimed, revolved around two axes: government and territory. Having demonstrated the universality of government (ranging from the rule of elders to a more firmly established chieftainship), he moved on to demonstrate the universality of notions of territorial ownership. "As Maine justly points out," Holsti wrote, "during a large part of what we usually term modern history no such conception was entertained as that of 'territorial sovereignty'. Indeed, "even today there does not exist unanimity with regard to the true character of 'territorial sovereignty'" (1914:266). Until this point Holsti used the phrase *territorial sovereignty* in quotation marks—not surprisingly, perhaps, considering the actual tussle underway between British and German jurists at the time. Conflict over tropical possessions in eastern Africa had led the imperial powers to contest new forms and definitions of sovereignty (Vincent 1988a).

Holsti used ethnography to answer three questions raised by the juristic and sociological literature:

Which theory of the origin of the state is in best agreement with ethnographic facts?
Is war the normal condition of savage society?
Are the origin and development of primitive integration and submission to chieftainship to be ascribed mainly to the influence of warfare? (1914:10)

Three chapters (nearly a hundred pages) delineated the character of primitive warfare. The slip system permitted Holsti to review the entire ethnographic corpus, regardless of its provenance or focus. At the end of the long day he suggested that his predecessors had erred in basing their general arguments on highly selective cases. Far from warfare being universal in simple societies, he found a lack of indiscriminate slaughter, low death rates from war, the killing only of adult males directly involved in combat, institutionalized inviolability of go-betweens or messengers between potentially hostile groups, and the prevalence of peace making and treaty keeping. He supported the view that the beginnings of international law could be discerned in savage society, although he referred to the work of neither Royce at the Bureau of

American Ethnology nor Gerald Camden Wheeler in London.

Holsti then examined the very cases used by Spencer, Vaccaro, Letourneau, Steinmetz, Gumplowicz and others who had focused on the more bloodthirsty peoples of the world to the neglect of others: the Maori of New Zealand, Fijians, Tongans, Dyaks of Borneo, Galla of Ethiopia, Masai, "Kafirs" (of southern Africa), and Native Americans, particularly the Iroquois. His reappraisal of the sources led him to suggest that "according to trustworthy statements, there is good reason to believe that the warlike aspirations of these races were of relatively late growth" (1914:107). He attributed bellicosity among them to various causes: the arrival of Europeans (Maori), the introduction of firearms (Fijians), the events of the last century (Dyaks), the domestication of cattle (Masai), the spread of Islam (Galla), and the demand for slaves ("Kafirs"). Having provided these ad hoc explanations for the emergence of militarism among the various peoples, he quoted John Wesley Powell to the effect that it was only after the arrival of the whites that warfare took place on any large scale among Native Americans. Holsti drew the conclusion that warfare was in no way a "normal condition" of savage society. The content of Holsti's study was ethnographic; its intellectual context was western Europe embroiled in one of its most savage wars.

Correlating Government, Law, and War

The most ambitious attempt to correlate slavery, government, law, and war, and to place them in the context of "economic culture" resulted from the collaboration of three London scholars: Leonard Trelawny Hobhouse, Gerald Camden Wheeler, and Morris Ginsberg. Hobhouse was Professor of Social Thought at the University of London, Ginsberg his young assistant. Gerald Camden Wheeler (whom we have already encountered as an authority on the Australian aborigines) was a student of Edward Westermarck and a part-time lecturer at the London School of Economics.[11] Their book *The Material Culture and Social Institutions of the Simpler Peoples* was published in 1915. Again, like the work of Nieboer and Holsti, its existence appears to have been quickly forgotten—if it was ever acknowledged—by the newly professionalizing field of anthropology.

The opening sentence of *Simpler Peoples* established its scientific credentials: "Theories of social evolution are readily formed with the aid of some preconceived ideas and a few judiciously selected corroborative facts," but the "voluminous results of anthropological inquiry" made such a procedure untenable (Hobhouse, Wheeler, and Ginsberg

1915:1). Unlike Nieboer and Holsti, Hobhouse and his collaborators (Ginsberg the sociometrician and Wheeler the ethnologist) restricted their inquiry to "the simpler peoples," setting apart their institutions from those of "national government."

At the time, their action called for little comment apart from a discussion of the difficulties of method. "We have called such governments national," they wrote, "and have not sought to correlate them further in detail with the simpler kinds, as a new nomenclature would be necessary which would not run on all fours with the old" (1915:49). What a theoretical impasse that innocuous idiom "run on all fours" concealed. Ginsberg returned to the sticking point in an introduction written for a reprint of *Simpler Peoples* fifty years later—significantly, the *first* reprint. He wrote of a *necessary* distinction between "civilized" peoples—that is, "broadly, peoples who have a recorded history"—and preliterate peoples. Hobhouse had dealt with the former in *Morals in Evolution* (1906). "In dealing with preliterate societies," Ginsberg wrote, "the historical approach has only a limited scope. Anthropologists provide at best only fragments of history, and, for the most part, they confine themselves to a description of the lives of the people they deal with as they see them at a given moment of time" (1965:x). Whether this was as true in 1915 as it was in 1965 is open to question. Nevertheless, a distinction between national (or complex) and simpler (or small-scale) societies had become by the Edwardian era the basis of a recognized division of academic labor between historians and classical scholars, on the one hand, and social scientists, on the other. It bequeathed to British anthropologists a portion of the social-science pie that was, indeed, ethnographic and comparative but above all else, ahistorical.

Their classification of the more than six hundred "simpler peoples" was derived directly from Nieboer. Their "stages of economic culture" built upon Nieboer's classification of methods of obtaining food, but as they advanced along the economic scale to the threshold of civilization, they added industrial arts. The result was a schematic classification (Fig. 2.1).

Government and Economics. The first question they asked was "how people are governed at the various levels of economic culture . . . how order is maintained, and justice administered" (1915:46). They began by distinguishing between the *form of government* and the *administration of justice*; they concluded by investigating the relation between the two. A chapter on the family stood between those on "Government

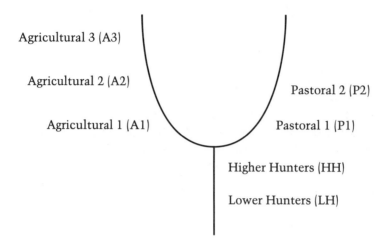

Agricultural 3 (A3)

Agricultural 2 (A2)

Agricultural 1 (A1)

Pastoral 2 (P2)

Pastoral 1 (P1)

Higher Hunters (HH)

Lower Hunters (LH)

Figure 2.1.   Hobhouse, Wheeler, and Ginsberg's diagram of
the evolution of simpler peoples
(adapted from Hobhouse, Wheeler, and Ginsberg 1915:29)

and Justice" and "War and Social Structure," though they did not make
it clear why they used this structure.

They found that the simpler societies of hunters and gatherers had
little or no formal government:

> They are in a measure self-dependent. They own a definite area of land.
> They join, more or less effectively as the case may be, in repulsing the
> assaults of any other group; and, again, in varying degrees of energy and
> community of feeling, they will protect their members against others. They
> may have a chief or council, formal or informal, of the older men. . . . But in
> the main they are self-dependent, owing no allegiance to anyone beyond
> their limits. Yet they do stand in social relations to neighbouring groups.
> A number of such groups probably speak the same dialect, and call one
> another by the same name, intermarry freely, perhaps meet at certain times
> for religious or ceremonial purposes, are generally on friendly terms, and
> perhaps are ready to cooperate for mutual defence. Such an aggregate of
> groups is generally known as a tribe, even if it possesses no common
> government or corporate individuality. (1915:47)

As a tribe ascended the economic scale, tribal unity became more
clearly defined. Often a tribal council or chief existed; when it did not,
a problem arose as to whether the tribe or the local group was the
"true" social unit. The authors decided to consider the various groups
one society even though they had no "common government." The local
groups they called primary groups (i.e., "the smallest organization

above the simple family which has a recognized unity and a measure of self-government") (1915:48). The secondary group was an aggregate of primary groups.

Ascending still higher in the scale were societies that could no longer be called tribal. "When government becomes so far *civilised* that local divisions have lost their independence and local chiefs have become or are replaced by heads of districts appointed by a ruling individual or council, a more *regular* form of government has arisen" (1915:49).

On the basis of their statistical evidence, the authors concluded

> that there is a tendency both to the consolidation of government and to the extension of the area of organised society as we advance in the economic scale. In the lowest societies there is in nearly half the cases no organised government at all, and in three out of four cases no government at all beyond the primary group. In the highest pastoral and agricultural societies there is organised government in all cases, and in three cases out of four the organised government includes more than one "primary" group, and extends to a large village, a tribe, or perhaps a "nation." (1915:52)

Two questions then arose: (1) What forms did organized government take and with what were these different forms correlated? and (2) How was order maintained in societies where there was no organized government? Finding an answer to the first question was hampered by inadequate data—the poor descriptions and lack of concepts in many ethnographies. No problem arose where there was no government or where there were chiefs, but the grey area in between defied statistical analysis. As the authors put it, "Our main difficulty here has been that government may be exercised by a council whose powers are often so loosely described that we have great difficulty in deciding whether they should be regarded as an original form of government or not. We have therefore ended by leaving the council out of the question and confining ourselves to the power of the chief alone" (1915:81). But leaving the council out of the question meant disregarding data from more than 18 percent of the primary groups and almost one third of those with tribal government.

No doubt the ethnography available at the time drew attention to the presence of chiefs and neglected less visible forms of authority. That this was no small matter in practical terms for the peoples among whom the ethnographers worked is apparent from the colonial record. For anthropology it was an imbalance that could not be corrected until a different kind of ethnography became available, an ethnography derived not from the reports of travelers, missionaries, police agents, and colonial officers but from continuous, prolonged observation in the field by anthropologists trained to discern more subtle forms of leadership, authority, and power.

Justice. As with the economic foundation of government among the simpler peoples, so with justice in Hobhouse, Wheeler, and Ginsberg's essay in correlation. They made no explicit reference to the vast amount of evolutionary thinking on "primitive law," simply dismissing it in their first sentence. The publications of Johann Kohler appeared in the bibliography; the work of Sir Henry Maine did not, presumably because it related to archaic societies, a matter that Robert Redfield had to explicate for nonanthropologists a few years later. They mined Powell's account of Wyandotte government and Dorsey's of Omaha law for isolated facts, along with a considerable amount of Native American data from other sources, including Bancroft and an ethnographer they called Boaz. But they totally disregarded the conceptual frameworks of the original sources.

The authors defined law as "binding custom." "All societies," they wrote, "recognize certain customary rules as binding their members, and at least within the society custom alone has a sufficient power to secure observance in normal cases" (1915:53). Differences arose in the rules themselves and in the punishments for their breach. They addressed three questions:

1. To what extent or in what cases does society act as a whole or through its heads or through some definite institution to restrain or punish the wrongdoer?
2. What methods of punishment are in use?
3. What procedure is employed? (1915:53–54)

Their findings were less valuable than the problems to which they drew attention. Self-help predominated among the lower hunters, and self-redress among the higher. As social organization was extended and society became more complete, it increasingly took upon itself the redressing of wrongs and the maintenance of order. Hobhouse, Wheeler, and Ginsberg were not prepared to call the latter *law* in line with Powell's definition of law as a rule of conduct that organized society endeavors to enforce. Nor were they prepared to move toward comparison with the civilizations among which Edward Brabrook was most at home. In the final analysis, they "proved" statistically Hobhouse's earlier conclusion in *Morals in Evolution* (1906) that justice is universal, law is emergent. And law had not emerged in the simpler societies.

They then turned their inquiry to three methods of dealing with crime. Crime might be treated as (1) an aggression to be revenged (retaliation); (2) a trespass (against an individual, the community, or the gods) to be atoned (atonement); or (3) something wrong to be put right (compensation). In the 201 societies they examined, they found adequate references to 330 instances of the application of justice. The distribution of the three modes of application was as shown in Table 2.2.

Table 2.2. Hobhouse, Wheeler, and Ginsberg's Findings on the Application of Justice

	Retaliation	Atonement	Compensation
L.H.	34	4	0
H.H.	53	5	3
A1	17	6	6
P1	5	5	2
A2	36	31	21
P2	5	3	7
A3	14	37	36
	164	91	75

SOURCE: Adapted from Hobhouse, Wheeler, and Ginsberg 1915:69.

Material on judicial procedure, they noted, was scanty. Among the lower peoples, "what sort of enquiry is held, and by what means guilt is ascertained, we are not informed. . . . [T]rials are hardly mentioned until we reach the Agricultural stage." And again, "information about procedure is often very defective. We sometimes hear of a man being 'found guilty,' but with no indication of any trial which precedes the verdict" (1915:61). This deficiency in the ethnography of law was not redressed for many decades (Chapter 6).

Discussing the relation between the development of justice and "government in general," they again set aside data on councils because they were so ambiguous. Focusing on the power of the chief alone, they concluded that there was "a certain correlation *but not so much as might have been anticipated a priori*" (1915:81, emphasis added). In general, and not surprisingly, "both in extent and in internal quality, the development of social order is roughly correlated with advance in economic culture" (1915:82). Nevertheless, this was a significant finding that led ethnologists to inquire more closely into the nature of chiefship.

En route to these conclusions, Hobhouse, Wheeler, and Ginsberg discussed in considerable detail the problems involved in analyzing the politics of simpler societies. They distinguished between (1) retaliation and self-help, (2) composition (i.e., compensation), and (3) regulated fight. Feuds and revenge involving individuals and kindreds were considered private justice (Fig. 2.2). Public justice arose only at higher levels of development, when "the public authority, be it what it may, may concern itself only with offences held to injure the whole community" (1915:54). Many cases fell along a continuum between self-help and regular public justice, and the authors discussed doubtful and peculiar cases in detail.

When they attempted to ascertain whether there was any "real advance" in the public enforcement of justice as they ascended their institutional scale, the authors again ran up against the central problem of the sociological comparative method: the unit of analysis. Their discussion is valuable, however, in light of the later emphasis in political anthropology on "the problem of the tribe" (Helm 1968). They noted that

in many cases the question whether self-redress is classified as internal or external depends on the classifier's selection of the social unit. In the case of the ordinary Australian tribe, we could produce solid reasons for taking the local group as the unit, and solid reasons for taking the tribe as the unit. On the former view we could produce a large number of cases of partially developed public justice or of assisted and controlled private redress. . . . On these lines we should regard the typical Australian community as very small, consisting often of not more than 20 to 40 or 60 individuals. . . . The society would figure as tiny but as relatively well organized internally.

   On the other hand the whole tribe might with equal appropriateness be regarded . . . as a single, larger, but less well organized society. . . . So treated an Australian tribe would be analogous to some more advanced society, comprising clans, villages, or other divisions. Within such a society, there is very possibly impartial justice, while between the clans there is only collective self-redress. (1915:63–64)

To document this last point, the authors set W. F. Roth's Queensland ethnological studies against Powell's description of the gentile system among the Wyandotte. Roth's aborigines "can make themselves mutually intelligible, and possess in common trade-routes, markets, hunting-grounds, customs, manners, and beliefs. They intermarry and would make common cause against an enemy. Mr. Roth speaks of them as messmates. His statement defines very fully what we mean when we speak of a single society in the absence of a common government" (1915:64).

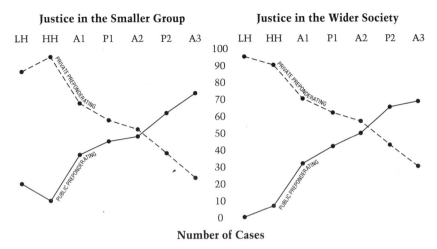

Figure 2.2. Hobhouse, Wheeler, and Ginsberg's comparison of private and public justice   (adapted from Hobhouse, Wheeler, and Ginsberg 1915:74)

Perhaps we can envisage at this point in the analysis a disagreement between the two sociologists, who favored the "tribal group" unit of political organization, and the ethnologist, who favored the primary unit. The issues they raised would haunt the study of Australian society and "amorphous polities" for many years to come. Their solution was to use both. When the local group is viewed as the society, all retaliation beyond its boundaries becomes "external"; when the tribe is considered the political unit, feuds between groups constitute a form of internal self-redress. In a long note (1915:66–67) they discuss the difficulty of applying the distinction consistently but conclude that the second alternative provides a better basis of comparison between societies of different types. The note also set a precedent for considering feuds a mode of attaining justice (see Chapter 4, on the work of Evans-Pritchard and Colson, and Chapter 5 for the synthesis and extended argument of Black-Michaud).

War and Social Structure. The third issue Hobhouse, Wheeler, and Ginsberg addressed was the relation of war to social structure. They began by noting that "the question has been raised whether the traditional view of early society as one of constant warfare is really justified by the facts" (1915:228). Again, they made no reference to earlier writers on the subject; the era had arrived when "social facts" were made to speak for themselves. Past voices were superfluous. In the creation of the new *science*, an age of ignorance of humanistic predecessors had dawned.

From a review of German, French, British, and American ethnographic literature published between 1744 and 1914, Hobhouse, Wheeler, and Ginsberg arrived at a distinction between *war*, "an operation conducted in the name of the community as a whole" and *feuds* or *external retaliation*, "a quarrel exercised by a part of a community only upon members of another community" (1915:228). They found that there were a few very primitive societies, mostly of the "jungle folk," that were quite "peaceful" but that there was no indication of "any association of peaceful propensities with the lowest stages of culture as such. At most it may be said that organized war develops with the advance of industry and of social organization in general" (1915:228).

Differences in the treatment of the vanquished enemy affected the organization of society. They recognized four variations: (1) societies in which there was no war, (2) societies in which prisoners were slain, (3) societies in which prisoners were enslaved, and (4) societies in which prisoners were adopted, exchanged, or set free. Statistical correlations indicated that the practice of killing some or all of the vanquished predominated "till we reach the highest agricultural stage where it drops by 50 per cent." Apart from the capture of wives, the enslavement of captives was very rare among the lower hunters, rising to about 20 percent of the cases among the higher hunters and remaining at that level "until we come to the Highest Agriculture, where it becomes the normal method."

The authors were then led to the question of ranks. They found an almost uniform increase in ranking as one moves up the economic scale, as might be expected, but also, and less to be expected, a greater tendency to distinction of rank among pastoral than among agricultural peoples. In neither case, however, was ranking directly related to warfare. Slavery was unambiguously correlated with more advanced "economic culture." They arrived at no firm correlations with property, but they did find that private property was negatively correlated with neighborliness, mutual aid, and customary distribution, "tending towards but not reaching communism" (1915:244). Private and communal land tenure coexisted, and there were only four cases of land belonging to a special class. Among these, interestingly enough, were Swanton's Tlingit and the Igorots of the Philippines. The communal principle did not lose out to the purely individual, however, which was nearly stationary throughout. Economic differentiation reflected in land ownership began to set in only at about the second stage of agriculture, although social differentiation preceded it. Their findings supported the speculations of Morgan and Engels, although they nowhere stated this. The authors concluded that

> Economic causes are . . . associated with the development of organised warfare and the substitutions of the enslavement of prisoners for their slaughter, liberation, or adoption. With the decline of infanticide, the better security for food, and the extension of order, we may infer a growing population, in some cases a desire for territorial expansion, in others a demand for slave labour. The mere extension of regular industry makes for social differentiation, since the effects of energy and thrift become cumulative. Hence we have the partial rise of a nobility and the more extensive development of a servile or semi-servile class. Hence, also, the communal tenure of land gives way, and while in some cases it blends with individual occupation or ownership, in others it passes more or less effectively into the hands of a chief or a nobility. On all sides social and economic differentiation replace the comparative equality of the hunting peoples. The extension of order is also, upon the whole, an extension of subordination. (1915:254)

The book's evolutionary veneer and the emergence of functional analysis as the dominant mode denied *The Material Culture and Social Institutions of the Simpler Peoples* the acknowledgment that was its due. It was, nevertheless, always there like a poor relation, providing the paradigmatic statement, its premises unquestioned, which underlay the study of political organization for the next several generations.

Common to all three scientific works discussed in this section was acceptance of the need to contextualize the object of analysis whether it be slavery, warfare, or justice. For better or worse, this was to remain the hallmark of political anthropology as it developed within the competitive environment of the professionalizing academy. Not surprisingly, all three works were strategically ignored or set aside by the most influential practitioners of the Edwardian era, diffusionists and functionalists alike. *Material Culture* remained a source book in its homeland, Ginsberg's distinctively interdisciplinary London School of Economics, but elsewhere, particularly in the United States, a great deal of time was spent reinventing the correlational wheel, even into the 1980s.

SCIENTIFIC SOCIOLOGY: DURKHEIM'S VISION

The students and colleagues of Steinmetz, Westermarck, and Hobhouse adopted scientific procedures in accordance with the tenets of comparative sociology, but their studies were essentially genetic or evolutionary in spirit. They sought the origins as well as the correlates of political institutions. Functional analysis set itself up in opposition to such trends.

The paradigm that shaped the anthropological study of politics in Britain, that dominated it from 1920 until 1953, and that is still highly influential in some quarters was fashioned in France between 1898 and 1913. Originating with Emile Durkheim and Marcel Mauss, it entered British anthropology through the teaching of Rivers and Marett and the lectures and publications of A. R. Radcliffe-Brown and Bronislaw Malinowski. Rivers drew Brown's attention to the recent work of *L'Année Sociologique* as early as 1906, and Marett later claimed that he had introduced the work of the French sociologists to Oxford even earlier. Certainly the sociological method was found acceptable when the young Mr. Brown delivered his first lectures at the London School of Economics and Political Science in 1909. His course of lectures was called, simply, Comparative Sociology.[12]

To ask why Radcliffe-Brown's brand of sociological anthropology, so influential in Britain for half a century, contained no politics is to ask why Durkheim and the *L'Année Sociologique* had not.[13] One reason lay in the emergence of a political science engaged in consolidating its own identity. The existence of politics at the margin of several sciences of society—economics, for example—was clearly recognized, and its emergence as a speciality appeared natural to all: the science of politics (Favre 1983:199). In Britain it was institutionalized in the very naming of the London School of Economics and Political Science, founded by the Webbs in 1895. But for Durkheim in France the political sciences were "bastardized speculations, half theoretical and half practical, half science and half art" (Durkheim 1890, quoted in Favre 1983:200). Politics proved to be Durkheimian sociology's blind spot; "political organization" had no place in its categorization of the subfields of comparative sociology.

Durkheim divided each subfield into two parts, "genesis" and "functioning," and always treated "political organization" solely under the first rubric. "Legal and moral rules" appeared under both, but "war," "revolution," and "class conflict" were problematic for Durkheim because they reflected not political organization but disorganization. The rubric "war" was used in one volume only; after that, books on war were reviewed as "international morality" (Favre 1983).

A sociogram by Philippe Besnard (1983) reveals how marginal to *L'Année* were its few contributors on politics. Georges Davy's *Sociologie Politique* (1924), in spite of its lengthy analysis of the potlatch, has never been translated into English and has had no direct impact on political anthropology. Emmanuel Levy and Paul Huvelin, young jurists, contributed an article and a handful of reviews on works in constitutional history, but only 2 percent of *L'Année's* reviews were even remotely connected with politics (Favre 1983).

Besnard's sociogram reveals the power of Marcel Mauss, Durkheim's nephew, whose work Malinowski much admired. Some years later, Mauss clarified (as Durkheim had never done) their view of the relationship between the study of society and the study of politics. "Politics is not part of sociology," he wrote, but is "that other discipline . . . in which we do not engage." They were, in fact, locked in territorial combat because, Mauss wrote, "Politics and Sociology have but one and the same object: societies" (quoted in Favre 1983:211–212). Here is the grounding of the Radcliffe-Brown program (Chapter 4), and its legacy is still to be found in the observations of such eminent anthropologists of politics as Edmund Leach and F. G. Bailey.

The Durkheimians began by studying modern Europe but ended up studying it hardly at all. Instead they worked with primitive societies, where "the facts are much simpler," in order "to find solutions to contemporary European problems," predominantly the "crisis" of twentieth-century European civilization (Vogt 1976:33). The bundle of methods and concepts that went along with the primitive shaped the form that the social anthropological study of politics took in the Edwardian era—a form that remains largely unquestioned.[14] It included (1) the sociological comparative method, (2) techniques for the study of correlations among the statistical regularities of "social facts," (3) an emphasis on places rather than eras, (4) a homogenizing notion of "collective consciousness" that was antipathetic to historical or evolutionary analysis, and (5) conservatism.

Ethnography: An Alternative Vision

There were alternatives within the French tradition on which Radcliffe-Brown might have drawn. Maurice Leenhardt and Arnold Van Gennep both valued ethnographic detail above generalization, and both carried out intensive fieldwork over long periods in one place. Both fit the anthropological mold that we have begun to discern: outsiders in their own societies whose careers were spent on the fringes of academic life, isolated from the seats and corridors of power Durkheim established through the dominance of his brand of functional sociology.

A missionary and practitioner of *ethnologie active*, Leenhardt faced in New Caledonia a field situation of colonial brutality and native depopulation similar to that which led Rivers, Wheeler, and Hocart away from evolutionary and sociological theory and into the study of diffusion. Today Leenhardt provides genealogical legitimation not as yet for a colonial ethnography but for a phenomenological study of politics, particularly myth as political charter (Clifford 1982).[15] Arnold Van Gennep carried out field research in a complex society, Algeria, in 1911 and 1912. He explained: "I counted on doing as one does when studying the Masai or the Australians, the Eskimos or the Indians: going into the villages themselves, staying there for some time and so conducting complete inquiries step by step" (quoted in Zumwalt 1982:300–301). Not surprisingly, Van Gennep was highly critical of the secondhand analysis of documents, texts, and ethnography-by-mail that characterized the work of many of his contemporaries. He was scathingly critical of theorizing based on the Australian materials. In a review of *Elementary Forms of the Religious Life*, he drew attention to the unreliable nature of many of the colonial sources Durkheim had used:

> Since I have gone through the same documents as M. Durkheim in the course of the years, I believe I can assert that their theoretical value is less than the author thinks; he treats them as commentators treat sacred texts, elucidating them with the aid of great erudition, but without asking whether three-quarters of the raw data are even worthy of confidence. . . . This abundance of references to documents provided by sundry informants, police agents, unspecified colonists, obtuse missionaries, etc., is not worth much, for there are pages of M. Durkheim's book in which the impartial ethnographer is bound to put question marks beside each line; "Is this certain? What is the value of the informant? What is the value of the document, or what exactly does it say?" . . . The idea he has derived from them of a primitive man . . . and of "simple" societies is entirely erroneous. The more one knows of the Australians and the less one identifies the stage of their material civilization with that of their social organization, one discovers that the Australian societies are very complex, very far from the simple and the primitive, but very far advanced along their own paths of development. (Quoted in Lukes 1973:524–525)

Van Gennep was among those who sought to found a new twentieth-century ethnographic science, convinced "that if the nineteenth century was the century of historical science, our own century will provide a conception of much greater breadth, derived from the detailed and systematic observation of living evidence, a conception that one may term *the ethnographic sense*" (quoted in Belmont 1971:115). Political divisions in the French academic world led Van Gennep to call himself a folklorist, not a sociologist, but to him folklore was not an armchair science but an open-air and laboratory science. In due course, folklore would be resurrected as popular culture, the lore of the people as opposed to the lore of the educated elite, their governors. But at the time, Van Gennep stood as a member of a dissenting academy, opposed to the functional sociology that came to dominate British political anthropology in the interwar years.[16]

THE FIELDWORK REVOLUTION

During the Edwardian era, it was still often very difficult to tell a professional sociologist from a professional anthropologist. Anthropology had clearly "drawn on the same intellectual capital as sociology," its success showing "what a high rate of interest that capital can be made to pay" (Macrae 1961:9). Philip Abrams (1968) attributed the problems of academic sociology in Britain to the growing administrative and intelligence functions of government itself, its social and economic involvements expanding at a unique rate in the twentieth century. In the colonies, on the other hand, anthropology found "a social structure in which simple political responses to social problems were less available and less plausible than they were in Britain, and in which, conversely, social problems were more fundamentally problematic" (Abrams 1968:153). "Useful to colonial administration and dangerous to no domestic prejudice" (Macrae 1961:9), Edwardian anthropologists sought to bring their skills to bear not on social and moral problems in general but specifically on those of their colonized contemporaries. Savages were fast disappearing even from the far corners of the twentieth-century globe, and this was clearly the result of the brutal expansion of European commerce and colonization.

A second step held the potential of conflict with the bookish scholarship of comparative sociology in both its genetic and functional forms. This was the sanctification of intensive field research, the adoption of genealogical recording, and an explicit scientific method grounded in the observation of activity, interviews, note taking, and the analysis of "fiches." It is hard now to appreciate the ardor with which these systematic methods were promulgated: *how* to interview, the *art* of notetaking; *firsthand* observation and quantification. Researchers quoted erudite French and German scholars at length in an effort to persuade the recalcitrant "accomplished graduate of Oxford or Cambridge that an indispensable instrument in the technique of sociological inquiry . . . is the making of notes, or what the French call 'fiches'" (Webb 1926:364). Beatrice Webb wrote passionately of her apprenticeship in the new science, which she used to study the poor and the working class with all the perceptiveness of a political anthropologist (genealogies and parapolitical interaction and all).

Nothing changed the course of the anthropological study of government more than this early Edwardian innovation in research procedure and epistemology. It entailed two shifts in perception: first, that intensive field research was more productive of results than survey techniques and, second, that what actually happened in the field situation was as legitimate a form of anthropological data as the delineation of formal governmental structures.

The Genealogical Method

Contrary to received knowledge within the discipline, the fieldwork revolution was instigated in Britain by W.H.R. Rivers. It began with his paper "A Genealogical Method of Collecting Social and Vital Statistics" (1900), written after his participation in the Cambridge Expedition to the Torres Straits, and was fueled by his field monograph *The Todas*, (1906). It reached its apogee in 1912, a decade before Malinowski's celebrated *Argonauts of the Western Pacific* (1922). Having begun by advocating "the genealogical method" of inquiry, Rivers was thereafter stuck with the label, although the method he fleshed out in 1910 and 1912 was something much more.

Rivers urged the collection of pedigrees for an entire specific population cluster of peoples located in time and space. For each individual, a range of data was to be recorded. Rivers considered that a most important feature of the method was to record as far back as possible the social condition of each individual included in the pedigrees. The locality to which each person belonged was to be obtained, and often he found it necessary to record not only the district but also the name of some smaller territorial group, whether village or hamlet. If the people belonged to social divisions, these were to be given. He urged the fieldworker to record any other facts about each person that might have social significance, taking special care to record the origins of those who had married into the community from other tribes or places. Both natural and adoptive parents were to be recorded. The fact that genealogies collected in this way from each individual overlapped provided an opportunity for cross-checking for trustworthiness (Rivers 1910).

Genealogies differ greatly from the charts of kinship terms obtained from the ethnography-by-mail of Rivers's predecessors and peers. First, his unit of data collection was a named individual, and the ethnographer aimed to collect genealogies from every named individual in a locality. This would embrace both kin and non-kin. Rivers was sensitive to the importance of place in the expression of individual and social identity, and to the existence of social divisions of various kinds. He emphasized the systematic collection of data about named individuals even if its significance would not be fully appreciated until later. They became, he wrote, "real personages to me although I may never have seen them, and the whole investigation proceeds in a manner which interests both me and my informants far more than if the personages in the account had been x, y, and z" (1910:8). The method also had an advantage that Rivers did not foresee. After the publication of *The Todas*, he began to receive letters from Indian catechists and missionaries who knew the individuals named in his genealogies and could both corroborate and add to his data.[17]

The genealogical method was invaluable for the study of what was later called "law in action." Rivers advocated its use for the investigation of laws regulating descent, the succession of chiefs, and the inheritance of property. The *concreteness* of the method was its greatest attribute. It was possible, Rivers asserted, "to take a given piece of land and inquire into its history, perhaps from the time when it was first cultivated. The history of its divisions and subdivisions on various occasions may be minutely followed, and a case of ownership which would have seemed hopelessly complicated becomes perfectly simple and intelligible in the light of its history, and an insight is given into the real working of the laws concerning property which could never be obtained by a less concrete method" (1910:7).

The genealogical method made it possible to investigate abstract problems "on a purely concrete basis. It is even possible by its means to formulate laws regulating the lives of people which they have probably never formulated themselves" (Rivers 1910:9). This formulation held the potential of moving anthropology from the study of rules to regularities, from structure to organization. Rivers's contribution to the analysis of the politics of kinship and the processual analysis of politicking in general made the analysis of genealogies quintessential to the study of politics.

Rivers constantly added to the uses to which the genealogical method might be put. These included the study of population movement, demography, and the effectiveness of law. All reflected social problems encountered in the colonial situation at the beginning of the century. Moreover, Rivers suggested, a statistical count and comparison of the data over generations permitted the analysis of change resulting from European contact. His pioneering methodological directives and his actual field research revolutionized the analysis of politics.[18]

Politics Among the Todas

Rivers undertook five months of intensive research among the Todas of
the Nilgiri Hills in southern India in the winter of 1901–2. He was
supported by the Gunning Fund of the Royal Society and the British
Association. He chose the Todas specifically for the manageable size of
the population for an observer's fieldwork and the inextricable confusion in the literature on adelphic polyandry, which they were known to
practice.[19]

For Rivers, as for his fellow Edwardians, political anthropology was
part and parcel of social organization. The subheadings of his chapter
on Toda social organization were as follows:

The Clan
The Kudr [moiety]
The Polm [lineage]
Laws of Descent
Adoption
Government
Crime
Suicide
The Monegar [government headman]
Headmen
Property
Debt and Servitude
The Position of Women

The most striking feature of Rivers's description of Toda government
was his continual contrasting of the formal with the actual. The dis-
crepancy between them revealed the political. Discussing the Toda general council, for example, Rivers first delineated its constitution: the
representation of the four Toda clans and a Badaga village. He then
named the men on the council at the time he was staying among them,
identifying each man by reference to the seventy-two genealogies contained at the back of his monograph. He noted where the council met,
both in public and in private, and he attended some of their sessions.
Most of the time they were engaged in the settlement of civil disputes,
but he noted that the committee was also responsible for the management of many important Toda ceremonies, including the now-classic
ceremony associated with the migration of the village buffaloes. For
the next two generations, Rivers's account of the ceremony entered
anthropology textbooks; by the third generation it had become little

more than a set of footnotes for Levi-Strauss. Few read the original weighty book, and fewer still would have been prepared to reevaluate Rivers's account of the Todas for its political content.[20]

Petty Despotism on the Administrative Frontier

Rivers wrote a detailed ethnography of the actual historical situation among the Todas at the time he was among them. Toda politics during 1901–2 largely revolved around the respective struggles and alliances of the *monegar* (or government headman, appointed by the imperial power for the collection of taxes from the administered population) and the clan and lineage headmen.[21]

Clan leaders were men in the prime of life chosen for their character and ability. The first *monegar* had been appointed by the British, but the office had become hereditary. The headman Rivers encountered was a classificatory brother of Kuriolv, a petty despot who was able not only to dominate the Toda council but in the past had been responsible for actually altering its constitution, expanding the council and placing on it certain of his friends. Rivers described several instances when Kuriolv interfered in the "normal" course of affairs. He was told that "in several instances the Todas would revert to their old customs as soon as Kuriolv died" (1906:553).[22]

Rivers tended to attribute Kuriolv's leadership and power to his forceful character, but so detailed is his ethnography that it is possible to suggest the structural and processual issues involved in the power struggle. Genealogy 52 (see Fig. 2.3) shows Kuriolv to be the eldest son of the son of Teitchi, the first headman. At the time of Rivers's field observations, Kuriolv was the "big man" of the largest lineage of the Teivali clan, the Kuudr. He lived at Kuudr village. The clan had at least sixty-three male and thirty-five female members. Kuriolv's support group consisted of eight lineage heads. His village had substantial huts, built in the Tamil style by Kuriolv, as well as two dairies and buffalo enclosures. One classificatory brother, Tcitnir, was reputed to be a sorcerer, and another, Ivievan, was the headman.

Kuriolv had made strategic marriages. He had two children by one wife (Punaveli, gained in brother-sister exchange with the Kusharf clan) and three by Sintharap (of the Keodr), who was also the polyandrous mate of a clan brother by whom (according to the genealogy) she had no children. Kuriolv's son Kulpakh similarly shared his wife Toridz (Kusharf clan) in a polyandrous relationship with his clan brother Kiladvran, the younger brother of Ishkievan, from whom Teitnir, the sorcerer, said he had learned his art. All these complex genealogical relationships

The Kuudr Lineage

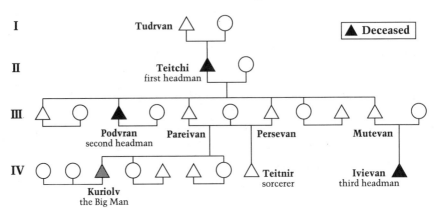

Figure 2.3. W.H.R. Rivers's diagram of the genealogy of a Big Man among the Todas
(adapted from Rivers 1906, genealogy no. 52)

became relevant when a problem arose over the distribution of a piece of property.

Rivers wrote of a situation "out of which a lawsuit may one day arise" (1906:564). We may call it "The Case of Kiugi's Buffaloes":

In all cases of distribution of property, inheritance depends on descent as determined by the *pursutpimi* ceremony, and not on the real descent, even if this should be well known. Thus the boy Meilitars, who is really the son of Kuriolv, but is legally the son of Pepners, should not inherit any of Kuriolv's buffaloes, but will receive those of his legal father, Pepners, of whom at present he is the only son. . . .

Several interesting features of Toda law are illustrated by a case out of which a lawsuit may one day arise. If the family of Kiugi should become extinct, there would arise a dispute about the succession to the property, which would turn largely on a case in which the *pursutpimi* ceremony was performed several generations ago. When the eldest child of Tudrvan was about to be born, Tudrvan was away from home, and had not performed the *pursutpimi* ceremony. There was a danger that the delivery might take place before the ceremony could be performed and Kors was therefore called in to give the bow and arrow, and Teitchi, who was born soon afterwards, was, according to Toda custom, the child of Kors. When Teitchi grew up, however, he decided to regard himself as the son of his real father, Tudrvan, and being a powerful and influential person like his grandson Kuriolv, he appears to have had his way, and his descendants have been regarded as the descendants of Tudrvan. Tudrvan himself gave the bow and arrow in the succeeding pregnancy, and there is therefore no doubt about the legitimacy of Pusheiri and his younger brothers and sisters.

Owing, however, to the part played by Kors before the birth of his grandfather, Kuriolv has lately directed that Kiugi, the son of Kors, should belong to the same *polm* as himself in order that he or his family may succeed to the buffaloes of Kiugi's *polm* if this should die out. It is known, however, that Kiugi's *polm* is closely related to that of Tuliners, so that should the *polm* of Kiugi become extinct, there would arise a lawsuit between Kuriolv and Tuliners or their representatives for the possession of Kiugi's buffaloes.

The essential point of the situation is that Kuriolv is trying to make use of his double position as the descendant of Tudrvan by real paternity and of Kors by virtue of the *pursutpimi* ceremony. According to the latter he is of the same *polm* as Kiugi, but if equity prevails in the decision of the *naim* which may have to settle the dispute, Kuriolv or his representative will have to decide whether he is descended from Tudrvan or Kors, and will not be allowed to take advantage of both lines of descent.

As a matter of fact, I was assured by several Todas that though they have apparently fallen in with Kuriolv's wishes, they still regard Kiugi's *polm* as most closely allied to that of Tuliners, and if Kuriolv should die before the extinction of Kiugi's family, I have little doubt that the *naim* would decide that the buffaloes of Kiugi should go to the family of Tuliners.

This potential lawsuit is important as showing the role played by the genealogies in the social regulations of the Toda community. We see that an eventuality which may never arise and probably will not arise for many years to come is already the subject of consideration and discussion, that the crucial point upon which the lawsuit will turn is an event which occurred probably about 120 years ago, and that the ties of kinship which will be involved in the dispute are carefully preserved in the memories of the people.

The history is also very interesting in showing that a century ago a man of force was able to set aside a fundamental regulation of Toda society, and that his grandson, who has apparently inherited the powerful character of his ancestor, is following in his footsteps, and, is able to put on one side Toda customs or laws when they conflict with his interests or desires. (Rivers 1906:564–565)

Rivers presented detailed cases not to document an argument but as an integral part of his analysis. His knowledge and interest in law were grounded in the work of Frederick Maitland, whom he knew personally. Harold Laski pointed out to Justice Oliver Wendell Holmes that Rivers's "scientific work was broad enough to make him see its bearing on law and history," and he described him as "probably the best living anthropologist and a very delightful person" (Howe 1953:253). A phrase of Maitland's might well have struck a chord with Rivers as it did with later political anthropologists: "Substantive law has at first the look of being gradually secreted in the interstices of procedure." "The Case of Kiugi's Buffaloes" provided just such a treasury of substantive law.

The folk traditions of social anthropology have long attributed "the fieldwork revolution" to the happy accident whereby during World War I, Bronislaw Malinowski, an alien, was immersed in lengthy and intensive fieldwork as a result of his internment in the Trobriand Islands by the Australian government. Malinowski himself provided such a charter in *Argonauts of the Western Pacific*, which appeared in 1922. Research suggests that the instruction both in theory and method given to Malinowski and Radcliffe-Brown by their teachers has been somewhat underestimated.[23] Malinowski himself called Rivers "his patron saint in fieldwork" (Langham 1981:173).

But the question was not simply one of intensive participant observation replacing the ethnographic reporting of amateurs. What was really at issue for the anthropological study of politics was the theoretical framework within which ethnographic reporting might be placed, the hypotheses it might generate, the "knowledge" it might accrue, and the purpose to which it might be put. The fieldwork revolution promised a new body of data to replace the conjectures about origins that had dominated the nineteenth century and the comparisons of political institutions that had opened the twentieth. These new data were the political actions of observed named individuals. For this brief moment, such reporting did take place, and today we may draw upon it to re-evaluate the colonial era. The political detail such studies provided, however, was very quickly stigmatized as theoretically naive by the dominant functionalists. Constructed models of political constitutions and academic reconstructions of the political organization of societies no longer in existence appeared in its stead.

A FIELDWORK MANUAL

Any suggestion that Rivers was singularly unsuccessful in his propagation of fieldwork methods (Rooksby 1971) has to be set alongside the important contributions he made to the highly innovative fourth edition of *Notes and Queries*, published in 1912. His chapter on methods (giving advice on language learning, note taking, pictorial notes, questioning, corroboration, and confidentiality, as well as the genealogical method) was the most substantial in the manual.

The handbook was a response to a shift in anthropological research interests that occurred around 1900. So successful had earlier editions of *Notes and Queries* been in stimulating amateur inquiry into ethnological matters that the Royal Anthropological Institute (the RAI, which acquired its honors from King Edward VII) started a new journal, *Man*, to publish the results. Contributions between 1900 and 1919 indicate a trend away from missionary contributions on language and belief systems and toward the interests of military and administrative officers in law and political organization (Urry 1973). The combination of these two factors—Rivers's insistence on fieldwork techniques and the greater participation of soldiers and bureaucrats stationed in colonial possessions—augured well for the anthropological study of politics.

The committee for the fourth edition of *Notes and Queries* consisted mainly of former members of the Torres Straits Expedition: Seligman, Haddon, and Rivers. The president of the RAI, Sir Hercules Read, was chairman, and Myres, assisted by Barbara Freire-Marreco, was its secretary. The volume they produced was "not so much a guide for travelers as a manual of advice for more highly trained observers; a handbook for a new era of anthropological research to be based on more exact methods" (Urry 1973:51–52). This was the handbook that Malinowski took with him to the field in 1914. The committee rearranged its contents in accordance with a "scientific scheme of classification," and included a general chapter on method. They took care to define technical terms and to provide precise English nomenclature; narrative replaced lists of "leading questions." The framework of the new science entailed a division into four parts: physical anthropology, technology, sociology, and arts and sciences.

A breakdown of the sociology section is shown in Table 2.3. Within "Economics of the Social Group" the last two topics were "Property and Inheritance" and "Slavery," and the remaining headings reflected something of the catchall character of the study of as yet unrelated political topics. The order in which the handbook treated the various

Table 2.3. Size of Subsections in the Sociology Section of Notes and Queries, *1912*

Subhead	Number of pages
A General Account of Method	19
Population	2
Life-History of the Individual in Society	14
Social Organization	17
Economics of the Social Group	12
Government: Politics	33
Morals	1
Warfare	3
External Relations Between Communities	2
TOTAL	103

topics indicated the primacy placed on social organization. Yet the Morganian view of property (one might better call it Morganitic, considering the illegitimacy accorded it within the establishment) as the litmus test of political evolution was still evident. Rivers contributed the essay on "Property and Inheritance."

The first edition of *Notes and Queries* (BAAS 1874), treated slavery as a somewhat anomalous topic; the 1912 edition viewed slavery exclusively as an economic institution. To this day, slavery has not been as prominent in political anthropology as its institutionalization warrants. The politics of enslavement was pre-empted by the idea of the slave as property. Thus, in 1912 the researcher was urged to specify the exact legal and social status of a person described as a slave because, it pointed out, the term was often widely applied to a condition like "slavery" as it existed in recent times in Europe and America. What was involved was persons who did not have the status of freemen "but (in the old phrase) are 'disabled from belonging to themselves'" (BAAS 1912:170).

Notes and Queries directed inquiry toward nine clusters of interest: the historical origins of slavery and its demographic imprint; the categorizations, appearance, and purpose to which slaves were put (domestic and industrial slavery were distinguished from serfdom); the rights of ownership and the treatment of slaves; the sale of slaves; slaves' rights and responsibilities; the social and group relations of slaves; and finally, manumission. The most marked difference from the nineteenth century was the added emphasis on the legal aspects of slavery. The concluding instruction read: "Collect evidence as to public and religious opinion in relation to the custom and law of slavery" (BAAS 1912:171). This reflected perhaps a change in the real world of slavery, a significant merging of the Anti-Slavery Society and the Aborigines' Protection Society in 1909.[24]

For the first time, the 1912 edition of *Notes and Queries* separated inquiries concerning government and politics from those on social organization, suggesting a more technical and specialized interest in them. Barbara Freire-Marreco, the author of this section, was Marett's student and one of the first scholars to be awarded the diploma in anthropology at Oxford. In 1912 she was a research fellow of Somerville College; her field interest lay in the American Southwest.[25] As befitted the goals of the new scientific anthropology—to "make a true record of a *living* society" (Freire-Marreco 1912:173, emphasis added)—her discussion of government and politics rested on instruction in fieldwork methods. Since reconstruction was not the anthropologist's objective, she immediately addressed problems of working in a "simple society which has been exposed to European contact." Among the points she made were the following:

1. *Informal as well as formal authority should be recognized.*
"[T]he authority by which uncivilized communities are regulated is often very slight and informal. . . . [I]t is as well to record every exercise of authority, including family discipline and social influence or prestige."

2. *Appointed as well as indigenous chiefs should be studied.*
"[T]he men who seem to be 'chiefs' may have gained their prestige quite recently, by being chosen, or by taking on themselves, to be intermediaries between natives and foreigners. These cases of present-day chiefs 'in the making' are none the less interesting and worth recording; but if the observer accepts them without further inquiry, he may get a wrong idea of *native* political organization.

3. *Views across generations should be sought.*
"Naturally you will wish to hear the views of leading men, and not only those of a young interpreter; though the young men's views must not be overlooked if you wish to make a true record of a living society."

4. *Informants' biases should be recognized.*
"[Y]ou will hear much of questions now in dispute or lately settled, but very little of the normal working of customs which are generally accepted. . . . [M]en who feel keenly on these subjects will often tell you of exceptions rather than of rules. . . . An earnest politician of this sort is a valuable informant, but you need a sympathetic understanding of his temper and of the circumstances which bias his view, and information from other sources to balance it."

5. *Political situations cannot be studied cursorily.*
"[A] hasty inquiry will teach you scarcely anything of native government. You must stay long enough to grasp the political situation, living at close quarters with the native authority, if not under it. As emergencies arise and are dealt with, you will learn the normal working of institutions; your informants will explain, amplify and correct; you will see the process by which custom is enforced or modified, the balance of power, the checks and limitations of authority." (Freire-Marreco 1912:172–174)

The ethnographic record was thus to include, for the first time, not simply the institutional forms but also the informal processes of both government (authority) and politics (influence, prestige, and power). Freire-Marreco made no absolute distinction between the social and the political realm, as the topics suggested for field observation made clear. These included

> authority within the family, the position of women, personal and social prestige; social ranks and grades; political authority; delegated authority; provision for enforcing authority; religious and magical aspects of authority; public property and revenue; councils and assemblies, popular elements in government, secret societies; laws, legislation; crimes, vengeance, public justice, lynch-law, courts; covenants and oaths, ordeals, curses. (Freire-Marreco 1912:174)

The inclusion of "Law" and the position of women under the rubric of "Government/Politics" is noteworthy. The list did not reflect, however, the interest in external relations among communities that also existed in British anthropology at that time. The *method* of study—close and prolonged observation—was beginning to shape the *field* of study; the closed system was in the making.

THE BRITISH COLONIAL MILIEU

As it became a profession and a distinctive academic discipline, anthropology began to aspire to the training of civil service officers and the appointment overseas of government anthropologists. Because of the language skills required of both the anthropologist and the colonial administrator, anthropology became a specialization. It also acquired a problem orientation. Not incidentally, anthropologists paid increased attention to law and order. Ties with folklorists, classical scholars, philologists, historians and archaeologists—all critical affiliates of earlier practitioners—gave way before the onslaught of practical anthropology.[26] Along with the change came the loss of a reading public.

Yet, once again an attempt to engage the Colonial Office in the funding of anthropology failed. Rivers and those who advocated practical anthropology were operating in a political context of public concern over the moral and practical defects of imperialism. The Fabian Society came into existence in 1900, at the beginning of Britain's monopoly capitalist era. Fabian assaults on the economic concentration of wealth began to have some effect around 1903 when H. G. Wells's *Mankind in the Making* appeared. C.F.G. Masterman's persuasive *The Heart of the Empire* (1902) argued that since London lay at the heart of the empire and was the source of its vitality, scholars should turn their attention to the city's social problems and away from the imperial periphery. Manuals revealing imperial exploitation in the Congo and South Africa such as Edmund D. Morel's *Red Rubber!* (1905) and Henry N. Brailsford's *The War of Steel and Gold* (1914) were more influential than the "radical" anthropologists of the day.[27]

Nevertheless, between 1900 and 1920 the RAI made several attempts to win recognition for their involvement in imperial affairs.[28] In June 1900 it petitioned the secretary of state for the colonies to appoint a commission to inquire into the condition of the native races of South Africa and the relations of the European colonists to one another. In 1905 it requested a Civil List pension for Rev. Lorimer Fison (whose Australian aboriginal studies had been so important to the profession); in May 1908 it petitioned the government to establish an ethnological bureau like the BAE. In 1910 it collaborated with the Royal Colonial Institute in the training of probationers in the African service; in October 1913 the RAI appointed a committee to carry out Sir Richard Temple's scheme for the establishment of "applied Anthropology," and in the same year it sought to have a government anthropologist appointed to British East Africa (Kenya) and Uganda.

The dons were singularly ill placed to plead the cause of a practical anthropology in the service of the state. Few Edwardian anthropologists were members of the establishment: many came from families dissenting from the established Church of England (Haddon was the son of a Baptist printer; Tylor, a Quaker; Hocart, a Wesleyan Methodist; Spencer a nonconformist; Seligman, a Jew). Several of them were outsiders in a geographical sense (Marett and Hocart were from the French-speaking Channel Islands, Elliott Smith was from Australia, and Westermarck was a Finn). The dons' passionate involvement earned the disapproval of the Colonial Office. Marett and Balfour were on one occasion referred to as "wild enthusiasts," and Haddon and Read on another as "crazy Ethnologists." But above all, the Colonial Office was not prepared to rate professional expertise in the customs and cultures of native peoples above the quietly understood prerogatives of patronage and birth: when push came to shove, the Honorable Charles Dundas was given the plum job, not the better qualified R. S. Rattray.[29]

Sandal-Clad in Africa

In 1910 the fieldwork of one of Rivers's students, Northcote Thomas, provided something of a test case for anthropology as a profession.[30] His career represented a transition between comparative sociology and the fieldwork tradition, because prior to undertaking field research, Thomas, like so many scholars of his era, had written on kinship and group marriage among the Australian aborigines. His was the volume

The Natives of Australia (1906) in The Native Races of the British Empire series. In that same year he accepted an appointment as government anthropologist in Nigeria, where he served until his transfer to Sierra Leone in 1912. He was appointed to Nigeria because "the information collected in a questionnaire sent to District Officers was insufficient and it was necessary to have it studied and elaborated by an expert" (Lackner 1973:133). Thomas's two-volume report on the Edo-speaking peoples of the colony was published in 1910, and six volumes on the Ibo-speaking peoples followed in 1913 and 1914. The first and fourth volumes dealt with law.

Thomas approached African peoples through language, making, in these exploratory days of colonial administration, no use of the concept of the "tribe." His first report dealt with language, religion and magic, marriage and birth, inheritance, adoption and property, and law and kinship, in that order. His practice was to tour a region inhabited by the speakers of one language. Stopping in towns and villages, he then, with the help of interpreters, quizzed their inhabitants on their customs. He then made a general statement, accompanied by a scrupulous recording of local variations. He made no attempt, however, to analyze or account for the differences he found. As a student of Rivers, he collected genealogies wherever he went (and reproduced some). He strongly advocated the use of the genealogical method for the collection of "concrete details" and "reliable information." His best use of it appeared in a section on demography in his Sierra Leone report alongside village plans, an account of the derivation of wives, and a reference to problems encountered because several men had become labor migrants. Clearly he was recording the current situation, not a reconstruction of the past.

Thomas provided another early use of a specific case in the anthropology of law. We may refer to it as "The Case of the Costly Lawsuit," since this was the aspect of the judicial procedure that most struck the eminently practical Thomas. That litigation brought profit to the legal profession rather than to the litigants was the gist of his summary: "[T]he debate went on for nearly three days, each side being mulcted by the two chiefs who heard it, firstly 15s. for the summons and the answer, secondly 4s. for subsistence money for the chiefs, and thirdly 10s. hearing fee, in all 29s. each. They also deposited £2 each security for the fine to be imposed on the loser, the whole £4 to be adjudged to the winner." Yet, "the case was an exceedingly simple one" (1916:153–154). As Thomas described the case,

Mela, a fisherman, gave six pennies worth of fish on credit to Sedu who subsequently refused to pay. Mela took him to court asking the chief justice Seka to recover the money. Seka received an axe worth one shilling, and a gown worth two shillings and six pence from Sedu in settlement of the debt. This however, he refused to hand over to Mela, denying even that he had received it.

Mela then went to Sedu and in some fashion persuaded Sedu to pay him the sum owed directly, in spite of Sedu's complaints that he had already paid the equivalent to Seka. Mela said that he didn't care about that, do what you will with him.

Sedu then summoned Seka before Bai Lanteli. Bai Lanteli, however, summoned before him not Seka but Mela and ordered him to return Sedu's money, as Seka had no quarrel with him. Bai Lanteli gave the case against Mela on the ground that "you cannot crown a chief and then uncrown him."

Thomas was perplexed by the case: "I made more than one effort to understand the point of view and to discover why Seka was able to summon Mela at all, but without success. "Finally on coming into another chiefdom, I was told by the chief, who had some reputation as a jurist, that the decision was wholly wrong" (1916:153–154). We will return to the pragmatics of justice in the next chapter.

The Colonial Office itself was not completely convinced of the usefulness of Northcote Thomas's researches, in spite of argument that they furnished material "for the compilation of a code of tribal usage which will be of considerable value for administrative purposes and may hereafter form the basis of positive legislation." This was the first (but certainly not the last) occasion in which an anthropologist was involved in the codification of so-called customary law in a colonial territory, and the committee set up to evaluate his work expressed its emphatic opinion that "in the interests of the efficient administration of these territories it is most desirable that enquiries of the kind carried out by Mr. Thomas should be undertaken on a large scale and for an extended period. They are convinced that *as the country is opened up and properly increases in value* there will continually be greater need for accurate knowledge of the people and their usages if mistakes which may entail serious consequences are to be avoided [emphasis added]."[31] The interests of commerce as well as social control would appear to have been uppermost in their minds.

Practical Anthropology

Appeals to imperial responsibility and to the practicalities of finding employment for anthropologists in Britain aside, practical anthropology, as it was called, was not without its opponents. Matters came to a head around 1912 (not in relation to the patronage of the Colonial Office, although the pure-and-applied argument was brought to bear) when the possibility was held out of obtaining funding for the new discipline from the American philanthropical financier Andrew Carnegie. In a report to the Carnegie Foundation, W.H.R. Rivers drew attention to the fact that in the world at large, the new imperialisms of Europe and the United States wrought, as he put it, "rapid and destructive change" (1913:6). Year by year, knowledge of other cultures was expanding in academic circles at a geometric rate, and ethnology, the young science, was "in the stage at which it [was] seeking for principles and methods by means of which to obtain a firm footing amidst the vast complex of facts with which it [had] to deal."

Rivers made two recommendations. First, that research be conducted on islands, where conditions would be relatively simple and favorable, rather than in continental areas; and second, that it be conducted by professionally trained anthropologists carrying out intensive rather than survey investigations, not by government officials and missionaries. The report heralded an era of private anthropological financing that escalated as the United States became more and more involved in European and global business matters.

In 1917 Rivers made a second appeal, which was more narrowly directed. It appeared in a short paper entitled "The Government of Subject Peoples." One of the problems with the management of colonial peoples, as he saw it, was the false and inadequate knowledge that administrators had of the people they had to govern. They lost respect because of their ignorance: "It is not good that a people should daily see men, who hold themselves to belong to a superior race, believing firmly in a code of knowledge which every native knows to be only a mongrel version of the truth" (1917:309). Moreover, given that reforms had to be carried out, there was a lack of appreciation that they might have unintended consequences. "[I]t is one thing to destroy or modify in ignorance, and it is quite another to do so with a knowledge of the consequences which must inevitably follow these courses of action" (1917:314). Rivers hinted at the intelligence function of anthropology, observing somewhat sarcastically that the British Empire had been built up by character rather than by intelligence. "The great success of this mode of growth in the past," he warned, "should not blind us to its insufficiency for the future" (1917:327).

Rivers's class-consciousness was out of step with the academic needs of his time. He turned to lecturing for the Workers Educational Association and stood for Parliament as a Labour party candidate in the election of 1922. His death in that year coincided with the publication of Malinowski's *Argonauts of the Western Pacific* which he helped arrange.[32]

Diffusionism and the Imperial Cosmos

Opposition to anthropology's colonial trajectory was voiced most audibly by those not in positions of academic power, Rivers's diffusionist colleagues Grafton Elliot Smith and William J. Perry. Who, then, were these Edwardian diffusionists who seemed so out of step with the needs of the state and how important were their academic politics?[33] Eminent scholars showing an interest in diffusion have been treated as if they had turned aside from the paths of righteousness, straying into ignominious fields, yet critical issues underlay the dissension between functionalists and diffusionists.[34] Their resolution, and the form it took, led British anthropology along a particular, narrowly defined path. The outcome established the power holders of British academic anthropology for the next two generations and allocated the auspices and funding of all field research.

Truly explosive issues tend to burst the bounds of chronology. The origins of the diffusionists' battle with functionalism lay in the distinction made in 1879 between historically oriented ethnology and a sociology that dealt with social systems. The distinction lasted until at least 1934. For our present purposes the confrontation may be traced to 1911, when Grafton Elliot Smith's *The Ancient Egyptians* gave rise to what its detractors called "The Heliolithic School."[35]

The quarrel had many arenas. It could be recognized in the affairs of the Royal Anthropological Institute, where two of the main protagonists, Perry (a diffusionist) and Malinowski (a functionalist) were elected Ordinary Fellows in the same month, November 1910. It was fought out in the offices of publishers and in the book-review columns of professional journals. It had a regional dimension, with Elliot Smith at Manchester University observing that "the people down south" were not prepared to publish "heterodox views."

From the moment in 1911 when Elliot Smith framed his first theoretical statement, his work was continually caricatured by his detractors, and the diffusionist approach was simply damned for its speculative excesses. Momentarily, as their problematic gained legitimacy in academic discourse, "moderate diffusionists"—Rivers, Hocart, and Wheeler—were distinguished from the demonic "hyper-diffusionists" — Perry and Elliot Smith. But (as Rivers's biographer, Richard Slo-bodin, has pointed out) the idea that diffusionism was "a litany of futil-ity has been accepted by generations of students" ever since (1978:73).

At the heart of the struggle lay the subject matter of anthropology, then in the process of definition. Was it to be the study of closed, small-scale societies or was it to represent the human aspects of global con-cerns, the diffusion of "races" and the emergence of "mixed" cultures? Budding professionals like Alfred Reginald Brown, C. Daryll Forde, and Gerald Camden Wheeler were caught between the two. Rivers had begun to draw a distinction between "mixed" and "unmixed" cultures after his field experience in the western Pacific, where "blackbirding" (labor recruitment) had led to extreme population movement. Between 1863 and 1914, some 100,000 Pacific islanders had been shipped as indentured plantation laborers to Queensland, Fiji, Samoa, and New Caledonia. In a letter to Brown, who was struggling to write up his Andaman Islands field data in Birmingham, Rivers expressed disquiet at his student's treating as a simple society one that seemed to him to be clearly the complex result of historical contacts and the mixing of races. Even the sociologists recognized that "culture contact, direct or indirect [was] in fact the normal, not exceptional, process throughout human history" (Hobhouse, Wheeler, and Ginsberg 1915:28).

The issue was parochial, and several imperial powers arrived at simi-lar modes of scientific conceptualization. The contact of peoples was already on the agenda of cultural anthropology in the United States, as we have seen, and was elaborated in a schema that Powell called "accul-turation." Acculturation theory challenged the evolutionary tradition because the diffusion of capital around the globe, often encapsulated in the colonial situation, demonstrated clearly that savages could become civilized without the passage of thousands of years. Theories of cultural diffusion first emanated from Germany during the last quarter of the nineteenth century. Besides being clearly more compatible than evolu-tionary theory for scholars whose nation had been formed only fifty years previously, they also reflected the character of Germany's early engagements in sub-Saharan Africa.

In challenging the arguments of evolutionists and sociological an-thropologists, Elliot Smith argued that civilization arose in historical circumstances. Neither evolutionary theory nor visions of the psychic unity of mankind could account for where and when it appeared. Differ-ences among existing cultures could be attributed to the movements and settlement even of small groups; the stimuli of contacts between them were fundamental in the development of distinct cultures. Often this movement was related to the exploitation of different natural re-sources. Thus for Elliot Smith diffusion was not simply an abstract concept but was, like the migration with which it was associated, an historical process. A localized past and present could only be explained by reference to the wider world in which they had developed. Elliot Smith, as Elkin put it, stood for the large concept and vision (1974:153–154). "He saw the whole civilized world as one Oikoumene (using Kroeber's term), of which diffusion, or the interpenetration of culture traits and complexes, was the means of ensuring continuity in space and time." So commonsensical did the idea of the migration of aspects of culture seem by the 1970s that anthropologists like Elkin (1974) and Burridge (1973) found it necessary to account for the poor reception it had once received.[36] For those interested in Oceanic interisland phenomena, culture history was revitalized. To some extent this may have been a self-defining stance adopted by Australian scholars. On the other hand, the revitalization included a new interest in Kroeber's work as well as that of Hocart and a reaching out to Immanuel Wallerstein's newly published book *The Modern World-System* (1974b).

The Open Society

The major contribution of diffusionist theory to political anthropology has not yet been fully explored. Its latent function in countering the dehistorization of a dominated people clearly failed. Nevertheless, the particular contributions of three of its practitioners proved of lasting value. All were converts to diffusionist theory, and all worked in Oceania. Rivers's work has already been discussed. Both Arthur Hocart and Gerald Camden Wheeler pursued, for example, the theme of politi-cal heralds and envoys through several of their works (e.g., Hocart 1913; Wheeler 1910). Intergroup relations played a role in the conceptualiza-tion of political units. Their ethnographies of island communities in the Pacific that had trading and diplomatic relations with each other shaped their analyses, as did their compliance with Rivers's insistence on intensive fieldwork and the genealogical method.[37]

A year after Wheeler's return from the Pacific, his book *The Tribe and Intertribal Relations in Australia* (1910) was reviewed by a fellow stu-dent, who described it as a sociological, contemporary, problem-ori-ented study "without entering into any questions of origins, develop-ment, or any prehistory at all," in short, a "good, really scientific, ethnographic monograph"—just what the discipline needed. The re-viewer was Bronislaw Malinowski (1911:25–26). Wheeler himself de-scribed *The Tribe and Intertribal Relations* as a study in the primitive

jurisprudence of international law.[38] Wheeler derived his view of international law from the jurist Ludwig Oppenheim and found many of the
ideas of international law already clearly developed in Australian
aboriginal society, including territorial sovereignty, the diplomatic im-
munity of messengers and envoys, and the rights of asylum, domicile-
ment, and hospitality. He considered the group relations of the Australians to be "the true units in [which] we may trace the beginnings of
International Law" (1910:22).

Malinowski appreciated Wheeler's concrete detail and sense of problem but could not resist casting the fluid, open-ended analysis in his
own terms: "The local, territorial distribution of the natives; the con-
notation of the group living together, being in actual daily contact; the
boundaries of a track of country over which a group roams; all these
questions are involved and form together the problem of tribal constitution." Wheeler, having "fixed the forms of social organization," went
on to show their "working" (Malinowski 1911:27–28).

Wheeler did this by elaborating on war and justice. The most consistent manifestation of tribal unity, he argued, was that local groups did
not carry on unregulated warfare with each other. Justice he defined as
"those more or less regulated methods by which differences either between groups or between individuals are composed" (1910:116). Anthropologists later used this same dichotomy—law within and war
without—to underpin political anthropology in its classical era.[39]
Wheeler, like many who followed him, grappled with the problem that
much of the fighting among the Australians was really a form of justice:
"The first blood that flows puts an end to the fight" (1910:148). The
blood feud was thus a form of legal warfare and only "indiscriminate
vengeance" leading to carnage was really war.

Wheeler's anthropology, published and unpublished, contained all
the contradictions of the Edwardian era. Echoes of evolutionary stages
accompanied his synchronic Australian sociology, and their reconciliation was diffusionist. Foreshadowings of functionalism, and even of
structuralism, appeared, but there was one quintessential difference.
Wheeler insisted,

> The study of cultures cannot but be followed from the historical standpoint,
> that is, they will be looked on as always in process of change in time and
> space; fundamentally the method must be historical. . . . If Ethnology is
> essentially historical in method, we have to assume a theoretically endless
> possibility of movement, and of action and reaction, direct or indirect,
> between culture groups. On the postulate of unlimited movement and
> interaction we reach a conclusion where the question of independent

origins for culture elements [i.e., evolution], or of their spread from definite centers [i.e., diffusion] has no fundamental importance; the range of man becomes in the limit itself one organic whole. Theoretically, every point is or has been in contact with any other. The two doctrines [evolutionary and diffusionist theory] become one only; and the historical, or culture contact theory is mainly a point of view, or methodological principle—without losing in this aspect any of its fundamental importance. (Wheeler 1926:xiv–xv)

Although Wheeler's field notes indicate that he was a keen observer of the colonial situation, his published work remained conventional. The text quoted above, pregnant in its reference to historical *or* culture contact theory and its tracing of the processes of change, was published in his somewhat obscure *Mono-Alu Folklore* in 1926.

What was distinctive about diffusionists such as Rivers, Hocart, Wheeler, Perry, and Elliot Smith was their uncompromising insistence that anthropology study not only primitive or savage peoples but the whole world, ancient and modern, in its historical complexity.[40] To those who argued that this would not be scientific, Elliot Smith quoted the words of historian Frederick J. Teggart, Kroeber's colleague at Berkeley. "The widening outlook of both anthropologists and historians, *as well as the requirements of science*, demands the coordination of these two phases of humanistic inquiry" (Teggart 1916:276, emphasis added). These words were to be reiterated many times on both sides of the Atlantic as an opposition developed between those who analyzed law, government, and politics *within* society and those who studied them *among* societies, particularly societies unevenly positioned within the global power structure.

AMERICAN ANTHROPOLOGY: BEYOND THE RESERVATION

The first two decades of American anthropology in the twentieth century have long been seen as dominated by the Boasian ascendancy, but this was never the case as far as the study of politics was concerned. One of the many paradoxes of anthropology is that some of the men most involved in national or international politics paid little attention to the political organization of those whom they studied. Franz Boas of Columbia University was one such scholar, and his cultural anthropology was apolitical in the extreme. This was in striking contrast to his scientific activism in the politics of his day. Both as an authority on race and as a victim of discrimination, Boas was active in opposing racial segregation, writing for the popular press, mobilizing philanthropy for Negro education, and speaking at Atlanta University on the invitation of W.E.B. DuBois (Beardsley 1973; Stocking 1979b).

The most adventurous work was done by those outside the formal academy at the Bureau of American Ethnology and in museums where men and women who were interested had the opportunity to explore politics. The political analyses of James Mooney and John Reed Swanton have been underrated; only in the academy with the training of graduates was the reproduction of ideas fully realized.[41]

The institutionalization of anthropology owed much to Frederick Ward Putnam, who in 1886 had assumed a chair attached to the Peabody Museum of American Archaeology and Ethnology at Harvard. Under his aegis, Boas was appointed to the American Museum of Natural History and Columbia University. Boas viewed museum collections as potentially the basis for university instruction, so gaining a toehold for the discipline in the academic world (Darnell 1971). At first dependent on, and in collaboration with, the Bureau of American Ethnology, Boas's academic anthropology gradually ousted it from prominence, although their common subject matter, Native Americans, made the paradigmatic shift that occurred gradual rather than revolutionary. In the struggle in 1919 between Boas and the Washingtonians, only two men at the bureau refused to take sides: Swanton and Mooney.

Boas "consciously envisioned a social network" of university departments chaired and staffed by his students (Darnell 1971:99). A beginning was made at Berkeley, to which Alfred Kroeber was appointed in 1901. Unlike Columbia, Berkeley attracted mostly students from midwestern and western states. With the legacy of Powell's Colorado studies on the edges of its domain, its intellectual thrust soon diverged from that of Boas.

Outside the Putnam-Boas orbit of luminaries and satellites, Frederick Starr owed an appointment at the University of Chicago to its president, William Rainey Harper. Starr's part in the development of anthropology in America is usually viewed negatively: he is most remembered at Chicago for *not* having established a department at a time when funds in plenty were flowing into anthropological coffers elsewhere.[42] Whig historicism makes him reactionary: "Because Starr refused to abandon evolutionary theory and to cooperate with other scholars or disciplines, the program [at Chicago] was a great disappointment, particularly to Boas" (Darnell 1971:98). Nationally, Starr's political stance was progressive. A somewhat idiosyncratic character, he engaged in anti-imperialist activities that at times embarrassed his university. His large, popular classes were given sporadically on his return from photographic and ethnological expeditions to Africa, the Philippines, Japan, and elsewhere. The part he played in shaping Philippine legal ethnography is the subject of a later section.

Politics at the Bureau

Regardless of the intellectual and political predilections of its researchers, the main responsibility of the Bureau of American Ethnology to the taxpayers who funded it was to make available to the public syntheses of the nation's ethnological findings. After years of travail, the bureau's encyclopedic *Handbook of American Indians North of Mexico*, under the editorship of Frederick Webb Hodge, began to appear in 1907. Its chief contributor on subjects of a political nature was John Napoleon Bonaparte Hewitt. Described by Swanton as "a kind of Bureau institution" (n.d.:45), Hewitt claimed descent from the Bear clan of the Tuscarora, founded by a captive white woman. Prior to his recruitment by Powell, he had been a conductor on the New Jersey railway system. His *Handbook* entries (Hodge 1907) dealt with chiefs, clans and gens, and confederation and government. Government policy toward the Indians was outlined by A.C.F. (Alice Fletcher?). Although the pen was Hewitt's, in most cases the words might have been those of Powell himself—an indication of the intellectual stagnation that set in at the bureau after 1898.

For the first two decades of the twentieth century, Hewitt's *Handbook* entry on government served to crystallize the ethnography of political organization among Native Americans. The political leagues of the eastern seaboard were given prominence, with the Iroquois confederation taking pride of place. "Looser confederations" were recorded among the Chippewa, Ottawa, and Potawatomi. Political features were not clearly adumbrated. The seven council fires of the Dakota, the Powhatan, and the Caddo confederacies were said to be all "held together largely by religious affiliation" (Hewitt 1907:337), but what else might hold them together was not reported. The reader interested in government was advised to turn to entries on the clan and gens, social organization, and the tribe.

The vision of Native American government presented in the *Handbook* was patchy, unsystematic, and lacking in theory. It compares unfavorably with Nieboer's comparative research using Native American data. In part this was because Native American ethnography continually threw up cases that challenged his argument, but it was due even more to the systematic and comprehensive nature of his causal inquiry. Finding considerable differences in the abundance of food, fixed settlement, size of group, preservation of food, trade and industry, property, and wealth between the peoples of the Pacific Coast and those of the central states, Nieboer was led to explore why the former had slaves and the latter did not. In the course of his questioning, he systematically reported on the nature of power and influence among specific Native American groups in a manner that was far more perceptive than Hewitt's idealistic rendering of their forms of government. Nieboer's analysis of power and influence was not, as far as I know, used by either Boasians or bureau ethnologists; it is summarized in Table 2.4. The superiority of Nieboer's work lay not simply in his collation and application of ethnographic data culled from amateur sources but also in his implicit application of the theories of classical political economy. The bureau's ethnology, without Powell, was theoryless.

Table 2.4. Nieboer's Analysis of the Nature of Leadership Among Central North American Indians

Group	Attributes of Chieftainship
Montagnais	rhetoric, eloquence. "They have no other law than his word."
Algonquins	bravery in war, personal prowess, and tact
Ojibway	wisdom, courage, hospitality
Blackfeet	prowess, self-denial, disowning of property; no power unless distinguished as a warrior
Kutchin	(1) elected for wisdom and courage (2) power depends on number of beads he owns (3) chiefs hold position by periodically redistributing their chattels
Cheyenne	bravery and wisdom
Sioux	bravery
Apache	(1) wealth, bravery, wisdom, with some succession to office (2) bravery (3) succession, bravery, wealth
Comanche	war leader, knowledge, cunning

SOURCE: Derived from Nieboer 1900.

Bureau workers contributed most to the anthropology of politics not in Washington but in the field. The disproportionate time Mooney spent there recording but never allowing time enough to collate and analyze his data was criticized by a committee appointed to look into the bureau's affairs in 1902.[43] Certainly Mooney's field research was not scientific in the same way as Rivers's. His major goal was to salvage culture in the form of material objects, texts, and ceremonials. The demands of the Smithsonian Institution and the museum world left him rudderless in a sea of theoretical and methodological frustration. And yet, his innate ethnographic sense won through.

Several of Mooney's published contributions between 1899 and his death in 1921 touched on politics. In 1907 he provided an entry on the Ghost Dance for the *Handbook*. In this he took the occasion earlier denied him by Powell to elaborate on the belief in the coming of a messiah as "a natural human longing" among peoples long subjected to alien domination (Mooney 1907:492). After Powell's retirement, Mooney focused increasingly on Indian political relations as he began to publish on the Kiowa and Cheyenne. He also engaged in the practical politics of representing the "peyote" case to the government.

John Swanton, Mooney's colleague at the bureau, had very different work habits. Much more of his political data entered the published record: first, ethnohistorical analyses of the political organization of several Indian tribes of the Southeast and the Lower Mississippi Valley, among them the Natchez (1907), Creek (1917), and Caddo (1931); and second, succinct reviews of political studies by others, notably Sir James Frazer and the American sociologists of primitive society Hutton Webster and Eben Mumford.

As is often the case, the field situation in which Swanton chose to work, first among the Native Americans of Mississippi and Oklahoma and then elsewhere in the Lower Mississippi Valley and the Southeast, shaped his contribution. This region had suffered Spanish, French, and English incursions, so he was led to primary ethnohistorical sources. Because Native American organization in these regions took the form of large-scale confederacies, his ethnography was integumentally political. That it never fed into the mainstream reflected the academic dominance of the Boasians, their success in redefining anthropology in their own image, and their transmission of this image as a legacy for later generations. Only in one instance did Swanton's ethnohistory enter the record, and then as a political enigma.

The Enigma of the Natchez State

The Natchez have proved peculiarly troublesome for political anthropology. A group of Native Americans first described by travelers along the Mississippi in the eighteenth century, the Natchez were almost entirely exterminated by French colonists. When Swanton worked among them, only five families remained. But as Swanton noted, "Aside from their temple nothing attracted more attention from visitors to the Natchez than their peculiar strongly centralized form of government" (1911:100).

The Natchez polity was composed of two classes: nobility and stinkards. The nobility was further divided into suns, nobles, and honored people. The rank of a Natchez individual, according to Swanton, was based only on descent. The nobility was exogamous, and children's rank was determined by the rank of the higher ranking parent. If this was the mother, the child took the rank of the mother; if it was the father, the child took the rank *below* that of the father.

Swanton drew on French sources for his reconstruction of a form of government in which a ruling class provided a great chief, who had despotic powers of life and death. He compared him with the first Ottoman emperors. Members of the great chief's family were treated as chiefs if they were genealogically close. Something akin to slavery existed (the Natchez provided Nieboer with one of his "anomalies"), and outlying villages sent tribute in the form of produce. The great chief's power was as absolute as a king's, and his sister or mother in the matrilineally organized state was given the title of woman chief. Though, as Swanton put it, "she does not meddle with the government, they pay her great honors. She has also, as well as the great chief, the power of life and death" (Swanton 1911:101).

The great chief nominated other important officers of state: two war chiefs, "two masters of ceremony for the worship of the temple, . . . two officers who preside over the other ceremonies which are observed when foreigners come to treat of peace, another who has the inspection of the public works, [and] four others charged with the arrangement of the festivals" (Swanton 1911:103). The great chief had a council to advise him, and "sometimes his authority was considerably curtailed by it, as well as by the more prominent and the energetic village chiefs." Both the sun (chief) and the war chief could also be controlled by the principal warriors, to whom the young people listened as if they were oracles—"a very important fact" (Swanton 1911:107). Swanton nowhere referred to Morgan's work, in spite of the commonalities of matrilineal descent reckoning and conciliar government shared by the Natchez and the Iroquois.

The Natchez have been subjected to continual primitivization since Swanton first wrote their ethnohistory. In the process, his data have been laundered to accord with the prejudices of others (in the sense of Gadamer 1976). Following his sources, Swanton described the Natchez state quite clearly as a two-class society comparable with early European states in its political complexity. Encountering such polities, eighteenth-century European travelers recognized them as nations with whom diplomatic relations might be established. In the course of the twentieth century, however, Native American polities were gradually downgraded to the level of tribal organizations. Swanton's two classes within a tributary state were watered down by successive generations: by William Christie Macleod in the 1920s, by C.W.M. Hart in the 1940s, by E. Adamson Hoebel in the 1950s, and by Elizabeth Tooker in the 1960s. They all reflected the ethos of their times. Only in the class-conscious 1930s was Swanton's analysis left unquestioned.

The Berkeley Adventure

The underpinnings of anthropology at Berkeley lay in the work of the California historian Hubert Howe Bancroft, who in 1859 began to collect material on the Pacific states of the Americas. By 1869 he had accumulated some sixteen thousand books, manuscripts, maps, and files, and by 1874 he had begun to publish five volumes on *The Native Races of the Pacific States of North America*. The first, on "wild tribes," provided the substantive basis for the first ethnological survey conducted by professional anthropologists in California.

Bancroft's legacy to Berkeley anthropologists was fourfold. First, he bequeathed a sense of domain that reached inland from the Pacific Coast as far as Utah and Colorado, thus bringing under the Berkeley survey peoples as far east as the Utes and Shoshoni. Second, along with this sense of space he brought a sense of time, even of urgency, "to gather and arrange in systematic compact form all that is known of these people; to rescue some facts, perhaps, from oblivion, to bring others from inaccessible nooks, to render all available to science and to the general reader" (Bancroft 1874:x–xi). Bancroft's third legacy was a vast array of "facts" about the "wild tribes" of California, presented without apology. Last, he bequeathed a turn of phrase that encapsulated what became their "problematic." By 1906 it was part of Kroeber's stock-in-trade: a characterization of the California Indians as being "degraded in the midst of plenty."

Bancroft "often wondered why in some regions nature is so niggard of her bounties to man that savagery and barbarism had not devised means to enable their sons to dwell there in organized political communities" (1882:53). The backwardness of the Native American in California had to be explained:

Although the poverty and barrenness of his country account satisfactorily for the low type of the inhabitant of the Great Basin, yet no such excuse is offered for the degradation of the native of fertile California. On every side, if we except the Shoshoni, in regions possessing far fewer advantages than California, we find a higher type of man. Among the Tuscaroras, Cherokees, and Iroquois of the Atlantic slope, barbarism assumes grandest proportions, but if we continue the line to the shores of the Pacific we find this intellectual dawn checked, and man sunk almost to the utter darkness of the brute. . . . The Californians . . . wear no clothes, they build no houses, do not cultivate the soil, they have no boats, nor do they hunt to any considerable extent; they have no morals nor any religion worth calling such. . . . We must look, then, to other causes for a solution of the question why a nobler race is not found in California; such for instance as revolutions and migrations of nations, or upheavals and convulsions of nature. (Bancroft 1874:324–325)

All the elements of Bancroft's musings—features of the environment, material culture, contact with Europeans, revolutions, and migrations—entered into the political studies developed at Berkeley over the next fifty years. California's historical demography challenged evolutionary theory; its native inhabitants were hunters and gatherers, yet the region supported the greatest density of population anywhere north of Mexico. But it also challenged a new environmentalism—a political ecology—developing under Kroeber's guidance as he took up Bancroft's "problematic."

Political Organization Among the Californians

If part of Kroeber's legacy came from an historian, another part was handed him by the politicians and taxpayers who supported his state university system (Heizer 1978).[44] In the first two decades of the twentieth century, the white population of California was small, but Native American settlements were to be found in almost every valley. With fewer people relocated to reservations, environmental conditions loomed large. Their propinquity to the Berkeley anthropology department also engendered a continuous intensive field experience.

In spite of environmental diversity, Kroeber found all California political organization to rest on similar forms of social structure, which were simple and loose. There was no clan (gens) organization, and there were no tribes.

The lack of organization generally made the systematic classification of the divisions of any large body of Indians difficult; in population and social life the village approximated a localized clan, but, being the largest political unit, it corresponded in a measure to a tribe. In so simple a condition of

society difference of rank naturally found but little scope. The influence of
chiefs was small, and no distinct classes of nobles or slaves were known.
(Kroeber 1904:83)

Kroeber's generalization was based on the findings of Goddard (1903)
and Dixon (1905) among the Hupa and Northern Maidu. Their common
checklist required them to report on both the units of social organization and the "authorities" (chiefs, headmen, shamans, and councils).
Kroeber's overall assessment of Native American culture is notable on
two scores: first, its somewhat negative tone and, second (apart from
a perplexed reference to wealth), its comparative lack of political content. A lack of bellicosity, intensity, and pride rendered the Californians, for Kroeber, "among the least characteristic of the Indians of
North America" (Kroeber 1904:103). Such political data was certainly
at odds with Powell's reconstruction of Wyandotte political organization and with the eastern ethnographies of leagues (Morgan 1851), confederations (Hewitt 1907), nations (Mooney 1894), and tributary states
(Swanton 1911), though Powell's Shoshoni and Ute might have been described in similar terms in 1861 and were indeed to be described in just
this way a few years later by Julian Steward, one of Kroeber's students.

The native peoples' own history did much to shape their political
condition. Some had been in contact with Euro-Americans since the
early sixteenth century; mission records date back to 1769. Others
remained autochthonous until 1851, when California achieved state-
hood. Between 1851 and 1880 prospectors and settlers instigated widespread persecution of the native peoples, culminating in a series of "Indian wars." A Ghost Dance (an offshoot of that studied by Mooney east
of the Rockies) swept northern and central California in 1870.

The federal government took responsibility for Native Americans in
California only in 1900. By the time Berkeley anthropologists knew
them as individuals, many were on reservations and rancherias. Some
were engaged in wage labor on the smallholdings and commercial enterprises of Euro-Americans. Others survived in shanty settlements by
scavenging, begging, and prostitution. The human condition of California's poor was later to become part of the Berkeley anthropological tradition (Chapter 4), but for the first twenty years reconstruction and
classification were the order of the day.

Kroeber perceived his task as publishing a complete account of the
California Indians, assembling data by what Cora du Bois later called
"the old ethnographic dragnet system of classification" (1980:82). As
the editor of the *University of California Publications in American*

Archaeology and Ethnology (UCPAAE), he established a format "tailored to the requirements of diffusionary historical reconstruction" (Hanc 1981:47). This format dragooned the political data into shape, and when a student wished to deviate from it, he was obliged to seek Kroeber's permission (Drucker and Heizer 1967).

The *UCPAAE* format evinced "a fractured, atomistic view of culture" (Hanc 1981:41). Each table of contents listed some thirty to forty topics, beginning with geographical facts about the region in which a tribe was to be found and going on to report aboriginal conditions, internal and external territorial relations, linguistic factors, food supply, the seasons, house types, pottery, basketry, weaving, songs, games, leadership, sibs, personal names, initiation rites, transvestitism, warfare, creation stories, medicine and magic, mourning ceremonies, and so on. In this passage from material to spiritual traits, museum concerns are apparent. A discussion of leadership might appear between "Games" and "Sibs"; "Warfare" follow "Birth Customs" and precede "The Creation." Nevertheless, all the monographs published between 1903 and 1939 reported, if cursorily, on political organization. The four studies that contributed most to political ethnography all found it necessary to deviate from the *UCPAAE* format, as we shall see in Chapter 3.

The American Colonial Milieu

During the first two decades of the twentieth century, "dollar imperialism" grew at the expense of Britain's more overt political empire. Indeed, since 1865 the United States had increasingly been challenging Britain's imperial dominance—a state of affairs only fully apparent after 1946. Within both the British imperial state and the American-dominated global economy, the empire bore the costs while finance capitalists reaped the profits.[45] This is not the place to discuss their relative merits from the perspective of either imperial power or the colonized world, but certainly as far as anthropology was concerned, the strength of one in part determined the weakness of the other.

When the chairman of the National Research Council of the United States suggested in 1902 that American anthropology should "follow American interests overseas," he was echoing popular sentiments (MacCurdy 1902:534). His suggestion provoked some anti-imperialist sentiments both in Congress and among anthropologists, but by and large, the expanding academic discipline was approving. The Bureau of American Ethnology attempted to extend its scientific frontier. It sent J. W. Fewkes to Puerto Rico "to investigate the aboriginal economy of the island, and to report just how America could use her new acquisition" (Noelke 1974:175). McGee proposed a new research program in applied ethnology, arguing that "many of the practical problems connected with immigration, Chinese exclusion, the occupation of Puerto Rico, Hawaii, the Philippines, and the education of the colored race can be finally solved only in the light of ethnologic principles" (1906:466). In neither case was the bureau successful in changing its image. Yet some of the most significant anthropology of this era was practiced not among Native Americans but overseas—in the Philippines, in particular. Roy Franklin Barton's ethnography of Ifugao law (1919) reflected neither the dominance of Boas nor the tradition of the bureau but rather a mixture of evolutionist and diffusionist ideas characteristic of British intellectual thought. Frederick Starr and R. R. Marett were his avatars, although two more uneasy bedfellows would be difficult to imagine.

The international context of anthropology changed considerably between 1900 and 1920. Publications such as the Native Races of the British Empire series, a handbook series edited by Northcote Thomas that dealt in turn with Australia, British Central Africa, North India, and British North America were all reviewed in the United States, often by Philippines experts. An ethnological survey of the Philippine Islands had been organized in Manila by the U.S. Philippines Commission in 1901. Its goals were (1) to explore among the wild peoples, (2) to investigate and report on the practical implications of all legislation affecting the non-Christian peoples and to recommend new legislation for such peoples, (3) to publish scientific ethnological data, and (4) to collect museum specimens.

The relationships among anthropology, education, and administration were close. The use of administrators and schoolteachers during their vacations as ethnological researchers was, of course, deplored by professional anthropological bodies. As in Britain, conflict between professionals and amateurs developed quickly. Indeed, the American Anthropological Association had been formed in June 1902 by some forty professional anthropologists when it was felt that Section II of the American Association for the Advancement of Science (which contained twice that number and included amateurs) was no longer serving emergent interests.

Anthropology served the American foreign service's needs in the classroom as well as in the field. As an academic discipline, anthropology was inaugurated at Columbia University in 1894 by Livingston Farrand and W. Z. Ripley, who gave a combined course in general ethnology. Franz Boas, appointed as a physical anthropologist in 1896, was teaching the ethnography of America and Asia by 1899. Berthold Laufer, a Sinologist, gave instruction in Asian ethnology. The Midwest captured the Philippines academic market, but the Ivy League universities held the Open Door to Chinese ethnography. In 1906 Columbia joined with Yale to offer ethnography courses in preparation for the foreign service.

The potential for research in Sub-Saharan Africa was also recognized. The Peabody Museum began publishing *Harvard African Studies* in 1917. The second volume contained two articles of political interest: an account of the Kababish Arabs (Seligman and Seligman 1918) and a comparison of the military systems of the Zulus and Spartans (Ferguson 1918). On June 20, 1912, the peripatetic Frederick Starr sailed for Africa. His journey took him to the hinterland of Liberia, the "colonial estate" of the Firestone Rubber Company. Starr was a leading spokesman for the Anti-Imperialist League and used his lecture tours to argue against American involvement overseas.

In Britain, anthropologists worked at the heart of empire and, however indirectly, overseas expansion buttressed their endeavors. For American anthropologists looking overseas, a more nebulous setting contained the subtle forms taken by commercial and missionary expansion. An address by George MacCurdy to Section H of the AAAS (1902) brought out the lion-and-fox approaches to overseas adventures that reflected at least the superficial differences between British and American imperialism. MacCurdy observed how European anthropology took on a cosmopolitan character in direct ratio "not only to the area of the *colonies* and dependencies of the several countries, but also to the tonnage of their merchant marine engaged especially in the foreign *trade*. The anthropologist's horizon is constantly under limitations imposed by his government's colonial or commercial policy." As for the United States, he observed that although it had only recently become a world power, "if we expand along with our opportunities, it is safe to say that an analysis of the work we shall do in the next twenty years will show different results from that of our record for the epoch just closed" (MacCurdy 1902.534). MacCurdy's prophetic vision became a reality in the Philippines.

Law Among the Ifugao

The greatest contribution to the anthropology of politics between 1898 and 1919 came from the pen of one who was neither an academic nor a professional anthropologist. It was the work of a schoolteacher whose sole ambition at one time had been to be a "data-collector," an ethnographer working in the field for the ethnologist Frederick Starr.[46] His work was distinctive because, in the fashion of other Edwardian ethnographers and in spite of its mishmash vocabulary, it was an analysis of a contemporary colonial situation, not a reconstructed primitive past. His legal ethnography was commissioned, moreover, not in the Cinderellalike context of colonial Africa but in the richly funded and generously endowed American colonial territory of the Philippines.

The American presence in the Philippines epitomized what Americans liked to believe was a very un-American situation shaped as much by the Department of Commerce as by the State Department or Congress. Having never formulated an imperial policy and lacking a "colonial office," and "colonial service," American activity (the Filipino historian Salvador Lopez has suggested) was largely guided by "motives of calculated self-interest and deliberate exploitation" justified by "a belief in the manifest destiny of the United States . . . as the new bearer of freedom and democracy to 'benighted peoples' outside the pale of Western civilization" (Lopez 1966:9).

The American rationale for an interest in global affairs was that the heirs of those who had cast off the yoke of British imperialism were dedicated to the revolutionary proposition that government gains its sanction from the will of the people. "This gave Americans the sinews and armor of righteousness when their explorers, followed by exploiters and exterminators of the aboriginal population, prepared the way for the expansion of settlement across the vast continent" (Perkins 1962:7) and then throughout strategic regions of the globe.

After initially supplying the Filipinos with arms so that they might throw off the colonial yoke of Spain, the United States intervened with force to prevent their victorious leader from entering Manila. In negotiations from which the Filipinos were excluded, a peace treaty was signed in Paris in which Spain ceded the Philippines to the United States for twenty million dollars. A Philippine-American war broke out less than two months later. As American troops left for the islands to take up the White Man's burden, President McKinley assured them that "The Philippines are ours as much as Louisiana by purchase or Texas or Alaska" (Lopez 1966:12). By 1901 the war was over, and four months later, in an experiment unique in colonial history (Keesing 1937), troopships landed nearly two thousand American schoolteachers on the islands. American political sovereignty and capitalist cultural hegemony thus provided the context in which researchers conducted anthropological research throughout the Philippines between 1901 and 1916.

As a member of this expatriate force, Roy Franklin Barton worked in the Mountain Province of northern Luzon continuously from 1905 to

1908 and for six months during four visits between 1910 and 1912. His ethnography, *Ifugao Law* (1919), written at the request of the government, was based on his intimate knowledge of Kiangan, a small town in the eastern part of the subprovince of Ifugao.[47] Here resident magistrates and the constabulary were active, and Barton was sometimes called upon to act as a defense attorney in legal cases (Barton 1930a). Barton took an Ifugao wife (as did other American officials) and appears to have encountered no problems in making his inquiries throughout an extensive region. It has been said of Barton that he "produced some of the most gifted ethnography ever written in English" (Kroeber 1949:91). Kroeber's choice of the word *gifted* expresses, I believe, a sentiment that Barton's work was not the result of training or craft but was the on-the-spot recording of an observer. He was recognized among his peers as "an outstandingly fine fieldworker" while at the same time receiving from an increasingly theoretically minded profession the accolade of empiricist par excellence (Du Bois 1950:81–82). Throughout the time he was in the Philippines, Filipino nationalists were concerned with the primitivization and commercialization of the Mountain Province peoples. Barton avoided this trap.

Barton's role as a pioneer of legal anthropology has been widely recognized. *Ifugao Law* was called "a pioneer study in legal anthropology" (Nader, Koch, and Cox 1966:288), a "landmark" (Gulliver 1969:11), and "a classic study" (Conklin 1960:5).[48] Yet, through academic transmogrification it suffered the same fate as Swanton's Natchez, with evolution erasing class (Vincent 1987). Bohannan's criticism that Barton reported all his ethnography as if it were law (1965:42) was simply Oxbridge scholasticism. Barton, indeed, made no attempt to divorce law from economy, class, or warfare, although he wrote separate books on Ifugao law, economics, and religion. He discussed slavery, political inequality, political brokerage, war, and the feud as aspects of Ifugao law. *Ifugao Law* also provides further ancestral legitimation of the use of the case method in legal anthropology.

The American-Filipino war did not greatly affect the Ifugao, although at least one local scholar (Dumia 1979) sought what connections there were. The first government school was opened in 1903, and during the first two years of Barton's residence, the area was governed from the lowlands through a detachment of the Philippine Constabulary, a small body of thirty-two enlisted Ifugao. On the establishment of the Mountain Province, an American military commander, Lt. Jeff D. Gallman took up residence in Kiangan. His activities greatly facilitated Barton's ethnographic work. The great public feasts he threw at government expense provided Barton with an opportunity to travel widely and safely, to be seen as a benefactor, and to take superb photographs of the events of which he wrote.

Barton's ethnography of Ifugao politics will be discussed in relation to property law, class, slavery, the political broker or go-between, feuds, and the historical context of political change. These categories are, for the most part, imposed upon his data. It should be stressed that, apart from one citation of a Dublin jurisprude, Barton refers to no authorities, no ethnologists. He does, however, preface his study with a quotation from R. R. Marett.

Property Law Among the Kiangan Ifugao. *Ifugao Law* (1919) has four parts: Family Law, Property Law, Penal Law, and Procedure, looking like something out of a law school curriculum (Nader, Koch, and Cox 1966). The format of the monograph reflects its American origins, and its substance reflects the degree to which Ifugao was part of a modern colonial possession. A compact geographic region, the Mountain Province lies at an elevation of over 7,000 feet. Ifugao, one of its seven subprovinces, lay in the southeast, its mountains rising sharply from the plain below. The Ifugao grew irrigated rice on terraced mountain fields with a skill and artistry that led Barton to claim they had no peers in mountain husbandry. His photographs bear him out. All land around the long-established population centers had been claimed for terracing by 1909. Rice was the most valued crop and had economic, social, ritual, and political significance. Sweet potatoes provided a second staple. Population density was up to 400 people per square mile. In spite of nearly three hundred years of Spanish rule and proselytizing by the Roman Catholic church, the people were dispersed in small hamlets and had no apparent allegiances greater than those to family, kin, and neighborhood. They had a reputation as headhunters.

It is not without significance—substantively, methodologically, and theoretically—that Barton began his monograph by writing of contract law among the Ifugao as it was manifested in property law, family law, and the law of irrigation, sale, and indebtedness. The most valued property was land, which might be bought and sold. Water rights accompanied a land transfer. Family property (land, forests, and heirlooms) could not be alienated by an individual holder alone, nor could moveable personal property. Both required kin approval and a public ceremony. Land might be pledged, and brokers (*monbaga*) were used to arrange both the pledging and the sale of property of all kinds.

Indebtedness, Barton noted, was widespread. He attributed it to the ceremonies required for marriages, funerals, and other rites of passage, and the large-scale borrowing that this involved. The minimum interest rate even for short-term loans was usually 100 percent. Marriage was a business transaction, with bridewealth payments varying according to class. The monbaga also negotiated settlements for divorce and desertion. The Ifugao are a property-minded people and always there is the lance in the background. All aggressive acts that were penalized Barton called crimes. Some aggressive acts went unpunished, because there was a privileged class in Ifugao society that flaunted any law. At Berkeley, Max Radin tried to persuade Barton to write of torts rather than crimes, but Barton stood firm (Kroeber 1949:19). Torts, a term in Anglo-Saxon law, are private or civil wrongs. Whether a distinction should be made in ethnography between torts and crimes later became one of the debating points in the anthropology of law (Hoebel 1954) that served to render it an arena of common discourse and, for a while, a specialization in its own right.

The Monkalun, or Political Broker. Barton's rigorous attention to procedure in his analysis of contract law contained the potential to move anthropology in two directions: first, away from the ethnological concept of "self-help" to account for order in societies that were seen to be lacking in law, and second, away from a blinkered focus on kinship as the bedrock of social control. Barton's data revealed more negotiation than self-help, more brokerage than kinship.

Ifugao mediators were of two kinds. A monbago negotiated contracts and a monkalun, litigation.[49] They might be the same man, but the two roles were distinct. The Ifugao monkalun epitomized contingent officialdom. He was always a member of the upper class (Kadangyang) and usually a man with a reputation as a headhunter. As such, he could always muster kinsmen to support him. Chosen by the plaintiff, he was not related to either party in the litigation. He acted, however, not as an advocate but as a mediator. Barton judged him to lack authority if the "accused be not disposed to listen to reason and runs away or 'shows fight' when approached, the monkalun waits until the former ascends in his house, follows him, and *war-knife in hand*, sits in front of him and compels him to listen" (1919:94, emphasis in original). Once he had been called in, the monkalun saw to it (Barton does not say how) that the litigants dealt only with him. At stake was a not inconsiderable fee made up of pigs and other valued property. Success redounded to the credit of the monkalun, who built up a reputation and a career.

Success was not the inevitable outcome of his efforts, though various pressures worked toward the reconciliation of the antagonists. "The kin of each party are anxious for a peaceable settlement, if such can be honorably brought about. They have feuds aplenty on their hands already. Neighbors and co-villagers do not want to see their neighborhood torn by internal dissension and thus weakened as to the conduct of warfare against enemies. All these forces make for a peaceful settlement" (Barton 1919:95). Should a litigant persist in flaunting the intervention of the monkalun, he would find the monkalun's kindred aligning with that of his opponent, thus adding to those "feuds a-plenty" with which he already had to deal. When mediation failed, feud prevailed. That feuds were so numerous attested to the frailty of mediation as a legal instrument among the Kiangan Ifugao.

When he successfully brought the two parties together, the monkalun arranged damages acceptable to both. This was the matter of skilled negotiation in which the reputations of litigant and mediator alike might be seen to rise or fall in the most public of arenas. Two principles operated: (1) scales of payments and damages were fixed for each kind of transgression or transaction, and (2) different grades of penalties existed for each of the three Ifugao classes. Within the possible range of payments and damages, legal outcomes rested on five factors: the nature of the offense, the relative class position of the litigants, the solidarity and behavior of each of the factions involved in the dispute, the personal reputations and tempers of the main litigants, and the geographical position of the neighborhoods involved. To these must be added the ability and intentions of the monkalun.

We can reconstruct the class structure of Kiangan Ifugao society from the scale of fines and from Barton's accounts of day-to-day behavior in which class differences were manifested. Within the framework of this class structure, the *monkalun* operated as a thermostat; the outcome of his negotiations provided the sensate, visible effect of the class system in operation.

Class and the Organization of Inequality. Class distinctions were recognized in early-twentieth-century Ifugao.[50] Described in most detail by Barton was the *kadangyang*, the wealthy class. Of the middle class, the *natumok*, he said little, and of the *nawatwat*, the poor, little more. An underclass of slaves also existed. The three classes were distinguished by their differential ownership of access to land and water: "A man's social status is fixed by the amount of rice he harvests; his wealth is in his rice fields" (Barton 1922:400).

Barton suggested that, among the Kiangan Ifugao, the term *kadang-yang*, the wealthy, "signifies about the same that the word *illustrado* [an illustrious person], robbed of its reference to education and enlightenment, does in the lowlands: a wealthy, influential man" (1922:418). The wealth of these illustrious men rested on the possession of rice lands, forest lands where hogs might be grazed, and heirlooms such as gold necklaces, gongs, rice wine, jars, glass beads, and strings of agates or bloodstones. Rice lands were acquired, for the most part, through premortem inheritance; the eldest child (son or daughter) acquired the land of the parent who had the best fields; the second child acquired the land of the other parent. Heirs gave some land to their siblings.

A man might be born of a kadangyang family, or he might be recognized as a kadangyang after giving a feast and carving out an elaborate lounging bench for himself at which he might hold court. Since genealogies were reckoned back some ten to fourteen generations, bilaterally, so it was hypothetically possible for all men to claim kadangyang ancestry. Although Barton wrote at times as if they were a class of nobles, his ethnography suggests that emphasis should be placed on the claiming and validation of the privileged position. This might be done by holding a feast, with those attending providing public recognition of the achievement of kadangyang status. Clearly, however, elements of class reproduction were also present.

The Ifugao lived in small hamlets made up of some six to twelve houses occupied by both kin and non-kin. Personal kindreds included all the descendants of eight pairs of great-great-grandparents, extending laterally to include third cousins. These were the exogamous units of Ifugao society, and members were dispersed over fairly wide territories. Each kindred had at its center an individual of high social and economic status. This was the *gaowa*, or "the center," "the head of the family who unites all the members of a given family around himself" (1938:6). Such men advised their kinsmen and settled disputes among them. They also gave feasts that brought honor to their kindred. Family heads loaned goods to their kinsmen at lower rates of interest than they charged to others, and in return, kinsmen were obliged to support them in feuds and litigation (Barton 1919; J. Starr 1958). While all "centers" were kadangyang, not all kadangyang were "centers."[51]

Kadangyang as a class had considerable privilege in Ifugao society. As the word suggests, the privileged man stood above the law. Where wealth and power rested on the cultivation of a good crop, as among the Ifugao, the acquisition and control of labor was critical. Ifugao expended more labor per capita on rice cultivation than any other peoples in the Mountain Province, and women and children, valued resources, worked alongside men in the terraced fields (1922). Barton noted: "Any Ifugao, except one of the most powerful, who might try to take a plural wife would only bring upon himself heavy punishment—punishment that would be administered by the kin of the first wife" but "men who are very wealthy . . . *make* polygamy legal for themselves" (1919: 10). He cited the case of a man who paid an indemnity to the kin of his first wife, kept a second, and, we learn later, even contemplated a third (1922:415).

Kadangyang betrothed their first-born and perhaps even their second-born children while they were still young to other individuals of high rank. Siblings were shed off every generation "so that in the main only first or second born children" attained the rank of kadangyang (1949: 145). Kadangyang controlled the courtship behavior of their children; youths of other classes ranged near and far to visit girls' dormitories. Kadangyang also placed a high price on bridewealth and remarriage. The kadangyang thus practiced exclusion to maintain power, authority, and privilege. The operation of Ifugao law, Barton showed, served both to maintain these privileges and to ameliorate the conditions to which abuse of privilege might give rise.

From Barton's ethnography, *natumok*, the middle class, was clearly a residual category. Some natumok became kadangyang as they acquired wealth, and others became impoverished and sank into the poor but respectable lower class. At any one time, the natumok were comprised of (1) those who had a surplus of rice but were not kadangyang; (2) those who had enough rice for the year but no surplus; and (3) those who ran out of rice and had to work for it or borrow it at high interest rates (Barton 1919, 1922, 1949).

The analysis of middle sectors within a political structure provides insight not only into the actuality of power but also into its ideological conceptualization and the political ideology of those who describe it. Like later American commentators on his work (Keesing 1934, J. Starr 1958) Barton assumed "upward mobility" for the middle class. Yet the likelihood of this occurring was not supported by other features of the colonial Ifugao power structure. Starr (1958) believed that the middle class formed a majority in Ifugao society, but Barton at one point (1922:399) stated that more than half of the population were nawatwat, poor. His account of the Ifugao middle class belongs to the "good citizenship and individual ambition" school of American thought in the Philippines, to which Keesing (1937) drew attention. Yet, good ethnographer that he was, Barton's documentation of the lowest class, the nawatwat, and of an underclass of slaves below them, suggests a much more pervasive inequality in Ifugao than either their, or his, dogma would permit.

More than half of the population fell into the category of *nawatwat*, or lower class. Within it were recognized the "poor but respectable" and the "very poor or poverty stricken" (Barton 1922:418, 410). Nawatwat had very small rice fields if they had any at all. They were the tenants of the kadangyang and were often obliged to pawn both women and children in order to settle their debts. Lower-class children were adopted by the wealthy, who also employed the men as their servants. Nawatwat could be enslaved for theft and for spitting on a member of the kadangyang class, even accidentally, or for insulting them in any way.

Slaves could be acquired from warfare, by purchase, and in the settlement of debts incurred by members of the lower class. Had he known, Barton's Ifugao ethnography would have contributed an excellent test case for Nieboer's hypothesis that slavery would not be found where land was plentiful. According to Barton, in the past male captives were beheaded and only women and children taken as slaves. Children were also sold to slave dealers. Slaves were valued at between five pigs and five carabaos in Ifugao and at between five and twenty carabaos in the lowlands. In the lowlands the children of slaves remained slaves; in Ifugao a slave's children were free and were presumably categorized as members of the nawatwat. The ordering of political inequality clearly had some degree of flexibility within it, but it also had mechanisms that supported the maintenance of power by a privileged few, not least the existence of this underclass of slaves, replenished from both within and without the local system of kinship and neighborliness.

The Taking of Life. An important question about any culture is whether legal systems are more protective of persons or property. In a section on penal law, Barton discussed homicide, executions (i.e., feuds), and war among the Kiangan Ifugao. He argued that "war, murder and the death penalty exacted in execution of justice are so near each other as to be almost synonymous terms" (1919:69).

The death penalty was incurred for the practice of sorcery, murder, persistent and willful refusal to pay a debt, adultery when discovered *in flagrante*, theft by a foreigner, and refusal to pay a fine. Since the kindred of an offender rarely considered the death penalty justified, any execution was likely to start a feud. "The Ifugao has one general law," Barton noted, "which with a few notable exceptions he applies to killings, be they killings in war, murders or executions, which public opinion would pronounce justifiable and legal. That law is: *A life must be paid by a life"* (1919:69). Blood feuds, he noted, were almost as numerous as the kindreds themselves.

Barton saw the feud as a mechanism within, or an extension of, customary law. War was a very different matter. It usually took place between comparatively distant localities and took the form of a series of head takings. These were carried out by individuals who lay in wait for their victims alongside well-traveled paths or sought them out near enemy villages. The heads of women served as well as those of men. Distant localities were almost continually at war. Whether heads were taken always, sometimes, or not at all served to discriminate among political groupings that were at war, were feuding, and were at peace. Relationships could be joined or severed by merging or murder. Neighboring villages and unrelated kindreds recognized different (and to varying degrees distinct) affinal, feuding, and war zones.

Barton's ethnography leaves the reader with a problem: if feuds "exist [where] to a certain extent ties of blood and marriage exist" (1919:70), and if head taking occurs in a feuding zone where there are no such ties, what is the political community? If the maxim "Law within and war without" applies, does head taking denote war? Is feuding war or law? At the time of Barton's inquiry, homicides were rare in Ifugao. Six were recorded in 1911, two in 1912, seven in 1913, four in 1914, and four in 1915 (Dumia 1979:42–43). Barton attributed the low rate to the colonial government's prohibition against spear carrying, yet a built-in mechanism also existed that might prevent a feud from breaking out. Involuntary coughing (and tuberculosis and persistent coughing were both common ailments in the mountains) was used as an omen to provide face-saving conditions for those who sought not to fight. Thus was the supernatural brought into play when political conditions proved intolerable. As in the case of a later ethnographer (Evans-Pritchard), Barton probably never saw feuding in operation, and in this rare instance, he was reconstructing a remembered past.

The Historical Context of Political Change. For the most part, Barton provided a systematic account of Kiangan Ifugao society. He was recording, however, a political system in which economic change was occurring rapidly even as he wrote. Kiangan had been a center of both Spanish and American colonial administration. Barton believed that, as a result, an old system of government, "a system of feudal lords and feudal land holdings" found elsewhere in the province had "vanished almost completely" from Kiangan (1922:412). He did not describe this feudal form of indigenous government, since he was not interested in reconstructing the past. He did, however, explain how it was that Pax Americana had brought about its decline. First, peace and the equality of rich and poor before American law made it unnecessary for poor men to have a kadangyang protector. Second, the introduction of money replaced rice as payment for labor and so undercut the monopoly of that commodity by kadangyang. Third, the opening of trails encouraged labor migration to the plains and the earning of cash for buying land. Fourth, the development of wage porterage for government officials, missionaries, traders, and foreign residents similarly freed the poor from their dependence on the kadangyang. Finally, the availability of permanent wage labor for government in the administrative station and the police constabulary further eroded the old ties.

While he is clearly alert to the process of making labor into a commodity in Kiangan, Barton's model of political change related specifically to land shortage and applied to both the old feudal system and the new American colonial free enterprise system. Barton believed the old feudal system still operated in more remote districts where, under a sharecropping system, a lessee was "practically a serf."

To what extent Barton's view of the Kiangan Ifugao as "lacking government" (1919:6, 9, 11) is related to their being under American sovereignty is not clear. Whether the Ifugao of Barton's ethnography might better be viewed as peasants in a colonial dependency, as primitive foodgetters or as savage headhunters has never been raised. Nor has Barton's contribution to political anthropology as a genre been recognized. His pioneering work on Ifugao law has received considerable acclaim, but in truth, anthropologists have made little use of it. His corpus of Ifugao ethnography has been neglected even where it might be most informative—in the analysis of political inequalities, political economy, and the feud.

Barton has been described as "an anthropological behaviorist and a jurisprudential realist" (Eggan 1969:viii). His contribution to legal realism is in the tradition of the greatest writers on law from Justices Holmes and Cardozo to Karl Llewellyn, Malinowski, and their successors. Law is embedded within society, a dimension of political power. In the context of what has come to be called "imposed law" in the colonial setting (Chapter 6), Barton's study is of prime significance.

Primitive Society Enthroned

At the end of one era and the beginning of the next, a textbook appears. Just as the professional ethnologists at the Bureau of American Ethnology worked on the production and accumulation of an ethnography of Native Americans for the general public, so the academics around Boas were no less concerned with the consolidation and reproduction of their labor for the new discipline of cultural anthropology. Professionals fed on monographs; students on textbooks. The training of graduate student observers stood high on Boas's agenda; the production of the textbooks was left to these students. In 1920 Robert Lowie's *Primitive Society* was published, a year after Barton's *Ifugao Law*. Its title reflected the academic stance of the new profession. Both in Britain and the United States the role of the primitive was on the rise.

From the outset, *Primitive Society* was a denial of Lewis Henry Morgan's *Ancient Society* (1877), which Lowie considered hopelessly antiquated (1920). At the heart of the text (following seven chapters on kinship structures and preceding three on rank, government, and justice) two chapters lay in opposition to each other. One, on property, refuted Morgan; the other, a rather pretentious chapter on associations, presented Lowie's own alternative. To attack Morgan was by 1920 a well-established Boasian practice, but the origins of the theory of associations were less well known. Boasian mythmaking has tended to obscure two historical facts. First, a different style of work was executed by students trained by Boas before and after 1915. Second, the contributions of some of his students derived as much from other sources as from Papa Franz. This was particularly evident in the Boasians' approach to political matters. In this instance, Lowie derived his theory of associations from the German ethnologist Heinrich Schurtz. He was also provoked by Rivers's unwitting revitalization of Morgan's ghost.[52]

Schurtz bridged geography, economics, and ethnology. An Africanist of the *Kulturkreislehre* and a diffusionist, his *Alterklassen und Männerbünde* (1902) had presumably been known to Lowie for a long time. Schurtz argued that the basis for social institutions lay in gender and age. He suggested a universal process whereby oppositions were constantly at work dividing and reuniting individuals into social groups. The generational separation of society into age classes of boys, youths, and married men was accompanied by customs designed to prepare youths for war, hunting, and marriage. Secret societies, far from being a degeneration, as earlier scholars had believed, were in fact correlated with the rise of patriarchal family heads who strengthened their control through priestcraft. "Natural" kin organization, based on family and clan (gens), was opposed to, and conflicted with, the integration of males into classes based on gender and age. Through family and clan, elders countered the weight of the young men's societies and restricted their influence to the military domain.

Schurtz elucidated cultural variables such as age, gender, family, and clan in order to measure interrelatedness. Nieboer, it will be recalled, tested the possibilities of interrelationships among slavery, land resources, ownership, and power. Lowie offered no such analysis.

Primitive Society fell far short of scientific rigor. Written as an undergraduate text, it barely drew upon the existing literature, and its main virtue, or vice, was that of simplification. In 1917 Lowie, called upon to teach a one-semester course at Berkeley, chose to call it "Primitive Society." On his return to New York, he turned the lectures into a book. A contract and an advance on royalties saw the manuscript ready in four months even though, as Lowie recalled, he was almost totally unfamiliar with what others might consider basic elements of the subject: the division of labor, property, law, and government. He read for the first time the work of Sir Henry Maine and, for his chapter on government, scraped the barrel for relevant ethnographies.

Lowie's major contribution to political studies was his demonstration from comparative ethnography that "even in very humble cultural levels . . . local contiguity is one of the factors determining social solidarity independently of blood relationship" (1920:394). He first used Barton's Ifugao data to suggest that their "bilateral group" corresponded "sufficiently well to the general concept of a kinship group as the governmental organism" (1920:391–392). Later, in *The Origin of the State* (1927b), he sifted Barton's material more thoroughly to suggest the importance of territorial factors.

Primitive Society synthesized in its pages a totally Boasian view of government and politics. The most striking conclusion to be drawn from it perhaps is that there were cultures wholly lacking in institutionalized government.[53] Functional equivalents were to be found in such "agencies" as genealogies (pedigrees), taboos, and ghost societies. Lowie set himself the task of elaborating a cross-cultural survey of such governmental forms. He began with a disingenuous opening paragraph in which he suggested there had been "a rather persistent attempt to deny the very existence of such a thing as political organization properly so called in the ruder cultures." Lowie recognized that this was "a point of primary importance" but temporized, considering it best "to view the facts without theoretical prepossession of any sort and to include merely *governmental agencies in different areas and how they are correlated with features of aboriginal life* (1920:358, emphasis added). His essential nominalism led Lowie to shun any exploration of causal relations. This was followed by an even more disingenuous and even more disastrous sentence: "In the present chapter we are more particularly concerned with the question of the existence and character of a central governing agency; for practical reasons the administration of justice will be treated separately in the one following" (1920:359). In this deft blow, for practical reasons of book making, the political dimension of law was set wholly apart from political organization.

The most striking features of Lowie's survey of primitive government was how little he knew of the work of contemporaries in England and France and how poor was his own compared with that of the Edwardians struggling to produce a science of politics. Kroeber praised *Primitive Society* as "modern, American and pragmatic," and commended Lowie's comparative method. The book, he pointed out, was descriptive, not interpretive. What, then, was the value of the method? "This admission seems inevitable," he concluded, "that though the method is sound, and the only one that the ethnologist has found justifiable, yet to the worker in remote fields of science, and to the man of general intellectual interests, its products must appear rather sterile. . . . There are . . . no causal explanations" (1920:380).

CONCLUSION

The uneasy years between 1898 and 1918 saw continued unrest at home in Britain and America, colonial wars throughout much of the globe, and a struggle for preeminence in anthropology among three competing paradigms: evolutionism, diffusionism, and functionalism. The victory of functionalism narrowed the scope of the anthropological study of politics to primitive society in the ethnographic present. Evolutionary theory was not to become prominent again until the 1950s (Chapter 5), and diffusionism reemerged as a framework of inquiry only in the 1970s (Chapter 6). Five components of Edwardian functionalism—admired by some, deplored by others—have persisted to this day. These are the sociological comparative method (with its denial of causal explanation), a delineation of interdependencies among "social facts" (i.e., closed-systems thinking); an emphasis on place rather than historical phase; the notion of "collective consciousness" (leading to homogenization); and political conservatism.

Colonial subject peoples in India, Oceania, and the Philippines, along with Native Australians, provided localized settings for the study of political leadership, domination, law, and intertribal relations. Several studies became the classics of a political ethnography engendered by a fieldwork revolution. The most important element in this for the study

of politics was Rivers's genealogical method, although its full significance for the analysis of law in action, political competition, the structuring of political relations, and the recognition of political change was
not spelled out until the 1950s (Chapter 5).

Operating within an intellectual milieu in which the analysis of imperialism provided an alternative framework, Edwardian anthropologists divorced themselves from the historical realities of the colonial
encounter. Diffusionists concerned over the impact of colonization on
administered peoples and those (like Leenhardt and Van Gennep) who
deplored the objectification of "the simpler peoples" were marginalized
within the expanding scientific profession. Political anthropologists
also turned aside from involvement in practical or applied anthropology.

There probably never was another time when anthropology was as
international as in this era—as demonstrated by the literature on slavery, war and its relation to the origin of the state, and statistical correlations among types of economy, government, warfare, and justice in
primitive societies. These treatises had uncertain futures, as the following chapters show. Nieboer's work on slavery is still valued; the correlations of Hobhouse, Wheeler, and Ginsberg tend to be overlooked, and
there has been much reinventing of the evolutionary wheel; Holsti's
analysis of war and the state has been superceded.

Paradoxically, the fourth edition of *Notes and Queries*, the fieldwork
manual intended for amateurs, contained a major contribution to the
academic anthropology of politics. A section by Barbara Freire-Marreco
laid out the revolutionary methods advocated by Rivers and Marett for
studying government and politics in a "living society." It set out an
agenda that few anthropologists, then and since, have been able to do
justice to in its entirety. It directed inquiry toward (among others) contact situations, colonial chiefs, informal authority, the views of the
young, the position of women, informal political processes, influence,
prestige, and power—all of which, as we shall see, entered political
anthropology as it developed into a subfield specialization (Chapters
4–6).

At the Bureau of American Ethnology, where intensive fieldwork had
long been practiced, the study of politics declined in importance between 1898 and 1918. Within the academy, Native Californians, the
least typical of the natives of North America, attracted the most attention as anthropologists at Berkeley embarked on the task of classifying
their various forms of political organization. But the ethnographic
classic that emerged in the Progressive Era came not from Native American studies but from American involvement in the Philippines. It took

the form of Barton's minutely detailed, honestly nuanced—yet today little read—*Ifugao Law* (1919). Here I have chosen to focus only on Barton's political accounting of property laws, class, slavery, political brokers, feuds, and political change. This paradigmatic pathbreaker for a contested legal tradition centered around law in action, political process, and the seamy side of law (Chapters 3–6). It was a blend of ethnographic romanticism and legal realism. In a sense, it epitomized this transitional yet formative era in the anthropology of politics.

3 Promise, Depression, and New Deals, 1919–1939

On the stage of colonial imperialism the rights and objects of subject peoples has become the central issue of world politics, short only of the nationalistic rivalry over the state of imperialism itself.

—ALAIN LOCKE AND BERNHARD STERN

The period following the defeat of Germany in 1918 saw the end of European dominance and the emergence of the United States and the USSR as major world powers.[1] Both marched to different drummers from the industrial imperialists of turn-of-the-century Europe. The late entry of the United States into the war and the failure of disarmament proposals after it were both largely due to American commercial interests in arms manufacture. The Versailles Treaty left numerous national minority and border problems unsolved, and the failure of the United States to join the League of Nations contributed in no small way to its inadequacy.

The Russian Revolution of 1917 marked the beginning of a new phase in imperial affairs. Expansion and conflict between the European powers over the redistribution of colonial territories gave way to a new form of imperialism in which the rivalry over carving up the world gave way to a struggle against the contraction of the imperial system. The United States emerged as the organizer and leader of a modern world system based on the rise of an international technology.

Throughout the 1920s for four-fifths of the globe the flow of arms was controlled, and bloodshed contained, within the British Empire. The engagement of Britain in war had made practical sense of Lord Lugard's principle of indirect rule within colonial territories, and the formation of the International Labour Organization placed economic development first on their agendas. Such political instability as existed in these years was to be found not in the imperial world but within the territorial boundaries of the two emergent world powers. Famine and civil war tore Russia apart and were followed by the dictatorship of the Communist party, Stalin's purges, and in 1923, a new constitution. Lenin died in 1924. In the United States a Red Scare in 1919 was characterized by strikes, bombings, and violent crime, which led to searches and seizures, investigations, and the deportation of suspect elements. The mounting power of labor was accompanied by harsher government handling of political unrest, particularly after the brief depression of 1921. A quota on immigration was introduced, and from 1925 on, Rockefeller funds began to finance research into American immigrant groups and their European backgrounds. Most anthropological research, however, was carried out in colonies where relative stability reigned. Between 1924 and 1926 the Ku Klux Klan was rampant in the South and the Midwest, campaigning in the name of morality against Negroes, Catholics, Jews, intellectuals, and critics of Prohibition.

Britain also witnessed the growing power of labor. The period between 1919 and 1922 was marked by a series of strikes by railmen, dockers, and other transport workers. Conservatives held office from 1924 to 1929. Ireland was divided by civil war, and in 1922 a Free State was established, with six northern counties remaining under the British crown. The dismantling of the British Empire had begun. In 1921 Afghanistan gained its independence, and in 1922 Egypt was declared an autonomous republic. Lebanon was established in 1926. Contrary to these trends, however, a British mandate was established over Palestine in 1920. The European model of the nation state was adopted throughout the Arab world. Mahatma Gandhi returned to India from South Africa to lead his first civil disobedience campaign in 1920. None of this was reflected in the anthropological study of politics.

We have seen how anthropology became a profession by excluding amateurs, by fostering within universities the reproduction of the discipline, and by establishing fieldwork as a rite of passage. By the 1920s field research was sometimes of as much interest to an expanding business community as to the government. The point must not be overstated. The new discipline had, indeed, begun to build up a corpus of studies and restudies on the basis of intellectual problems within anthropology itself. Nevertheless, one of the characteristics of this era, unlike that in which Powell, Boas, or Rivers operated, was the funding of research by organizations other than those connected with government. Jessup became the rule rather than an exception. The transition from government sponsorship to that of big business, produced violently competing paradigms within anthropology (Dupree 1957).

Business funding was most marked in the United States. In 1919 John C. Merriam, chairman of the National Research Council, declared that anthropology should no longer be preoccupied with Native Americans but should follow American interests overseas. The council, funded largely by the Carnegie Institution, already supported research in Central America, and in 1925 anthropology joined the Social Science

Research Council (the SSRC, funded largely by Rockefeller money) and began to embark on interdisciplinary research even farther afield. As the United States became a global power, its business arena expanded and research funds began to flow even to Britain. The fieldwork revolution required the routinization of international funding, and access to Rockefeller support often made the difference between success and failure for research there.

Funds such as these led to an orientation toward the social sciences and sometimes a commitment to social or welfare goals—what in earlier times might have been considered social engineering. Anthropology began to define itself as a social rather than a natural science, becoming a more conspicuous force in American life and reaching a wider public. Its separation from biology (particularly in the peculiar form of anthropometrics) and psychology was assured. The setting was ripe for the fieldwork monograph in which anthropologists gave well-rounded accounts of exotic societies and cultures the intricacies of whose forms and patterning had never been delineated.

In the United States the interests of the National Research Council and the SSRC in practical social problems encouraged research into race and immigration problems. In England, where the immigrant experience had been less severe and the race issue less prominent, the practice of "applied anthropology" was confined to colonial territories. Although the first government anthropologist had been appointed in 1906, the greatest impact of government on the profession came after 1919 when Lugard's program of indirect rule became a desirable practice throughout the empire. It was not, however, the British taxpayer who supported research in the colonies in these years, nor was the expense borne by the taxation of the subject peoples. Funding came from industrial and commercial philanthropists, British and American, among whom the Rockefeller interests were again prominent. No rigid distinctions can be maintained between political anthropology and "applied anthropology," "acculturation," and "culture contact" at this time. Contact and conflict were dominant themes in the twenties both at home and abroad. It escaped no one's attention that the main cause of a great deal of this conflict was the global expansion of big business.

By 1929 American science in the universities and in government had become so interlaced with the business economy that the Depression affected the whole research structure of the country (Dupree 1957). President Franklin D. Roosevelt introduced measures to reorganize industry and agriculture and to revive the economy by spending public money. Critically important for anthropologists was the government's perception of science as a substitute frontier (Dupree 1957). The Depression brought a New Deal for anthropology. Through federally funded projects, anthropologists began to research rural communities, communities overseas, urban conditions, and ethnicity among both new immigrants and African-Americans. Social complexity and class began to appear on the agenda.

If anthropology in the United States was at a crossroads, in Britain the way ahead seemed clearer than before. It moved either with Radcliffe-Brown toward greater and greater abstraction in search of the natural laws of society or with Malinowski toward concrete situations and applications. The canons of ethnographic fieldwork led the aficionados of both schools to sub-Saharan Africa (whither Rockefeller money took them) and it was this, in the end, that held them together. Rockefeller funding also brought British and American anthropologists more closely into dialogue than ever before under the umbrella concept of acculturation or, in its British variant, culture contact.

In 1931 the appointment of A. R. Radcliffe-Brown to the University of Chicago brought with it an alternative to the unquestioned concentration of American anthropology on "cultures." Little of the intellectual baggage he carried with him to America was as new as he thought, but Radcliffe-Brown's comparative sociology did call forth a response from the Boasians. This took the form both of a reassertion of the importance of history and a glissading into the term "socio-cultural." In the Boasians' study of politics, this brought about a more self-conscious analysis of groups and institutions. Not all the credit should be given to the catalytic qualities of social anthropology, however. As in Britain in the Edwardian era, a strong and vibrant sociology affected the course anthropology took. This was more evident at Chicago and Harvard than at Berkeley and Columbia, but those institutions underwent a transition as well. The distinctive contribution to political anthropology of Duncan Strong and Alexander Lesser alongside Steward at Columbia initiated intellectual developments that were fulfilled only after World War II.

In both America and Britain the study of the political was better achieved overseas than at home, and it was in America's backyard—"following capital" as Redfield put it (1928)—that Mesoamerican village studies elevated the political domain out of the Kroeberian morass of holistic cultural description. Following capital, however, it was not always at this early stage of professionalization the university anthropologist who most usefully delineated the politics of the peripheral societies. The anthropology of politics penetrated each continent in the wake of earlier professionals—traders, missionaries, and administrators.

Paradigmatically, American political anthropology was at its furthest remove from that in Britain in this phase. It remained a four-field discipline in most universities, and interest in state origins was a collaborative effort between archaeologists and German-born cultural anthropologists, neither of which groups showed much interest in developments in Britain, where Malinowski was pioneering the observation of subtle and often power-political ongoing actions and events. Radcliffe-Brown was out of England for much of this time, establishing or consolidating anthropology departments in several colonial outposts, "the Jonathan Appleseed of social anthropology" (Stocking 1985:3). Most of those who received anthropological training at LSE and Oxbridge during these years were not doctoral candidates but young men going out to govern the colonies. The profession expanded very slowly, and the British tradition was carried to foreigners to a greater extent than to those at home. Scholars made no significant contribution to the anthropology of politics in a formal sense, apart from Malinowski's statements about war and an iconoclastic confrontation over law between the two masters. The era was not distinguished by a mainstream contribution in the British tradition and was, in fact, brought to a conclusion by the somewhat controversial fieldwork of a young South African woman.

Within American anthropology, as always, native American political organization provided a battleground of contrasting ideologies and methodologies. The typological approach of the Boasian school was confronted by the work of a marginal practitioner. William Christie MacLeod's study of the American frontier (1928a) led him into an historical narrative of contact and conflict combined with an ethnological sense of political structure. Had David Easton's 1959 appreciation of MacLeod's work been shared by his contemporaries, MacLeod would have been recognized not simply as a most prolific but also as a most productive political anthropologist. As it was, his specialization in political ethnology was virtually ignored.

THE SEARCH FOR ORDER

Since it is now generally recognized that social forces play a part in the emphasis placed on one line of inquiry rather than another, it is no surprise to find that the 1920s and 1930s in both Britain and the United States were characterized by an interest in law and disorder. The search for order was an abiding characteristic of the functional tradition (Murphy 1971) that became dominant at this time, an intellectual response to growing dissatisfaction and unrest in the British colonies and restlessness in the urban and industrial work force of the United States. These unhappy historical conjunctures brought forth a coherent statement within the anthropology of law.

As early as 1899 in an address delivered before the New York State Bar Association, Justice Oliver Wendell Holmes, dean of the United States legal profession, stamped on anthropological jurisprudence a hallmark of academic respectability. "It is perfectly proper," he said, "to regard and study the law simply as a great anthropological document. It is proper to resort to it to discover what ideals of society have been strong enough to reach that final form of expression, or what have been the changes in dominant ideals from century to century. It is proper to study it as an exercise in the morphology and transformation of human ideas. The study pursued for such ends becomes science" (1899:441). For Justice Holmes, a great admirer of Maine, anthropological jurisprudence was historical. But not until the 1920s, with the institutionalization of functional anthropology, was jurisprudence given full recognition in anthropology, and the labels applied then reflected the elastic (and perhaps inchoate) character of the legal domain: primitive law, social control, anthropological jurisprudence. Each label reflected a slightly different perspective.

Contributions to the developing anthropology of law came from three main sources. First there was comparative or historical jurisprudence, represented by such differing scholars as Vinogradoff, Cardozo, Hohfeld, Hartland, Pound, Jhering, Jolowicz, Allen, and Jackson. Which of these contributions entered anthropology, which were deliberately discarded by it, and which found that their time had simply "not yet come" has yet to be explored. Certainly, however, any evolutionary approach was given short shrift in these function-ferment years. Goldenweiser, for example, in reviewing Hartland's *Primitive Law* (1924), found occasion both to regret the English scholar's apparent ignorance of American criticism of evolutionary theory and to lament that he still chose to "orient his course by the stars of the classical heavens." (1924:445). Hartland was shortly afterward the butt of Malinowski's comments too (1925, 1926a, 1934). Anthropologists tended to deplore jurisprudes' lack of distinction between law and custom in primitive societies.

A second source for the anthropology of law was colonial law. The work of Dundas (1921), Ajisaje (1924), Bullock (1928), Driberg (1928), Danquah (1928), Rattray (1929), and Harries (1929) united in one endeavor African jurists and British administrative officers. The British colonial product was, however, a very different construction from Barton's Philippines study of the previous decade. It was based more on inquiry than observation and smacked of constitutional law. Insights may be gained from these studies, but they had little collective impact on the study of law as it developed in anthropology.

Academic anthropology itself contributed the third and quantitatively slightest strain to the study of law at this time, but as this chapter argues, its controversies encapsulated critically divergent stances. Thus "law" was the arena in which Malinowski chose to confront Durkheimian sociology in the shape of Radcliffe-Brown. American legal studies continued to fight old battles. Native American reconstructions differed little from those produced by ethnographers with the Bureau of American Ethnology at the turn of the century, but they centered on aspects of law that tested the tenets of Morgan and Marx rather than Durkheim. Thus property was of major concern, given its explanatory prominence in nineteenth-century analyses of civilization and capitalism. Quite prominent, too, was the analytical significance of the individual, where formerly custom and culture had held sway.

A lineage unrepresented in the anthropology of law in the 1920s and 1930s was that of the German scholar Max Weber, whose *Wirtschaft und Gesellschaft* was first published in 1925. The reason for this neglect, even among those who relied heavily on German scholarship for their ethnography, was simple. Weber, like Marx before him, was largely concerned with law in "historical societies" and with capitalism. By the 1920s anthropology had firmly established that its object of inquiry was primitive, tribal society, and it was the rare stalwart souls—most of them amateur ethnologists—who contributed to anthropological knowledge their data on, for example, Bedouin justice (Kennett 1925) or Balkan law (Durham 1928).

Authoritative statements about law appeared in introductory texts and in essays by anthropologists in the interdisciplinary volumes spawned by the emergence of the social sciences. In spite of its quixotic nature, Lowie's contribution (1927a) was most frequently singled out for appreciation (see, for example, the praise Cairns lavished on it in 1931). After doffing his cap to evolutionary forebears Maine, Maitland, and (surprisingly) Morgan, and lauding the synthesizing contribution of Johann Kohler, Lowie briefly summarized what he called the four main "problems" of legal theory. These were (1) family law, in which he attacked theories of matriarchal and communal stages in the evolution of law; (2) property law, in which he discussed where and when individual and communal claims might be made; (3) associations; and (4) the state. He would appear to have moved onto the last two topics somewhat absentmindedly, forgetting his interdisciplinary brief and returning to old, familiar stomping grounds. While his action redeemed his earlier separation of law and justice from politics, he provided no explanation of either associations or the state as the recipient, originator, or context of law.[2]

Lowie's review of primitive law drew on incidental cases the ethnographic provenance of which he never cited and the historicity of which he never considered. The Pueblo Indians, Polynesia, the Algonkians, Queensland, the Vedda of Ceylon, the Andamanese, Papuans, the Nootka, Mexico, New Zealand, the Kirgiz, Eskimo, and Melanesia are the identifications made to bear the burden of his discussion of family and property law. Only in one respect has Lowie's contribution to the anthropology of law endured, and this, paradoxically for the phlegmatic Lowie, in the form of a metaphor. "The jurisprudence of advanced civilisation," he remarked, "refined by centuries of acute intellects, is marked by a clarification of basic concepts such as the student of anthropology may well envy. There are obvious pitfalls to be avoided. Primitive customary law does not present the rigid formalism of codified law. It would surely be the acme of artificiality to pigeon-hole the rules of inheritance in an aboriginal community according to the standards of English jurisprudence" (1927a:51). Thus he voiced what became known in anthropological discourse as the formalist-substantivist controversy. In the anthropology of law this is couched in terms of pigeonholing.

Writing for this particular social science audience, Lowie cut his cloth accordingly. Victorian ethnography had contributed to the corpus of primitive law such exotic practices as sorcery, feuding, self-help, cursing, pawnship, and slavery, and Lowie was reluctant to sacrifice the distinctive caliber they bequeathed anthropology on the altar of the social sciences. A decade earlier in the Philippines, Barton had had no problem in locating all the activities of his "headhunters" within the rubrics of Western law. The professor of jurisprudence he cites (like Maine) recognized the relevance of Irish Brehon law for law in contemporary tribal societies. By the time Lowie was writing, however, the anthropology of law was moving away from historical jurisprudence just as anthropology was moving away from history. Lowie's gesture toward the great jurisprudes of the turn of the century was a wave not of greeting but of farewell.

Law in Action

"One of the reddest herrings ever dragged into the working of orderly jurisprudence," Paul Bohannan once wrote, "was Malinowski's little book called *Crime and Custom in Savage Society"* (1965:36).[3] Bohannan's opinion has been shared by formalist practitioners in the anthropology of law ever since. Towering above most contemporary works, Malinowski's contribution became a target for criticism. At the time, however, although it was received appreciatively by laymen and jurisprudes, Malinowski's study of law was almost entirely ignored by anthropologists. When scholars speak so vehemently we may sense either that we are in the middle of some kind of row—a paradigmatic challenge, perhaps—or that they really are not looking deeply enough into, or adequately contextualizing, Malinowski's work. The truth of the matter is that Malinowski's work, like Barton's, will not let the *politics* of law—the seamy side of law, Malinowski called it—be set aside so easily. The formalists were attempting to attain cultural hegemony, to use Lowie's term (1920:388). Here I argue that Malinowski's *Crime and Custom in Savage Society* (1926a) was not a red herring dragged across the path of forward-looking gamedogs, but a seminal work in an alternative anthropology of law.

For nearly thirty years the folk history of British social anthropology has made it quite clear that Malinowski, while he certainly wrought a methodological revolution, was no theorist. Adam Kuper charged him with theoretical naïveté, crude utilitarianism, and blindness to the notion of a social system. Some ambiguity creeps into the first charge since Kuper also credited Malinowski with "a grasp of the complexity of social reality which amounted—almost—to a theory" (1973:31). The last charge suggests that Kuper considered it a weakness not to operate in terms of systems thinking and reflects Kuper's intellectual heritage rather than Malinowski's failings as a theorist. *Crime and Custom* was substantive, not formal; processual, not structural. Its ethnographic integrity frustrated scholars like Bohannan and Pospisil when they began to develop the new subfield of legal anthropology in the 1950s.

Malinowski's interest in law was both deep and extensive. *Crime and Custom* was a collation of a lecture and two articles written between 1923 and 1926. His interest in family law began with his work among the Australian aborigines when he noted that "in treatises on primitive law and on family law such general concepts as 'legal' or 'law' are never explicitly defined" (1913:9). He then set aside the problem in Australian society on the grounds that it merited a separate treatise. He wrote instead of social norms "enforced by a direct, organized, and definite social action," classifying these according to the sanction they enjoyed: religious rules (sin), customary rules (improper conduct), or legal norms (crime). Crimes, he observed, were punished "by the decision of the community acting as a whole, or by its central organs, or certain groups" (1913:15). When he came to write his treatise on law some ten years later, Malinowski took a different position. As Schapera has pointed out (1957), his perception of law changed several times during the course of his career. Schapera wrote as if this were reprehensible, but it might also be viewed as a testament to the success of the seminar method at the London School of Economics, where Malinowski was such an engaged teacher.

The notion of "invisible realities" underlay Malinowski's ethnographic method.[4] This premise is both central to an appreciation of the anthropology of law as distinct from lawyers' jurisprudence of constitutional law and critical to the analysis of politics in general. The principle that lay behind observed behavior, action, and events subsequently rendered the anthropological study of politics distinct from that of other disciplines such as political sociology and political science in an increasingly interdisciplinary age. Later it was to give it common ground with the study of politics by historians.

The concept of "invisible realities" appeared most explicitly in Malinowski's discussion of land laws in *Coral Gardens and Their Magic* (1935). Malinowski argued forcibly that it is not what local practitioners might say in response to persistent inquiries that should become codified law but what the inquirer observed people to do. He stressed the significance of the distinction by referring to what in common colonial parlance had become known as "customary law." Land policies in British colonies—"Ireland in the past, or present-day India, certain East African dependencies or the Union of South Africa" (Malinowski 1935:317–318)—were uppermost in his mind at the time. Malinowski, the academic, was very much a participant in the political world. The Irish Free State had newly won nationhood; Mahatma Gandhi's civil actions against oppressive landlords were the order (or the disorder) of the day in India; East African governments were in the process of codifying colonial law. The Union of South Africa was in the forefront of his mind because his research assistant for *Coral Gardens* was a young South African, Hilda Kuper, and another of his students, Monica Hunter, had just completed research into land hunger in that country. Malinowski recognized that colonial cultures were in the process of rapid change and regretted that he had not placed more emphasis on the colonial situation. This he later called "perhaps the most serious shortcoming of my whole anthropological research in Melanesia" (1935:318).

As with his teacher Rivers, considerations of method and technique brought about conceptual innovation:

The main achievement in fieldwork consists, not in a passive registering of facts, but in the constructive drafting of what might be called charters of native institutions. The observer should not function as a mere automaton; a sort of combined camera and phonographic or shorthand recorder of native statements. While making his observations the field-worker must constantly construct. . . . To put it paradoxically, one could say that facts do not exist in the sociological any more than in the physical reality; that is they do not dwell in the spatial and temporal continuum open to the untutored eye. The principles of . . . legal constitution . . . have to be constructed by the observer out of a multitude of manifestations of varying significance and relevance. It is these invisible realities . . . which are scientifically important in the study of culture. Land tenure is typical of such "invisible facts." . . . The sanctions of law, the economic principles of production, the political institutions of a tribe, are all "invisible facts." (1935:1:317)

Malinowski's perception of law in society emerged within historically changing contexts, first between 1913 and 1923 and then between 1926 and 1935. In his concern with law, economic production, and politics, was Malinowski following a hidden agenda? While Barton, the autodidact, was struggling to place the observed "facts" of Ifugao law within the framework of conflicting theories of ethnology, was Malinowski, the Central European intellectual par excellence, struggling to place his anthropological contribution within the context of conflicting traditions in European intellectual thought? How consciously was he addressing, and thereby taking sides in, one of the major theoretical controversies of his time: whether Marxist analysis could be applied not only to capitalist but also to precapitalist societies? Was this what Alvin Gouldner (1970:448) had in mind when he wrote of Malinowski's "subterranean dialogue" with Marx?[5]

By the mid 1930s Malinowski was conscious on all sides of what today are called "legal pluralism" and "imposed law" (Chapter 6). Within Trobriand society he recognized a multiplicity of legal systems: one relating to kinship, another to the village community, another to the district system, another to magic. These he saw as being at times in harmony and at times in conflict with one another. To understand how this "composite body of systems behaves under the strain of circumstances" (Malinowski 1926a:76) he posed three questions: (1) What is the nature of criminal acts and procedure and their relation to civil law? (2) What are the main factors active in the restitution of the disturbed equilibrium? and (3) What are the relations and possible conflicts between the several systems of native law? None of these concerns was recognized by the formalists who set about codifying the anthropology of law in the 1950s. As they ordered their myths, Malinowski's most productive years became, for them, a legal vacuum.

The Seamy Side of Law: On Reading *Crime and Custom*

In the rushed partisan world of academic scholarship and the production of textbooks, Malinowski's words and ideas were too often abstracted from the text in which they appeared. Critical analysis requires a close following of the text, the perception of its logical passage, the weighing of words, and the recognition of juxtapositions. This is no mean task with *Crime and Custom*, for Malinowski could not always resist the temptation to stray off his path to savage both his forebears and his contemporaries.

"Primitive Law," Malinowski stated at the outset, is "the study of the various forces which make for order, uniformity and cohesion in a savage tribe. The knowledge of the forces should have formed the foundation of anthropological theories of primitive organization and should have yielded the guiding principles of Colonial legislation and administration" (1926a:2). Malinowski's disdain for "kinship algebra" is well known, and we have seen Lowie and Goldenweiser challenge the nineteenth-century evolutionary view that stressed kinship over territorial contiguity. Rivers's shift from kinship primacy to diffusionism opened a Pandora's box of possibilities for political anthropology, and Malinowski here put his own stamp of approval on "other-than-kinship" concerns. It would be a long time, however, before it was explicitly recognized that much of what was conceived of as kinship might have been more usefully scrutinized as constructed law. Malinowski echoed the strains of Central European philosophy, Simmel particularly, when he introduced the concept of social "forces," with all the connotations that later led anthropologists to abandon "social systems" for "social fields" (Chapter 5). To see this only as a contest between Malinowski and Radcliffe-Brown, as some have done, trivializes the issue.

The forces that make for order (used by Malinowski to mean regularity), uniformity (achieved by "socialization"), and cohesion (i.e., integration) do not neccessarily move in step, so *Crime and Custom in Savage Society* contains both a study of "law and order" and an analysis of "crime and punishment." Malinowski's critics seldom pay equal attention to both parts. Malinowski declared his position very early in the pigeon-holing controversy. His procedure was to approach the facts with a very elastic and wide conception of the problem before us. In looking for 'law' and legal forces, we shall try merely to discover and analyse all the rules conceived and acted upon as binding obligations, to find out the nature of the binding forces, and to classify the rules according to the manner in which they are made valid. We shall see that by an inductive examination of facts, carried out without any preconceived ideas of ready-made definition, we shall be enabled to arrive at a satisfactory classification of the norms and rules of a primitive law from other forms of custom, and at a new, dynamic conception of the social organization of savages. (1926a:15–16)

"Binding obligations" was Malinowski's key phrase, and to "discover" them in the Trobriand Islands he turned to a *situation*, bounded with all the unity of Greek drama, to find out what held people together in a task that required regularity and cohesion: fishing in the lagoon of Kiriwina. He thus began his analysis of law with production—with relations of production—in a task critical to the society's existence and involving one of the cornerstones of a legal system: property. "The ownership and the use of the canoe," he wrote "consist of a series of definite obligations and duties uniting a group of people into a working team" (Malinowski 1926a:18). Both ownership and crew membership were also matters of privilege. The term itself indicates a relationship to law. In this way Malinowski approached the study of law through contract law; Malinowski was a legal realist.

As Malinowski developed his analysis of "the binding force of economic obligations" in the Trobriands, he moved from the act of fishing to the exchange of fish. As the activity expanded to involve more than its immediate participants to become a series of transactions linking the coastal with the inland villages (from the arena to the field), he distinguished more clearly between activity as an economic arrangement and its ceremonial and legal aspects. The inland villagers required fish for their ceremonial feasting, while the coastal villagers required vegetables for theirs. The dependence of the two districts upon each other, in Malinowski's view, was "severely penalized" (1926a:23). Again, the verb is significant. Reciprocity serves as "a weapon for the enforcement" of rights, and the ceremonial manner in which the transactions were carried out, entailing public control and criticism, added still more to their binding force.

Much that Malinowski said of law in the Trobriands would apply to commercial law in the United States. Both rest on notions of reciprocity, and as Elizabeth Colson has pointed out (1974), Malinowski recognized that these depend not simply on rewarding interpersonal relationships but also on a fear of penalties. It is, however, not always clear in either legal environment what the penalty is and how the penalty fits the crime—or tort. Consumer and tenant grievances bear testimony to this. In civil law, sanctions are not as systematically codified as they are in the criminal division. And Malinowski forcefully insisted that it was in civil rather than in criminal law that his interest lay, in legal hegemony rather than in the lawful use of power.

Malinowski's interest in civil law rose, indeed, out of his reaction to a legal anthropology "still almost exclusively studied in its singular and sensational manipulations . . . blood-curdling crime, vendetta, criminal sorcery, incest, adultery" (1926a:73). Thus he chose to describe "the ordinary, not the singular; . . . the law obeyed, . . . not the law broken" (1926a:73). Law in action revealed the maintenance not simply of duty, law, and order but of privilege. This, we recognize more explicitly than did Malinowski, is indeed the politically soft underbelly of society, as distinct from its more visible armor of criminal law.

Again and again in *Crime and Custom* Malinowski drew attention to links in the chains of mutualities, to arenas of public life and to fields of social forces, fields of tension that were the Trobriand legal system. Ultimately, to Malinowski (entrapped in a colonial situation) this "whole system is in balance" (1926a:41), and yet, clearly it was not, as his own ethnography showed. Problems of child beating, wife brutalization, palimony, and the like pale into insignificance alongside the Trobriander's structural dilemmas with matrilineal descent, inheritance, patrilocality, and relations with a mother's brother. All these problems, Malinowski showed, were normally worked out in a public arena of penalty and humiliation, satisfaction and reward. The norm, however, was not always operative. Some Trobrianders had recourse to the resident magistrate for the resolution of their legal tangles; others chose to ignore their obligations and become outcasts and hangers-on to Europeans. Not until 1942 did Malinowski confront this "historical element" head-on in an address to the American National Lawyers Guild.

Malinowski adopted the case method, or as he called it, the analysis of certain *events* (1926a:77), to address such issues. The suicide of a youth, Kima'i, who had committed incest, revealed how deviations from the ideal were widely accepted unless it was in someone's interest to make a public issue of them. In Trobriand society, without courts or constabulary, public opinion was neither greatly outraged by the crime nor did it react directly. It had to be mobilized by a ceremonial pronouncement and insults hurled by an interested party. Malinowski was as interested in law methodically evaded as he was in law upheld.

Malinowski's discussion of sorcery in *Crime and Custom* proved pathbreaking. In the Trobriands, sorcery was both a criminal practice and a method of administering justice. Which it was in any particular instance depended on who was practicing it on whom and when he was doing so. On the one hand, sorcery was "the main criminal agency" (1926a:85); on the other, the Trobriand chief used sorcery to punish offenders. Malinowski was very clear and very emphatic about sorcery's political import: "[B]lack magic is regarded as the chief's principal instrument in the enforcement of his exclusive privileges and prerogatives. Such cases pass, of course, imperceptibly into actual oppression and crass injustice. . . . [S]ince it invariably ranges itself on the side of the powerful, wealthy and influential, sorcery remains a support of vested interest; hence in the long run, of law and order. . . . In whatever way it works, it is a way of emphasizing the status quo, a method of expressing the traditional inequalities and of counteracting the formation of any new ones" (1926a:92–93). Thus, he concluded, where there was no *formal* code or administration of justice, it was very difficult to draw a line between the "quasi-legal" and the "quasi-criminal."

Malinowski forcefully urged recognition of the dynamic aspects of law. On one occasion an ongoing but tolerable quarrel became a crisis when a chief's son, Namwana, charged his adversary, the chief's nephew, Mitakata, in the resident magistrate's court. In Omarakana village the chief withdrew into his hut; as night fell "the subdued village settled down to a silent supper, each family over its solitary meal" (1926a:102). Suddenly, the chief's heir apparent, elder brother to the imprisoned man, crossed to Namwana's hut and, in ringing tones, told him to leave the village. His command was followed by similar demands from Mitakata's sisters and a maternal nephew. "Before the night was over, Namwana Guya'u had left Omarakana for ever," left his father's village and returned to that of his mother's brothers, where he should, by custom, have resided. The chief mourned the departure of his favorite son for three days but could not deny the legality of his kinsmen's action. His resentment, however, remained deep and lasting. Two years later, when Malinowski returned to the village, the marriage tie between the clans had been broken and "there was a deep rift in the whole social life" (1926a:105). Malinowski knew that such tensions between sons and maternal nephews of chiefs were not rare; he recognized, moreover, the fact that colonial practice accentuated the problem, because he had reported an instance in which the chief had actually ousted his sisters' sons, "supported in this by European influence, which naturally worked for patrilineal claims" (1926a:106).

The clash of maternal and paternal interests, Malinowski suggested, was probably the most important consequence of contact with Europeans. Out of such clashes were law and order engendered:

> Law and order arise out of the very processes which they govern. . . . They obtain . . . as the result of a constant struggle not merely of human passions against the law, but of legal principles with one another. The struggle, however, is not a free fight: it is subject to definite conditions, can take place only within certain limits and only on the condition that it remains under the surface of publicity. Once an open challenge has been entered, the precedence of strict law over legalized usage or over an encroaching principle of law is established and the orthodox hierarchy of legal systems controls the issue. For as we have seen the conflict takes place between strict law and legalized usage, and it is possible because the former has the strength of more definite tradition behind it, while the latter draws force from personal inclinations and actual power. There exist thus within the body of law not only different types such as quasi-civil and quasi-criminal, or the law of economic transactions, of political relations, etc., but there can be distinguished degrees of orthodoxy, stringency, and validity, placing rules into a hierarchy from the main law of Mother-right, totemism, and rank down to the clandestine evasions and the traditional means of defying law and abetting crime." (1926a:122–123)

Operating within the colonial milieu, Malinowski was, in a sense, in competition with administrative officers, missionaries, and teachers who, in achieving their goals—the maintenance of law and order, conversion, transformation—similarly needed to understand the working of the indigenous society. Malinowski savaged them remorselessly, demonstrating *why* their efforts were unrewarding, if not damaging. He noted, for example, that in the study of "customary law," what he called "Hearsay Anthropology" had "taken over the orthodox native doctrine or rather their legal fiction at its face value, and (had) been thus duped by mistaking the legal ideas for the sociological realities of tribal life" (1926a:112–113). "Hearsay Anthropology," he concluded, was constantly exposed to "the danger of ignoring the seamy side of savage law" (1926a:121). Malinowski's recognition of this other side of the law and his conceptualization of systems of law in conflict comprised his dual contribution to political anthropology, in part as a legal realist but even more as an expounder of agency.

Law in the Abstract

As a theorist, Alfred Reginald Radcliffe-Brown derived his intellectual sustenance from the French sociologist Emile Durkheim. He was what William Watson (1964) has called a spiralist.[6] Born in 1881, he entered

Trinity College, Cambridge, in 1901. In 1904 he became Rivers's first anthropology student, and from 1906 to 1908 he worked among a relict population of Andaman Islanders in the Bay of Bengal. Returning to England, he taught comparative sociology and ethnology at Cambridge and the LSE before engaging in an inquiry into Australian aboriginal society from 1910 to 1912. During the first two years of the war, he lectured in Birmingham and Australia; in 1916 he became the director of education in Tonga. In 1920 he went to South Africa, where he held the chair in social anthropology at the University of Cape Town. He then moved to the University of Sydney (1925–1931) and thence to Chicago (1931–1937). He did a spell of summer teaching at Columbia University. Between 1935 and 1936 he was at Yenching University in China, and finally he took up the chair in social anthropology at Oxford in 1937.

During the period with which we are concerned (1919–1939), Radcliffe-Brown formulated a programmatic statement for the anthropology of law. It has been said that a science in its early stages is both ambitiously profound in its aims and trivial in its handling of details. Barton's and Malinowski's studies of law were ethnographic, born out of a perception of the complexities and contradictions of social life. Radcliffe-Brown's contributions were, in contrast, abstract, shallow, and simplistic.[7] They consisted of a logical series of classified definitions—primary and secondary sanctions, positive and negative sanctions, general or diffuse sanctions—all framed within notions of social euphoria and dysphoria. Law was "social control through the systematic application of the force of politically organized society" (1933a:202), a definition derived from Roscoe Pound's idea of social control through law and introduced to anthropology a short time before by Richard Thurnwald (1932). In the two authoritative articles that appeared in 1933, one on "Primitive Law" and the other on "Social Sanctions," Radcliffe-Brown presented living societies as dead cultures; ethnographic data became "social facts." Kroeber's Yurok appeared alongside Barton's Ifugao, Dunbar's Akikuyu, and Rattray's Ashanti in a timeless schema, and from these few instances he drew "developmental" conclusions based on a relationship between subsistence technology and political organization. Following Durkheim, Radcliffe-Brown concluded that "In its most elementary developments, law is intimately bound up with magic and religion; legal sanctions are closely related to ritual sanctions. A full understanding of the beginnings of law in simpler societies can therefore be reached only by a comparative study of whole systems of social sanctions" (1933b:206). He did not refer to the comparative sociology of Hobhouse, Wheeler, and Ginsberg (1915) or to Malinowski's ethnographic and theoretical work. Nor, apparently, did he doubt the universal application of European legal concepts.

The developmental classification he had arrived at through a concern with public delicts suggested to Radcliffe-Brown that further research was needed into what he termed "diffuse negative sanctions"—hostile reactions toward behavior and judgments of disapproval. He suggested that they might conveniently be studied, in the first instance, through vocabulary. Diffuse negative sanctions would then presumably be correlated in some way with the public negative sanctions he had already set out. Although Radcliffe-Brown was no fieldworker and there is mounting evidence that his contribution to both ethnography and theory was somewhat derivative (Needham 1974; White 1981; Stocking 1984), he did have a tidy mind, and it is in concepts and in the classification of problems that his contribution lies.

The only application of Radcliffe-Brown's schema was by John H. Provinse in a doctoral dissertation at the University of Chicago in 1934. It was never published, but a summary may be found in Provinse's article "The Underlying Sanctions of Plains Indians Culture" (1937). The Plains Indians had the potential of being "highly instructive with regard to legal sanctions and political development" (1937:341). They provided an intermediate case between a noncentralized authority that lacked a law of public delicts and a centralized authority in which such law had developed. After reinterpreting the Plains Indians data in the light of the Radcliffe-Brown schema, Provinse was, however, able to come up with a conclusion no more inspiring than that, "One does not find in these Plains military societies the germs of law and of the state" (1937:365).

A fair amount has been written about Radcliffe-Brown's impact on anthropology at Chicago, less on the impact of Chicago's intellectual milieu on Radcliffe-Brown. Fortes has suggested that in 1931 he moved away from Durkheimian functionalism toward a more structuralist view of how institutions function in a social system adapted to a particular environment (1969:45). Stocking points out that in 1931 Radcliffe-Brown was in Chicago, and he suggests that it was in close proximity to the Chicago Law School that he "first felt the direct intellectual influence of Sir Henry Maine in a significant way. Maine's concept of 'corporation' provided the basis for a view of the individual in more clearly structural terms" (1984:172). The influence may well have been mediated through Robert Redfield. At Chicago at that time he probably encountered, too, the sociologist E. A. Ross's textbook *Social Control*

(1901), with its conceptualization of social sanctions virtually identical with that Radcliffe-Brown came to formulate in his encyclopedia essay on the subject.

Legal anthropology, as a subdiscipline, has focused more on the "great men," Malinowski and Radcliffe-Brown, than on the intellectual currents to which they were exposed. Abel (1973:205) has set out Malinowski's and Radcliffe-Brown's positions as antagonists in the following manner:

RADCLIFFE-BROWN	MALINOWSKI
negative sanctions	positive sanctions
sanctions subsequent to act	sanctions antecedent to act
emphasis on law in the breach	law as observed
mandatory law	facilitative law
mechanical solidarity	organic solidarity
externalized sanctions	internalized sanctions

Anyone viewing Radcliffe-Brown as a Horatio to Malinowski's Hamlet might choose to question this series. A structural opposition between Radcliffe-Brown "the thinker" and Malinowski "the doer," along with the higher status accorded to the first, has led to the underestimation, even the misrepresentation, of Malinowski's contribution to political anthropology. The entire edifice may indeed be viewed as a product of the cultural hegemony later established by the Oxford School. The American E. Adamson Hoebel found more similarities than differences between them, but his observation that both focused on cultural integrations and homogeneity at the expense of conflict and dispute (1954:296) seems singularly misguided. For Malinowski, the very systems of law were in conflict. Radcliffe-Brown's "model of society" led him away from an appreciation of both the historicity of social facts and their complexity.[8] The same can hardly be said of Malinowski.

Radcliffe-Brown's definition of law and the conclusion predicated upon it—that some societies have no law—was initially adopted by E. E. Evans-Pritchard as he began work among the Nuer of the southern Sudan in 1933. The "fact" that the Nuer had no law led Evans-Pritchard to inquire into other modes of social control in the acephelous pastoral society. Later, he changed his mind and "found" that there was law among the Nuer (1940b). Feud provided the sticking point. Sorcery as a political phenomenon also provided a litmus test of law in action, and the work of Malinowski's students and the ethnography of Evans-Pritchard provided a lively discourse on law in action. Malinowski and his students followed in the tradition of Marett and Rivers: individuals in society exercised options and flaunted laws—the Kuriolv tradition, as I have called it (1986a:337), after the notorious law flounter of the Nilgiri hills. In 1936 Malinowski chose the anthropology of law as the ground on which to face Radcliffe-Brown's "rattling of typological antitheses," prefacing a student's monograph (Hogbin 1934) with a developed reiteration of his own views.

NATIVE AMERICANS: THE ETERNAL FRONTIER

The lawlessness and unrest of the British colonies as they experienced the almost revolutionary changes that accompanied the Depression led British anthropologists to focus on law and order. The same forces operating within the domestic economy of the United States engendered a less controlled response. Alternative paradigms and alternative anthropologies almost came into being, many of them inspired, if not funded, by the government's perceptions of the nation's social problems or by radical responses to them. As always, the nation's eternal frontier—Native America—predominated, but it was not quite the same. Three new traditions emerged in Native American scholarship in this interwar period of domestic disorder. The earliest contained a conservative critique of Boasian functional abstraction, captured here in a contrast between the work of Robert Lowie and that of William Christie MacLeod. The last entailed the study of Native Americans on their reservations. In between, a great spearheading of field studies disciplined (perhaps overdisciplined) a near revolutionary paradigmatic shift. Romanticism, realism, and revisionism coexisted.

Democracy and Individualism

"The Indians of North America generally incline to democracy and thus contrast sharply with the Negroes of Africa." Thus Robert Lowie began his review of government in *Primitive Society* (1920:383). His sources were of two kinds: literary and ethnographic. The former consisted of cigthteenth- and nineteenth century classics such as John Adair's *History of the American Indians* and the *Jesuit Relations*. Bancroft's California materials were not cited. Apart from some slight references to three Bureau of American Ethnology reports, Lowie's ethnography was derived solely from his fellow Columbians, Boas, Kroeber and Goldenweiser, as well as his own work among the Plains Indians. Such insular practice became common among anthropologists and indeed was characteristic of a discipline in which an individual's fieldwork became not only the hallmark of his professionalism but the arbiter of his critical faculties.

Hermetic pragmatism led the anthropology of politics to center on classification and structure at the expense of criticism and evaluation. This had a particular impact in Britain. Lowie was highly regarded by his British contemporaries, and his dismissal of so much Native American ethnography as "reconstruction" was accepted without question. The rationale for this treatment in the 1920s lay in the fact that Native American peoples were no longer living under conditions in which they experienced a fair degree of continuity with their precontact situation. Their societies had undergone tumultuous changes as they encountered Euro-American expansion across the continent, and by 1920, when Lowie was reviewing their forms of government, most Native Americans had been behind the "iron walls of reservations," as Mac-Leod put it, for at least three generations. Functional anthropology was prepared to deal with none of this.

Lowie's central orienting antithesis of democratic individualism and central authority was implicitly a frontier theme. Any deviation from individualism he attributed to the inequality of stratification (which he called "the caste system") that came about with centralization. In the individualistic and dismissive spirit of his age, he focused on authorities rather than authority, on the political power of leaders rather than on sovereignty. The continuum that emerged is diagramed in Table 3.1. Thus was the Native American tribe shorn of both its historicity and its provenance. Neither its cultural past nor its environment were relevant. Reified, it became the conceptual unit the sociological comparative method required.

Yet, given Lowie's thesis of democratic individualism, the tribe alone was not enough. Existing ethnography demanded that Lowie take into account political units other than the tribe, both lesser and greater. Lowie argued that on the Northwest Coast the notion of the tribe had no meaning because only the encampment or village was recognized as a political unit. Elsewhere allegiances between distinct language groups created political units without any attempt at political integration or centralization. Both the Creek and the Iroquois "founded something after a more pretentious pattern" (1920:388).

Lowie made it clear that, in his opinion, democratic individualism was the natural order of things among Native Americans. It was certainly not due to the breakdown of ancient chieftainships through contact with Euro-Americans. Quite the reverse, he suggested that the federal government had tended to enhance the powers of native chiefs. That Native Americans in their "natural" state were able to do without a powerful executive arm of government and without penal institutions

Individualism Democracy Egalitarianism Separatism		Authority Oligarchy Stratification Centralization
Democratic individualism	Separatism	Centralism
Plains Indians	Northwest Coast Indians	Natchez
Crow Hidatsa Northern Maidu Cheyenne Omaha Dakota Mandan Hopi Maidu Shasta	Tlingit	
Titular chiefs only Valorous warriors	Chiefs with limited political power Rigid class distinctions Tribute Collective deliberations of a council	Monarchy Noble-caste councilors Power of life and death Tribute Corvée labor Officials appointed
Contingent authority, e.g., the Plains police	Customary law in the hands of family heads The Potlatch	
Centrifugal Forces Dominant		Centripetal Forces Dominant

SOURCE: Compiled from Lowie 1920.

Lowie attributed to "the tremendous, not to say terrific, force of established custom and public opinion" (1920:385).

The Plains Indians of Dakota among whom Lowie did fieldwork became for him, like the Trobrianders for Malinowski, an ethnotype in the scenario of political development. But whereas Malinowski, who did so much to advance methodologically the study of agency and the individual, referred to savages and tribes to the end of his days (ensuring for himself a popular readership), Lowie, who did so much to advance conceptually the study of society and its institutions, had before him only disoriented individuals, inaction, and decay. If Malinowski projected a Trobriand past onto the present, Lowie projected a Native American present back into the past.

Quite different from both was the vision of their contemporary, William Christie MacLeod. MacLeod's *The American Indian Frontier* (1928a) was "ahead of its time" in both anthropology and American history. Until his death in 1932, Frederick Jackson Turner's frontier thesis, first expounded in 1893, had been widely accepted and applied. Then young Depression-era liberals and Marxist historians began to challenge it. MacLeod's work (which may have been influenced by Charles Beard's economic revisionism) took a completely novel stance. He began by reporting the decimation of some 800,000 Native Americans following contact with whites. He proceeded to blend history with ethnography in a study that political scientist David Easton, called upon to review political anthropology as a subfield in 1959, praised for its rare distinction in focusing on exclusively political data in a disciplined and profitable manner. At the time, however, MacLeod's work received bad reviews from professional anthropologists.[9]

That MacLeod's work was not well received by professional anthropologists in Britain and the United States tells us a great deal about the successful establishment of functionalism. Wilson D. Wallis, an Oxford-trained American, observed that its theme would probably attract historians rather than Americanists, "for the approach is fundamentally regional and historical rather than ethnological." In a rather unfortunate phrase, Wallis concluded "The anthropologist does not care who destroyed the Indians or how the job was done" (1931:631). These contemporary evaluations were not borne out, and MacLeod's synthesis of American frontier relations became a sourcebook in less complacent periods (Mead 1932; Lesser 1933; Lewis 1942; Leacock 1954).[10]

MacLeod found nothing strange in comparing the Native American tribe with the Roman gens, or the English conquest of the Scottish highlands with the Euro-American conquest of the Plains.[11] His Indians and whites faced each other in one conflict-ridden situation after another, and his use of ethnography suggested not differences but parallels between European and Native American forms of government and similarities bred of circumstance. Time and the sequencing of events were of the essence, as were diplomacy and economics.

Lowie's sociological paradigm compared abstract political forms, contrasting the democratic individualism of "the Native American" with the despotic monarchism of "the African." MacLeod, on the other hand, compared Native American indigenous political organization with the highly developed oligarchical and state-socialist governments of the Inca, Maya, and Aztecs, which he believed were akin to those of the native peoples of northern Europe before their conquest by the armies of Rome.

This led him—naturally, as it were—to a discussion of "the tribe," in which he questioned the term's usefulness:

> The word "tribe" has been used to describe so many various types of human groupings that it is on the point of losing all scientific validity. I shall use the word, as consistently as may be, to mean a sovereign political unit. This restores to the word a degree of preciseness and usefulness. In this sense, then, the Delawares, the Mahickans . . . the Natchez, and so on, were tribes, that is sovereign states. The Sioux, the Haida, and many other so-called tribes, had better be called peoples, inasmuch as they were merely large groupings in independent political units who spoke dialects of the same language. The Iroquois, the Creeks, and so on, were confederations of tribes, each a sovereign state just as was each of the United States under the Articles of Confederation. (MacLeod 1928a:21)

MacLeod arrived at a taxonomy of political forms: peoples (without sovereign states); tribes (sovereign states); confederations of tribes; and empires. This classification of Native American political organizations was based on political rather than cultural or environmental criteria, resting as it did on the ethnohistory of the bureau ethnographers and Boasian historical reconstructions.

MacLeod then weighed the outcome of the United States' encroachment on the sovereignty of indigenous nations. This resulted in an ordering of the complex and variable political ethnography of the continent. First, he suggested that the political organization of Native Americans had *specific* geographical and regional roots. Five areas experienced state formation: (1) the uplands and mountain valleys of eastern North America, where democratic confederacies and consolidations of tribes were to be found; (2) the Atlantic tidewater, with undemocratic consolidations of tribes and petty empires; (3) coastal New England, where quasi-formal pyramidings of chiefs through various levels to a "king" or head civil chief had grown up; (4) northwestern North America, with forms similar to those in coastal New England; and (5) the Carolina coastal regions, Florida, and Louisiana, where royal kingdoms were to be found. Among them the Natchez reached "the acme of centralization" (1928a:22).

Larger than state forms of political organization, great oligarchical republican confederacies arose under certain conditions. MacLeod described the Hurons of the St. Lawrence waterway (Powell's Wyandotte); the Iroquois of New York (Morgan's League); the Cherokee of southern Appalachia (so important to Mooney's ethnological vision); and the Creek, Chickasaw, and Choctaw confederations of the southern Piedmont (of whom Swanton wrote). All transcended the bounds of locality, language, and culture and were at least as well knit, in MacLeod's judgment, as the thirteen colonies prior to their secession from Britain. In this emphasis on confederations rather than peoples and tribes, MacLeod clearly placed himself at a remove from the ethnological trend that had come to focus on "the primitive." Easton (1959) saw the major contribution of political anthropology as it came of age (Chapter 4) to be its scientific analysis of *nonstate* political forms and their acephalous dimensions. Constructs of political confederations drew attention to cultural heterogeneity rather than the homogeneity of "the simpler peoples."

Nor could a closed unit of analysis serve MacLeod's ethnography of politically organized forces, Native and Euro-American, in historical contact and conflict. At the heart of MacLeod's model of political society lay sovereignty; it is this in his synthesis in *The American Indian Frontier* that is contested. Nothing could be more removed from the increasingly dominant functional mode of representing the indigenous polities of conquered peoples. Instead of a bounded unit, he addressed a moving frontier; instead of a closed political system of interdependent parts, he wrote of contingent alliances and conflict; and instead of "primitive" political forms, he described states, confederacies, and empires. *The American Indian Frontier* also stood apart from the hegemonic functional anthropological mode in its perception of relevant data. Academic anthropology was fast moving toward nearly complete reliance on observed field material and complete disregard of the written word. Observations, descriptions, and the analyses of the on-the-spot fieldworker were considered vastly superior to all secondary sources, and MacLeod was no fieldworker.

Even with all these indications of maverick scholarship, MacLeod's study of the American frontier would probably not have been found so irrelevant to the developing discipline had he stopped at this point. But having set the scene for the contact of races, he proceeded to analyze the political interests of the Euro-American conquerors: the seventeenth-century Scottish frontier, the traders, joint stock companies, business corporations, the sweep of empire, mission interests, plantation systems, reservations, and the pauperization, as he called it, of the Native American. As a political economist, MacLeod traced the historical roots in Europe of successive waves of colonial expansion from the metropole—a transatlantic political setting that featured colonist and native alike.

Global and imperial economic enterprise, political conquest, and consolidation were thus placed squarely on the agenda of American political anthropology in 1928. No clearer challenge was ever offered within the academy to the understanding that somehow overland expansion—such as was practiced by the new twentieth-century global powers, the United States and the USSR—was essentially different from the overseas expansion of the older European powers. In its time, however, MacLeod's vision proved neither enlightening nor subversive of old ideas—it was, by and large, ignored.

African Models in the American Southwest

The most specialized and productive Native American studies carried out between 1919 and 1939 originated not on the eastern seaboard but at Berkeley, and yet, paradoxically, those that contributed most to the anthropology of politics were all marginal in some way to the mainstream Berkeley adventure: an ornithologist whose highest academic qualification was a high school diploma, a woman relegated to the art history department, a British geographer, and a midwesterner whose field research was conducted outside of California.

The plethora of small California tribes without clearly bounded political organization was, as we have seen, a matter of some concern for Berkeley ethnographers. Several of their contributions relate to the nature of political organization without the state. Kroeber himself coined the word *tribelet* to indicate the small, autonomous political units found throughout California. The tribelet consisted of the aggregation of people living in two or more separate villages who recognized the leadership of a chief. While satisfactory for descriptive purposes, this concept did little to advance analysis of the composition of politics itself.

At this point, Edward Winslow Gifford, Kroeber's colleague at Berkeley, shifted attention from the localized tribelet to descent. Gifford practiced a way of life that was to become orthodox in the new profession. He was teaching a course in world ethnography, continuing to reconstruct the social and political organization of the Miwok of the Sierra Nevada (his previous fieldwork), and about to engage in field research in Tonga in the South Pacific.

Gifford introduced the concept of lineage to Native American studies very consciously, suggesting that it referred to what Rivers had called a "patrilineal joint family" and what he himself had earlier called a clan.[12] The Miwok term *nena* stood for both the lineage itself and the ancestral home in which the lineage was supposed to have arisen. The nena was headed by a chief, who was the patriarch "so to speak" of the lineage. Succession to this office was from father to eldest son. The lineage was a landowning group, "the limited real estate which was held by it being used in common by all members of the lineage." Each lineage was exogamous. Gifford emphasized that the essential feature of the Miwok lineages was that although their members were scattered throughout California, they were bound together genealogically. "From all the information that can be gathered," Gifford asserted, "what is today only a social group was anciently also an autonomous political unit, maintaining . . . friendly relations with other nena, particularly those from which wives were drawn and those whose members attended ceremonial gatherings" (1926:389).

Gifford suggested that the Miwok lineages were landowning because they practiced transhumance. Their hamlets were located by springs or streams in an "every-man's land" where there was a "mutual recognition of the international right" to hunt and gather. But in the summer the Miwok moved into the higher mountains, returning to delimited holdings, their ancestral dwellings. Gifford attributed the amalgamation of lineage hamlets into villages to the pressure placed on the Miwok by Spanish and Mexican settlers in the San Joaquin valley.

Whether Gifford's analysis of his sparse ethnography is wholly convincing, or whether his interpretation was overly influenced by his knowledge of Tonga, must be left for specialists to decide.[13] A great deal of prestige later became attached to the delineation of modes of political organization that exist where there is no state, and a cluster of anecdotes, reports, and genealogies developed around Gifford's discovery.

When comparing Gifford's analysis of lineages with better-known studies of lineage systems in sub-Saharan Africa, three basic differences in perception stand out. First, Gifford, using historical sources as well as informants, found lineages coming together over time to form more complex systems, while the Africanists, writing in an ethnographic present, placed more stress on lineage segmentation. Second, Gifford speculated on pressures at work within and upon lineages. He drew not only on his own Miwok data but also on Kroeber's extensive researches among the Yurok, and in so doing, he came both to echo Micronesian and Polynesian diffusionist studies and to anticipate processual reevaluations of the African data by a later generation. These dealt with differential access to wealth and economic advancement. "To a certain extent," Gifford speculated, "the bonds of obligation created by the wealth concept subverted the bonds of lineage." But, he also noted, "a favorable living environment would indirectly operate against the continuance of localized autonomous lineages inasmuch as it would make possible the living together of two or more lineages. Such co-residence carries with it a surrender of a certain autonomy. . . . Wherever the lineages dwell together . . . certain territorial ties are present which must be regarded as over and above the kinship ties which operate within each lineage and serve to make each a compact consanguineous group" (1926:398–399). As lineage theory progressed, its pretensions diminished, although kinship and territoriality, jural relations, and material forces remained constantly in the foreground.

A turning point came in the ethnological study of the Californians when Alfred Kroeber began to recognize several Southwests. What was needed, he suggested, was more an intensive knowledge of the area as an ecological setting. This had a clear political dimension and was concerned, furthermore, with processes rather than political forms. Kroeber argued that, while anthropologists had paid a great deal of attention to culture, they had virtually ignored economics and politics.

The work of two of his colleagues, Gifford and a young archaeologist, G. Duncan Strong, encouraged Kroeber to sketch in the outlines of such a modern, nonsimplistic environmental study. Its features contrasted sharply with both Lowie's sociological approach and MacLeod's historical endeavors, yet it contained elements of both. Kroeber used economics (i.e., landowning) to generate a dynamic model of political organization that contained notions of generation, reconstitution, and change. These were systemic elements: Kroeber remarks on the interlocking relation of the social and political aspects of institutions, and the intermeshing of religion with authority. Legacies of evolutionary thinking remain: a theoretical assumption that lineages are the smallest building blocks in the construction of local groups and that social forms such as lineages reconstitute themselves. Kroeber thought that groups with more complete structures once had a "status" similar to that of the Shoshoni or Paiutes, official functions becoming differentiated as organization became more "elaborated" or complex. He might almost have been rewriting Herbert Spencer or John Wesley Powell. Most challenging, however, was his readiness to speculate, to formulate conjectural history, to attempt causal explanations of the processes he discerned. This was subsequently to lead him to work on civilizations and global trends in world history.

Until the end of the 1920s, Native American studies were for the most part concerned not with political origins but with historical reconstructions of what may have been presented as a timeless natural state but was in actuality the second half of the nineteenth century. Appreciation of functional wholes and cultural configurations gave way to one or several of their interdependent parts, so attention came to be paid, almost apologetically at first, to "the particularly political."

The "Particularly Political"

The transition from a cultural to an ecological approach to Native American political organization—and beyond—was pioneered by Anna Gayton, who attempted to reconstruct political life in the San Joaquin valley and foothills of California. The inhabitants of the northern part of the valley had been extinct for nearly a century; in the central valley, two Yokuts were to be found "huddled on a rancheria," one a woman who recounted "the customs of her people" and the other a man who was senile in 1925 when Gayton began her research. In the mountains and foothills, still on their old village sites, a few representatives of almost every known Yokut tribe remained. Her notebooks of her fieldwork, carried out between 1925 and 1929, contained the personal names of over 700 Yokuts and Western Mono inhabitants. Across the mountains from the San Joaquin valley, Steward worked among the Shoshoni; to the south, Daryll Forde worked among the Yuma; and both Gifford and Kroeber, Gayton's mentors at Berkeley, had been conducting research among the neighboring groups for many years.

The political life that was being reconstructed, as Gayton made explicit (1931:80), was that of the childhood of her oldest informants, sometime between 1855 and 1875. Whether they generated her interest in political conflict or she intended from the onset to explore Yokut political behavior is not clear. For reasons that cannot be explored here but which may tend to be characteristic of women anthropologists whose husbands are on the faculties of major departments, Gayton's academic career was patchy. Kroeber clearly respected her as a collaborator on material culture, but any instruction she gave at Berkeley was in the art history department, not anthropology. Her publications on

Yokuts-Mono appeared over a long period (between 1930 and 1948), and it is necessary here to draw on the later work to do justice to her insights. A manuscript entitled "Yokuts and Western Mono Ethnography" has never been published (see Gayton 1945).

In the swampy valley floor of the San Joaquin River, fishing was the main Yokut occupation. Trade routes passed from north to south. To the west, barren, treeless, and waterless slopes climbed to the Coast Range crest and were little used except for rabbit hunting. To the east of the swamps lay the oak-covered valley floor, rich in game and vegetable foodstuffs. Farther east, and still providing good sustenance, were the Sierra Nevada foothills. The 12,000-foot-high Sierra Nevada divided the Western Shoshoni inhabitants, the Mono, from their kind in the Great Basin.

The Yokut economy rested on fishing, hunting (deer, rabbits, ground squirrels, and quail), gathering (acorns, berries, and wasp grubs), and trading in baskets, pottery, salt, tanned skins, and blankets. As we have seen, the richness of the Californians' environment and their paradoxical lack of political development had already contributed to an abstract discussion of the influence of habitat on organization and progress toward civilization. Anna Gayton entered into the controversy somewhat sourly in 1945 in response to the idealism of those who considered the environment to be of minimal importance in shaping culture. Gayton's spirited reply was characteristic of what we may recognize as the Depression cohort at Berkeley. She found "an intimate relation between important immaterial phases of the culture and the environmental setting"; the "function" of the environment was that of "a cultural stabilizer," possibly even "an active integrator" (1946:253). Shunning what she perceived to be extreme positions, she set out not to argue but to document "the determination or non-determination of culture by environment" (1946:268). She approached the topic tentatively in a monograph, "Yokuts-Mono Chiefs and Shamans" (Gayton 1930a). "The purpose of this paper," she wrote,

> is not exactly what the title perhaps implies: it does not purport to be a
> discussion of social organization, nor of religion as such. While descriptions
> of political organization and the chief's place in it, of religious ideas,
> concepts of the supernatural, and the shaman's relation to them, of cere-
> monial activities, and of other cultural miscellanea, must appear here, they
> are not offered as topics of primary interest, but rather as stage settings and
> properties against which the chiefs and shamans play their interacting roles.
> It would no doubt be simpler to define the chiefs as legal officials in a static
> social setting, and to relegate the shamans to their place as professional
> doctors; but in so doing we would have only a partial picture, and that a

conventional one, of these functionaries. Native informants on first inquiry invariably describe their chiefs as the official leaders of the political unit, adding as other officials messengers, dance managers, and in some instances, subchiefs. Shamans are never recognized as officials. Yet all informants supply anecdotal evidence which shows that the shamans, unofficially, were political factors of tremendous power.

Her intent was "to show the chiefs and shamans not as categorized functionaries, but as individuals of elevated powers operating in a given social setting" (Gayton 1930a:361–362).

Gayton provided a conventional account of the formal political structure. She grouped the Yokuts and Western Mono into units that, she argued, could justifiably be called tribes, made up of families, living in villages, possessing one to three chiefs, and with a distinctive dialect and name. "Members of each tribe occupied roughly defined areas, spoke a distinctive dialect, practiced their daily pursuits and ceremonies, gave allegiance to their chiefs, and were self-consciously aware of the political unity which was expressed in their tribal name" (1930a:367).[14] The chief

> held directive control of the great mourning ceremony, an intertribal affair of extensive proportions, authorized the movements of families on seed-gathering and trading expeditions, sanctioned reprisal killings of asocial persons, provided food and shelter for the indigent or helpless members of his community and advised people in domestic quarrels. He was aided by brothers, sons and daughters, and also by his wives. These persons all bore the title of chief although the women did not transmit it. . . . Considerable wealth accrued to the chief through the advantages of his position, i.e. he profited in many trading transactions, shared payments received by his shamans or entertainers, and loaned money at high interest. However, his patriarchal responsibilities far exceeded those of his fellow citizens, and he was not necessarily the wealthiest of men. (1945:417)

When Gayton turns from formal office to actual behavior, she makes it clear that chiefs accumulated great wealth and achieved considerable aggrandizement, though she only hinted at the mechanisms of aggrandizement. The people were, as Gayton put it, "taxed" through ceremonial dances at which spectators were required to contribute money or foodstuff to pay for the entertainment. Even more important was trade, which was controlled by the chief. Traders from other tribes "would first go to the chief's house to state their business, as was customary with all outsiders, and to receive the welcoming meal. Hence the chief had first chance to buy the wares they brought and retail them to his neighbors if he so wished" (1930a:374). One commodity strategically controlled by the chief was eagle down. The eagle was sacred to his lineage and could not be killed without his permission. Yet demand for eagle down was constant since it was used in a medicine. It is not insignificant, given Gayton's analysis of the political relations of shamans and chiefs, that this particular eagle-down cure could be used by the public at large without the intervention of a spiritual intermediary.

The same was true of shamans. Access to shamanic powers was attained by dreams, and Gayton, with the easygoing psychological explanations that were a feature of her time, suggested that many persons were just too lazy to acquire supernatural help (1930a). Close study of her genealogies shows, however, that the sons of shamans became shamans, and Gayton delineated the respective spheres of interest of shaman and chief within the exploitative arena they controlled. A chief who was not a good man at heart, she observed, "and who had a desire for personal aggrandizement, attained it through illegitimate arrangements with malevolent shamans" (1930a:385).

Gayton was almost apologetic about making these observations because, as she put it, the fact "that chiefs were not always the benevolent officials which Yokuts and Mono ideals claim them to be, either was not generally known or was not readily admitted" (1930a:401). A tension clearly existed between the people's presentation of their political culture and Gayton's appreciation of the invisible realities of political life. It is a dilemma of professional discourse shared by every fieldworker, who is indebted to the confidences of his respondents. The leadership potential of shamans or medicine men had long been discussed in the ethnological literature, as we have seen, but the activities of shamans within the political community had not been sketched out before. Gayton collected a series of anecdotes about "the sinister activities of evil shamans" and "evidence of the baleful role which doctors played in aboriginal life" (1930a:392, 398). She argued that in spite of the possibility of being sentenced to death for evil practices, shamans considered the possibility of the acquisition of wealth and power worth the risk. What then was the relationship between chiefs, who wielded legal powers, and "these impressive non-officials of anti-social activities" (1930a:398)? She suggested that it was, in fact, symbiotic: "There seems to have been more harmony than conflict owing to a system of reciprocal services; a system which greatly increased the wealth of the chief on the one hand, and protected the shaman from the violence of avenging relatives on the other" (1930a:398–399). Their cooperation extended from the local mourning ceremony to intertribal killings undertaken when a chief was jealous of a neighboring rich man. At this point Gayton provided a case study. Nothing could more clearly signify that the ethnographer was beginning to move away from idealized reconstructions of customs toward the grim realism of Native American life among Euro-American settlers. Below, the case is given a title, and an abridgment is presented solely in Gayton's own words.

Motsa, A Poisoner Chief

Motsa [a Poisoner Chief, to the north of Tulare Lake across the trade route] . . . had the status of a chief but [his] attitude towards others was that of a malevolent shaman. . . . [H]e injured members of his locality largely by the use of poisons though he possessed some supernatural power. That he openly victimized his fellows was due, perhaps, to the fact that his valley had been the first in the region to suffer from the encroachment of white settlers. He was neither the son or nephew of the previous chief but was simply chosen as one of these men to act as the next chief upon the death of the last influential chief at the Lemoore rancheria.

Motsa first lived at Wallace's ranch . . . [where] he killed an Indian by putting poison in his shoes. He was paid to do this. The night the man died Motsa [set out for] the Lemoore rancheria where [members of his tribe were living]. [His son was still there in the 1930s, but Gayton was unable to obtain him as an informant.] The fact that Motsa ran away was considered proof of his guilt. . . . At Lemoore [ranch] Motsa settled down and married. Thereafter began his dominance over the local group. Motsa had some supernatural power which he gained in the usual manner. He ate wild tobacco to help his dreams at night. . . . When he wanted to make himself invisible in order to go about eavesdropping or to place poison on people's clothes he took out his jimsonweed talisman and held it in his hand. Nobody could see him then.

He had a coyote assistant just like a doctor. He had a coyote song. . . . [When the coyote appeared,] Motsa would get on the coyote's back and wrap his arms around the animal's neck. . . . If people looked outside their houses at night and saw a coyote they knew that Motsa was about. . . . [Motsa had among his friends] many professional doctors from whom he learned much. . . . [Motsa was not regarded as a doctor but as a poisoner. Many deaths were attributed to him: that of a young girl whom he had threatened to kill; that of the big chief of a neighboring moiety who was hardworking and saved the money he earned; that of Josie Alonzo's brother; Josie's mother; her maternal grandfather; and others. Josie Alonzo was Gayton's informant at Lemoore ranch.] Everyone referred to Motsa as . . . bad chief or . . . a person who would rob anything from anybody. He didn't care for he was not afraid of any one. He never expressed any sorrow over any one's death but just went about his own business as usual. . . . [Motsa was finally killed by magic or poison by a man whose daughter-in-law he had tried to seduce.] (1930a:400)

Gayton concluded: "However, how much is fact and how much is prejudice in this informant's tales of Motsa, is of no moment in the present discussion. All our accounts of the activities of malicious doctors and chiefs which are given here represent native attitudes toward these men as a class rather than as individuals" (1930a:401–407).

Gayton found a complete lack of formulated law among the Yokuts-Mono. Peace and public satisfaction were maintained by means of influence sanctioned by the fear of sorcery. This both worked for public good and served as a tool for chiefs when exercised through their shamans; "sorcery as a deterrent of crime kept a balance of peace in everyday life" (1930a:409).

A chief who hired a shaman to sicken a rich but mean man was performing a public service even if he himself profited, but he could not make unrestrained use of malevolent supernatural power. He was a public figure and open to censure. Though he acquired his position by inheritance, its retention depended on his conduct. Popular sentiment turned against the chief who gave unfair decisions or was suspected of self-aggrandizement.

Gayton related the lack of codified law to easy subsistence and generosity as an ideal. An abundant food supply (before white intrusion) accounted for the lack of territorial bounds and property laws. Giving food away reduced the possibility of theft. "Viewed from another angle these cultural habits may be regarded as laws," she suggested. "They were such in effect, but were not verbally formulated. From the point of view of their own culture . . . [they] were customs of courtesy expressing the ideal of generosity. Equality of rank among the people at large, that is, the absence of a class system, expressed the nullity of codified social law" (1930a:414).

Gayton concluded her account of Yokuts-Mono chiefs and shamans with a discussion of the impact of the Ghost Dance of 1870, which was diffused throughout much of the San Joaquin valley. Chiefs stepped in to control the new dance form and handled the social problems its large assemblies created. They were also active in diffusing it.

Anna Gayton's study of shamans and chiefs among the Yokuts and Western Mono reflected not only a shift away from the constraints of the *UCPAAE* format but a paradigmatic shift of the first order. Idealism gave way to realism as she presented an analysis of the actions of individuals who were, as she put it, "role-playing." Even more important, she set informants' structural categories and definitions on one side as she strove to present an organizational account of real power holding in the San Joaquin valley. These are matters to which we shall have occasion to return many times.

Political Ecology of the Hopi and Yuma

Like Anna Gayton, Cyril Daryll Forde was marginal to the mainstream of academic anthropology in the 1920s and 1930s in several ways. A Londoner and the son of a clergyman, he was educated at a county school and at University College, London. In 1924, at the age of twenty-two, he was appointed lecturer in Elliot Grafton Smith's department. His first publication, *Ancient Mariners* (1926), belonged to the diffusionist genre. Two years later he met Robert Lowie, who was visiting Britain, and on completing his doctorate in geography and being awarded a Commonwealth Fellowship, he went to Berkeley.

Forde was antipathetic to the dominant theoretical position of Radcliffe-Brown (Lowie 1959; Fortes 1976). He knew Rivers and was a close friend of both V. Gordon Childe (whose contribution to the anthropology of politics will be discussed shortly) and Lord Raglan, the staunch advocate of an anthropology that dealt with nonprimitives. He was outside the circle of functional social anthropologists associated with Malinowski at the London School of Economics, and indeed, as Meyer Fortes (himself a student of Malinowski and a colleague of Radcliffe-Brown) put it, "as a member of the research group attached to Elliot Smith and Perry, and later as a student at Berkeley under Kroeber and Lowie, he would have been regarded as belonging to the antifunctionalist movements of the 1920s and 1930s" (1976:475). The temptation to explore further Fortes's use of verb tense and his choice of words in the phrase "anti-functionalist movements" must be resisted in order to make the point directly that Daryll Forde represented both a tradition and vision of anthropology that contested the dominance of the hegemonic functional "school." His training as a geographer and an archaeologist, along with his field experience in the Southwest, shaped his very distinctive ecological contribution to the anthropology of politics.

Forde appears to have thrown himself wholeheartedly into the Kroeberian enterprise at Berkeley. His *Ethnography of the Yuma Indians* was published in 1931. In it he adopted the *UCPAAE* format in its entirety. This meant that after a brief discussion of the region, territory, and settlement pattern of the Yuma, Forde noted their external and linguistic relations with other tribes, which were manifest through war, barter, and festivals. A description of the food supply followed, with brief but meticulous descriptions of agriculture, planted grasses, landownership, gathered seeds and fruits, tobacco, hunting, feasts, and fishing, in that order. He next described seasonal activities and then material culture: houses, pottery, basketry, and weaving. Sections on river navigation, songs, and musical instruments preceded a discussion of leadership. This was followed by an account of social organization, clans, genealogy, kinship, personal names, boys' initiation rites, girls' puberty observances, tatooing, marriage, transvestitism and birth customs. Warfare appeared next—captives, weapons, shields, and training—followed by discussions of the creation, the soul and afterlife, prayer, medicine, magic, cremation rites, and mourning ceremonies. There was no discussion of law. Apart from an initial focus on subsistence economics, neither rhyme nor reason seemed to order the ethnography. There was certainly no sense of "functional interdependence" or "organic whole" such as had appeared by 1931 in the work of Malinowski's students, or the primacy Radcliffe-Brown attributed to kinship.

Forde described the political organization of the Yuma as "stable anarchy" (1931:134). He quoted at length one informant who told of Yuma settlement in small groups along the river at the foot of the mesa. Each group had its own leaders, who were, in essence, the more active heads of families. They met as a "democratic village council" to run the settlement's affairs—Forde used the terms *group, village,* and *band* interchangeably—coming together "whenever anything big was planned, a battle or a feast" (1931:135). Men were retired from this executive body of leaders if they became senile. At this point, he shifted from reconstructing the past to describing the present (i.e., 1928–29) as he observed public events being run by men in their forties and early fifties. Although the Yuma sense of tribal solidarity was strong, American culture had penetrated deeply into their material life. Many had sold their land to Euro-Americans, and the irrigable terrain was dotted with cotton ginneries. "The aboriginal cultivation [had] necessarily been supplanted and the social organization of former times [had] largely disappeared" (Forde 1931:85–86). Their ceremonial and religious life was unaffected by a thin veneer of Methodism and Catholicism.

Forde had considerable difficulty in extracting information on past organization from the Yuma. While they would go into "elaborate and even fanciful detail" about magical and mythological events, they were indifferent to "the mechanics of life" and the "details of everyday existence." He did learn, however, that besides the village leaders the Yuma previously had a tribal leader (*kwoxot*), a man of power who gained this title by telling his dreams and by giving feasts so that his fame would spread. Forde also noted that most successful dreamers and feast givers came from the "more powerful" families, which "had a lot of good men" (1931:135). The functions of the kwoxot were minimal. His house was a communal gathering place for feasts, funerals, and meetings; he stored food and distributed it to the poor; he was a rainmaker and an orator; he was not a war leader but was responsible for the care of scalps and the guarding of captives. A war leader or *kwanami* (brave man) deferred to the kwoxot.

Forde was able to determine that economic and military organization was not based on, or even integrated with, clan organization; nor were there lineages. Like his fellow Berkeley fieldworkers Gayton and Steward, Forde's object was to reconstruct the aboriginal political organization of the Yuma prior to the advent of Euro-American colonial powers, and we may see in his Yuma ethnography a mix of four generations' history presented as a "cultural product." In the long run, what was important about Forde's research among the Yuma was not so much his ambivalence about the ethnographic product, nor the findings themselves, but the fact that he was there in the Southwest, because it was out of this experience—his "transAtlantic novitiate," as he called it (Fortes 1976)—that he became a catalyst for an alternative vision of anthropology in Britain in the 1950s.[15]

Archaeology's Contribution

Anthropology at Berkeley, as at the Bureau of American Ethnology, was essentially historical, challenging the search for universals and suspicious of overly sociological abstraction. A leading spokesman for its views, in opposition to the increasingly sociological study of Native Americans developing at the University of Chicago, was William Duncan Strong. His insistence on the quintessential unity of archaeology, history, and ethnology influenced the anthropology of politics at the Bureau of American Ethnology, where he was director from 1921 to 1927, and at Columbia University, where he later taught. After combining ethnology with his archaeological findings in the Southwest, Strong began to sound a methodological clarion call in 1935. Its notes were ecological, historical, and ethnological. His *Introduction to Nebraska Archaeology* (1935) discussed the cultural adaptation of Plains Indian tribes to their environment, described their horse culture as "a thin and strikingly uniform veneer over the central plains" (1935:298), and concluded by insisting on "the basic importance of the prehistoric record in checking or corroborating the work of the ethnologist" (1935:300).

Strong predicted that the application of archaeological techniques would "overturn one of the most strongly held ethnographic concepts in the area," the view of the Plains Indian as, from time immemorial, a nomadic hunter and warrior (1936:362–363). The political significance of such inventions of tradition is explored in Chapter 6. Here it is sufficient to observe that the "myth" of the Plains Indian as exposed by Strong must surely be related to the self-serving stereotype of nomadic peoples as warrior hordes whose own aggressive behavior justified "civilized" retaliation. That culture was not simply acquired but produced was also an essential component of Strong's thinking.

Although much of Strong's perception, and certainly his professional status, was based on his field research and his critical appreciation of Native American ethnology, he also moved within an orbit best delineated through the work of V. Gordon Childe, whose *Man Makes Himself* (1936) appeared in the same year as Strong's programmatic essay "Anthropological Theory and Archaeological Fact." In his essay Strong argued for the superiority of archaeological over ethnohistorical (documentary) research in the analysis of Native American–white contact because the ethnohistorical documents were so often consciously or unconsciously biased.

Childe's academic career is discussed here in some detail because of his influence on Kroeber and the Berkeley anthropologists and because few lives so captured the spirit of the 1930s in its political, institutional, and scholarly manifestations.[16] Vere Gordon Childe was born in Sydney, Australia, in 1892. He studied classics and philosophy at the University of Sydney and classical archaeology at Queen's College, Oxford. Among his supervisors was Sir John Myres, whose close political and academic influence we have already noted (Chapter 1). He joined Oxford's Fabian Society in 1914, numbering among his friends Rajani Palme Dutt (founding member and leading theoretician of the British Communist party), Raymond Postgate, and G.D.H. Cole. A pacifist, Childe returned to Australia in 1917, first to teach and then to enter left-wing politics as private secretary to the leader of the Labour opposition party in New South Wales.

In 1921 Childe returned to London, settling close to the British Museum and the library of the RAI. Among his friends was Daryll Forde. From 1921 to 1914 Childe spent his time in research in the libraries and at left-wing clubs while looking for a job. He worked as a translator, a temporary lecturer at LSE, and as the librarian at the RAI in 1925.[17] His innovative book *The Dawn of European Civilization* was published the same year. Within anthropology, his work was more influential among American than British scholars. The young Berkeley crowd welcomed a new paradigm, while the apparent affinities of his work with that of Elliot Smith and the diffusionists made his a losing cause in Britain. By 1926 the institutional powers of Myres and Seligman were on the wane, Malinowski was selected as director of a well-funded African research program, and the gulf widened fast between archaeology and social anthropology on the one hand and the ethnology of Europe and the tribal world of the tropics on the other.

It is tempting to read in a carefully constructed passage in *Man Makes Himself* an explicit challenge to dominant Malinowskian anthropology in Britain similar to what Strong offered ethnologists in America. In a manner reminiscent of Malinowski's dramatic opening to *Argonauts of the Western Pacific* (1922), Childe described how an economy, a social organization, and a system of production may be inferred from a canoe, and how changes in technology can lead to changes in an economic system over time.

Childe argued further that the age of ideological, unscientific political history was over and that "cultural history" should be recognized as a respectable academic field. "Marx insisted on the prime importance of economic conditions, of the social forces of production, and of applications of science as factors in historical change," he wrote. "His realist conception of history is gaining acceptance in academic circles remote from the party passions inflamed by other aspects of Marxism" (1936:12). This was more true in Britain than in the United States at the time.

In 1939 Childe was a visiting professor at the University of California, and his paper "Archaeology and Anthropology" was published in that year. Childe's work appealed to Berkeley-trained and subsequently Columbia-routinized anthropologists on several counts. First, he supplied a precedent: a history of man's social evolution from a hunting-gathering stage to civilization. Second, he was concerned with the application of knowledge: one of the major effects of the class division in his eyes was the separation of theoretical from practical knowledge. He argued that while the theoreticians, the kings, the priests, and others were members of the upper classes, the craftsmen—exponents of practical knowledge—were relegated to the lower classes. As a result, the new learning of the upper classes was "all too often fettered by subservience to superstition and divorced from the applied sciences that produced results" (1936:262). Third, Childe emphasized cultural materialism rather than economic determinism and thus met Boas's objections while at the same time providing a way out of the morass of "party passions inflamed by . . . Marxism," as he himself put it (1936:12). He produced a materialist history, not a Marxist economic analysis, through his use of the concept of culture. Finally, Childe reenergized this core concept of American anthropology—culture—at a time when sociologizing trends were becoming manifest in all the major departments.

Thus Childe provided an alternative to Radcliffe-Brown's grand vision at a time when it seemed to be peaking.

Childe's work was highly regarded not only by Strong but also by Alexander Lesser and Julian Steward, two up-and-coming practitioners whose impact on the anthropology of politics is discussed next. All shared his vision of cultures not as static but as changing systems. All were outspoken critics of British social anthropology, derogating its notions of functional integration, its static analyses, and its lack of historicity. All took markedly materialist approaches, though with less consciousness of Marxist scholarship than Childe himself. Marxism was, as Alvin Gouldner put it, "part of a suppressed underculture" in American sociology and anthropology . . . for those who matured during the 1930s" (1970:158). All recognized diffusion as an important part of cultural evolution. Childe shared with Strong an attachment to the importance of history and with Steward a conviction that all human behavior is explicable. Differences among them were largely related to whether priorities in explanation were best accorded to history, social organization, or the environment.

If the Boasian thesis, which dominated American anthropology from 1903 to 1927, is seen to coexist with its antithesis, most clearly formulated by MacLeod, then the work that emerged after that date provided their synthesis. The normative focus on cultural traits and historical reconstruction in the first and the combination of economic and historicopolitical considerations in the second produced a political anthropology that was grounded in history, ecology, and politics. Its bedrock was materialism, and it became associated in the popular mind with the name of Julian Steward. Whether this was entirely justified is questioned in the next section as we look at the contribution of Alexander Lesser.

The Historicity of Political Facts

In Europe, Childe was able to advance his ideas of culture history by the motor of Marxism, but the American academy was less tolerant of historical materialism. Or perhaps it was that in American anthropology there was scope, as in Germany, for a different kind of political activism, that of the citizen-scholar. At Columbia, Boas led his colleagues and students into the political arena, supporting socialist and communist organizations fighting Fascism and racism (Beardsley 1973; Stocking 1979b). He was, however, antipathetic to Marxism as an intellectual vehicle, viewing it simply as economic determinism. Many American anthropologists have found it difficult to separate the ideas of Marx the nineteenth-century intellectual from those of the political parties and associations that drew on his ideas. An intellectual iconography and a reliance on the "sacred texts" of Durkheim and Weber (particularly in sociology departments) does not incur the same political scrutiny, although perhaps it should.

During the 1930s several Columbia anthropologists were left-wing political activists. Elman Service and Clifton Amsbury, along with John Murra of Chicago, fought in Spain. Melville Jacobs, Alexander Lesser, Bernhard Stern, Morris Swadesh, and Gene Weltfish turned to socialism or communism at home. The choice of problematics in the dissertations of 1930s graduate students suggests the exceptionally tolerant ethos of the anthropology department in the face of—or perhaps fueled by—the hostility of the university administration, a stress not lessened by the killing of Henrietta Schmerler, inexperienced Columbia student fieldworker, on the Fort Apache reservation in 1931.[18] The clearest evidence to date of the political ethos in which intellectuals operated is to be found in the publishing histories of several Columbia dissertations (Chapter 4).

The threads of the Marxist tradition in political anthropology are still difficult to discern, let alone unravel. The public debate over sociological functionalism that took place in the halls of the American Anthropological Association meeting at Pittsburgh in 1934—and that redounded rather emptily elsewhere—is one place to start. Its beginnings were inauspicious. Alexander Lesser had presented a paper that unwittingly challenged the functionalist theory of Radcliffe-Brown.[19] As Lesser himself recalled, he thought he was addressing American ethnologists and was objecting both to the kind of things that Kroeber, Wissler, and Spier were doing in historical reconstruction and to the sociologically oriented studies of Benedict and Mead. The choice before Native Americanist scholars, as he saw it, was between historicism and functionalism; Lesser argued that it was not functionalism per se that was in error but synchronism.

An earlier statement of Lesser's position appeared in his Plains Indian acculturation study published in 1933. There he argued that, methodologically speaking, "time perspective or historicity is essential to an understanding of culture whatever special approach is taken. . . . I think the primary principle of our methodology must lie [in] the fact [that] historicity is neither an end nor by itself a means but a condition which must be recognized at every step" (1933:336). By comparing the distribution and function of the elements in a hand game that accompanied the spread of the Ghost Dance, Lesser was able not simply to document political change over time but also to account for the directions that change took. His monograph opened with a fierce denunciation of recent contacts between the Pawnee and the American government. It was, indeed, an implicitly political monograph about the conquest of the Pawnee and "the whole abysmal record of their subjection to the United States Government and its caprices" (Mintz 1985:105).

In 1935 Lesser squarely addressed the opposition between his own historical position and functionalism. "How are . . . functional relations to be established?" he asked.

> First of all, we begin, as in any science, with observation. We see such and such events going on. Many things are always happening at the same time, however. How are we to determine whether or not those things which happen at the same time are related to one another? For it is obvious that they may be contemporary events, or even serial events, not because they are related to one another but because their determinants, unknown and unobserved, have caused them to happen at the same or subsequent times. In short, contemporary or associated events may be merely coexistences. *Culture, at any one time, is first and foremost a mass of coexistent events.* . . . As soon as we turn to prior events for an understanding of events observed, we are turning to history. History is no more than that. It is a utilization of the conditioning fact of historicity for the elucidation of seen events. (1935:391–392, emphasis added)

In 1939 Lesser warned his colleagues that anthropology would have to become both problem oriented and broader in scope if it were to survive. He referred to the disapprobation other social scientists expressed for anthropology's pursuit of cultural relativity and the primitive. The falsity of cultural isolates—what Lauriston Sharp later called "the cookie cutter concept of culture"—did not receive explicit exposition in Lesser's work until his neglected but most important paper "Social Fields and the Evolution of Society" (1961). But it was perhaps no coincidence that he recalled the early influence on him of Wheeler's *The Tribe and Intertribal Relations in Australia* (1910).[20] Lesser viewed a cultural institution not as a thing or an aspect but as "a manifold which is not a unit system, but a combination of meanings which have tended to become associated" (1933:336). His choice of the term *manifold* emphasized the process of the coming together of disparate elements. In material terms a manifold is a pipe fitted with several lateral outlets, or a metal chest with many valves, or the third stomach of a ruminant—hardly the images that come readily to the mind of a political anthropologist. Derived from Kantian philosophical usage, the concept was later to be employed by two of Lesser's erstwhile students, Sidney Mintz and Eric Wolf (Chapter 4). "Every perspective," as Kenneth Burke asserted, "requires a metaphor, implicit or explicit, for its organizational base" (1957:132). Not until the 1980s was the metaphorical value of the manifold made explicit (Chapter 6), and then it was in opposition to sociological notions of an all-pervading modern world system.

It might have been expected that the intellectual opposition that Lesser mounted to functionalism, British and homegrown, as well as its concentration on primitive societies, would have sparked an alternative tradition in American anthropology. His historicism, and his view of culture as a dynamic continuum, led him to advocate the application of anthropology's distinctive field methods to modern complex societies. His aversion to timeless and placeless abstractions ultimately led him to the analysis of social fields.

That no such alternative tradition emerged can only be attributed to the man and the times. A dedicated citizen scholar, Lesser's honest and radical appraisals were often unwelcome to the establishment, whether the federal government or the academy. In the years following the Depression, when the academic labor market was flooded and so many of his peers were obliged to work in the public sector, Lesser remained on the sidelines. Lacking opportunities for sustained graduate teaching and training, Lesser's vision was not translated or reproduced by a following generation of students. Its indirect impact—a largely oral tradition, perhaps—was nevertheless on the record.

Shoshoni Revisited: The Politics of Band Society

Few careers better exemplified the tendency in political anthropology to shift from the particular to the general than that of Julian Steward. His monograph, *Basin-Plateau Aboriginal Sociopolitical Groups*, based on field research among the Shoshoni, was not published until 1938, although he carried out the fieldwork much earlier. The rich detail of his analysis of the natural habitat of the Great Basin, the settlement patterns of the Shoshoni he encountered and mapped, and the observations he made of local groupings and leadership provided a unique contribution to the political ethnography of band society. This was not reconstruction, nor a mix of reconstruction and reality, but an observation of ongoing action within a carefully depicted environment. Steward also took into account all the available historical sources and linguistic data. He used Powell's published materials but apparently not his unpublished manuscripts. The monograph is a classic in political ethnography, a transition between Boasian historical reconstruction and sociologically oriented functional ethnography.

By the time his monograph appeared, Steward had already published papers on the economic and social bases of primitive bands (1936), linguistic distributions and political groups of the Great Basin Shoshoni (1937b), and ecological aspects of southwestern society (1937a). Some were published in rather obscure places (including abroad), which reflected the reluctance of professional American anthropologists to welcome a new approach, particularly one that was considered radical and overly deterministic (Turney-High 1940).[21] The first paper introduced what Steward suggested was a methodological innovation: "the assumption that every cultural phenomenon is the product of some definite cause or causes" (1936:344). This is a necessary presupposition if anthropology were to be a science. By "cause," Steward meant not "what brought primitive bands into being" but rather, form following function, evidence of the pervasive influence on his work of a social science paradigm that he shared with Radcliffe-Brown, among others. What Steward did not adequately appreciate, R. F. Murphy has suggested (1977), was the extent to which the culture of the Shoshoni he observed was a response to the Depression, which both they and he were struggling to survive.

Steward's so-called causal analysis resulted in a simple taxonomy based initially on kinship features and then on locality. First he distinguished between patrilineal and composite bands. (He identified matrilineal bands but did not discuss them.) Patrilineal and composite bands were to be found in association with scarce resources, low population density, and simple technology. Patrilineal bands were small, and they jointly owned hunting territory and practiced patrilocality and band exogamy. Composite bands were larger and nonexogamic, and they practiced bilocal residence. Steward explained the difference between them in ecological terms: composite bands were to be found where people hunted abundant large, migrating game throughout a wide territory. The ecological factors that produced primitive bands included the need for families (1) to join with others both for enhanced productivity and as a kind of subsistence insurance, (2) to gain access to a variety of foods from different regions, and (3) to gain security and support in warfare and feuds. The band type of political organization was thus contingent on local resources: social organization was contingent on economy.

Political unity was very similar in all bands. Centralized control existed only for hunting, rituals, and other communal activities. Leaders had temporary and slight authority. In patrilineal bands, the leader was usually the head of the lineage; in bilateral bands, he was simply a prestigious person. Chiefs were rare; the influential leaders were often shamans. Steward observed that although bands were ordinarily autonomous, they might temporarily unite for special purposes. The larger unit on such occasions could be called a tribe. Steward suggested that "It is not wholly revealing to record merely that a group had a chief or considered itself a band, for neither the nature and extent of the authority delegated to the chief nor the kind of solidarity among members of the band is self-evident. Moreover, novel conditions and concepts introduced by the white man often radically altered native groupings, bringing solidarity and chieftain's authority where it had not previously existed" (1937b:628). He warned, too, that the political unity of a past age might be exaggerated by contemporary Native Americans, suggesting "the need of careful investigation of the dynamic aspects of native political institutions" (1937b:630).

Steward then turned to the "causes" of two distinct forms of political grouping he found among the Shoshoni. His explanation drew on both historical and locational factors. He distinguished village organization, in which habitual association and cooperation were limited to the inhabitants of a single village, from band organization, which was variable in its social and economic foundation but always entailed cooperation, a degree of centralized political control, and a sense of solidarity among the inhabitants of a well-defined territory. Village organization rested on a gathering economy in valleys where game was scarce. The Basin-Plateau Shoshoni held "no concept whatever of group ownership of food territories" (1937b:629). Apart from short communal rabbit and spring antelope drives, communal gatherings did not occur, because of the difficulty of transporting sufficient food; few Shoshoni he observed had horses.

Steward did not set out to produce a holistic description of Shoshoni society in *Basin-Plateau Aboriginal Sociopolitical Groups* (1938). He took great pains to document how band organization varied in different parts of the country, attributing this to whether a band had horses. Horseless gathering villages were to be found in the north of the region and mounted hunting bands in the south. The distribution of the mounted bands was governed by an eastern limit to salmon fishing and a western limit to lowland "bottoms" where horses could be grazed. "The importance of the horse in primitive economy and the consequent social and political effects should not be underestimated," Steward insisted. "The western limit of the horse was the western limit of the [patrilineal] bands" (1938:377).

The horseless western bands' political unity resulted from their proximity to more or less permanent habitations and habitual cooperation in drives, hunts, irrigation, seed gathering, and dances, all under the direction of a band chief. In the mounted eastern bands, he found political control to be vested in one or more chiefs, with authority for warfare, hunting, dancing, and other activities divided among them. Each band occupied a fairly well defined territory but traveled great distances on horseback and thus had frequent contact with other bands. Among those Shoshoni influenced by Plains Indians, war honors carried great prestige and won their holders civil as well as military authority. Although Steward was clearly aware of the historical contingencies that shaped Shoshoni political organization—the advent of the horse, the spread of firearms, the dislocation and amalgamation of tribes, all "factors incident to the coming of the White man" (1938:378)—his appreciation of temporal factors was outweighed by spatial environmental ones, and his ethnography remained essentially descriptive and functional.[22]

Steward was not an intellectual, and his upbringing and education encourage our viewing him as a kindred spirit in many ways to John Wesley Powell. His contribution lay in his basic fieldwork method and the kinds of data he collected. Like Gayton and Forde, and progressively moving beyond their uncertainties as a less marginalized Berkeley student was better able to do, he lived and worked among groups of Native American respondents rather than the scattered and isolated individuals they had encountered. Steward's was the most grounded investigation possible and was well within the Kroeberian environmental problematic that Berkeley anthropologists inherited from the state of California. Yet the format of *Basin-Plateau Aboriginal Sociopolitical Groups* (1938) has only to be placed alongside Steward's 1933 *UCPAAE* ethnography of the Owens Valley Paiute (where political organization was dealt with in a little over two pages) to indicate how far he had come in his thinking and the extent to which he was pioneering a new paradigm.

Ironically, however, Steward's generalizing tendencies led him toward the neo-evolutionary surge that welled up after the war. Its trivialization of field research and the "thick ethnography" he was so well placed to write changed the orientation of his work. Like Powell before him, Steward left the Shoshoni to direct the team research of others (Chapter 4).

THE POLITICS OF ACCULTURATION

No other paradigm held so much potential for an anthropology of politics as did that surrounding the concept of acculturation. Concern with "the interaction of cultural groups," to use Herskovits's deceptively simple definition (1938a), had long existed within anthropology. Powell and McGee used the very term at the bureau, and it underlay the research of diffusionists, who were caught up in the eugenics revolution and who were fearful of the fate of Oceanic peoples swept up in the fervor of economic imperialism. But it was not until the 1930s that acculturation became the central organizing concept of an anthropology that was beginning to question the never-never land of isolated primitive peoples and the analytical unit of the tribe.

Anthropologists of all nationalities converged in their adoption of the term. Richard Thurnwald, a German, defined acculturation as "a process of adaptation to new conditions of life" (1932:557) and clearly recognized that domination was an important aspect. So, too, did Linton, for whom acculturation referred to "those phenomena which result when groups of individuals having different cultures come into continuous first-hand contact, with subsequent changes in the original culture patterns of either or both groups" (1940:501). Other anthropologists viewed acculturation as a unidirectional process imposed on a political minority (Mead 1932; Lesser 1933; Parsons 1936), challenging those who laundered the global experience to make it one in which donor-recipient cultures were in reciprocal exchange. Leslie Spier, editor of the *American Anthropologist* (and the husband of Anna Gayton), argued that acculturation studies were really political science and had no place in anthropology (Kelly 1985).

The Clash of Cultures

In Oceania, contact between Europeans and local populations had long been known to have had disastrous results. Rivers, as we have seen, edited *Essays on the Depopulation of Melanesia* in 1922. From the European point of view, high mortality was a component of what was called in the 1920s "the Native Problem." But as George Henry Lane-Fox Pitt-Rivers reminded his readers in *The Clash of Culture and the Contact of Races: An Anthropological and Psychological Study of the Laws of Racial Adaptability, with Special Reference to the Depopulation of the Pacific and the Government of Subject Races* (1927), there were two sides to the Native Problem: "There is the problem of realizing the white man's interests in a black man's country, that is the former's aspect of the problem; and there is the black man's problem, the problem of maintaining his own existence, identity and welfare" (1927:25). Pitt-Rivers's study, conducted under the sponsorship of Marett at Oxford, was dedicated to Malinowski and drew upon Trobriand ethnography as well as the author's own experience in several Pacific islands.

"The great world-shattering changes of the past decade," wrote Pitt-Rivers, "the War, the Russian Revolution, the Treaty of Versailles and the consequences of these events, have led men to question for the first time many of the previously unchallenged assumptions implicit in their own civilization, whilst it has prompted them to regard with real concern and a desire to understand civilizations unlike their own" (1927:xii). The shattering world of which Pitt-Rivers wrote was one of disintegration and decay, for which Europeans were responsible. He believed that "native" culture should be left as untouched as possible and was thus prepared to defend headhunting, sorcery, and indigenous slavery. He questioned missionaries being given a legal monopoly to practice an alien and competitive magic in the Pacific islands and asked, "On what grounds of policy or ethics can we, who exclude Asiatics from Australia, defend our one-sided penetration by Christian missionaries into China, forced on the unwilling Chinese?" (1927:240). Anthropology's academic bias against missionaries reflected, perhaps, the struggle between them for the control of knowledge as power.

Pitt-Rivers was advocating a "right sort" of anthropology, functional and practical, and he addressed central political issues that did not reappear for another fifty years in political anthropology, and then not conjointly and systematically. These were (1) the status of a political unit, (2) the related issue of sovereignty, and (3) European domination in most of the imperial world. As culture contact became a funded field of inquiry, as we shall see, its belligerent, political dimensions were lost.

The global context of Pitt-Rivers's clash of cultures was "the almost ubiquitously existing state of unrest among subject races under European tutelage": the South African miners strike that "developed into an abortive revolution in March 1922"; the role of the Communist International in serving as "a pillar of fire leading on the rebellious peoples in Asia and Africa"; and the movement of "world-wide unrest among subject races against European tutelage . . . led to a marked degree by those [who have] assimilated most 'successfully' European education, European religion, and European blood" (1927:25, 29, 31). All of this was far closer to a political anthropology in the making than to the new subfield of acculturation or culture contact studies that in fact emerged.

When Peoples Meet

An alternative political anthropology did, however, almost emerge from the accumulation of ethnographies that acculturation, as a concept, had engendered or embraced. It even achieved that subfield phase of development marked by a classroom textbook, *When Peoples Meet: A Study in Race and Culture Contact* (1942). Published under the auspices of the Progressive Education Association, then chaired by Ruth Benedict, an associate professor of anthropology at Columbia University, the volume was coedited by Alain Locke, a professor of philosophy at Howard University, and Bernhard J. Stern, a lecturer in anthropology at the New School for Social Research and in sociology at Columbia. Almost half the extracts used came from anthropologists. Others were derived from the work of historians Jacques Barzun, Frederick J. Teggart, and Arnold J. Toynbee; psychologist I. D. MacCrone; writers on politics Leonard Woolf and Hans Kohn; and sociologists Everett V. Stonequist, Isaac A. Hourwich, Caroline F. Ware, E. Franklin Frazier, and John Dollard. The project was conceived by Alain Locke, an African-American philosopher, critic, and spokesman. His objectives were similar to those of Jomo Kenyatta, who in 1938 said that anthropology could be used as part of a growing African challenge to colonial rule (James 1973). Locke's collaboration with Stern—the biographer of Morgan, collaborator with Ross, and active socialist—personified the kindred of the Red and the Black that had developed with the onset of the Depression.

The five parts of *When Peoples Meet* and the distribution within it of anthropological extracts were as follows:

		No. of extracts
1.	Culture Contact and the Growth of Civilization	11
2.	Varieties of Culture Contact	2
3.	The Ways of Dominant Peoples: Devices of Power	2
4.	The Ways of Submerged Peoples: Tactics of Survival and Counter-Assertion	2
5.	The Contemporary Scene in Intercultural Relations	2

The anthropological extracts fell mostly into Part 1, with the work of Benedict, Boas, T. T. Waterman, and Linton placing the subject matter in a global cultural setting. A section on the universality of cultural interchange drew upon Westermann, Herskovits, and Wissler. A third section, on European aims at dominance, included Harry L. Shapiro's "The World in Motion," Margaret Mead's discussion "Some Problems of Culture Contact," George Pitt-Rivers's "Types of Culture Contact," Firth's "The Effects of Western Culture upon Primitive Peoples," and Redfield's "Culture Contact in Central America." Part 2 dealt with power politics and dominance, the role of imperialism, types of social cleavage, and the economic basis of culture conflict. In the last appeared Monica Hunter's "Contemporary European-Bantu Relations in South Africa" and George Pitt-Rivers's "The Detribalization of the Natives of the Pacific Islands." Essays in physical anthropology by Boas and Shapiro represented the anthropological contribution to Part 3. They were included to point up the manner in which the fallacies of a concept of "pure races" and ethnic stereotyping were devices of power, providing "superiority creeds" for the dominant. Most of the anthropologists documented the tactics of survival and the counterassertion of "submerged peoples" such as South African nationalists (Hunter), African-Americans (Powdermaker), Australian aborigines (Elkin), and Native Americans (Linton). A final section contained Schapera's discussion of "The Outcome of European Domination of Africa" and Sapir's of "Language and National Antagonisms."

All twenty-one essays had first been published between 1925 and 1939, a clear indication of anthropology's initial appreciation of the integumental political nature of culture contact. The volume had the potential of crystallizing domestic political consciousness in the United States just when the country was about to step openly onto the global stage. It also held the promise of synthesizing the anthropological contribution to the politics of domination in the contemporary world, since it contained the clear statement that modern societal complexity arose from processes emerging in the pursuit of colonial and capitalist goals. It was exactly this conceptualization (but with somewhat different values placed on the colonial and capitalist impact on "other races") that gave rise to a more acceptable main branch of acculturation studies.

The Rockefeller Incentive

The institutional response to the global unrest of this era rose not in the empire but in the shaken financial center of the industrialized world, New York. In 1922 Beardsley Rummel, a University of Chicago psychologist, was appointed to head the Rockefeller Foundation with the mission of shifting its emphasis from social services to primary research. The foundation was somewhat hostile to American anthropology, conceiving it to be antiquarian, and so was particularly receptive to an appeal for funding from William Beveridge, the director of LSE. This provided Malinowski (who had had previous contacts with the foundation) with an opportunity to direct his students on a research project the foundation desired: field research into what the British called culture contact, what the Americans called acculturation. The challenge of the new domain led to a questioning of the closed-society thinking that the comparative method had imposed and a rethinking of fieldwork methods. The "study of culture contact as a dynamic process" (Fortes 1936) promised a greater focus on the political.

This institutional support for field research was unprecedented in Britain. The International African Institute was founded in 1926 with financial support from Germany, France, Belgium, Italy, Britain, South Africa, and the International Missionary Council, as well as the Rockefeller Foundation. Malinowski provided the blueprint and dispatched a team of fieldworkers from his LSE seminar to Africa. Certain problems were central to the culture contact studies—the codification of traditional law, with special attention to land tenure and marriage; the position of chiefs; labor migration; and household budgets—issues, one might say, of political economy, especially in colonial Africa, where the policies and practices of the colonial government penetrated into the innermost recesses of domestic life.

Publication outlets for the culture contact studies were provided by the Oxford University Press and the journal *Africa*, the organ of the Royal African Institute, which appeared for the first time in 1928. From this moment on, anthropologists studying politics found a ready outlet for their work. Between 1929 and 1939, forty of the fifty-eight articles in *Africa* were on political topics. Its contributors included not only the leaders of the field (Malinowski and Seligman) and their junior colleagues (Fortes and Schapera) and professional protégés (Mair, Richards, Read, Krige, Forde, Wilson, and Beemer) but also German, French, American, and Canadian scholars (Thurnwald, Lestrade, Warner, Gutmann, Hofstra, Oberg), and colonial authorities (among them Margery Perham and R. Meek) as well. Not least among the contributions to the study of politics were eight articles that outlined research methods for the study of culture contact.

Commercial, not imperial, resources funded culture contact studies in Africa. Both the Carnegie Corporation and the Rockefeller Foundation provided general support for research and publication, and business interests in South and Central Africa (where American mining interests were well represented) supplied local support. The Colonial Office gave no financial support to anthropological or any other kind of social science research and was, indeed, notorious for not doing so (Richards 1977). The Rhodes-Livingstone Institute in central Africa was founded in spite of Colonial Office opposition (Brown 1973). The Sudanese government, it should be pointed out in light of the political significance of Evans-Pritchard's Leverhume-funded studies (Chapter 4), was not under the jurisdiction of the Colonial Office. As for commercial funding of American research on acculturation, Rockefeller, Carnegie, and Ford money was "responsible in one way or another for almost all American research in non-Western areas" (Domhoff 1969:39).

The American Vision and Its Critics

"When William Rainey Harper accepted the challenge of converting Rockefeller millions into a major university in the Midwest, one of his first acts was to appoint an anthropologist" (Stocking 1979a:11). This was, as we have seen, Frederick Starr, who was attached to the sociology department. In 1897 two of his students, David Prescott Barrows and Morton Leland Miller, received their doctorates and embarked on professional careers in the Bureau of Ethnology of the Philippines. In the 1920s the department produced studies of various immigrant groups in America, including the Japanese, Czechs, and Italians. Redfield's dissertation, "A Plan for the Study of Tepotzlan, Mexico," was completed in 1928 (Faris 1967). A separate anthropology department was established at Chicago in February 1929. "Within six weeks [its] three anthropologists [Cole, Sapir, and Redfield] had sent off to the Rockefeller Foundation a five-year plan for anthropological research, which was quickly funded to the tune of $75,000" (Stocking 1979a:19). This vision grew into the momentous *Memorandum on Acculturation* (1936) (coauthored by the triumvirate of Redfield, Herskovits, and Linton), which set American anthropology on a new paradigmatic path—one along which many of its practitioners march to this day.

The concept of acculturation brought together many who had broken away from the intellectually dominant Boasian reconstruction of Native American cultures. The first task of its advocates, therefore, was the construction of a respectable genealogy. They found ancestral legitimacy in the early use of the term by bureau ethnologists to refer to the transference of arts and industries from one Native American people to another, which, they stressed, captured a process leading to the emergence of a common culture, with no implication of one culture being dominant and the other subordinate. When Powell used the term in 1880 for Native Americans borrowing traits from the Euro-Americans, he did not intend to imply dominance. His colleague, W. J. McGee, however, suggested that since "human development is essentially social, and may be measured by the degree in which devices and ideas are interchanged and fertilized in the process of transfer—i.e., by the degree of acculturation," it was possible to recognize a progression from what he called martial and piratical acculturation to commercial and educational acculturation (1898:243). This paradigm, published in 1898 on the eve of the dispatch to the Philippines of boatloads of American teachers, might well have provided the new colonists with a reassuring sense of mission. The umbrella concept that had first been introduced to advance the scientific study of the Native American minority thus followed the flag overseas. Gifford analyzed Euro-American acculturation in Tonga in 1924.

The Depression and the government's greater concern with social problems brought about a surge of acculturation studies. The sociologist's lexical armory—assimilation, minorities, marginality—had failed to move understanding beyond the static condition of American society. Now the people were restless and social dynamics were required. Characteristically, the root of the problem was thought to lie somehow in those who expressed the restlessness (the "blame the victim" syndrome) so the SSRC began to fund acculturation research as a branch of culture and personality studies. Linton outlined the problem most succinctly:

> Prior to the World War it was assumed that the absorption of minority groups into the American population required nothing more than time and not a great deal of that. European immigrants of all nationalities would be fused in the melting-pot. Indians would die out, with the few survivors losing themselves in the White population. The Negro problem would take care of itself somehow although meanwhile they must be kept in their place. None of these comfortable assumptions have been borne out in practice. . . . [M]any of the European immigrant groups . . . show a strong tendency to survive and encyst themselves in the body politic. . . . [T]he Indians have become the only racial element in our population with a birthrate above that required for replacement and have postponed their transformation into Whites indefinitely. . . . [T]he rise of racial consciousness and pride among the Negroes and the increasing bitterness of economic competition has widened the gap. . . . The need for intelligent handling of all these situations is obvious and it is equally obvious that the first step towards successful planning must be to ascertain the general factors present in all contact situations and how they operate. Only when this has been done can we hope to control and direct the forces at work. (Linton 1940:vii–viii)

The rising tide of racial consciousness and bitterness among African-Americans was particularly problematic, and the government sponsored research into colonial practice in Africa in order to reconstruct the African-American educational system in the United States—a hint of American "internal colonialism" later to be clearly delineated by some political anthropologists. At the time, some anthropologists also moved into the study of the African-American population through the back door (West Africa and the Caribbean), arguing that it was necessary to understand the "cultural backgrounds" of the various elements of the American population. By the 1930s they were arguing that the sociological analysis of assimilation had failed, not recognizing, perhaps, that it was assimilation itself, not the concept, that had failed. Some also began to study immigrant Europeans, with pioneer research being carried out by Wilson D. Wallis (1923) in his work among the Armenians. But it was the study of Mexicans and Mexican-Americans, then as now, that was most heavily laden with political import, so it is to this outreach of the acculturation paradigm that most attention is paid here, not least because the major contribution was made by a leading member of the acculturation triumvirate, Robert Redfield.

America's Backyard: A Chicagoan in Mesoamerica

For scholars with an affinity for America's own brand of sociology—a vibrant, resonant, urban brand quite unlike the role and rule abstractions of Radcliffe-Brown—there was a living society to be observed. It was being spawned in the 1920s in the city streets of Chicago and New York and was made up of "colored" immigrants. For such scholars, a new anthropology was in the making, one that turned aside from the study of Native Americans on their reservations to collaborate with ecologically minded urban sociologists. Anthropology's role in the collaboration was to study the "folk" end of the process that brought immigrants to America.

Robert Redfield has proved to be one of the few anthropologists to embark on overseas field research not to produce an ethnography but to initiate a program in nomothetic studies. He carried out his inquiries first in the Mexican districts of Chicago under the direction of sociologist E. W. Burgess. He then applied to the SSRC for funds, suggesting that "a description of the life of such Mexicans in their home communities would facilitate an intensive study of the problems arising out of the growing Mexican immigration into the United States" (Godoy 1978:55). Redfield asserted that anthropology could make "scientific studies of foreign populations who do now and who promise even more to present practical problems to the people of the United States." As he put it, "Following capital, we go abroad to meet these people in their own homes, and pursuing employment and a higher standard of living, they come into our country; and in both cases problems arise—of politics, of administration, of immigration, of social welfare" (Redfield 1928:243, quoted in Godoy 1978:47). Following capital, Redfield left for Mexico. There he worked in the small town of Tepoztlán a few miles southeast of Mexico City. Taking up residence with his wife and mother-in-law, his field observation lasted eight months in 1927.

Trained as a lawyer, Redfield was philosophically an idealist. His training in anthropology was slight: major influences were his father-in-law—sociologist Robert Park—and Fay Cooper-Cole, an archaeologist at Chicago. In his first published paper he cited Rivers approvingly: "I am one of those who believe that the ultimate aim of all studies of mankind, whether historical or scientific, is to reach explanations in terms of ideas, beliefs, sentiments and instinctive tendencies by which the conduct of man, both individual and collective, is determined" (Cline 1952:212). This might appear to us today to be a highly selective use of one of Rivers's many statements about what he thought he was about. Be that as it may, Redfield sought in Tepoztlán "the geographic distribution of culture and mentality," and thus he came to distinguish a central or inner zone of "los correctos" (the more sophisticated city-wise persons, who were often shopkeepers, artisans, or schoolteachers) from a marginal or outer zone of "los tontos," who lived "only in the mental world of Tepoztlán; [ate] the old food in the old ways; and [kept] up the religious festivals of their grandparents" (1930:150).

This is a prime example of the emasculation of politics in the anthropological study of Mesoamerica. The spatial distribution of culture traits and mentalities was conceptualized sociologically and functionally without reference to historical events or political relationships. Later Redfield was to say that he focused on what people enjoyed and what enriched their lives, not on their suffering. Tepoztlán was, for Redfield, a place of harmony and consensus, isolated from the unpleasantness of Chicago or Mexico City, with a population little interested in politics or national affairs. It says a great deal for Redfield's ability to sustain his nomothetic goals that such a portrayal of peasant life came out of Tepoztlán in 1927.

On January 14 of that year, Redfield received a letter from the American consul general in Mexico City, telling him of the Zapatista insurrection in Morelos and urging him to move to the safety of the capital. The people of Tepoztlán, Redfield knew, "were very Zapatista in sentiment." Shortly afterward, according to Redfield's papers and his wife's diary,

> about 40 rebels entered Tepoztlán at 2 o'clock Friday morning. Greta [Mrs. Redfield], removing fleas, heard rifle fire and the yells—quite horrible. We dressed, and carried the children out the back way to the Condes. We stayed there an hour while the rebels and some of the townspeople shot it out in

the plaza. Conde got excited and Mrs. C. was at first almost hysterical. Greta calmed her. The children rested on the Conde bed. Conde and I went down to the plaza after the invaders retreated, in time to stop a riderless horse, examine a rebel lying in the gutter, shot through the chest, and talk with the excited Tepoztecos. Two natives were shot; one seriously. All quite peaceful next day—business as usual . . . [the rebels who had entered the town] . . . were shouting 'Viva Cristo el Rey', 'Muera el Gobierno'. As it turned out later, they had come into town to steal horses. They went to the houses of the Bolshevik members of Tepoztlán, took horses, shot and wounded two Tepoztecans. Most of the townspeople hid themselves away prudently in their houses but the Bolsheviks (perhaps about a hundred) were fighting it out in the Plaza. (quoted in Godoy 1978:67–68)

Mrs. Redfield left for Mexico City, accompanied by her husband; shortly afterward he returned to Tepoztlán to complete his fieldwork, with the town again in the throes of carnival.

To what extent was Redfield's apolitical stance in his creation of field data itself a political position? Godoy has argued (1978) that the scientific model he presented of "deculturated" Mexican rural society at far remove from (North American) civilization served unconsciously both to dispossess the Mexican people of their history and to provide an ideology of superiority for North Americans engaged in business, diplomacy, and scholarship there. Redfield's nomothetic anthropology denied the fact that Mexico had been a colonial society, had experienced one of the first successful revolutions of the twentieth century, had been the home of even older civilizations than those of western Europe, and was, at the time of his field research, a literate society with its own social scientists. These realities distanced him from his scientific objective: the analysis of sociological facts, timeless and placeless, related not to historical contingencies but to the timeless processes of the universe. It would be half a century before the world in which Bolsheviks fought in the streets of Tepoztlán became the global village of political anthropology. Even then, Redfield's vision would remain dominant in the discipline, its strength lying (in part) in the fact that it seemed to be not politically engendered but scientifically objective. Paradoxes more than principles shaped Redfield's nomothetic contribution. These led him from folk to peasant society and ultimately back to his own starting point following global capitalism.

Between 1930 and 1933 (the Depression years) Redfield carried out research in three Yucatan communities: Chan Kom, a Maya village; a small railroad town; and its capital city. The concept of modernization began to replace acculturation in his thinking, and the three communities exhibited it in varying degrees. As he translated space into time, they became stopping places along a Yucatan continuum—a "process of transition" (1934b).

Redfield's schema was to become extremely influential in providing one of two competing paradigms for the study of politics in peasant societies and must therefore be subjected to close scrutiny. Redfield thought of process as

> a shift from one type of society, which the most isolated village represents, toward another type, illustrated by the Yucatan capital city but even better by our more mobile northern cities. But the process is also . . . in large measure an actual historical process, in that the sequential changes made manifest by the comparison are actual events that have taken place in the chronological development of certain members of the series. . . . The description may be understood . . . either . . . as an account of a general trend in social or cultural type as Western civilization has entered Yucatan, or as a somewhat schematic recapitulation of the cultural history of any town in Eastern Yucatan that began as an isolated homogeneous village and became progressively modified by contact with the city and the wider economy and society. (1934a:167)

Nowhere in his description of the transitional process did Redfield refer to anything governmental or political. His closest approach was an observation (1934a:168–169) that godparental or compadre relations became less important as such institutions of control as class and wealth differences developed. Yet, fundamentally, as his research proposal to the SSRC initially suggested, Redfield had always—or nearly always— at the back of his mind a vision of the processes involved in the expansion of global capitalism. "This particular historical change that has taken place and is taking place in one particular place, Yucatan," he wrote, "need not be regarded as *a unique series of events. It can be compared with the effect of white civilization upon peripheral peoples in other parts of the world and it can be compared with the gradual civilization of Europe as known to us from history*" (1934b:68, emphasis added). He simply laundered capitalism to make it *white* civilization.

Was Redfield's view of Yucatan as politically insensitive as his vision of Tepoztlán? Suffice it to note that Yucatan's regional economy rested on the plantation production of sisal in the north (producing revenues for the U.S. firm International Harvester) and that it had been the locale for the so-called Caste War. On the eve of Redfield's field research (1930–1934), a socialist party flourished. A socialist had been elected governor in 1922, but a counterrevolutionary "movement" succeeded in having him arrested and shot. The Depression brought decreased market demands for sisal, and among the sufferers were the striking unionized railwaymen who had transported it. Public demonstrations must have been part of Redfield's everyday life during the years he was in Yucatan, many of them controlled by the military arm of the landlord class. Inevitably, anthropologists were quick to reevaluate Redfield's ethnography of both Mexico and Yucatan (Chapter 4).

Behind Mud Walls in Imperial India

Karimpur is a village near Agra in northern India with a population of 754, made up of members of twenty-four castes. As members of the North India Mission of the Presbyterian Church of the United States of America, William and Charlotte Wiser lived in the village during five seasons between 1925 and 1930. Thereafter they maintained close contact with the villagers from their mission headquarters in a nearby town. Their first account of life in Karimpur was published in 1930 as *Behind Mud Walls*. Later William Wiser became a resident scholar at Cornell University, where, with the guidance of the rural sociology department, he prepared *The Hindu Jajmani System: A Socio-Economic System Interrelating Members of a Hindu Village Community in Services* (1936). A generation later both books were reprinted, the latter with a foreword by Oscar Lewis, and the former with a foreword by David Mandelbaum and with additional chapters written by Charlotte Wiser after revisiting Karimpur in 1960.

Behind Mud Walls is of value as an anthropological study of politics largely because of its lack of pretension. Its opening chapters, which deal with the leaders, those who follow, and the untouchables (those outside the caste system), plunge directly to the heart of the complex of domination in the villages. Until they understood the power structure in operation, the Wisers were unable to carry out their mission. Unlike anthropologists later, they gave no primacy to caste. Rather, they observed: "If we were to limit our experiences to our own village, we should be tempted to interpret leadership as being synonymous with caste prestige. If caste precedence and economic power rest in the same men, their leadership is assured. If the two qualities are separate, villagers follow the man who can grant or withhold their daily bread" (1930:19).

The leaders of the village happened to be Brahmans; agents represented its two absentee landlords. "One would judge from the titles and duties of these agents that they were here simply to serve as links between the village and officials or landowners. But the villager has learned to his sorrow that the chief interest of most of them is their own profit and that of certain men directly above them. Their offices of trust are used to gain a formidable hold over the villagers whom they nominally serve" (1930:100–101). "We might as well try to help the farmer rescue his field from a storm of hail or a swarm of locusts," they wrote. "When a clever agent makes use of a villager to further his own ends, he takes care to leave no trace of his activity other than the straightened circumstances and bitterness of his victim. It is the story of the unscrupulous strong taking advantage of the ignorant weak, which might be heard anywhere" (1930:100). The Karimpur villagers were fortunate enough to be served by a government-appointed village headman who did not exploit his office, and the Wisers provided a description, full of circumstantial detail, of the difficulties encountered by an interstitial officeholder (as later jargon has it) such as he.

An abundance of cases revealed abuses of power by the watchdogs of law and order: two village watchmen, untouchables, who received honoraria for reporting to police headquarters in a neighboring town. The Wisers also detailed numerous dramas of extortion, exploitation, and corruption involving two brothers who served consecutively as *patwari* (village accountant). "Their joint household," they observe, "is more like the stronghold of a prosperous money and grain lender than the home of low-paid agents. The stores of grain, the animals, the jewelry of the women, everything betokens wealth far beyond that of the people whom they serve" (1930:111).

Most important, the Wisers *looked behind* these situations in which agents abused their power, seeking deeper knowledge and understanding. They were sufficiently well placed outside the system itself (and the hegemony that veiled political reality from those within it) to see farther than the villagers themselves:

> Illiterate, ignorant of their rights, dominated by the fear of the known and of the unknown, our more simple minded villagers are an invitation to oppression. They are the ones who suffer most from the tyranny of unscrupulous agents.
>
> On the other hand, there are the men accustomed to lead, fairly well informed as to their rights, and well acquainted with the tactics necessary to increase their own wealth and power. They are too sophisticated to be awed by the underofficers of authority whom they meet in the village. Instead, they use these agents to serve their own ends. With the simple minded farmer, the accountant is the one who takes the initiative in threatening to change the records. But often it is the leaders who make the overtures to the accountant. They offer to pay him liberally if he will change the records to their advantage. If the change goes undetected, their gain is beyond the payment they have given him. If it is detected, they quietly watch him suffer the blame, knowing that he cannot safely acknowledge the acceptance of bribes. The representatives of the police in the village are still more accessible as tools of the powerful. Being of

untouchable origin, they take for granted that they are to follow the bidding of the leaders. The result has been that on several occasions our original condemnation of agents has had to be transferred to more clever men behind them. Where clever leaders and clever agents are combined, they are a menace to simple, self-respecting all-fearing villagers. (1930:113–114)

The Wisers did not simply analyze the behind-the-scenes actions of participants in these dramas of corruption and exploitation; on occasion they also intervened to authorize defensive action or to inform higher authorities. The Wisers were, according to Mandelbaum (1963), pioneers in working out approaches to village development in India that were of lasting value. In a sense, they personified with Christian zeal an action anthropology that was particularly sensitive to political realities. The value of their political ethnography lies above all in the high quality of its detailed reporting. They spent a long time living in the village, learned and used the language, observed events, and came to know residents as individuals—the necessary grist of the field anthropology on which political studies depend.

The Wisers' study was in the tradition of Marett, Rivers, Barton, and, let it be said, Malinowski. They wrote explicitly of "the village" in the Indian tradition, however, and did not generalize their findings to larger abstract entities such as "cultures" or "societies." Later the community study method, as it came to be called, earned praise, particularly for its reporting without any theoretical preconceptions and therefore in such a way that the information contained within it may be subjected to constant renewed analysis on the basis of hypotheses and theories that later emerge (Bell and Newby 1971). *Behind Mud Walls* was exceptionally strong in this regard and cast a quite different light on culture contact in colonial India, viewing it not simply as the impact of American Christian missionaries on Hindu society but also as the penetration of Indian state bureaucracy into the countryside.

When Lewis wrote a foreword to the second edition of *The Hindu Jajmani System* (the first anthropological monograph on a patron-client system), his praise of the work was tempered by criticism of what can only be attributed to the influence of the Cornell sociologists on the amateur missionary observer. Lewis contrasted what Wiser presented analytically with what he had earlier reported ethnographically: "Wiser's definition of the jajmani system stresses the element of reciprocity between jajman [patron] and kamin [client] and the stabilizing and integrating aspects of the system, but his data also points to the asymmetrical nature of the power relationship. Landownership is clearly the most important determinant of power in the jajmani system.

Indeed, a major function of the system is to assure a stable labor supply for the dominant agricultural caste in a particular region by limiting the mobility of the lower castes, especially those who assist in agricultural work" (1958:xii). In spite of Wiser's benevolent interpretation of the jajmani system, he was not unaware of the harsh realities that underlay it.[23] Indeed, *Behind Mud Walls* had been quite explicit about them. Wiser's own analysis of earnings from jajmani in Karimpur showed that out of the 161 families in the village, 44 (all of them menial caste families) were completely unprovided for by the system. Further, 81 families, 38 of them Brahman, did not reciprocate within the system: "they are served but do not serve"; their relation to others was asymmetrical (1936:120). For individuals in all these families (i.e., over half of the total in the village), "The industry of the individual rather than the interest of the community plays the largest part in [their] lives" (1936:117).

Evaluating the Hindu jajmani system from the point of view of the nation, the village community, the functional group (i.e., the caste), and the individual, Wiser was sensitive to the value Indian scholars placed on the autonomous village community but noted that it "causes a conflict with centralization of power and national loyalties" (1936:123). He assessed its advantages and disadvantages at the village level in terms of E. A. Ross's five canons of social control, paralleling Radcliffe-Brown's apparent use of the same resource at Chicago at more or less the same time.

Wiser premised his evaluation of the jajmani system on a belief that the caste system was rigid and not receptive to change. Since it was hereditary, he viewed it as rigidly feudal. The position of the lowest groups was, as he saw it, still akin, in social attitudes if not in actual practice, to that of slaves. Valuable as Wiser's field analysis is for the study of patron-client politics, his adoption of sociology's formalistic functional organization was a retrograde step. As a field anthropologist, however, his ethnographic data provided the kernel for reevaluations by generations of Indianists to come.[24]

DEADLY ISSUES: WAR AND FREEDOM

Between 1919 and 1939 wars of conquest became things of the past for most of the imperial world as it entered a phase of consolidation: not war but *pax imperium*. By the early 1930s, however, the slow movement toward war in Europe, fired by the nationalistic fervor of Hitler's Germany, began to call for a response from anthropologists. Some became authorities on "the deadly issue," teaching the public that the belief that war was somehow a natural, and perhaps even a desirable, condition of mankind was a scientific fallacy.

Malinowski Looks Back

In 1936 Malinowski was invited to speak at the Phi Beta Kappa exercises at Harvard. His speech was published in the *Atlantic Monthly* under the title "The Deadly Issue." He began: "I have chosen to discuss what to me appears the most vital and, as it happens, also the most deadly issue of the day: war as a menace to our immediate future. I speak as an anthropologist of sorts. Now to be an anthropologist really means to be a citizen of the world, past and present. For *anthropology, the science of Man, embraces the study of human civilizations within the widest compass, archaic and modern, primitive and developed, exotic and those around our own parish pump.* The anthropologist should be able to perceive the cultural reality of war as it really is, objectively and dispassionately; to see it in its true perspective across the widest distances of time and space" (1936:659, emphasis added). Malinowski defined war as "an armed contest between two independent political units, by means of organized military forces, in the pursuit of a tribal or national policy" (1936:659). He then set out to answer three questions:

Is war a biological necessity?
Has war a constructive and cultural value?
Has war always been an effective instrument of tribal policy, economic and political?

After surveying the type of fighting that occurs among "the lowest primitives," Malinowski found no "organized clash of armed force aiming at the enforcement of a tribal policy. War does not exist among them" (1936:660–661). He suggested to his psychologically oriented American audience the need to distinguish between individual human behavior and institutionalized organization. He urged a functional appreciation of peace in society, pointing out that peace is not a negative state: a mere absence of fighting. "It is a dynamic condition. . . . If we want to prevent war we must replace the part which it plays by a powerful and effective machinery which would take over some of its functions. . . . The real road to peace . . . lies in the creation of an international super-state for the use of force in the maintenance of peace" (1936:661).

Malinowski then moved to an ethnographic review of fighting at "a somewhat higher level." He found "a bewildering variety in modes of fighting, raiding, and wholesale murder, neolithic worlds in which head-hunting, cannibalism and nocturnal raids wiped out whole villages" (1936:661). Intellectually, he drew on the contribution not only of Hobhouse, Wheeler, and Ginsberg but also the exciting new ideas of V. Gordon Childe, his colleague in London. To give concrete examples, he examined the case of his "friends," the Kiwai Papuans of southern New Guinea and the Trobrianders, concluding that for them fighting was not politically constructive since it led neither to the development of political power nor to the fostering of military virtues. The Trobrianders he considered "typical pacifists of the neolithic state. . . . They know nothing of raiding and fighting on a large scale and their hostilities never lead either to conquest or to loot, or even to head-hunting" (1936:662–663), even though they were surrounded by aggressive headhunters on all sides.

Comparing the Trobrianders with the Kiwai Papuans, Malinowski found "a most unexpected correlation, or absence thereof. The general idea which we all have is that military efficiency is 100 percent correlated with high political organization. This is completely controverted by our evidence from eastern New Guinea. The peaceful Trobrianders have developed chieftainship, are organized in enormous political units, and are, in every way, the most advanced natives of the whole area," whereas the warlike Papuans "have no political units, are divided into small tribelets, and are in every respect culturally inferior to the Trobrianders" (Malinowski 1936:663). A survey of fighting in the archipelagoes of Indonesia and among the hill tribes of India, Africa, Polynesia, and America would, Malinowski assured his audience, lead to the categorical conclusion: "Those who seek for the origins of the state in military aggression are certainly mistaken" (1936:663).

Malinowski then discussed slavery as "perhaps the first really constructive advantage derived from inter-tribal war" (1936:663). Again he may be quoted at length, this time for both the content and tone of his remarks.

> Slavery is an institution which is as little instinctive or innate as war itself.
> A few generations ago, serious arguments were advanced that slavery had been ordained by God, implanted by Him in the heart of man, that it was an established law of nature. Similar arguments are now advanced in favor of war.
>
> Slavery, like war, can be shown to have been absent from the earliest stages of humanity, and to have come to fruition at a certain epoch; to have fulfilled a valuable function then, and to have become entirely useless after. When it ceased to pay, theologians discovered that it was immoral. Slavery

and war are, moreover, closely intertwined. The first element in the history of cultural development, indeed, which makes war a really effective instrument of tribal policy is precisely slavery. Human material was the first to be effectively looted. At the stage when the producer can only feed his own mouth, slavery is obviously unprofitable. It is no good having a hundred slaves if these hundred slaves can achieve only the feeding of a hundred mouths. As soon as the foodgetting industries developed sufficiently to make slaves profitable, wars of slave raiding started. Thus was inaugurated the long epoch in which war becomes economically profitable and politically constructive. (Malinowski 1936:663–664)

Malinowski noted that this process was not necessarily associated with agriculture; slave raiding on the Northwest Coast provided the labor needed for the fishery, metalworking, and textile industries. These he considered "perhaps the most primitive slave owners on record" (1936:664). Indigenous slavery was also to be found in Central and South America and in Africa, where it was necessary to distinguish it from slave wars for export. Africa became disorganized, many of its cultures extinguished, and the life of the whole people darkened not because of indigenous slavery but because two higher cultures—Islam and Christianity—opened a worldwide market for slaves and organized fratricidal warfare among the Africans.

Wholesale robbery or looting by war developed, as Malinowski told it, when the sedentary agriculturalist populations of southern Asia and the Near East became prey to the pastoral tribes surrounding them. "Under such conditions war with a purpose, war as a profession, makes its appearances on the historical stage" (Malinowski 1936:664). The next significant phase came when warfare combined looting, slave raiding, and territorial acquisition. Permanent rather than temporary exploitation was thus established, and conquest became the main factor in "political reconstruction and cultural progress" (1936:665). Malinowski gave as examples the Ashanti, Dahomey, Yoruba, Baganda, and Zulu states in Africa; in the Americas the Iroquois League; and elsewhere the Maori, the Tonga, and the kingdoms of Mexico and Peru.

Malinowski then spoke of the nonprimitive world, rapidly surveying the military history of Europe from the Middle Ages to Hitler's Germany. "The wars of today and tomorrow," he observed, "have become a contest between machines, industrial enterprise, and financial organization. The hero of the next war, the man who from the air destroys a whole peaceful township in its sleep with poison gas, is not expressing any biological characteristics of his organism, nor showing any moral virtues," nor can warfare be regarded as a source of cultural values.

Furthermore, he argued (and here the reader is urged to turn to Malinowski's argument in its entirety), "the preparedness for war, far from being functionally profitable, is merely destructive. . . . [T]he world organized, or rather disorganized, for the future war is moving inevitably toward economic catastrophe" (1936:668).

Finally, Malinowski answered his third question, concluding that mankind had reached a stage of evolution in which war had again ceased to be a culturally constructive force. In short, he had proved to his own satisfaction that war is not and never has been a biological necessity, that the cultural value of war is not universal but limited to a well-defined period in human development, and that war has become merely destructive and demoralizing, "the most cruel and imbecile expression of the dominance of the machine over man" (Malinowski 1936:669).

There is no record of the reception given Malinowski's remarks by either his Harvard audience or the readership of the *Atlantic Monthly*. As he himself suggested, he was hardly an authority on warfare. He had not observed it or written much about it. He spoke rather as a European anthropologist and citizen of the world, aware of the dark clouds of war daily gathering.

An Argument Ex Silentio: Pax Imperium

For most of the interwar years, the anthropology of war was an argument *ex silentio*. Given the holistic requirements of functional anthropology, scholars routinely made reference to war in the ethnographies of societies in which warfare was, or had recently been, a feature of life. This was particularly the case in Oceania (Malinowski 1920; Perry 1923b; Barton 1930a, 1930b; Wedgwood 1930a; Hocart 1931; Warner 1931; Bell 1935; Fortune 1939), where a shift may be discerned from reports of headhunting and insecurity from the point of view of individuals to the function of warfare for society itself. Fortune, describing an Arapesh battle against the Germans in 1910, suggested it differed from traditional warfare in being not for territory but for women. Tribes engaged in headhunting, pig stealing, raiding for cannibalism, and expeditions of revenge for sorcery. W. Lloyd Warner, a student of Radcliffe-Brown, analyzed Murngin (Australian) warfare in structural-functional terms: "If it were not for warfare Murngin society as it is now constituted would not exist" (1931:457). He enumerated six varieties of fighting among them and demonstrated dialectically that warfare was directly opposed to ceremony since it tended to destroy the solidarity of the larger group. As one of the mechanisms on which polygamy was based, however, warfare in the aboriginal tribe was "partly responsible for the solid foundations of the smaller kinship structure" (1931:482).

In an introduction to Warner's monograph *A Black Civilization* (1936), Lowie, his teacher at Berkeley, pointed out that Radcliffe-Brown had supervised Warner's thesis. Comparing it, particularly the chapter on warfare, with studies being made in America at the same time, Lowie concluded that Warner "cannot be considered a servile follower of Durkheim," remarking provocatively: "Personally, I prefer to judge anthropological productions without reference to their author's 'political' affiliations" (1936b:xix). So strongly was the sociological tradition followed in Warner's monograph that Lowie sought compromise by suggesting that it also had American origins. He was not very successful. It seems fitting somehow that it was in the analysis of warfare that the American and Durkheimian traditions so clearly clashed.

The seeds of a third tradition were also being carried on the wind. These were implanted neither by colonial wars nor by World War II but by lesser-known military events between 1918 and 1920. The intervention of British, Canadian, and French troops in the Balkans during the Russian Civil War seems to have fostered a more cynical understanding of war. When the Allies declined to support Marshal Foch's call for an all-out crusade against the Soviets, Leninist centralism was assured victory. The repercussions of this earthshaking event, the culmination of the Russian Revolution, reach far into the depths of anthropology as a discipline. Clausewitz's realistic precept that war is the continuation of politics by other means challenges any notion that warfare may be developed as a subfield of anthropology independent of politics. It also suggests the incompleteness of a political anthropology that does not view war as an integral part of its subject matter.

The South African Connection

With rare exceptions, anthropology's emphasis on "social control" and newly funded research into "culture contact" or "acculturation" led away from an explicit focus on warfare, especially in colonial territories. "Social disorders," as they were called, engaged attention more. A rare study that combined the analysis of changing institutions with an implied critique of the society in which they operated came from the pen of a young South African, Hilda Kuper (née Beemer).

Kuper conducted field research in Swaziland and published a study of Swazi military organization in 1937. The Swazi had conquered and incorporated neighboring clans and had established a kingdom in southern Africa toward the end of the nineteenth century. Ultimately they submitted to what Kuper described as "paper conquest." Recognizing the superior military strength of the Dutch, the Swazi ceded their lands to them and were incorporated into the Afrikaner Lyndenburg Republic. British victory in the Boer War led to the establishment of a colonial protectorate over the 6,704-square-mile territory of Swaziland, and its population became members of the British Empire.

Up until this time, Kuper wrote, the "co-ordinating basis in Swazi society" was its army. Regiments were age-based, cutting across kin and local loyalties to integrate the nation around the throne, barracks being centered at the royal villages. The two major activities of the regiments were warfare to extend the nation's boundaries, retain independence, and secure internal solidarity (by the distribution of captured cattle and booty) and routinized agricultural labor to sustain the king and his people. Since Swaziland was a protectorate to be developed in the interests of its own people, not settlers, the Swazi Nation was maintained as the most extensive administrative unit under colonial rule. Under such circumstances, the mobilization of labor was of utmost importance, and Kuper recorded that both local contingents and the regimental labor centralized at the royal court carried out fifty hours of national service per man per year. At court, the young soldiers received an education in legal procedure, public speaking, and bureaucratic administration, returning to their villages as loyal, useful, valued king's men. Much of the sovereign's power over them was vested in his control over their right to marry, since this was organized on a regimental basis.

Kuper compared the former role of the military in Swaziland with what she observed in the 1930s. At that time food was scarce, and some 40 percent of the men were away, laboring in the mines. Another 40 percent were, as she put it, "controlled by different organizations": two-thirds of the country was in the hands of European farmers, traders, miners, and administrators, and there were twenty-three mission stations.

Military training was not encouraged by the protectorate administration, and mission schools did not have cadet forces. The sale of firearms to "Natives" was tightly controlled. The maintenance of law and order rested with 23 European and 107 Swazi policemen, but "the 'big stick' [lay] outside the protectorate's boundaries in South Africa and the metropole" (1937:189), a fact of political life known to every Swazi. An emotional paragraph addressed the contradictions:

> The European has not in his practice attacked militarism, has not shown that fighting is bad, that bloodshed in war is brutal, nor that nationalism is dangerous. The Europeans have fought against themselves, have fought against the natives and have even asked the natives to help them in the

fight. They have increased, rather than decreased, the importance of armed strength as a source of national unity and individual security. But they have monopolized the power of force. (Kuper 1937:189)

At this point in her argument, Kuper contrasted the death toll from nineteenth-century internecine warfare with that from recruitment into twentieth-century industry. Warfare had been an intermittent activity; mortality at the mines was both high and regular. Kuper suggested that what was important was not

> the factor of numbers alone, but the effect and meaning of those numbers. *Much of the change observable in Swazi culture and, I venture to suggest that this is not true only of the Swazi but of more primitive tribes brought into contact with the Westerner, is the result of the introduction of new types of death and the attitude to the dead.* . . .
> The values of life and living are largely dependent on the means which are sanctioned for the destruction of its members, and on the social reactions to death. Death by disease, death under the baton of the police, the whip of the farmer, or the chain and knife of the Amalaita gang, is neither a noble sacrifice, nor is it regarded as a politico-economic venture which will benefit the people and maintain the culture of the dead worker. . . .
> The European has crushed intertribal wars . . . has introduced a new, *and false,* security of life on the one hand, while on the other the new milieu stamps on the Swazi mind the cheapness of individuals. (Kuper 1937:193–194, emphasis added)

Here, indeed, was something new coming out of African ethnography. Kuper's work far exceeded in analytical significance its context within the Swaziland Protectorate and the Swazi Nation.

Kuper was also sensitive to divisions within the colonial power structure. She reported that when King Sobhuza II (1899–1982) attempted to reintroduce age regiments into protectorate schools, he was encouraged by some British administrators but opposed by others, as well as by missionaries and mission-educated Swazi. In true colonial fashion, a commission of inquiry was set up to determine the feasibility and desirability of the monarch's scheme. Kuper made the memoranda submitted to the commission an integral part of her analysis. Several anthropologists proposed the Pathfinder Organization of African Boy Scouts as an alternative to the revival of age regiments, among them Winifred Hoernle, Schapera, Malinowski, Basil Mumford, and J. D. Rheinalt Jones. Allan Marwick, then an administrator in Swaziland, argued in favor of the "traditional" institution. The question, as Kuper pointed out, was who should exercise control. Since the Pathfinders would be under European direction, possibly from South Africa, the colonial government agreed that the regimental educational system might be incorporated into national taxpayer-supported schools, although mission schools would not be compelled to follow suit. The government viewed this as a "compromise experiment," but Kuper made it clear that it was a signal success for the Swazi nationalist movement. Future constraints, as she saw them, were set by the overall nature of black-white relations and the possibility of cooperation between "different classes developing among the Swazi. Even if the new [age-regiment system] fails, it should at least have made clear the necessity of some such organization. Consciously, and unconsciously, the Europeans are disrupting the nation, and are pressing disorganized bands and maladjusted individuals to become the drones in the European economic-social milieu, an aimless and disharmonious proletariat with no effective link with their traditional leaders, no appreciation of their own cultural heritage, and no equality in western culture" (Kuper 1937:204).[25] Thus, from an analysis of "primitive" warfare and military organization in the Swazi situation, this rare anthropologist was led to a perception of culture contact that was quite distinctively and explicitly focused on force and the value of human life among subject peoples.

Hilda Kuper's analysis of Swazi militarism, Swazi internal politics, the politics of the colonial state, the surrogate colonialism of South Africa, and colonial militarism in the service of capitalist economic development were indeed revolutionary. A new paradigm might have been based upon the idea that an installed government might "declare war" on its own people and might, moreover, co-opt some of the people's leaders in order to succeed. This was a much more dynamic view of warfare than that to be found in the literature, as we have seen. Her study was clearly political anthropology in the modern vein, based on intensive and prolonged fieldwork and the analysis of both structure and event. The door was opened for an anthropological analysis of war in all its configurations.

But the door was closed again almost immediately, first, as we have seen, by those who adopted the concept of culture contact, in which scholars almost always assumed that such contact between peoples of different cultures was pacific and productive, and second, by structuralists, who required a closed unit of analysis, puzzling over whether feuds between "warring" groups were to be considered law or war. For this structuralist persuasion, the sociologist Stanislaus Andrejewski provided a systems analysis of warfare that seemed to take into account everything with which they could ever possibly be concerned. It was, perhaps, so overwhelmingly comprehensive that it nailed shut the systems coffin, at least temporarily. This grand schema having been achieved, ethnographers could concentrate again on feuds and law (Chapter 4). Certainly none followed Hilda Kuper along the path to "internal war."

CONCLUSION

The period between the wars (1919–1939) was one of great promise for the anthropology of politics. An essential realism, which may have been bred of a certain disillusionment with the unfulfilled promises of capitalism and colonialism, led to a concentration on the actual as opposed to the ideal, and the material as opposed to the ideological. This led to strident challenges in the study of law (where Malinowski confronted Radcliffe-Brown), the study of war (where Malinowski appeared to be taking on uninformed public opinion), and the study of contacts between peoples of different races (where political sensitivities were at variance). Native American political enthnography documented the apparent soundness and scholarly advantages of the new realism.

Functional theory was paramount throughout this period. Although it encouraged tautology and synchronism, it also demanded comprehensive and reliable fieldwork, and this in itself led to an exposure of functionalism's deficiencies. Toward the end of the period, anthropologists trained as functionalists, such as Alexander Lesser in America and Monica Hunter and Hilda Kuper in Britain, were producing political ethnographies that were considerably more sophisticated than those of the earlier generation.

And then came World War II and the disruption of the anthropological study of politics. Many prewar concerns were not picked up again; others were, but only so that they might be repudiated. Malinowski's vision of law in action, with its distinctive features, was called a red herring by one leading legal anthropologist (Chapter 4). As we shall see in Chapter 4, Malinowski won the battle but lost the war to the combative followers of Radcliffe-Brown.

Anthropologists in the 1930s also set out contesting frameworks for the study of Native American political organization. MacLeod's narrative of the conquest and political reorganization of Indian peoples reflected his wide reading in European economic history and political economic theory, but it failed to enter the mainstream. Instead, Lowie's idealistic portrait of democratic individualism prevailed. Nor did Anna Gayton's subtle analysis of political manipulation by chiefs and shamans enter the canon of political anthropology. Ironically, Gifford's delineation of lineage politics was quickly overtaken by Californian ethnography but reemerged as the preeminent component of Oxbridge structuralism fourteen years later. What became institutionalized in America was the ecological, historical materialism of Steward, Strong, and Lesser. Their pioneer ethnographies appeared in the 1930s; the pay-off, in the dissertations of their students, came after the war.

But the dominant paradigm of these years between the wars was built around the concept of acculturation or culture-contact. In its political dimension this idea addressed the *clash* of cultures and was in a direct line from George Pitt-Rivers's work of that name (1926) and the anxiety of Edwardian diffusionists over the plight of subject peoples. Few of the anthropologists who worked within the paradigm, and certainly not its most prominent figures—Redfield, Linton, and Herskovits—claimed this genealogy. Margaret Mead, as we shall see in Chapter 4, was to prove the exception. Yet acculturation theory contained, albeit implicitly, the attack on racial domination, imperialism, and monopoly capitalism that has been a subterranean trend within the discipline on both sides of the Atlantic from the beginning. This, too, was a casualty of the discontinuities created by World War II, lost to the collective memory of textbook writers until its rediscovery in the 1980s (Chapter 6).

Part 2
Political Anthropology

4 Classical Simplicity, Complexity, and Class, 1940–1953

> No single thing abides; but all things flow.
> Fragment to fragment clings—the things thus grow
> Until we know and name them. By degrees
> They melt, and are no more the things we know.
> Globed from the atoms falling slow or swift
> I see the suns, I see the systems lift
> Their forms; but even the systems and the suns
> Shall go back slowly to the eternal drift.
>
> —TITUS LUCRETIUS CARUS

World War II was a "lesson in cultural dominance on a scale never seen before" (Wolf 1964:13). Although sharing victory as allies, Britain and the United States entered the postwar era more estranged intellectually than they had ever been before. The war's impact on each country was very different. Britain was drained by its six long years of mobilization; the United States moved in one small stride from the dropping of the atomic bomb and the decisive holocaust of Hiroshima and Nagasaki to war in Asia—in Korea from 1950 to 1953.[1]

Britain, like France, had been ravaged by the sheer manpower requirements of modern warfare; institutions not geared to the war machine had ground slowly to a halt. Britain's economy continued to feel the effects of the war, including food rationing, well into the 1950s. Anthropologists who had spent the war in the armed forces or at work in government bureaus moved back into professional life, picking up the pieces, rebuilding university departments, issuing new journal series, reestablishing anthropology as one of the social sciences. At the end of the war, a Labour government came to power, the first wholly untethered opportunity for the Labour party to put its policies into practice. Among them were the gradual dismantling of the British Empire and the reform of education to permit more working-class youths a toehold on the ladder of advancement. One immediate impact was the admission of war veterans into the universities.

The anthropology that was consolidated in British universities between 1940 and 1953 was conservative in orientation: the 1930s generation of fieldworkers had been waiting too long for it not to be. When the Association of Social Anthropologists was formed in 1946, according to Raymond Firth, Radcliffe-Brown "naturally was elected as President" (1986:5). Membership was by invitation, and the criteria, not very precisely stated, were "a teaching or research appointment in so-cial anthropology in the Malinowski-Radcliffe-Brown tradition." The ASA was set up to be independent of the Royal Anthropological Insti-tute as a vehicle for "a new order in anthropology" (Firth 1986:5). The leaders of the new order were E. E. Evans-Pritchard, Meyer Fortes, and Firth himself. From the start, tensions within the association reflected differences of theory and application between Oxbridge and the London School of Economics. These had repercussions on research and publica-tions about politics. Oxbridge productions were universally recognized as mainstream political anthropology and, indeed, established the legitimacy of the subfield. An LSE trajectory challenged the dominance of Oxbridge structuralism in a less cohesive and less coherent form.

Paradigmatic competition within British anthropology found both ideological and material expression. Ideology took the form of Firth's disagreement with orthodox structuralism, going against the grain of the first ASA meeting in January 1947 and Max Gluckman's assault on the theoretical contribution of Malinowski and his students (1947a, 1947b, 1949a). Under Evans-Pritchard's direction, *l'affaire Anglaise* with the *Annales* school of turn-of-the-century French sociology con-tinued in a series of translations by Oxbridge students and dons of the work of Mauss, Hertz, and Durkheim. Material competition was re-flected in squabbles over colonial SSRC funding. Here anthropologists associated with LSE held the advantage (Richards 1977; Firth 1986).

American contacts and influences were minimal in Britain during this period, particularly after Radcliffe-Brown's unwilling retirement from Oxford in 1946. This effectually isolated Daryll Forde at Univer-sity College, London. Not until the late 1960s, when the Oxbridge pro-gram began to flounder, were transatlantic acknowledgments again made. Two attempts to place the British structuralist taxonomy of Afri-can political systems within a more global perspective (Lowie 1948a; Forde 1948) fell on deaf ears, and the protective isolationism of the Africanists was sundered only when attention shifted to the subconti-nent of India.

The beginnings of this change may be discerned in the work of the graduate students brought into the expanding programs funded by the Labour government. Many were war veterans, most were men, and most worked (inevitably) with professors whose field research had been car-ried out in the Pacific or Africa. Between 1945 and 1953 new fieldwork in these regions, and in India too, reached an all-time high (Ardener and Ardener 1965), as did the number of undergraduate degrees obtained in anthropology. Until this time, most British anthropologists had gained their first degrees in subjects other than anthropology, with history predominating. Malinowski (philosophy) and Radcliffe-Brown (biology and engineering) were exceptions.

A new feature of late 1940s and 1950s fieldwork, paralleling a trend in the United States, was the amount of research carried out in Europe. A large portion of this was conducted in the more exotic Mediterranean countries, but part reflected close ties with sociology and the application of anthropological methods to problems of educational, industrial, and rural change. This necessarily had political dimensions, although these tended to be muted.

The ultimate domination of the Oxbridge structural-systems approach to primitive government and small-scale societies was manifested at the end of the era, when the first textbooks appeared, each with its mandatory chapter on political organization. These drew on the same "classic" ethnographies—Tallensi, Nuer, Bushmen, Bemba. Three were Oxford products (Bohannan 1963; Beattie 1964; Lienhardt 1964); the fourth was Lucy Mair's *An Introduction to Social Anthropology* (1965a). Yet even in this LSE textbook, Mair's synthesis of political anthropology reflected the intellectual hegemony of Oxbridge structuralism, showing few signs of the more original work that was shortly to come from her pen. The textbooks accommodated political anthropology to one dominant framework in which polities were placed according to the degree to which political centralization had occurred and bureaucratic complexity had developed. No acknowledgment was made to Herbert Spencer or any other predecessor, and *African Political Systems* (Fortes and Evans-Pritchard 1940) was projected as *the* seminal work. Each textbook contained analytical chapters on kinship or social structure, economics, political organization, and religion (the labeling and order reflected slight differences of perspective). These were followed, unhappily for the most part, by a descriptive chapter on social change. Thus it was that the subfield of political anthropology, born in 1940 (Cohen 1965; Balandier 1967; Coloon 1968), was consolidated by the 1960s. "The 'professionalization' of the discipline for which the pre-war generation had worked, was overwhelmingly realized in the post-war 'bulge' group" (Ardener and Ardener 1965:303), and the main intellectual beneficiaries were anthropologists interested in the study of politics.

The situation was quite different in the United States. Anthropologists emerged who had served the government in various professional capacities during the war, having learned that "their skills could be applied fruitfully to problems affecting modern societies and the deliberations of national governments and nation states (Mead 1973:1–2). Ralph Beals in his presidential address to the American Anthropological Association, inaugurated, as he saw it, "a period of the rebirth of theory in anthropology" after its long preoccupation with fieldwork on relict cultures (1951:3). "Where before the war the point of reference for the anthropologist had been the native culture, after the war the point of reference increasingly came to be his own culture" (Wolf 1964:14). Many aspects of American society came under scrutiny—but not its politics.

Ties with sociology became closer than at any previous time, but it was area studies that became the focus of government and commercial funding. The anthropology of law saw the collaboration of a young anthropology student and one of the country's leading commercial lawyers, resulting in a distinctive blend of antiformalist legal realism constantly at odds with ingrained formal evolutionism. Scholars viewed this rising "ethnological jurisprudence" as quite apart from the anthropology of politics. Wartime inquiries had been at the national level, studying one's enemies and allies; after the war they followed American interests abroad to Mesoamerica and Puerto Rico—but not, significantly, to Korea or Vietnam.

Within the academy itself, and customarily in the field of Native American studies, continuity was the order of the day as Duncan Strong's students accepted his challenge to rethink Native American culture history. Even this endeavor, traditional as it might be thought to be, was threatened by the investigatory powers of Senator Joseph McCarthy. The American trauma over the loss of China to the Communist party of Mao Tse-tung, along with the falling in Europe of what Winston Churchill, with characteristic rhetoric, called the Iron Curtain between East and West, had repercussions in the American domestic arena. The House Un-American Activities Committee disillusioned many professional anthropologists with government (Mead 1973) by hounding left-wing academics, sometimes with their university's compliance. A certain "laundering" of dissertations took place when their authors later published their work.

"In the late 1940s and the 1950s," Eleanor Leacock recalled, "a wide range of evolutionary issues were taken on as problems for doctoral research by students interested in Marxism and in the political activities of the times. However, it was still not possible to identify oneself in professional publications as taking a Marxist approach" (1982:251–252). Leacock remembered dissertations as being concerned with evolutionary theory, but those most closely related to the analysis of political matters were in fact historiographical. The overall impression left by the 1950s dissertations reviewed in this chapter is their indebtedness not to the evolutionary theories of Morgan and Engels but to the historical materialism of Marx.

Such has been the sea change experienced by American anthropology in its Marxist voyage since the late 1960s that close textual and historical inquiries must be carried out to distinguish Marxists and shades of Marxist scholarship within the American academy. Contemporary authorities on the subject are tentative in their judgments, not wishing to offend those who would like to be called Marxists and not wishing to disown those whom tradition has so identified. "I can only make surmises about the formulations of others," Leacock writes, "but I can speak with assurance about myself on this point. When I discussed the impact of the fur trade on native Canadian society and the significance of the transformation from production for use to production for exchange, I cited, not Marx as I should have, but a chance statement of the far-from-Marxist Herskovits" (1954:7; 1982:255). Not until the 1960s was it possible for an academic to discuss "Marxism as such" (Leacock 1982:249).[2]

In the 1950s, when Marxism itself became a political issue within American anthropology, its tradition was extraordinarily diffuse. Today a minimal definition of Marxist scholarship might involve sharing "Marx's understanding of capitalism and history," using "his general method of analysis," historical materialism and dialectical reasoning (Ollman and Vernoff 1982:7). By these criteria, few anthropologists before 1940 could be considered Marxists; by the 1950s they existed. There are three main reasons for this. One lies in the publication history of Marx's writings, particularly as they were translated from German and French into English. A second lies in the genealogical happenstance that traces the foundation of ethnology to Morgan and hence recognizes its heritage in Engels and evolutionary theory at the expense of Marx and historicism. This distinction was touched upon in Chapter 1, when the village community of East and West was under discussion. It continued, engendering a lack of attention to capitalism, history and dialectics, and the success of neo-evolutionism as the new anthropology in the postwar period. Yet historicism continued to offer an alternative to evolutionary theory—not among the dons, perhaps, but among students in the field, and not in the primitive societies on which taxonomies were built but in the complex setting of urban America. A third reason why few anthropologists could be considered Marxists before the 1950s might be the anti-intellectualism of anthropology itself.

A kaleidoscope of possibilities for the emergence of a distinctive anthropology of politics had existed, as we have seen, on the eve of World War II:

1. *The diffusion-to-acculturation route.* This was proving abortive, since only Lesser emphasized the political nature of assimilation, conquest, and domination. Most anthropologists viewed the contact between groups as pacific and productive, if somewhat problematic intellectually. Monica Hunter's book *Reaction to Conquest* was considered inappropriate and not within the British academic tradition. Yet only in South Africa was political ethnography centered on colonial domination and the impact of government policy on subject peoples. (Not until the 1970s was an attempt made to pull together the strands of South African anthropology to provide an alternative to the structural functionalism of this consolidating era.)

2. *The urban studies viaduct.* Harvard's prestigious ecology/ethnicity/urban studies were, on the whole, apolitical, although politicians' careers might be exposed somewhat incidentally in the course of constructing systems of social order. Community studies might take government as a framework but were essentially not concerned with community or local politics. No muckraking tradition entered American anthropology. In marked contrast, it was from urban studies that anthropologists launched criticisms of South African government policy.

3. *The materialist trajectory.* Depression-generated studies encouraged a focus on material factors, with politics viewed as competition for access to scarce resources. Steward's Shoshoni sociopolitical groups had appeared in this context. Walter Goldschmidt (1946, 1947) and John Bennett (1969) analyzed agrarian society in the United States and Canada and were prepared to criticize and condemn big business, but no political anthropology of complex societies emerged.

4. *The Native American parochial tradition.* Native American ethnology was full of political content. Mead provided an analysis of observed political behavior on an Indian reservation; others reconstructed Plains Indian political economy. The marginalization of Native American social anthropology and ethnology from comparative political anthropology was due to the incoherent, sprawling overabundance of American anthropology at the time, contrasted with the tightly controlled, small but productive group of British anthropologists.

5. *Law as a mode of entry.* Legal realism became prominent and influential. Within anthropology this led to the formal adoption of the case method, but this did not pay off theoretically in the analysis of politics until the late 1950s (Chapter 5). Law was studied sui generis. In

neither Britain nor the United States was ethnological jurisprudence an attractive field of specialization for the new postwar generation.

None of these five trajectories led toward a recognized subfield of political anthropology, although they did provide resources upon which such specialization might draw. Instead, political anthropology emerged almost retrogressively as a deflection from the experience of the war veterans who entered the profession in 1946. Initially, its basis was the accumulated ethnographic field data of the earlier generation; its paradigm, a construct for societies that no longer existed.

The hegemony of British structural functionalism in establishing this paradigm—in the face of opposition—finds witness in the testimony of Georges Balandier, a French sociologist. Balandier described political anthropology as both a very old project and a recent specialization. He defined it as "a subdivision of social anthropology or ethnology . . . concerned with the description and analysis of political systems (structures, processes and representations) proper to societies regarded as primitive or archaic" (1967:1). Clearly, classical simplicity had won out over the political complexities of the modern world.

RETHINKING NATIVE AMERICAN POLITICAL ORGANIZATION

Studies of Native Americans between 1920 and 1939 had formed, as we have seen, a somewhat eclectic field. The horse-and-buggy era of fieldwork was well on its way out. Kroeber was openly criticizing the Boasian school in which he had been trained. The Californians had begun to move toward the particularly political and the ecology and economy that appeared to underpin it, but their Depression-bred materialism lacked a theoretical focus.

In 1946 a new act allowing Native Americans to present evidence to the federal government to support their claims for compensation for the loss of tribal lands (Horr 1974) diverted many Berkeley-trained anthropologists from purely academic pursuits. At the same time it provided them, as expert witnesses, with an occasion for synthesizing their half century's findings.[3] As it turned out, much of the evidence they presented simply testified to the inadequacy of much of their earlier work and provided an impetus toward synthesis and generalization on quite other theoretical grounds.

Most of the anthropologists were employed not by the Native Americans but by the federal government. Their voluminous reports and opinions described individual Native American tribelets and were full of unrelated facts and compendious detail. Hearings were conducted between 1949 and 1956, and the case was finally decided in favor of the Native American plaintiffs. Their success was actually more significant in the informal political arena than in the courts, because it led to the formation of the California Intertribal Council, a new all-embracing contemporary political organization. The hearings did not do a great deal for the anthropological profession, which has yet to mend its fences with Native American political activists.

The political dimensions of the ethnology presented to the hearings followed the pattern of previous decades. Kroeber's evidence (revised and published in 1962) dealt with landowning patterns, defined the tribelet as the basic landholding unit, and documented this from the Yokuts and others. He described the constituent units of the miniature tribes, discussed the role of "chiefs," and introduced the concept of "nonpolitical ethnic nationalities," which he compared with political units in feudal European society.

A small group of anthropologists provided an exceptionally valuable, wide-ranging synthesis with ecological depth by breaking away from the closed-unit tribal paradigm. These included Ralph L. Beals, Harold Driver, Walter Goldschmidt, Abraham Halpern, Herbert R. Harvey, Joseph A. Hester, Ernest R. Neasham, Julian Steward, William Duncan Strong, Erminie Wheeler-Voegelin, and Nona C. Willoughby.[4] Yet none of their work entered the mainstream of political anthropology at this time, in part because it was not made available to the profession in a cohesive form. Its methods and the premises on which it rested nevertheless spilled over into American anthropologists' concern with politics, reaching into the various local, regional, and state levels in the complex societies in which they began to work more intensively after 1946. By and large, however, it was not the Berkeley scientific laboratory-in-the-field Native American ethnography but an historically oriented political economy that emerged at this point. Perhaps this, too, was one of the scars from the specialists' legal battle.

William Duncan Strong's graduate seminar "Time Perspective and the Plains" at Columbia University restored a strong sense of ethnohistory to the study of political organization. Several dissertations written by participants resulted (Holder 1951; Jablow 1951; Lewis 1942; Secoy 1951; Codere 1950; Faron 1954; Friedl 1950; Leacock 1952; Service 1950; Wike 1951; Willis 1955). All were based on direct field research. Alexander Lesser directed the 1935 Ethnology Field Study Group of the Laboratory of Anthropology at Santa Fe, out of which the first two dissertations came. Jablow's thesis owed much to the recent archaeological findings of the Columbia University–North Dakota Historical Society

Expedition of 1938. But as important as the forebears and the elders was the academic fraternity that the theses themselves created so that a coherent reevaluation of Native American political economy developed.

The Columbia monographs fell into two overlapping categories. Several dealt with Plains Indian culture history and the political economy of groups undergoing changing patterns of contact with each other and with Europeans as the American frontier moved west. Leacock's *The Montagnais "Hunting Territory" and the Fur Trade* (1954) and Preston Holder's dissertation, "The Role of Caddoan Horticulturalists in Culture History on the Great Plains" (1951), fall into this category. Most important, however, was the interrelatedness of Bernard Mishkin's *Rank and Warfare in Plains Indian Culture* (1940), Oscar Lewis's *The Effects of White Contact upon Blackfoot Culture* (1942), Joseph Jablow's *The Cheyenne in Plains Indian Trade Relations, 1795–1840* (1951), and Frank Secoy's *Changing Military Patterns on the Great Plains* (1953). Jointly they provided a coherent reevaluation of the static-culture-area concept favored by the Berkeley anthropologists and a consistent critique of culture, history, and political economy.

A second category included Jane Richardson's *Law and Status Among the Kiowa Indians* (1940) and Helen Codere's *Fighting with Property* (1950). Here the influence of Columbia faculty members other than Strong and Lesser is more clearly seen, Ruth Benedict and Ralph Linton foremost among them. These monographs were more concerned with law, ranking, and stratification in contrast with the first group's interest (explicit in the case of Bernard Mishkin) in the economy and class. Steward's interests overlapped the two groups.

The Changing Political Economy of Plains Indians

The students of Plains culture history drew heavily on the Lesser-Strong paradigm outlined in the previous chapter.[5] Apart from Oscar Lewis, whose work was more eclectic, they made no use of the then ubiquitous acculturation theory, despite a concern with peoples in contact. In accordance with the paradigm, they viewed no group in isolation from others, and they traced historical phases of change triggered by economic—usually technological—innovations. Ecological variation underlay all the analyses. No taxonomies resulted, religion and kinship were slighted, and the culture-area approach was substantively challenged. Through a combination of oral history methods and field and documentary research, they recast the political economy of the Plains. What did not appear, however, was any tendency (such as in the Berkeley work) to link the past with the present. All the Columbia monographs dealt with the economic and political dismantling of Native American political organization prior to the reservation system.

A controlled progression was contained within the four Plains Indian theses, as the last of them makes clear (Secoy 1953). Mishkin (1940) outlined the part the horse played in the economic life of the Plains people and the degree to which it affected their culture. He viewed Kiowa culture in terms of interworking influences and complex relations rather than culture traits. He demonstrated how in Plains society the horse, rank, warfare, and to a lesser extent trade were "inextricably interwoven" (1940:63). Social position hinged mainly on achievement in war. Mishkin questioned the widely accepted psychological view of warfare as a game (Lowie 1920), arguing that it must be viewed within its economic framework. The key to the economic situation was the advent of the horse, which had entered the Plains from the Spanish settlements in the Southwest in about 1600. By the middle of the eighteenth century, the horse had passed through Shoshoni hands and on east to reach the northern Plains. The importance of the horse in the Plains economy could not be overstated, Mishkin argued; the military assigned to crush the Plains Indian had first to exterminate his horses, a political barbarism characteristic of frontier expansion.

The introduction of the horse into the Plains stimulated intertribal trade, visiting, and intermarriage. It transformed an economy that had been based on hunting buffalo on foot with packs of dogs, and it provided transport and saddle animals. Since the horses were unevenly acquired within a population, they transformed political organization. The horse industry affected societies that did not have them as well as those that did; overnight, peaceful neighbors became aggressive, nomadic marauders. "The ability to move quickly over a wide area in order to follow the migrations of the buffalo gave the Indian a sense of power," Mishkin concluded. "The goodly number of meat parfleches which could be carried around released him from constant economic pressure and permitted the enjoyment of a highly developed social life. . . . [T]he frequency with which people came together in inter-band or inter-tribal contact immeasurably strengthened political and tribal solidarity" (1940:2). Native Americans in the north and southwest had the largest numbers of horses. One Blackfoot was reported to have owned between four and five thousand; the Crow, on average, were probably the richest horse owners; the Kiowa had surpluses; the Pawnee were horse-poor.

Among the Kiowa, the advent of the horse brought a new standard of wealth, measured by the possession of herds of broken and unbroken horses. Unbroken horses were not simply for prestige or exhibition but were used to replenish the active herd. They "opened a new source of revenue and provided the means for operating in a new field of economic endeavor—trading" (1940:22). The Kiowa, some 1,600, had an extensive range in the early nineteenth century. The tribe was divided into from twelve to fifteen bands, made up of extended family groups under a headman. These roamed after buffalo during the summer and settled within relatively stationary camps during the winter. The whole tribe convened only during the month or two of the Sun Dance, when "unity was achieved and political solidarity received its foremost and, in fact, its only formal expression" (1940:26). Revenge parties, raids, the meetings of societies, tribal hunting, and most marriages took place then. At other times, each extended family group "operated as a self-contained unit economically, socially, politically and even religiously" (1940:27). The composition of the family was fluid; marriage and residence regulations, Mishkin asserted, "must be generally viewed against the background of political and economic considerations" (1940:26). The remaining two-thirds of Mishkin's monograph traced the impact of raiding and trading horses on the Kiowa hierarchy of ranks.

To Mishkin's ethnographic reappraisal Oscar Lewis added history. A history major before he entered anthropology, he prefaced his culture history of the Blackfoot with a charge that anthropology neglected written history. "The history of anthropology," he suggested, "thus presents the paradoxical picture of great pre-occupation with historical problems, and no end of historical interpretations from ethnographic data, with only a minimum of use of documented history" (Lewis 1942:1–2). Lewis deplored the relegation of documentary history to a minor position (1942:3). Even contemporary acculturation studies, he noted, had for the most part "employed history merely for background purposes" (1942:2–4).

Using traders' journals, travelers' reports, fur company records, government papers, and a host of secondary sources, Lewis set out to show the changes that occurred in economic structure, social organization, marriage, and warfare following Blackfoot involvement with Canadian and American fur traders. Lewis then pictured differences in government policy and adjustments on the reservation, as well as preservation treatment, as shaped by differences in the policy and character of the two fur companies involved, the Hudson's Bay Company in Canada and the North West Company in America. The unique position of the Blackfoot, straddling the international boundary, made the study of their acculturation exceptionally useful for attributing cause and effect.

Whites involved in the acculturation process had already appeared in the contrast, pointed out by MacLeod and Mishkin, among others, between southwestern contacts with agents of the Spanish government and eastern Native American contacts with French or American private individuals or companies. But Lewis's insights rested on ethnography, not acculturation theory. He was, indeed, as critical of the before-and-after approach of acculturation theorists as he was of "logical and functional" analyses of a process that he believed had to be analyzed temporally; specific dates became important—1730, 1754, 1830. Above all, Lewis supported Strong's perception that culture areas (or at least three of them: the Northwest Coast, the Plains, and the Woodlands) were recent historical products. He argued further that they were due in large measure to the operation of the fur trade as an agent of diffusion.

Lewis's Blackfoot ethnography was detailed, and only a few points can be abstracted here that contribute to the general picture of political change presented by the Columbia quartet. The Blackfoot were a buffalo-hunting Plains Indian group located, at the end of the eighteenth century, east of the Rockies and north of the Yellowstone. Numbering some 9,000, they were made up of three tribes: the Blood and Siksika in the north, and the Piegan in the south. Around 1728 the Blackfoot had received guns through the Cree Indians, and a few years later, horses from the Shoshoni. Hudson's Bay traders, unable to persuade them to bring in furs, set up their own trading posts on the edge of Blackfoot territory. Differences in the rate of arming the various tribes were crucial in determining the balance of power in the area. The Cree, whose beaver furs were in demand, were armed at the expense of the wolf- and fox-hunting Blackfoot. In competition with each other, traders began to supply liquor to those who brought them furs. Only when the companies united in 1821 did the supply of liquor dry up. By about 1830, however, the beaver was exhausted east of the Rockies, and the heyday of the Canadian trade was over. About this time, the Blackfoot approached an American Fur Company trader who had set up a post in their area and who was seeking not beaver pelts but buffalo hides. But closer trade relations were accompanied by a smallpox epidemic; by 1837 over two-thirds of the Blackfoot had died.

To support the network of trading posts throughout the territory, the traders relied on the Blackfoot, because of their control of the rich buffalo grounds, as a major source of provisions: dried and pounded meat, pemmican, backfat, and dried berries, as well as tallow. The traders treated some Blackfoot groups differently from others; the favored Piegan undertook large-scale trapping, and the company established trading posts within their territory. Within the tribe, the increased demand for buffalo hides stimulated the accumulation of horses for raiding, hunting, and bridewealth payments. Polygamy increased, as women were employed in the preparation of the hides. Horse herds increased greatly in size, and this in turn "perpetuated and intensified" the social gradations that already existed. Men with large herds could purchase many wives and "in the exchange thereby transform idle capital (surplus horses) into productive capital (women)" (1942:40). Age at marriage dropped.

The fur trade stimulated intertribal contacts. The Blackfoot, according to Lewis, "borrowed" age-gender societies from the village tribes to the south, whom they met at the trading posts, although they apparently had a rudimentary age organization of their own which performed policing duties. Lewis thought the expansion of herding and polygamy and the increased number of age societies all occurred around 1830. "The borrowing of age grades at this time," he argued, "is intelligible in that they were an ideal mechanism for expressing and channelizing the vertical mobility which came with the increase in wealth" (Lewis 1942:41–42).

The authority of chiefs varied at different times according to whether competition or monopoly prevailed in the fur trade. Monopoly increased, and competition weakened, their authority. The Hudson's Bay Company made it a policy to deal only with chiefs and headmen, conferring many honors on them, whereupon their competitors sought out the younger men. By undermining the chiefs' authority, the competitive traders contributed to the instability of bands. Raiding under temporary leaders replaced large war masses under central leadership. A show of numbers was replaced by stealth, secrecy, and ambuscade. "Casualties increased and warfare became a serious and deadly affair" (Lewis 1942:59).

The third member of the dissertation cohort, Joseph Jablow, set out to "define the structure and function of intertribal trade" among the Plains groups "against the background of the influence of the horse and the fur trade" (1951:5). His monograph *The Cheyenne in Plains Indian Trade Relations, 1795–1840* (1951) focused on a group of strategic middlemen in the horse and gun trade.

Finally, Frank Secoy's work traced the moving frontiers of trade in horses and guns and the concomitant patterns of military organization and activity on the Great Plains. The essence of his argument was that the culture of any Native American society at any time reflected its position in relation to two moving economic frontiers, the trade in guns, which penetrated the region from the northeast, and the trade in horses, which moved across the region from the southwest. The Apache provided the core of his western ethnographic data, and the Sioux of his northeastern. The complex cultural patterning of such groups as the Shoshoni in different localities and at different times during the two-hundred-year period with which he was concerned could then be accounted for in terms of a dynamic model of the historical process. The importance of intertribal relations, which Lesser had always stressed, as well as contacts among groups within dominant societies (such as traders and missionaries) and groups within the tribes with which they were in contact (intermediaries, medicine men, ecologically advantaged sectors of the population, and the like), was shown to analytical advantage in Secoy's work. His thesis was, in a sense, the culmination of the cohort's shared endeavor.

The Columbia corpus received a very mixed reception at the time of its first appearance. Scholars from abroad appeared to welcome its originality more than did Americans. No attempt seems to have been made to trace its roots in American ethnology, so thoroughly had the work of MacLeod been forgotten. Critics suggested that "economic determinism" was overemphasized (Eggan 1965:517). Hoebel intimated that most of the Columbia studies were ideological in content when he wrote a mixed, and on the whole co-optive, review of Jane Richardson's *Law and Status Among the Kiowa Indians.* He observed that "it will come as something of a shock to most Americanists to read of the strong class divisions and attitudes which are presented as characteristic of the Kiowas. Yet the materials substantiated the thesis, and one feels that this author [unlike the others?] has not worked under the compulsion of any pet ideology" (Hoebel 1941:645–647). Hoebel left the pet ideology unnamed.

Jablow's study of the Cheyenne as middlemen on the Plains, trading horses and guns, was reviewed by F. G. Bailey, whose own first monograph, *Caste and the Economic Frontier* (1957), was to open up a new processual paradigm in political anthropology. After two paragraphs in which he summarized Jablow's argument, Bailey concluded:

> This is the first systematic study of trade in the Great Plains. Apart from its originality, the importance of the book lies in its conclusive refutation of two common assumptions: that Plains warfare was little more than a game; and that Plains societies had subsistence economies. In fact, as the author shows, warfare was mainly an economic activity by which men obtained horses for trade. And, the use of horses made possible a surplus which was used for trade.

The author deals briefly and clearly with a complicated subject. His book, taken with those of Mishkin and Lewis (Vols. III and VI in the same series), makes intelligible the relations between the tribes of the Great Plains in the early 19th century. (1951:173)

How much this early reading may have influenced Bailey's conceptualization of the economic and political systems he was later to discern in his fieldwork in Orissa in India can only be surmised. Certainly no British reviewer was worried about "economic determinism" or the cohort's "pet ideologies," and failure to incorporate these writings into a developing political anthropology specialization has to be explained on other grounds. Certainly an alternative was emerging at the time— and also at Columbia—in the form of a comparative jurisprudence that was much better placed to gain and hold the academy's attention. Nevertheless, antipathy to the materialist interpretations engendered by the Depression but reproducing themselves through Marxist philosophy was a feature of the anti-intellectual America of the 1950s. So much of the innuendo of the times remains to be explored that a case may better be made by quoting passages from the text of Preston Holder's dissertation (deposited at Columbia in 1951) alongside the revised text of his book *The Hoe and the Horse on the Plains*, published by the University of Nebraska Press in 1970 (Table 4.1). The political language of the dissertation—references to evolution, class, the program of colonialism, and power—was transformed into discussions of development, status, pattern, and "those in high places." V. Gordon Childe was no longer cited, being replaced by two of Holder's contemporaries.

Since one of the main values of these earlier studies in political economy lies in their historical specificity, it is difficult to summarize their contribution to political anthropology in general terms. They delineated the features involved in a process, recognizing that the weighting of these features and their involvement in sequences occurs differently at different times and in different places. But this leaves open the possibility that causal determinants lie outside the system in which interrelationships are being recognized, a fact that all clearly recognized. Holder (1951), for example, in describing how conflict between nomadic and horticultural groups finally came to an end with the disarming of the equestrian nomads, couched his perception in ever-expanding circles of causality. The quality and consequences of this conflict, he concluded, were intensified by the emergence of the United States as the single "European" power to be dealt with in the area. This in itself was only partly a result of the consolidation of the new continental culture.

Table 4.1. Comparison of Holder's Marxist and Conservative Discourse

Marxist	Conservative
From: "The Role of Caddoan Horticulturalists in Culture History on the Great Plains." Ph.D. diss., Columbia University, 1951 (emphasis added).	From: *The Hoe and the Horse on the Plains: A Study of Cultural Development Among North American Indians.* Lincoln: University of Nebraska Press, 1970 (emphasis added).
In North America, as elsewhere in the world, the *evolution* from small roving hunting and gathering units to large sedentary villages accompanied the appearance of horticulture (Childe 1936, 1946). (p. 32)	In Native North America stable villages of horticulturalists were a relatively late phenomenon. Here as elsewhere in the world they were the result of some thousands of years of *cultural development* from simple bands of roving hunters and gatherers (Wedel 1961, Willey 1966). (p. 23)
Not only, therefore, is the horticultural village an ancient reality on the Plains but also these villages were class stratified and economically atomistic with resources channelled inward to maintain *the class lines.* In using this term "atomistic," I do not mean to imply a lack of trade relations between villages. Indeed, the widespread "Calumet" ceremony so often reported in early historic accounts is one indication that there were extensive inter-group relations on the pre-horse Plains. (p. 71)	Not only, therefore, was the horticultural village an ancient reality on the Plains, but also these villages were socially stratified and were economically autonomous with resources channeled inward to maintain *the status lines.* The term "autonomous" does not imply a lack of trade relations between villages. The widespread calumet pipe ceremony so often reported in early historical accounts is one indicator of extensive intergroup relations on the prehorse Plains. (p. 65)
I have shown that the Europeans appeared in the New World with a *program of colonialism* which called for the exploitation of the movable wealth by the labor of the inhabitants, their final removal and the ultimate occupation and utilization of the land. (pp. 130–131)	The Europeans appeared in the New World with a *pattern of colonialism* which called for the exploitation of the movable wealth by the labor of the inhabitants, the final removal of the people, and the ultimate occupation and utilization of their land. (p. 140)
Even in the face of these severe stresses the Caddoan horticulturalists did not become horse nomads. It was to the complete disadvantage of *those in power* to institute a totally nomadic existence. Those elements of the villages, the commoner men, who might see advantages to becoming nomads were in the least favorable position to voice or to implement their wishes, or to crystalize them into any organized group activity in the face of the weight of tradition and authority. (p. 133)	Even in the face of these severe stresses the horticulturalists did not become horse nomads. It was to the complete disadvantage of *those in high places and their supporters* to institute totally nomadic existence. Those elements of the villages, the commoner men, who might be advantaged in becoming nomads, were in the least favorable position to voice or to implement their wishes, or to crystalize them into any organized group activity in the face of the weight of tradition and authority. (pp. 142–143)

More important were the sweeping internal effects of the Industrial Revolution on Europe and the New World, which dictated a changed and accelerated pattern of colonial expansion throughout the world. In the new situation, only the more technologically advanced native peoples could continue to contribute as producers of wealth. The more "backward" groups, which included the Native Americans, had to be displaced, isolated, or destroyed to make room for the expansion of European culture bearers on a new level of exploitation of natural resources. By the last half of the nineteenth century, the natives could no longer make significant contributions to the growth in European industrialization within the framework of their own culture except perhaps in the areas exploited by technologically backward European countries.

Since this group of anthropologists did not extend their analysis to the outer circles of causality, the analyzed system remains open-ended. Above all, there is no sense of self-adjustment within the system. The very fact of the conquest of the Native Americans by the Europeans and their encapsulation on reservations made conflict and division, decline and fall, the seemingly inevitable outcome of the political process. When processual analysis reenters political anthropology in the 1960s (Chapter 5) we shall be able to make comparisons with these earlier endeavors.

Fighting with Property

Only one work from the Columbia corpus entered fully into the mainstream of American anthropology, Helen Codere's *Fighting with Property* (1950). Although most of the Columbia students worked among the Plains Indians, Codere's study of the Kwakiutl of British Columbia was largely a reevaluation of Boas's early ethnography combined with a rigorous searching of historical materials. Tracing Kwakiutl acculturation over 150 years as it was expressed in potlatching, Codere argued quite simply that between 1837 and 1924 warfare declined and potlatching—fighting with property—became more important in Kwakiutl society. Codere found the Kwakiutl to be "remarkable for the degree of their preoccupation with social rank," with every part of their culture seeming to focus on this (1950:5). They recognized a hierarchy of more than six hundred social positions, each one accorded titles, crests, and ceremonial privileges, and each upheld by means of property distributions, or potlatches. With the introduction of infectious diseases by whites, population declined. Thus, while the number of potlatch positions remained the same, it became easier to gain access to them, even to the point that there were more positions than people to fill them. Further, potlatching escalated as European trade goods were introduced into the system. Warfare, carried out largely to gain social prestige, had been suppressed by the Europeans, but since its ends were achieved by trade, it also became redundant for the Kwakiutl themselves. Warfare was thus "domesticated" into the service of "the all important rivalry for social prestige in which the potlatch was the primary method and test of achievement" (1950:129).

Codere's analysis was immediately popular among anthropologists, intrigued as ever by what appeared to be a very peculiar, even unique, irrational institution. The idea of fighting with property entered into the literature as a distinctive blending of historical functional interpretation. Homer G. Barnett's 1938 study of the same institution paled into insignificance beside it and was, indeed, not resurrected until the 1960s, when, amidst other competing approaches, the whole notion of fighting with property was challenged and potlatching was found to be not an adjustment to European domination but a form of resistance to it.

Only Codere's monograph was immediately accepted into the American mainstream (in part because of its legitimating reevaluation of Boas's work), but in Britain the value of the Columbia anthropologists' political-economy approach was more clearly acknowledged. The reviews invited by *Man*, the journal of the Royal Anthropological Institute, are of interest in the genealogy of political anthropology as a specialization. Stanislaus Andrzejewski, whose work on military organization Radcliffe-Brown praised highly, reviewed Secoy's monograph on Plains military patterns very favorably. He took pains to point out that it was not a piece of conjectural reconstruction but that its "solidly based findings confirm the theories about the relations between warfare and social structures propounded by the students of comparative sociology" and stated that he considered it "a valuable contribution to our knowledge of the history of peoples without history" (1954a:173).

PRIMITIVE LAW: HENCHMAN OF LEGAL REALISM

Political anthropology's debt to Karl Llewellyn needs to be placed within a larger context than that of law alone. Legal anthropology in the United States was as convoluted in its relationship with jurisprudence as was social anthropology in Britain. The last quarter of the nineteenth century had seen a major effort to render the study of law a "legal science," and its major proponent was the dean of the Harvard Law School, Christopher Columbus Langdell, whose introduction to his casebook on the law of contracts asserted:

Law, considered as a science, consists of certain principles or doctrines. . . . Each of these doctrines has arrived at its present state by slow degrees; in other words, it is a growth, extending in many cases through centuries. This growth is to be traced in the main through a series of cases. . . . . [T]he cases [that are useful in discovering legal doctrines] bear an exceedingly small proportion to all that have been reported. The vast majority are useless, and worse than useless, for any purpose of systematic study. Moreover, the number of fundamental legal doctrines is much less than is commonly supposed; the many different guises in which legal treatises are a repetition of each other, being the cause of much misapprehension. If these doctrines could be so classified and arranged that each should be found in its proper place, and nowhere else, they would cease to be formidable from their number. (Quoted in Heffernan 1983:136–137)

While Langdell's emphasis on legal science may well have been connected with a desire to "domesticate" the training of lawyers in university departments (Heffernan 1983:136), the gradualism of the growth of law as he saw it had more in common with the evolutionary theories of his day than with the historical comparative approach of Britain's foremost jurisprude, Sir Henry Maine. This evolutionary legacy has remained surprisingly strong in American anthropology right up to the present.[6]

As the social sciences changed from a natural-science to a sociological orientation, so too did jurisprudence. Roscoe Pound launched an assault on Langdell and the formalistic type of analysis his teaching had engendered, urging on his profession "a pragmatic, sociological legal science" (1908:608–609), embracing the pragmatic ideas of Pierce and James and the sociological functionalism of Albion Small. There was a firm tradition of reading both English and American anthropology and sociology. We know, for example, from Justice Oliver Wendell Holmes's correspondence with the young Harold Laski (Howe 1953) that Spencer's *Principles of Sociology* was held in high regard and that Sumner's *Folkways* and Lowie's *Primitive Society* (with its running battle with Morgan, whom Holmes admired) were favorably reviewed.

With this intellectual heritage, Karl Llewellyn contributed his genius not simply to legal but to political anthropology as a whole. In 1915 Llewellyn entered Yale Law School, which was always more responsive to the broader currents of social thought than other Ivy League schools. On its faculty he encountered Wesley Hohfeld, Arthur Corbin, and Walter Wheeler Cook, legal realists all. But even more influential on Llewellyn's thinking (and certainly on legal anthropology) was Benjamin Cardozo's *The Nature of the Judicial Process*, published in 1921. One of its central tenets—that judges were concerned not simply with legal rules within a hierarchical system of ideas but also with their social consequences—Llewellyn carried immediately into his teaching at Columbia Law School, where he obtained an appointment in 1924.

Between 1924 and 1940, Llewellyn became one of the most vibrant and vitriolic proponents of legal realism; after 1940 he readjusted his perspective to reassert the importance of normative issues. His conversion followed an exposure to two "other cultures," those of Leipzig in 1928 and a Cheyenne reservation in 1935. Llewellyn wrote,

> The law of the Cheyenne Indians made clear to me what I had never before dreamed, to wit, that law and justice had no need to be in conflict or even in too much tension, but could instead represent a daily working harmony. For in common with most lawyers, and indeed with most jurisprudes, I had mostly taken for granted a sort of perpetual struggle between the needs of regulation and form of the precedent-phase of justice on the one side and, on the other, any dynamic readjustment of a going system to just what needed to be done. Pound had rightly stressed shifting tides in the struggle, and that I had seen. But I had to get to the Cheyennes in order to wake up to the fact that tension between form, or precedent, or other tradition and perceived need requires, in nature, to be a tension only for the single crisis. It does not have to be a continuing tension in the legal system as a whole, because an adequately resilient legal system can on occasion, or even almost regularly, absorb the particular trouble and resolve it each time into a new, usefully guiding, forward-looking felt stand-for-action or rule-of-law. (1960:513)

Both elements in Llewellyn's "frozen dialectic" (Murphy 1971) entered political anthropology. Llewellyn-of-the-Cheyennes was dominant in the American branch for some time, largely through the undergraduate texts of his collaborator, E. Adamson Hoebel, who applied an evolutionary-functional model to both law and ethnology at large. Llewellyn-the-legal-realist was resurrected by British political anthropologists in the following generation and thus reentered an American legal anthropology that had shifted its focus from function and system to structure and process. Critiques of both followed.

The initial collaboration of Llewellyn and Hoebel has become the stuff of legend for legal anthropology. Llewellyn, Betts Professor of Jurisprudence at Columbia, in effect sponsored Hoebel's doctoral study, published as *The Political Organization and Law-Ways of the Comanche Indians* (1940). He also served on Jane Richardson's doctoral dissertation committee for "Law and Status Among the Kiowa Indians" (1940). Both arose out of ethnology field study groups of the Santa Fe Laboratory of Anthropology, the first directed by Linton in 1933 and the second by Lesser in 1935. As Hoebel was fond of noting, "Three days before departure for the Comanche field I received a simple note. 'I understand you are interested in American Indian Law', it read. 'So am I. Could I talk to you?'. Out of that has grown a stimulating association of the sort that is one of life's rare pleasures" (1940:5). What stimulated Hoebel's own interest in law is not clear. Benedict professed "both ignorance and disinterest"; Boas believed Native American culture to be "devoid of legal aspects," although it was he who had spoken of Hoebel's interest to Llewellyn in the first place; Linton was apparently prepared to go along with the arrangement, grudgingly perhaps, because Linton believed at the time—even with Richardson and Hoebel's fieldwork under way—that "many American Indian bands . . . have no regular legal procedures and, in many cases, no officials" (1936:228). There is much yet to be learned about the "two Columbias" that existed within the anthropology department in the 1930s and 1940s.

The anthropology of law lacked ethnography, methodology, and theory, as the publications of Lowie (1920) and Kroeber (1925) evinced. There had been no articles on law in the *American Anthropologist* between 1888 and 1928, and only two monographs, neither by a professional anthropologist (Barton 1919; Moss 1920). English and German jurisprudes had "formalized primitive law into unrealistic code-like edifices" (Kayakawa 1964:737). What could not be overlooked, of course, was Malinowski's *Crime and Custom in Savage Society* (1926a), and it was this work (with anything but codes and full of the minutiae of realism) that had "caught Llewellyn's interest and stimulated his concern for the possibilities of a fruitful joinder of legal realism and anthropology" (Hayakawa 1964:737). Llewellyn's later understanding that "the nature of institutions [such as law] is that they grow around our needs and partly serve them" is wholly Malinowskian. But, he continued, "the nature of institutions is also that they never serve these needs to satisfaction" (1951:40).

In all likelihood, it was Llewellyn's early reading of Max Weber, the German historical sociologist, that led him to advance processual rather than evolutionary arguments. He lived in Germany during his undergraduate days and fought on Germany's side in World War I, the only American citizen to receive the Iron Cross. On America's entry into the war in 1917, he attempted to enlist in the American army. Llewellyn read and cited Weber's work long before it was translated and became fashionable in American anthropology.

Legal Realism

To limit political anthropology's debt to Llewellyn to an appreciation of his interest in the law of Native Americans and his utilization of the case method in its study would be to trivialize it. The debate over legal realism was a political battle couched in methodological terms, and those who learn about Llewellyn only through Hoebel—whose work tends to be atheoretical and apolitical—miss a great deal. It is not insignificant (given our earlier observations on Malinowski) that Llewellyn's special expertise was in the field of commercial law.

Roscoe Pound was somewhat bemused by Llewellyn's passion. "I have received," he wrote, "books and letters on legal themes from professors and others, . . . but I was particularly struck by the tone of a New York professor—Llewellyn, that I think I have noticed in one or two of the others. They utter harmless things that I should not think could provoke antagonism, and that do not seem to me dazzlingly new, as if they were voices crying in the wilderness—or heroes challenging the world. I say to myself, 'Why so hot?'" (Howe 1953:1296). Llewellyn answered the question a few years later. "The young man who wrote these lectures," he recalled, "had sense enough to know that he was offering no original ideas, that he was merely drawing on and attempting to shape into a thing seen some stuff from a great and noble common reservoir of observation" (1951:8). Llewellyn undoubtedly had in mind the work of Pound himself, as well as the writings of Cardozo. Laski was able to tease the aging dean along these lines. He had just attended a lecture by Goodhart entitled "Recent Tendencies in American Jurisprudence," and he wrote to Pound in January 1932 that Goodhart had declared that "the realists à la Karl Llewellyn of Columbia were just wicked; that you and Cardozo had undermined that faith in the place of inescapable logic in the law which was fundamental to security" (Howe 1953:1955). In spite of the teasing tone, Laski, who knew New York well in these years, would have appreciated that a realism expressed by Pound in the 1880s would have been a very different realism from that of Llewellyn in the depressed 1930s.

What then was this "teapot tempest" (Llewellyn 1951:9) over legal realism all about? First, the roots lay in the crisis through which the American legal system passed around the turn of the century. According to one recent scholar, this crisis involved "the breakdown of the common law system: the removing of the theory of precedent, the abdication of judicial power to innovate, the replacement of decisional law by statute, the attempt to achieve nationally uniform state laws, the current indications of a federalization of even one private law [and] the tendency to promote statutes to a code status," all of which was part and parcel of one of the major political events of this century, the "massive intervention of the Federal government in all areas of social and economic life" (Gilmore 1961:1046–1047). This was itself a response to America's almost uncontrolled growth in immigration between 1880 and 1920, its expanding industrial economy and labor movement, and above all the political upheaval that threatened.

At the beginning of this period, questions of private law had been left to the states, and the states had left them to the courts; this was an era par excellence of judge-made law. Until around 1880, case law evolved fairly smoothly, although indications that it was breaking down under its own weight could be seen as early as midcentury, when the law profession first showed an interest in codification. Not until the 1890s, however, did the federal government act, appointing a National Conference of Commissioners on Uniform State Laws. With this Holmes and his peers sounded the first expressions of realism, giving rise to some of the epigrams beloved of Llewellyn and a succession of political anthropologists ever since:

The life of the law has not been logic, it has been experience.
The common law is not a brooding omnipresence in the sky.
Prejudice is the term we use to describe our opponents' facts; fact is the term we use to describe our own prejudices.

Legal realism thus emerged to contest the rigidification of American law, which it found to be overly complex and unworkable. It was a social movement. Llewellyn sounded a clarion call in May 1931 that found its response not only among lawyers but also among anthropologists, although those familiar with Malinowski's writings may have felt a slight sense of déjà vu. "Ferment is abroad in the law," wrote Llewellyn. "The sphere of interest widens; men became interested again in the life that swirls around things legal. Before rules, were facts; in the beginning was not a Word, but a Doing. Behind decisions stand judges; judges are men; as men they have human backgrounds. Beyond rules, again, lie effects: beyond decisions stand people whom rules and decisions directly or individually touch. . . . *Beyond rules lie effects* but do they? Are some rules mere paper? And of effects, what effects? Hearsay, unbuttressed guess, assumption or assertion checked by test—can such be trusted on this matter of what law is doing?" (Llewellyn 1931:1222).

The legal realists of the 1930s included Max Radin, who at Berkeley had been a reader of Barton's Ifugao manuscript, and Jerome Frank, whose *Law and the Modern Mind* (1930) was later to influence both Max Gluckman and Simon Roberts, author of *Order and Dispute: An Introduction to Legal Anthropology* (1979). Llewellyn's readiness to embrace anthropology lay, if William Twining's perception (1967) is accurate, in his early "private practitioner orientation," acquired as an office lawyer for the National City Bank who was rarely involved in litigious business but was well placed to look at problems from the point of view of typical clients in large business concerns. His position in the legal profession bore similarities to that of Hoebel, much the younger man, of course, in anthropology. Llewellyn's *Cases and Materials on the Law of Sales* (1930b), which followed *The Bramble Bush* (1930a), his 1929–30 Columbia lectures, had established his reputation in the United States as a controversial figure with the reputation of a giant; in Britain he had "scarcely any reputation at all, except as an occasional Aunt Sally" (Twining 1967:515).

By the 1940s Llewellyn's intellectual radicalism was fading, to be replaced by a new romanticism in the form of a seeking out of the simpler, clearer evocation of universal principles of justice among the "untouched" Cherokee. A far cry from the legal realist who taught his students that iconoclasm could be

> a sport as well as a condition; even when not so viewed, the fact of smashing calls disproportionate attention to the broken pieces; revolt is seldom accompanied by balanced judgement. We of the teaching world are still as full of our discovery as once was tortured Galileo: move, move it does, the law. And if to make you see the movement we must shout down the pious words with which courts have pretended that no change occurred—then we must shout, shout disbelief. We must blaspheme the legal oracles. Well, then, we do. We strip the trappings, verbal and other, off the courts. We turn the spotlight on the places where the tinsel gaps, where you see cheap cotton, or see sweaty skin beneath. (1951:124)

It is difficult to see how the scholar who cried out for the study of legal process in such an impassioned manner could have derived satisfaction from working with four eighty-year-old Cherokee respondents recalling the "law-ways" of their past—but he did. Such contradictions abound: neither Llewellyn nor Hoebel were participant observers of law-in-action on the Native American reservations. His behavioral law—"the behavior-side of matters legal," as he often called it—derived from four books. These were Sumner's *Folkways* (1907), which had first drawn him to ethnology as an undergraduate at Yale, Ross's *Social Control* (1901), Bentley's *Process of Government* (1908/67), and Rattray's *Ashanti Law and Constitution* (1929). He deplored the loss of interest in law as a field of anthropological study in the complex American society. When Middletown came to be surveyed and revisited by the Lynds, the legal aspect of behavior there "did not seem worth canvass" (Llewellyn 1941), an observation repeated a decade later by Julian Steward.

Llewellyn was not well placed to make the point, and his advocacy of the study of behavioral politics lost out to functionalism, scientific classification, comparison, and generalization, as we have seen. When he set out to reconstruct a genealogy for legal anthropology (1941) he began with Barton's *Ifugao Law* (1919), Malinowski's *Crime and Custom in Savage Society* (1926), Barton's *The Half-Way Sun* (1930a), Malinowski's introduction to Ian Hogbin's *Law and Order in Polynesia* (1934), Rattray's *Ashanti Law and Constitution* (1929), Spieth (1911) on the Ewe, Gutmann (1926) on the Chagga, Dundas (1921) on the Kikuyu, Hoebel's *The Political Organization and Law-Ways of the Comanche Indians* (1940), and Richardson's *Law and Status Among the Kiowa Indians* (1940). Llewellyn also thoroughly approved Huntington Cairns's observation that "to make behavior in the legal aspects of life the subject matter of a 'science' is to overcome the obsession that *only the State* can have significance in this connection, and so to open up the closely comparable phenomena of primitive law in primitive societies, and of sub-group 'by-law' within our own society, for the revealing light they shed on legal phenomena in general. Gurvitch has in good part gone this same road, as had Ehrlich, and especially Max Weber. It is a good road" (1941:8).

This is a far cry from his ethnologist collaborator Hoebel's view of evolutionary stages and his primitivization of contemporary peoples in his many textbooks. Yet Hoebel appreciated that, for Llewellyn, law was process. Society was always in flux, and form existed only "in enduring relationships of flowing action" (Hoebel 1961b:742). Custom was therefore not a satisfactory tool for inquiry into legal phenomena. "It is vague, diffuse in reference, misleading as to content, and involves a peculiarly vicious indiscriminate fusion of 'practice' and 'accepted standard for practice'. If one is interested in process, especially in a society at all mobile and non-homogeneous and with specialized bodies of ways (i.e., almost any known society) then 'custom' belongs, as a working tool, with the firelock smooth-bore. a good instrument, in its day, worth preservation in an intellectual museum" (Llewellyn and Hoebel 1941:10). Anthropologists, however, clearly were not prepared to jettison so lightly a concept with such a noble pedigree. Malinowski had used it as a straw man, but Gluckman, the preeminent legal anthropologist of the next generation, was to use it to some effect in *Custom and Conflict in Africa* (1955a).

Llewellyn was, as we have seen, a battler who believed that things should be better for those at the mercy of a legal system. His battle as a lawyer had been directed toward ending hypocrisy and abuse; his vision as a lawyer-turned-anthropologist was of a society in which the finest values of humankind could be realized. This he thought he had found among the Cheyenne. After his Cheyenne fieldwork in 1936, he spent five full summers (1945–1949) working among the Keresan-speaking Pueblos of New Mexico. Llewellyn himself said that he got "a new pair of eyes" from work among Native Americans (Hayakawa 1964:725), but a long-promised monograph never materialized. Much of Llewellyn's legal realism entered the anthropology of law, but not in the 1940s. For the Kiowa, Comanche, and Cheyenne of the Plains, the days of living Indian law had long since passed.

The Law-Ways of the Plains Indians

E. Adamson Hoebel's *The Political Organization and Law-Ways of the Comanche Indians* (1940) opens with an anecdote. "On the second day of our field work with the Comanches," Hoebel recalled, Ralph Linton " 'empirically' demonstrated the non-existence of law-ways by asking one informant, 'What kind of law did you have?'. 'We didn't have any law in the old days.' Whereupon Linton closed the issue" (1940:21).

Hoebel reopened it. He patiently questioned and requestioned his Comanche informants (old men and women who could reconstruct Comanche folkways between 1820 and 1880) until all disagreements and contradictions were eliminated and he could present what he called the "least common denominator" (1940:7). His goal was to construct a comparative jurisprudence. "The Comanche and the case-trained American lawman proceed in like manner," he observed in one of the earliest formalist statements in the anthropology of law (1940:17). "What holds perforce for the Comanche should hold for the study of all primitive law. Legal behavior is behavior and should be treated as such" (1940:6). He thus accumulated case histories to show legal mechanisms at work. His procedure was to put "pump-priming questions" to the informant "designed for the most part to probe into dispute situations, since most law is concerned with definition of conflict of interests" (1940:17).

The fruit of Hoebel's later collaboration with Llewellyn appeared as *The Cheyenne Way* (1941). The Cheyenne were chosen over other Plains Indians because they were said to have formal government. The period for which most of the tales were recalled was one in which military societies were challenging the power of the chiefs. The work thus became "a study of men in conflict, institutions in tension, and laymen or craftsmen at work on resolution of tension" (Llewellyn and Hoebel

1941:viii). Throughout the study they denied that modern American and Cheyenne law differed greatly, although their American law was of the twentieth century and that of the Cheyenne of the nineteenth. They accordingly dismissed as unnecessary controversies many problems previously addressed in comparative jurisprudence—distinctions between torts and crime, public and private enforcement of law, group responsibility, "levels of law-stuff," and the origins of law in religion.

In the discussion that preceded the general analysis of the law-ways of Cheyenne society, Llewellyn contributed two observations that (because of the nature of the Cheyenne data—the oral recollections of four main informants in their eighties) he was not able at that time to elaborate. First, he made it clear that the case was to be viewed as a public representation of a crisis situation. He cited (Llewellyn and Hoebel 1941:42) *The Polish Peasant in Europe and America* (Thomas and Znaniecki 1918) to make a methodological point about "situations."[7] Second, Llewellyn noted that American legal procedure was made up of five steps: (1) the operative facts, which had occurred before the lawsuit began, (2) the setting up of legal proceedings in proper form, (3) the proof of the claim and an opportunity for challenge, (4) the official judgment, and (5) the preservation of a record. Such analytical apparatus and elaborate procedural machinery did not exist among the Cheyenne and would not have been expected to exist. Llewellyn's romanticism over the Cheyenne and Hoebel's sociological evolutionism proved easy bedfellows.

Another contribution, again not worked out fully because of the nature of the Cheyenne data, lay in Llewellyn's discussion of the problem of jurisdiction among various coexistent "and often essentially competing, legal schemes" in a society (Llewellyn and Hoebel 1941:60). Llewellyn's approach to legal pluralism was based on his knowledge of modern American civil law, which, as he noted, "has been moving uninterruptedly into expansion of group relations and of group responsibility . . . the party, the corporation, the union, the cooperative, workmen's compensation, and *respondent superior*." The "going total 'legal' structure of the culture" was to be understood, in his view, "only by getting on down into the intra-group regulations as well" (1941:52).

Llewellyn thus recognized different coexisting types of effective regulatory and trouble-settling devices and diverse and sometimes conflicting levels of "law-stuff" within any complex society. Morals and custom were thus "effective devices of group self-regulation without whose aiding presence the devices of official law would falter and fail"

(1941:52). In *The Cheyenne Way*, however, the official law of the total society is the subject of the inquiry. Law channels conduct in such a manner as to prevent or avoid conflict. Furthermore, law "cleans up social messes"; it consists of rules, practice, motivation, and result; it involves rights and remedies.

Yet Llewellyn was constantly aware of law-as-process and could not let a systems model alone suffice. "Not only multiple schemes of normation grow in a culture, but within groups and across groups. . . . [B]ut law itself may grow up in complementary or rival systems. . . . There will develop then nice questions as to which system of law-stuff a litigant can wangle himself into or under, making careful anticipatory weighing of the advantages to himself" (1941:60). He appreciated that this kind of data appeared in the Ifugao and Trobriand ethnography of Barton and Malinowski while regretting that it was not brought into specific focus as a "problem of jurisdiction among the various co-existent, and often essentially competing, legal schemes."[8] Their material, he believed (1941:60), had a surface confusion that the material internally denied.

The Case Method

The case method is based on the premise that formal law comprises principles contained in the decisions that solve (adjudicate) disputes (Pospisil 1971). We have seen the early use of cases by Northcote Thomas, Rivers, Barton, and Malinowski, but it was through the work of Llewellyn and Hoebel that the case method formally entered political anthropology.

Hoebel (like those before him) began by reporting cases to document Lowie's contention that the germ of the state was to be found among the Cheyenne in the military societies. Llewellyn suggested that he look not for their coercive aspects but for their civil activities. The "cases," incidents that supported the argument, were presented anecdotally. Anyone who disagreed with Lowie's contention was at liberty to present (if he or she could) "cases" that would negate it. In the later monographs on the Comanche (1940) and Cheyenne (1941), cases were used "as a working matrix from which [legal] principles could be rigorously abstracted" (Pospisil 1971:13), a shift to a structural technique, as Van Velsen discerned (1967). A methodological emphasis on "trouble cases"—the dramatic rather than the routine—became Hoebel and Llewellyn's legacy not simply to the anthropology of law but to political anthropology in general.

PRIMITIVE WARFARE

During this period, structural studies of closed societies, especially African "tribes," dominated political anthropology. Warfare became an indicator of the bounds of a political unit (Radcliffe-Brown 1940), and the anthropological study of warfare became increasingly marginalized. V. Gordon Childe (1941) continued to relate war in prehistoric societies to the stages of evolution delineated by Hobhouse, Wheeler, and Ginsberg. Ranging himself alongside proponents of diffusion, he demonstrated that most "savages" were pacific and that warfare, a perversion, was a by-product of "civilization." Within the British ethnographic tradition, Evans-Pritchard wrote up his material on Zande border raids and warfare (1957a, 1957b), and Reo Fortune contributed a further analysis of Arapesh warfare in New Guinea (1947).

In a more analytical vein, Max Gluckman (1955a) struggled with the comparative politics of rebellion, revolution, and civil war. Drawing on his own work and that of Hilda Kuper among the Swazi (1947), he discerned in both states rebellions to replace the king but not revolutions to destroy the monarchy and replace it with a different form of political government. Ethnographies of other African states (Schapera 1940; Richards 1940; Oberg 1940; and Nadel 1940) indicate that this was true of all. Gluckman later (1963:9) suggested the relation of his theory to isolated ideas in Aristotle's *Politics: A Treatise on Government*, Marxist-Leninist writings on rebellions, and Weber's work on traditional authority.[9] Redfield similarly observed that in European history "no peasant revolt had revolution for its goal" (1956:35). Still, twenty years later Eric Wolf addressed the issues anew in *Peasant Wars of the Twentieth Century* (1969).

Gluckman asked (1956) why most civil wars were expressions of a cyclical process and why rituals of rebellion, or what Hilda Kuper called "the drama of kingship" (1947), exhibited a similar process—a cycle of rebellion and restrengthening of the monarchy. He tried to connect a series of facts: the Swazi and Zulu had stable subsistence economies but lacked good communications, highly productive tools, widespread trade, or luxuries that would enable the ruling group to establish itself as a class distinct from commoners. The economy necessitated widespread dispersal of the population and the division of the nation into counties. All men owned their own weapons, so every county had an army. These counties developed strong loyalties to their leaders and hence local autonomy. Leaders had to support followers to maintain their own power, and they and their kin intermarried with these followers. This often resulted in hostility to the central government and a desire for independence. Yet there was no secession. Instead, the various sections of the nation supported different princes in their struggles to gain the throne and thus were involved in fighting not against the king but against each other for the kingship.

Radcliffe-Brown welcomed a now forgotten work by Stanislaus Andrzejewski, *Military Organization and Society* (1954b), as a theoretical inquiry within comparative sociology. In its preface he deplored the preference among social scientists "for facts over theories"; only studies such as Andrzejewski's, Radcliffe-Brown maintained, held promise of "a really scientific understanding of human society" (1954:vii). Andrzejewski set out to explain the importance of military factors in shaping societies. He acknowledged a debt to Spencer, Mosca, and Weber; the contributions of Steinmetz, Oppenheimer, Sorokin, and Thurnwald were also important for his work because his explanation encompassed social stratification and the conquest theory of the state. The monograph itself is a sustained, abstract, analytical thesis that cannot be so simply reproduced.

At the opposite pole from Andrzejewski's theorizing was the multitude of data provided by ethnohistorical accounts of Native American fighting patterns, particularly in the Southwest (Linton 1944; Swadesh 1948; Ellis 1951; Fathauer 1954) and on the Plains (Newcombe 1950). Of all the Native American polities, the Iroquois continued to excite the most interest (Snyderman 1948; Scheele 1950), historian George T. Hunt's *The Wars of the Iroquois* (1940) having stimulated an ethnohistorical response. Of course, rethinking Native American political organization in the 1950s called for considerable attention to its military aspects, as we have seen. The migration and displacement of peoples, competition for access to scarce resources—particularly horses, weapons, and shrinking hunting grounds—and the machinations of traders were most critical.

A volume of a very different sort—and one that might be taken to challenge the political reconstructions of both the rethinkers of American ethnography and Radcliffe-Brown's program at Oxford and Chicago—was Harry Holbert Turney-High's *Primitive War: Its Practice and Concepts* (1949). This study was based on library research, and although the author thanked Melville Herskovits and Ralph Linton for their "sound criticism" (1949:xv), it owed more to military science than to anthropology. Iconoclastic as it was, it was not well received within the academy, and later surveys of the anthropology of war (Fried,

Harris, and Murphy 1968; Otterbein 1973) either failed to mention it or were dismissive.[10]

One of the few contemporary ethnographies to draw heavily on Turney-High's paradigm was John C. Ewers's *The Horse in Blackfoot Indian Culture* (1955). The strengths of the volume for a political anthropologist lay in Turney-High's reintroduction of primary sources (even if they were penned by amateurs) and his knowledge of military principles. He dealt with the actual conduct of war—war as action—thus his pointed criticism of ethnography: "The typical field report makes a fine description of attitudes, values, ceremonials, personnel and motives for war. Indeed, the *avoir du pois* weight of excellent material about all behavior leading up to an engagement and that immediately following a fight would make an impressive recording. Only the actual conduct of the fight is missing. . . . The field researcher has been meticulous regarding the icing and has overlooked the cake, which is not ordinarily the way the typical field ethnographer works" (Turney-High 1949:21). Turney-High thus devoted two-thirds of his study to the *practice* of primitive war: the form and function of weapons; the theory of war and the military horizon; formations; discipline and command; the functional desiderata (tactics, the offensive, and protection, for example); intelligence, surprise, and countersurprise; and battle plans. Only then did he discuss what had been the mainstay of work on warfare by most anthropologists: sociopsychological and economic motives; military values and attitudes; and the relation of war to the organization of society.

POLITICS IN THE COMPARATIVE MODE

The year 1940—the year that saw the publication of both *African Political Systems*, edited by Meyer Fortes and E. E. Evans-Pritchard, with a preface by A. R. Radcliffe-Brown, and Evans-Pritchard's *The Nuer*, a monograph on a tribal population in the southern Sudan—opened the classical period of British political anthropology. Oxford's anthropology became the established mode. Its dominance was buttressed by the prestige of England's oldest university, the concentration on fieldwork in Africa, close links with the International African Institute, and the establishment of the Association of Social Anthropologists of Great Britain and Northern Ireland (ASA). The moving spirit of the era was Evans-Pritchard, successor to Radcliffe-Brown and the Oxford chair.

The strength and cogency of the Radcliffe-Brown program and the caliber of the field research it engendered led to almost universal acknowledgment of its excellence within the discipline. It was, nevertheless, in essence a conservative nineteenth-century program, and derivative at that. Maine's *Ancient Law* (1861) and Durkheim's *Division of Labour* (1893) provided its intellectual nourishment. As Edmund Leach described the program's approach:

> Individuals were presumed to be born free into a society composed of corporate institutions, the relations within which and between which provided a paradigm of social existence. The structural shape of such a corporation is intrinsically self-perpetuating and is independent of the individual life-span of its particular members. Social structure is thought of as a network of relationships between "persons" and "roles." The stability of the system requires that the content of such relationships shall be permanent. In such a society every individual who fills a role finds himself under jural constraint to fulfill the obligations inherent in that role. More crudely, the customs of a society are seen as providing a body of moral norms worked out in behaviouristic form; the discrepancies between individual behaviour and customary behaviour are due simply to the inability of the average man to live up to the moral demands of his society. He is represented as knowing very well what ought to be the case, but as devising immensely complicated fictions which will absolve him from the inconveniences of virtue. (Leach 1968b:296–297)

It is common enough for anthropologists returning from the rich and often confusing experience of field research to look around and seize upon tightly argued systems of thought that will help them order their data. Such had been the case with the young A. R. Brown when on his return from the Andaman Islands he had turned aside from the complexities Rivers offered to embrace the tailored logic of French sociology. Yet even in 1922 the enveloping hegemony of Durkheim's sociology had begun to decline in France itself. In 1934 Jean Izoulet, professor of social philosophy, wrote the damning phrase soon to be quoted by Durkheim's adversaries: "the obligation of teaching the sociology of Durkheim in 200 Normal Schools in France is the gravest national peril that our country has known for some time" (quoted in Clark 1968:39). Malinowskian functionalism proved inadequate for the analysis of culture contact and change, and Radcliffe-Brown's systemo oriented structural functionalism filled the void.

The dominance of Radcliffe-Brown's structural anthropology by no means implied monopoly, although this might be overlooked by outsiders taken in by hegemonic utterances. The editors of *African Political Systems*, for example, claimed, "We speak for all social anthropologists when we say that a scientific study of political institutions must be inductive and comparative and aim solely at establishing and explaining the uniformities found among them and their interdependencies with other features of social organization" (1940:2). That they did in fact speak for the dominant strain in British social anthropology may be inferred from the number who rallied to counter Lord Raglan's charge (made repeatedly between 1943 and 1955) that the discipline was defining itself in an unnecessarily limited manner, neglecting history, stressing the "primitive," and serving colonial administration. Raglan was polemical, hyperbolic, and inaccurate in many of his statements, but they provoked replies from H. J. Braunholtz (president of the RAI), J. H. Hutton (former India administrator-turned-anthropologist at Cambridge), Lucy Phillips Mair (then reader in colonial administration at LSE), Margaret Read, and J. L. Myres. Mair did, indeed, speak for all when she clarified the type of analysis the discipline practiced: "It is a close study of the norms of social behavior, and the degree of conformity with those norms, with the forces operating for and against conformity, in the societies we study and in their various social groups and institutions" (1955:70). Opponents within the system, like Lord Raglan, understood the governing interest of the new anthropology; outsiders (particularly Americans) thought it obsessed with kinship. In fact, its obsession was with politics "and with kinship only insofar as it was politics" (Jarvie 1974:304). It would be easy to dismiss Lord Raglan as a folklorist, an amateur, even a crank, were it not that he was a close and respected friend of Daryll Forde. As a knowledgeable amateur, he had the freedom to voice muted discontents more widely felt within the profession at large.

To explain the dominance of the paradigm it is necessary to account for the dominance of Radcliffe-Brown, particularly since his actual practice of anthropology ran so against the grain of the discipline's distinctiveness.[11] In the mid 1930s Westermarck had expressed surprise and concern at his attachment to Durkheim: "It seems to me rather singular that Radcliffe-Brown should have been so fascinated by the theories of Durkheim and his school of sociologists, who have been so reluctant to embark actively on field studies" (1936:240). Several incidents in his early career indicate that Radcliffe-Brown was not a good field worker, as we have seen, but it seems likely that the influence of Durkheim and the *Année Sociologique* was not simply, or even primarily, intellectual. He was already using Durkheimian insights in a course of lectures at Trinity College in 1909, although as Goody (1973) pointed out, many of his ideas might just as likely have come from Spencer as from Durkheim. Durkheim's *Division of Labour* (1893) was, after all, a direct polemical attack on Spencer. But what Radcliffe-Brown might also have learned from Durkheim was the importance of impression management, administrative organization, and public relations.

The Radcliffe-Brown Program

The essence of the Radcliffe-Brown program lay in its goals of comparison, classification, and generalization. Underlying it was intensive ethnographic fieldwork of the kind pioneered by Marett and Rivers, the techniques of which were set out in the revolutionary *Notes and Queries* of 1912 and were followed by Malinowski in the Trobriands. What distinguished Radcliffe-Brown's vision from that of Malinowski was his scientism, his need to establish a natural science of society with its own body of sociological laws. His political anthropology had to be nomothetic, and its main tool was the sociological comparative method. His preface to *African Political Systems* (1940:xii) established this at the outset:

> The task of social anthropology, as a natural science of human society, is the systematic investigation of the nature of social institutions. The method of natural science rests always on the comparison of observed phenomena, and the aim of such comparison is by a careful examination of diversities to discover underlying uniformities. Applied to human societies the comparative method used as an instrument for inductive inference will enable us to discover the universal, essential, characters which belong to all human societies, past, present and future. The progressive achievement of knowledge of this kind must be the aim of all who believe that a veritable science of human society is possible and desirable." (1949:12)

The establishment of general sociological laws required some sort of classification of empirical polities. Fortes and Evans-Pritchard developed the theme: "A comparative study of political systems has to be kept on an abstract plane where social processes are stripped of their cultural idiom and are reduced to functional terms. The structural similarities which disparity of culture conceals are then laid bare and structural dissimilarities are revealed behind a screen of cultural conformity" (1940:3).

The Impact of *African Political Systems*

Ronald Cohen has described *African Political Systems* as "the first serious attempt to define a field of political anthropology" (1973:866), a judgment shared by Mair, who described the work as "the first attempt of British social anthropology to isolate the political aspects of the societies they studied and present these in a form that would make comparison possible" (1975:8). It was the most widely known, and in some quarters the most notorious, product of British political anthropology in the 1940s. Ironically, it was, according to Fortes, "originally inspired" by Isaac Schapera, a South African anthropologist. In the spring of 1937 Fortes had the occasion to visit Cape Town, where he saw the proofs of Schapera's *Handbook of Tswana Law and Custom*. Struck by the contrast between Tswana and Tallensi political organization, Fortes arrived at the idea of a wider comparative study. We may infer from Schapera's later actions, both in a "semi-public critique" at Chicago and in his own regionally discrete comparative study of South African political systems, that the volume did not come up to his expectations. It is, indeed, tempting to see Schapera's *Government and Politics in Tribal Societies* (1956) and Mair's *Primitive Government* (1962), an equally controlled regional comparison of indigenous political organization in eastern Africa, as LSE alternatives to the Oxbridge model.

African Political Systems was not a well-planned, coherent volume with each contributor testing the hypotheses or working within the framework of the editors. It was not a British equivalent of *Acculturation in Seven American Tribes* (Linton 1940). The editors' simple-minded division of the societies into the two categories of state and stateless highlighted the originality of their own contributions but hid the value of several others, undermining the dynamics that underlay them. Of the eight essays in the volume, only those of Evans-Pritchard and Fortes were wholly in the Oxbridge kin-centered mode; the others reflected the diverging approaches to politics extant at the time.

Most studies of more complex political systems than those of the Nuer and Tallensi inclined toward narrative history rather than sociological analysis. Max Gluckman, for example, wrote an account of political organization in two periods of Zulu history, 1775 and 1936–1938. A probably apocryphal story has it that he offered *An Analysis of a Social Situation in Modern Zululand* to the editors, but they declined it. He then presented them with the historical account. Schapera, the most established among the contributors, stuck very much to his own lathe (to use a Kentish idiom) discussing sovereignty in an African chicfdom in the context of its ethnic and territorial constitution. He was one of the few contributors to use the term *constitution*, although the goal of structural analysis as a genre was, in effect, to describe and analyze constitutions, or ideal structures. The political scientist David Easton singled out Schapera (along with Macleod, it will be recalled) as one of the few anthropologists ever to have "directed their attention to strictly political phenomena" (1959:210).

Audrey Richards's account of Bemba political organization was the most ambitious in the volume. She particularly addressed the colonial administration's perception of the Bemba state and appeared to be somewhat at odds with the editors, who distanced themselves from the practical tasks of administration. S. F. Nadel, like Richards but even more explicitly, chose to write of the problems of colonial administration in the riverine state of Kede in northern Nigeria, although he denied that this was his main intention. Kalervo Oberg, an American-trained anthropologist who wrote of the Ankole kingdom in Uganda, clearly marched to a different drummer. He singled out for attention elements of Ankole cultural idiom. His interest in the domination of agriculturalists by pastoralists and the emergent conquest state derived from literature other than that with which the editors were most at home. For Gunter Wagner, writing of the Luhya (the Bantu peoples of the Kavirondo in Kenya), the logical starting point of any study of political organization was the demarcation of the political unit, and he proceeded from this to analyze ways of gaining political prominence among the acephalous peoples. The final classic papers in the volume, those of its two editors, also dealt with nonstate societies. Fortes described the Tallensi clans as maintaining their own submerged political institutions in spite of the strong penetration of British rule; Evans-Pritchard's Nuer emerged as "anarchic" pastoralists.

In spite of its success within the closed ranks of social anthropology in Britain, *African Political Systems* was not well received elsewhere. The South African political philosopher Julius Lewin recognized it as "the beginning of a new development" in anthropology and lauded it as a pioneering study of so-called stateless societies, "where political organization is such as to make some of the normal concepts of political science quite inapplicable" (1940:455–456). But he criticized the book for (1) its neglect of forebears, specifically Hobhouse, Wheeler, and Ginsberg; (2) its neglect of other social sciences and its "gratuitous criticism of political science, which serves only to indicate that they have not really looked into the modern literature on the subject." (He suggested that there was a considerable interdisciplinary lag between anthropology and political science), (3) its neglect of such questions as how the economic life of the peoples described has influenced their political institutions;[12] and (4) its lack of agreement as to what to include and what to leave out. He cited law as an example of a topic treated ambiguously. Lewin, until 1967 a professor of African law and government at the University of Witwatersrand, later became a lecturer in colonial administration at LSE and Manchester University. The tenor of his criticism of *African Political Systems* and the political implications of the structural analysis of African politics, particularly South African politics, later formed the basis of a bitter ideological conflict between his compatriot Gluckman and the collateral heir to the Oxbridge program, Edmund Leach.

The dean of American Africanist anthropologists, Herskovits, was even harsher in his review of the volume. The author of *Dahomey: An Ancient West African Kingdom* (1938b) proceeded to castigate the contributors for their ineptitude "in handling such an historical problem as that of cultural change," an ineptitude he considered characteristic of "the functionalist group." Like Lewin, he regretted their lack of attention to studies of African political organization by previous scholars. "It should not have been difficult," he wrote, "to include recognition of the existence of such works, and it would have been gracious for some of the authors, at least, to have written without such utter disregard of the research of their older colleagues. No mention of Roscoe or Meek or Labouret or Gutmann, for example, finds its way into these pages. It would have been even better had the contributions of such students been used as comparative data; or if, at the very least, the existence of works such as theirs had been indicated by a check-list of those volumes in which expositions of the political life of African people are to be had" (1941:466). Oxbridge anthropology, as we have seen, was characterized by lineal, not lateral, thinking. Herskovits also judged it a defect that the essays dealt only with political organizations in British colonies, and like Schapera later, he was critical of the planning that had gone into the comparative volume. Oxbridge anthropology ran a tight ship.

Herskovits sought to move beyond the book's simple state-stateless dichotomy to explain the patterning of the two types of polity. He did not make it clear where his perception came from but suggested that "the distribution of each . . . must be established as a necessary first step to further understanding [because] these distributions are not of a broad, contiguous character. Rather the societies having the second, looser type of control are interlarded among those groupings whose political structure . . . is termed that of "primitive states" (1941:466). It seems likely that he had in mind something like the "shatterbelt" concept familiar from historical and anthropological work on civilizations. He may well have known James Fairgreaves's *Geography and World Power* (1915).

Herskovits recognized, nevertheless, the pioneering quality of the analysis of acephalous societies. This was, he wrote, "untrod ground, and perhaps this is why two of the three contributors who are concerned with tribes of this kind give the impression of being uneasy over the absence of specific categories" (1941:467). Wagner's discussion of "internal political structure," for example, was merely a compilation of comments on social organization, gift exchange economies, religion, and (finally, and more to the point), quasi-legal processes. Similarly, Oberg's discussion of Kavirondo "external political structure" was nothing more than a report on warfare.

Herskovits was appreciative of Evans-Pritchard's own move beyond Radcliffe-Brown, a move toward process as he saw it. Clear statements of Nuer "political relativity" revealed, he suggested, the inadequacy of "the functionalist position, which holds that no cultural institution can be understood except in terms of its interrelations with all other portions of the culture of which it forms a part. This approach is shown to be impossible when dealing with shadowy, amorphous canons of regulation such as are to be found in 'non-political' African groups. And in Evans-Pritchard's thesis that the consistency we perceive in Nuer political structure is one of *process rather than one of morphology* . . . we see reflected the importance of studying a given aspect of culture in terms of the special problem it poses" (1941:467, emphasis added). Herskovits did not seem to know that Evans-Pritchard had in fact arrived at processual analysis much earlier (1937) in his study of witchcraft, sorcery, and magic in the Azande state. This is entirely consistent with the distinction that was also emerging at this time—but less programmatically—between social structure (constitution, morphology) and social organization (activity, process).

C. K. Meek criticized many of the same things as Lewin and Herskovits, finding the ahistoricity of some of the essays troublesome and deploring the lack of reference to existing standard works and the degree of conceptual obfuscation, particularly in the work of Fortes that adhered most closely to the ideas of Radcliffe-Brown. He also drew attention to the neglect of topics such as the relation between intertribal groups and intratribal relations, the role of pantribal secret societies, and the use of ambassadors and arbitrators, which were found in the work of the "diffusionist and institutional anthropologists" among Radcliffe-Brown's peers. Meek was particularly skeptical of the state-stateless dichotomy, noting that numerous so-called stateless societies displayed some of the features of so-called primitive states. His own knowledge of Ibo society and other riverine West African polities acutely raised the problems inherent in the dichotomy.[13] As a former administrator, Meek was also critical of the "perhaps over pessimistic" view of most of the writers who "seem preoccupied with the destructive influences at work in African society and fail to give weight to the new forces of integration" (1941:42). Edmund Burke once observed that political theory limped behind political practice by about fifty years. That was just about the length of time that the polities described in *African Political Systems* had been colonies. Only Fortes addressed himself to this historical reality. The indigenous political constitution, he suggested, existed in a layered juropolitical situation, submerged beneath the imposed colonial administrative structure.

According to the Radcliffe-Brown program, comparison was to be followed first by classification and then by generalization. The 1940 comparison gave rise to a very simpleminded three-part classification of African political systems: (1) primitive states (e.g., Zulu, Ngwato, Bemba, Kede, and Ankole), characterized by centralized authority, administrative machinery, and judicial institutions; (2) stateless societies (e.g., Logoli, Tallensi, and Nuer), characterized by "ordered anarchy"; and (3) band societies (e.g., Bushmen and Bergdama), in which the political unit was the kinship unit. Later, in an introduction to *Tribes Without Rulers* (Middleton and Tait 1958), Evans-Pritchard gently suggested that the typology of *African Political Systems* had not been as important as people seemed to think. It had been no more than a stepping-stone to classification. What was important, he suggested, was the consideration of African political systems as indigenous systems, unaffected by European contact. Given the more than eighty years of colonial rule in Africa at this time, this can only be construed as placing priority on reconstruction and the "discovery" of the importance in political constitutions of unilineal descent groups. Only many years later, as we have seen, did Radcliffe-Brown recall Gifford's part in this "discovery."

Generalization, the third stage of the scientific endeavor, was modestly achieved by Fortes in response to a series of reevaluations of his and Evans-Pritchard's work (Worsley 1956; Smith 1956). Fortes suggested in 1953 that unilineal descent groups were to be found in a middle range of relatively homogeneous, precapitalistic economies in which there was a degree of technological sophistication and rights in durable property. His description of these as precapitalistic economies was novel in 1953 and may have been a response to the fact that political anthropologists were beginning to throw open again the doors that Radcliffe-Brown and his Oxbridge apostles had closed. The history of the subfield was itself in the process of reconstruction.

As is so often the case, the theoretical challenge to the Radcliffe-Brown program of comparison, classification, and generalization was couched in methodological terms. On the surface it took the form of questioning the basic first step—comparison—but beneath the surface was a fundamental questioning of the program's "dependence on abstract units and processes rather than on real units and processes" (Balandier 1970:31). Two critics of Radcliffe-Brown's Comtean comparative method, Schapera at LSE and Eggan at the University of Chicago, followed Maine rather than Comte. Schapera's critique of Radcliffe-Brown appeared in 1953 at the time of the latter's advocacy of comparative community studies, and Eggan introduced his method of controlled comparison to the profession in his presidential address to the AAA (1954). Both argued for comparison only within given ecologically and historically delineated regions. Schapera referred disparagingly to the correlations of Hobhouse, Wheeler, and Ginsberg, which he saw in a modern form in Murdock's mining of the Human Relations Area Files. Eggan referred back to Kroeber. Their joint insistence on comparison only after intensive field research within a region delineated in ecological and historical terms heralded a new political ethnography for the next generation.

Political Structures and Constitutionalism

In later years, British anthropology's own hagiography of the Radcliffe-Brown program found that its origins lay in the study of unilineal descent groups in three seminal works that appeared in the 1930s. These were Evans-Pritchard's early accounts of Nuer lineage organization (1940b), Raymond Firth's monograph on the Tikopia (1936), and Forde's work on the Yako of West Africa (1938, 1939). This co-optation of markedly different nuances in political anthropology was achieved by recognizing that in all three, descent rules and institutions were seen as belonging as much to the political domain as to kinship. The essays of Evans-Pritchard and Fortes in *African Political Systems* were then seen to be crystallizations of this achievement, and finally *Tribes Without Rulers* (1958) its culmination. Godfrey Lienhardt best captured the success of the paradigm:

> A good anthropological monograph looks as though it might have been produced without great difficulty, for it has already reduced to order the complications and problems presented by the mass of material collected piecemeal in day-to-day inquiries. Once the lineage principle in political structure has been elucidated, for example, it seems obviously possible as a basis for *political relations*. People who are politically organized on this principle, it will be remembered, unite with those nearer to them in their genealogical tree, at every point, against those who are more remote. *The elements in this political structure then are lineages (themselves conceptual)*, and the nature of the relationship between them is simply

expressed as 'fission and fusion'. That does not seem as though it should have been hard to discover.

But the members of any lineage may be individually widely dispersed, and in any case they usually bear no external mark of their lineage membership. *A lineage system* is not apparent to the eye. It *is a theory of political behaviour*, according to which lineage members act by a kind of rule-of-thumb knowledge, which the social anthropologist expresses in more comprehensive and abstract terms. He thus represents *the principles behind the political behaviour* of the people he has studied, and in doing so hopes to provide a model to which political behaviour in other societies may be referred. This is not achieved without systematic study and considerable comparative knowledge, and in fact the nature and importance of lineage segmentation were for long obscure to knowledgeable students of politics, whose only model of political structure was that of the state. (Lienhardt 1964:194–195, emphases added)

Three monographs by Evans-Pritchard, all of them political and all based on both field and library research, encapsulate Africanist political ethnography in this most vibrant era. These are *Witchcraft, Oracles and Magic Among the Azande* (1937), *The Nuer: A Description of the Modes of Livelihood and Political Institutions of a Nilotic People* (1940b), and *The Sanusi of Cyrenaica* (1949). The impact of each on the developing political subfield was very different. The methodological and political import of the first was not appreciated until some twenty years later, and then indirectly, through the processual analysis of Victor Turner (Chapter 5). The third remained less influential than it might have been, although the rebellious discerned its potential for changing the field around. *The Nuer* (1940b) and its unlikely-sounding "political" successor *Kinship and Marriage Among the Nuer* (1951) dominated the intellectual arena between 1940 and 1953 and, indeed, foretold the paradigmatic shift that was to bring it to a close.[14]

In 1940 Evans-Pritchard described the political system of the Nuer as relations within tribes, between tribes, and between the Nuer and all foreigners with whom they come into contact (since a timeless politi cal constitution is being described, I employ the ethnographic present tense here). Distinctions are made in the method of fighting in each case. The tribe, of which there are fifteen in Nuerland, is the largest political community. Within it, the use of force is governed by rules and conventions, and there is a recognition that compensation should be paid for homicide. Members of a tribe inhabit a recognizable territory with exclusive rights. The tribe and the area are named after a dominant clan, upon which a political aggregate is built up.

Within each tribal area, boxed into each other in a nesting fashion, are primary, secondary, and tertiary sections. The last named, equivalent to districts, are made up of groups of interacting villages. These sections are conceptualized and spoken of in genealogical terms following the structural arrangement of the dominant clan in each tribe. Thus the primary tribal section parallels the maximal lineage; the secondary section parallels the major lineage; the tertiary section parallels the minor lineage; and the village parallels the minimal lineage.

The political system mirrors the territorial and kinship structure. The political groups are corporate lineages of patrilineal kin, which thus recognize mutual rights and obligations *as a body*. Each comes into effective political action only in opposition to a comparable balancing group in the total kinship structure in a given social situation. In other words, if a fight starts, certain men are duty bound to rally to the support of the person involved, depending on their position in the total strucutre of the society.

Two tribal norms govern political behavior. One is the right of the corporate group to demand compensation for injury; the other is the obligation of the corporate group of the aggressor to pay compensation. Because of the high value placed on immediate vengeance as a principle, a face-saving institution in the form of the Man of the Earth allows a settlement to be negotiated.

The ecological restraints upon Nuer society demand that there should be peace and cooperation between tribes and within the tribe. Because of the need for a seasonal migration to a limited number of waterholes, members of Nuer villages—which are the chief interacting groups in the society—have to be on friendly relations with each other to cross neighboring tracts of land, share cattle camps, and distribute cattle.

There are also social restraints on violence. These include the principle of exogamy, the ready acceptance of strangers into a village group, clustering around a dominant lineage, the acceptance of the ritual sanctions of a common mediator, shared age-set membership, and joint attendance at feasts and ceremonies—all of which link the members of one village with members of others. Many of these ties extend even across tribal boundaries, but it is in neighboring villages that they function most effectively and are most necessary. Above the tertiary, or district, level, although the principles remain, practice may be moderated by expediency.

The right to form a vengeance group if compensation is not paid is recognized throughout the Nuer tribes. This group is made up, in principle, of the close agnatic kinsmen of the injured party, around whom rally their fellow villagers. The size of the group depends, as has been said, upon the relative positions of the aggressor and the victim in the total kinship structure. In practice, because of the distances involved, the groups are rarely drawn from above the level of the tertiary section. Beyond that level the feud is allowed to perpetuate, and the fission of sections may result.

Vengeance groups are restrained from carrying on a feud by the balance of force, by the many cross-cutting links between the individuals and groups involved, and by the mystical sanctions that uphold the ideals of mediation and compensation. Due to the practice of exogamy, both feuding groups have kinfolk living among the opposition. On the one hand, these people will put pressure on the villagers to pay or accept compensation quickly, and on the other hand, their very position will cause their own kin also to consider a peaceful solution to the potential feud. Ritual sanctions—such as the curse of the mother's brother, which will fall on a village *as a whole* and which is stronger than a father's curse; the pollution of the earth; and the dangers of sharing food vessels within the village—lead antagonists to avoid conflict. These sanctions are both ritually to be feared and socially and economically inconvenient, as normal village life and the interaction essential to the economy cannot go on while groups are in a state of feud.

The Man of the Earth, usually of a neutral lineage with respect to both parties in the dispute, acts as a mediator, the channel of communication necessary to restore peaceful relations. By giving sanctuary to the killer, he provides time for arbitration, and backed by ritual sanctions, he presides over the reconciliation, decision making, and agreement while also acting in an executive capacity in collecting and delivering an agreed number of cattle, which form the compensation.

Thus, although the right to vengeance is recognized, feuds can only be waged at the higher levels of tribal structure, where injuries need not be recompensed because the groups live far apart and peace is not necessary to preserve life. At lower levels, where there are more conflicting loyalties, the right of an agnatic group to vengeance is balanced by many cross-cutting ties, which encourage compensation and the maintenance of peace. In Herskovits's judgment, *The Nuer* marked Evans-Pritchard as "a major figure in the field of contemporary social theory"; no more important work in social analysis, he wrote, had appeared in recent years (1944:396). The first step had been taken along the road leading from the functional analysis of political organization to structuralism.

Structuralism has become a many-faceted phenomenon, and it is necessary to clarify the concepts and theory expounded in its name by the Oxbridge political anthropologists of the 1940s. Its adherents saw political structures as composed of the reciprocal relations between kin groups and territorial groups, between localized lineages and dispersed clans, and between local and wider communities. Their structural analysis of African political systems was an amalgam of three well-established ideas: (1) Durkheim's segmental societies, mechanical solidarity, and collective consciousness; (2) segmentary opposition, as in William Robertson Smith's *Lectures on the Religion of the Semites* (1894) and Gregory Bateson's *Naven* (1936), for example; and (3) "fusion and fission." One of the clearest statements of their application appeared in a paper Fortes presented at the American Anthropological Association meeting in Chicago in November 1951. In discussing the post-1940 contribution of African ethnography to anthropological theory, Fortes delineated its major achievement, the analysis of unilineal descent groups (UDGs). His argument (Fortes 1953) is presented at some length:

<<< The most important feature of UDGs is their corporate organization (Maine 1861; Weber 1947). The way a lineage system works depends on the kind of legal institutions found in a society; and this, we know, is a function of its political organization. Lineage organization is most developed in segmentary societies (Durkheim 1893) where the lineage is not only a corporate unit in the legal or jural sense but is also the primary political association. . . . All legal and political relations in the society take place in the context of the lineage system.

Lineage grouping is also the basis of local organization and political institutions in societies which have national government centered in kingship, administrative machinery, and courts of law. The primary emphasis, in these societies, is on the legal aspect of the lineage. The political structure of these societies was always unstable and this was due in considerable degree to internal rivalries arising out of divisions between lineages. The more centralized the political system the greater the tendency seems to be for the strength of descent groups to be reduced or for such corporate groups to be non-existent. Legal and political status are conferred by allegiance to the State not by descent, though rank and property may still be vested in descent lines. In centralized societies there is a clearer structural differentiation than in segmentary societies between an internal field of domestic relations (based on kinship and descent) and an external field of jural-political relations.

The characteristics of unilineal descent groups as political corporations (or interest groups) come out in monographs through discussions of (a) their assumed perpetuity in time which is a conservative or stabilizing factor in political relations, (b) the fact of jural equality that underlies lineage membership and which is manifested in collective responsibility in blood-vengeance, self-help and the feud, (c) their existence in a complementary relationship with or in opposition to like units; lineage membership is exclusive and exhaustive, (d) lineage genealogies as pseudo-history, as charters or dogmas making up constitutional theory, (e) a tendency for a society made up of corporate lineages to split into rival lineage factions and the countering of this tendency by an extension of the ideology to the widest political unit [the war/law definition of the political unit becomes critical here] by religious institutions and sanctions.

Fortes suggested that social anthropologists had begun to think of social structure in terms of levels of organization. We can investigate the total social structure at the level of local organization, at that of kinship, at the level of corporate group structure and government, and at that of ritual institutions. We see these levels are related to different collective interests, which are perhaps connected in some sort of hierarchy. And one of the problems of analysis and exposition is to perceive and state the fact that all levels of structure are simultaneously involved in every social relationship and activity. This restatement of what is commonly meant by the concept of integration has the advantage of suggesting how the different modes of social relationship distinguished in any society are interlocked with one another. It helps to make clear also how certain basic principles of social organization can be generalized throughout the whole structure of a primitive society, as for instance the segmentary principle among the Nuer and Tallensi.

What is the main methodological contribution of these studies? Fortes answered: the approach from the angle of political organization to what are traditionally thought of as kinship groups and organizations: We see that descent is fundamentally a jural concept . . . (Radcliffe-Brown 1935). Why descent rather than locality or some other principle forms the basis of these corporate groups is a question that needs more study. He suggested, however, the priority of descent over residence on the grounds that it was "legally superior." >>>

This was about as far as structural studies could go. The Radcliffe-Brown program called for attacking problems that were in a sense repetitious—the same structural problematic, different locales; the application of discerned principles or laws to each fresh body of field data. Researchers worked within the scientific tradition, attempting to adjust either existing theory or existing observations in order to bring the two into closer and closer agreement. Thomas Kuhn has pointed out the paradoxical nature of such a procedure: "Clearly . . . [it was] neither intended nor likely to produce fundamental discoveries or revolutionary changes in scientific theory. Yet—and this is the point—the ultimate effect of this tradition-bound work has invariably been to change the tradition. Again and again the continuing attempt to elucidate a currently received tradition has at last produced one of those shifts in fundamental theory, in problem field, and in scientific revolutions. At least for the scientific community as a whole, work within a well-defined and deeply ingrained tradition seems more productive of tradition-shattering novelties than work in which no similarly convergent standards are involved" (1977:234).

That this was indeed the case with the Oxbridge paradigm was proved by the superb reevaluation of the ethnography of Evans-Pritchard and Fortes by Michael G. Smith, Peter Worsley, Kathleen Gough, Aidan Southall, and Keith Hart in the years immediately following. Its overthrow was imminent as early as 1949, when Fortes's *The Web of Kinship Among the Tallensi* appeared. The book revealed, Leach suggested, "both the value and the limitation of structural concepts. What Dr. Fortes has really described is the moral code of the Tallensi with all its logical ramifications. . . . [H]e has shown, if only in passing, that the Tallensi do not observe their own moral rules" (1950:22). This is the route toward agency taken by political anthropology in the next decade.

An Asiatic Intervention:
Political Systems of Highland Burma

Before agency—or, as it came to be called in political anthropology, action theory—could emerge full-blown, the structural components had to be contested from *within* the paradigm. The publication of Edmund Leach's *Political Systems of Highland Burma* in 1954 was immediately heralded as revolutionary, in part because that is what Leach himself said it was and in part because Raymond Firth proclaimed it so. It was, in fact, a rebellion within the functional framework similar to that Gluckman initiated in his critique of Malinowski (Gluckman 1947a, 1949a).

In 1954 Leach was forty-four years old and had just left a readership at LSE to take up a lectureship at Cambridge. As early as 1940, after field research in Kurdistan, he began questioning anthropology's emphasis on social forms. The discipline's interest, he wrote, "tends to be so exclusively on the abstract concept of social structure, that the coexistence of a formal material structure is sometimes forgotten." He concluded that, since "structural pattern affects the interests of different individuals in widely different ways, . . . there can never be absolute conformity to the cultural norm, indeed the norm itself exists only as a stress of conflicting interests and divergent attitudes" (Leach 1940:62). Both Gluckman and Leach worked toward "the diachronic variant" (Banaji 1970) of functionalist theory, but their diachronics were cyclical rather than historical.

Political Systems of Highland Burma opens with the question of how Kachin identity was established among the congeries of hill peoples in a northeast frontier region of Burma. Leach discerned a shared ritual language among them, an ideological system of political categories. Given this commonality (a "grammar" of ritual action), he then interpreted local variations as elements of the political structure and historical change as a form of transformational logic. The resulting model of political change in the Burma highlands then described alternating cyclical change within a system in which ideological feedback tended to prevent crystallization into either of two polar types of political organization. The types—*gumsa* and *gumlao*—are both full of contradictions. Leach's explanation of political change from an egalitarian (*gumlao*, anarchic) to a ranked (*gumsa*, hierarchical) political society (to use the generic terminology that became common in America at this time) was ideological. At all times, groups and individuals were undertaking actions, for various reasons, that moved them away from their present political condition and toward its opposite. Leach lost his field notes and, as both his admirers and critics observed, his ethnography is very thin.[15]

Leach's book met with muted reviews at the time of its first appearance. While not all would have accepted Maurice Freedman's 1954 description of it as the most brilliant monograph to appear in recent years, its scholarly contribution was generally accepted. A few wondered what all the fuss was about. John F. Cady, for example, wondered why, when the Kachin situation seemed so easily understood on political and geographical grounds, Leach shrouded it in jargon and dwelt so much on the novelty of his analysis (1954). Most important for the development of political anthropology in the next decade, the first critics of Leach's monograph questioned the analytical significance Leach attached to individuals. He had suggested that individuals' choices are the result of "a conscious or unconscious wish to gain power" (Leach 1954:10); people (not simply the Kachin) "will seek to gain access to office or the esteem of their fellows which may lead them to office" (1954:10). This is pursued further in Chapter 5 when action theory is under consideration.

Every generation reappropriates its intellectual heritage in line with its own priorities, and critics of the next generation (Banaji 1970; Nugent 1982) showed that Leach failed to take into account both punitive colonialism and indigenous resistance in arriving at his timeless cyclical model of alternating political forms. This critique of political ethnography gradually became central to the subfield. What is most striking here is the artifice of the abstract theoretical problem that concerned him compared with the work on real political change being conducted *at the same time* by the RLI-Manchester anthropologists discussed shortly. Later, indeed, Leach himself did some rethinking on this score.[16] If the appearance in 1954 of *Political Systems of Highland Burma* did indeed mark "the beginning of a trend," as Leach himself believed (1964), it could only have been a trend away from the study of politics per se and toward the study of systems of ideas, language, thought, and myth.

Talal Asad (1979:615) struck even more deeply and even included Leach's critics in his broadside when he raised the post-Orientalist question of "how anthropological texts construct for a whole society, or even for a group of it, a total integrated semantic system, which defines for that society what its essential identity is." Further, he suggested that Leach's ideological definition of the Kachin system missed the question of "whether there were not specific political economic conditions which make certain rhetorical forms objectively possible and *authoritative*" (1979:616). Neither Leach nor his critics, Asad observed, made "any attempt to explore the systematic social connexions between historical forces and relations on the one hand, and the characteristic forms of discourse sustained or undermined by them on the other" (Asad 1979:616). Asad's comments, made in his 1979 Malinowski Lecture at LSE, rendered parenthetical almost the entire subject-matter of political anthropology for the twenty years following the publication of *Political Systems of Highland Burma*, the subject matter of the next chapter.

Uninformed Criticism and Informed Elegy

Never were American and British anthropology as far apart as in the years following the war. Considerable criticism of the British emanated from the United States on much more extensive grounds than that directed in the 1930s against the functionalism of Malinowski and Radcliffe-Brown. This may have been due in part to the British closure of ranks in the ASA, since few Americans were eligible for membership, but the indictment launched was intellectual. Murdock (1951) summed it up in six points: (1) the primacy attached to kinship; (2) fieldwork conducted solely in British territories; (3) academic tribalism (i.e., limited citation of works written by other than British colleagues); (4) a lack of history; (5) a lack, therefore, of an interest in change; and (6) indifference to psychology. All, he concluded, reflected the overwhelming influence of Radcliffe-Brown.

American reviewers of British work in political anthropology had been making similar charges for a long time. Elizabeth Bacon (1941), for example, commented on Leach's lack of reference to other studies of Asian chiefship in his *Social and Economic Organization of the Row-anduz Kurds* (1940), his failure to appreciate the roots in the past of the contemporary conflict he described, and his lack of citation of other than sociological literature on the Middle East. Cline's review (1942) of Evans-Pritchard's *The Political System of the Anuak of the Anglo-Egyptian Sudan* (1940a) was devastating.[17]

Firth responded (1951b) to Murdock's criticism. Several of his remarks indirectly suggested the existence of an alternative, even an oppositional, anthropology in Britain. As a non-Africanist, he supported many of Murdock's strictures. "Even in the field of lineage analysis," he noted, "more consideration of the material of Gifford and other Oceanic investigators might have led the Africanists to pay more heed earlier to definitions of such groups in terms of the rights exercised in residence, land use and status" (1951b:475). As one who favored the analysis of social organization over social structure, Firth included in his own genealogy not only Durkheim, Frazer, and Morgan but Marett—a significant indicator of an alternative to structuralism, as we shall see. Nevertheless, Firth remained defensive of Radcliffe-Brown and elaborated on his relationship to Malinowski, Murdock's erstwhile colleague at Yale. Of them he wrote:

> Viewed very broadly, the contrast can be epitomized from the aesthetic angle as the difference between the romantic and the classical modes of thought. With Malinowski, form was less important than content; the realities of human behavior were what mattered. He aimed at reduction of behavior to rule, but he considered that all the diversities of the human creature should be taken as far as possible into account. He sought for wide generalizations, but not for their formal expression. He was prepared to find the beauty of his scientific propositions in irregularity, if regularity meant forcing his knowledge or his imaginative insight into an artificial mold. Hence his impatience with the neat verbal definition, his inclusive treatment of the notion of law, his insistence on the elementary family as the basis of kin group structure.
>
> With Radcliffe-Brown, this has seemed too imprecise, a blurring of patterns, a lack of that restraint necessary in science as well as in art. To him proportion has seemed of primary importance, and this has implied that social relations should be arranged in order. The notion of system has been paramount, to the neglect if necessary of the full content of phenomenal reality. (Firth 1951b:480)

Closing ranks against American critics, Firth thus argued that "the approaches of Malinowski and Radcliffe-Brown are at bottom complementary rather than antagonistic. This has come to be realized by those who are not afraid to be called eclectic. But the contrast between them has affected British social anthropology deeply for more than twenty years, and continues to serve as an index, even symbol, of other differences" (1951b:480). These other differences were, indeed, about to bring about a major paradigmatic shift in political anthropology (Chapter 5).

Two notable attempts were made during this period to maintain a transatlantic dialogue, one by Robert Lowie, who was invited to give the RAI's Huxley Memorial Lecture for 1948, and the other by Daryll Forde in his presidential address to the same body. Lowie called his talk "Some Aspects of Political Organization Among the American Aborigines" and, by direction and indirection, contrasted American studies of states and stateless societies with the "illuminating studies on African politics edited by Drs. Fortes and Evans-Pritchard" (1948a:11). In his introduction he gave a nod to French scholarship in Africa and acknowledged the value of viewing such terms as *the state, law, government, political*, and *sovereignty* as implying "the control of physical force so far as a given society recognizes it as legitimate." He was, again, international in his citation, attributing this usage to Weber, Radcliffe-Brown, and Thurnwald. Lowie then took it upon himself to analyze trends toward state evolution in the Americas.

Like Herskovits earlier, Lowie chose not to focus on the forms of stateless societies but on the processes whereby they might or might not be integrated into states. He pinned his argument to political demography, indirectly contesting Fortes's and Evans-Pritchard's statement that population density had nothing to do with state formation.[18] He then documented and classified the range of coercive authority adumbrated in American aboriginal politics, drawing attention with self-conscious teleology to "sundry gropings towards the establishment of political authority, which, however, lose themselves in blind alleys" (1948a:21). A ninety-four-item list of references (the longest surely ever provided for a Huxley lecture and the longest ever published in *Man*) not only documented his case but exposed the British to a vast literature in political anthropology from Dorsey to Steward.

The second attempt to bridge the Atlantic void—Daryll Forde's presidential address to the RAI in the same year—had a dual focus. First he took up his running fight with Firth over the future, advocating a return to the grand vision of Tylor, Huxley, and Spencer in which anthropology was an integrative, holistic discipline. He then argued for the ecological approach, showing how specific interpretations by Morgan, Malinowski, and Radcliffe-Brown would have been enriched had they paid attention to the relation of material techniques. But, he observed, "Marx's contemporary emphasis on the importance of techniques as determinants of economic relations, of political and even ethical systems seems to have evoked little response in Anthropology" (Forde 1948:3).

Knowing his audience, Forde chose to illustrate the importance of ecology by referring to "our" understanding of unilineal kinship groups. He referred to a fundamental "lack of empirical study of the processes which brought such corporate groups of kin into being and of the factors underlying the operation of unilineal principles of succession. The first modern advances in this field were made by Gifford and Steward in their studies of the structure and ecological context of village communities and bands among the peoples of Southern California and the Plateau-Basin region of western North America. It was from this work that the importance of ecological determinants of the small lineage of personally linked unilineal kin became apparent" (Forde 1948:7). Forde then went on to describe, in considerable detail, the processes by which a centralized state brought about the atrophy of the wider system of unilineal grouping, drawing on Gluckman's ethnography of the Lozi (1941) and his own knowledge of West Africa. "It is not suggested," he concluded, "that political centralization and economic specialization are themselves simple products of local ecological conditions. . . . [T]hey point to the significance of the prior operation of other ecological processes elsewhere from which technical, economic or political penetration of a new area follows. Thus, ecological factors always affect cultural patterning and social organization whatever the other specific elements in the situation. They do so because culture and social organization are to a significant degree adaptive mechanisms whereby aggregates of human beings adjust their behaviour to the material situation in which they find themselves" (Forde 1948:9).

In the course of his address, Forde digressed, as he put it, to make a forceful statement that owed a great deal to his transatlantic cultural novitiate and his friendship with V. Gordon Childe. It sounded personal, but his words might better be viewed as the voice of a past generation that had lost out in the struggle to make British anthropology an historical discipline: diffusionists, cultural archaeologists, political economists, and cultural historians. Most important, it sounded the death knell for Durkheimian sociology as it was perpetrated in the Radcliffe-Brown program.[19]

At the time, both Lowie's and Forde's words fell on deaf ears in spite of their labored attempts to speak the common language of unilineal descent groups. *Tribes Without Rulers* (Middleton and Tait 1958)—

which, as we have seen, was portrayed as the last word on unilineal descent groups and as a culminating achievement within political anthropology—completely ignored their contribution. Orthodoxy reigned and it was as if they had never spoken.

CENTRAL AFRICA AND THE MANCHESTER SCHOOL

The extent to which both Robert Lowie and Daryll Forde accepted the arena of discourse defined by the Oxbridge structural functionalists is striking. Neither referred to an equally stimulating body of field inquiry that had developed in central Africa and that would have been more to their liking, particularly since American ethnology was quite well known to its practitioners (Kuper 1982; Colson 1985a). The dialectic of the changing field situation and the contradictions in Oxbridge theory bred an early opposition that became institutionalized in 1942 in a newly founded department of anthropology at Manchester University in the English midlands. This developed in three phases, two of which are dealt with in this chapter. The first (1937–1942) centered on the Rhodes-Livingstone Institute of Social Studies (RLI) in Northern Rhodesia.[20] This was established on the initiative of the governor of the protectorate, Sir Hubert Winthrop Young, and in spite of the lack of interest and even positive opposition on the part of both the Colonial Office and local settlers and industrialists (Brown 1973). The institute, housed in Africa and not attached to any university, seemed almost destined to produce a sustained alternative to Oxbridge political anthropology.

A second phase (1942–1954) began in Northern Rhodesia and ended at Manchester with Max Gluckman ensconced in the chair. Here he embarked on the training of the next generation of researchers into political problems. The essays he wrote between 1940 and 1954 were collected into one volume, *Order and Rebellion in Tribal Africa* (1963), which had an autobiographical introduction. A school was in the making.

Phase 1: Colonial Controversies and the RLI

The first director of the RLI was Godfrey Wilson. His appointment was controversial. Among the reasons for it were his "wide outlook, often alleged to have been absent from colonial anthropology; his refusal to see any significant differences between social anthropology, sociology, and history; and his determination to bring economic and administrative factors into his analysis of central African society" (Brown 1973:187). Wilson's central African anthropology also owed a great deal to the Depression, which impressed upon him the value of Marxism for understanding industrial capitalism. Here, however, the industrial setting was the copperbelt of central Africa. Unlike Marx and Engels in Manchester, however, Wilson's devout Christianity and pacifism led him not to radical political analysis but to scientific pedestrianism. He instituted a three-pronged research program in Northern Rhodesia: in the industrial copperbelt, among migrant laborers, and in the impoverished rural areas. All three trod delicate ground. Six miners had been killed by police action in 1935, and seventeen were killed by the military when strikes by black and white miners broke out in 1940. Opposition to the institute's politically sensitive research led to calls for Wilson's resignation. It was suggested that his stance as a conscientious objector might affect native morale and interfere with the military recruiting underway for the war effort. Wilson left in April 1941.[21]

At least three themes in Wilson's work had implications for political anthropology. First, he stressed the interconnectedness of countryside and town. This encouraged a focus on regions rather than particular African tribes and tribal locations, and the movement of men and women between towns and rural homelands in response to both the labor demands of the protectorate and their own social and economic needs. Related issues of social control and public administration were clearly spelled out. Second, he discussed the place of Northern Rhodesia within a global economic system. Thus, in his "Essay on the Economics of Detribalization in Northern Rhodesia," Wilson wrote of its Africans not as tribesmen but as "members of a huge worldwide community . . . their lives . . . bound up at every point with the events of its history. . . . Their standard of living now depends on economic conditions in Europe, Asia and America, to which continents their labor has become essential. Their political development is largely decided in the Colonial Office and on the battlefields of Europe, while hundreds of their onetime separate tribes now share a single destiny. They have entered a heterogeneous world stratified into classes and divided into states, and so find themselves suddenly transformed into the peasants and unskilled workers of a nascent nation state" (1941.12). Finally Wilson's writing embodied the sense of historic change taking place in the industrializing country, almost a sense of inevitability: "In the structure of Northern Rhodesia (as of the world at large) radical social contradictions are evident today; and . . . in consequence, that structure must be changed, in one way or the other, so as to resolve them. This necessity is not a moral necessity; it is objective and material" (1941:82). In short, Wilson attempted, consciously or unconsciously, a marriage of Marx and Malinowski. Wilson's work was castigated by those of his contemporaries who were unwilling to have anthropology address social problems. Particularly damaging to his reputation, certainly in Northern Rhodesia if not in the academy, was the use made of it in Leonard Barnes's book *Soviet Light on the Colonies* (1944).[22] Wilson died in 1944.

Phase 2: From Field to Academy

In 1942 Max Gluckman succeeded Godfrey Wilson as director of the RLI. When he left in 1947 he was banned from returning to Northern Rhodesia because he had helped African politicians who opposed plans for a federation of their country with Nyasaland and settler-dominated Southern Rhodesia. The institute's Seven-Year Program, as it developed, combined Wilson's agenda with an elaboration of interests drawn from Gluckman's South African experience. Most salient were a predilection for seeing anthropology address contemporary problems; a recognition of global forces impinging upon and shaping particular local situations; attention to conflict between groups; an appreciation of the role of the environment; the heuristic primacy in causal explanation of economic, and to a lesser extent political, factors; and finally, the use of a dialectical method.

Born in Johannesburg in 1911, Gluckman as an undergraduate at Witwatersrand University was considerably influenced by Winifred Hoernle—who had him read Maine, Morgan, and Robertson Smith—and Isaac Schapera, who lectured on law (H. Kuper 1984). He then went to Oxford as a Rhodes scholar. Wilson appointed Gluckman as a specialist in political institutions. His chapter on "The Kingdom of the Zulu" was about to appear in *African Political Systems,* and he was appointed to make a similar study of the Barotse—"how the political organization . . . came to be what it is" was the way Gluckman phrased it (Brown 1979:528). His first RLI publication, *Analysis of a Social Situation in Modern Zululand* (1958) [or The Bridge, as it is familiarly known] became one of the methodological sourcebooks of political ethnography in the twentieth century. Situational analysis and a concern for process march side by side; contradiction, cooperation, and conflict run coterminously through its pages. "The whole is achieved in an analogous manner to Marx's *18th Brumaire* and Goffman's *Encounters,* by theoretically informed, detailed direct observation" (Frankenberg 1982:4).

The starting point of the analysis in The Bridge was a series of events Gluckman recorded on a single day in January 1938. He described the car journey to the ceremonial opening of a new bridge. Photographs and a sketch map portray the scene. As the morning wears on, Zulu assemble at the north end of the bridge, officials (Europeans and Africans) at the south end. Speeches are made, songs sung, and salutes exchanged. Led by singing Zulu warriors, the chief native commissioner (a European) drives his official car across the bridge, followed by others. They then ceremoniously turn around and return to partake of refreshments. The Europeans have tea and cake. A European—but a missionary, and a woman—carries the same food to the Zulu king. Other Zulu are feasting in groups, Christians and missionaries apart from the rest. Gluckman and his companions leave the celebrating, which was to last all day.

These seven pages of narrative description were followed by twenty pages of close analysis—situational analysis, as it came to be called (Van Velsen 1967). Gluckman analyzed Zulu social structure as a functioning unit in a temporary equilibrium. As he pointed out, it is of fundamental importance to recognize that the factor maintaining this equilibrium—the superior force of the white group—did not appear in the analysis (1958:25). Unequal opposition between the two "color-groups," Africans and whites, pervaded all activities and all institutions, yet they were bound together by conflict and cooperation. An individual's membership in a particular group in a particular situation was determined by the motives and values influencing him in that situation. Individuals could thus live coherent lives by situational selection from a medley of contradictory values, ill-assorted beliefs, varied interests, and techniques (Gluckman 1958:26). Gluckman remained at the RLI until 1947, when he returned to Oxford for two years before becoming the first head of the newly established Department of Social Anthropology and Sociology at Manchester in 1949, a position he held until 1965.

The Wilson-Gluckman Program

The research program initiated by Wilson at the Rhodes-Livingstone Institute and continued by Gluckman at Manchester University had five outstanding features: (1) a modern problem orientation, (2) a global dimension, (3) a bias toward conflict and conflict revolution, (4) a focus on the economy and the environment, and (5) a dialectical method. During the period in which the RLI anthropologists were conducting field research in Northern Rhodesia, the formal political system of the colonial protectorate consisted of the colonial administration, responsible ultimately to the Colonial Office in Britain, where sovereignty lay in the Crown; local government, in which African chiefs and headmen participated; and as independence neared, national political parties embracing both indigenous Africans and white settlers. All these entered into the Manchester studies, as well as what Bailey later came to call "parapolitical" systems: union politics, village factionalism, competitive struggles for leadership, and resistance movements.

The uneasy relationship between the colonial administration and local politics was encapsulated for Gluckman in the intercalary position of the village headmen and the interstitial roles that developed within a changing political economy (1949b, 1963, 1968). Weberian models of bureaucracy, in his view, distracted attention from the realpolitik of power in which the headmen's dilemma, "ground between the upper millstone of a colonial government and the lower of their own people," was set (Lienhardt 1964:86). There were several ways his initial analysis of the problematic could go, and in the succeeding years political anthropologists pursuing the problem took many tacks. Just as in his earlier analysis (1960) of Shaka, the Zulu monarch caught between European intruders and a dispersed following of pastoral warriors, Gluckman now resorted to psychological explanations. Later he offered an explanation in terms of a conflict of values.

Lloyd Fallers of the University of Chicago developed the intercalary theme further (1955), although he chose to credit Weber rather than Gluckman with impetus in this direction. Later, the concept of intercalary roles (paralleling Nadel and Wolf's vision of the interstitial, as we shall see) did much to make Mancunian perspectives hegemonic in political anthropology in the 1960s and thus, inevitably, to subject it to critical reevaluation. Adam Kuper, on the basis of his own study of Kalahari village politics, suggested that the modern village headman's position was not necessarily as untenable as Gluckman's analysis suggested, because he underestimated the officeholder's room for maneuver (Kuper 1970b), an argument following Lucy Mair's long-standing concern with local bureaucracies and local politicians (1965b). Had Gluckman used the extended case method, Kuper suggested, he would not have found the headman as hamstrung as he had supposed. My own analysis of subaltern officeholders in colonial Uganda suggested that Kuper's focus was overly directed toward the local situation of the headman and 'his people.' The rapid turnover of colonial chiefs in Teso suggested that the officeholder there was extremely vulnerable, perhaps because his function was less one of maintaining law and order than of mobilizing labor and mediating agricultural change (Vincent 1971, 1982). Martin Southwold's Buganda analysis (1964), which supported Gluckman's interpretation, suggested a greater need to focus on differences among colonial states rather than among headmen.

Elizabeth Colson, Gluckman's successor as director at the RLI, had earlier drawn attention to the "Janus-faced" native authorities among the Plateau Tonga and provided a sophisticated analysis of politics within their ranks. Above all, however, she explained that, "surprisingly enough," the system worked, because of the administration's ultimate sanction and a court system that rested partly on the indigenous political structure (1948:92–98).

Important for our present purpose was the significance of the RLI's focus on the modern colonial officeholder rather than on the reconstruction of an historically past tribal authority. The meaning of *custom* and *tradition* in the modern setting were the subject of inquiry, not themselves explanatory scientific concepts. In this the legacy of Rivers, Marett, and Malinowski was most apparent. Here again the most sophisticated statement came from Colson. "It is . . . over a hundred years," she noted, "since [Tonga] indigenous organization could operate undisturbed from foreign attack or from foreign control. The Tonga may once have had a more complex structure which perished during the period of the raids. I am not prepared therefore to argue that the system which I am now presenting was workable in the days before the European peace established a general community of law. But it is the system which the Tonga today conceive as their indigenous one and which therefore presumably conditions their response to the new system introduced by European administration" (1948:86). Such a perception of the relation between indigenous and modern political organization in sub-Saharan Africa stood in stark contrast to the political reconstructions of the Oxbridge school.

Structural contradictions expressed in rituals of rebellion, revolution, and civil war continued to engage Gluckman throughout his career, the inherited antithesis, perhaps, of his much-loved research into law. He later deplored the way in which the dominance of "lineage theory" had distracted "young Africanists" in the 1950s from examining the nature of civil war in the politics they were discussing. He urged them—Fallers, Southall, and Barnes, in particular—to "drop this preoccupation with lineage theory which can blind one to the problems of state power" (1963:31).

The Seven-Year Plan, introduced in 1943, set out to study the colonial protectorate of Northern Rhodesia as a rapidly changing, industrializing society in which problems of urbanization, migration, and labor drew attention to its innate tensions and stresses. It had several features in common with Steward's design for the anthropological study of Puerto Rico as a modern society but was essentially different in its selection of particularly stressful political situations for close analysis. The plan distinguished six types of region on the basis of whether subsistence or cash cropping predominated, whether labor was imported or extracted, and proximity to the line of rail. It pictured the relationship between town and countryside as asymmetrical: the focus was on land tenure, labor, depopulation, and markets in the rural areas and on migration, problems of order, and unionization in the urban setting. It treated labor migration and urbanization in each of the sample studies as independent variables and described their effects on kinship organization, political values, and religious beliefs. As Richard Werbner noted in 1984, both anthropologists and historians have come to appreciate the controlled comparison that resulted. It provided a corrective to the application of such sociological megaconcepts as "peasantization" and "proletarianization." The RLI survey of Lambaland in 1946, for example, focused on a region of postfamine resettlement. Within this spatial unit, researchers surveyed twenty-seven villages and collected quantitative data on demography, settlement, and social organization. They grouped the villages into three areas, characterized by differences in resettlement patterns, soil types, and agricultural potential. Relocation was problematic in the new area because the people resisted government-imposed rules on contouring and planting.

Three aspects of the work broke with the assumptions then prevailing in Africanist political ethnography. First, the unit of analysis was a region and its villages, not a tribe. Second, kinship was taken to be a contingent factor, not a primary one. Third, the village centered on its headman, not a traditional community, proved to be the characteristic feature of the region. The headman, recall, was a modern functionary introduced by the colonial administration. (Gluckman, in effect, won for political ethnography the battle Sol Tax lost in Mesoamerica to have the contemporary administrative unit recognized as a political unit.)

Reception: Political Anthropology on the Ramparts

Gluckman himself thought that very little of the work of the RLI anthropologists was read by the administrative officers it was written to inform. If their view of Audrey Richards and him, quoted by Brown (1979) from confidential memoranda, is anything to go by, anti-Semitism and anti-intellectualism would go a long way toward accounting for this.[23] Wilson's and Gluckman's history of questionable loyalty to the Crown-at-War and their (and later fieldworkers') support for African political opposition to the proposed federation of the two Rhodesias with Nyasaland would have tainted their judgment in the eyes of conservative settlers and administrative officers.

Within the academy, the distinctive ethnographies of the Manchester school won them professorships and chairs at newly built provincial universities in Britain and in the Commonwealth. None attained appointment to Oxbridge or London, except at the School of African and Oriental Studies. Adam Kuper's slighting reference in his *Anthropology and Anthropologists: The British School* hardly reflects their impact in more adventurous and relevant domains: political anthropology in the United States, central African historiography, and above all, the independent nation of Zambia. Within a few years, the Manchester style of political ethnography would bridge the gap that earlier Africanist studies and Oxbridge political structuralism had done so much to create. In short order it became the mainstream of political anthropology as a specialized subfield on both sides of the Atlantic.

LOCALITY, REGION, AND STATE

While the study of political organization by British anthropologists was becoming both more specifically focused on kinship and blood and more abstract in its attention to political constitutions, the anthropological study of political matters in the United States was becoming both more broadly focused on territory and on earthly domains and more oblique in its attention to the specifically political. Out of the first was born a recognized subfield of political anthropology; in the second, the subfield lay buried.

The strength and intensity of the sociological contribution in Britain was partly attributable to its concentration on the colonial peoples of sub-Saharan Africa rather than upon the great civilizations of China and India. This was the kinship-centered political anthropology of "tribal peoples"—envisaged as having an existence apart from the colonial territory in which they were to be found—that Adam Kuper called the "never-never school of political anthropology." In the United States, on the other hand, one legacy of the nation's military and financial investments throughout the globe was the consolidation of anthropological research throughout its unsung empire. This challenged it to move beyond Native Americans, its own "tribal peoples."

The resulting divergence of British and American anthropologies of politics was in marked contrast to their collaboration in acculturation studies in the prewar years. One key figure who might have held the two schools accountable to each other, Malinowski, followed his own predictions for the advancement of his discipline into formerly colonial peasant Mesoamerica, crossing the Atlantic to join the Yale department and, between 1937 and his death in 1942, carrying out field research in Mexico. None of his British colleagues or students followed him.

In practice, British and American anthropologists did much the same thing in their fieldwork. Most Africanist ethnographers conducted their systematic research in quite small villages and then generalized their findings to an abstract homogeneous "tribal" society to which, they maintained, the villagers belonged. The more sophisticated work of some—S. F. Nadel's *Black Byzantium* being the outstanding example—could equally well be viewed as a study in "locality, region and state" rather than as a somewhat anomalous LSE ethnography of a Nigerian tribe.

Political Organization in Nontribal Societies

The most visible American academic activity of the period from 1940 to 1953 lay in the culmination of Redfield's nomothetic endeavors to characterize "folk society." His contribution was subsequently dismantled on both ethnographic and epistemological grounds, but it contained elements that decisively influenced political anthropology in the generation that followed and that are still unquestioned by scholars in cognate fields. We may characterize it as a continuum from "tribal" to "peasant" political anthropology, distinguishing a subspecies that still has not been succinctly delineated and characterized to this day.

The anthropological study of peasant political organization began as the study of folk society. Redfield first delineated the concept in a lecture to Chicago undergraduates and then published it in Spanish in Mexico in 1942. The editors of the *American Journal of Sociology* solicited it for republication in 1947. Of special interest to us now is an excerpt from Redfield's original course material, published for the first time in 1962.

The "folk society" is a mental construct, an ideal type with several distinctive characteristics. It is

> small, isolated, nonliterate, and homogeneous with a strong sense of group solidarity. . . . Behavior is traditional, spontaneous, uncritical, and personal; there is no legislation or habit of experiment and reflection for intellectual ends. Kinship, its relationships and institutions, are the type categories of experience and the familial group is the unit of action. The sacred prevails over the secular; the economy is one of status rather than of the market. In a 'folk society' people know each other well and remain in long association with each other; there is little communication with outsiders. They have a strong sense of 'we' against 'they'. There is no marked division of labor and society members consume what they produce. Technology is simple and there is little change.

Behavior in the folk society is highly conventional, custom fixes the rights and duties of individuals, and knowledge is not critically examined or objectively and systematically formulated; but it must not be supposed that primitive man is a sort of automaton in which custom is the mainspring. It would be as mistaken to think of primitive man as strongly aware that he is constrained by custom. Within the *limits set by custom* there is invitation to excel in performance. There is lively competition, a sense of opportunity, and a feeling that what the culture moves one to do is well worth doing. (1947:300, emphasis added)

At this stage in his thinking, Redfield was clearly characterizing what in other circles was called "primitive society," and he drew on the ethnography of hunting and gathering bands—the Andaman Islanders, Californian Indians, Australian aborigines, and Trobrianders, among others—to document his presentation. He spoke of "tribal groups that still remain around the edges of expanding civilization" (1947:306) and drew on his own Yucatan field data to discuss the degree to which "folk" characteristics existed in different communities. The less isolated and more heterogeneous communities were more secular and individualistic. In this way he presented an argument about the disorganization of culture as civilization expanded. He owed an intellectual debt to sociologists Tönnies, Durkheim, and Sumner,[24] and he used global ethnography for apt illustration. The diagram Redfield used to accompany his lecture on 'folk society' is reproduced in Figure 4.1. It illustrated some of the ways in which, historically, "primitive societies had become transformed into different types of societies" (1962:253). It is a little unfair to use as a basis for discussion a blackboard diagram intended only for use in the classroom and possibly not for publication, but as an historical document Redfield's diagram provides rewarding insights into his vision of anthropology and his conceptualization of the actualities of the world around him, including—or excluding—its political realities.

Redfield's categorization of societal types was global; moreover, he saw their production as the result of three dynamic processes: conquest, urbanization, and migration. Each produced distinct forms of society. He considered urbanization to be clearly the nature of things, with tribal peoples becoming transformed into peasants and city dwellers. Some of these might, through occupational specialization, remain "quasi-folk," backwoodsy frontiersmen. More would migrate to become pioneer or immigrant communities in alien lands. Where conquest ensued, aboriginal peoples might be assimilated, colonized, or encapsulated; some might then, in a next phase, similarly become

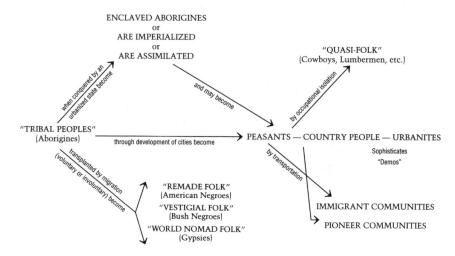

Figure 4.1.   Robert Redfield's diagram of the folk process

(from Margaret Park Redfield 1962:253)

peasants or city dwellers. Those tribal peoples transplanted by migration appeared destined to coexist with peasants as marginal folk. Redfield considered African-Americans, Bush Negroes, and Gypsies marginal. (This is an interesting reflection of his view of the place of African-Americans in American society in the 1930s). In his publications Redfield was taxonomical, and the processes generating the typology he suggested were nowhere explored. His classroom diagram provides a window on his thinking.

Major critiques of Redfield's "folk society" model appeared almost immediately (Tax 1941; Murdock 1943; Herskovits 1948; Steward 1950; Lewis 1951; Miner 1952; Sjoberg 1952; Mintz 1953a). Horace Miner, a Chicago-trained anthropologist then at the University of Michigan, had done fieldwork in Tombouctou, and he chose to comment on the effect of technological change on societal forms, particularly the introduction of the plow, which disrupted group solidarity, fostered individualism, and led to unbridled competition—a very Mainean observation. He saw culture change as introducing new conflicts, and he concurred with Herskovits (1948) in regretting Redfield's focus on form rather than process. His highest praise for the folk-urban continuum was that it provided a framework within which various theoretical fields might be integrated to provide greater understanding of the nature and course of culture change. He did not raise the question of alternative frameworks already in existence.

That is exactly what Gideon Sjoberg did in delineating feudal society in contradistinction to Redfield's "folk." Sjoberg considered the neglect of feudalism prior to this in the United States understandable; the current focus of attention was, he believed, due to the political changes that had placed the United States in a position of world leadership, engaged in "reform" programs in many "backward" countries. He did not suggest that the idea of the folk society should be discarded but that its "indiscriminate application" should be questioned. The model might fit so-called primitive or tribal societies but not complex societies in Asia, Europe, or—dare he say it—Latin America. Distinctions between "folk" and "peasant," "literate" and "nonliterate" societies were already widely recognized. The latter could better be understood if the concept of "feudal society" were adopted. Sjoberg based his comments largely on historical materials from China, Japan, India, and France.

Feudalism is predicated on a large peasant population that produces a surplus to support towns—political, religious, and commercial centers—in which reside the most important members of the elite. "The ruling stratum," Sjoberg wrote, "is at the very least composed of a governmental bureaucracy and a priestly and/or scholar group. In addition, a nobility, a landlord group, and militarists or warriors, among others, may be present in various combinations" (1952:233). A small minority is supported by and "exploits" a large subservient populace, which passively accepts its role. A closer examination of the ruling minority is essential. As noted, political functionaries are one of the constituent elements. Aside from exerting legal control, they exact some kind of tribute from the peasantry. This serves to perpetuate the elite and support such groups as an army, which protects the society from external aggression. Political functionaries are recruited from the upper class and thus reflect an inherently conservative tradition that preserves the status quo (1952:233). Sjoberg then went on to discuss the scholars and priests, landlords, merchants, and military. He noted that peasants are not the only components of the masses; craftsmen, artisans, and guilds complement them.

Sjoberg clearly considered many societies described by anthropologists to be feudal. No internal evidence suggests that he viewed feudalism as an historical phase in the development of capitalism, and he wrote mostly of China and India. He derived his analysis of political change from the impact of Dutch and British colonialism on Asian societies (Boeke 1948; Furnivall 1948). Feudal-like structures tended to resist industrial urbanization, whereas folk or primitive societies rapidly disintegrated in response to the same process. This is due to the efforts of the elite to survive and preserve feudal traits even within colonial situations.

Sidney Mintz's critique of Redfield's folk society offered yet another conceptual alternative: the rural proletarian community.[25] He drew attention to the incompleteness of Redfield's ethnography of Yucatan, on which so much of his view of folk society was based, noting that he had completely ignored the existence there of vast henequen (sisal) plantations, the backbone of the region's economy. These rural industrial organizations surely played some part in the agrarian society, and they certainly threw into confusion Redfield's urban-rural and industrial-agricultural polarities.

Mintz drew on his own Puerto Rican field data to characterize the rural proletarian community in which

> the vast majority of people is landless, propertyless (in the sense of productive property), wage-earning, store-buying (the stores being a chain owned by the corporation, with few competitors), corporately employed, and standing in like relationship to the main source of employment. These rural proletarian communities might also be considered class isolates, in the sense that economic alternatives to wage labor in the sugarcane industry, other than via migration to the United States mainland, are very scarce. The working people stand in like relationship to the productive apparatus but are also interacting in reciprocal relationships with members of higher classes (such as the managers). The rural proletarian community associated with the plantation emerges as isolated in a very different way from that of the folk society. In the latter the isolation is primarily geographic, and the society can be discussed almost completely in terms of itself. In the former the isolation is socioeconomic. The rural proletarians form a part-society, and they are members of a class which can be analyzed adequately only with reference to other classes. (Mintz 1951:139–140)

Mintz then summarized the similarities between rural proletarian communities and folk societies before returning to those features that made it more like the urban end of Redfield's folk-urban continuum. This meant a return to class and capitalism. As Mintz observed:

> The same forces which made of its people a class isolate also revamped and reorganized its way of life. The plantation exists to satisfy needs outside the local milieu—the national or international market. In the local setting it requires for its successful operation a large working-class population; a monopoly over the land; a standard medium of exchange (money); standardized rates of pay; a purely impersonal set of relationships between employed managers and employed workers; means of maintaining control and discipline over the labor force; . . . and the efficient regulation of work procedures, usually involving the reduction of tasks to their simplest

essentials, any job being easily learned, and any laborer therefore easily replaced. In short, the successful plantation requires all those features of economic operation which have come to be called rationalized, or "high capitalistic." (Mintz 1951:142)

Mintz then called for a typology of plantations, taking into account both form and process, and derived from field studies and careful historical research. Mintz's work and that of his colleague Eric Wolf were later to establish a new paradigm for the political analysis of agrarian society, proletarian and peasant. This was originally sparked by a lecture Redfield delivered in Chicago in 1954 on "The Peasant's View of the Good Life" (1956). This stimulated a "symposium-by-correspondence" (Silverman 1983:11) among nine scholars which led ultimately to the replacement of the "folk society" concept with that of "peasant society."

Idealism Revisited

Oscar Lewis's *Life in a Mexican Village: Tepoztlán Restudied* was recognized at the time of its publication in 1951 as signifying "the crumbling of an old shibboleth: the assumption that a newcomer should not check or criticize another anthropologist's work, because such handling somehow seemed to impugn the veracity of the first work and somehow stigmatize the whole guild" (Cline 1952:212). Lewis was, in fact, encouraged to work in Tepoztlán by Redfield himself, the assumption being that the earlier work could be simply and easily updated. But Lewis was not a student of Strong and Lesser for nothing.

Lewis's contribution to the study of politics has gone largely unrecognized, perhaps because he flaunted so many anthropological canons. His fieldwork was conducted in an idiosyncratic fashion, drawing on teams of investigators, working closely with local intellectuals and experts (who usually did not know the language of his informants), and above all, preferring a problem focus to the classic monographic inquiry. Lewis saw himself as engaged in reporting ethnographic facts, not in giving way to the cultural idealism first of Ruth Benedict (in his Blackfoot reevaluation) and then of Redfield (in Tepoztlán). His career between 1941 and 1966 reflected the path that political anthropology itself had taken, from the study of tribal societies to peasantries and thence to complex urban settings. An interlude with the Ford Foundation in India (discussed in the next chapter) that followed immediately on the publication of his Tepoztlán reevaluation was innovative in shifting American interest from Mesoamerica to South Asia. For most of his life Lewis was a well-funded field researcher; he held academic posts only for short periods and never at what were then major universities. He trained no graduate students, and his problem orientation prevented his contribution from being recognized until the very end of his career. Lacking an institutional base, Lewis's contribution to political anthropology remained inchoate, yet today any reader of his collected essays (1970) must appreciate very clearly that it is the work of a skilled political ethnographer and an acute political analyst.[26]

Words written in retrospect expressed most clearly his inherently political philosophy. Lewis was recalling his restudy of Tepoztlán and Redfield's suggestion that their respective findings depended on the hidden questions that guided their research. Redfield asked, What do these people enjoy? Lewis asked, What do these people suffer from? "It seems to me," Lewis wrote, "that concern with what people suffer from is much more important than the study of enjoyment because it lends itself to more productive insights into the human condition, the dynamics of conflict, and the forces for change" (1970:252).

Not surprisingly, therefore, Lewis found in his Mexican ethnography that both local and national politics were of extreme concern to the people of Tepoztlán. Moreover, in focusing on the individual and the family rather than the barrio, Lewis found intense conflict among the villagers. His more politically attuned perception of Tepoztlán led him to question Redfield's ethnography in several critical areas. He drew attention to the role of land and collective labor, the prevalence of crime, the effects of the revolution on the class structure and other social institutions, the new cultural florescence under President Díaz, and above all the high degree of active participation in politics. Above all, Lewis challenged Redfield's "ideological localism" and his failure to account historically for why Tepoztlán was the way it was. Redfield's taxonomic schema whereby changes in the past were represented as different forms in the present was, for Lewis, a confusion of form and content with structure and process.

Thus ethnographic research in Mesoamerica gradually moved out from under the umbrella of acculturation and toward the study of localized communities, but its passage was not easy. It is salutary, for example, to observe what happened to the *municipio*, or small town, as a unit of analysis when Mesoamerican experts got together for a weeklong seminar sponsored by the Wenner Gren Foundation for Anthropological Research in 1949.

Sol Tax's "discovery" of the municipio as a political unit in Guatemala was the first sign of a possible shift in the thinking of anthropologists in Mesoamerica. His suggestion necessarily began with a disclaimer referring to the problems involved in using archival and ethnohistorical sources whereby linguistic groups at the time of the conquest too easily became "kingdoms" at the time of the conquest: "[O]ne is led to infer that the Quiche, for example, are an ethnic entity with one definable culture and a political and social organization comparable with that of, say, the Iroquois" (1949:423). Tax isolated "quickly and certainly—groups of people who do represent, without question, social and cultural units. . . . The people of Guatemala live in municipios which are territorial, administrative divisions commonly recognized in all governmental matters, but which are also—as it happens—the basic ethnic divisions and cultural groups into which the country is divided" (1949:425). Here, then, was no reconstruction of Guatemalan Indian societies but a practical recognition of contemporary political forms.

Yet Tax's municipio disappeared after page 45 in the seminar proceedings. A footnote (1949:69) explained why. One of the goals of the conference was to reach agreement on several propositions, and there was general resistance to Tax's proposal that the municipio provided the most useful unit for political analysis:

> Whetten: I am wondering whether the people working in Mexico wouldn't define specializations by the village, where you don't have this vacant town type of thing, rather than by municipio as you do in Guatemala.
> De la Fuente: I would say that in Oaxaca you can substitute village for municipio.
> Beals: If you use municipio in Michoacan you may get five villages in one municipio.
> Tax: We would have to define the different political units in these countries. I know that in Mexico the municipio means something different from what it means in Guatemala.
> Stone: The word village is better in the east.
> Tax: Village doesn't mean much in Guatemala. What we can say is the local cultural unit . . .
> Paul: The village is a more constant unit.
> Tax: I agree that if we are talking about middle America we don't use municipio.

A footnote to the footnote followed: "In the remainder of the paper following this footnote, the term municipio has been changed to the more generalized term 'community'—Ed." (1949:69). Thus the historical municipio gave way to the generic village community as the unit of political analysis.

The concepts of folk society and village community carried the flag of Mesoamerican scholarship into anthropology at large, providing an alternative paradigm to the dominant tribal model. Critiques led to a refined conceptualization of "peasantries" and, less successfully, to the recognition of historical process. Apart from this, however, the body of writings that emerged from Mesoamerican anthropology at this time had its own built-in limitation. This lay in the shift toward "problems." For us this poses a problem in itself, because few "problems" addressed by these anthropologists were defined as political. The recognition of "the waste" and "the sown," as Hexter put it in his vivid metaphor, requires consideration of the problematic itself in every case. As political anthropology moved into the study of peasant society, this new problematic moved away from governments, leadership, parties, rank, and stratification toward access to and control of land. For some, labor was also an economic, but rarely a political, issue. Redfield's idealized and romantic view of the peasant attached to his land was largely responsible for this. Not for a long time did the recognition of that other part of peasant society—the urban, commercial, and ruling sector—lead political anthropology to nationalism and the state.

In 1953 Redfield gave a lecture at the University of Stockholm in which he borrowed the concept of the moral order from C. H. Cooley and his father-in-law, Robert E. Park. For Redfield, conflict in the peasant village was a conflict of values as the traditional moral order came into conflict with new moral orders introduced from the city and the improved technical order, which the peasant could not resist. Finally, the Huxley Memorial Lecture at the RAI in March 1956 provided an occasion on which Redfield, talking about "Societies and Cultures as Natural Systems," praised the "competent formulations" of social structural analysis as "the consideration of political life as a balance of forces" (1962:122–123) in simple societies.

Area Research: Theory, Practice, and Politics

The United States entered World War II after the Japanese bombing of its fleet in December 1941. Her major theater of war lay in the Far East. Entry into the war made it "painfully clear that there was a severe shortage of people trained in both the social sciences and area studies. ... Academics ... with first hand knowledge of Asia and the Pacific were in great demand" (R. J. Smith 1974:11–12). For anthropology, the most valuable of these programs were supported by Carnegie or Rockefeller money; all were problem oriented rather than encouraging "purely" ethnographic or ethnological research, and all provided training for those who became contributors to the anthropological study of politics in the era that followed.

In areas, however, where field experience resulted from a military presence, whether Japanese or American, ethnographic studies were more focused on crisis and change. Those with the greatest significance for political anthropology were the Cornell University Studies in Culture and Applied Science, which provided an umbrella for research in North India and Thailand (as well as in Peru and among the Navajo); the Cornell-Thailand Project, initiated in 1947; and the Cornell Southeast Asia Program of 1950.

The connection between governments and anthropologists with skill in particular languages and a knowledge of particular regions received a new legitimacy with the establishment after the war of area institutes and university programs of area studies. The USSR, Latin America, the Middle East, Africa south of the Sahara, Eastern Europe, the Pacific, China and Japan, southern Asia, and Southeast Asia all became foci of such institutions, clearinghouses for research and the dispensation of knowledge to government and business as well as the academic community.

The institutes usually provided facilities for language training, and the anthropologists found themselves to be part of an interdisciplinary community of political scientists, economists, historians, sociologists, geographers, and others, all rapidly acquiring expertise in non-Western countries that had formerly been almost the sole preserve of colonial administrators, missionaries, traders, and anthropologists. At the same time, natives of those regions were brought to the institutes, not as informants but as co-professionals. The objectives of such institutions, it was clearly recognized, were generally political rather than scientific.[27] The course of their establishment reflected the changing concerns of, first, the United States and European governments in the rest of the world and, much later, the desire of the wealthier nations of that world, such as Israel and the oil-rich states, to accumulate and engender information to guide foreign relations. This section deals with the first phase of this international accumulation and exchange.

In 1950 Julian Steward undertook an appraisal of area studies. He began by pointing out that "The effort to put area research on a solid scientific basis does not signify a retreat from the rather grim realities of the contemporary world into a realm of pure academic fancy. It means simply that opportunity has come to carry out the fundamental precept that practical needs will be better served by better science"

(1950:xiii). There was, he argued, no special *area discipline*, whereupon—having reviewed the practice of area research in a manner that
clearly established anthropology's preeminence in the field—he rendered area studies practically synonymous with American anthropology itself.[28] This he then subjected to critical appraisal, ultimately rec-
ommending a "problem" approach. This followed the lines of a research
design he had initiated at the Smithsonian Institution in 1942, when
an attempt had been made to categorize a range of community types.
Research began on the northern coastal plain of Peru, in the only village
thought of as Indian, a village already in "the final stage of being assimilated to modern Peru," and continued in the highlands, where the Indian villages were rapidly losing their Indian characteristics "to become
'mestizos'." In broader terms, Steward noted, "this might be called proletarianization" (1950:34–35). The final study in the project, Harry
Tschopik, Jr.'s *Highland Communities of Central Peru: A Regional Survey* (1947) dealt with "the effect of nationalizing and proletarianizing
processes on individuals who left their home communities and were
subjected to national influences" (Steward 1950:35). This was surely a
more ambitious study in political structure and process than had previously been attempted. A cynic might attribute Steward's advance to the
shift that had occurred in the intervening years. The pressures of war
clearly revealed to American business interests in South America that
they needed to know more about the national sector. It is something of
a paradox that Steward clearly admired the work of Owen Lattimore,
whom he described as "one of the strongest advocates of an area approach . . . interested in the postwar development of nationalism"
(1950:19). The ecological bias of his own research encouraged him to
explore the economic changes that were transforming the rural areas of
whole continents, particularly after 1945 as American capitalist enterprise began to oust more socialistically oriented programs associated
with colonial and revolutionary governments.[29] He thereupon established a paradigm for the exploration of the relationship between the
village, community, or locality and global political and economic
processes.

In Lattimore's China, questions concerning political ideology led directly to questions of economic adjustments, which in turn required
analysis of the effects of industrialization; the possibilities for coopera-
tives or other kinds of collectivization; the economic and social basis
of nationalism; the importance of propaganda, organization, and tactics
in the development of political ideologies; and the sources of power,
which in any government resides in industrialists, workers, landlords,

or peasants.[30] Inquiries into these and many other subjects, Steward suggested, would give greater meaning to a community study in Mexico, Ireland, Peru, China, Brazil, or India, for all these areas were experiencing similar trends. All showed the effects of industrialization; all were affected by the dissolution of empires and the rearrangement of centers of economic, political, and military power; and all showed the deep stirrings of nationalism (Steward 1950). Within political anthropology, the writings of Wolf, Bailey, and Geertz stand as testimony to his vision. Steward offered scholars at work in complex societies an inclusive conceptualization of "socio-cultural levels of development," a synchronic model that suggested that evolutionary categorizations were truly in the past, along with contemporary man's primitive and savage forebears. Most of them by now, after all, had witnessed the arrival of landing craft on their beaches and the warships of great powers in their lagoons. "The contemporary world," Steward wrote,

> has become an integrated whole, that is, one area or "one world" to the extent that events in each region, nation, or area affect and are affected by events in many other places. A study of Pan-Islamism cannot be separated from British colonialism or from nationalism in India, and developments in India deeply affect England's external economic and political developments. If one studied Chinese peasants instead of Pan-Islamism with its socioreligious focus, the subject would also have international ramifications: the meaning of Chinese communism and nationalism to the peasant population; the locus of political power; how communism and nationalism are related to internal factors of demography, food supply, social structure, governmental forms, and processes of revolution; and to external factors of foreign trade, infiltration of political ideologies, military power, and international policies. (Steward 1950:84–85)

Seeking a unit for ethnographic analysis, Steward arrived at the nation state. Sovereignty was its defining feature for Steward because definite boundaries, a central government, and a set of laws that produced certain regularities in the functions of national institutions underpinned the nation. It was a natural unit of investigation for the ethnographer, Steward asserted, because census data, statistics, and so on were available on a national basis. Existing approaches to nations as culture areas or as embodiments of national character were inadequate because neither paid much attention to formal political, economic, military, educational, and other national institutions. For Steward these four institutions were emerging as key points of concern; all were aspects or expressions of centralized power and authority.

Within this context, it was something of an advance on earlier dichotomous models of complex society that Steward recognized a regional dimension at all. He required in regional studies something more than already existed in U.S. regional geography or the concept of the culture area. One of the principal problems, he thought, was the nature of the linkage of a region with the larger structural whole and the analysis of the "developmental processes" involved. A descriptive awareness that within the nation some regions were more "backward" than others, along with his overriding interest in ecological zones, led to his praise for the Tarascan project and North Carolina's sociological studies of the southeastern United States. Both, however, had certain weaknesses; the former failed to analyze "the dependency relationships of the community and the region to the larger Mexico" (1950:62), and the latter failed to specify the extent to which the Southeast was "economically and politically dependent upon a larger society" (1950:71). The extent to which Steward, true to his holy grail of comparison, had wrestled existing ethnography into a global discourse in which no analytical distinction was made between "complex societies" at home and "simpler" societies in the rest of the world was quite remarkable.

The People of Puerto Rico:
A Study in Political Economy

Locality, region, and state provided the internal dimensions of a joint Chicago-Columbia study of Puerto Rico under the direction of Julian Steward in the immediate postwar years. A cohort of anthropology doctoral students set out to study the major regional variants of its rural population, selected on the basis of their agricultural specializations. Although Steward "provided the initial theoretical orientation, . . . his students—particularly Eric Wolf and Sidney Mintz—carried it forward in ways that Steward himself neither anticipated nor perhaps even fully understood" (Silverman 1981:61).[31]

The students carried out their research between February 1948 and August 1949. Participants included Columbia students Mintz, Wolf, Robert Manners, and Raymond Scheele, along with John Murra and Elena Padilla from Chicago. Isabel Caro and Robert Armstrong (both from Chicago) participated for some of the time. Four Puerto Ricans cooperated in the research: Angelina Roca, Charles Rosario, Delia Ortega, and Edwin Seda. The project was funded by the SSRC and the Rockefeller Foundation. Prior to field research, each worker was required to have knowledge of the fundamental institutions of Puerto Rico as a dependency of the United States, a familiarity with earlier sociological and cultural studies of the island, knowledge of its cultural history, and a working knowledge of the Spanish language. The Columbia members of the team prepared for fieldwork in a seminar in which cultural history, demography and statistics, the sugar industry, other economic activities, U.S. policies, social structure, race relations, and ideologies were examined. The project paid considerable attention to the selection of communities in which field research would be carried out.

The study viewed communities as "adaptations of productive complexes" (Steward 1950:133). The team saw its task as accounting for regional variations among the coffee, tobacco, sugar, and mixed-crop areas. The communities were selected after preliminary research into differences in production, land use, land ownership, and size. Some were ruled out because of local attitudes and political restraints; some Puerto Ricans saw the students as agents of American imperialism (Mintz 1977). Four communities were finally selected:

1. A sugar-growing community on the south coast characterized by corporate ownership, large-scale irrigation, and mechanization. This community was typical of several south-coast municipios and also of the culmination of a trend in national culture toward absentee ownership. Its population consisted largely of laborers and resident managers, the older middle and upper classes having moved away.

2. A north coast community where the government was the main owner of land and sugar mills but where there was no irrigation and little mechanization. Like the south coast sugar community, this consisted largely of laborers, but there were also several small resettlement communities, some quite large homesteads, and large, plantation-type profit-sharing farms.

3. A coffee-producing community in the western mountains. This municipio was characterized by traditional face-to-face relations between owners and workers, a general lack of mechanization, a concentration of land in the hands of Spanish-born owners, and considerable survival of old Hispanic patterns.

4. A tobacco and mixed-crop community in the central mountains. This region had privately owned farms, most of them small.

Two aspects of the Puerto Rico study were innovative in political anthropology: the conceptualization of the integration of local-national relations as problematic; and the project's causal explanatory goals. The concept of levels of sociocultural interpretation was on the face of it "an extremely simple concept, and at the same time a concept which—in all of its simplicity—recommended itself then because it allowed recognition of a certain measure of complexity in society"

(Wolf 1978:20). Steward was conscious of the defects of community studies, including the false assumption of homogeneity that underlay so many of them. Wolf believed that Steward "first formulated his version of the concept of levels of sociocultural integration as a reaction to acculturation studies" (1978:20–21).[32] In stressing complexity and variation, Steward argued against some of the major orientations in political anthropology in the late 1940s. Internal evidence in *The People of Puerto Rico* (1956), Steward's later autobiographical comments, and inferences that can be made from the historical context of the man and the book support William Roseberry in his distinguishing among the various approaches used by the participants in the Puerto Rico project. Wolf's contribution to the anthropological study of politics, like that of Mintz, requires separate recognition. Roseberry has made a point-by-point comparison of the "two introductions" to *The People of Puerto Rico*, the first by Steward, looking backward, as it were, over his shoulder at anthropological contributions to the study of cultural change, and the second by "the Staff" called "The Cultural Historical Approach." Inevitably a question arises about the extent to which *The People of Puerto Rico* is a Marxist study; Roseberry argues succinctly that it is not (1978:32–36).[33]

Because of the significance of this issue in the historiography of political anthropology, the focus here is on the chapters by Mintz and Wolf. Mintz, as an undergraduate student of Lesser and a socialist by upbringing, had the most strongly historical orientation toward his subject matter—sugar, slavery, and the contemporary rural proletariat. His field research in Canamelar investigated the subculture of what he called "a rural sugar plantation proletariat" that had come into being in response to the United States' capital investment, political occupation, and demand for sugar. He set out first to reconstruct the preexisting family-type hacienda way of life and then to describe and analyze the changes that had occurred.

Mintz's ethnography argued the falsity of "primitivizing" or "tribalizing" the municipality of Canamelar: "corporate stockholders in Boston and New York played a vital role in the way of life of the people" (1956:316). Throughout his analysis, Mintz searched for similarities and differences that had meaning historically, politically, and culturally. The first third of his study provided an ecological and historical account of the municipality and the barrio in which he lived. Much of the analysis of "the past" centered on the plantation system and "labor power," drawing on Nieboer's *Slavery as an Industrial System* (1900) (discussed in Chapter 2 of this study) and on Marxist perceptions of rent, appropriation, and exploitation. Technology was not neglected. "The history of the rural people of Canamelar," Mintz argued, "can be written in terms of the relation of labor to the land" (1956:343). The history was one of conflict and resistance. "The sociopolitical atmosphere was menacing—dependent on the corporation [the land-factory combine that replaced the hacienda] for credit, housing, and labor, workers could not organize easily. But a strong spirit was not long in developing" (1956:346). An account of strikes and, ultimately, union and Socialist party organization followed.

Mintz adopted eclectic language to describe "the reality of a class culture, or subculture, within the larger society" (1956:351, following Kroeber 1948), the people standing "in a uniform relation to the means of production and in a like relation, economically and socially, to one another" (1956:351). He then described what might be called "the labor process" in the community. Clearly approving Steward's interest in analyzing the social organization of work (discussed in Chapter 3), Mintz and his team members were clearly operating under a Kroeberian-style mandate, required to provide ethnographic data for comparative purposes as well. He handled material on the social functions of the family, the socialization process, urban occupations, health, folk medicine, food habits, and folk arts and science with less analytical extemporization than Wolf was able to achieve in the coffee-producing peasant community of San Jose. Their joint 1957 publication, "Haciendas and Plantations in Middle America and the Antilles" (Wolf and Mintz 1957), continued the dialogue they had clearly enjoyed in the field.

Eric Wolf was twenty-five years old at the time of his field research in Puerto Rico. Born in Vienna, he entered the United States via an internment camp in England in 1940. He entered anthropology at a time when, as he put it, "V. Gordon Childe's *What Happened in History* (1946) was required reading and graduate education included an obligatory immersion in Kroeber's rewritten *Anthropology* (1948)" (Wolf 1981:395). His professional work was grounded in the dialectic between plantations and peasantries which arose out of the Puerto Rico discourse. The consistency of Wolf's vision of culture, peasant society, and political interdependence may be traced from his Columbia dissertation of 1950, which subsequently became a chapter in *The People of Puerto Rico* (Steward 1956). From the beginning he stressed that culture has a temporal dimension: "different cultures grew up in the course of time, with each major change in the cultural equipment available for the exploitation of the environment. While each previous culture entered into the making and development of the new, the character

of each culture was novel and different from that of its predecessor. . . .
Yet, each culture, once established, developed rigidities which limited
its capacity for further change." He also emphasized that change came
from the outside. "Puerto Rico," he wrote, "has never been completely
isolated from the modern world market. . . . Its culture has always been
linked to the prevailing commercial purposes of the day. The local culture always had to interact with a larger economic, social, and *political
system, of which it formed a part.*" Recognizing the methodological
problems this created for the anthropologist, he suggested that, nevertheless, he might "assess the mechanisms which link the community
to the city, the island, the nation, or the world" (1956a:172, emphasis
added).

Wolf wrote an ethnography of the municipality of San José, the coffee-
producing community in the western mountains. It had a population
of 19,423 in 1950, divided among 3,805 households. About 18 percent
lived in the growing town, the rest in the eight mountainous barrios
around it. "The anthropologist attempts to study culture by everyday
observation of actual behavior," Wolf wrote, "as well as by recording
statements and impressions on ideal norms in the context in which
they are made." For such purposes, Wolf needed a smaller "unit of concentration," so he chose two neighborhoods in one barrio to "furnish
both evidence of a functional kind and insight into historical relationships." He studied the town "in terms of . . . its relationship to the
rural areas" (1956a:174). Direct participation, indirect and unguided
interviews, formal interviews, genealogies (for eighty-three households), historical reconstruction from nine old informants, and data
from historical documents in the town archives provided Wolf's field
"data." Much of it he quantified through the use of a questionnaire
toward the end of the field inquiry. Respondents comprised 17.5 percent of the landowners and 15 percent of the landless population.

After sketching the town and barrios, Wolf concluded: "Each of these
aspects of culture, such as the contrast between country and town, the
isolation of the rural neighborhoods, the social status involved in own-
ing a horse with a leather saddle, the sexual division of labor, the system of ritual godfatherhood and co-fatherhood—*represents a problem
which must be discussed and analyzed both historically and in terms
of functional relationships*" (1956a:178, emphasis added). Here Wolf
set out the Lesserian principles that molded analysis of political culture
in the years to follow.

To abstract for discussion the "particularly political" is clearly in violation of the monograph's spirit, for the work is one of political economy in the anthropological usage of that term. Under the subheading "Politics and Law," Wolf dealt with the organization of political power, agrarian reform, and law. His analysis of these topics was based on public knowledge, a few key inquiries, and some calculations; it presaged the type of inquiry into local politics that anthropologists made in the 1960s (Chapter 5).

Wolf's discussion of law in San José centered on the police and the illegal activities of the people: brewing rum, the illegal lottery, and cockfighting. He showed the importance of the first two in the rural economy. A similar analysis of cockfighting has yet to be made. From court records he discovered that breaches of the peace were urban crimes, while assault was rural. Prosecution of the latter was hampered by the reluctance of witnesses to testify against kin and ritual-kin. Since the people did not trust lawyers, informal legal advisers and witnesses had come into being, but everyone viewed the biweekly court sessions in San José largely as entertainment.

Thirty years later Wolf perceived three major shortcomings in *The People of Puerto Rico*, including the fact that the study was apolitical: "There is no analysis of the structure and function of the state, and no question or query about the nature and the characteristics of the 'national institutions'. These are taken at face value, and not analyzed— for instance, with regard to the way in which they both serve and hide the forces which underlie and organize them" (1978:28). Nor was there any formulation of what came to be known as dependency theory, although as Wolf later recalled, it was emerging strongly in the work of Gunnar Myrdal at the time. Marxist analyses of imperialism and internal colonialism might also have provided alternatives to Steward's sociocultural levels of integration.

Wolf concluded in 1978 that "perhaps none of this could have been said twenty-one years ago. These remarks are predicated on the renewal of political economy and the breaking down of conceptual and method ological boundaries among the social sciences" (1978:25). Certainly a great deal must be attributed, within the United States and particularly, perhaps, within the Columbia and Chicago departments, to the need to establish and legitimate a specific role for anthropology, as distinct from sociology in postwar Third World research. "Re-reading the book," Wolf concluded, "I was amazed how close we often came to opening paths towards this new ground, and chagrined as well that we did not go further at the time" (1978:25).

In the years that followed, Wolf established himself as a leading authority on the politics of peasantries. Much of his ethnographic endeavor focused on Mexico and Central America, but his goal of clarifying the nature of peasant resistance both locally and globally led him to a more general historical comparison (Chapters 5 and 6). Sidney Mintz continued to center his attention on political and historical problems arising out of his Caribbean field experiences. His emphasis, with its different starting place in the Puerto Rico study, developed along different lines from that of Wolf, parallel and always complementary: the study of lower-class rural people, proletarian rather than peasant but equally a product of the capitalist world.

Community Power Structures

Anthropological studies of communities tended to lack a significant political dimension. Certainly the nineteenth-century issues that lay between Maine and Baden-Powell in the understanding of the nature of the village community in India and medieval Europe were far removed from their intellectual concerns. Two species of community study could be distinguished by 1940, one generated by Latin American and Asian ethnological field research and another spawned by sociologists interested in social relations, class structure, race relations, and social stability in the United States. Steward criticized both for treating communities as tribes.[34] His sweeping indictment rightly (although implicitly) castigated Radcliffe-Brown's suggestion that communities were microcosms of the societies in which they were situated, but it less justifiably dismissed Redfield's work, which had surely moved as far in this direction as had Steward's own.

Steward drew on particular deficiencies of a political nature to make his point. He noted a lack of attention to warfare, although, he said, it is "perfectly clear that each contemporary community has been very much affected by warfare and may be again" (1950:23–24). Both the demographic profiles resulting from conscription in peasant societies and village war memorials attest to the validity of Steward's observation. He tabulated the amount of space given to different topics in nine community studies, indicating how obliquely politics and national influences were discussed. In Latin America, economics loomed large; in China and Japan, social and political issues.

John Embree's perception of the Japanese village as a peasant community anticipated by almost a decade Kroeber's now classic description of peasantries as "part-societies with part-cultures" (1948). The Chicagoan's study set out the national-local dimension quite clearly. "A

peasant community," he wrote, "presents many important differences
from the simpler societies; each little peasant group is part of a larger
nation which controls its economic life, enforces a code of law from
above, and, more recently, requires education in national schools. The
economic basis of life is not conditioned entirely by local requirements.
. . . The farmer's crop is adjusted to the needs of the state" (1939:xvi).
His community study countered Steward's critique that the genre
lacked the exhaustive coverage of economics, politics, religion, and society of the orthodox ethnographic monograph but failed to meet his
stipulation that the community be studied in historical depth and comparatively. Radcliffe-Brown's preface to Embree's study was disarmingly
out of touch with the trendsetting work.[35]

It did, however, reflect the premises underlying W. Lloyd Warner's
team research in Newburyport (Warner 1963); the seven-volume Yankee City series; the selection of ethnographic sites in middle America
(Warner 1941, Hollingshead 1949) and the Deep South (Davis, Gardner,
and Gardner 1941) by his associates; and the American community
studies done independently of his auspices by Elin L. Anderson (1937),
John Dollard (1937), and Hortense Powdermaker (1939). Three features
potentially of political import characterized the independent studies:
first, field research among African-Americans; second, a regional focus
(e.g., Useem, Useem, and Tangent 1942; West 1945); and, third, an appraisal of social class, most distinctively in two studies by Walter Goldschmidt, *Small Business and the Community* (1946) and *As You Sow*,
(1947). Goldschmidt, like Steward, criticized community studies for
their "implicit analogy of community to tribe" (1950:485). What concerned him most was their inadequacy for analyzing social class in
America. He drew attention to the emergence, as he saw it, of "a four-
class system," which studies of homogeneous communities obscured.
Pioneering as they were in the anthropology of complex societies, these
community studies were relegated to the ranks of "rural sociology" by
most anthropologists. Their impact on mainstream political anthropology at the time was absolutely nil.

As for the Yankee City study, it is ironic that this work—born presumably out of concern over the growing union organization of the
workingman and the loss of gemeinschaft in a modern industrial city—
focused *at the outset* on class differences within Newburyport, but it
ended up legitimating ethnic stereotypes. The Yankee City concept of
class was purely subjective, derived from informants' own views of
their social stratum.[36]

The Lynds' study *Middletown* (1929) also received impetus from anthropology—in their case W.H.R. Rivers. They carried out their initial fieldwork in Muncie, Indiana, for eighteen months in 1924 and 1925. Its goal was to describe what had taken place in Muncie between 1890 (when the population was 11,000) and 1924 (population 35,000). The Lynds adopted a simpleminded dichotomous class division between a working class "who dealt with things" and a business class who "dealt with people." Their work was wholly atheoretical. In 1935 Robert Lynd revisited Muncie for ten months. By this time he was prepared to write "a hard-hitting exposure of the sources of power in what he regarded as a typical American small town. . . . [H]e packed into *Middletown in Transition* all his militant and evangelical feelings about what was wrong in American society" (Bell and Newby 1971:84). In particular, he made visible a large and powerful family of wealthy manufacturers who dominated the town. The 1925 work devoted twenty pages to government; in 1935 this more than doubled. The greater visibility of a politically dominant family in the Depression decade was accompanied by an increase in space devoted to institutions "caring for the unable," since most working-class and some middle-class families had during these years become unable to care for themselves. The Lynds thus recorded what they called "the pervasiveness of the long fingers of capitalist ownership" and expressed surprise that there was no overt class conflict (1937:451). Both workers and management rejected unionization. This would appear to support Marx's observation that loss of community was a consequence of capitalism (Bell and Newby 1971:25), and indeed, Lynd "admitted" to reading Marx prior to his restudy of Middletown.

By this time it is clear that three concepts relating to "class" were in use in American tribal, peasant, and contemporary anthropology. The first involved "social stratification"; the second was a Marxist usage relating "class" to the means of production; the third was the concept of "social class." Democratic ideology reaching back to de Tocqueville (1862) and James Bryce (1888) denied the existence of class in America. It was recognized, nevertheless, that "the total absence of rank and universal acceptance of equality do not . . . prevent the existence of grades and distinctions which, though they find no tangible expression, are sometimes as sharply drawn as in Europe" (Bryce 1888, 2:752). This, to the anthropologists, was "social class."

What had happened in these years, and what became manifest in the Yankee City studies, was the appearance of Max Weber on the intellectual scene. There are numerous references to Marx in Warner's *Social Class in America*, but it is the influence of Weber rather than Marx that is to be seen in the ethnography of political power. The unraveling of Weber's "class," "status," and "power" is almost a preoccupation in the community studies that followed. The choice of "social stratification," "class," or "social class" terminology tended to reflect, at this time, a scholar's institutional and personal political preferences. The first, much in vogue among evolutionists, tended to be conservative, the second radical, and the third fell somewhere in between. Not until much later did a Weberian-inclined political anthropologist, Lloyd A. Fallers, redirect the discipline to the analysis of inequality pure and simple (Chapter 5).

Yet, out of the vast Yankee City project came a subterranean stream of political ethnography that not only sabotaged formal structuralism of the Radcliffe-Brown variety but also merged with a new processualism developing in Britain. Even more critically it challenged, toe to toe, the newly emergent "American science of politics." The approach was variously labeled *interactionism, behavioralism,* and *ethology,* and was associated with Conrad Arensberg, Eliot Chapple, and William Foote Whyte. The broader paradigm of which it is a part is known as *small group theory,* a discussion of which Mullins (1973) subtitles "The Light that Failed." The connective tissue of Kurt Lewin's posthumous *Field Theory in Social Science* (1951) grafted together a generation of Harvard and Manchester political ethnographers (Chapter 5).

The historical roots of the small-group theorists lay in a "revolt" (Mullins 1973:122) against nonempirical, armchair theory.[37] Whyte, whose three-and-a-half-year study of an Italian community in Somerville, Massachusetts, began in 1937, published a methodological appendix in *Street Corner Society* (1943a) that has itself become a minor classic. In it he acknowledged his debt to Arensberg, a full-time Yankee City researcher. On the basis of this research Whyte issued "A Challenge to Political Scientists" (1943b), which he had the audacity to publish in their leading journal, *The American Political Science Review.* This sparked off a correspondence that revealed the methodological distinctiveness of political anthropology vis-à-vis the science of politics— a contrast that stands to this day.

Whyte described his procedure as "building up the structure and functioning of the community through intensive examination of some of its parts *in action,* . . . relating the parts together through observing events between groups and between group leaders and members of the larger institutional structures [of politics and the rackets], . . . seeking to build a sociology upon observed interpersonal events" (1943b:69). He challenged political scientists (1) to take an interest in politics rather than ethics, (2) to study politics by becoming participant observers in political machines, and (3) to build up a conceptual scheme that would permit them to analyze political behavior in terms of the social structure of American society. We are not concerned here with the polemical exchange that followed but with the responsive chord that Whyte's article struck in political scientists swept along by the "wartime push to demote theory, to be practical and descriptive," and to turn aside from ethical disputations among themselves (Garson 1978:63). The challenge of political realism proved compelling, and the new American science of politics became, in essence, a behavioral science (Eulau 1964). Anthropologists, if any read the article (for nowhere have I found it cited by them), appear to have been quite untouched by it.

Politics, for Whyte, was "a struggle among individuals and groups for power and prestige" (1943b:697). In his field research he drew attention particularly to its extrasystemic features, those that Bailey later called parapolitical. In street-corner society these were such "extra-legal," "unofficial," and "irregular" practices as patronage, corruption, and political bossism. "The politician does not build up his organization out of an undifferentiated mass of people. He grows up in a society which is complexly organized. To be successful in his career he must be familiar with its ramifications and know how to win the support of the groups which make it up" (Whyte 1943a:209). At every stage there is an actual or potential conflict of loyalties, and Whyte provided superb ethnography to arrive at an analysis of frequencies of interaction that accounted for observed outcomes. He analyzed campaign meetings as "events" and focused attention on the interactions required to achieve community and personal political objectives—securing local improvements or personal favors.[38]

CONCLUSION

In the years after World War II, political anthropology came to be recognized as a distinctive subfield of British sociological anthropology. Its canon was made up largely of monographs on the constitutions of African political systems, and its greatest advance was in the study of so-called stateless societies. This I have called the Radcliffe-Brown program, tracing its development from the Durkheimian legacy described in Chapter 3 to the new structuralism of Fortes and Evans-Pritchard. *African Political Systems* headed the structural canon, but in the long run, the critics who deplored its parochialism and neglect of history held the candle to the future of political anthropology. Leach, although he was unable to move beyond the parameters of the structuralist paradigm, provided much-needed criticism from within.

Yet, even in the years from 1940 to 1954, an alternative vision to Oxbridge structuralism existed within British anthropology. This had much more in common with developments in the anthropology of politics in America than was appreciated at the time or since. This alternative also emerged out of Africa, by way of Wilson's program for research at the Rhodes-Livingstone Institute. Gluckman, his successor, established the same program at Manchester University, where the next generation provided political anthropology with fresh political ethnography from Asia and a coherent new paradigm based on action theory.

A focus on space and time was common to both Manchester and American anthropologists at this time, although their different ethnographic sources—central Africa and America and its backyard—continued to sustain the transatlantic gulf that Lowie and Forde had deplored (Chapter 3). Redfield's ideal "folk society," which in effect collapsed time into space, came under strong attack. Feudalism, rural proletarian communities, and national politics appeared on the agenda in its place. The students of Strong and Lesser, pioneers in the 1930s (Chapter 3), rewrote the political ethnography of Native America, accounting for its changing forms of adjustment and resistance to contact and domination. Steward's students embarked on fieldwork in Puerto Rico, producing a classic study that proved to be the forerunner of political anthropological engagement with dependency theory and the world-systems model in the 1970s (Chapter 5). Anthropologists also began to study politics in U.S. communities and even challenged political scientists to do the same. Behavioral politics developed within the sister field a few years later.

Legal anthropology became a strong contender for separate status within the discipline between 1940 and 1953, and Hoebel's 1954 textbook on primitive law marked its success. The stimulating vision of the lawyer Karl Llewellyn provided legal anthropology with a cosmopolitan genealogy, but because of his own involvement with the legal realism movement, his more lasting impact proved to lie in his advocacy of the study of law as behavior. In this, he found his ethnographic roots in the work of Barton and Malinowski (Chapters 2 and 3). The future of this realistic, action-centered legal paradigm lay with the Mancunians and processualism (Chapters 5 and 6). In contrast with the study of law, warfare suffered badly during this period, because structuralism defined it as external to a polity. A beginning was made, however, in distinguishing rebellion from revolution, a subject that will appear in Chapter 5.

5   Romanticism, Boom, and Bust, 1954–1973

Far-called, our navies melt away;
On dune and headland sinks the fire:
Lo, all our pomp of yesterday
Is one with Ninevah and Tyre.
                —RUDYARD KIPLING

I care nothing for the systems—only for the insights.
                —OLIVER WENDELL HOLMES

The decline of European imperialism around the world brought into being a second era of uncertainty and indeterminacy fraught with possibilities and potential disasters for the anthropology of politics. Unlike the Edwardian era, when alternative definitions of the field gave way under the functionalist onslaught, the postimperial years saw regicidal competition not within political anthropology itself but from other ascendant disciplines—political science, political sociology, and political economy, all creatures of the American science of politics and the cold war. In 1953 the Korean War came to an end, and in the twenty years that followed, Third World countries moved to center stage in global politics, leaving the major powers—the United States and Soviet Russia, and to a lesser extent, Britain and France—to react to their initiatives.[1]

Britain, after its announced dismantling of the empire, began to put its own house in order. With Labour governments in office, new universities were created in the provinces, and opportunities for higher education were broadened through increases in government scholarships. Departments at Sussex and Kent universities began to coordinate new scholarship in the anthropology of politics and Western European studies. Warwick established an interdisciplinary program in comparative law. Class issues were, as ever, contested in the political arena, but by the end of the decade a swing to the right was apparent throughout Western Europe. Conservatives were elected to office in Britain in 1970.

The dismantling of the British and French empires brought independence to many (a subject Lucy Mair investigated in *New Nations*, her contemporary anthropological textbook published in 1963 and Clifford Geertz examined in *Old Societies and New States* the same year). Peter Lloyd's 1966 study of the new elites revealed that in several countries they included anthropologists and academics turned politicians. Jomo Kenyatta came to power in Kenya; Busia in Ghana. Elsewhere anthropologists became ministers of culture. Independence left in its wake political instability as well as change. In sub-Saharan Africa, for example, rebellion and revolution dominated the political process in the Belgian Congo (Zaire), Zanzibar (united with Tanganyika to form Tanzania), and Southern Rhodesia (where the white population unilaterally declared their independence from Britain). In Ghana, Nkrumah was overthrown in a bloodless coup. Confronted by the "wind of change" sweeping through Africa in the 1960s, the Republic of South Africa moved to the right. Greater intolerance of black political participation followed the election of B. J. Vorster as prime minister in 1966.

The "first new nation," the United States, had its problems, too. Black protest entered both the national arena and public consciousness in 1955, when African-Americans in Montgomery, Alabama, boycotted segregated buses. It reached a climax eight years later with a Freedom March on Washington. Almost immediately this success was overshadowed by increasing U.S. military involvement in Indochina. African-Americans became more organized within the profession, but the anthropology of politics tended toward the study of ethnicity, with its frequent sidelining of both race and power. The powerlessness of the black minority throughout the country became fully evident when the "long hot summer" of 1964 brought race riots to several American cities. The assassinations of Malcolm X and Rev. Martin Luther King fueled a search for new political initiatives.

The United States established a military council in South Vietnam, a former French colony, in 1962. A year later a Buddhist-led coup overthrew the government of that country, and by 1964 the United States was heavily involved in resisting the North's efforts to reunify the two Vietnams. In the course of the nine-year war (1965–1973) the United States expended $109 billion; combat deaths numbered some 1,150,000; and some 425,000 civilians were killed. Protest demonstrations against the war spread from the universities to the streets. Anthropologists throughout the country engaged in "teach-ins" on Vietnam.

In 1968 political discontent in its many forms took to the streets in the United States, Britain, and France. Student rebellions closed universities. For a short while, an aroused consciousness of the politics of race, big business, imperialism, poverty, and above all, American involvement in Southeast Asia, led to a questioning of capitalist and communist ethics alike. Partly in response to a search for alternative values (a search generated for many by participation in President John F.

Kennedy's Peace Corps), enrollment in anthropology departments surged. Responding to the issues students raised, many in the profession began to explore the contribution of intellectual Marxism to political anthropology. Some focused on French structural Marxism, but others responded also to nonacademic influences, reading Marxist and socialist texts more familiar to their friends and colleagues in sociology and history departments. By the end of the era, anthropology departments were domesticating the fledgling scholars by recruiting new members with "qualifications" in Marxist theory.

In 1973 the Vietnam War came to an end. The participation of anthropologists in intelligence activities during the war had threatened to disembowel the American Anthropological Association, but the most lasting effect on political anthropology came from the critical writing of Kathleen Gough (1968), which legitimated a new paradigm, opening up to anthropology the study of imperialism.[2] Its reflexive form, the critique of past practice, appeared in two edited volumes, Dell Hymes's *Reinventing Anthropology* (1969) and Talal Asad's *Anthropology and the Colonial Encounter* (1973a).

Gough's challenge that political anthropology embrace the study of socialist and communist political systems was not taken up. Events behind the "Iron Curtain" had shaken British intellectuals—the march of Soviet troops into Hungary in 1956 being the most critical, perhaps—but the power vacuum created by decolonization provided funds for increased anthropological field research in Third World countries. This culminated in 1973 with the International Congress of Anthropological and Ethnological Sciences (ICAES) in Chicago, out of which arose a mammoth series of weighty tomes. Many of these (but particularly *The Politics of Anthropology* [Huizer and Mannheim 1979] and *Political Anthropology* [Seaton and Claessen 1979]) reflected new political paradigms. An underpinning may be discerned in such Third World events as the war of France, England, and Israel against Nasser of Egypt over the Suez Canal in 1957, the establishment of the West Indian Federation in 1958; Fidel Castro's overthrow of the Cuban dictator Fulgencio Batista in 1959; the emergence of the parapolitical organizations Al Fatah in 1964 and the Palestine Liberation Organization in 1969; the Six-Day War between Israel and the Arab nations in 1967; the election of Salvador Allende, a Marxist, as president of Chile in 1970 and his overthrow three years later; the establishment of martial law in the Philippines by Ferdinand Marcos in 1972; and the war between India and Pakistan and the creation of Bangladesh, also in 1972.

The post-independence period for most new nations saw two transnational migratory trends that were ultimately to affect the anthropology of politics. As the United States and Britain became more racially heterogeneous, new immigration laws redefined those eligible for citizenship. In the Third World, as class differences grew, successive elites began to send their children for further education to European and American universities. This was happening in a world clearly recognized as a "company town" (Idris-Soven, Idris-Soven, and Vaughan 1973), in which business and military interests were becoming multinational. In the world of realpolitik an era ended and another began. An Arab oil embargo precipitated an energy crisis throughout the industrialized world. In the academy, Immanuel Wallerstein's *The Modern World-System* (1974b) marked a crisis in disciplinary specialization, redirecting energies toward a new set of political questions.

The period from 1954 to 1973 was one in which the history of anthropology was only just beginning to be obscured by tradition. It was a humpbacked era, its turning point appearing around 1965. In 1954 the Oxbridge paradigm still dominated British political anthropological thought to the extent that it was in danger of paralyzing young workers. Yet at the same time, in seminars and classrooms an opposition was quietly voiced. The work of Isaac Schapera and Edmund Leach, whose theories confronted problems of change, carried political anthropology out of the Durkheimian era and away from its long infatuation with the sociological comparative method.

Reevaluations of past paradigms accompanied the emergence of the new. Tribesmen gave way to peasants in a contemporary world, in which peasants—some peasants—were fast becoming capitalist farmers. Structure and stability gave way to organization and change, with Raymond Firth issuing the catalytic statement in 1954. This, in turn, provided a platform from which to shift the focus away from constitutions and toward political activity. S. F. Nadel, along with two students of Schapera and Leach—Fredrik Barth and F. G. Bailey—brought about an entrepreneurial rebellion that led to the explicit formulation in action theory of ideas that might be traced back to the revolutionary *Notes and Queries* of 1912. Legitimation came in 1965 at the Oxford meeting of the ASA, to which the older generation invited younger scholars—including some from the United States who were not members of the association—to assess the state of the discipline. This gave rise to *Political Systems and the Distribution of Power* (Banton 1965) and *The Social Anthropology of Complex Societies* (Banton 1966).

At more or less the same time, participants in an invited session on political anthropology at the 1964 annual meeting of the AAA produced a volume of essays, *Political Anthropology* (1966), edited by Marc J. Swartz, Victor W. Turner, and Arthur Tuden, of Michigan, Cornell (late of Manchester, England), and Pittsburgh respectively. This was followed a year later by *Local-Level Politics* (Swartz 1967). Both volumes reflected a new rapport among British and American anthropologists, which was strengthened operationally by the appointment of several leading British academics, most of them Africanists, (including several on the cutting edge of political anthropology) to American and Canadian universities. They included Victor Turner, Aidan Southall, William Watson, Philip Gulliver, and later F. G. Bailey. It also reflected the growing influence of the American science of politics and, within it, the subfield of behavioral politics.

The first decade saw the spate of introductory textbooks referred to in Chapter 4. Each was organized along institutional lines and so included a chapter on political organization. Most came from the pens of Oxford anthropologists (Bohannan 1963; Beattie 1964; Lienhardt 1964) and reflected the vital legacy of Evans-Pritchard. Novel syntheses were produced in certain aspects—Bohannan on law and war, for example, and Lienhardt on political ideology. Two more specialized texts came from LSE anthropologists Schapera (1956) and Mair (1965a) both of which contained more penetrating alternative views of political change than their generic titles would suggest. All these writers, in spite of a knowledge of trends in the United States, appeared to have as their goal the consolidation of a political anthropology that was peculiarly nationalistic. It drew largely on the analysis of British-trained anthropologists and a body of ethnography generated within the British Commonwealth.

In the United States two completely opposed paradigms emerged. The neo-evolutionary vision of politics of Elman R. Service (1962), Morton H. Fried (1967), and Marshall Sahlins (Sahlins and Service 1960) provided a popular and simple taxonomy (to be discussed shortly) into which the entire political anthropological corpus since 1879 could be placed. This served in much the same way as the evolutionary paradigm of Powell, Spencer, Hobhouse, Wheeler, and Ginsberg had served earlier. Deriving as it did from the work of Leslie White, Julian Steward, and Karl Polanyi, it ordered ethnography in a manner that gave offense to few; certainly for teaching purposes the simple four-part division of all the world's polities into bands, tribes, chiefdoms, and states imposed order. In Fried's formulation it also raised important questions about political units and sovereignty. Neo-evolutionism did, however, further encourage anthropologists to dwell on timeless universals.

The coming of age of culture history in the mid 1960s provided an alternative American paradigm. Unlike neo-evolutionism, it was concerned with the complexity of ongoing contemporary politics in Third World peasant societies—with the asymmetry of power, wars, and the human condition (Wolf and Hansen 1972). It raised and reflected the political questions of the age—Cuba, China, Vietnam—building on the anthropology of the peasantry that had begun to overtake the seminal work of Redfield and Steward in the 1950s. It also continued to address the issue of complexity, which had arisen earlier. A major trend was toward Nadel's "interstitial structures" (1957), quasi groups and fields of social relations existing within the matrix of the state's formal institutional structure (Mayer 1966; Mitchell 1966; Wolf 1966a). Here British and American political anthropology converged.

By 1969 more than two hundred academics in the United States were declaring a specialized interest in "political anthropology"; that same year one in four of the academics in Britain listed politics among their chief theoretical interests. Shifts were taking place within the emergent specialization. Thus it was rare to find any political anthropologists using the terms "primitive" or "social control" to describe their interests. Most referred to "politics," "political organization," and "political systems." Very few expressed interest in law in one form or another. Only two members of the ASA, both teaching in American universities, actually described their specialization as political anthropology—and one was Victor Turner.[3]

As higher education expanded, more textbooks and edited readers were produced, and political anthropology, solidifying as a subfield, had its share. They reflected shifts from orthodoxy to heterodoxy, from Oxbridge dominance lingering on in *Comparative Political Systems* (Cohen and Middleton 1967) to four alternative paradigms. These centered upon (1) process: *Political Anthropology* (Swartz, Turner, and Tuden 1966); (2) agency: Bailey's *Strategems and Spoils* (1969); (3) neo-evolutionism: Fried's *The Evolution of Political Society* (1967); and (4) humanism: Wolf's *Peasants* (1966b) and *Peasant Wars of the Twentieth Century* (1969).

The period from 1954 to 1973 was characterized by advanced fissioning into regional and subfield specializations. A question arises as to the extent that particularistic problem orientations within specific areas (such as Oceania, South Asia, and Latin America) gave rise to particularistic conceptualization and theory and the extent to which new paradigms of global theory articulated them. Indications of proliferating and advancing specializations are not hard to find. Regional and subfield journals began to appear after 1946 and increased threefold after 1960. In both *Man* and *American Anthropologist*, dissatisfaction was expressed with their reviewing procedures, reflecting the advance of specialized knowledge on both sides of the Atlantic.

With the decolonization of anthropology, training courses for civil servants diminished in number, but new courses for "industrialists" and "expatriate experts" were engineered (Richards 1961). Area specializations both fostered and required a problem-solving orientation which, it might be thought, would challenge conventional fieldwork methods.

THE CHALLENGE OF DEFINITION

Between 1954 and 1965 anthropologists groped for a definition of the subject matter of political anthropology and a subfield specialization. They addressed three audiences: the general public, practitioners of other social sciences, and their fellow anthropologists. As late as 1964, Morton Fried, in a radio talk on "Anthropology and the Study of Politics," still felt free to talk about his own interests—the study of power, conflict over scarce resources, historical jurisprudence, politics in contemporary China, and the state. Other anthropologists, he noted, were interested in studying functional relations between particular polities and particular economies, religions, or social systems. Still others specialized in the study of secondary states newly generated as a result of the retreat of imperialism and colonialism. Anthropological interest in the study of political systems, he concluded, "is not limited to simple societies, to the evolution of ancient states, or to modern problems of political enculturation. We may look forward to increasing interaction between scholars specializing in the realm of politics and those who take wider behavioral or cultural frames as their system of reference" (Fried 1964:7).

Max Gluckman similarly addressed the public through a broadcast on the British Broadcasting Company's "Third Programme." He alerted his listeners to the problems ahead in Third World politics. He talked of European ignorance of how African societies were held together without the formal apparatus of government, but he went on to observe that "the major political difficulties with primitive societies today are created by a different kind of ignorance: the European failure to realize that Africans and other primitive people are today so deeply involved in our own social system that they are moved by the same political forces which are at work around us at home" (1956:80).

Clearly, at this point political anthropology was still defining itself by what had been distinctive in the past, "primitive societies," but the nature of future practice was clearly on their minds. A major impetus to introspection was a long, critical, and wholly unsatisfactory review of the field by David Easton (1959). Easton was a political scientist at the University of Chicago, and his essay dealt largely with *African Political Systems* and its derivatives. The essay proved important not for its intrinsic quality but because it made political anthropologists face up to the question of self-definition. They were not political scientists, nor, in spite of statements to the contrary, were they political sociologists. What, then, was the difference?

The Rejection of Systems Theory

Systems theory was an attempt to provide a universal framework for political order and political change. The term *system* had long been employed descriptively, from Powell to *African Political Systems*, but the systemic interdependence of the parts—kinship, economic, religious, and political structures—had been assumed rather than demonstrated. Easton apparently took *African Political Systems* very seriously. Just prior to his review he had published *The Political System* (1953). A few years later his *Framework for Political Analysis* (1965a) and *A Systems Analysis of Political Life* (1965b) began to appear on anthropologists' bookshelves. His ideas were attractive for two reasons. First, he provided a simple model of a political system (any political system) which placed within one genus the political systems of both Western and non-Western societies. Second, he made it clear that this was no accident; he had learned from anthropology how ethnocentric were the views of most political scientists, and he shared the nomothetic, scientific goals of Radcliffe-Brown, Fortes, and Evans-Pritchard. In short, his later work was itself derivative of *African Political Systems*.

A more immediate stimulus for Easton's vision surrounded him at the University of Chicago. He was in essence a man of his time, when what was known as general systems theory was abroad in the United States. Based on the World War II sciences—cybernetics and information and communications theory—general systems theory continued to be heavily funded in the universities by the American government even after the war (von Bertalanffy 1956; Boulding 1956, 1968).[4] The growth of these sciences marked a transition from a concern for the dynamics of energy transformation to a focus on the dynamics of organization and the "triggering" effects of information transmission. The distinction was recognized more clearly in the developing subfield of economic anthropology than in the study of politics (apart from law). There, however, it was couched as a *controversy* between formalist and substantivist approaches, not as a shift from one to the other. When the shift did occur in political anthropology, it was due to more sensitive work than that of Easton. Nevertheless, the overall gross simplicity of his model attracted anthropologists during what was, for many of them, something of a crisis period. It replaced the old organic and mechanical uses of the "systems" metaphor with what appeared to be a scientific breakthrough.

General systems theory faced four scientific problems: wholes and how to deal with them; the analysis of the complex and dynamic relations of parts, especially when parts were themselves complex and changing; interchange with an environment; and the mechanics of control, of self-regulation, and self-direction. Anthropology was eager to define itself as a social science in this intellectual milieu, and many aspects of general systems theory worked themselves into the discipline both self-consciously and unself-consciously during the next decade.[5] But it was the simplicity of Easton's model of the political system that made it attractive, not refinements he tended to overlook even as he minimized that other contribution to his political thinking, the work of A. F. Bentley (1908).[6]

Easton defined a political system as "those interactions through which values are authoritatively allocated for a society" (1965b:21). It exists in an environment composed of other social and nonsocial systems. Political science—and political anthropology, in Easton's view—derive their intellectual coherence from the effort to identify the internal features of political systems, the politically relevant features in their environments, and the nature of the linkages between the two. Political process was then "the translation of politically relevant characteristics of the environment into inputs of support and demand to the political system, the conversion of these inputs into outcomes through consensus and conflict at the core of the political system, and the output of values and costs to the environment" (Winckler 1969:302).

Easton provided a series of diagrams to make his exposition clearer, and his succeeding works elaborated the metalanguage of the first. There is little reference to the real world in his systems analysis, apart from the occasional mention of changes in government. Government, however, is located in Easton's system inside the black box, into which the systems thinker does not look. A student of Fortes, Adam Kuper,

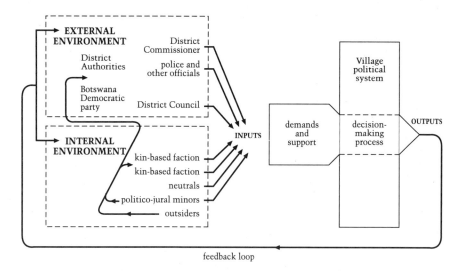

Figure 5.1. Kuper's diagram of the Kalahari village political system
(adapted from Kuper 1970a:173)

adopted Easton's systems model. His diagram of the political system of a Kalahari village (Fig. 5.1) is accompanied by a much more complicated analysis in his book *Kalahari Village Politics* (1970a). Kuper was perhaps less critical of political systems thinking than many of his peers, but he shared with them a concern for "the daily stuff of modern politics" (Kuper 1970a:3).[7]

The matter came to a head at the important Conference on New Approaches in Social Anthropology, organized by the ASA and held at Jesus College, Cambridge, in June 1963. Two of the volumes that resulted, *Political Systems and the Distribution of Power* (Banton 1965) and *The Social Anthropology of Complex Societies* (Banton 1966), provided a new roster of anthropologists interested in politics. Among them were Britishers (F. G. Bailey, Peter C. Lloyd, Aidan Southall, and Adrian C. Mayer) and Americans (Ralph W. Nicholas and Eric R. Wolf). Both Lloyd and Southall questioned Easton's critique of the field, as well as his central focus on authority. Their inclinations lay more toward Max Weber than general systems theory. Nor were the editors of the volumes, Max Gluckman and Fred Eggan, prepared to accept his criticism without a murmur: "We are tempted to point out that in the kinds of societies traditionally studied by social anthropologists, political, economic, religious, and social systems are in fact often not differentiated, and to reply that political scientists have not themselves made so clear a definition of political systems" (Banton 1965:xx). The second point is valid; the first, less so. Political scientists of Easton's time were no clearer than political anthropologists about what constituted the essence of "the political" and clearly recognized their own provincialism.

Easton's review of political anthropology served more to distinguish boundaries between anthropology and political science than to critique the field. He was aware of what was actually being studied in the late 1950s: "the sources of social conflict and the integrative devices for muting it; the nature and function of law and legal processes; the impact of complex societies upon primitive ones, with special attention to the consequences for political structures; the transformation of political elites; the application of available anthropological data to the solution of urgent issues of political policy; and the introduction of anthropological concepts and methods into the study of modern complex societies" (1959:210). Yet he chose to concentrate on unilineal descent groups and segmentary lineage organization. This had certainly been a major contribution to political theory in the 1940s, but it was hardly of central importance in 1959. He then proceeded to delineate as an alternative his own model of the political system instead of acknowledging the paradigmatic shift that had occurred and addressing it.

Anthropologists themselves both criticized and condemned the midwife who had brought their own disciplinary offspring into the light of day. Bailey noted how "even resolute frontiersmen like David Easton do not quite disencumber themselves of the notion that in the last resort politics is a matter of governments. Easton builds the concept of 'authorities' into his definition of politics, and he cannot bring himself to countenance any but the supreme authority as truly political. What goes on in lesser arenas—in villages or universities or professional associations—he calls 'parapolitical.' He has hung himself on a quite unnecessary hook" (Bailey 1968:281). Abner Cohen was even harsher, charging that Easton's 1959 review was both damaging and irresponsible: "he neglects whole streams of thought within anthropology whose contribution to the study of politics have been immense. Worst of all, he completely misunderstands the nature of the central theoretical problems with which social anthropology deals" (1969a:215).

Criticisms of Easton's political analysis flowed fast and furious within political science too. Condemned were his holistic mode of conceptualizing "the political system"; the reductionism involved in treating it as "a necessity system"; the model's high level of generality; its presentism; its concern for the "power-house" rather than the "public"; his failure to address the disjunction between "the goals of the system" and the "purposes of political actors"; and the homeostatic assumptions (Crick 1959; Evans 1970). There was thus both external criticism of the Easton model in terms of its range and application, and doubts about the scientism of the whole endeavor. What is missing from systems analysis is the study of individuals, agency, and groupings. Easton failed to address the relation of the system to the purposive actions of political actors, and this is exactly where political anthropology took off between 1957 and 1973. By the end of the period, its successes and failures were themselves being assessed.

Constructing a Charter

The first encyclopedic review of political anthropology as a subfield appeared in 1968. Its author, Elizabeth Colson, neatly shelved the previously dominant Oxbridge paradigm and set up a new one in its place. Since she provided the emerging paradigm with both a genealogy and a charter, it will be presented at some length. First, however, what of Colson's credentials? Having earlier conducted field research among the Makah Indians of Washington state and at a Japanese-American internment camp in the 1940s, Elizabeth Colson became firmly established as a leading political anthropologist through her work among the Plateau Tonga of Zambia, her directorship of the Rhodes-Livingstone Institute, and teaching and publications on both sides of the Atlantic. Her political analyses were always contemporary: the conditions of colonial overrule and the penetration of industrial capitalism, the state, and the global economy were on the agenda for Colson long before others formulated the new problematic they embodied.[8] Colson's uniquely transatlantic voice limned both the practice of political anthropology and its underpinning in the history of ideas, specifically those of Durkheim, Weber, and Simmel. Political anthropology in its last hundred years (since Maine's *Ancient Law* [1861]) had largely been concerned, in Colson's view, with matters of definition and the creation of typologies: "They clarified the characteristics that distinguished different systems and used these as the bases of typologies useful in comparative work. Inevitably they dealt with descriptions of political groups and political roles as these ideally functioned. This directed attention to 'constitutions' and mechanisms for social control rather than to the competitive aspects of politics" (1968:189–190).

The main controversy within the discipline focused on the relation of kinship to territoriality, and Colson reviewed the contributions of Maine, Morgan, and Lowie to the subject. "The truth appears to be," she concluded, "that people who have much the same degree of technical and economic development may vary in the way in which they conceptualize their political relationships, which are always territorial in nature. Some express them in kinship idiom; others use some other model. The differences, whatever they are, that distinguish highly developed political systems from simpler systems do not rest upon so easily formulated a dichotomy as kinship versus territoriality" (1968:190).

Malinowski's creation of the functional school of anthropology cleared the way, Colson suggested, for a study of political action as well as political structures, although he himself "contributed little directly to the development of political studies. . . . Political anthropology received its real emphasis when students trained by Malinowski and Radcliffe-Brown encountered still functioning large-scale political units when they began to work in Africa in the 1930s. . . . [T]hey were forced to study government, whereas their predecessors, who had dealt with small-scale societies, had studied social control" (Colson 1968:191). Political anthropology *as a distinctive branch of social and cultural anthropology* was a late development stimulated by the publication of *African Political Systems* in 1940.

Colson drew attention to the way in which the ethnography of successive continents gave rise to new issues within political anthropology, a subject about which she had more to say in her lecture to the American Anthropological Association (1976). North American ethnographers, she noted, had little to say about Native American political organization, because it could only be reconstructed from the memories of a demoralized conquered people. The development of Australian and Melanesian ethnography in the early twentieth century strongly influenced studies of religion, kinship, and social structure but failed to stimulate research on political problems. In Africa, Colson suggested, Radcliffe-Brown's minimal working definition of political organization as the maintenance or establishment of social order within a territorial framework by the organized exercise of coercive authority through the use, or the possibility of use, of physical force, although strongly criticized, as we have seen, was useful for analyzing the mechanisms that underlay cohesion and the control of violence in seemingly amorphous stateless societies (1968:191). Prior to this, Durkheimian theoretical influences—which treated societies as moral systems, emphasizing common values, integration, equilibrium, and continuity— had been paramount. Max Gluckman found conflict "an integrative device serving to maintain existing systems of political relationships" (1968:192), but after most African nations had achieved independence, a shift in interest became apparent. This reflected a change in the type of data now available for observation. Colonial authorities used and maintained indigenous political institutions where these were adaptable, but as administrative institutions rather than as a means whereby competing interests and dissent could be expressed. Political dissent was not recognized as legitimate within the subordinate political units that most anthropologists studied. The decline of colonialism, the rapid growth of political parties, and the emergence of new political regimes after World War II radically altered the anthropologist's conception of the field of study.

Anthropological studies dealing with national political parties and their impact on local political events began to appear. "In a period of contending interests," Colson concluded, "most studies deal with competition, with conflict, and with rapid change [and] political maneuver in systems whose stability is no longer a given" (1968:192). This shift toward conflict and change Colson dated to 1954. "If the period from 1940 to 1960 was dominated by the synchronic study of political structures in a state of assumed equilibrium and by the creation of typologies, the period after 1960 showed an increasing interest in the development of a theory that could deal with change, faction, party, and political maneuver" (1968:90). The work of Leach, Barth, and M. G. Smith contributed to this.

Colson's essay provided a pedigree for the emerging paradigm in political anthropology just at the moment when its political science rival was about to celebrate its entry onto the Third World stage by institutionalizing itself as comparative politics.[9] It marked the end of the new paradigm's first phase; by 1968 anthropology already stood at a crossroads and was in a revisionist mood.

A PLACE IN THE SUN

The 1960s was a decade of academic turmoil as universities in the new nations began to restructure their curricula and Western social scientists moved in to carve out research territories. British and American scholars differed somewhat in their responses to the new intellectual frontier. The British more explicitly recognized that any demarcation between the social science disciplines was purely conventional (Runciman 1970), a matter of past academic politics, as we have seen. The Americans, meanwhile, concentrated on carving up the pie. Most adopted a field method of inquiry (in some manner and to some extent), relegating anthropology to local-level analyses. Political anthropologists responded by asserting that its distinctive contribution lay in neither methods nor content but in intellectual sophistication. It contested the narrowness of the space allocated to it by a political science that was itself developing factional interests. Indeed, subfields such as behavioral politics, comparative politics, and political culture seemed very close to anthropology (Fallers 1963b; Cohen 1965; Weingrod 1967; Vincent 1969). Only after a decade of jostling for distinctiveness were political sociology and political anthropology eventually seen to be "like trains on different tracks, each moving speedily away from the other" (Weingrod 1967:122–123).

Political anthropology's effort to assert a separate identity was reflected in three concurrent trends. First, many British anthropologists and former colonial service officers began to take teaching and research posts in American universities. Second, there began to emerge a generation of scholars with higher degrees in both political science and anthropology. Finally, the vacuum left by the imperial retreat was entered by global agencies that funded new research.

That political anthropology monopolized knowledge about the local level was unquestioned, but its expertise in topics such as national integration, cultural pluralism, and elite structure was less apparent. Scholars made several efforts to address the methodological question of how anthropology could span the "levels" being imposed upon it by other disciplines, particularly development economics and political science.[10] This led to important conceptual innovations. Political development, as the anthropologist defined it (Richards 1960; Smith 1960), referred to a major discontinuity in political structure, that is, a change of system, not change within a system. Scholars identified distinctions between repetitive, structural, gradual, and radical change (Fortes 1958; Bailey 1960; Firth 1964; Gluckman 1968), as well as the difference between rebellion and revolution (Worsley 1961). In part this reflected concern *in the field* with the rapid changes introduced in the 1960s—the "development decade" of many new states—but it also rested on a long tradition of sociological evolutionary thinking. Within a structural framework, too, change and stability were understood to be corollary concepts. From this firm platform, anthropologists were equipped to offer not simply local-level analyses, but the political ethnography of contemporary Indonesia, a country of over 97 million people (Geertz 1963a) or of West African states in the nineteenth century (Forde and Kaberry 1967). Reluctant to accept a place defined for it by others, the discipline began to expand more and more into the realms of political science and history.

But, above all, political anthropology elevated problems of national integration from a shallow, utilitarian, presentist concern (itself a function and dimension of great-power politics) to one of indigenous concern and historical proportions. Evans-Pritchard's (1971) dynamic account of the political development of the Zande state, incorporated into the Anglo-Egyptian Sudan in the 1920s, was one such work. The indigenous polity had a population of over three million, covered between 60,000 and 100,000 square miles, and contained within its boundaries more than twenty culturally distinct ethnic groups. Evans-Pritchard looked at problems of succession; personal allegiance to a charismatic leader; the questioning of relationships of authority and subordination; variations in the degree of autonomy between provinces; the relation between a communications system and governmental effectiveness where great reliance was placed on the personal control of the leader; the differential rate of expansion in different parts of the polity; problems of stability; relations between the central authority and the judiciary; general mobilization; intelligence; the spoils system; the balance of power; assassinations; reciprocity as a political mechanism; and so on.

Similarly, the contributors to a symposium on West African kingdoms in the nineteenth century (Forde and Kaberry 1967) compared their historical development, territorial structures, control and exploitation of resources, tribute and trade, and modes of incorporating subject peoples. Principles of succession and appointment at various levels in the hierarchy and modes of competition for power were also central themes. The contributors related them to ideology and the ritual of kingship, the administrative machinery of the state, and the organization and control of military forces. Since the external relations of the kingdoms had, in some cases, played a part in determining their internal structure and bringing about change, they also delineated these factors. Clearly, political organization as well as structure, competition, ideology, and extrasystemic features were coming to be recognized as integral to the anthropological perspective.

Yet it was still not clear whether political anthropologists viewed their contribution as a subfield of political sociology (Goody 1966a) or political science (A. Cohen 1974a), or as an enterprise of a sufficiently distinctive kind to be recognized as qualitatively different. What *was* proving to be distinctive as the 1960s progressed was its objective: to bring historical and contemporary societies into one coherent discourse regardless of whether they were situated in northern Europe or the Third World. This inevitably led it to question the ideological implications of much contemporary Western social science as the era came to a close (Sahlins 1972; Asad 1973b). Knowledge, ideology, and power were striving toward synergy.

Just as they resisted being assigned exclusively to the grassroots level of contemporary states, so political anthropologists refused to be relegated to the "traditional" as opposed to the "modern" sector. For the most part, they considered the traditional-modern dichotomy to be of very little use. In their place they proposed to distinguish systems of social relationships that contradicted one another from those that did not. They took contradictions to indicate the increasing complexity of social interaction (Bailey 1963; Garbett 1967). They employed the constructs of equality, ranking, and stratification to make developmental distinctions if the focus was upon the political community (Fried 1960, 1964, 1968), and if the focus was on the development of governmental forms, on minimal, diffuse, and expansive political organization (Mair 1962). Mair showed how some (traditional?) stateless systems contained the prototypical (modern?) governmental forms out of which states might develop. Having described how they functioned in relative autonomy, Mair then demonstrated how they had been articulated with colonial regimes.

The major contribution of political anthropology in this era, and the one that contributed most to its survival, was its study of institutionless arenas (Zolberg 1966). Whereas political scientists tended to work downward, dealing with vertical structures, anthropologists were concerned to work outward, horizontally, from any point within a political arena. The interstitial, informal aspects of government and politics were what the anthropologists considered most crucial (Nadel 1956; Wolf 1966).

Political anthropology was also concerned with a topic of primary interest to the newly installed Third World governments of this era and to the foreign policy experts of the major powers: nation building. Political anthropology tended to have a more populist orientation than political science because, in a sense, it controlled the data on the populations that had to be mobilized in support of the new regimes. Yet it was inhibited by its past treatment of such political elements as "tribes," "races," and "ethnic groups." Anthropologists did not sufficiently acknowledge at this time that the colonial state, under the sovereignty of a European power, had already gone a long way in the process. Nation building was not, as Lienhardt suggested (1964:78), a problem of "converting a political system of relations between once sovereign peoples within its boundaries into a more comprehensive political organization" but one of succession to the mantle of colonial resistance. As always, Evans-Pritchard came up with the timely monograph. His book *The Sanusi of Cyrenaica* (1949) described how a congeries of North African tribesmen had been melded into one state organization through the centralizing strategies of an Islamic confraternity, but for some reason (perhaps because it was as much a political narrative as a structural analysis) it never entered into the mainstream of political anthropology.

Working within the stable administrative framework established by the colonizing power fostered an emphasis on stability and unity. Researchers saw indigenous political organizations as frozen at a particular moment in time so that instead of looking at the changing politics in terms of a moving frontier, as on the American Plains in the 1950s or in Asia (Bailey 1957; Leach 1960; Lattimore 1962), they became, virtually, historical reconstructions. The emphasis on static studies and the presentation of political constitutions was implicit in the sociological concept of an "ethnographic present" introduced, as we have seen, by John Wesley Powell. Because researchers had described most of the political systems as ideal types, not as political forms integrating marginal peoples into a colonial state, they lent themselves only to taxonomy making, not to the analysis of the political process.

ON TAXONOMY

Just as the mass of ethnographic detail that had emerged from Victorian scholarship had led to earlier systems of classification in political anthropology, so the impetus of *African Political Systems* (1940; hereafter *APS*) and the inadequacy of its taxonomy produced renewed efforts to impose order. Political anthropology, after all, hoped to become "the comparative science of politics and modes of government" (Balandier 1970:159), encapsulating political science and defying any restriction to primitive systems. Yet the classification of simple political systems (as opposed to complex ones), and the study of indigenous political institutions (as opposed to colonial ones), continued to occupy the field. There was some effort, as we shall see, to take into account more and more content and context with each successive taxonomy. Four taxonomies will be discussed here. Three of them (Figs. 5.2–5.4) were based on *APS*; the fourth (Fig. 5.5) came out of a different tradition.

Two classifications fleshed out the "noncentralized" wing of the *APS* dichotomy (Figs. 5.2 and 5.4). Typology building sometimes became an end in itself (Owusu 1975) even though Leach roundly condemned it as butterfly collecting (1961). The hunt was pursued most avidly by Evans-Pritchard's Oxford students until eventually even he was obliged to say

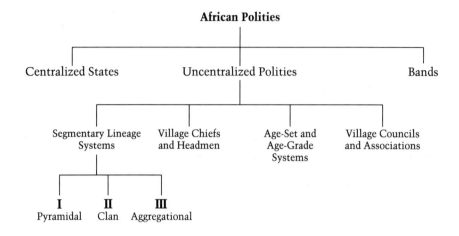

Figure 5.2. Middleton and Tait's taxonomy of tribes without rulers
(based on Middleton and Tait 1958)

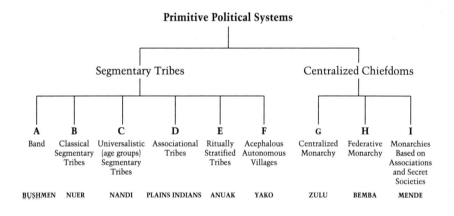

Figure 5.3. Eisenstadt's taxonomy of primitive political systems
(based on Eisenstadt 1959)

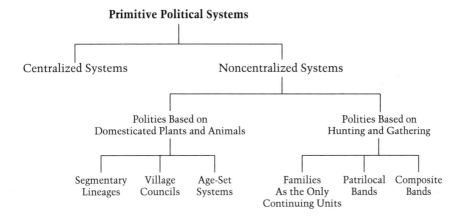

Figure 5.4. Cohen's taxonomy of primitive political systems
(adapted from Cohen 1965:120)

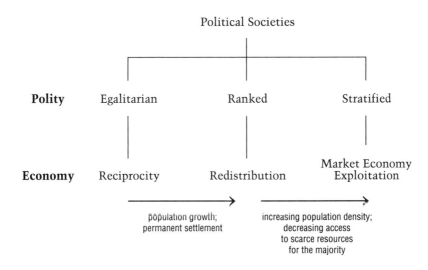

Figure 5.5. The Polanyi-Fried taxonomy of political societies
(based on Polanyi 1968 and Fried 1967)

publicly that he thought the intuitive *APS* taxon had been taken far too seriously. The editors of *Tribes Without Rulers* (Middleton and Tait 1958) traveled farthest in pursuit of the elusive noncentralized political systems, recognizing subtypes of subtypes, as can be seen in Figure 5.2.

Scholars in cognate disciplines found the unacknowledged primordial attachment to kinship disconcerting and volunteered alternatives. S. N. Eisenstadt, an Israeli sociologist, devised his own preliminary comparative analysis of primitive political systems (1959). He found the earlier dichotomization of centralized and acephalous political systems inadequate but was prepared to work with it (Fig. 5.3). In his discussion he focused instead on conflict, social control, and crosscutting alliances. He drew largely on the work of Colson and Gluckman. Eisenstadt suggested that thus far anthropologists had placed too great an emphasis on groups and that there should be closer scrutiny of governmental functions.

Eisenstadt suggested the adoption of a sociological paradigm derived from Weber, calling for the analysis of the political system as a subsystem within society: "[T]he representative organization of a territorial society . . . has the legitimate monopoly of the use of force within the society which it regulates; in its representative function it uses this monopoly for the implementation of those goals which are held to be most important for the society by its influential members and groups and to some extent by all members of the society" (1959:61). Anthropologists, Eisenstadt believed, had been too preoccupied with the extent to which specialized political roles had developed within the societies they studied and had ignored other important criteria, such as the relative emphasis within each system on the four main types of political activity (administrative, executive, party-political, and juridical-cultural), the scope and nature of the political struggle, and the extent and nature of possible changes. Above all, they had neglected "the various social conditions which are related to different types of political organization" (1959:204).

It was perhaps an indication of the insecurity felt by American anthropologists that such an article should have been published in the association's professional journal. The work Eisenstadt reviewed was done entirely by British scholars. Moreover, the comparative analysis he advocated was being carried out at the time both by sociologists such as Marion Levy and Talcott Parsons and by a new breed of political sociologists, including Gabriel Almond and James S. Coleman. Like Easton earlier, these social scientists were taken very seriously by political anthropologists seeking to maintain an ordered progression in their theoretical discourse: all were systems men, and functioning systems at that.

The next contributor to political anthropology's attempt to set its house in order was also, like Eisenstadt, an insider-outsider. Ronald Cohen, a Canadian teaching at an American university (Northwestern) and one of a handful of scholars with a familiarity with both political science and anthropology, became in the 1960s the leading authority in the United States on political anthropology, its practice and potential. He had the advantage over Eisenstadt of drawing upon both British and American anthropological traditions.

In "Political Anthropology: The Future of a Pioneer" (1965), Cohen provided a considerably more sophisticated taxonomy of primitive political systems (Fig. 5.4). It was based not on functional systems analysis alone but on a combination of sociological and ecological criteria. APS had questioned the relevance of demography and modes of livelihood for political analysis; Cohen restored them. Like Eisenstadt, he did not question the APS distinction between centralized and non-centralized political systems, but he blended an APS-derived recognition of lineages, councils, and age-set systems with Julian Steward's discriminations of hunting and gathering bands. These he called non-centralized systems (Fig. 5.4). Centralized polities, Cohen suggested, should be differentiated according to some of the variables he had found to be significant earlier in an analysis of the feudal Nigerian state of Bornu. These were the degree of control by the center and the nature of succession.

Cohen shared Easton's anxiety over the lack of theory in political anthropology but disavowed his recommendations. He expressed every confidence that "as more and more cases are examined, it is expected, *within the framework of the traditional wisdom*, that what is political and its exact nature will emerge. Indeed to define it too clearly ahead of time might conceivably direct observation away from some unsuspected source of political organization in any particular society," (1965:117, emphasis added). As Max Weber had urged half a century before: "[T]he final and definitive concept cannot stand at the beginning of the investigation, but must come at the end" (1902/1976:47).

The fourth taxonomy (Fig. 5.5) came out of the Weberian tradition. Weber's legacy was, by now, shared quite widely among scholars engaged in the study of kingdoms and empires. A volume edited by Karl Polanyi, Conrad Arensberg, and Harold Pearson, *Trade and Market in the Early Empires* (1957), was extremely influential. Polanyi, an economic historian, distinguished four modes of economic integration:

market systems, reciprocity (a symmetrical movement of goods between individuals or groups), redistribution (the channeling of goods to
a central authority), and householding (1968). His own work focused on
redistribution in kingdoms and empires (Weber's "traditional" polities)
and was integumentally historical. Because of this, his very real influence on political anthropology tended to be both subtle and diffuse. It
came at the very time when the new subdiscipline needed a quick fix
for its ethnographic dazzle.

As so often happened when historical processes proved hard to grasp,
the quick fix was provided by evolutionism. Deriving sustenance from
the writings of Leslie White at Michigan, particularly his *Evolution of
Culture* (1959), the neo-evolutionists Marshall Sahlins (1968, 1972) and
Morton Fried (1960, 1967) began to apply Polanyi's typology to so-called
pre-state societies. Sahlins later gave up evolution for history, but
Fried's adaptation of the schema took American political anthropology
by storm. He simply combined Polanyi's classification with an argument about the growth of inequality reminiscent of Engels's *The Origin
of the Family, Private Property and the State* (1884/1972). Fried's
evolutionary schema was a stage model (Fig. 5.5), a universal progression from egalitarian societies characterized by reciprocity through
ranked societies, where a redistributive economy was to be found, to
stratified market-based political economies.

Fried's evolutionary schema was attractive in its simplicity. Most
existing political ethnographies could be placed in one of three boxes:
egalitarian, ranked, or stratified. Where this raised questions, a minor
industry developed around, for example, the concept of exploitation
(Harris 1959; Dalton 1974), affluence (Sahlins and Service 1960;
Sahlins 1972), or (as with the *APS*) the relation of population density to
state formation (Stevenson 1968). The publication of Marx's *Grundrisse*—introduced to most political anthropologists, remember, in
the form of Eric Hobsbawm's *Pre-Capitalist Economic Formations*
(1964)—along with the impact of French Marxist ethnography (Terray
1969; Godelier 1973a, 1973b), particularly in the dissenting years following the student rebellions of 1968, led some political anthropologists away from simple taxonomy per se toward the significant theoretical questions it raised.

Others remained to draw up fresh battle lines on the taxonomic front.
Elman Service focused on cultural integration rather than political inequalities and unequal access to scarce resources. His taxonomy elaborated on Fried's "long" middle portion between the egalitarian band
and the stratified state occupied by the tribe and the chiefdom. Many

anthropologists could work with the notion of the chiefdom but, as always, took up battle-axes over the problem of the tribe. Neo-evolutionists, materialists, and Marxists fought academically (Fried 1967; Helm 1968; Sahlins 1968; Godelier 1973a, 1973b). More important, the offensiveness of the term *tribe* to the citizens of new nations (Southall 1970) and the legal difficulties its use raised for Native Americans (Sturtevant 1983) led to an unhappy juxtapositioning of its use in undergraduate texts with its jettisoning in more advanced circles.

In an era when Third World "modernization" was high on the agenda, social scientists required a categorization of "traditional" societies as a baseline for measuring development, progress, and political advance. From the time of Morgan, taxonomies had revolved around economic as well as political features. Until 1954 they had been either evolutionary or superficial or both. Those of Hobhouse, Wheeler, Ginsberg, and Childe fell into the first category; the classification offered in *African Political Systems* fell into the second. It is one of the ironies with which political anthropology abounds that Morton Fried, who had provided the field with its most pervasive taxonomy of political forms, also chided the discipline with failing to recognize the significance of where sovereignty lay. The colonial state and the new nation featured in none of the taxonomies produced in the turbulent years from 1954 to 1973.

REEVALUATING

The path to the reevaluation of the constitutional paradigm was marked by Raymond Firth's distinction between structure and organization:

> In speaking of social organization we are not dealing with any isolable, concrete social identity. Our analysis refers to a field of social action which is identified in terms of pattern-sequence. . . . In the concept of social structure, the qualities recognized are primarily those of persistence, continuity, form and pervasiveness through the social field . . . [T]he concept of social organization . . . recognizes adaptation of behaviour in respect to given ends, control of means in varying circumstances, which are set by changes in the external environment or by the necessity to resolve conflict. . . . If structure implies order, organization implies a working towards order—though not necessarily the same order. (1955:3)

From Malinowski's first student at LSE, political anthropology thus received its charter to engage more rigorously in the study of political process.

But first the productivity of the new organizational paradigm had to be demonstrated. This was done through reevaluations of the "classics."

A series of reanalyses of the political *organization* of the Nuer, as opposed to its political *structure*, focused on leadership and support groups, on the source of political authority, on political choice and political manipulation, and subsequently on political ecology and the politics of ethnicity (Beidelman 1971; Gough 1971; Greuel 1971; Glickman 1972, 1974; Haight 1972; MacDermott 1972; Newcomer 1972; Burton 1981). The interests of the actors involved in the political situation at any point in time became a prime concern (Schapera 1956; Barth 1959a, 1963; Bailey 1969).[11] A reexamination of the literature on segmentary lineages (such as those Evans-Pritchard described among the Nuer) similarly suggested that the processes by which they developed might be discerned by viewing them as organizations of predatory expansion and placing them within a wider ecological-historical perspective.[12] Sahlins (1961) and Southall (1976b) viewed competition and external threats as a necessary condition in the political economy of any people if segmentary lineage systems were to develop. The first group moving into an area was unlikely to develop a segmentary lineage system, whereas the second to enter the area was more likely to do so. This emphasis on structured sequences had been most clearly set out, remember, in the 1940 textbook *Principles of Anthropology*, by Eliot Chapple and Carleton Coon.

The political ethnography of Fortes's Tallensi and Malinowski's Trobrianders were similarly reevaluated. Worsley's Marxist reexamination (1956) drew attention to Fortes's predilection for equilibrium analysis and a neglect of historical change. The kinship polity was under attack. "Tale society has now become part of the world economy," Worsley suggested (1956:72), and the impact of labor migration, wage labor, and production for the market had to be taken into account. He drew up a new agenda that would entail the political anthropologist leaving the field for the study: "Detailed field work studies have been accumulating for two decades and more; there is now a danger that we may become submerged under a flood of specialized and limited monographs. Further progress in scientific anthropology demands a break with empiricism, and the clarification of general theory, utilizing the rich field-material that exists" (1956:74).

Roger Keesing called for theoretical rethinking of a different kind. Comparing Tallensi descent models with those of the Kwaio of the Solomon Islands, lineage with Big Man models, he observed that "the gulf between the way Kwaio (and I as their ethnographer) conceptualize their system and the way Fortes and Goody conceptualize the African systems seems far wider than the gulf between what the Kwaio and the

Africans do" (1970:765). The gulf, he suggested, was generated by the structural models, not by the "facts," by which he meant what people did. He set out his own vision and in so doing clearly enunciated political anthropology's emergent paradigm: "Instead of seeing societies *as composed of groups*, we see individuals *moving through situations*, with different groups crystallized in different contexts according to rules not unlike those of a grammar" (Keesing 1972:23–24, emphasis added). The focus was on individuals, agency, and process.[13]

The larger dimensions and methodological implications of a processual approach—a political anthropology of action or agency, to use the terms adopted for it toward the end of this era (A. Cohen 1974a; Bourdieu 1977; Vincent 1978)—were clearly spelled out by S. F. Nadel.[14] Nadel suggested that the particular expertise of anthropologists working in contemporary complex societies lay in field research directed toward the discovery and analysis of the interstitial. The anthropologist's main concern, he wrote, "is with the 'interstitial spaces' of the social structure, where the other disciplines concern themselves primarily with the gross structure itself, with specific institutions, associations, with legal machineries, and so on. By 'interstitial spaces' I mean simply the inter-personal relations between the human beings who make up the society, and the day-by-day interactions and communications through which institutions, associations or legal machineries operate" (Nadel 1956:171–172).

Eric Wolf emphasized a similar point in his important contribution to the transatlantic ASA volume *The Social Anthropology of Complex Societies* (Banton 1966). Anthropologists, he suggested, study the terra incognita existing within the larger political system. Under the rubric "Core and Periphery in Complex Societies," he noted:

> There are political resources which are essential to the operation of the system, and the system will try to remain in control of these. But there are also resources and organizations which it would be either too costly or too difficult to bring under direct control, and in these cases the system yields its sovereignty to competitive groups that are allowed to function in its entrails. . . . [W]e must not confuse the theory of state sovereignty with the facts of political life. Many organizations within the state generate and distribute and control power, in competition with each other and with the sovereign power of the state. As examples one might cite the Teamsters' Union of the United States, the Mafia, or the American Medical Association. Thus we could also draw a map of political power for any complex society in which the key centers of control—Lenin's strategic heights—appeared in red—showing strong concentrations of sovereign power—while other political regions appeared as grey or white. We thus note that the formal framework of economic and political power exists alongside or

intermingled with various other kinds of informal structure which are *interstitial*, supplementary, parallel to it. Even the study of major institutions, such as of the American and German armies during World War II, or of factories in Britain and the United States, or of bureaucratic organizations, has yielded statements about the functional importance of informal groups. Sometimes such informal groupings cling to the formal structure like barnacles to a rusty ship. At other times, informal social relations are responsible for the metabolic processes required to keep the formal institution operating, as in the case of armies locked in combat. In still other cases, we discover that the formal table of organization is elegant indeed, but fails to work, unless informal mechanisms are found for its direct contravention, as in the network of *blat* relationships among Soviet industrial managers.

   The anthropologist has a professional license to study such interstitial, supplementary, and parallel structures in complex society and to expose their relation to the major strategic, over-arching institutions. (Wolf 1966a:1–2, emphasis added)

The more subtle and penetrating understanding of politics that began to emerge led to further "scientific" attempts to limit and define the field. Bailey introduced the concept of "parapolitical structures" (1968), taking the concept from Easton (1965a) but redefining it as "the kind of political structures . . . which are partly regulated by, and partly independent of, larger encapsulating political structures; and which, so to speak, fight battles with these larger structures in a way which for them seldom ends in victory, rarely in dramatic defeat, but usually in a long drawn out stalemate and defeat by attrition" (1968:281). A preliminary to his political manual, *Strategems and Spoils* (1969), Bailey's work gained a large following among political anthropologists in the 1970s, while at the same time its tendentiousness rendered it central to critical theory (Silverman 1974; Barrett 1984). This was probably the most expansive moment in Bailey's middle-range theorizing. In 1958 he had written a paper for *Closed Systems and Open Minds* (Gluckman and Devons 1964) that marked off social anthropology from history and the study of culture on the one hand and economic and political science on the other. Thereafter his "encapsulated politics" shrank further, finally to end up within the walls of the academy itself, whither the "duty of abstinence" (1964:168), a disciplined refusal to trespass on the fields of the others, had in effect logically led him.

By 1968 political anthropology's stance was almost wholly revisionist. It began to move from a concentration on popular or local-level politics to elite politics. It began to question its cultural units of analysis. The politics of ethnicity emerged and began to replace what had previously been called tribalism (Moerman 1965; Fried 1966; Barth

1969; Southall 1970; Vincent 1974). Ideology and cultural categorization began to receive more attention, complementing the earlier primary focus on groups and group interests, and the attention then being paid to individual political actors.

Clifford Geertz's essay, "Politics Past, Politics Present" (1967) discusses the role of empirical research in contemporary polities and the need to distinguish the ambitions of leaders from the social instrumentalities by means of which their ends are sought. Mair discussed African socialism (1967) and Worsley elite ideology in the Third World (1964). Geertz grappled with the problem of analyzing the relation of past political culture to current political ideology, a concern Bailey also broached in an essay on conceptual systems (1972). The notion of political culture never did become quite as prominent in political anthropology as in political science. Political scientists drew on anthropological research in education and socialization to buttress their analyses (Coleman 1965; Bender 1967), but these tended to be neglected within political anthropology itself.

A questioning of past practitioners' understanding of the context of their political ethnography led to a recognition and exploration of the by then mostly historical colonial situation (Balandier 1951; Steward 1955; Worsley 1957; Geertz 1963b). But the greatest failure, as Kathleen Gough pointed out in 1968, was political anthropology's failure to take into account the global context of both "Western" imperialism and Communism. It was in this direction that political anthropology moved in the following decade (Chapter 6).

ACTION AND PROCESS

To characterize the processual analysis that provided political anthropology with its dominant paradigm after 1965 as revolutionary would be to misjudge its roots and to ignore its continuity with the past. Its practitioners struck a new pose and so drew attention to a whole series of problematic concerns that had previously been overshadowed by closed-systems thinking within structural functionalism. Systems thinking predominated in political anthropology between 1940 and 1954, as we have seen, and systems metaphors tended to be hegemonic, a propensity to systematize being ever present (Barrett 1984). By 1957 it became apparent that an alternative—process thinking—was in the making. It became most visible in the work of the Manchester School, but it also had a significant LSE component.

It was generally recognized that a focus on political process demanded consideration of political structure as well, yet the relationship between structure and process was a particularly touchy matter in political anthropology. As the new subfield began to acquire what Aidan Southall perceived to be a Madison Avenue veneer, he considered it necessary to remind everyone that function and structure are both dynamic, are both processes of long duration. "This particular piece of biological wisdom," Southall wrote, "should not have been thrown overboard along with the cruder aspects of organic analogy" (1968:44). Southall was doubtless right to emphasize that structural analysis could be the vehicle for the study of structure and change, but the fact remained that it had rarely been so.

An overly sociological conceptualization of structure had clearly crept into the anthropology of politics. Researchers saw social groups and categories as units of structure rather than as the epiphenomena they really were. In conversation, Levi-Strauss once silenced a critic who charged him with finding structures, structures everywhere by responding that he considered there to be but small islands of structure amidst seas of probabilities. It was the latter that processualists tried to change. They groped their way toward the analysis of unstructured forms and "institutionless arenas," as Aristide Zolberg called them (1968).

In 1957 S. F. Nadel's *The Theory of Social Structure* was published posthumously. It made concrete the paradigm that had been developing at LSE as action theory, which was highly compatible with the Mancunians' situational analysis. The focus of analytical attention was individual and group interaction. The analysis of the political thus set aside configurational analyses of institutions and categories and placed the emphasis instead on relationships obtaining between actors—transactions. This was important for, as Arensberg observed: "Systems are all too often invoked in which every other factor is coded, but the flow of action among the system-elements which are live persons is ignored" (1972:11). Inquiry started not from structural rules or social roles but from the observation of interpersonal events. This shift from role players to individual actors carried political anthropology into a study of individuals' movements in time and space and away from individual decision making and behavioral psychology, which it had been in danger of taking over from American political scientists.

This again was highly compatible with the type of processual analysis being developed at Manchester, where structures of social relations, ideas, and values were still delineated but in relation to processes of which they were both the products and regulators. "Process-theory involves a 'becoming' as well as a 'being' vocabulary," wrote Victor Turner. It "admits of plurality, disparity, conflicts of groups, roles, ideals, and ideas, and, since it is concerned with human beings, considers such variables as 'goal', 'motivation', 'intention', 'rationality', and 'meaning'" (1964:314). For nearly eighty years anthropologists had labored to make their study of politics a science, although an historical connection with the humanities had constantly struggled to assert itself, most conspicuously in folklore (popular culture), ethnohistory, and the romance of fieldwork. Processual metaphors remained historically subordinate because they were in large part "non-scientific" (Bernstein 1978; Hunter 1982). Only in the study of judicial process (Gluckman 1955b) and ritual process (Turner 1969) did a body of comparative writings develop. Elsewhere nomotheticism was better served by action theory.

The Manchester School

By 1955 it was apparent that Radcliffe-Brown and his scientific reconstructionist program of comparison, taxonomizing, and generalization faced an alternative. The tightly knit cohort of anthropologists and sociologists who worked around Max Gluckman at Manchester were a solidary team, provoking the red-baiting jibe, "We are all Maxists here." Jibes were offered in retaliation: Oxbridge's "delusions of grandeur" were exposed as its "lamentable reign of error" drew to a close.

Of the three distinct phases in the politics of the Manchester School,[15] some were more oppositional to the dominant paradigm than others. The "school" itself was not monolithic; the very fact that Gluckman was a Rhodes Scholar at Oxford (although his teachers sent him to attend Malinowski's fieldwork seminars at LSE) in part accounted for his ambivalences and ambiguities. The impact of the school on institutionalized anthropology may be measured by the fact that eleven of the anthropologists who held full appointments at the RLI—Colson and Wilson were exceptions—attained professorships in Britain. Of these, the scholars whose work contributed most to the maturation of processual theory in political anthropology were J. A. Barnes, Ian Cunnison, A. L. Epstein, Max Gluckman, J. C. Mitchell, Victor W. Turner, J. van Velsen, and William Watson. Barnes, Mitchell, and Cunnison obtained doctorates from Oxford between 1950 and 1952; the remainder earned the first doctorates in social anthropology granted by Manchester after 1954. Besides the Africanists, the first generation of the Gluckman seminar included F. G. Bailey (India), R. J. Frankenberg (Wales), and Emrys Peters (Cyrenaica).[16] The cohesiveness of the group rested on similar fieldwork chronologies, the application of a specifically designed field method, and a graduate seminar at which the microscopic analysis of field data bred common discourse. Most important were their "situational" approach, and what came to be called "the extended case method" (Van Velsen 1967). The collegiality of the center and the extension of the discourse to three continents (Africa, Asia, and Europe) in part accounted for the hegemonic influence of the processual approach to politics after 1965.

One monograph above all encapsulated the promise that Mancunian anthropology held: Turner's *Schism and Continuity in an African Society* (1957), "a high-water mark in that Manchester mainstream which derived from Malinowski's *Crime and Custom* [1926a] and his notions of endemic conflict and the social or life situation" (Werbner 1984:176). Around the concept of the social drama and life microhistories of fully fleshed individuals interacting as intricately with each other as in a Russian novel Turner erected a framework for the analysis of political process. Other Mancunians—and most notably F. G. Bailey—took up the *routine* of political strategizing, manipulation, and the advancement of interests—the Machiavellian moment, to coin a phrase. Turner himself chose to structure process, exploring culture rather than polity, and finally, almost as a historian or novelist, cherishing the primacy of field data for all its real and apparent contradictions.

The 1957 season was excellent for Manchester's first-division team. It saw the publication not only of Turner's *Schism and Continuity* but also Frankenberg's *Village on the Border: A Social Study of Religion, Politics and Football in a North Wales Community* and Bailey's *Caste and the Economic Frontier*, set in Bisipara, an Indian village. In all three, political actors maneuvered in small localities, and competition, conflict, and change were as noteworthy as custom and continuity. An epigram from William Blake prefaced Turner's book: "General forms have their vitality in Particulars, and every Particular is a Man." No clearer disavowal of Radcliffe-Brown's anthropology could have been made.[17]

Schism and Continuity presented the structuring of individual action and processes of interaction as integumentally conflict ridden. Yet, as W.E.H. Stanner pointed out in a long critical review (1959), Turner's view of conflict and conflict resolution, although processual, was not dialectical. Much of Turner's extended case analysis of the Ndembu centered on "attempts made by parties who have secured social gains in preceding social dramas to consolidate their position, and attempts by defeated parties to repair their damaged prestige, attach to themselves fresh supporters, and win over to their side members of opposing groups" (Turner 1957:132–133). But, wrote Stanner, in a true Malinowskian vein, "It can be argued sensibly that it is precisely this, the manipulative, bargaining, transactional approach to life, which *is* the system of their life. In other words, that the 'endemic conflict' is not an upset or a defect or an aberration or a friction of some idealized or perfect system, but is *itself* the system, together with the accompaniments and consequences which, logically, follow when most interests can only be attained through other people, i.e. on terms either of agreement or of force" (1959:216)—the seamy side of life, as it were.

Many of these selfsame issues were discussed in the Manchester seminars of the late 1950s and 1960s, foreshadowing by some thirty years both much of what Anthony Giddens, a Cambridge sociologist, came to write about structure and agency and a heated debate in Marxist circles over the rival merits of historian Edward Thompson's and structuralist Louis Althusser's models.

The Shrinking Political Arena

As processual anthropology moved out of the field institute and into the academy, a tendency set in for some of the RLI field researchers to articulate their publications with those of the mainstream, which by the 1950s was structured along the lines of Fortes's exposition of "the developmental cycle of domestic groups" (1958). At what cost this was done is explored by Werbner, who convincingly shows how village studies by Mitchell (1956) and Marwick (1965) increasingly "blocked out phenomenological questions of selective perception and the present reconstruction of the past" (1984:166). These RLI concerns, superbly addressed by Barnes (1951) and Cunnison (1951) in their studies of history and the invention of tradition, were themes later taken up by John Comaroff (1982) and Richard Werbner (1969, 1977), as well as by Manchester's leading historian, Terence Ranger (1982; Hobsbawm and Ranger 1983). A further indication of defection from the Manchester stable was the use of the names of "tribes" (the Yao and the Cewa respectively) in titles. The Mancunian vision focused on locations—Barotseland, the Luapula River, Plateau Tonga, Gwembe (a town), an urban African community, the valley Korekore, a Zambian rural community, lakeside Tonga, and the like.

With Gluckman's own move back into the academy and with his field researchers committed to writing up their materials in Manchester, further shifts occurred. These may have been affected by the disciplinary pressure of Evans-Pritchard; the carrot of ASA membership for academics; a spate of academic posts opening up in Britain and the Commonwealth, which encouraged greater conformity; or the expansion of the student body in both Britain and the United States. Whatever the precise causes, the problem orientation of the central African field-workers gave way in part to an ivory-tower intellectual struggle for rigor and the simplification of complexity. Those RLI fieldworkers with whom Gluckman had already found himself to be most at odds method-ologically—Barnes and Mitchell—increasingly turned, once their Afri-can monographs were written, to more general methodological themes. Of the early researchers at the RLI, only Elizabeth Colson continued to do central African fieldwork, and she continued to demonstrate her paradoxical ability to bring conflict and change into historical perspec-tive by always focusing on the contemporary. Studies of resettlement (1971), prophets (1977b), and education and elite formation (Scudder and Colson 1980) in Zambia followed.

As units of study began to shrink, researchers addressed the prob-lematic relation of the locality to the "outside" world. The seminal statement was made by John Barnes (1954), writing of class and com-mittees in Norway. He was followed by Frankenberg (1957), Bailey (1957, 1960, 1963), and Van Velsen (1964). Their observations were based on fieldwork in Europe, Asia, and Africa respectively. Both Bailey (1971) and Geertz (1972) elucidated the difference between working *in* communities and working *on* communities.[18]

Among the second generation at Manchester, a social fields approach, with its open-endedness, kept the global dimension clearly in view. Norman Long's monograph *Social Change and the Individual* (1968) concentrated the attention of the school's critics on action theory and methodological individualism in spite of his own greater emphasis on problems of rural change in political economies that were becoming capitalistic. Their myopia later led the Dutch anthropologist Van Bins-bergen (1981) to disinter the global dimension in the local situation described by Long. None of the Mancunians confused "isolation, for analytical purposes, . . . with *de facto* isolation" (Van Velsen 1967:145). The legacy of Maine and Marx and the long debate over the Indian village community were once again invoked.

The most important contribution of Mancunian political anthropol-ogy was, perhaps, its demonstration that rigorous anthropological research could be carried out in modern, rapidly changing complex so-cieties across the globe. During this period, its two related paradigms—processual theory and action theory—were developed not only in trop-ical Africa but also in Norway, Wales, India, Lebanon, and Israel. It distinctively stressed the anthropologist's perception in "civilized societies" of what its own members were blind to. The underlying structures of political action were revealed in everyday parish pump politics. Regardless of cultural particulars and formal political institutions, the art and science of politicking was gradually made transparent through the analysis of situations, events, and processes. This "political anthropology" bridged the transatlantic divide in a way that *African Political Systems* (1940) never could. Whereas *APS* was divisive and was received with hostility in the United States, the Mancunian vision, with its two texts—the introduction to *Political Anthropology* and *Stratagems and Spoils*—bred a new and extraordinarily lively shared subfield that all were prepared to call political anthropology.

ACTION THEORY

Action theory in political anthropology was characterized essentially by a focus on individual actors and their strategies within political arenas.[19] In its formative phase (1965–1973) it was associated with a range of theoretical frameworks, among them those built around transactions, symbolic interaction, systems analysis, methodological individualism, game theory, interaction theory, and political clientelism. It differed from the behavioral approach in political science, in which the analysis begins with the individual and his or her motives, proceeds to emphasize choice, and concludes by inferring structural limitations from behavior. Action theory in anthropology began by locating the individual within the framework of both formal and interstitial social organization and then proceeded to the analysis of political action and interaction. It paid particular attention to the sequence of events and to political formations other than categories and corporate groups. Most significantly, it demanded a particular mode of field observation that resulted in a distinctive form of fine-grained political ethnography. Its adherents developed a series of related concepts. Some concerned the political forms generated out of the coalescence of individual actors, others related to modes of political behavior, and still others related to the context (both spatial and temporal) of political action.

The action approach developed largely in the development decade of the 1960s in conjunction with the analysis of "social change" in the Third World. In Africa, researchers placed emphasis on the contemporary social situation in which political actors met in face-to-face encounters. A coherent body of literature developed, as we have seen, around the theme of the village headman and the conflict of roles arising out of his intercalary position in the colonial administrative structure. In India, the problem of relating the village to its wider administrative and political context and the task of studying national political parties, elections, and structural change inspired not only a comprehensive systems analysis of political action within the nation-state but a conceptual tool kit for the elaboration of principles of competitive political behavior in discrete arenas. In Latin America—where researchers no longer placed an emphasis on the national context and historical conditions—the marginalization of rural communities and the role of cultural brokers were major interests. In America, Chapple and Arensberg's delineation of interaction theory was a contemporaneous trend (Arensberg 1972), but whereas the Harvard scholars explored emergent structures and industrial relations, those at the LSE were concerned above all with Third World societies and rural change.

From this shared concern with the substantive conditions of societal change, two themes emerged that came to dominate this approach within political anthropology: (1) the face-to-face encounters of particular individuals and (2) the particular setting of these encounters within encapsulated or closed communities. These two themes were brought together in Bailey's *Strategems and Spoils: A Social Anthropology of Politics*. In creating and transmitting its genealogy, action theorists highlighted the extent to which their approach to politics through the manipulative ploys of individuals contained its own dialectic: the manipulation of "symbols" and the manipulation of "material resources." Underlying both was what has been called "the Malinowskian impulse": "early programmatic exhortations to record ordinary day to day activities . . . and to search for explanations by the way of evident facts of observable behavior before invoking the weight of the past to account for the actions of the present" (Dyson-Hudson 1972:7). Action theory's younger practitioners sometimes presented it as having emerged in opposition to the structural functionalism of *APS* (Van Velsen 1964), but others (Kuper 1973; Boissevain 1974a) found its origins with Herbert Spencer and R. R. Marett. Marett, for example, wrote in 1912 that

> even where the regime of custom is most absolute, the individual constantly adapts himself to its injunctions, or rather adapts these to his own purposes with more or less conscious and intelligent discrimination. The immobility of custom is, I believe, largely the effect of distance. Look more closely and you will see perpetual modification in process; and, if the underlying dynamic be partly due to physical and quasi-physical causes . . . there is likewise at work throughout the will to live, manifesting itself through individuals as they partly compete and partly cooperate one with the other. (quoted in Wallis 1957:90)

It was, however, at the London School of Economics that the individual-action-oriented approach to politics was formulated. Appearing early in the work of Mair and Leach, its conceptual design was first clearly set out by Firth in his essay "Social Organization and Social Change" (1954b). Not, however, until the publication of Nadel's *Theory of Social Structure* in 1957 and Firth's *Essays on Social Organization and Values* in 1964 were its theoretical underpinnings made apparent. What strikes one in retrospect is the extent to which both were in a dialogue with Weber and Marx. Both marked, as major works often do, the end of one era and the beginning of another.

Mair had consistently reiterated the necessity of studying individuals within a "constitutional" framework, but her appointment as a reader in applied anthropology in 1956 (before this she had been a reader in colonial administration) gave institutional recognition to the roles of individuals in a complex society and the impact of government policies on the lives of its citizens (Mair 1965b, 1969; Owusu 1975). For Mair, changes in society rested on "changes in the rules that govern social relationships—rules about the ownership of property, the right to exercise authority, the duty to cooperate with particular people in particular circumstances" (1965b:21). All social roles, she argued, allowed players room for maneuver, a freedom of choice that they used to further personal interest. When she asked what they might be expected to aim at in the choices they made, her answer was *power*, the ability to control the actions of others. Edmund Leach, her colleague at LSE, took a somewhat different tack, as we have seen, stressing surface material factors, whereas she chose to focus on the less well recognized effects of changes in law and the expectations of the privileged.

Leach's model, in all its manifestations, while further establishing choice-making individuals and their purposive actions within political anthropology, remained essentially consensual, equilibrated, and overly concerned with "rational" man. Ultimately having recourse to explanations in terms of environmental adaptation, he failed to recognize the materialist dialectic.[20] It was under the cover, as it were, of Firth's formulation of social organization that action theory in political anthropology finally emerged. Firth distinguished between two aspects of social action: structure and organization. "The structure," he wrote, "provides a framework for action. But circumstances provide always new combinations of factors. Fresh choices open, fresh decisions have to be made, and the results affect the social action of other people in a ripple movement which may go far before it is spent" (1964:35). An anonymous reviewer of the field (whom we may take from internal evidence to be Bailey) wrote of a political anthropology that viewed political activity as essentially competitive. *"Sometimes referred to as* '*social organization*'," he noted, "this is best perceived by considering the actors not to be so many faceless automata, moving to and fro at the behest of structural rules, but as manipulators choosing within a range of possible tactics and asking themselves not only what they ought to do, but also what they can do" (SSRC 1968:19–20, emphasis added).

There is a sense in which all these scholars—Mair, Leach, Firth, and Nadel—were speaking political anthropology all along. Easton, recall, deplored the anthropologists' inability to separate out "the political" from other aspects of society. Well might a purist be offended by Leach's casual footnote: "By 'polity' I mean 'society'" (1954:5), or Nadel's statement that "if . . . it is argued that the 'social structure' I am envisaging is little more than a power, authority or status structure, I would reply that this seems to me the only 'dimension' both sufficiently abstract for our purpose and still sufficiently relevant, in the sense of being important in human and social existence" (Nadel 1957:121–122).

For all these pathfinders for action theory in political anthropology, structure and organization were complementary, standing respectively for form and process in social life. Structure involved role-playing; organization involved both roles and more spontaneous, decisive activity that did not follow simply from role-playing. Social organization is ordered activity. Firth saw as the greatest problem in anthropology the translation of the acts of individuals into the *regularities of social process*; this was in marked contrast to those who, following Durkheim, considered it to be a search for *rules of social order*. Many ideas crystallized by Firth can now be seen to have contributed to the yet amorphous action theory of political anthropology. Processes, contradictions, choices, above all the purposive goal-oriented actions of individuals, characterized the developing field from the beginning.

Critics of this view of society pointed to its tendency to foster a consensual equilibrium model of political society, overly dependent on notions of "rational" man. The dangers of "methodological individualism," its tendency to sink into ethnomethodology and a microsociology devoid of any concept of level, were also noted. Above all, its neglect of history—a result, perhaps, of its initial Malinowskian impulse—was also remarked. The major contribution of the approach lay in its focus on purposive action.

Out of these beginnings, then, action theory developed in the late 1950s and early 1960s. From field research into economic and political change, political anthropologists moved toward a more explicit concern with structural principles ordering action—that is, of systems (Bailey 1957), nongroups (Boissevain 1968, 1971, 1974b), invisible organizations (A. Cohen 1974), and comparison, and thence to renewed aquaintance with processual and historical analysis (A. Cohen 1974a; Turner 1974). Their adoption of a common terminology, a fair degree of cross-referencing to each other's work, and above all, their overall impact on political anthropology made for a coherent and incrementally growing body of conceptualization and dialectical theory. It nevertheless concealed the fact that two contradictory paradigms were emerging: action theory and processual theory.

If the contribution of *African Political Systems* to the study of politics had been the delineation in 1940 of nonstate political *structures*, the contribution of action theory in this era was to delineate forms of competitive political *organization*. Action theorists moved beyond the study of encapsulated communities and marginal politics in preindustrial nations to engage in the pursuit of parapolitics in the grey areas of modern, industrial capitalist and socialist states. Cohen's fear that the microscope of action theory was so powerful in disclosing the details of face-to-face political interaction that it might be "powerless, or out of focus, to reflect the wider structural features of society" (1974a:41) was allayed by political ethnographies from Latin America and Europe. Action theory within political anthropology moved from the study of the manipulative strategies of a rather narrow range of political actors to a greater clarification of the particular settings and circumstances in which they operated. This opened the door to regional, national, and transnational inquiries, which in turn fostered the further development of fields analysis and the adoption of a processual political unit made up not of localized individuals but of men in movement and actions and enterprises that were dependent for their success on operations across space and over time. The political situations and encounters that had long characterized the approach led, eventually yet in a seemingly inevitable way, to a concern with the processes of domination and exploitation and the transformation of societies within a modern global political system (Chapter 6)

Strategems and Spoils

Bailey's *Strategems and Spoils* (1969) set out to provide a model of political behavior of universal application: a tool kit, as he put it, for general discourse on the principles of routine competitive political action. Bailey believed that "beneath . . . contextual variations and cultural differences, political behavior reveals structural regularities" (1969:ix). It was thus on the structural regularities (limitation 1) of political competition (limitation 2) that he focused. A third self-imposed limitation was a focus not on benevolent, altruistic politicians but on politicians who "encounter others whom they perceive as motivated by self-interest, who advocate opposing policies, and who therefore must be tripped up, knifed in the back, or in some other way disposed of so that the general good may be served. No statesman is effective unless he knows the rules of attack and defense in the political ring. *Our interest is in finding out what these rules are*" (1969:xii, emphasis added).

Bailey expressed a personal preference for compromise rather than passionate politics and so to a repugnance for disorder. "My central situation," he wrote, "is not the *game* (which connotes only orderliness) nor the *fight* (where no holds are barred) but competition which, unlike the game, lies close to the edge of anarchy because the contestants do not 'lack all conviction', because, in other words, they think that what is at stake is important. This edge of anarchy is fenced off by rules: and this book is about *the rules which regulate political combats, and about the regular patterns which exist within them*" (1969:xiii, emphasis added).

Bailey could not have been more open in the bounding of his contribution, yet he was assailed as if he had claimed that *this* (this limited interest) was the whole of politics. Nevertheless, because of its narrow focus on what we may call "practical politicking," Bailey's paradigm was found to be extremely useful. His attempt to "discover some of the general principles in political maneuver which transcend cultures and which provide questions which could be the tools of research in a variety of different cultures" (1969:xiii) was widely taken up, and his success may be measured by the large number of political analyses that utilize his "bag of tools." Encompassed on all sides by a generation of younger scholars engaged in cosmopolitical concerns, Bailey himself applied his tool kit to the politics of reputation (1971), the politics of innovation among European peasants (1973), the folklore of academic politics, and committee maneuvering (1977).

Assessing the success of Bailey the ethnologist in *Strategems and Spoils* (1969) requires looking at Bailey the ethnographer of *Caste and the Economic Frontier* (1957), *Tribe, Caste and Nation* (1960), and *Politics and Social Change* (1963). Conducting field research in India for a total of thirty-eight months between 1952 and 1959, Bailey analyzed politics in three arenas: the encapsulated village of Bisipara, the Orissa state, and the nation. He also distinguished three levels of explanation: first, the cultural level, the actor's own model of his political actions; second, the sociological model of groups and their interrelationships within the village; and third, the understanding arrived at by looking at relationships outside the village. These show how certain groups within the village are enabled to challenge, and to some extent to overthrow, the established order. These three explanations—cultural, structural, and external—are complementary. The structure of groups and the institutions that regulate their interrelationships forms the core of analysis from which it is necessary to move outward into ideological and ecological fields.

In spite of Bailey's own concentration on the second sociological level, as time went on political anthropology itself moved more toward political culture and value systems, on the one hand, and the recognition of ecological and historical factors, on the other. There were several reasons for this. First, Bailey's narrow restriction (1964) to arenas of multiplex relationships threatened to limit political anthropological study to villages, small communities, and small-scale societies and to those areas in complex societies where multiplex relationships were to be found. For Bailey,

> The difference between anthropology, and political science or economics, lies in the type of relations studied. Both the latter disciplines work at a higher degree of abstraction than social anthropology. They concern themselves with specialised, or single-interest, relations; in the one case relationships involving power, and in the other case relations involving the exchange of goods and services. We do not abstract to this level; indeed our whole attention is focused on the way different relationships—economic, political, and ritual—are linked to one another. In other words, we are interested in social systems in so far as actual relations between persons tend to carry more than one interest—in so far as they are multiplex. (1964: 72–73)

Because of his sensitivity to disciplinary boundaries, Bailey described his 1963 study of Orissa villages within the framework of Indian national politics as badly integrated. The first part of his book, he suggested, "resembles social anthropology; the second looks like political science; and the third part might have been written by a somewhat hasty historian with sociological leanings" (1963:219). A concluding chapter therefore laid out a single conceptual framework into which the three parts would fit.

Bailey was extremely explicit about his problem orientation, the criteria on which he decided closure, and the necessary artificiality of analytic research. This enabled critics to mount a detailed attack against his minimalist political anthropology. They deplored local or village studies, arguing that the only true political unit of study was the seat of power and sovereignty: the state. They noted his omission of Europeans, aliens to the cultural system but politically an influential minority. They questioned the definition of the system in terms of the actor's model and suggested that by focusing on small-scale multiplex relations Bailey had conveyed a false notion of gaps between the urban and rural which ignored the movement of material commodities and people between the two. Above all, they criticized Bailey's political paradigm for its perception of all change as externally induced. Bailey analyzed the politics of small-scale actors with considerable insight, but he never placed the politics of the powerful under the microscope.

Criticisms of Bailey's model of encapsulated politics were mounted in several arenas, both regional (for example, the Middle East and Europe) and topical (peasant societies). In the history of ideas we can find the issues first raised in the late Victorian literature on the "village republics" of India (Chapter 1), but by the late 1950s and the 1960s the issue was as much one of political anthropology's distinctive methodology in the face of other disciplines' incursions into its field and its arguable superiority over "Indology."

The continuity of Bailey's work with that of his structuralist predecessors was apparent from his citations, but a subtle shift had nevertheless occurred from a view of structure as a system of continuing relations between social groups with a high degree of stability à la Radcliffe-Brown to an explicit perception of structure as a body of rules, a constitution.

On Concepts

Perhaps the most important aspect of political anthropology between 1954 and 1973 was the body of concepts that became widely accepted by a large number of its practitioners. Introduced in both monographs and articles, the concepts generated a large secondary literature as their implications and usefulness were weighed and refined but above all as they were used in fresh ethnographies. So extensive was this—almost as expansive as some of the claims for one concept vis-à-vis another — that the discussion that follows centers only on the most often cited usages. The definitions provided are attributed to specific individuals, but around each there grew a halo of secondary meanings and nuanced commentary.

Yet, in spite of this there emerged no coherent body of interrelated concepts—no theory of political action or of political process—but only clusters of concepts. The first cluster surrounded the political forms generated out of the coalescence of individual actors. Among these were quasi group, action set, clique, gang, faction, coalition, in-

terest group and party. The second related to modes of political behavior: choosing, maximizing, decision making, strategizing, interacting, transacting, manipulating, career-building, spiraling, recruiting,
maneuvering, competing, fighting, dominating, and encapsulating. The
third related to the context (both spatial and temporal) of political action: event, situation, arena, field, environment, power structure. Researchers applied the first and second sets largely in synchronic analysis, and the uses were action oriented, particularly in the work of Bailey
and Jeremy Boissevain. The third cluster moved toward replacing synchronic with diachronic or processual analysis and was most strongly
entrenched in the work of Victor Turner.

If the most remarkable feature of this most remarkable era was its
practitioners' adoption of a common vocabulary, its second most remarkable feature was their extensive cross-referencing of each other's
work. There was also a concerted effort to adopt new procedures, new
units of analysis, and new language for the particularly political. This
made it acceptable to a whole generation of political anthropologists on
both sides of the Atlantic. Most significant of all, however, was the new
common understanding of what politics was all about. As Lucy Mair
put it, "There are always and everywhere persons with conflicting and
competing interests, seeking to have disputes settled in their favor and
to influence community decisions (policy) in accordance with their interests. This is politics" (1962:10).

Bailey's Tool Kit

The concepts Bailey came to employ in his analysis of political action
became widely accepted within political anthropology and must be presented with some specificity.[21]

> <<<Politics may be thought of as a competitive *game* characterized by
> agreement about the prize and rules which regulate conduct. Without rules
> politics ceases to be a competition and becomes a *fight*. Players must be
> evenly matched. There is an idiom of confrontation and encounter.
>
> *Normative rules*—rules based on cultural values—may be distinguished
> from *pragmatic rules*—how to get things done. Pragmatic rules represent
> one useful analytical tool for understanding social change. Another is the
> idea . . . that an environment may contain rival political structures, thus
> making up a political field.
>
> A political structure, then, contains rules about prizes and values (i.e.
> following Easton, what is valued); personnel; leadership (teams); competi-
> tion and control. There are never enough *prizes* to go around; values both
> create and regulate political competition. They are symbolized.
>
> Every political structure has rules about *personnel*, which say what
> qualifications a man needs to occupy a political role. Roles are assumed to

be compatible or incompatible with political activity. Most structures identify at least three categories of personnel: the political community, the political elite (the competitors), and political teams. The political community is bounded by identifying rules which mark off members from outsiders. A right to "fair play" is linked with symbolically communicated roles. In some communities roles are played out under duress.

The political *elite* are those in the community qualified to take an active part in competition. Political contestants mobilize supporters as a *team*. Rules allocate authority (leadership) within a team. There are also rules in any political structure about how the *competition* should take place. These constrain behavior and regulate *confrontations* and *encounters* (agreed tests of strength).

Some roles are too important to allow them to become fouled and confused by political competition. Some people are above politics; some are mediators; some are referees. The game-politics analogy is now stretched, for . . . very often the political referee is in an ambiguous position. In games the referee is clearly and unambiguously *not* one of the players: he can never win the prize.>>>

In elaborating his paradigm of politics as a competition, Bailey made it clear in response to those who considered him to be taking politics too lightly that he believed:

there is a sense in which politics *are* secondary. When politics interfere with raising families or producing enough to eat, then people say that something has gone wrong with that political structure. . . . Some of my readers may already be thinking that "real politics"—the politics which matter—are what I have just been calling fights. . . . But what is the meaning of "important"? Coups and revolutions are certainly more violent and more dramatic than the Westminster routine. But surely it is impossible to assert, in any absolute sense, that they are more important. Importance is relative to the values of whoever is making the judgement: it is not an attribute of events themselves. (1969:2)

What was required, perhaps, was a greater scrutiny of types of political action rather than any further taxonomic efforts to arrive at general, universally applicable concepts. Bailey's tool kit was designed for middle-class, gentlemanly politics, in which the rules of the game did indeed, on the surface at least, set boundaries for political action; it was less useful for other purposes.

Groups and Nongroups

In 1965 Lucy Mair, the voice of clarification and clarity for this generation of young political anthropologists, set out in an introductory textbook a formal definition of the group as an analytical construct. It was derived from the work of Maine, Weber, and Nadel. "The word *group*," she wrote, "does not mean, as it does in everyday speech, any collection of people. It means a *corporate body* with a permanent existence; a collection of people recruited on recognized principles, with common interests and rules (norms) fixing rights and duties of the members in relation to one another and to those interests. The common interests can be called property interests, if property is very broadly defined" (Mair 1965a:15). This definition lay at the heart of a political anthropology centered on individual actors and their strategies in political arenas. The further conceptualizations that developed out of it were largely directed toward clarifying political forms between the sociological or structured individual and the group.

Thus in 1968 the American-Dutch anthropologist Jeremy Boissevain laid out a continuum of nongroups that imposed a degree of order and relatedness on the usages of his British contemporaries—Bailey, Barnes, Barth, Bott, Epstein, Mayer, and Peters—while at the same time including the Americans Whyte and Wolf. Boissevain traced the ancestry of nongroup thinking to Morris Ginsberg's coinage of the term *quasi-group* thirty years earlier. Ginsberg defined quasi-groups as "portions of the community which have no recognizable structure, but whose members have certain interests or modes of behaviour in common, which may at any time lead them to form themselves into definite groups" (1934:40).

Boissevain's continuum of nongroups (individual-centered interaction systems, for the most part) is shown in Figure 5.6. It derived its ethnographic legitimacy from his work on the Mediterranean island of Malta on factions, parties, politics, patronage, and poverty (1964, 1966). The continuum immediately evoked a critical response, to which Boissevain responded. The most positive outcome of the exchange was a closer generic definition of a coalition as "a temporary alliance of distinct parties for a limited purpose" (Boissevain 1971:470). In the immediate past, anthropologists had applied terms such as *action-set, clique, gang,* and *faction* to this configuration.

Boissevain's position on quasi-groups changed as he came to see that two existing concepts—category and coalition—adequately covered the political phenomena involved. Bossevain saw factions as the basic units of conflict in society yet hardly made them distinctive units of analysis when he placed them "one step beyond divided public opinion and one step this side of corporate groups" (1968:551). In this phase his work was primarily taxonomic, but his later ethnographies suggested that factions might usefully be viewed not as universal phenomena but as contingently emergent threshold phenomena.

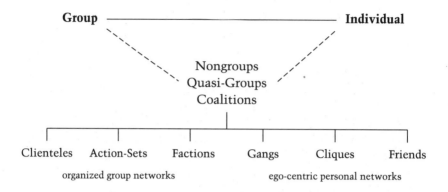

Figure 5.6. Boissevain's continuum of nongroups
(adapted from Boissevain 1968)

In *Friends of Friends: Network Manipulations and Coalitions* (1974b)
Boissevain applied the tools afresh. The individual was structured not
by role playing but by the structural and interactional character of
his network. This then became the basis for his analysis of communication paths, action sets, cliques, and factions. If these were involved
in competition for scarce resources in the public arena, then they were
political.

Much of Boissevain's ethnography dealt with the noncorporate clustering of personnel, but he also contributed to political anthropology a
dynamic analysis of political entrepreneurs (brokers and patrons) and
political coalitions. This he framed within a political theory of conflict,
law, and order derived largely from western European ethnography—in
reality although he did not at the time couch it specifically as such—
from contrasts in political institutionalization in the core and on the
periphery (i.e., in northern Europe and the Mediterranean).

Boissevain clearly set out his contribution to the theoretical edifice
of action theory. "By beginning social analysis with the interacting
individual," he wrote, "movement is built into the analytical model,
for individuals move constantly. Their relations with others are constantly re-arranged. As they advance in years, move up or down their
chosen career ladder, change residence, they make new contacts, and
discard or are discarded by older ones. Ultimately they die, and the
various ego-centric interaction systems of which they were the focal
point dissolve" (1968:546).

Extremely important to later developments were brokers and other
manipulators. These developed "at points where networks intersect,"

such as "villages, towns and even cities ... where communication channels such as roads, rivers and seas meet. [They are] specialists in network relations who often make use of their special manipulative talents. They bring together people: buyers and sellers, people with problems and those with power, knowledge or specialised networks that can help resolve them. They even bridge the distance, sometimes narrow, sometimes immense, between differing value systems. They transmit, direct, filter, receive, code, decode, and interpret messages. If they are astute they can convert the talent they have into power, which in turn helps them to expand their network. They can also use their network to recruit coalitions of persons who serve their interests directly" (1968:549).

Boissevain distinguished his approach from Bailey's. By the term *individual* he meant not the actor but the individual interacting purposively with others. He rejected Nadel's term *person* for the individual actor, and along with both, the tethering implications of roles, rules, and norms. Boissevain's individual was structured not by role but by network. Adrian Mayer's ethnography of an Indian election (1966) provided an excellent demonstration of the value of the concept, although his usage differed slightly from Boissevain's. Indeed, Boissevain's vision of interstitial politics was not well received everywhere. Abner Cohen, for example, suggested that he was flogging a dead horse (networks) and missing a vital body of theorizing (transactionalism) that had much greater explanatory power.

PROCESS THEORY: FIELDS, DRAMAS, METAPHORS

In 1966 Victor Turner took a large hand in writing an introduction to *Political Anthropology* (Swartz, Turner, and Tuden 1966). This set out what was called a processual model of political change, focusing on the relations between personalities and groups that made up a *political field*. Politics was defined as "the *processes* involved in determining and implementing public goals and in the differential achievement and use of power by the members of the group concerned with these goals" (1966:7). The key element of the processual paradigm was quite similar to the concept of revitalization set out by Anthony Wallace a decade earlier (1956). In both, a process comes into play after a crisis, which restores an unstable structure to equilibrium. Both Wallace and Turner worked with notions of structure and antistructure. Both developed ideas originally found in Van Gennep's *Rites de Passage* (1909), in which process involved separation from normalcy, a transition phase, reincorporation, and a return to normalcy. Both drew on event analysis.

Wallace's study was heavily psychological, explaining a religious movement such as the Ghost Dance as "a deliberate, organized, conscious
effort by members of a society to construct a more satisfying culture"
(1956:265). Since such an effort brought forth resistance, his model included power struggles in a conflict situation.

Later Turner moved away from this equilibrium-disequilibrium system relationship, turning to chains of events such as pilgrimages and
revolutions. His reputation had been made, as we have seen, with his
study of conflict among the Ndembu of central Africa and their ritual
solutions. Subsequent publications established him as a leading figure
in the emergent subfield of symbolic anthropology. His book *Dramas,
Fields and Metaphors* (1974) interrelated the manipulation of symbols
with the struggle for power. This permitted the incorporation of a range
of structural elements—position, stratum, and class—that had previously been somewhat neglected. His study of the Hidalgo insurrection
in Mexico displayed the working definitions later adopted (with some
idiosyncratic variations) by political anthropologists within this genre.

Turner provided an extended case history of the insurrection, a sequence of political dramas taking place in a series of arenas in an expanding political field. Arenas are frameworks, institutionalized or not,
that manifestly function as settings for antagonistic interaction aimed
at arriving at publicly recognized decisions with respect to prizes and
values. Social dramas are units of aharmonic or disharmonic process
arising in conflict situations; harmonic processual units are termed
social enterprises. (Like Leach and Nadel, Turner tended to use "social"
and "political" interchangeably.) A political field is "the totality of relationships between actors oriented to the same prizes or values" made
up of "purposive goal-directed group action. . . . Though it contains
both conflict and coalition, collaborative action is very often made to
serve the purposes of contentious action" (1974:127–128).

When characterizing a political field, "relations of likeness such as
classes, categories, similar roles and structural positions" are of prior
sociological importance. When successive arenas are characterized, systematic interdependencies in local systems of social relations from demography to residential distribution, religious affiliation, and genealogical and class structure become significant. Corporate groups, factions,
and the ego-centered networks of leaders are also important in arena
analysis. On the national level, fields, categories, class structure, cultural universals, and church, state, sect, and party are the subject of
inquiry. At the regional and township (municipio) levels, arenas, corporate groups, alignments cutting across class boundaries, cultural speci-

ficities, and patterns of local hierarchies have greater relevance. Turner's challenge is to grasp, coherently express, and analyze the interdependence of field with arena.

Although it is clear that Turner built a great deal on the work of his colleagues, he also moved process theory in new directions. Political fields, he suggested, overlap and interpenetrate; some are organized and purposive; others contain much that is arbitrary and accidental. This important notion allows for the manipulation of the ambiguous, which is so important in politics. Turner also added the idea of the possibility of a primary political process (in the Mexican case, the power of myth), which so influences political behavior that it "acquires a strange processual inevitability over-riding questions of interest, expediency, and even morality, once it gains truly popular support" (1974:110–111, 122–123).

Turner provided a paradigm that moved the political anthropologist far beyond the confines of game theory, transactionalism and action theory itself. He was interested not in gentlemanly competition but in the kind of political changes that "shake the very premises and foundations of the social order" (1974:141). And, as he went on to note, "in historical practice, it is, as Weber would agree, the educated middle classes that in their competition, whether violent or peaceful, like to introduce rules to which both parties subscribe" (1974:141). The politics of class struggle, he suggested, do not go according to commonly accepted rules, for none such exist.

The ideas of Max Weber had by this time, as we have seen, been widely if selectively incorporated into political anthropology. The Weber of Talcott Parsons entered through the ethnography of political integration and bureaucracy in new nations in studies contributed by Geertz (1963) and Fallers (1963a). A second Weber, who deduced every important general sociological concept from the notion of action or agency, was clearly familiar to the elders of action theory, Firth and Nadel. This Weber entered the work of Abner Cohen (1969a, 1969b, 1979), particularly in his analysis of symbolism and ethnicity.

A third Weber, the Weber of a historical bent, did not enter political anthropology until Turner called on him in 1974 in his processual analysis of the Mexican insurrection. This Weber hit hard at those action-oriented political anthropologists who leaned toward ontological individualism, because this Weber showed how misleading abstract formulations like "economic" or "political" man could be. "He urged that the sociologist should go beyond saying, 'This is how it would be, other things being equal' to saying, 'This is how the thing works in this case,

given its peculiar historical setting.' He wanted his types to be illuminating in unique and specific historical circumstances" (Rex 1969:172).
This far no political anthropologist went between 1954 and 1973.
Turner was himself on the threshold of such a politically sensitive cultural historical paradigm on the eve of his untimely death in 1975.

The Processual Paradigm

No clear statement of the processual paradigm that emerged out of the
RLI field researches and that of the Mancunians is to be found in the
publications of any of the anthropologists involved.[22] It is therefore
necessary to turn to the philosopher Stephen Pepper, whose description
of what he called the contextualistic root metaphor comes closest to it.
He wrote:

> The point of origin of contextualism is probably the historic event. . . . By
> this the contextualist does not mean primarily a past event, one that is, so
> to speak, dead and has to be exhumed. He means the event alive in its
> present. What we ordinarily mean by history, he says, is an attempt to
> represent events, to make them in some way alive again. The real historic
> event, the event in its actuality, is when it is going on *now*, the dynamic
> dramatic active event. . . .
> These events are all intrinsically complex, composed of inter-connected
> activities with continuously changing patterns. They are like incidents in
> the plot of a novel or drama.
> . . . [D]isorder is a categorical feature of contextualism, and so radically so
> that it must not even exclude order. That is, the categories must be so
> framed as not to exclude from the world any degree of order it may be found
> to have, nor to deny that this order may have come out of disorder and may
> return into disorder again—order being defined in any way you please,
> so long as it does not deny the possibility of disorder or another order in
> nature also. . . .
> Change in this radical sense is denied by all other world theories. . . .
> Contextualism is constantly threatened with evidences for permanent
> structures in nature. It is constantly on the verge of falling back upon
> underlying mechanistic structures, or of resolving into overarching implicit
> integrations of organicism. Its recourse in these emergencies is always to
> hurry back to the given event, and to emphasize the change and novelty
> that is immediately felt there, so that sometimes it seems to be headed for
> utter skepticism. But it avoids this impasse by vigorously asserting the
> reality of the structure of the given event, the historic event as it actually
> goes on. The whole universe, it asserts, is such as this event is, whatever
> this is. (Pepper 1942:232–235)

As we have seen, for the processualists in political anthropology the
equivalent of the historic event of the philosopher was the analysis
of the social situation, such as the opening of the bridge in Zululand

observed by Gluckman (Chapter 4) or the social drama created by Turner. Their method, event analysis, recognized large casts of characters and interpersonal relations as complex as those in any Russian novel. They attached significance to individual actors and to agency. They recognized disorder both in the political form of rebellion and revolution and in the theoretical form of antisystem and nonsystem.

And, like the contextualists the philosopher describes, Gluckman and Turner were "constantly threatened with evidence for permanent structures in nature" (Pepper 1942:235) even as they focused on radical change. This led them to discern contradictions and emphasize conflict. Gluckman studied rebellion more than revolution and recognized, ultimately, a constant tendency toward equilibrium in all social systems. Turner initially envisaged the prevalence of crisis resolution in social life but later recognized the possibility of irreconcilable conflict.

Finally, the contextualism of the political processualists was limited in the way the philosopher suggests. Turner did, indeed, avoid the impasse of utter skepticism by turning to "the historic event as it actually goes on"—the Mexican revolution or the murder of Becket, for example—arguing, as Pepper says, that "the whole universe is such as this event is, whatever this is" (1942:235).

Process and Form in Political Life

No one individual more than Fredrik Barth, a Norwegian scholar born in Germany, contributed to the generation of the new paradigms that developed within political anthropology between 1955 and 1973.[23] Yet, unlike Gluckman at Manchester, he did not, as Paine (1974) and Evens (1977) have suggested, engender a school. True to his own biography, his academic career, and the cosmopolitics of the time, Barth's contributions to both theory and ethnography reached across nations and continents to consolidate the new paradigm-in-the-making.

Although Barth himself thought his theory derived from the field rather than the academy (1981a:1), he appears to have been considerably influenced, consciously or unconsciously, by his early training at LSE under Leach and Schapera.[24] LSE had developed a focus on individuals in action and political leadership since the days of Malinowski. Schapera's *Government and Politics in Tribal Societies* appeared in 1956. As an institutionalized maverick at LSE, Schapera's idiosyncratic use of the Americans F. J. Teggart and William Christie MacLeod, as well as H. J. Laski, had long held the promise of an alternative political analysis to the Oxbridge party line. Barth drew on both his field experience of the Swat state in Pakistan and Schapera's argument in his 1956 monograph to rebut Radcliffe-Brown's view of a political system as resting on "the organized exercise of coercive authority through the use, or possibility of use, of physical force" (1940:xiv). Thus he followed Schapera's advocacy of the study of political organization as "the whole system of communal leadership and all the functions (as well as the powers) of the leaders [including] such activities as the organization of religious ceremonies or collective hunts, or the concentration and redistribution of wealth, [as well as] the administration of justice" (Barth 1959a:1). Like so many of his peers at LSE and Manchester, Barth frequently made an "aggregate reference" to Malinowski, which we may take (given the nature of the seminar and research assistantships at LSE) to include the ideas specifically from Schapera (1956), Leach (1954), and as I have suggested (1978), Lucy Mair. The inspiration of Nadel (1951, 1957) may also have shaped the formulation of his transactional theory, with its attention to the choice-making, risk-taking individual.

Barth's neostructural monograph *Political Leadership Among Swat Pathans* (1959a) developed from Firth's vision of structure as a framework setting a limit to ranges of choice in behavior. It proved to be a pathbreaker. It made structure a setting, like ecology and demography, for a different problematic. Unfortunately Bailey's later incorporation of Barth's Swat materials into *Strategems and Spoils* and its use as legitimating data for action theory in political anthropology deflected attention from Barth's much more significant contribution to processual theory. Indeed, Barth later wrote that he felt that the thrust of his model building had been misread, largely because of the discipline's taking up and working to death the least revolutionary aspect of his paradigm—transactional theory.

Yet Barth's plea, as he himself later put it (1981a:76), was in fact for a paradigmatic shift under a banner bearing the key words *generative* and *process*. A reanalysis of his ethnography actually makes clearer the difference between the transactional and processual paradigms. In a commentary on "Event vs. Aggregate," Barth suggested that the impasse that troubles anthropological thinking is where to locate endogamous sources of change within a system. The answer, for him, lay in the recognition of two levels within the system. Since "aggregate outcomes, and emergent properties on the macro level [tend] to be at odds with individual and collective intentions, [they] elicit dissatisfaction and innovative action from individual actors and parties—i.e. events which entail change" (1981a:81–82). Barth framed the issue in dialectical and processual but not historical terms. A significant shift in questioning occurred in political anthropology only when the ethnographer also began to ask how and why *that* behavior rather than any other was taking place, so taking up again the concepts of culture and historical process.

Barth's work was central to the development of political anthropology between 1955 and 1973, not simply for its immanent value but also because it generated a theoretical discourse that was not to be found in the rest of the discipline at that time. This addressed two methodological issues: (1) the challenge offered to structuralism by ontological individualism, and (2) the concentration on political actors' manipulative strategies and the aggregate consequences of such strategies. Not surprisingly, Barth's political ethnography of the Swat state generated one of the largest bodies of reevaluative literature in political anthropology.

By 1972 the impact of Barth's work led Ian Jarvie, the discipline's semiofficial mediating philosopher, to write at length on ontological and methodological individualism, because he believed that critics of the "new" approach were misunderstanding its premises.[25] Ontological holists (including Durkheimians), he explained, argued that groups combine and organize individuals into a new entity, a superindividual, from participation in which the individual gained his sole reality. Ontological individualists, on the other hand, argued that the only real entities in the social world are individual persons. Social structure and social organization are patterns of interrelatedness between persons, not over and above persons.

In his reaction to Durkheimian ontological holism, Barth thus belongs to a category that tended toward ontological individualism along with—at times somewhat uneasily—the team from LSE led by Firth, Nadel, and Schapera, as well as several Mancunians. Lucy Mair, structurally playing her gender role, attempted to mediate between them, much as the philosopher Dorothy Emmett did at Manchester. Barth became the leading exponent of ontological individualism in its purest philosophical form. As Barth himself tried to emphasize in his rebuttal of his critics in 1981, this did not negate the equal reality of social contingency.

Barth's monograph initiated a transactional approach to politics. His analysis treated what he perceived to be the acephalous political organization of a Swat valley in Pakistan. His argument was, briefly, that against the formal frameworks of society (the network of kinship and ties to a locality) dyadic relations linked paired individuals in relations of dominance and submission. Primary political groups developed around single leaders, who were aligned, along with their followers, into a larger political system. All relationships implying dominance were dyadic and contractual in nature. Political action was the art of manipulating such relations to create corporate political followings. Jayawardena characterized this as "the follow-my-leader approach to politics" (1960:302).

Reevaluations of Barth's paradigm flowed in. In 1974 Robert Paine suggested, from within the fold of transactionalism, that Barth neglected power as a variable of exchange. Attention to the different contexts of power, dependent on the positions of actors in the power structure, could lead to a perception of the strategies of underdogs as well as the powerful. Paine also commented on the "market philosophy" and "normative morality" of transactional theory. Although they deplored these aspects of his work, Paine and his Canadian colleagues followed closely in Barth's footsteps, producing finely honed monographs and collections of essays on patrons, political brokers, and go-betweens in the Arctic. Paine's own work (1971) also brought Wolf and Barth into dialogue, as it were.

On a completely different trajectory from Paine, Lawrence Krader also noted Barth's inattention to power: "the focus is on a 'theoretical' problem, eschewing the current political scene" (1961:1122). *Eschewing* is a significant choice of a term, raising yet again the issue of political anthropology's practical relevance. Like American critics of Leach's work earlier, Krader implied that the problematic recognized by the action theorists and processualists was much too narrowly conceived:

> The larger issue, the situation of the Yusufzai of Swat in the Pathan social and political system, in Pakistan, and in Afghanistan-Pakistan relationships, is a mighty topic, relevant to the book and important for theoretical ends despite its practical side. The existence of tribal enclaves throughout southwest Asia calls for our attention and most careful analysis, for much political time and energy is devoted to this issue in that part of the world. This is so in part because it is usually unmentioned. Since the relations between the central authority and the tribal enclaves within the larger political body are of great antiquity and of wide distribution today, many problems, both theoretical and applied, remain to be studied. (1961:1122–1123)

This is, in fact, a topic taken up by the next generation, who posed it as the impingement of heroic tribal peoples on archaic agrarian societies in South Asia.

Barth's monograph sparked from Talal Asad a reevaluation that marked the decline of action theory in its several guises. Asad laid bare the theoretical assumptions underlying Barth's model of politics in Swat. It consisted, he said, of "a number of closely interconnected theoretical elements: (1) rules (legal, moral, prudential); (2) individual

motivations (specific purposes and general strategies); (3) the formation
of fluid interest groups through multiple dyadic transactions (as in a
free marketplace); (4) the systematic compulsion to expand one's control of resources in order to survive (as in a self-regulating capitalist
system); (5) a dynamic equilibrium underlying the concrete manifestations of political strength and weakness" (1972a:80). To the question,
Who defines and applies the rules of the game? the answer for Asad was
clearly a dominant class of landowners who exploited the landless. The
agrarian class structure was the fundamental political fact. Opportunities and disabilities were structured by an individual's class position. Small landowners were being progressively eliminated; the class
structure, based on the ownership of land, was revealed in an historical
process of polarization.

Asad gave his reevaluation the title "Market Model, Class Structure
and Consent: A Reconsideration of Swat Political Organization"
(1972a). His perspective was clearly very similar to that of Worsley and
Gough in their reevaluations of the classic Tallensi and Nuer ethnography. There was, however, a fundamental difference. Whereas they, in
1957 and 1971 respectively, had chosen to rebut Fortes's and Evans-
Pritchard's *interpretations* (using data these anthropologists had themselves published and hinting at an alternative analysis that owed more
to Marx than Durkheim or Robertson Smith), Asad chose to challenge
the Barthian paradigm itself. As a rebuttal of "the modern interaction-
ist approach, . . . a dominant intellectual tradition in contemporary
political anthropology," (1972a:74, 93) he offered an overtly Marxist
interpretation of Swat Pathan politics.

In 1956, prior to the publication of his monograph, Barth had discussed the political ecology of Swat, relating ethnicity to the exploitation of ecological niches. If competition arose among ethnic groups for
the same niches, those militarily more powerful replaced the weaker
unless the weaker were better able to utilize marginal environments
within the ecological niche. Thus he accounted for political/ethnic distributions, the "mosaic" co-residence of western and southern Asia in
a manner quite different from that of Leach in highland Burma. Three
years later (1959b) he used his data to present a game theory alternative
to the then dominant structuralisms.

Barth himself reviewed how this happened (1981a, 1981b), responding to his critics in the process. Perhaps the key statement he made was
one in which he attempted to clarify what he saw as the relationship
between the "individual" and "a status." For him, political organization was not underwritten by self-interested, choice-making political

entrepreneurs but by structural and contextual constraints on political action. As Bailey perceived in reviewing Barth's 1981 volume, this underplayed politics and competition—for which read, surely, politicking and competition—and moved Barth back toward the structuralists, whose work he had consistently opposed (1982:585). What Bailey was missing here was what Sydel Silverman had pointed out in a critique of Bailey's own politics: "In any event . . . the most decisive causes are in the 'environment' (which includes other social institutions and other political structures). . . . [T]hus we are faced with the predicament of having the major problems—the most critical causes—ruled out of the range of study" (Silverman 1974:112). Barth's political ethnography had more in common with Wolf's dialectics and Turner's processualism than with the behavioral politics of action theory as practiced by Bailey.

THE PACKAGING OF POWER

Because of its intellectual coherence and its organizational success, action theory was most visible in political anthropology between 1965 and 1974. Processual theorists operated less rigorously. Their perceptions often derived from a large corpus of works, eclectic in conceptualization and catholic in ethnography, that broadly dealt with the issue of power, usually in its more institutionalized and centralized forms.

Three tough-minded notions guided those who focused on power. First, within any society an objectively exploitative relationship binds the lower strata of producers to the upper strata. Second, this relationship involves the routine use of coercion in its maintenance if not in its instigation. Third, the critical political process involves the extraction of the productive surplus resulting from the labor of the majority of the population and its allocation among the minority. It was left to the next generation (Chapter 6) to explore notions of hegemony, class, and underdevelopment.

The tough-minded model clearly had its roots in classical political economy, and anthropology's most distinctive contribution at this time was to focus on elites. Again, Nadel's theoretical influence was formative, but the concept was most successfully applied in the mid 1960s in the anthropological study of new nations. Aidan Southall (1966) related the emergence of elites to principles of stratification. For him, the elite was a boundary-straddling category of social actors between the center and the periphery. Stratification was a matter of formal institutional structures and the elite a dynamic organizational phenomenon, requiring parallel but independent study. This distinction between "elite" and "establishment" was important. The concept of the elite came into prominence at a time when the stratification systems that corresponded to the ideology of colonial rule, and that the colonial authorities had attempted to create and maintain, ceased to be effective. Rapid economic development in the new nations brought into prominence persons who only a short time previously had been of low status, as well as another set of people who were already challenging their newly asserted authority. Political, as opposed to economic, development received its impetus from those segments or groups strategically placed to move up in the system. The elite concept operated in precisely this sphere, where, as Peter Lloyd (1966b) pointed out, because of social change or rapid social mobility, appropriate norms had not been clearly defined.

Elites form "the growing edge of social activity, . . . that which at any time is not yet institutionalized (although it inevitably will be if successful)" (Southall 1966:344). Political anthropology, as we have seen, was especially interested in such interstitial groups; those with influence but not yet power or legitimate authority, those in the process of politicization, particularly in conjunction with "those dynamic aspects of power and influence which are liable to elude formal analysis" (Southall 1966:326), such as patronage and corruption. They also formed the basis for a comparison of political development. The political scientist W.J.M. Mackenzie, who discussed the notion of men in movement at some length, concluded that it had "certain advantages, tactical, conceptual and ideological for the study of political change in new nations" (1967:353). Yet, in spite of this, analysts placed most of the emphasis on the continuities of the development process rather than on change.

In practice, the concept of the elite contained, indeed, all the contradictions of its intellectual origins. Those who used it to delineate structures or systems had much in common with Gaetano Mosca, Vilfredo Pareto, and Robert Michels, and their use of it was equally conservative. Those who used it processually were attempting to capture the political movement of flux and the failure to routinize power that characterized so many new nations. Manghezi (1976) later described both applications as deflections from class analysis. In evaluating this judgment it is necessary to reconstruct the somewhat mechanistic, economistic vulgar Marxism of this era, when class formation and class consciousness were seen to be not processes but stages in political evolution.

Political anthropologists adopted the notion of ethnicity, like that of the elite, to replace the study of the systemic with the study of the processual. Very quickly, however, both concepts were domesticated. Cultural pluralism—the rubric under which ethnic studies first appeared—was also an innately conservative concept, and it, too, was related to ideas of stratification and class. Within political anthropology this came to be known as the "Plural Society" debate. It was initiated in the Caribbean by a British-trained Jamaican anthropologist, M. G. Smith, and it gave rise to a vast literature.

An early essay on the plural society in Malaya suggested the dangers inherent in a facile use of the idea of pluralism. It was simply as a matter of convenience, Freedman suggested in 1960, that three societies were recognized in Malaya—Malay, Chinese, and Indian—as a preliminary to the useful fiction that it was a plural society. None of the ethnic divisions was politically autonomous; none constituted a unit; none was a valid group. The Malay and Chinese might be described as meaningful cultural categories, all the members regarding themselves as belonging to an ethnic community, but the communities were not organized entities.

A distinction such as that made above between *valid groups* (a collection of individuals who stand in regular and relatively permanent relationships to each other [Nadel 1951; Mair 1965a]) and *cultural categories* (mental constructs only) underlay most objections to the plural society model. Without the distinction, one was tempted to argue from cultural and racial appearances to political realities. In its purest form, the plural society model ignored all other cleavages between individuals and groups, including class cleavages. It also tended to preclude any temporal perspective, denying change and process. Political analysis was concerned with the process by which categories were transformed into groups; that is, with the politicization of ethnicity. Cultural pluralism became politically relevant only when differential access to positions of differing advantage was institutionalized in ethnic terms (Vincent 1969). The mere existence of social or cultural categories in the population was not enough to account for political cleavages; there had to be the politicization of ethnicity before one could talk about the politics of ethnicity. Ethnicity per se was a cultural, not a political, variable. One had, therefore, to inquire into the process of politicizing ethnicity and the ideology that validated it.

The political anthropologist in the 1960s was strategically placed to analyze society in terms of its openness for the individuals and groups that comprised it. The earlier assumption that society was always, and was by definition, integrated began to be questioned, and once the integration of society was regarded as questionable, the door lay wide open for an empirical inquiry into how varying degrees of integration were produced and maintained. This problematic was set forth most clearly by Barth in his essay on the "Processes of Integration in Culture" (1966). For those influenced by Gluckman, of course, the explanation required a recognition that conflict in roles played a critical part in preventing the mobilization of clear-cut groups with divergent interests that might threaten the integrity of the state. Thus Colson: "The tough society with the greatest chance of survival through time without major internal struggles is the one in which members are knit together by a large number of different ties, where the adherent in one set of relationships is an opponent in another and the lines of battle are not easily drawn" (1985b:65).

Stratification tended to be the political root metaphor for those concerned with whole societies and abstract structures; others, involved in the contemporary politics of new nations, operated more freely with the ideas of center-periphery relations and processes of integration. Less in evidence in these heady post-independence days of nation building was the prospect of political instability and devolution, although Zolberg's anxiety over the salience of violence and disorder in contemporary African life (1968) encouraged me in 1969 to speculate on the potential of political anthropology for the analysis of guerrilla insurgency, for example. In the embryo state-nations that decolonization spawned, anthropological analyses of nativistic or millenarian movements, barrio solidarity, cargo cults, revitalization, prophets, witchfinding movements and the like had helped political anthropology to understand the dynamics of irredentism, liberation movements, rebel uprisings, and peasant revolts in groups that did not participate fully in the civic culture of the state.

From the time of Mooney on, as we have seen, charismatically led millenarian movements had been described as characteristic forms of political development among those subject to colonial rule and other suppressed peoples. Political anthropologists were familiar with pastoralists and peasants who, when confronted with the need to take joint action, had thrown up political structures de novo. Recognition of earlier interstitial parallels led them to rediscover political history. Historians of medieval Europe and nineteenth-century nation building certainly were reading anthropology.[26] A reciprocal concern with the past political development of the new stable states of Europe never did provide the bridge between political science and political anthropology that had been anticipated (Vincent 1969). Political scientists remained defiantly ahistorical throughout this period, while political anthropologists marched in several different directions at once. Europe remained a disparaged frontier, and anthropology's growing rapprochement proved to be not with political science but with history.

At first, however, it was the immediate colonial past that engaged most political anthropologists, particularly those who had experienced it firsthand. Cunnison drew attention to the discipline's lack of tools for analyzing colonial government. "The two systems [indigenous and colonial] run concurrently," he observed, "and both have to be considered. [When] they are treated separately . . . their interactions in the present political field do not fully emerge" (1957a:70–72). As the colonial period drew to a close in much of the tropical world, it became clear that the development problems of the 1960s were "not completely unique nor peculiar to those countries in Africa, Asia and Latin America" where anthropologists usually worked. "Africa's wars, civil wars, coups, revolutions (or lack of them), agricultural reform programmes, rural-urban migration patterns, administrations, political parties (where they exist), presidents, trade unions, socialisms, capitalisms, churches, central banks, and so on are continuous as well as discontinuous with those in Eastern and Western Europe, North America, Oceania, Latin America and Asia" (Apthorpe 1970:1–2). In the colonial period, differences attracted the most attention; in the 1960s, political anthropologists began to focus on the continuities.

The most comprehensive statement along these lines came from John Barnes, who by 1958 held the chair in the Australian National University.[27] He described the colonial impact on indigenous political life, particularly the loss of sovereignty associated with the suppression of war-making powers and the historical development as a result of such forms of resistance to the imposition of colonial state power as revolt, rebellion, insurrection, sedition, terrorism, banditry, brigandage, mutiny, piracy, faction fighting, and murder. He thus attempted to delineate the outcomes of what had been obliquely addressed as culture contact or acculturation, focusing on its undersides. Published in the United States in *Comparative Studies in Society and History* (not a mainstream anthropology journal), Barnes's 1958 paper made no impact on the discipline.

Some fifteen years later, the anthropological analysis of colonial ideology and practice was successfully masterminded by Talal Asad. Asad conducted his own field research among the Kababish of the Sudan, publishing a monograph on political leadership in 1970. As he established a growing reputation as a critic of Eurocentric social thought, Asad showed (1973b) how different images of non-European rule in African and oriental societies reflected the nature of their colonial encounter with the academy. In the decade that followed, his edited volume *Anthropology and the Colonial Encounter* (1973a) launched a significant critique of both political anthropology and the history of the discipline.

Historical contextualization encouraged a vision of continuities that served to widen even further the scope of political anthropology, restoring the lost vision of that Edwardian generation that had hoped for something more. Researchers saw the politics of the so-called Third World countries as continuous with those of the West, not only historically but also in the present. They viewed much of the political development—or underdevelopment—of the new nations as a continuing function of the external political designs of the European powers. The shrinking arena of political anthropology (from processualism to local-level analysis to face-to-face politicking) was engulfed in a totally new paradigm—or so it appeared to those who had forgotten, or had never known, the lost battles of their forebears.

An Alternative Paradigm

Perhaps the most striking feature of this period was how out of step anthropologists writing about politics in Latin America were with their colleagues conducting research in other regions. It was as if the much longer history of colonization and the more distant achievement of independence raised different questions. Certainly a different paradigm emerged to challenge the parochialism and presentism of the political anthropology of "new nations."

The early 1950s had seen critical reevaluations of Redfield's research in Mesoamerica (Lewis 1951; Cline 1952; Miner 1952; Foster 1953). Redfield was criticized both for his conceptualization of what he at different times called folk, little, or peasant communities and for his particular descriptions of specific settings (Lewis 1951; Mintz 1953a). In response Redfield set out to clarify his conceptual framework in *The Little Community: Viewpoints for the Study of a Human Whole* (1955), and *The Little Community and Peasant Society and Culture* (1960). His response was better received in Britain than in the United States, where critics led by Julian Steward were beginning to label his work descriptive, lacking in any attempt at causal explanation.

In 1956 Redfield used Chan Kom, the village in which he worked in Yucatan, as a litmus test for various approaches then current in anthropology, viewing it in turn as an ecological system, a social structure, a test of psychological and statistical approaches, biography, and finally history. He discussed Oscar Lewis's conflicting interpretation of Tepoztlán, but his response was, in effect, not a defense of a paradigm but a demonstration of eclecticism. His view of the community remained unchanged, yet the day of "the little community" and "the human whole" was over—apart from its echoes in philosophy and the humanities. The anthropology of this era of new nations within a global pantheon of the United Nations turned away from ideal-type formulations and toward studies of localities and levels of organization within the nation-state. Rural proletarians (Mintz 1953a) took their place alongside communities of peasants.

Anthropologists grew "increasingly sophisticated about the relationship of nation and community," while "national elites (began) to reassess the human resources at their disposal and to encounter their peasants, often for the first time" (Wolf 1956b:1065). This conjuncture inspired several competing classifications of types of peasantries (Wagley and Harris 1955; Wolf 1955; Adams 1956). The taxonomies were based on community studies and attempted to rise above them.

The Wagley and Harris taxonomy made no attempt at an analytical framework: Indian, peasant, and city dweller remained as separate as they usually were in Latin American ethnography. Adams's contribution was more like political sociology than anthropology, exhibiting an overwhelming interest in political stability and change that surely reflected the anxieties of the United States over political events in its own backyard. He did, however, deal explicitly with class. Wolf's typology was both more limited and more ambitious. His goal was to reorient inquiry, moving from typologies based on cultural content to typologies based on similarities and dissimilarities of structure. Given his structural definition of a peasant as an agricultural producer who retains effective control of land and aims at subsistence rather than reinvestment, the political content of his taxonomy was assured. He confined himself to peasants, noting (as had Redfield, Kroeber, and Steward) that the very term *peasantry* indicated a structural relationship, not a particular culture content.

The distinctive features of Wolf's (1955:455) typology of peasant groups were as follows:

1. The subject matter was defined as narrowly as possible.
2. Structure, not cultural content, was preeminent.

3. The initial criteria for the types was primarily economic or sociopolitical, but other features were included.

4. The types were component parts of larger wholes.

5. There was an underlying notion of historical trajectory.

What was *most* distinctive about Wolf's typology was that "the character of the larger whole and the mode of integration of the part-culture with it" were given "primary weight" in its construction. The different forms of peasantry were, in other words, generated by forces within the state; they were articulated with different urban forms (i.e., different town-country relations), and the state itself existed within a growing world market. Wolf was at pains to stress that he was dealing with *modern*, post–Industrial Revolution peasants: "There have been different types of industry and markets, different types of industrial expansion and market growth. These have affected different parts of the world in different ways. The peasantries found in the world today are the multiple products of multilineal growth" (1955:453).

Wolf described two types of what he called peasant segments: (1) those practicing intensive cultivation in the highlands of nuclear America and (2) those found in humid low highlands and tropical lowlands. The first form he called *closed corporate community peasantries* and the second *open cashcrop peasantries*. The first was frequently encountered in Latin American ethnography; the second was exemplified by San José, the coffee region in which Wolf had worked in Puerto Rico. Other types of Latin American peasants existed but, lacking ethnography at that time, Wolf simply delineated them as (1) cash crop peasants who marketed 90 to 100 percent of their total production and enjoyed a greater stability of market than most and more extensive outside capitalization; (2) peasants who produced for stable local urban markets, or were, perhaps, near former political and religious settlements; (3) peasants in a region that once formed a key area of the developing system of capitalism whose holdings were residual bits of former large-scale organizations; and (4) foreign cash-cropping colonists often in forested buffer zones.

This brief listing suggests the tenor of Wolf's argument. The market was the motor of integration, operating at the local, regional, national, and international level. No terminology has yet emerged to embrace all these species, although the distinctions among subsistence production, simple commodity production, and capitalist production appear to be related. Nor has there been any attempt to classify peasantries worldwide in structural terms such as these, although it might be thought to be necessary for the analysis of peasant politics. Wolf continued to develop his analysis of closed corporate communities, using Southeast Asian as well as Latin American ethnography, moving concurrently toward the study of the nation-state and political symbolism (1953, 1956b). Later he published a synthetic study, *Peasants* (1966b), and then a controlled comparison, *Peasant Wars* (1969).

Wolf later argued that primacy belonged to "the *forces* generating the processes." Structure, he observed, "becomes a temporary accommodation to these forces, which extend their pressures from within or from without the system. It is thus not enough to describe the cultural forms (e.g., the hacienda or the closed corporate community) making that temporary intersection. We need to identify also the pressures and forces at work" (1964:65). Wolf's analysis of political processes is thus much more comprehensive than action theory (the analysis of observed action occurring within a structure at any one time in any one place). What becomes critical for Wolf is whether the observed action is translated into cultural, racial, or human psychological terms or whether it is seen to be an epiphenomenon of historical processes. The dilemma is an old one, of course: All men shape their own history but not on their own terms.

Two observations are, surely, in order. First, we observe how parallel are the objectives of Bailey and Wolf. Both attempt the structural analysis of global phenomena. Wolf, however, focuses on processual forces rather than activity or political forms. Second, we note the cultural hegemony in political anthropology of the British paradigm. Yet the writings of Eric Wolf, from *Sons of the Shaking Earth* (1959), a culture history of Mexico and Guatemala, to *The Human Condition in Latin America* (1972), coauthored with Edward Hansen, provide a key trajectory not simply for the political anthropology of the region but also for the ethnography and theory the dominant British practitioners ignored. This was greatly appreciated in other fields and by other disciplines.

Wolf's politics were comprised of the analysis of people doing things to people, and he relied on historical and ethnographic detail, not abstract theoretical formulations, to make his case. He was, for example, critical of Redfield's view of social structure "devoid of a sense of the dynamic inter-relationships of social groups" and of an ecology "more concerned with how men view nature than with how they master nature or are mastered by it in turn" (1964:60). For Wolf, "the understanding of the process of cultural development . . . must involve not only a knowledge of aggregated forms, of style, or of world view, but also a sense of the relation between environment and culture, of the struggle of social groups and their dynamic accommodation to one another, and, implicitly, of the emergence, distribution, and containment of power in a system" (1964:61). That last phrase, "implicitly, of the emergence, distribution, and containment of power in a system" leads one to suggest that Wolf has been, continuously and consistently for over thirty years, one of the most political of all anthropologists. Yet his work is rarely recognized as mainstream political anthropology.

What then of Wolf's writings on power? For Wolf anthropology is, above all else, a humanistic discipline. He first deals with power and symbolism—the dramaturgy of power, as Abner Cohen was later to call it—when he comments on Redfield's neglect of "the study of the great collective social myths that serve to draw large strata of the population toward collective goals." Here, Wolf suggests, "the anthropologist must join hands with the political scientist and the intellectual historian. What the anthropologist can contribute to such a study is not so much the definition of the elements contained in the myth, or a knowledge of their checkered histories, but a sense of where—in real life—the myth finds its points of reference, in what specific acts and problems the mythic elements lie anchored" (1964:77–78). One can see the sleeping Malinowski nodding his head in approval, but Wolf chooses rather to join hands with a contemporary, Leach, as he notes that "characteristically [the American anthropologist] has been uneasy or imprecise in his understandings of the power aspect of social organization. These are, in turn, the fields cultivated by our British colleagues" (1964:62).

It is significant that Wolf refers his reader on this occasion to his 1958 essay on the Virgin of Guadalupe as a national symbol. It was published in the *Journal of American Folklore*, and we have seen how frequently folklore or popular culture have provided a window on politics for anthropologists—James Mooney, Mary Kingsley, G. C. Wheeler, Arnold van Gennep, and Alexander Lesser among them. Here is a truly subterranean tradition yet to be mined.

Wolf's *Sons of the Shaking Earth* (1959) is an analysis of the dynamics of colonial rule and the development of nationalism characterized by constant attention to the formation of institutions, contradictions within them, and the paradoxes that contain the seeds of processual and historical developments. Compared with other Latin American studies of the time, Wolf's analysis of the formation of the colonial hacienda and the closed corporate community of the Indian; of the destruction of the indigenous Mexican state and its aftermath; and of the political resilience of the Indian village is methodologically distinctive. It stands in marked contrast to studies of petty capitalists and the middle class.

Wolf was always conscious of history. On the subject of class, he noted that "superficially, the rise to power of the mestizo resembled the experience of the European middle classes and their emancipation in a series of 'bourgeois' revolutions." But the mestizo mass was not a middle class, or a class at all if class be defined in terms of differential access to the means of production. He wrote:

> The mestizos, . . . comprised both men who worked with their hands and men who worked with their wits. They shared not a common stake in society but the lack of such a stake; they shared a common condition of social alienation. Relegated to the edges of society, living in permanent insecurity, their reactions were akin not to the firmly anchored, substantial European middle classes but to the groups which Karl Marx called the "Lazarus-layers of the working class" and to the rootless, underemployed, unemployable intelligentsia-in-rags of post-1929 Europe who furnished the condottiere of the European Right and Left. In their common estrangement from society, the petty official, the political fixer, the hard-pressed rancher, the hungry priest, found a common denominator with the Indian bereft of the protection of his community, the artisan burning his midnight oil in poverty and religious devotion, the petty trader or cattle-rustler, the half-employed pauper of the streets, the ragamuffin of the Thieves' Market. Such men constituted neither a middle class nor a proletariat; they belonged to a social shadow-world. (1959:242)

Wolf, along with the other contributors to *The People of Puerto Rico* (Steward 1956), had begun edging toward a more satisfactory methodology in his doctoral dissertation, and *Sons of the Shaking Earth* began to flesh it out more fully. Some critics may have felt that his vision of the sociohistorical process was engendered by European Marxism, but the strength of Wolf's work lay in its adopting the dialectical method while refusing to assume that the Latin American historical process necessarily followed a European path. His analysis was formulated out of Mexican ethnography and projected a vision of a society that was autochthonous, culturally distinctive, revolutionary, and resilient.

Wolf's scholarship, while it included Marx, was much richer. He drew on German, French, Spanish, and English sources much as did the cosmopolitan Edwardians who were seeking to maintain the complexity of anthropology among the disciplines. *Sons of the Shaking Earth*, wrote one British reviewer, "is a triumphant example of the combined use of anthropological and historical methods" (Mendelson 1960:246). Wolf was not unique in this, but once again it is striking how it is method rather than subject matter or theory that creates a distinctive paradigm.

The use of archives and historical sources did, indeed, characterize Latin American political ethnography at this time, and it has continued to do so since. The close reading by historians and anthropologists of each other's work (Cline 1952; Zunz 1985) is much less prevalent elsewhere. This made it possible for Wolf to start not simply with a distinction between Ladinos and Indians, urban and rural, plantations and villages as they existed in the 1950s ethnographic landscape, but with an explanation of how they came to be there. Responses to depression in seventeenth-century Spain led the gold-seeking colonists to turn to hacienda agriculture for survival, and the Indians who did not succumb to the related labor demands placed on them established defensive communities in the mountains. Similarly, his account of Mexica (Aztec) empire building and the empire's dismantling by the Spanish led to his explanation of the making of a peasantry, the crafting of the religious complex, and the leveling of class within the Indian community. The same concern was expressed by Wolf's colleague, Sidney Mintz, when he engaged in a methodological debate over cultural as opposed to structural explanations of the emergence of early yeoman communities, peasant villages, and runaway-slave communities in the Caribbean in response to changes in plantation systems.

The scientism of Julian Steward has already been discussed, and it is perhaps necessary to dissociate both Wolf and Mintz from their professor's goals and concerns, although Wolf himself does so only by indirection. Wolf was Steward's doctoral student and later his research assistant at the University of Illinois. In his earliest papers he adopted Steward's vocabulary to some extent, using, for example, *multilineal evolution* and *horizontal segments* as parallel terms to others that might have been more in keeping with the structural analysis that underpinned his anthropology. Whereas Steward, looking back, was concerned with the breakthrough from "primitives" and "communities" to "social groups" and "nations," Wolf, from his Puerto Rico work on, was looking forward not to what was but to why it was and how change came about— the dynamics of the situation. And every situation was, integrally and integumentally, dialectical. What is common to Gluckman's analysis of a social situation in Zululand and Wolf's analysis of hacienda-community relations in Mexico (and perhaps to Marx's analysis of Eighteenth Brumaire) is what I label here *processual political analysis*. Wolf was ahead of the Mancunian processualists like Victor Turner (who was also later to write on Mexico) in seeing the ethnographic conditions under which most of them had worked as colonial and postcolonial situations in which explanation had to be provided in terms of the historical development of European capitalism. This is a step that Gluckman and his students failed to take.

Wolf (like his brother-in-arms Sidney Mintz) was never pretentious about making a contribution to either the theory or the methods of political anthropology. Indeed, one may assume that both abhor the vacuums that subfield specializations tend to become. This was not true of other Latin Americanists in the 1950s and 1960s, some of whom seemed much more attuned to sociological than to cultural analysis. Their work tended to refer more to the British subfield and to be more closely in dialogue with U.S. policy agencies, applied anthropology, and political science.

Outstanding among them was Richard Adams, whose *Crucifixion by Power*, a large volume on the Guatemalan social structure between 1944 and 1966, appeared in 1970. Adams's theory of politics rested on a series of concepts and definitions:

> A *level of articulation* is of equal (coordinate) power. A *domain* is a separable hierarchy. A *structure* is "a set of conditions" within which *organization* (rules and behavior) takes place. The struggle for power generates *confrontation*, which leads to *structural escalation* (better known to anthropologists, perhaps, as asymmetrical schismogenesis). Power may be *independent* ("grass roots") or *derivative* ("by appointment"), *unitary* ("monolithic") or *multiple* ("pluralistic"). Underlying these (and implicit in the definition of "structure") is a thoroughly materialistic view of what constitutes power. (Edmonson 1972:77)

Adams's theory of politics was applied by a cohort of his students at the University of Texas who in effect charted the manner in which, to use his jargon, the "assumption of regnancy" by the Guatemalan military came about with the blessing of the United States. "The late 1960s, a period of severe political repression in Guatemala, marked a turning point in anthropological work. National events and politics took center stage [focusing] on national institutions to the virtual exclusion of traditional concerns with Indians and small villages" (Smith and Boyer 1987:205). But the earlier history of the country may have been more important than Adams allowed, and, following Wolf, at least one reviewer deplored his neglect of cultural mechanisms in the acquisition and consolidation of power. That same reviewer (Edmonson 1972:79) concluded: "It is quite clear from this book whose power is crucifying whom. But the book is much too polite to say so, and consequently it obfuscates the data."

There was nothing polite about the writings of a group of Latin American scholars who came to be called Dependistas. Among them Andre Gunder Frank (1969b) made it quite clear that liberal North American intellectuals supported, in effect, an antirevolutionary bourgeoisie and contributed to keeping Latin America in a state of underdevelopment. This work and others are placed in the context of cosmopolitics in Chapter 6.

THE JUDICIAL PROCESS

Between 1954 and 1973, legal anthropology emerged as a distinctive subfield, respected by lawyers but neglected, for the most part, by anthropologists.[28] Its distinctive feature (which Easton would surely have deplored) was its tendency always to see the legal system as embedded in a wider social milieu. Its exact relationship to politics per se was subject to debate among legal specialists. Researchers made studies of the manipulation of courts and other processes of dispute settlement in struggles for political power (Barnes 1961; Gulliver 1963; Nader 1965). Property law provided a central concern (as for Morgan and his successors at the Bureau of American Ethnology). By implication, kinship, inheritance, marriage, divorce, and so on should therefore all have been part and parcel of the *content* of law, but so strongly established was the earlier subfield specialization of kinship and social organization that Leach considered iconoclastic his observation that "kinship systems have no 'reality' at all except in relation to land and other property" (1968b:305).

Three visions of legal anthropology began to appear. The first was the most conservative within the traditions of both historical jurisprudence and structural-functional anthropology. Paradoxically, given the work of RLI as a whole, this was practiced almost exclusively by Max Gluckman, and it was practiced virtually as a hobby.[29] The second, a cognitive and substantive approach to law, was developed by Paul Bohannan largely in opposition to Gluckman's universalizing tendencies. Finally, and also largely in reaction to Gluckman's work, a third vision of legal anthropology focused on what Gluckman considered extrajudicial processes, processes of dispute settlement or conflict resolution in societies that lacked courts and a formal judiciary (Gulliver 1963, 1978). By the end of this era, this became the dominant and most distinctive contribution of anthropology to the study of law. It was also closest, within political anthropology, to the analyses of action theorists and processualists. All three legal advocates—Gluckman, Bohannan, and Gulliver—were Africanists. The field situation in which each worked—among the Lozi of Barotseland (central Africa), the Tiv of Nigeria (western Africa), and the Arusha of Tanganyika (eastern Africa) respectively—accounted for some of the differences among them. Gluckman died in 1975, but his legal writings from 1955 to 1974 provided the touchstone for this era in political anthropology. The transatlantic subfield specialization that developed did so around the common discourse generated by his ethnography.

The Reasonable Man

Gluckman's study of Barotse law was out of step with the political anthropology Wilson had established at the Rhodes-Livingstone Institute. His concerns were twofold, the first (in the colonial African context) was politically radical, the second, evolutionary and conservative. Gluckman never reconciled the tensions between the two (Moore 1978a).

The concept of the Reasonable Man that Gluckman saw in use in Lozi courts was, he suggested, an indication that African law was of the same caliber as Western legal thought, an argument that it was important to make in Northern Rhodesia when so many whites opposed independence on the grounds that Africans were unfit to rule themselves. Gluckman was one of several South African anthropologists (in particular) who "saw their commitment to anthropology partly in political terms" (Kuper 1973:178). The concept of the Reasonable Man as a standard figure in Barotse court trials against which, in cross-examination and judgment, councilors assessed the behavior of disputing parties aroused considerable debate at the time. Perhaps the happiest reconciliation was achieved by Moore, who suggested that "the Reasonable Man is best explained not as critics take him—but as a concept enunciated by Barotse judges to encompass and cope with a whole variety of awkward judicial problems and standards. He is a device, a technical tool of the judiciary" (1969:264).

It is difficult to reconcile this aspect of Gluckman's legal anthropology with his simplistic, evolutionary view of archaic law. In his own words:

> We cannot understand any African tribe's law in isolation. . . . [W]e must see it in a comparative frame; and the main outlines of that frame have been drawn by Maine and other jurists. When we contrast any tribal society with modern society we are working with the difference between Durkheim's mechanical and organic solidarities, Tonnies' *Gemeinschaft* and *Gesell*-

shaft, von Wiese's sacred and secular societies, Weber's traditional and bureaucratic societies, Stalin's patriarchal and industrial societies, Redfield's folk-society and urban civilization. We neglect the comparative mode of analysis . . . at our peril. (Gluckman 1956:213)

Within this comparative framework, Gluckman reconstructed Barotse law as archaic law. I have been at some pains in this study to distinguish between evolutionary and historical approaches to politics, and remember that Maine's comparative jurisprudence was historical, not evolutionary. The same cannot be said of Gluckman. His procedure in documenting the Lozi past was Malinowskian; history was only what was retrieved from the memories of his oldest informants. Nor did he view his ethnography of the contemporary Lozi as a kind of social history, as some of his peers had begun to do. Gluckman's primary political model was that of *tribal* society. This led him to neglect the changing political economy of the region, the impact of the colonial legal system, and, most important, the actual power structures of Barotseland.[30]

Gluckman pioneered the observational study of law in the courtroom. His adoption of the case method (he held Llewellyn and Hoebel in high esteem) permitted the analysis of some sixty cases that came before the Lozi royal court. To be sure, he did not practice the extended case method, although he advocated it. The last volume of his proposed trilogy was to have been on the role of courts in Barotse social life, but this would have required a return to the field for the data his earlier, more constricted operations had excluded. Gluckman commented on this himself in a reappraisal of *The Judicial Process* published in 1967. "Trained in an anthropological tradition that sought norms, not case histories," Sally Falk Moore observed, "this attention to episodes and cases, not just to statements about customs and rules, presaged deep changes in social anthropology itself, many of which he was instrumental in generating" (Moore 1978b:65).

Lloyd Fallers's *Law Without Precedent: Legal Ideas in Action in the Courts of Colonial Busoga* (1969) took up where Gluckman left off. It is a study of court procedures informed by the ethnographer's intensive knowledge of Busoga society. Critical reviews of the monograph (Collier 1970; Moore 1970) marked, in fact, an end-of-the-era shift from the study of "legal ideas in action" to "people in action using legal ideas" (Collier 1970:854).

The new legal anthropology that was emerging expressed a general unease at the notion that any society's law should be conceptually consistent and a perception of the effect of local politicking on which cases actually reached court. Both Moore and Collier advocated that legal manipulation and maneuvering within the court of law be studied. "We need to look at courtroom performances," Moore wrote, "with the same attention to levels of meaning that we give to the performance of ritual" (1970:1480). Collier, remarking on how litigious the Basoga were (one in ten men appeared in court every year) and how many judgments (one third) were reversed, reinterpreted Fallers's rich data to show how Basoga litigants were gambling with the legal system and judges were playing politics with their decisions. "In a context where cash had replaced patron-client ties as the means for personal advancement," she suggested, "the high compensation offered to successful plaintiffs made the courts the best route to quick wealth" (1970:857). Collier's brilliant reanalysis of a marital dispute showed how the judge granting a wife the divorce she sought "took the advantage of an alternate set of values to justify knifing a political enemy in the back" (1970:857). Collier's review highlighted the strengths of a political ethnography of law and, indeed, in its sense of political realism recalled Oscar Lewis's reevaluation of *Tepoztlán*. In the decade that followed, both Collier and Moore began to reinsert legal anthropology into the mainstream anthropological study of politics—a project Gluckman clearly approved.[31] The degree to which private disputes between individuals had potential political structural importance was the key issue on which both the formal corporatism of M. G. Smith and Leopold Pospisil and the substantive constitutionalism of Gluckman and Fallers were eventually challenged.

Gluckman had begun to contribute to this discourse just before his death. He shared with Stanley Diamond (1974) the political goal of establishing quite clearly the coercive role of the state. "A private dispute becomes political when it comes to court," said Gluckman, "since it involves the power of the state; and the power of the state in this public arena brings in interests other than those of the immediate disputants." And later, "In a highly developed authoritative polity, the state tries to control, ultimately, what happens in the law of all its constituent groups with their own by-laws, and in relationships between them" (Gluckman 1975:327, 331). Gluckman described Yale jurist Charles L. Black, Jr.'s *Structure and Relationship in Constitutional Law* (1969) as "running along the lines certain of my colleagues and I were attempting to march on" (1975:334). This he believed brought together "problems of political struggle [the Civil Rights movement] and confrontations in forensic areas, *where the suits appear to be between individuals*, with basic doctrines in the structure of social relationships" (1975:337, emphasis added). This perception led him to suggest a new basis on which legal systems might be compared: "We have to see societies not as entirely different in kind, but as varying in the kinds of disputes between individuals, related in some specific way, which provoke major confrontations in the wider polity, and in the extent to which battles *vi et armis*, and what kinds of battles, are likely in each society. We have also to analyze types of public arenas in which battles can be fought without recourse to arms" (1975:337). Thus was "law" placed once again integumentally within the entrails of society at large.

The Terminological Approach

Gluckman's ethnography tended to overshadow discourse in legal anthropology, but there were also other items on the agenda. Paul Bohannan's distinction between "folk systems" and the "analytic systems" of the anthropologist, first set out in *Justice and Judgement Among the Tiv* (1957), reflected his Oxford training under Evans-Pritchard. When he began to argue procedural primacy for the folk classification, hackles were raised (Hoebel 1961a; Gluckman 1962), particularly those of political anthropologists who were busy elevating Firth's distinction between social structure and social organization into the judicial arena. Processualists (e.g., Epstein 1967) deplored Bohannan's stress on jural structure rather than jural process, and his use of Tiv cases — eighty in all — simply for apt illustration.

The terminological approach — whether to kinship or law — never sat well with most political anthropologists from Malinowski (1913) to Moore (1969). At Burg Wartenstein, Bohannan and Gluckman appeared to thrash out the old cultural-sociological debate yet again. There was, however, an additional factor: Evans-Pritchard and *his* students explored vernacular terminology to bring out contrasts with Western concepts; Gluckman explored them to bring out similarities (Moore 1978a). Gluckman's ethnography correlated legal culture with social and economic systems, Bohannan's ethnoscientific cultural approach viewed social organization as epiphenomenal.

Dispute Settlement: Process and Decision

A focus on dispute settlement in arenas other than those in which judges and courts operated released legal anthropology from the constraints placed on it by Gluckman's expansionist and Bohannan's myopic tendencies.[32] The need to extend legal anthropology to "extrajudicial" processes was recognized by Gluckman himself in his textbook *Politics, Law and Ritual in Tribal Society* (1965), but the breakthrough had come earlier, with the ethnographic field research of Philip Gulliver. Gulliver (1963) found that although norms and rules might be quoted or cited at length by the Arusha of Tanganyika among whom he worked, they were quite irrelevant to the actual settlement of disputes. The crux of the matter lay in the respective political strengths of the contestants. Procedure, action, and sequence of events were thus more analytically relevant than rules, norms, and folk categories.

In spite of minor differences between the main protagonists, common discourse rather than divergence prevailed in legal anthropology between 1954 and 1973 as a result of Gulliver's shift in paradigm. This was evidenced by modifications in the thinking of its most influential theorists: they learned from each other. Thus Gluckman rethought many of his arguments (1965, 1972), and Gulliver retracted his early (1963) delineation of a continuum between judicial, Lozi-like, and political, Arusha-like, processes of adjudication. Finally, Laura Nader's edited volume *Law in Culture and Society* (1969) led Bohannan, Gluckman, and Moore to thrash out anew the whole question of culture-bound concepts. Once again the female scholar served as go-between and peacemaker in the, at times, rancorous encounter.

For the last decade of this era, from 1963 to 1973, the analysis of dispute settlement became the hallmark of legal anthropology. It restored to the agenda informal mechanisms such as sorcery and witchcraft accusations (Collier 1973), shamanism (Butt 1960:66), moots (Gibbs 1963; Strathern 1972), and feuds (Pospisil 1965; Gluckman 1975; Hoebel 1977), to mention just some of the now familiar topics. Laura Nader, who quite distinctively drew on case materials from the American bar to set alongside those of "traditional" societies, stressed the fact that the *functions* of law could not be assumed to be the same in all cultures. Nor was the function of law assumed necessarily to be primarily the resolution of conflict: harassment and ruination, for example, provide two alternatives to litigation (Beals 1955; Cohn 1959; Nader 1965). She, like Victor Turner (but citing Thurmond Arnold) also drew attention to law as theater, an idea later developed with some effect by the British historian E. P. Thompson. Nader also shared unwittingly the cynicism of Northcote Thomas and Karl Marx about who gets rich from litigation. In the Mexican town in which she conducted fieldwork, it was certainly lawyers, but the town treasury also benefitted. Studies such as these placed legal anthropology in close proximity to political struggles and relative power. They appeared at the same time as further ethnographic analysis of corporations (Smith 1974), inheritance (Goody 1962; Smith 1965b), succession (Colson 1966; Goody

1966b), and family property (Lloyd 1962, 1965), although no explicit statement was made about breaking down the barriers between legal studies and kinship.

Comparative Jurisprudence and Historical Process

Participant observation in the anthropological study of law did not lead to the total neglect of past structures and historical processes. Both Sally Falk Moore and M. G. Smith evinced an ingrained knowledge of historical jurisprudence that, over time, provided an intellectual context for what threatened to become an actor-dominated field. Their appreciation of the historicity of specific legal systems was accompanied by an appreciation of the historicity of the study of law itself.

Moore's *Power and Property in Inca Peru* (1958) was reprinted in 1972. Originally a Columbia doctoral dissertation directed by Duncan Strong, the monograph reevaluated Inca village relations in the context of the state. Moore found the involvement of local leaders in its administrative bureaucracy to be critical. Structural-functional anthropology and Hohfeldian legal realism buttressed Moore's interpretation.

M. G. Smith nicely complicated the observational, situational understanding of the legal anthropologist by introducing the historical process (1965b). Smith, for whom history rather than evolution had always been bedrock, was led to align himself alongside Maine and Weber in the structural analysis of corporations as "modal units" of social and legal structure (1974). Weber began to stride the anthropological globe even as Maine's ghost became more visible on the ramparts. In a most important paper, Smith (1965b) demonstrated the value of comparative history for analyses of contemporary jural institutions and legal development. French, British, and Moslem law in Africa provided his ethnography, but his argument was applied more widely (Kuper and Kuper 1965). The degree to which a comparative ethnology of law was feasible remained debatable, however (Pospisil 1971; Moore 1985a).[33]

An issue that might have arisen at any time but which particularly caught the attention of both Moore and Smith in this transitional era was the relation of the individual to the group (Moore 1969; Gluckman 1975) and of privilege to justice (Leach 1963; Smith 1965b). Concern for the individual and his or her "civil rights" (Gluckman 1975) contributes, surely, to Moore's antipathy for evolutionary interpretations of law (1965), an antipathy she addressed even more forcefully as time went by (1978, 1985). It appeared in critiques of Hoebel[34] and Gluckman; in explorations of the concept of the social field for the analysis of change (1973); and in a sustained reanalysis of the ethnography of strict liability, self-help, and collective responsibility. It also appeared in an interdisciplinary context, in which lawyers and sociologists still availed themselves of evolutionary notions (Diamond 1971; Roberts 1979; Posner 1980; Stein 1980).

A characteristic passage sums up Sally Falk Moore's relentless argument, which by 1972 was both combative and programmatic. She wrote:

> It is clear from the ethnographic material available today that what Pound conceived of as four stages of legal evolution—payment instead of vengeance, strict law, moral law, and a combination of equity and certainty— can all be found together in pre-industrial systems. These pieces of theoretical pottery, while arranged by Pound in apparently successive stratigraphic layers, can be found glued together to form a single pot. This is not to say that all legal systems are alike, but that the criteria Pound used for differentiating them are not the most useful distinguishing features. His evolutionary criteria are not useful because they are not founded on societal characteristics, and are principles that exist together, not only in that ultimate compound, our own supposedly remarkable society, but also in technologically simple societies. Less severe strictures apply to the legal-collectivity, legal-individuality discussions of Maine, Durkheim and Malinowski, because they never abstracted legal principles altogether from the social context in which they occurred. But the analytic fault in their evolutionary statements lies in their being over-focused on particular elements. In the case of Durkheim and Maine their visions of ever-increasing individuality in legal matters was legitimate as far as it concerned the particular problems to which they chose to address themselves. Malinowski looked at quite different materials and redressed the balance somewhat. But surely collectivity and individuality in legal matters are aspects of all systems, not alternative systems. To speak of the temporal precedence in legal development, of civil or criminal law, of public or private law, or of collectivity and individuality, does not make sociological sense. The generalizations couched in these terms use one aspect of system to characterize the whole, which is a procedure of dubious worth. (Moore 1972:100–101)

The publications of Fried, Sahlins, and Service had led, remember, to a more or less unquestioning acceptance of neo-evolutionary categories in American political anthropology. Moore dismissed evolutionary theory for having *trivialized* ethnography.

Cultural and Legal Pluralism

In this age of rapid political and economic change for colonial states and new nations, various aspects of the legal infrastructure attracted the attention of government official, politician, and legal anthropologist alike. Among them were land law and the reform of family law.

Above all, however, were problems associated with multiple legal frameworks (Pospisil 1958a, 1959; Gulliver 1963; Nader and Metzger 1963; Bohannan 1965); the institutionalization of legal pluralism at the state level (Kuper and Kuper 1965; Schiller 1965); and so-called customary law.[35] Kuper and Kuper (1965) provided an ideational analysis of law in plural societies, comparing law in homogeneous societies with law in plural colonial societies. The proposed codification of customary law in African nations (Allott 1966) fostered academic interest in founding the Restatement of African Law project at the School of Oriental and African Studies in London, a project at odds with most anthropologists' view of the interrelatedness of law and society. Not until the 1980s did legal pluralism again appear on the agenda.

A Future Assured

The institutionalization of legal anthropology as a subfield was most striking, as was its dialogue with lawyers and political scientists, much of which was incorporated into conferences and edited volumes.[36] Africanists Antony Allott, J.N.D. Anderson, T. O. Elias, W.J.M. Mackenzie, Leslie Rubin, Arthur Schiller, and William Twining showed considerable familiarity with anthropology. Passages from Gluckman appeared alongside those of Malinowski in law school texts.[37] College and law school students in America read in both fields.

Conferences on various aspects of the anthropology of law were held at Los Angeles in 1963 (Kuper and Kuper 1965), Stanford in 1964 (Nader 1969), and at Burg Wartenstein (Nader 1969) and Addis Ababa (Gluckman 1969) in 1966. A bibliographic survey was published in *Current Anthropology* (Nader, Koch, and Cox 1965). A special publication of the *American Anthropologist* entitled *The Ethnography of Law* (Nader 1965) appeared in 1965. The interdisciplinary journal *Law and Society* first appeared in 1967. Reviews of the field were commissioned for the *Biennial* and *Annual Review of Anthropology* in 1969 and 1975. A memorial volume for Gluckman (Gulliver 1978) made visible to all the cadre of distinguished legal anthropologists who had brought the coherent and prestigious new subdiscipline into being.

No anthropologist could remain unaware of the confident new specialization. In the United States, funding agencies responded. Laura Nader was particularly successful in raising funds for team research by Berkeley students into comparative village law and law in Western societies (Nader and Yngvesson 1973). In the United States, legal anthropology had some 120 practitioners by 1973. But in Britain matters were very different. Gluckman died a prophet without followers within his own bailiwick. When an ASA conference was finally held on the subject of law and anthropology in 1974, it failed to attract more than a few members. Four years earlier a proposal to hold such a conference had been turned down because it was seen as reflecting only a minor interest (Gulliver 1978). In response to a continually expanding interest in law among academic anthropologists, however, several textbooks in legal anthropology were published between 1965 and 1973, among them Gluckman 1965, Bohannan 1967, Pospisil 1971, and Spradley and McCurdy 1971. The continued existence of the specialization was as-sured—in the United States at least.

POLITICAL ETHNOGRAPHY: SERENDIPITY AND SPITE

Anthropology, Elizabeth Colson suggested, has advanced "by spiralism, by moving to new areas which pose different problems, rather than by cultivating our gardens" (1976:269). Sub-Saharan Africa had so domi-nated political anthropology in the 1940s that one disgruntled critic complained of Afro-imperialism. In the 1950s first Asia and then New Guinea projected new ethnography into the anthropology of politics. In the 1960s it was the turn of Latin America and the Caribbean, and finally in the 1970s Europe and the Middle East became the hunting grounds for ethnographic and theoretical advance.

By 1973 there were few regions of the world where anthropologists had not worked for between three and eight decades. So vast was the increased production of anthropological scholarship that some feared that "the progress of anthropology displayed a proliferation and sprawl that threatened its advance" (Arensberg 1972:1). Yet while certainly the political ethnography of each region of the world threw up new data and new issues, cross-cutting concepts promised to emerge that would hold the fragmenting discipline together.

The conditions under which political anthropologists selected locales for field research had, of course, changed considerably from Edwardian times, when Rivers elected to work among the Todas because they had already been so well studied. Imperial and national interests had long been engaged—without much success, as we have seen—in harnessing ethnographic research. In the period from 1954 to 1973, which was char-acterized by a multidisciplinary scramble over funding and research in Third World countries, anthropologists—pragmatic, positivistically in-clined social scientists—were obliged both to define their own collab-orative role and to resist its definition by others.[38] Clifford Geertz put it well when he discussed the nature of government in peasant societies:

In becoming thus involved anthropologists have . . . been drawn willy-nilly into an enterprise far wider than the confines of their own discipline and so find themselves faced with the unforeseen question of what, *qua* anthropologists, rather than as self-made sociologists, historians, political scientists or whatever, they have to offer to this wider enterprise. The easy answer to this, still preferred in certain circles, is data, preferably anomalous data which will demolish some sociologist's highwrought theory. But to accept that answer is to reduce anthropology to a kind of *spiteful ethnography*, capable, like some literary censor, of disapproving of intellectual constructions but not of creating, or perhaps even of understanding, any. (Geertz 1967:4, emphasis added)

Most of the 1950s generation of international social scientists carried to the Third World academic setting their predilections for sacred texts and party ideologies. In such grand company, ethnographers began to clarify their distinctive research methods. Neville Dyson-Hudson urged:

If we are to build upon the gains of the fifties, we must pursue a behavioral and realist style of thought as systematically and as vigorously as possible. We should try (for working purposes) to cultivate assumptions of variability rather than invariance, of contingency rather than of regularity, of individuality rather than of typicality. We should try for realism and detail, and persistently fight the tendency to generalize too quickly from the data we collect. This is no plea for a fragmenting social science based on infinitely individualized cases. We can always simplify, generalize and modulate from our detailed cases; but we cannot extract causes, details, and variations from data acquired as general statements, modalities or norms in the first place. (Dyson-Hudson 1972:9)

This vision of field research as important to political anthropology had to be set against the need to counter "ethnographic dazzle" by providing intellectual frameworks, reviews of the literature, and the like.

These two endeavors coexisted in the regional political ethnography produced between 1954 and 1973. Local particularism, regional ethnologizing through the adoption of specific concepts "thrown up" by the specialized ethnographies, and a striving toward larger nomothetic frameworks characterized what was fast becoming a global academy. Traditions were reworked as political anthropology moved toward explanations of "cultural" variation in terms of two contradictory universal paradigms: the cosmopolitical framework of an expansive capitalist economy and the generic framework of universal politicking behavior.

Ironically, in spite of its rich catholicity and its everlasting obsession with comparison, anthropologists overlooked one quiet suggestion from Max Weber that might have solved many of their theoretical dilemmas as they moved into the postcolonial world. Weber encouraged scholars interested in comparative studies "to think in terms of concepts applicable to some, rather than all, societies. This strategy of analysis proceeds in the belief that concepts of universals—even if useful for certain orienting purposes—are so emptied of content that they require specifications in order to be applied to some body of evidence, and these specifications are concepts of more limited applicability" (Bendix 1971:218). Politics was crying out for such treatment by 1973 when this period of ethnographic abundance came to an end.

CONCLUSION

The period between 1954 and 1973 was one of the most vital ever experienced by political anthropology. It began with a struggle to define and legitimize the new subfield specialization and ended with a clear agenda for the future. The new political anthropology was defined in response to an anachronistic review of its subject matter by political scientist David Easton in 1959. Political anthropology's answer to the struggle taking place among several disciplines for a distinctive place in the study of new nations was to reject its earlier trend toward reconstructing and typologizing primitive political systems in favor of research into interstitial, supplementary, and parallel parapolitical structures and their relation to formal power. Elites and ethnicity in new nations attracted a great deal of attention. Colson's critical review of the field in 1968 placed conflict and change at the head of the agenda.

Both action and process theory—long in the making, as we have seen (Chapters 3 and 4)—took clearer form in these years, with action theory providing the dominant mainstream paradigm for the discipline. Political ethnographers, such as Bailey and Boissevain, studied individual actors and their strategies within political arenas. This continued awareness of spatial politics was enriched by detailed field studies from Europe and Asia as well as Africa. Related paradigms, such as transactionalism, game theory, and symbolic interactionism, also embraced politics. An interest in political change led some action theorists toward the study not only of contradictions and conflict but also of the immediate colonial past. Processual theorists, such as Turner and Barth, found it difficult to disentangle themselves from the new vocabulary of action and agency, with the result that processual theory remained in what appears to be an endless formative phase (Chapter 4).

Legal anthropology closely associated itself with action theory, and the study of dispute settlement flourished cross-culturally. A common discourse was established between the Africanists—who dominated the study of law (Chapter 4), particularly Gluckman and Fallers—and a whole generation of American scholars trained by Laura Nader at Berkeley, who worked in Mexico and the United States. Subterranean themes, such as the legal relation of the individual to the group, power structures, and the historical processes of legal change began to take shape (Chapter 6).

Parallel to these developments, the trend toward emphasizing the politics of peasantries in Latin America continued. The Latin Americanists' use of archives and historical sources contrasted with the anthropologists' parochialism and presentism in their study of new nations in the discipline at large. Wolf continued to craft a cohesive paradigm for the anthropology of peasant politics, but this did not capture transatlantic attention until after his publication of *Peasant Wars* in 1969.

Dialogue across the Atlantic, one of the major factors accounting for the success of one paradigm and the failure of another, began to increase between 1954 and 1973 due to an increase in regional specialization within the discipline at large. This is so important that it merits more than the space allotted to it in this chapter. The advantages and disadvantages of regional political ethnography have yet to be weighed. This specialization within a specialization became institutionalized in courses, seminars, conferences, and journals throughout the latter part of this period when funds were flowing—and it is surely here to stay. The extent to which regional specialization is contributing to the disappearance of political anthropology as a distinct subfield is touched on in Chapter 6. By 1974 its effects had only just begun to be felt, and political anthropology entered the 1970s with two contradictory universal paradigms: the generic framework of universal politicking behavior and the cosmopolitan framework of an expansive capitalist economy.

6   Crisis and Consolidation, 1974 to the Present

Social anthropology not only studies human culture; it is itself a part of human culture. It studies social processes, but it is also a product of social processes. Hence it has changed its material and developed its methods as world relationships have changed and developed. In the future it may do so even more, and may probably be expected to enlarge its scheme of values in doing so.

—RAYMOND FIRTH

In 1974 many practitioners considered anthropology to be in a state of crisis, but it proved to be not the beginning but the end of a crisis brought about by theoretical stagnation (Ardener 1971; Jarvie 1975). Political anthropology was about to enter a field of new, contested paradigms. If any elements of crisis remain today, they are those of overproduction and underconsumption.

Not only the discipline but the profession itself was in crisis for much of the 1970s and 1980s. Its main symptoms were fragmentation, specialization, politicization, and unemployment (Scholte 1981; Goldschmidt 1985). The year 1983 saw the largest number ever of unemployed anthropologists in the academy. The AAA restructured itself as an umbrella over eighty-six distinct subfield organizations. Robert McCormack Adams in his Distinguished Lecture at the AAA's annual meeting, "World Picture, Anthropological Frame" (1977), noted how even annual meetings of the profession had become boundary-maintaining mechanisms.[1]

Both the discipline and the profession experienced extreme politicization in the 1970s. I suggested in Chapter 4 that while radical political thought has invariably been identified and labeled as such within anthropology, conservative tendencies have generally entered the mainstream without tags attached. *Reinventing Anthropology* (Hymes 1969) was a culmination in many respects of American civil rights protests, the Vietnam War, and finally the international academic radicalism of 1968, and it brought the division within the academy—and between the United States and Britain—into the open.[2] It was also the opening salvo of a paradigm, neither wholly conservative nor wholly radical, based upon reflexivity. In the next few years this came to include the historicizing of anthropological theory and a masochistic fascination with ethnography and meta-ethnography, as well as a receptiveness to the challenges of Third World academics. Within political anthropology, the six relatively distinct approaches that had developed earlier gave way to near polarization into action theory, systems theory, and neo-evolutionism on one side and political economy and culture history on the other. Process theory (a potential bridge) remained, as was its nature, inchoate.

Trying to find its boundaries, the discipline as a whole began to break up into a variety of technical approaches. Within the anthropology of politics, changes in research methods both underlay and reflected the eclipse of community in favor of region and the rejection of the "ethnographic present" in favor of history. These shifts also reflected, to a degree, trends in the "real world" of respondents and analysts. The eclipse of community was also associated with changing paradigms of the economy. The emergence of regional analysis owed much to William Skinner's insights into both marketing systems and closed communities in China at a time when kingdoms and the state were reengaging attention. Carol Smith's two edited volumes on regional analysis appeared in 1976. Their happy conjuncture with a theoretical groundswell that accounted for present political and economic structures in terms of present and past dependency relations owed not a little to Smith's own engagement in Central American research.

Notions of uneven development and national inequalities within capitalist systems (sometimes drawing on Lenin and Luxemburg but just as often not) had entered the anthropology of politics with the publication of Andre Gunder Frank's essay (1967) on the sociology of development and the underdevelopment of sociology. Reevaluations of what community studies were all about by some of the discipline's leading practitioners (Bailey 1971; Geertz 1972; Mintz 1976) sanctified, as it were, the new trend. Thus Geertz, for example, advocated that anthropology "discard the community study genre . . . in favor of a regional focus that can include both rural and urban systems in a common framework, a larger system" (1972:464). In 1980 the editors of the *Annual Review of Anthropology (ARA)* introduced alongside the classical four-field headings (Archaeology, Biological Anthropology, Linguistics, and Cultural-Social Anthropology) a fifth, Regional Studies.[3]

The French historian Fernand Braudel's *The Mediterranean and the Mediterranean World in the Age of Philip II* (first published in English in 1972) gave shape to one such region and inspired sociologist Immanuel Wallerstein's *The Modern World-System* two years later. Wallerstein's modern capitalist world, with its delineation of dynamic cores, peripheries, and semiperipheries, provided political anthropology with a new taxonomy for political systems, accounting for variability and encouraging once again the comparative perspective on which the discipline had almost foundered. After its 1960s struggle toward studying the interrelationship of "levels" in the political structures of the new developing nations, political anthropology welcomed the world-system paradigm, believing that it explained why both those nations and the discipline had failed to attain promised goals. While Wallerstein traced the intellectual roots of his endeavor to the *Annales* school of Braudel, Marxism brought together under the new umbrella those who had always argued the necessity for a processual and historical dimension (Wolf 1956a, 1982) with those whose field inquiries had recently led them to pursue so-called multinational companies across the globe. Many of the latter were feminists concerned over the exploitation of women's labor in such enterprises. Marxists were, for the most part, critical of Wallerstein's paradigm, obliging counter-Marxists to shift ground. They argued that more attention should be paid to kinship, ethnicity, and nationalism.[4] Since Marxists, too, bemoaned the lack of attention to ideology in the modern world-system paradigm, these categories received considerably more attention (along with class) after 1974.

Several of anthropology's elder statesmen and stateswomen led in approving the global perspective, and this was probably decisive in establishing its hegemony. As Adams put it:

> When we step back to enlarge the field of vision, we do not retreat from phenomena but better perceive their significance. We have tended to define the groups we study largely on the basis of their self-constituted structure, their aspect as independent organisms. Increasingly, however, an approach based on the web of interrelations that individuals as well as groups maintain seems equally valid and more consistent with the main course of development of the world we know. (1977:276)

Similar sentiments were expressed by Colson (1976) and Goldschmidt (1976).

One inevitable result was the politicization of world ethnography and the decline of political anthropology as a specialized subfield. In 1986 many fewer academics declared political anthropology as a specialization, and fewer departments offered a rounded program in the four traditional domains of social or cultural anthropology (religion, politics, social organization, and economics), which might invite such identification. On the other hand, many more academics professed a specialization in gender studies and peasant societies. Given the high political content of these two fields, it would appear that interest in politics had itself simply become more specialized.

Out-of-step development within the various domains of study (Vincent 1986b) reflected the uneven impact of the new global paradigm, on the one hand, and its internally generated opposition on the other. This showed up in political ethnography. Regional analyses encouraged reaching out (again) toward history, political science, and economics. Researchers placed new emphasis on political economy, dependency, history, indigenous states, and women. At the same time, the difficulty of doing fieldwork in war-torn regions led to a greater appreciation of the contributions of indigenous regional scholars (Gilmore 1982; Halpern and Kideckel 1983; Smith and Boyer 1987). In the earlier part of the period (1974–1979), concern with community, ethnicity, stratification, acculturation, action theory centered on the individual, ecology, and—ironically, perhaps—warfare was most prominent. Law as a subfield became less distinct, while efforts to globalize the study of war reemerged.

Third World anthropologists, like Third World historians, tended to be less receptive to regional and global analysis, and alternative foci developed simultaneously in the discipline at large. Most powerful among them were gender analysis and an amalgam of interests that, following Foucault (1977), we can characterize as being concerned with the interrelationship of power and knowledge. Marxists who turned to Poulantzas and Gramsci also began to march to a different drummer, turning away from what began to be described as economistic, "orthodox" Marxism. This was most apparent, not surprisingly, in the anthropology of law.[5]

Perhaps the most divisive issue to emerge in this period was the acceptance of political commitment among young scholars. Its roots must certainly be traced back to protest in the United States against the Vietnam War, the reproduction of that protest within the academy, and its recurrent expression in protest against White House policies in Central America. As in the past, political issues that divided the American nation divided the anthropology of politics as well.

Anthropology as an endeavor was contextualized both within the academy and in the world outside. Its content as a cultural and ideological form and as literary expression was closely scrutinized. Analytical literary criticism found a new mark. Significantly for the anthropology of politics, self-scrutiny and historical deconstruction placed old knowledge and old issues back on the agenda.[6]

COSMOPOLITICS

The era began with a reevaluation of the dependency paradigm, which had preoccupied many economists, sociologists, and anthropologists in the 1960s and which had clearly spread from Latin American studies to political anthropology by 1974. The dependency paradigm was the other side, as it were, of theories of modernization in the development decade. Dependency theorists causally connected the two to argue not simply the economic, political, and cultural dependence of Third World countries on Europe (Frank 1969b) but also the development of underdevelopment within them by Europe.

The national focus of much dependency literature (a function, perhaps, of reliance on government statistics) tended to push into the background not simply anthropologists' local and regional studies but also their observations on the locus of causal change in the encapsulating capitalist system. Godfrey Wilson had noted the impact of the Roman Catholic church and international communism as well as the expansion of capitalism (Chapter 4). Political scientists, historians, and European ethnographers seemed quite content to delineate political relations that operated between nations (donor/exploiter and dependent) at the national and international levels. Marxists and the majority of political anthropologists were not.

The challenge to the dependency paradigm came mainly from members of the Latin American academy itself, and it was surely not unrelated to the rapid industrialization of certain of their own nations. For political anthropologists the concept of dependency provided a directive rather than a theory leading them to focus on the particular (the locale) as the epiphenomenon of an historical process. The dependency perspective directs "the attention of the analyst to certain aspects of an historical situation—the relation between the internal economic and political forces and the external powers that dominate the world economy—but it does not tell the analyst just what these relations will be. In other words, it tells him how to study history, but does not tell him specifically what he will find as he does so" (Kahl 1976:176). Norman Long, a Manchester-trained Africanist who carried out field research in Peru in the 1970s, had no difficulty in adapting the social fields approach of anthropology, and the entrepreneurial brokers of Barth and Bailey, to the dependency paradigm (see Long 1975, 1977).[7]

It quickly became apparent that the dependency paradigm had to be complemented by analyses of regional underdevelopment and class formation. Dependency theorists like Frank recognized the pluralism of the colonial structure, and political anthropologists were quick to specify alternatives to the "class structure" of the dependent nation: kinship, ethnicity, and nationalism itself. The very unit of dependency analysis, the nation, had perforce to be seen as a construct, not taken as a given. For a politically committed scholar like Frank, the very acceptance of the dependency paradigm by bourgeois U.S. intellectuals made it suspect. Thus in *Lumpenbourgeoisie: Lumpendevelopment* (1972) he took pains to point out that "today the word 'dependence' is no more than a euphemism that cloaks subjection, oppression, alienation, and imperialist, capitalist racism, all of which are internal as well as external" (Frank 1972:9).

Here then was a new agenda for political anthropologists. Some of those most politically committed took it up; many, however, were deflected from its emphases by the publication in 1974 of Immanuel Wallerstein's *The Modern World-System*, which took the world of social science by storm. Intellectual production was at last in step with the profit production of international capitalism, the multinational firms, and the international migration of labor. Paradoxically, scholars of contemporary capitalism found their model in a study of the expansion of Europe in the sixteenth century written by an American sociologist who had previously worked in the developing nations of twentieth-century western Africa. They were prepared for it, perhaps, by the historical trend already under way within the discipline. Over the next fifteen years, Wallerstein wrote two additional volumes, bringing his story of the modern world-system up to the decade of the 1840s—that is, to the eve of the genealogical depth to which anthropologists had become accustomed to thinking and the eve of the bureaucratic explosion in the administrative records that they had come to read.[8] A hiatus clearly existed.

Within political anthropology, *The Modern World-System* was cited more for its vocabulary than for its content or argument. In much the same way as Walters (1980) suggested that social historians quote Geertz, for legitimacy, Wallerstein's paradigm encouraged anthropologists to feel that their fieldwork data was on a par, not on a lower "local" level, with that of other social scientists who, by and large, were much more powerful within the academy. But, whereas Geertz was quoted a great deal, Wallerstein was more often cited, his terminology adopted to place the fieldwork locale within a global context. Indeed, critiques of his systems paradigm were probably as influential as the synthesis itself.[9]

Among the paradigm's shortcomings that concerned anthropologists were its focus on taxonomy rather than process, on exchange rather than production, and on nations rather than less anachronous political units. Above all, however, they were concerned about its Eurocentrism. Wallerstein was particularly weak in his understanding of social organization, from kinship to class, in both European and non-European societies. Yet the world-systems model served a familiar purpose. Just as the Victorians adopted evolutionary theory to order the accumulating data of primitive ethnology, so many political anthropologists in the 1970s adopted the world-systems model to order the complex ethnography accumulated after World War II.

The modern world-system, Wallerstein suggested, rests on a global division of labor mediated through trade related to, but critically not structured by, existing political units. It is not contained within any unitary political structure. At any one time, cores, peripheries, and semiperipheries may be distinguished within the system. These organize labor differently, contain different class structures, and profit unequally from the system's operation. Historically, all the regions of the world may be placed within one or another of these three categories. Wallerstein perceived three phases in the process of bringing into being the modern world-system: the long sixteenth century, 1640 to 1815; the period from 1815 to 1917; and that from 1917 to the present. Anthropologists were quick to embrace Wallerstein's categories, to explore his delineations with respect to labor, and to point out that class alone was inadequate to analyze political structures. Frequently they did all three quite unhistorically, simply focusing on the transition in Third World countries from a colonial past to a field-locale present. But the most important problem that Wallerstein's paradigm raised for political anthropologists was what June Nash in 1975 called the Problem of the Passive Periphery.

Two areas of debate stimulated by cosmopolitical paradigms were of particular interest to anthropologists concerned with political economy: first, the extent to which modern capitalism both requires and produces and reproduces a peasant sector and, second, the effects of capitalist development on labor in so-called peripheral regions—feudalization on the periphery, as it was called. The long-standing anthropological debate on whether *feudal* was a term that might usefully be applied ethnographically was thus given a new and dynamic analytical relevance. Like family and kinship forms, researchers found servile labor in many cases to have been a response to peripheralization and not an institution rooted in the "traditional" structures on which capitalism was seen to "encroach." Though it first developed as a theoretical issue in Latin America (Laclau 1971; Kay 1974), Dutch colonialism in Indonesia subsequently attracted anthropologists to the problem (Geertz 1963a; Kahn 1981; Stoler 1985), as did peripheral Eastern Europe (Chirot 1976; Verdery 1983). Coerced cash-crop labor lay at the heart of the problem: the creation of a rural proletariat, as Mintz had long ago demonstrated in his critique of Redfield's "folk society" (Chapter 4). By the 1980s peasants and rural proletarians were being compared within a general analytical framework, "the labor process," the process by which "people in social relationships with one another deploy labor and allocate its products" (Wolf 1981:46).

Anthropology's alternative cosmopolitical paradigm—accepted by some, opposed by others—appeared with the publication of Eric Wolf's *Europe and the People Without History* in 1982. Like Wallerstein, Wolf focused on the long sixteenth century, and his readiness to accept the systems premises underlying Wallerstein's paradigm to a much greater extent than might have been expected (substituting mode of production for exchange) may have reflected the difficulty of delineating historical processes in times as remote from the present as those about which both wrote. Mintz, in "The So-Called World System" (1977), concluded that the formulation was premature. In an important theoretical statement (1978b), he used the particularities of Caribbean plantation systems, slavery as process, the making of peasantries and a rural proletariat, and phases in the history of capitalism to question mode-of-production analyses per se. He criticized the concept for its aggregation of diversity, its neglect of shifts within the "periphery" of the world-system, and above all, its neglect of cultural values. Mintz, remember, along with Wolf and like Geertz and Turner, was of that 1950s generation whose first field experience was gained when closed, holistic systems models were found to be inadequate for the study of complexity and change.

Scholarly acclaim greeted Wolf's best-selling textbook *Europe and the People Without History*, which was reviewed at length by historians and social scientists. What the world-systems paradigm did, in the hands of both Wallerstein and Wolf, was to render endogenous that which had previously been treated as exogenous in the analysis of processes of change. Anthropology in the 1950s had moved from the local to the national in terms of encapsulated systems, discovering en route that causal explanation tended to lie in the environment (Silverman 1974). In now moving from the national to the global, political anthropology thus arrived logically at its ultimate system.

Anthropologists of politics have always been more prepared to view world-systems thinking as an intelligent, if obvious, framework than to structure their analyses *within* its demands. Peter Worsley, a strong advocate of substantive ethnography, urged in 1974 that the adoption of cosmopolitical perspectives be both restrained and thoroughgoing. "The analysis of situations," he wrote, "has always to be informed by an awareness of the world within which situations and encounters are located, and more than that, requires an explicit conceptualization of what that world looks like" (1974:10).

The arguments and counterarguments that had so recently been required reading for any political anthropologist (see, for example, Frank 1969a, 1969b, 1974, 1975; Furtado 1970; Amin 1974; Leys 1974; Wallerstein 1974b; Stavenhagen 1975; Brenner 1977; Cardoso 1977) already appear to have taken on a periodicity all their own. Problems of underdevelopment and multinational expansion are still with us, of course, but the economistic point of entry into the cosmopolitical world has been superceded by passage along routes both more subtle and more direct.

Within political anthropology the global perspective went through three phases. First, as we have seen, in the ethnography of central Africa and Puerto Rico in the 1950s, a world-system was juxtaposed with a more specific local study; then in the 1960s and 1970s, the locality was encompassed within the cosmopolitical arena; and finally in the 1980s, in response to the dependency and world-systems paradigms, political anthropology turned away from a sole reliance on synchronic analysis toward process and history, with a greater sensitivity to the cultural and ideological dimensions of expansion and global involvement. Methodologically, the first compatible step for anthropologists was to study political brokers linking the locality and the outside world. An old idea, the "world," took on a new complexity, but as political anthropologists began to place local political structures in the context of the modern world-system, they tended to forget the rich-grained political ethnography of the past. Megaconcepts like exploitation, domination, and imposition tended to take the place of both causal analyses and explanation. The promise of the processual political anthropology of Lesser and Turner, with their parallel adoption of the concepts of ever-expanding fields, was not fulfilled.

NEW TAXONOMIES AND STATES OF MIND

Political anthropology between 1940 and 1973 was engaged, as we have seen, in the proliferation of taxonomies to order ethnography. By the mid 1980s one taxonomy appeared particularly useful for relating political ethnography derived from field research in rapidly changing societies. This rested, as had most of the earlier classifications, on an economic basis—a mode of production, as some chose to call it. It sought to address complexity by recognizing the coexistence within one polity of several economic forms, and to address conflict and change by recognizing processes of transformation.

As with dependency and modern world-systems paradigms, its initial premise was the development and expansion of capitalism. But unlike these models, it sought to account for complexity and diversity through the pursuit of process. Rather than take nation-states as the units, as the two earlier paradigms had done, the new approach began with the concept of *social formation*. A social formation might contain within itself one or more modes of production. Usually the studies delineated three modes of production: one had as its most salient characteristic kinship relations; another, the extraction of tribute; and a third, capitalism. All might be found in the contemporary situation so that, although the development and reproduction of capitalism is dominant everywhere, the other modes continue to exist in a subordinate relationship. Indeed, capitalism, some argued, requires their coexistence.

Within anthropology the publication of Marx's *Grundrisse: Foundations of the Critique of Political Economy* in 1973 provided a new lens through which both ethnology and ethnography might be examined. And this lens was historical, not evolutionary. Modes of production do not, in evolutionary fashion, replace each other in the development of a society; rather, a new mode of production may emerge and establish its dominance on the basis of the continued operation of older, subordinated modes of production. In terms of observable politics in the twentieth century, this means that the political process can be viewed as a process in which the capitalist mode of production sought to establish dominance.

The ethnographically confined research of a group that came to be known as the French structuralist Marxists was critical in bringing coherence to the paradigm, and its application outside of former French West Africa and by scholars who were not structuralists or Marxists was rapid. In labeling the group, ideology rather than ethnography was the key—continuities with earlier Africanist scholarship tended to be pushed into the background.[10] For this the group itself shared responsibility since it claimed—in a structuralist and Marxist vein—to represent a universal paradigm. Subsequent struggles among structuralists (orthodox and interpretive) and Marxists (structural and cultural) reflected a move toward restoring ethnographic, historical, and cultural content. Not for nothing did Edwin Ardener in the 1971 Malinowski Lecture, "The New Anthropology and Its Critics," attribute so much of the current crisis in British anthropology to the French structural Marxists.

The three forms of polity are not new in name, but a body of concepts is now attached to each that is wholly innovative. The kinship polity, delineated clearly by Fortes (1969), is a general term used here for a series of tangential approaches by a group of French Marxist scholars that are based on refined delineations of a domestic mode of production (Meillassoux 1975; Rey 1975; Coquery-Vidrovitch 1975; Godelier 1977) and for reconstructions of them by scholars interested in gender (Gailey 1987) and historical process (Southall 1988b).

The second form of polity is the tributary state. In the delineation of this form, Africanist ethnography blended with earlier research into what was called the Asiatic mode of producton, or Oriental despotism. Amin's 1976 formulation of unequal development inspired both an archaeological and an ethnological reconsideration of so-called early states. Much of it was brought together in two volumes (again resulting from the path-breaking ICAES meeting in Chicago) edited by Claessen and Skalnik, *The Early State* (1978) and *The Study of the State* (1981). A corollary development was the reexamination of caste and feudalism in India (Mukhia 1981; Byres and Mukhia 1985; Leach, Mukherjee, and Ward 1985). Most challenging of all, however, was the reinterpretation of Middle Eastern history and ethnography along these lines. Here not only Marx but also Weber came into his own, provoked by the critiques of Talal Asad (1973b), Samir Amin (1978), and Edward Said (1978).

Finally, the third form of polity, the capitalist state, was, as we have seen, already a generally accepted unit of analysis in political anthropology. By 1973 an effort was under way to distinguish modes of production and phases within it. For political anthropology, the strength of the model lay in the introduction of new concepts that related that which, in its growth over more than a hundred years, had appeared disparate. Old wine was then decanted into new bottles. The new concepts were few and included capital encroachment, uneven development, mode of production, and articulation. The old subject matter included the peasantries and plantations, segmentary states, and feudal societies of the 1950s and 1960s; kinship, bridewealth, witchcraft, and the circulation of women of the 1940s; "culture contact" of the 1930s; and diffusion, revitalization movements, frontier entrepreneurs, and resistance to encroachment going back to the earliest days of professional anthropology. The relations between "independent" peasantries and a rural proletariat could be explored (Wolf 1981); the dominant role of kinship accounted for (Meillassoux 1975; Rey 1976; Gailey 1987); bridewealth could be seen to parallel feudal land-rent (Rey 1971); and above all, inequality (asymmetrical relations between categories of persons) (Moore 1978a, 1978b, 1986) could be explored within this one emergent paradigm. This, as we have seen, had long been the primary stimulus for a focus on the particularly political.

By the 1980s it was clear that the new paradigm could counter the global abstractions of the dependency theorists and Wallerstein's modern world-system. For anthropologists, the attraction of placing more emphasis on the analysis of noncapitalist features of modern society and politics was irresistible. Accept the processual premise that all states emerged through contestation with oppositional sectors — whether these be described as kinship communities, rural peripheries, or labor reserves — and the relevance of the new paradigm to the postcolonial Third World becomes clear. Subordinate relations of production served not simply for the expansion of the capitalist relations, which were dominant, but for their reproduction. The paradigm invited political anthropologists to explore *how* this was done in place after place, time after time.

CONFRONTING CAPITAL: A NEW CONSENSUS?

Wolf has suggested that American anthropologists "become engaged in broadly political issues, class, race, ethnic conflict, often in a simple-minded way, but with real commitment" (Friedman 1987:117). The same has been true in the past of British anthropologists — Rivers, George Pitt-Rivers, to some extent Malinowski, Gluckman — as previous chapters have hinted. What is distinctive today about that large segment of political anthropology based on field research is a common stance within its emergent centers of interest. Born, perhaps, out of the impact of the modern world-systems paradigm and in anthropological reaction to it, these are discussed below as subaltern studies, the weapons of the weak, law, Marxism, and gendered politics.

None of these configurations is simply an intellectual development contingent upon the political events of the day and age; as we have seen, all have deep roots within the discipline, though the roots have not always been well nurtured. What is distinctive about this generation is that their common sustenance may be recognized in the adoption of a single phrase: *confronting capital*. For a hundred years the anthropology of politics has, as Redfield put it, *followed* capital; in the 1980s it began to confront it head on. The phrase is an attractive one because it looks beneath the surface features and behind the adopted labels; it is analytical rather than representational.[11]

Yet until the late 1980s a term such as *confronting capital* would have raised hackles in anthropology at large; maybe in a few small circles it still does. But in an era when Prime Minister Margaret Thatcher's minister of education, Sir Keith Joseph, can write about the lack of capitalist or bourgeois values and about class struggles in Marxist terms, and one of America's leading conservative historians, Gertrude Himmelfarb, can entertain a fellow traveler by demonstrating how Marx took some of his best phrases from Carlyle, Proudhon, Blanqui, and possibly Jean-Paul Marat, one must surely recognize that there has been "a wider opening-up of the social vocabulary. Words that for so long at best enjoyed a shadowy existence (marginalized into purely academic discussions) and at worst were censoriously excised from public statements— words like *capitalism* and *class*—have become the commonplace of public statements" (Corrigan 1980:xviii).[12]

So successfully has this vision been internalized by political anthropologists that its technical concepts (jargon) have been set aside and forgotten and its theoretical unity destroyed. It simply provided, like evolutionary and functional theory before it, a "frame" for the ongoing circumstances in which political anthropologists worked. This might, indeed, be the definition of dominance in the history of a science: as the 1980s progressed, it became more and more apparent that one could find Marx's analysis valuable, and even know Marx's writings intimately, without being a Marxist.

Subaltern Studies:
Political Anthropology from Below

Political anthropology has never distinguished itself by researching the corridors of power; the challenge to "study up" was not widely accepted, and the heartland of capital remained elusive. Research in Europe and the United States remained marginalized within the discipline, so successful had first primitivization and then ethnicization proved. Moreover, anthropologists interested in the particularly political had inevitably pursued it across the globe among those at the grass roots where they conducted field research. What distinguished the years following 1974 was their being joined in the endeavor by revisionist historians and political scientists in what came to be called subaltern studies. Throughout the Third World most of the population confronts contradictions engendered by their objective position as labor in a transnational capitalist economic system and their subjective position as subaltern groups in a colonial or postcolonial system. Although the closure of a dominant class may well be underway in certain countries, the system as a whole is one without class, and conflict is not expressed as class struggle. "The unity felt by the subaltern groups," Hobsbawm wrote, "will be so global as to go beyond class and state. There will not be peasants, but 'people' or 'countrymen'; there will not be workers, but an indiscriminate 'common people' or 'labouring poor', distinguished from the rich merely by poverty, from the idle (whether rich or poor) by the compulsion to live by the sweat of their brow, and from the powerful by the unspoken or explicit corollary of weakness and helplessness" (1972:10). Hobsbawm saw this as a precapitalist societal condition, but today it would more accurately be represented as a nonstate phenomenon. Postnationalist politics and transnational capitalism generate a growing consciousness and active struggle not against a dominant ruling class and its control of a national economy but against exploitation along international lines.

Here we will focus exclusively on two fractions—enormous fractions—of that category. First, peasants who, according to Shanin 1987, make up half of mankind, and second, women, who in so many parts of the world remain politically subordinated jural minors. This is followed by a consideration of the anthropology of law, where the political relationship of the dominant classes with the subaltern classes is currently being exposed.

Cosmopolitan analysis in the hands of Wallerstein and Wolf derived in part from a common effort to produce "total" history. In 1978 Stuart Hall distinguished the "history of the whole" from "history from below."[13] He wrote of "the advantages, the immense strides possible once one seriously adopts the perspective of investigating history from below. . . . It eloquently exposes the inadequacy of conventional accounts of the historical process simply because of what [these accounts] leave out. Indeed, not what they leave out but what they systematically repress For the conventional wisdom has given us an account of capitalism without the working class, an account of imperialism without Blacks, and an account of the division of labour without women" (Hall 1978:9).

"An interest in history from below," as Hall argued, "has crucial political consequences. It can restore a sense of agency, a sense of activity, a sense of the capacity of the working class and the repressed. . . . Recognition of the bases of cultural resistance and opposition takes us back to the material basis of that culture, and the recognition that economy constantly speaks in cultural and political and ideological terms"

(Hall 1978:9–10). Greater attention to culture offered political anthropology the opportunity to move beyond the economistic concepts of both orthodox Marxism and evolutionary theory.

Wolf wrote *Europe and the People Without History* (1982) specifically to expose what historians' and sociologists' accounts of the historical process left out. The unconventional categories of history from below and history from the outside held the potential for bringing together within the academy at least the labor movement (strongly reflected in the United States in the academy but not in the workplace), independence movements of all kinds, and the women's movement. These "special interests," as they came to be labeled in the 1980s, moved toward unification as one failure after another in the civil rights struggle and one instance of economic injustice after another was exposed. At the same time, fragmentation was encouraged in the short run by the legitimacy accorded in the academy to black studies, women's studies, and ethnic studies, all of which tended to deflect political anthropology from Redfield's professed goal: following capital.

Two aspects of history from below provided an agenda for the anthropology of politics: the study of topics systematically repressed in conventional accounts and the recognition of the material basis of cultural resistance and opposition. Discussion of the first was postponed, requiring as it does the analysis of cultural hegemony. The second item was taken up in the case of peasants but not of women.

The institutionalized arena for the production and reproduction of a critique of colonially engendered anthropology that ignored the subaltern classes developed in India in the late 1980s. For anthropologists it is perhaps ironic that the subcontinent that was sidelined as anthropology professionalized and primitivized its subject matter constructed anew the bridge between Europe and India, colonialism and capitalism, that the discipline, to its loss, had dismantled in the Edwardian era (Chapter 2).

One of the main tasks of the subaltern studies group is to expose the failures of colonial capitalist domination, because most historiography dwells on its successes. The subaltern paradigm considerably refines the "great modes-of-production narrative," as Spivak (1985) calls it. It suggests that confrontations rather than transitions be scrutinized. The group's most important—and to anthropologists, most familiar—stress is on the *agent* of change (the insurgent or subaltern) and on *situations* of crisis. The tropical agrarian nature of most of the Third World in which anthropologists worked meant that inevitably most of their studies of subaltern classes involved peasantries.

Weapons of the Weak: Peasant Resistance

Within the setting of global capitalism, which was high on the agenda of scholars working among peasants after 1974, was the problem of explaining why peasants lacked class consciousness and why, given that their misery was so extreme, they did not do more about it. They addressed the questions (which many saw as related) by looking at the moral economy of the peasantry. Extremely influential in what was by now a multidisciplinary, international research field were the British historian Edward Thompson and the American political scientist James Scott. Anthropologists who had worked in peasant societies tended to use the ideas of these two scholars to launch the assault.

Thompson (1971, 1978) developed his vision of the moral economy of the crowd out of a knowledge of eighteenth-century English society, where he perceived "class struggle without class." This was immensely attractive to political anthropologists and quickly raised new questions about long-reported peasant activities. Thompson also revealed (1975, 1978) his appreciation of the increasing rapprochement between social historians and anthropologists, although his view of culture was very different from most of theirs. Nevertheless, the concept of the moral economy fitted well with Bailey's moral community, derived, as we have seen, from Redfield 1955. Most important, it provided a tool by which parapolitical actions could be analyzed systematically along a range of nonclass, preclass, and anticlass idioms of consciousness.

Following both Thompson and Eric Wolf, James Scott provided what was probably the best ethnography of a peasantry in action within the classical anthropological tradition in *Weapons of the Weak: Everyday Forms of Peasant Resistance* (1985). It was as if political science was at last heeding the message of Whyte and Arensberg, taking up the challenge issued in the 1950s (Chapter 4). Scott had sketched out his main argument in *The Moral Economy of the Peasant: Rebellion and Resistance in Southeast Asia* (1976), now he provided an extended case study of one landscape of resistance around a Malaysian village, taking up residence there for two years between 1978 and 1980.

Scott viewed everyday resistance as "a vast and relatively unexplored middle-ground of peasant politics between passivity and open, collective defiance" (1986:1). His distinction followed the one Worsley and the Mancunians made between rebellion and revolution. Scott, an optimist in a field of pessimists (in spite of Wolf's documentation of peasant successes), considered everyday forms of resistance to be ultimately revolutionary. Rebellions are repressed; prolonged covert resistance ensues and, like guerrilla warfare, eventually changes the system.

Peasant rebels are Scott's straw men to some extent, "enraged, inchoate rebels in the grip of a millenial vision" (1986:1). Yet perhaps his fundamental point is well taken: Even in Mooney's fine-grained analysis of the Ghost Dance (1896), it is the massacre of the Sioux by government troops that lies at the heart of the ethnography; the rebellion is the sign that all else has failed. Meanwhile, the everyday weapons of resistance range from clandestine arson and sabotage to footdragging, dissimulation, false compliance, pilfering, slander, and flight.

Peasant forms of resistance, as Scott delineated them, have specific characteristics: "They require little or no coordination or planning; they often represent forms of 'self-help'; they typically avoid any direct symbolic confrontation with authority; and they are generally underwritten by a subculture of resistance" (1986:1). The literature that developed around Scott's formulation addressed such issues as intent, unintended consequences, and conceptions of justice in the peasant community.

Scott also introduced two ideas that did not receive much attention. First, he viewed peasant resistance as a process of escalation. "When such acts are rare and isolated, they are of little interest; but when they become *a consistent pattern* (even though uncoordinated, let alone organized) we are dealing with resistance" (1986:26, emphasis added). Second, Scott emphasized that the parameters of resistance are set not only by the "social ecology" of the peasantry but also by "institutions of repression." Swings between formal and parapolitical activity, he suggested, may be due to changes in the intensity of repression (1986:28–29). Here lay the axial dimension that had been lacking in action theory in political anthropology.

Scott's timely intervention brought together common knowledge from several disciplines, several experiences: Lewis's *Pedro Martinez* (1964); Cobb's study (1970) of popular protest against the police in France in the period 1789–1829; Hobsbawm and Rudé's analysis (1968) of agrarian protest in nineteenth-century England; Genovese's perception (1974) of "pre-political" resistance among slaves; Hyden's ethnography (1980) of resistance to the state in East Africa; Foucault's perceptions (1980) of power and knowledge, strategy and resistance—all of which contributed to a mounting body of concern with forms of protest against imposed power.

Scott's incursion into village ethnography brought reminders from political anthropologists—who, after all, had been there before—that everyday forms of resistance are to a large extent generated by everyday forms of domination. Andrew Turton, for example, urged that the examination of power "should include the techniques and modalities of both more physically coercive forms of domination and more ideological and discursive forms, *and* the relations between the two . . . in which . . . fear may be a crucial factor" (Turton 1986:39–40). Everyday forms of domination require analysis as much as do everyday forms of resistance. As Max Gluckman insisted, it is the shift, not the strike, that is the more interesting phenomenon (Frankenberg 1982). Anthropological critics were also worried about Scott's emphasis on sheer survival at the expense of less material incentives to resistance: claims of assaults on "cultural forms of life . . . dignity and 'human' value in its specific cultural conceptions" (Turton 1986:37).

Several historians of peasantries and peasant resistance had already drawn most profitably on Gerald Sider's work along these lines (1976, 1980). Sider's paradigm of culture-in-the-making took on a much broader canvas. Focusing on transformation in the colonial mercantile and capitalist economy of Newfoundland, Sider placed more emphasis on localized, even personalized, perception, knowledge, and experience. In so doing, he provided a critique, indeed, of the central concepts of both social history and anthropology—class and culture—and such corollary concepts as agency and experience. As he put it, "people act in terms of what they cannot understand, or understand in radically different ways, and in terms of relationships they cannot form, or sustain, or leave, as well as in terms of what 'works', what they think they clearly understand and probably do. From this perspective we may better understand how time and history come also to be embedded in culture and class" (1986:10).

As Sider observed, when anthropologists focus on change, the concept of culture is often deemed irrelevant. The concept itself is ahistorical, nonprocessual, and totalizing. Its dynamic structure is not understood. On the other hand, the concept of class, so often integral to the study of political change, evades "questions of cultural variation and the impact of culture on history" (1986:7). By examining detailed social and historical processes within the working-class culture of fisherfolk in Newfoundland from the sixteenth century to the present, Sider reformulated a notion of culture as a particular, active force at moments of formation and transformation. This view of culture has been influential in historians' analyses of peasant rebellions in Europe and indeed has the potential for broad application to subaltern studies.

Certainly the demand that localized peasant actions and ideologies be placed in the context of state institutions, and hegemony in the context of the institutional vehicles of ideologies (Popkin 1979; Evans 1986; Turton 1986), has a long history. That regional and global factors are *effectively* part of the analyses of agrarian politics remains to be demonstrated. James Scott's influential study is, in this respect, retrograde. It may lead political anthropologists to make greater use of the thinking of interpretive and symbolic anthropologists; it may even lead to an alternative theory of culture and class.

Proletarian Politics: What of the Future?

Much of the debate among social historians and others on the subject of peasant ideologies and resistance must produce in many American anthropologists an enormous sense of déja vù. What is new in the 1980s is the labeling of positions taken as conservative, populist, Marxist, neo-Marxist, and so on. Not only are more scholars openly professing political commitment, on both the left and right, but more are labeling (and mislabeling) the commitments of others. As the literature on peasant politics suggests, labeling is, in fact, a way of attempting to control. In this case what is being controlled is, not only academic sprawl but the freedom to differ.

Andrew Turton asked the key question: Were not rural producers under a dominant form of capitalism better viewed analytically as part of a new working class in the making? If so, should not attention be focused on "a new class problematic" rather than on "the agrarian question" per se? (1986:37). As we have seen, the fact that "social control" is exercised by making workers produce for their own subsistence needs and so reproduce themselves had been recognized since the 1930s in central and southern African ethnography; much of the "town and country" debate hinged on it, as did the European debate over why capitalist states *needed* peasantries (Carter 1975). That labor seeks to control at least part of its own subsistence so as to assert autonomy and escape oppression was, remember, an underlying theme in studies of Latin American peasant communities and, later, of ethnicity in working-class neighborhoods.[14]

The new emphasis is on resistance but not simply resistance to being ruled but resistance to capitalism itself (Mintz 1974a). An even newer emphasis is on oscillation and change in the resistance process (Stoler 1986). This has been documented best not among peasants but among plantation workers. It was Mintz who first suggested that the plantation was the earliest form of industrialization. The plantation had long presented itself to political anthropology as a crucible, a catalyst, for analyses of slavery, race, colonial and capitalist domination, peasant-ries, and the proletariat.

The plantation is, indeed, a window on the world the colonialist and capitalist made. Nevertheless, a dimension is missing. Throughout its hundred-year history the anthropology of politics has never been in a position to prepare its readers for revolutionary change. The 1980s focus on agrarian societies, albeit reflecting the predominance of this sector of the world's population, may well be deflecting attention from critical national, industrial, and urban themes that will characterize the crucible of revolutionary change in the twenty-first century. In the 1980s the discipline moved toward the ethnography of Europe and Japan, but political research in those two regions lagged behind. Indus-trial "complex" societies tend to remain beyond the vision of all but those concerned with their social problems. The geopolitics of cities and towns, while strategic for nuclear and guerrilla warfare, remained elusive within political anthropology.

ENGENDERED POLITICS

The political commitment of feminist scholarship ensured its contribu-tion to political anthropology. Not all six paradigms developed within the subfield by 1974 proved equally receptive to its data, however. Ac-tion theory, so impressive in establishing the subfield's distinctive mode in the 1960s, was particularly unreceptive because it dealt almost entirely with the political actions of males, neglecting women's agency (Harris and Young 1981). Processual theory likewise tended to ignore gender differences in political processes in spite of its quite impressive record in the analysis of symbolism and ritual.

The neo-evolutionary paradigm benefited most from feminist schol-arship, in large part because of the stimulus provided by Engels's *The Origin of the Family, Private Property and the State*, first published in 1884 and reprinted in 1972 to meet the needs of women's studies pro-grams throughout the United States. The argument was straightfor-ward: the oppressed condition of women arose from the development of private property and the necessity for inheritance. This led to the emergence of monogamous marriage, the nuclear domestic group, and the subordination of women.

Eleanor Leacock had long been engaged in placing this argument on the agenda of political anthropologists (Chapter 4) based on her Algon-kian ethnography. Considerable debate had ensued (Leacock 1972, 1977, 1981; Rowbotham 1972; Gough 1975). Leacock's own focus had been on the impact of historical events such as the appearance of the Jesuit missionaries and fur traders on Native American society in the seventeenth century, but most feminists who used her work chose to place it within the evolutionary Polanyi-Fried taxonomy, generalizing about the egalitarian nature of band society. They were then led to the argument that gender subordination was related to stratification and the evolution of the state (Sacks 1975, 1976, 1982). For a few, this led to an examination of the impact of the colonial state or capitalist expansion on nonstratified societies (Boserup 1970; Stoler 1977; Etienne and Leacock 1980; J. O'Barr 1982).

This approach led to a reevaluation of neo-evolutionary models within political anthropology. It also served, however, to perpetuate the myth among nonanthropologists (particularly within women's studies programs that became interdisciplinary) that anthropologists were mainly authorities on non-Western societies and origins. At first, feminist anthropologists collaborated in this great conspiracy by turning undue attention to such topics as matriarchy, matrilineality, and matrilocality, failing to consider these as jural mechanisms and neglecting their underpinning by political structures.

A structural paradigm provided the chief modus operandi for most feminists, the main thrust of their analysis being to counter the political implications of biological explanations of women's subordination. Problematic in the approach, as Naomi Quinn made clear (1977), was the acceptance of a feminist political commitment to better the condition of women worldwide. This encouraged the study of women generically and cross-culturally, using such concepts as "female oppression," "male dominance," and the like.

Regionally, structural analysis concentrated on female subordination in Oceania, where the symbolic representation of engendered inequality appeared to be particularly rich. A cohort of female anthropologists had pioneered a Malinowskian functional analysis of secret societies and women's place in social organization in Oceania in the 1930s (Wedgwood 1930b, 1936; Blackwood 1934; Kaberry 1939), but Marilyn Strathern's *Women in Between* (1972) established the genre anew. Celebrated for introducing a women's perspective on sexual antagonism (Duley and Edwards 1986), the monograph was particularly valuable because it could be set against the ethnography of Strathern's husband, Andrew, who was conducting his own research in Mount Hagen, New Guinea, at the same time.

Annette Weiner's *Women of Value, Men of Renown* (1976) followed and was even more "revision-ary" since her Trobriand ethnography could be placed alongside that of Malinowski and his classic *Argonauts of the Western Pacific* (1922). Because both androcentrism and exchange theory lay at the heart of much political anthropology prior to this date (Chapter 5), Weiner's analysis called not simply for a reinterpretation of Trobriand political structure but a rethinking of political subordination and inequality generally. That it did not in fact have this effect was largely due to the gap that was rapidly widening in the 1970s between regional specialization and the recognized topical subfields.

In the decade that followed, the structural paradigm in Oceania and elsewhere focused more on the attributes of power relations than on power itself. Gender ideologies and symbolic representations captured attention (e.g., Goodale 1971; Lindenbaum 1976; Ortner 1974; Brown and Buchbinder 1976; Ortner and Whitehead 1981; Lutkehaus 1982; O'Brien and Tiffany 1984; Keesing 1985). The power of metaphors in engendering politics was the subject of significant conceptual statements by historian Joan Scott (1986, 1988).

Both the political economy paradigm and the culture history paradigm in political anthropology were extraordinarily receptive to feminist Marxist approaches, and both included a focus on the industrial United States (Susser 1982, 1986; Lamphere 1987; Zavella 1987; Bookman and Morgan 1988) and the changes in women's position that came about with the development of capitalism. These tended to be quite widely assimilated into women's studies, although psychological contributions also appeared (e.g., Chodorow 1978), which deflected attention from structural and historical features of inequality, subordination, and oppression. Because of increasing ideological polarization within the academy and the continued sidelining of U.S. and European ethnography within the discipline at large (which by now was something of a general imposition), much of this feminist critique was limited in its impact on political anthropology.

More succesful in gaining mainstream notice was the ethnography that resulted from the application of the political economy paradigm to Third World countries. This drew attention to ways in which women were placed and treated within the economic and political structures of new nations, particularly those that welcomed multinationals into their midst in the early 1970s (Nash and Safa 1986; Safa 1981; Beneria 1982; Fuentes and Ehrenreich 1983; Nash and Fernandez-Kelly 1983; Young, Wolkowitz, and McCullagh 1984; Ong 1987). It also suggested subtle ways in which women resisted exploitation. Structural notions of binary oppositions between public and private, culture and nature, sacred and profane collapsed under the onslaught of specific case materials on Third World women at work, although their political actions outside the workplace were less closely scrutinized. The development-decade work of Danish economist Ester Boserup was most influential in initiating this critique, which was then sustained through edited series emanating from such university presses as those of Rutgers and the State University of New York.

The cosmopolitan dependency model led several feminist anthropologists to examine how the penetration of capitalism into the Third World had affected women there. As with dependency theory itself, these arguments tended to be economistic, but regional variations threw up political issues—particularly jural issues—as well. These included foot binding in China, the fate of widows in India, clitoridectomy (often wrongly thought to be an Islamic practice), female infanticide, and the like.

A great strength of the feminist perspective was that it collapsed disciplinary boundaries; for political anthropologists the bonus was easy access to the data and thought of social historians. This was particularly the case in the political ethnography of "civilizations" (of China, India, and Europe) and to a lesser extent that of Latin America, where, as we have seen, sociologists and political scientists tended to predominate in the academy. In sub-Saharan Africa, because of the entrenched structuralism of the two previous generations, anthropologists interested in the engendering of politics tended to turn to historians' reevaluations of particular colonial encounters.

In many cases (although there appears to have been no explicit hijacking of Scott's phrase "weapons of the weak") women's political activities were frequently interpreted generically as "natural" expressions of resistance to subordination and oppression. The explicit role of women in historical political movements was less often studied, although the classic case of the Ibo women's "riots" in Nigeria (Green 1947; Van Allen 1972) proved an exemplary exception. Scott's own inattention to women in *Weapons of the Weak* (1985) was strikingly anachronistic. The book's index entries suggest how he saw them: economic role in the family, farm labor, farm work groups, heads of households, honorary men, ineligible for religious charity. There was little scope for political action here, even resistance, let alone instigation. The moral community would appear to exclude women—a theme admirably pursued in the ethnography of Oceania and lowland South America.

Culture history (or historical anthropology, as it was coming to be called in Europe) shifted feminist attention away from the origin of gender subordination and toward its historical construction. The oppo-

sition became not biological explanation but structural and evolutionary explanation. Most influential were several essays by Rayna Rapp
(first as Reiter 1975 and 1977, and then as Rapp 1977, 1978, and 1979)
that set out the paradigm most clearly. That which most caught public
attention was her argument that the nuclear family was an historical
formation closely related to the needs of the changing capitalist political economy within which it emerged. At the time, public officials in
the United States were concerned with the increasing number of so-
called single-parent families and their drain on public expenditures. A
great deal of feminist scholarship had a strong practical or applied component, which again served, as throughout the hundred-year history of
professional academic anthropology, to marginalize its subject matter.

On the other hand, it could be argued that it was its applied dimension that made anthropology such a force in women's studies generally
in the 1970s and 1980s. Its critical tone had been set by the first generation (primarily Eleanor Leacock and Kathleen Gough, both of whom
considered themselves Marxists rather than feminists). By 1974 a second generation was firmly in place and was particularly sensitive to
both the anthropology of politics and the politics of anthropology.
Women's studies programs were firmly institutionalized in schools and
colleges, mainly in the United States but elsewhere too. The women's
movement had an international dimension, albeit with internal tensions. Articulated most forcefully in Mexico City in 1973, the issue of
whether the movement itself was a middle-class Western luxury impos-
ing itself on Third World intellectuals who were more concerned with
poverty and class was one that feminist anthropologists in particular
constantly had to face head-on in both the field and the classroom.

Feminist scholarship had its own interdisciplinary journal in *Signs*,
first edited out of Barnard College in New York by Catherine Stimpson;
the Feminist Press was born at New York's City University. Professional and academic career ladders were firmly grounded in interdisciplinary feminist scholarship. Numerous informal associations and networks linked participants and provided a support group that was in
striking contrast to the oppositional stance that feminist scholars were
seen to take in mainstream political anthropology. Unfortunately for
the subfield, this led many anthropologists to direct their energies
solely toward women's studies, a tendency that led to a preference for
exposing ideas in general articles rather than through the intensive
analysis of field ethnography, hence the larger number of articles on
thematic issues that appeared in a multitude of edited volumes, the
most influential of which were *Women, Culture and Society* (Rosaldo

and Lamphere 1974) and *Toward an Anthropology of Women* (Reiter 1975). This had both positive and negative effects. Feminist anthropologists were bonded together through such canonical essays, but the anthropology of politics was denied the ethnographic data that might be expected to bring about this transformation.

After 1974 a rapprochement between some perspectives within feminist scholarship and Marxism began to pay off for political anthropology. At first this took the form of critical essays on engendered political structures, one of the most informative being "Engendered Structures: Some Problems in the Analysis of Reproduction" (Harris and Young 1981). This essay provided a theoretical statement that had immediate implications for the subfield, although it was probably picked up primarily by readers of Claude Meillasoux and Jack Goody, who were interested in the development of kinship forms of social organization.

Harris and Young first dissociated themselves from more orthodox Marxisms that focused on production at the expense of relations of social reproduction that they saw as politically engendered. They thus dissociated themselves from economistic Marxism, which up until this point had tended to predominate (as we have seen) in both feminist scholarship and political anthropology. They challenged the mystification produced, as they saw it, by the unproblematic unity of such categories as women, marriage, and the domestic while stopping short of the exercise in deconstruction their critique implied. Origins, genericism, and cross-cultural comparison set aside, they proceeded to outline an analysis not of the reproduction of labor in the orthodox Marxist tradition but of the reproduction of bearers of specific social relationships.

Another work that derived from kinship studies and political anthropology but that transcended both was Christine Gailey's *Kinship to Kingship: Gender Hierarchy and State Formation in the Tongan Islands* (1987). Its analytical achievements were due not least to its defined and systematically sustained use of critical concepts from feminist and Marxist theory. Gailey's starting point was the observation that the state and class formation cannot be understood as processes without concomitantly analyzing gender and the status of women. Women's authority and status necessarily decline with class and state formation.

The following presents Gailey's argument in her own words (1987:ix–44). In her argument she draws on the work of Rapp, Service, Bunzel, Diamond, Goody, and MacKinnon, as well as her own earlier papers (1980, 1983, 1985). She subjects to criticism arguments on class, state formation, and gender by structuralists (Levi-Strauss and Ortner) and the timeless frames of reference of symbolic interpretive anthropologists (Geertz and Sahlins).

<<<Gailey first distinguished between kinship society and civil society [the state]. In the former authority is embedded in relations expressed in the idiom of kinship. The relative authority of women and men rests on claims to the labor time and products of others implied by relations through birth, adoption and marriage. No kin relationship is neutral with regard to authority but these "hierarchies" are never consistent with gender, age, or any other single consideration. Some relationships continue through life; others are partial markers of maturation or increased status. No one can claim unlimited authority; no one is without authority. Kin relations are multiple and flexible.

Gender hierarchy emerges through a partial divorce of the division of labor from kinship considerations. The division of labor is the meeting point of social reproduction and socially necessary production. Division of labor by gender and age in kinship societies sets up separate spheres of productive activity for women and men *during certain periods of their respective life cycles.* The division of labor by gender in no way makes marriage essential; siblings or other kinsmen may discharge the labor necessary. [Here Gailey embarked on an extended critique of the connections structuralists make among marriage, exchange, and social authority.]

State formation generates systematic gender hierarchy. Those processes which most affect women's status are the restriction of use-rights, commoditization, and tribute extraction. In class and state formation (and the two are not necessarily coterminous) people's functions in the division of labor come to be discernible with reference to categories of gender, age, and skill *abstracted from their particular kinship connections and meanings.* In the attempt to construct and ensure the survival of a division of labor that provides for the fundamental differences in social power—the existence of ruling groups permanently removed from direct production—all aspects of social life are called into question, but especially the relations that organize the maintenance and continuity (production and reproduction) of the kin communities. Women become the particular focus of ideological and lived-through status diminution.

Conflict between kinship and civil society inherent in state formation politicizes and redefines kinship relations. The continuity of kin based communities is made dependent on emerging state institutions. The subordination of community reproduction is achieved through splitting the unity and autonomy of local kin groups. Kin relations are subjected to legal and ideological diminution and circumscription by non-kin institutions. Above all, supercessionary claims are made on labor time. All are contested by kinship communities but coercion lies with the State.

The emerging state society is reproduced partly through kinship ordered production. The reproduction of class relations, on the other hand, depends on non-kin institutions such as military or religious structures. These orchestrate political control. Thus productive and reproductive activities

become separated. The nature of kinship within each of the emerging
classes changes since kinship relations no longer re-create the entire society.

In the producing classes, kin relations continue to determine remaining
use-rights to land, the organization of subsistence production, household
and familial composition, and often technical division of labor in corvée
projects and tribute production. But each of these arenas is constrained by
demands from the civil sphere. In the ruling class and the classes associated
with the reproduction of state institutions (priests, merchants, warriors),
kinship has a different meaning. Succession, alliances, and claims to
extracted surpluses and labor predominate. The number of kin roles within
the producing classes is reduced. The encapsulation of kin groups and the
curtailment of their authority affects women and men differently.

State ideologies engender a mental versus manual dichotomy associated
with culture and nature. Women of the producing classes are ideologically
debased as doing manual labor. Work for the support of emerging class
relations is distinguished from work within the kin community thus
creating civil and kin-defined domestic domains. The privatization of
women's work accompanies state formation. Women become a special focus
of control. Civil/religious ideologies highlight women's role in sexual
reproduction as a primary determinant of their social identity; the control
of sexuality is part and parcel of state patriarchy. Patriarchy is the
characterization of relationships between rulers and subjects using gender
and kin roles as *metaphors* of politicized relations.

In the defense of kin communities against the extractions and exactions
of the emerging dominant classes, kinship relations become strained and
can become oppressive. Control over women's potential as both makers of
goods and makers of people becomes an issue in both the state-associated
classes and kin communities. A heightened emphasis on sexuality and
fecundity as power in state ideologies is paralleled in the community—but
for opposite reasons. In the civil sphere, control of women's dual potential
becomes an obvious metaphor for the appropriation of kin group continuity.
Kin communities are confronted with the unprecedented difference
between continuity and survival. They are forced to fragment women's
social personhood and reduce their identities at least partially to the
exigencies of sexual reproduction. >>>

Besides relating this highly political paradigm to the feminist literature, clarifying the terms of its arguments and weighing alternatives,
Gailey documented her theory with illustrative ethnography and then
applied it in depth to the Tongan islands. Her considerable contribution
lay in systematically viewing as constructed and temporally produced
everything previously described as form or structure. Her initial premise was that "the conflict between producing people, orienting their
work towards subsistence, and civil authority, protecting the classes
that syphon off goods and labor is a *continual, ongoing process*" (Gailey
1987:ix). The State is thus not a political form but a process, and an

inconclusive process at that, as indeed is class formation. Neither are one-way streets, as she puts it.

Following Amin (1976) in an analysis of uneven development, Gailey extended her argument to colonial state formation and contemporary states. What was initially illustrated from the somewhat ahistorical ethnography of kin-based societies and the archaeology of ancient civilizations took on new life when documented from the colonial and postcolonial Third World. Her argument also explicitly left many questions unanswered, calling for more empirical research.

From a wholly different trajectory from Scott and the "peasantists" (but not from Thompson and Hobsbawm), Gailey's model embraced the analysis of resistance. She set the concepts of ethnogenesis (Diamond 1970; Sider 1976) and Gramsci's hegemony (1971) alongside ethnocide and forms of state terrorism. Gailey thus provided what Stuart Hall had observed to be lacking in Marxist scholarship: an account of the division of labor *with* women that never relinquishes political anthropology's vision of "the whole."

LAW: THE RECEDING DOMAIN

So vast had been the production of legal anthropology that several calls were made for its cataloguing between the years 1973 and 1985 (Barkun 1973; Collier 1975; Snyder 1981b; Moore 1985a). Although each review took its own stance, there was a fair consensus on the labels to apply. The dominant paradigm at the outset of this period was clearly that of the dispute process (modeled on and replacing Gluckman's judicial process), and reevaluations of it began to appear around 1972. Felstiner (1974) distinguished between dispute processes and dispute processing. The first involved social relations in processes of conflict; the second, procedures for reaching an outcome. Apart from a sense of completion—or repletion—there was little that one more case study could add to the first; the second led to the demise of the paradigm. Political anthropology's focus on access to justice and its overemphasis on informal alternatives to courts were responsible for this—an outcome Weber would not have found hard to explain. From Maine to Northcote Thomas and from Marx to Weber a cynicism about the practices of lawyers and their sensitivity to status honor inhibited the anthropology of law.

I suggested earlier that a bias toward social control rather than law obscured law's political dimensions. In 1975 Jane Collier published a review essay, "Legal Processes," which may be taken to mark a phase in law's political demise as a separate, specialized field of study. The segregationist achievements of the legal formalists of the 1950s and 1960s (Chapters 4 and 5) were coming to an end, and the romantic substantivists, Barton and Malinowski (Chapters 2 and 3), were coming back into their own. The review began: "Legal processes are social processes. Law is not above and apart from society, but is an aspect of ongoing social life" (Collier 1975:121).

The dominant approach to law was through the settlement of disputes, an approach older than but extraordinarily compatible with the processual paradigm of the Manchester school. Its concern with conflict control at the micro level and the maintenance of order was conservative, as Felstiner (1974) demonstrated. There was some shift toward moving analysis beyond the bounds of the courtroom and toward its context both by rounding out the actors sociologically and by looking at a dispute before and after its day in court. Individuals other than litigants and lawyers entered the extended case as the spotlight rested not only on the dramatic but also on the routine (Moore 1973, 1978a).

Critics of the approach (Abel 1981; Snyder 1981b) noted that politics tended to be left out of such self-contained studies, but the most conclusive indictment came from Cain and Kulcsar (1981–82). They called for an end to what they saw as "the dispute industry." In the previous decade, fourteen dispute-oriented doctoral dissertations had been produced at Berkeley alone; enough was enough. By this time the use of disputes as windows on society had become fashionable throughout political anthropology, but Cain and Kulczar drew attention to several unintended consequences when law was involved. Anthropology's ramifying exploration of alternatives to courtroom litigation was subject to abuse by U.S. government agencies seeking to cut back legal-aid programs. Much federally funded comparative research grossly decontextualized the cases being used, implicitly suggesting that the functional equivalents of informal dispute processes reported from small-scale societies and parochial settings were or could be effective in a class-structured capitalist society such as the United States (Cain and Kulczar 1981–82). A delicate reminder that the state could *not* be so ignored appeared in Sally Falk Moore's sad and ironic tale "Dividing the Pot of Gold" (1985b), an analysis of negotiations between a local community and a university over a National Science Foundation grant. Given the institutionalized collegiality of lawyers and anthropologists, young American anthropologists like Carol J. Greenhouse and Sally Merry were poised to make their mark in U.S. ethnography; in contrast to their British colleagues, who tended to be engaged more with post-colonial states abroad and social history at home.

Law as Process

The processual approach to law received new impetus with the publication of a collection of essays by Sally Falk Moore, *Law as Process: An Anthropological Approach* (1978a). Its opening essay traces the roots of legal process theory from Mancunian action theory: social life is seen to be an arena of contestation between regularly patterned cultural and individual agency, its manifestation being either rule-congruent actions or choice-making, discretionary, manipulative actions. Attempts to control behavior through the adoption of rules include law (defined as rules enforceable by government) and other enforceable norms that result from the political process. These are seen to be always partial and always accompanied by counterprocesses.

Integrated systems of law were always the product of a specialist elite—which might include anthropologists. Such systems were built up by piecemeal aggregation, and Moore viewed as misleading any attempts to seek out core ideas expressing societal ideas or values. Legislation in colonial and newly independent countries is counteracted by the semiautonomous social fields on which it is imposed. The counter-currents of effective rules in semiautonomous fields are usually underestimated, and the power of law to bring about change is overestimated. Those with the power to make rules that are binding within the semi-autonomous fields—reglementation—are often dominant members of corporate groups. Here Moore at first followed M. G. Smith in her argument but then went beyond to pursue such powers in noncorporate, transactional arenas. The relationship between the individual and the group becomes most vulnerable to abuse when state and corporate group interests converge. Moore was concerned with the impact of legislated interventions and court rulings on the terms of asymmetrical relations within the semiautonomous fields. Class relations, she suggested, have been explored widely in political anthropology, but other asymmetrical relations have received much less attention. Moore was particularly interested in situations in which individuals are members of organizations and those in which they are not members but are instead, for example, employees or subjects. Law may uphold or change such asymmetries and may do so unevenly. Moore called for the study of its impact.

Moore's long-awaited ethnography, *Social Facts and Fabrications:*

"Customary Law" on Kilimanjaro, 1880–1980 (1986), was just such a study. She carried out fieldwork in Tanzania between 1968 and 1979, and in her book she analyzed the transformation of Chagga legal and political ideas and practices during colonial rule and then in the independent African socialist state that followed. She placed local events (disputes) in a broad historical context and worried that "fieldwork has become a peculiar form of current history" (1986:7). After examining the social foundations of the colonial Chagga legal order, she analyzed modern case reports that revealed the individualizing and decontextualizing process underway within the jural process. Her climactic extended case analysis demonstrated the ultimate importance of rounded, holistic ethnography: lineage chronicles revealed "what a finely edited version reaches the courts" (1986:243). Moore's Chagga ethnography pursued law and reglementation into every nook and cranny of nuanced relationship, perpetuating and revitalizing the rich tradition of Africanist ethnography of the 1950s.

I have suggested throughout this book that changes in political theorizing generally follow rather than precede methodological innovation. Toward the end of her monograph, Moore began to grapple with the methodological problem. First she looked back to observe that processual analysis is, in fact, neither model nor theory but rather a redefinition of subject matter accompanying a practical and analytical interest in change. Yet, she said, while change predominates, repetition (to the point of involution) and reproduction must also be explored. Moore viewed her own approach as a hybrid historical/ethnographic perspective, with politics, economics, and history providing a background and the fieldwork moment (conceived in temporal terms) a foreground. The tension that Moore recognized between "the fieldwork method and the historical questions into which it now inquires" (1986:321) seems likely to be the tension that will produce a new paradigm in the 1990s not simply in the anthropology of law but in political anthropology generally.

Legal Pluralism

In 1969 Laura Nader defined the anthropology of law morphologically and structurally as "the understanding and analysis of legal systems *as they operate in particular cultural and societal contexts*" (1969:viii, emphasis in original). Thereafter the most marked feature of the anthropology of law was its focus on historical materials, even among those who had earlier concerned themselves with, at most, short-term processes (Abel 1979; Pospisil 1979; Moore 1986). This new study of historical legal processes had several dimensions. Some researchers chose to focus on colonial legislation and its impact on specific peoples or localities (Chanock 1985; Vincent 1988d). Others chose to reconstruct historical change in what had until this time been almost uniformly called customary law. Still others focused specifically on the impact of new legislation on the old, with all the dimensions of center-periphery, state-locality, and town-country comparisons to the fore. Many did all three. What was important was that what had been studied disarmingly as legal anthropology freed of its political implications was sundered from its anachronistic, ahistorical base and brought squarely into the political anthropology of the 1980s. The term *social control* might still be used by lawyers (Kamenka and Soon-Tay 1980), but the issues addressed by legal anthropology were imposed legislation, discipline, and *how* law rules (Foucault 1977; Fitzpatrick 1980; Sugarman 1983).

Alan Watson's *Society and Legal Change* (1977) identifies four prevailing notions of law. First, a romantic view that law expresses the common consciousness or spirit of a people; second, an evolutionary view of law; third, a view of law as social engineering; and finally a Marxist view of law as coercion and violence, as class law. Watson, professor of civil law at the University of Edinburgh, gave jurisprudential examples of each type: Montesquieu and von Savigny; Maine and Diamond; Pound and von Jhering; Marx and Engels. Anthropologists could be pigeonholed similarly: Barton and Malinowski as romantics; Hoebel and Fried as evolutionists; Gluckman and Nader as social engineers; Childe and Snyder as Marxists. Watson argued that all four visions were wrong. All assumed that legal development was either a rational or a natural response to existing circumstances, an assumption he considered both inadequate and false. He argued that "though there is a historical reason for every legal development, yet to a considerable extent law in most places and at most times does not progress in a rational or responsive way, and that the divergence between law and the needs or wishes of the people involved and the will of the leaders of the people is marked" (1977:4–5).

Watson then set out a diffusionist thesis (although he never used the term), focusing on "legal transplants." He observed that "at most times, in most places, borrowing from a different jurisdiction has been the principal way in which law has developed." This, he noted, "is as true today when one state in the USA will take over what has been worked out in another, or when England follows New Zealand, or Scotland, Sweden or France, as in the centuries of the Reception of Roman Law and earlier" (1977:98). This, of course, in former colonial territories is what imperialism is all about and why its legacies are creating so many problems that cannot easily be solved by law alone. When Snyder (1981b) suggested that no satisfactory theory of legal pluralism existed, he in effect issued a challenge to those who were beginning to believe that the diffusionist vision (Chapter 2) might be revived in political anthropology.

There was, however, a fair amount of ethnographic reporting on legal pluralism, cultural pluralism, and legal transplants. Snyder (1981b) reviewed it at some length because he valued the light it shed on the ethnocentrism of his fellow lawyers. Moore (1985a) did so because she thought it would prove amenable to the application of the comparative method. She related legal pluralism to what has been described as the ethnic revival and to the work of Leo Kuper and M. G. Smith (1969) on plural societies, raising again, as among Smith's Caribbean colleagues (Chapter 5), the question of whether pluralism is more usefully viewed not as a structural form but as a phase in an historical process.

Relevant to much of the literature on legal pluralism is the distinction between system and nonsystem, and system and antisystem. Laura Nader and her students tend to focus on nonstate systems and, indeed, on litigants' preferences for not going to state courts. Their experience is captured in the quip, "All men are equal before the law, but they are no longer equal after it" (quoted in Collier 1975:126). Nader and Todd (1978) viewed homogenizing state law as a form of domination. In 1985 Moore, drawing on the South African case, suggested how pluralism can be used to segregate, "enslave," and exclude.

The system-antisystem distinction brings together those who see state law as imposed (Burman and Harrell-Bond 1979) and those who see "folk law" as cultural resistance. They include Pospisil, whose writings from the beginning focused on legal enforcement. In this period Pospisil began to crystalize his arguments within the colonial New Guinea setting (1971, 1979).

Law as Discourse

The culmination of the anthropological approach to law that developed after 1974 appeared in Sally Humphreys's exegesis on law as discourse. For Humphreys, "Law as discourse, as a combination of speech and action, is inherently historical and political" (1985:257). She set out the route toward this metaphor within the subfield: the distinction between the living law and the black-letter law of the state set out by Ehrlich and paralleled by the American legal realists, including Karl

Llewellyn (Chapter 4); Malinowski's argument that individuals choose among rules of law in action (Chapter 3); Gluckman and his Manchester school's vision that change and instability could best be analyzed through dispute settings in which contradictory norms and ambiguities surface (Chapter 4); and the appreciation that so-called customary law might better be viewed as a colonial creation (Chapter 5).

Three trends came together in the late 1970s. The first trend, and that closest to the political anthropology of the Mancunians and LSE's action theory, culminated in Pierre Bourdieu's *Outline of a Theory of Practice* (1977), a treatise that did not spell out its derivations as clearly as it might have done. Today Bourdieu's call for an alternative to seeking a pattern of rules in a theory of practice seems extraordinarily tame, and it may well be simply the novel Kabyle ethnography, Gallic provenance, and Cambridge-Princeton patronage that made it (on translation in 1977) seem more important than it really was.

A second trend toward increased research in complex societies, whether of the contemporary United States or of past colonial states, fostered greater appreciation of Max Weber's analysis of the emergence and role of legal specialists. Gilsenan (1982) drew out Weber's view that law is "structured by the competition between central rulers trying to maintain the maximum of power over their subjects and local powerholders trying to carve out their own domains of arbitrary power over their dependents and limit the central government's claims on them" (Humphreys 1985:246). Weber was most interested in "qadi" justice and law, politics, and bureaucracy in China and India, and Moore's work in modern socialist Tanzania echoed many Weberian concerns.

The third trend was the ethnography of law undertaken by Marxist social historians at the University of Warwick. E. P. Thompson's *Whigs and Hunters: The Origin of the Black Act* and Douglas Hay's edited volume *Albion's Fatal Tree: Crime and Society in Eighteenth-Century England* both appeared in 1975. D. Sugarman's *Legality, Ideology and the State* followed in 1981. Here we pick up again threads already appearing in political anthropology at this time—law as an instrument of coercion and punishment developed for the protection of property rights, and more innovatively, law as the redefinition of popular protest as crime. This linked up well with the tradition of exploration into popular culture that had done so much to create the rapprochement between political anthropology and the new social history out of which had come a newly self-defining historical anthropology. Indeed, Sally Humphreys's "Law as Discourse" appeared in *History and Anthropol-*

ogy, a new journal she was instrumental in founding in 1985.

In adopting the discourse metaphor, Humphreys drew together the following points:

1. Looking at law as part of the discourse about good and bad society permits us to eliminate Western ethnocentric ideology and dichotomizations of evolutionary theory.

2. A view of law as "a fight between alternative definitions of rights" (Thompson 1975:259), besides taking up the point often made before (Fallers 1969; Moore 1978a) that law is a form of socioethnological reflection, emphasizes the combination of utopian and polemical elements in both legislation and court practice. At all levels we are dealing with "competing attempts to impose models of what society should be on others" (Humphreys 1985:241).

3. Attention is thus drawn not simply to the coexistence of alternative competing models of society but to the "silences in codified law which have traceable motives" (Humphreys 1985:251).

4. The term *law* cannot be defined precisely; demarcation lines vary over time and between one group and another.

5. Law combines speech with action, and its study implies the analysis of the power relations structuring speech.[15]

6. Rules of law and legal arguments are formulated, approved, and cited in specific historical circumstances.

7. Law always has an external source of legitimation in conceptions of power and conceptions of justice.

8. It and they exist alongside alternatives.

9. Social discourse is a surface phenomenon (Comaroff and Roberts 1981). Processual studies are needed to reveal "the politics of culture in action. . . . Only a detailed historical analysis of the genesis, interrelations, power bases, interests, and social experience of competing classes, class fractions, and elites can explain how they will interpret each other's actions and structure their own discourse. . . . [Legal structures] cannot be understood without the event and processes which produced them" (Humphreys 1985:258–259).

In the late 1960s and early 1970s, recall, the study of law by anthropologists and academic lawyers developed in close harness in spite of lawyers' impatience with overly detailed ethnography and their own primary goal of contributing to comparative jurisprudence (Snyder 1981b). In the late 1970s and the 1980s, as the anthropology of law turned more to social history, the danger, paradoxically, was that anthropologists and historians would talk past each other. To this point historians have valued anthropologists for their synchronic analyses of cultures and mentalities (Humphreys 1985); now there appears to be a danger of their tramping the same turf.

Marxism and the Analysis of Law

After 1974 a new receptivity to the Marxist tradition surfaced among legal anthropologists.[16] Just as in the 1950s and 1960s scholars began to draw together the threads of Weber's discourse on law, so too in the late 1970s and the 1980s there were attempts to apply Marxist theory systematically (Cain and Hunt 1979; Hirst 1979; Sumner 1979; Hunt 1981; Spitzer 1983). The Weberian enterprise generated the legal anthropology of M. G. Smith and Lloyd Fallers, but no similar mainstream figures emerged in the Marxist anthropology of law, although E. P. Thompson may have stood in as a surrogate. The impact of Marxism on legal anthropology was much more diffuse, but it was clearly recognized by reviewers of the field (Snyder 1981b; Humphreys 1985; Moore 1985a).

Francis Snyder of the University of Warwick School of Law, an American trained in both law and anthropology, concluded that the significant Marxist contribution lay in "the relationship of law to class formation and the connections between changes in legal processes and the development of capitalism as a distinct historical form" (1981b:158). He traced both in his political ethnography of Senegalese legal change. Strikingly, in the anthropology of law capitalism rather than colonialism tended to become the object of study in non-Western societies, reflecting its own legal historical roots, perhaps, in the classic work of the Scots political economists. Snyder's *Capitalism and Legal Change: An African Transformation* (1981a) and Fitzpatrick's *Law and State in Papua New Guinea* (1980) were two such studies. Continuing practical involvement in the independent postcolonial nations seems logically to have encouraged the study of capitalism rather than what proved in many cases to be a somewhat short-lived colonialism, and the applied dimension of legal anthropology held considerable potential.

The political economy rubric often applied to Marxist studies of law is, perhaps, a misnomer, because anthropologists have tended to neglect the legal aspect of political economy and politics—as did Marx himself. This is somewhat paradoxical if Hall et al. (1978) and Hunt (1981) are correct in associating the emerging Marxist analysis of law with a growing law-and-order crisis in the United States and Western Europe. Nevertheless, the main thrust of Marxist analysis was to counter what has been labeled the consensus model of law (Hunt 1981).

This, as we saw in Chapters 3, 4, and 5, rested on five assumptions: (1) that law represents the value consensus of a society; (2) that law represents those values fundamental to the maintenance of social order; (3) that law represents values that it is in the public interest to protect; (4) that the state, which is represented in the legal system, is value neutral; and (5) that law mediates between groups in pluralistic societies, representing the interests of society at large (Hunt 1981).

Orthodox Marxists suggest, on the contrary, that law represents the interests of a dominant class within any society; that it is an agency of conflict, not integration; and that it is "the creator and amplifier of social inequality and disequilibrium, being the bearer of class bias and privilege" (Hunt 1981:95). Such was Barton's innocent finding among the Ifugao (Chapter 2), and Evans-Pritchard's data on Nuer crimes and compensation might have led to a similar conclusion had he not resisted it. Reevaluations of his work (Beidelman 1971; Gough 1971) skirted even the term *law*.

The Marxist perspective on law tends, first, to question the normative concept "social control" and, second, to explore the actual as opposed to the assumed relationship of law to the state. Within legal anthropology this has led to a reexamination of colonial states and their legal procedures and to an examination of law in postcolonial Third World states. Scholars put taxation, licensing, codification, and forestry legislation, for example, under a critical microscope, and this has proved to be a domain in which colonial policies can usefully be distinguished from capitalist practices. Thus a political anthropologist attuned to intraclass competitive interests might contribute critical ethnography to the abstract Marxist formulation according to which "(a) The 'capitalist state' may use law as a means of 'disciplining' specific capitals in the interest of capitalism as a whole, and (b) power groups in capitalist societies may use the state and its laws against the interests of both specific capitals and capitalism in general" (Spitzer 1983:113).

THE POLITICS OF THE ACADEMY

It would be too simple to characterize the 1980s as a period when two paradigms clashed: on the left, Marxism; on the right, interpretive anthropology. Certainly the days are long past when a Hoover Institution could be established at Stanford for the expressed purpose of countering the evils of the doctrines of Karl Marx. Yet it is necessary, I think, to ask why Marxist analysis has had such an impact in these years after its long history of subterranean dialogue, particularly in those areas of political anthropology—peasantries, women, and law—that have proved central to 1980s practice.

Part of the answer certainly lies in the close-knit body of ethnographic data that Marxist analysis has generated since the late 1950s, moving from reevaluations to primary research. Even more important, however, is the fact that Marxist analytical procedures start from the same premise as the political anthropology that became dominant at that time: the study of the concrete. It was Lenin, after all, who defined Marxism as "a concrete analysis of a concrete situation" (quoted in Hunt 1981:107 n. 17). This is not, I believe, the perception of Marxism held by most non-Marxists, because they may well fail to appreciate the extent to which Marx's objective was the practical analysis of the concrete phenomena that surrounded him. It is economic phenomena associated with capitalism that now engage contemporary Marxists, who operate with multiple perceptions of the concept, for Marxism is a dialectical construction, quarrelsome, always in the making.

Indeed, it might be truer to say that in the 1980s not Marxism but eclecticism predominates in political anthropology. Scholars who would not consider themselves Marxists have used elements of Marxist theory selectively as tools like any others to address particular problems. As Scholte pointed out, "After all, Marxism is the historical product of Western civilization; it may be radical in its analysis of capitalism (and, as Lukacs suggested, should be limited to such analyses), but it nonetheless expresses an intellectual consensus (anthropologically viewed) with bourgeois rationalism" (1983:263). And, of course, there is a plethora of Marxisms to choose from.

Marxist approaches in anthropology received legitimation, as it were, with the publication in the 1975 *Annual Review of Anthropology* of an essay by Bridget O'Laughlin. James Wessman's *Anthropology and Marxism* appeared in 1981 and Maurice Bloch's *Marxism and Anthropology* in 1983. They were strikingly different books. Bloch was most concerned with an evolutionary Marxist anthropology in which Engels loomed large; Wessman's book was about Puerto Rico and peasantries. Only Stanley Diamond's journal, *Dialectical Anthropology*, has sustained Marxist anthropology consistently in the United States. The *Critique of Anthropology*, a London-based production, was started by Americans in exile, as it were. The Council for Marxist Scholars was formed in New York in 1978, but for the most part, personal networks and receptivity to each other's publications provide the structure for academic Marxist political anthropology.

Within the generally polarizing view of popular anthropology in the

1980s, Marxist anthropology is pitted against interpretive anthropology, Eric Wolf against Clifford Geertz, prizewinners both. Wolf won an award for the best work in anthropology in 1985; Geertz, an award for literary criticism in 1989. Although interpretive anthropology currently attracts the attention of anthropology at large, its impact on the anthropology of politics has as yet been slight. Many of its practitioners have, indeed, been charged with being apolitical, a charge that Geertz (1983), one of its finest practitioners and one of its keenest critics (1988), has dismissed in magisterial fashion. A younger generation—more sensitive, perhaps, to its limitations (Dolgin, Kemnitzer, and Schneider 1977; Marcus and Fischer 1986)—has attempted to redress matters by relating the interpretive paradigm to world historical political economy.

Almost from the start, reviews of Geertz's work have been ambivalent, a reflection, perhaps, of his powerfully institutionalized position at the Institute for Advanced Study in Princeton. By 1988 some had become positively venomous (Gellner 1988), but reviewers most often have expressed regret not at the emergence of interpretive and hermeneutic anthropology per se but at the large number of practitioners inferior to Geertz that it has produced. The most sustained critique is that of Roger Keesing, whose introductory textbook, *Cultural Anthropology: A Contemporary Perspective* (1981), treated the tribal world as a legacy of human diversity, dealing with the expansion of the West, peasants, the creation of the Third World, cities, and the quest for human futures in a politically attuned vision of the discipline. Yet, as noted throughout this study, textbooks tend to mark the closing of a paradigm and the end of an era.

Keesing's critique of interpretive anthropology was grounded not so much on political ethnography as on a political reading of Michel Foucault, whose book *The Archaeology of Knowledge* (1977) suggested that knowledge is always distributed and controlled. This in effect negates an anthropology that takes cultures to be collective creations. Cultures as texts, Keesing pointed out, "are differently read, differently construed, by men and women, young and old, experts and nonexperts. . . . An anthropology that takes cultures to be collective creations, that reifies them into texts and objectifies their meanings, disguises and even mystifies the dynamics of knowledge and its uses." Furthermore, cultures "do not simply constitute webs of significance [as Geertz and his colleagues suggest], systems of meaning that orient humans to one another and their world. They constitute *ideologies*, disguising human political and economic realities as cosmically ordained. . . . Cultures are webs of mystification as well as signification" (Keesing 1987:161).

It is necessary to ask *who* creates and defines cultural meanings, when, for whom, and for what purpose. "One cannot merely define men and women in terms of the webs of significance they themselves spin, since . . . few do the actual spinning while the majority is simply caught" (Scholte 1984:140). In retrospect, the mounting critiques of interpretive anthropology take us back to Redfield and Lewis in Tepoztlán (Chapter 4) and to Sydel Silverman looking at Bailey's politics (Chapter 5). We are, in fact, back where this study began, in the Introduction, relating text to context, historically and politically.

Perhaps the problem for interpretive anthropology is that it was largely generated from a position of eminence. "Trends are generated from the bottom up, fads from the top down" (Hannerz 1987:218). The real question is whether the neglect of the issue of power and the promotion of myths of cultural unanimity are intrinsic to hermeneutics as a method. "*Of course* knowledge is situated. *Of course* access to knowledge and systems of symbols in which it is encoded is uneven. *Of course* some people have more power than others over these systems" was one reply to Keesing's critique of interpretive anthropology (Frankel 1987:170). It was nothing new in 1987 to be told these things. What was new was that all this was by then being taken for granted within mainstream anthropology.

CONCLUSION

Because this chapter carries our narrative of the anthropology of politics (Part 1) and political anthropology (Part 2) to the present, this conclusion to Chapter 6 is also the conclusion to the study. A reminder may be in order as to why I chose in the introduction to call this study a narrative rather than a review or a history. I suggested that only through narrative could one arrive at causal explanations, why this paradigm in political anthropology appeared and either succeeded or failed. We have arrived at the present, and we have arrived at a critical moment when scholars in anthropology, history, and literary criticism are rethinking historicism. They are turning back to the future and repossessing the past.[17] The Third World of criticism has had its effect.

I have argued that in the study of politics, paradigmatic change has usually followed changes in methodology rather than the reverse. The cosmopolitical paradigm that emerged in 1974 was no exception. It rested on the dependency theories of Latin American sociologists and economists, but it was when Immanuel Wallerstein turned from the study of contemporary new African nations to seventeenth-century historical sources that space, time, and a global perspective came together in *The Modern World-System*. This enabled anthropologists of all political persuasions (and we have seen how the discipline, throughout its history, has been characterized by rival ideologies) to recognize the value of a paradigm that placed Europe and the Third World in one global conceptual arena. We have traced this development through three phases in political anthropology: first, the 1950s ethnography of central Africa and Puerto Rico (Chapter 4); second, the local, regional, and national studies of the 1960s and 1970s (Chapter 5); and finally the cosmopolitical studies, reviewed in this chapter largely as they deal with the subaltern classes, peasantries and women.

Between 1940 and 1973, as we have seen, political anthropology produced a series of taxonomies to order its ethnographies. In the 1980s a new taxonomy came into being, distinguishing three types of social formation. These are the kinship polity (familiar to us from the work of the ethnologists of the Bureau of American Ethnology discussed in Chapter 1); the tributary state (largely based on the delineations of Samir Amin, as we have seen); and the capitalist state. Although the ethnographic fleshing out of kinship polities and tributary states continues, it is around the challenge of confronting capitalism that a new consensus has appeared. This has taken the form not of an exercise in reconstructing history but of an immediate exploration of the noncapitalist features of modern society and politics, of interstitial structures, and frequently of interests that are inadequately met by the organizational structures and harnessed power of the capitalist state.

Chapter 6 introduced five of the many configurations emerging in the anthropological study of politics in the 1980s. These arose from diverse wellsprings in the Third World, in other disciplines, in our own forgotten past. Subaltern studies are in the process of crystallizing around the concerns of historians and anthropologists in India: the nature of the colonial state and the failures of colonial capitalist domination. Political scientist James Scott called his 1985 ethnography of a peasant village *Weapons of the Weak*. Both his fieldwork methodology and his analysis were imbued with the spirit of political anthropology at its height in the late 1950s (Chapter 5). Shaped by the field techniques of Bailey and his colleagues, it brought to fruition W. F. Whyte's agenda for political scientists in 1943 (Chapter 4). Scott's work is now providing a catalyst for today's anthropologists studying innumerable varieties of peasant resistance and proletarian politics around the capitalist globe. Gough's admonition that anthropology has failed to study socialist and communist political systems is almost as true today as when she delivered it in the late 1960s, although there are signs that this may change with the ending of the Cold War.

The anthropology of law is moving away from its self-created exclusivity (Chapters 4 and 5) toward the rediscovery of its paradoxical roots in politicking and justice. Although it is almost totally removed now from evolutionary, functional, and structural concerns (a fact that lawyers appear not to have recognized), legal anthropology turns its attention to historical legal change and law's relation to power structures. Diffusionist theory—the loser in the Edwardian struggle against the theories of evolutionism and functionalism (Chapter 2)—again rears its head, this time in the guise of legal pluralism and legal transplants. The same has been true in many other domains of political anthropology now that the cosmopolitical system has been given academic respectability.

Throughout this study, beginning as it does in 1879, Victorian perspectives on politics, particularly evolutionary theory and Marxist theory, have exerted a continuous presence. A species of the former underlies today's sociobiology (reference to which can only serve to remind the reader of how much has of necessity been omitted from this narrative; my own candidates for inclusion, had it been possible, would be the anthropology of education and applied anthropology). Today's Marxist anthropology is very different from any that has gone before, not least because of the internal changes wrought in Marxism itself by the firsttime publication of Marx's *Grundrisse* in 1973. I have suggested in Chapter 6 that the political ethnography that Marxism has generated has considerable significance for Marxists in other disciplines, and the future may see a trend toward closer dialogue.

In the course of its perambulations over the landscape of complex societies, political anthropology has also intermittently drawn on the work of Max Weber. This is likely to increase in the next decade as research in civilizations (particularly China and Japan) receives more government and business funding. As this study has shown, political anthropology throughout its history has tended to follow the flag and the overseas investor.

As we have seen, by 1974 six varieties of political anthropological theory had evolved and were to be found in the subfield. These were action theory, processual theory, neo-evolutionism, structuralism, political economy, and culture history. Chapter 6 has shown how all six were challenged by the new wave of feminist scholarship, and questions on the gendering of politics and the politics of gender have not yet been satisfactorily answered. They remain on the agenda for the 1990s. This study has traced a concern with the politics of gender back to the 1930s, but this is one of several areas in which oral tradition has been more vital than the written record. Historians of science are now exploring the contributions of women to the discipline, permitting a new chapter to be written, shortly, in the critique of political anthropology. I have tried to suggest here that the structured position of women in the academy may well make them particularly sensitive to interstitial politics. Their published works are well represented in the bibliography not because I have sought them out to restore a lost record (as I did with other marginalized anthropologists of politics) but because they shone.

In conclusion, this study presents a case for a new historicism in political anthropology. It should be clear by now that this involves no disengagement from fieldwork and no retreat into reflexivity at the expense of the "real world." True historicism, like the dialectic, is immanent critique. In the introduction to this work, I suggested the importance to each other of anthropology, history, and literary criticism. As my study draws to a close, I chance upon a programmatic statement within critical theory which echoes my design. It is that an important place exists within political anthropology in the 1990s for "a historicist project when it is conceived and conducted as a reflexive affair and when reflection, an act of mind, is set in the field of material production, its cultural mediations and their hegemonic forms. . . . [A] reading of the past which is not also and integrally a reflected operation on the present betrays its received historicist premises: namely, to reveal the past, the object, either as it is/was in itself, or as it is intended in the sympathetic consciousness of the present" (Levinson 1989:2). The historicist project is at one and the same time a presentist project given meaning by way of the future (Vincent 1989b).

Historicism such as this will not replace contemporary political engagement, nor challenge fieldwork, nor lead to further fissures within the discipline. It holds the promise, rather, as the title of this chapter indicates, of consolidation. Anthropologists who study politics— whether of the discipline, the academy, or the world "out there"—have a future. In part this is, indeed, due to their newfound reflectiveness, but it is also, and largely, due to the distinctive anthropological practice, peculiar within the humanities, of carrying out fieldwork and producing ethnography.

Notes

INTRODUCTION

1. The practitioners of these cognate disciplines variously call them intellectual history, the sociology of knowledge, the science of society, the sociology
of science, the history of science, and literary criticism. They appear to maintain fairly strict boundaries, since there is little dialogue or cross-referencing
among them, although most recognize a German ancestry in the history of
ideas. Few seem familiar with anthropological analyses of phenomena identical
to those with which they are concerned. Compare, for example, Crane's "invisible colleges" (1972) and Kadushin's "networks" (1968) with the ideas of anthropologists Whitten (1970), Wolfe (1970), and Barnes (1972).

2. Colson (1985b) argues strongly against conceptualizing them as
"others." The issue is raised again in Chapter 6.

3. Neither colonial administration nor applied anthropology is discussed
here, but both clearly merit detailed study in their own right. General Pitt-Rivers (Chapter 1) coined the term applied anthropology in 1881 in order to classify
a paper by Sir Bartle Frere, an administrator, entitled "On the Laws Affecting
the Relations between Civilized and Savage Life" (Bodley 1988:2). Debates over
practical anthropology and development anthropology have pervaded the history of the profession, but they have not, so far as I know, been directly related
to the anthropological study of politics per se. Applied anthropology has, indeed,
been effectively marginalized by mainstream academic anthropology. Perceived
crises in the profession's employment structure have not yet changed this.

4. The most blatant Whiggism occurs in two areas: first, the unconscious
adoption of the categories of twentieth century functional anthropology when
writing about the anthropology of an earlier era (e.g., Burrow 1966); and second,
the unquestioning assumption that anthropology's subject matter is primitive
society. Both Redfield (1950) and Langham (1981), for example, took pains to
relate Maine's *Ancient Law* (1861) to nonliterate tribal societies in spite of
Maine's own recognition that notions of law were not of universal application
but related to specific forms of society. This study argues that both functionalism and primitivism are, in fact, positions achieved and maintained within
anthropology in the face of opposition: they are events (Vincent 1986a). So, too,
of course, is historicism—seeing events in their own context (Stocking 1968).

5. As, for example, the panelists on "Late Capitalism or Monopoly
Capitalism and Anthropological Studies in the 1980s," organized by Jeremy

Keenan (University of the Witwatersrand, Republic of South Africa) at the International Congress of Anthropological and Ethnological Science (ICAES) in Vancouver in 1983. The panelists were, besides Keenan himself, John Clammer, Claude Meillassoux, and Simon Clark.

6. Appadurai (1988b:40–41) compared his use of the genealogical method with Michel Foucault's archaeology (1977), "a practice which, when successful, uncovers not just a genetic chain, but an epistemological field and its discursive formations." He intends it "to occupy the middle space between the atemporal stance of certain kinds of contemporary criticism (especially those affected by deconstruction) and the exclusivist and genetic assumptions of most standard approaches to the history of ideas." My use is less metaphorical and is intended to expose agency as well as ideas.

7. The problem of selective inclusion confronts this text as much as any other, of course. Prior to 1940 the problem is not overwhelming with respect to professional academic anthropology. I have attempted to cover the literature comprehensively even while highlighting the contributions of those who have tended to be relegated to the margins or background, or even forgotten. These are frequently amateurs, women, and (in the United States, particularly) African-Americans. I attempt to restore their voices, first, because they belong in the repertoire of our predecessors in the discipline in its formative years. Restoring them addresses the process I call the manufacture of ignorance, which is both an historical and a political process. Second, they have made contributions to key problem areas in the anthropology of politics today—problem areas that were in many cases defined out of court in the "classical period" of political anthropology, from 1940 to 1954. I am very aware that the words of those most successfully silenced, the peoples we study, are not adequately represented in the pages that follow. The nondisciplinary regional specializations (discussed in Chapter 6) may bring them into greater prominence.

Certain approaches within political anthropology are not emphasized in this study, although I appreciate that in some cases I am thereby sidelining the "losers" in a methodological struggle. Because I concentrate on field research, such topics as the origins of the state, evolutionary theory, statistical analyses of the Human Relations Area Files, and, regrettably, ethnohistory receive only contingent attention.

8. These calculations are based on entries in the membership directory of the Association of Social Anthropologists (1988) and the American Anthropological Association's *Guide to Departments* (1988). I am indebted to Diane Ciecawy for the labor involved.

9. Many historians of anthropology follow an idea or a problem area over time, a mode of transmission of knowledge rendered au courant by invaluable periodic reviews. Yet reviewers tend to feel obliged to report only on what is and not on what is not or might be. Collini (1978) is surely exceptional in his exploration of the propriety of asking why something did not happen. Such a perception (along with research in several archives) underwrote my explanation of why diffusionists failed and functionalists succeeded in establishing a programmatic political anthropology in the Edwardian years (Chapter 2). Furthermore, a positive achievement in the anthropology of politics may be so recognized for reasons other than the merit of the ideas or applications in question.

Indeed, the inculcation and transmission of that recognition is itself subject to inquiry (Vincent 1987, 1988b) if the politics of anthropology itself is to be brought into the open.

10. I owe this observation to Stephen Rubinstein.

CHAPTER 1. THE MOVING FRONTIER, 1879–1897

1. This introduction draws on Mosse 1961; Jaher 1964; Burrow 1966; Collini 1978; Bannister 1979; Rich 1986; Collini, Winch, and Burrow 1984; and Stocking 1987. Intellectual histories of the social sciences in the United States between 1865 and 1914 (e.g., Furner 1975; Silva and Slaughter 1984) tend to deal with the professionalization of academic sociology, economics, political science, and education but explicitly exclude (on various grounds) anthropology. The intellectual milieu of the Bureau of Ethnology and the anthropological academy can be constructed from them, nevertheless, and existing heroic and institutionally focused studies of anthropology placed in context.

2. Biographical details on Morgan are to be found in Stern 1931, White 1940, Resek 1960, and Trautmann 1987. Particularly valuable are Tooker's account (1983a) of Morgan's research on the structure of the Iroquois league and Trautmann 1987, which does a great deal more than talk about kinship. On the interrelatedness of Morgan's business and scientific interests, see Benison 1953, particularly chapter 5. Benison attributes Morgan's decision to go into politics in October 1860 to his experiences in Marquette, Michigan, in that year. Morgan was nominated for the New York State Assembly on the platform of the newly formed Republican party. He regarded political office as a stepping-stone to the position of commissioner of Indian affairs in the Department of the Interior. Benison's chapter 6 deals with his role in the antislavery crusade and his criticism of the federal administration of Native Americans.

As recently as 1978, Tooker, a leading authority, suggested that Morgan's "classic work remains the best single description of the structure of the League" (1978:440). As a classic, it has been cast in the mold of successive traditions in anthropology. Powell (1880:115) described it as "the first scientific account of an Indian tribe ever given to the world." Compare Leslie White (1940:1–2) "Morgan . . . labored mightily to place anthropological investigations upon a strictly scientific basis." The Boasians virtually expunged Morgan's work from the record, but Fred Eggan resurrected *The League* not simply as "a pioneer ethnological monograph but [as] a contemporary classic in political anthropology" (1972:4). He may well have had in mind the fact that Morgan's work met the criteria set by his Chicago colleague, political scientist David Easton (1959), because it dealt with a purely political topic—the confederacy of fifteen Native American nations—in its own right. The Morgan Lectures at the University of Rochester in New York, although occasionally characterized by iconographic gymnastics, provide a valuable barometer of Morgan's place in political anthropology; see, in particular, Fortes 1969 and Colson 1974.

Hinsley views Morgan's description of Iroquois political organization as an allegory on American life in the 1840s, an era of "uncertainty, at times a haunting fear, that the young republic was fatally flawed, splintered by deep divisions—wealthy and poor, male and female, free and slave—that defied solutions"(1985:29). According to Hinsley, the central concern of *The League* is,

"What is the lesson of the Iroquois decline for the American republic?" (1985: 37). For the context of such questioning around Rochester, New York, see McElroy 1984.

3. After a long period of relative obscurity, the Scottish political economists have begun to come into their own. Marvin Harris devoted considerable attention to them in *The Rise of Anthropological Theory* (1968). Evans-Pritchard 1981 noted their importance. A softbound edition of Adam Smith's *An Inquiry into the Nature and Causes of the Wealth of Nations* (1784) was published in 1976, and Adam Ferguson's *Essay on the History of Civil Society* (1767) appeared in paperback in 1966. For a useful discussion of the tradition, see Michael Perelman's *Classical Political Economy: Primitive Accumulation and the Social Division of Labor* (1984).

A coherent anthropological adoption of political economic theory dates only from the publication in 1964 of Eric Hobsbawm's *Pre-capitalist Economic Formations*, extracts from Marx's *Grundrisse*. Somewhat disparate use has been made of its concepts. Neoevolutionists, for example, emblematically adopted the term *civil society* in the 1960s, and there are both non-Marxist and Marxist traditions of its use. Perelman 1984 discusses those of the Scots and Hegel. Morgan adopted the distinction between political and civil society from *Ancient Law* (Maine 1861).

Given the argument about primitivization that pervades this study, it is worth noting, perhaps, that it was Marx's translator, not Marx, who wrote of primitive accumulation. "The seemingly Marxian expression 'primitive accumulation' began with Adam Smith's notion that 'the accumulation of stock must, in the nature of things, be previous to the division of labor'. Marx translated 'previous' as *ursprunglich*, a word that Marx's English translators rendered as "primitive" (Perelman 1984:6).

4. Several writers, using various terms, have distinguished a processual or historical tradition from the dominant evolutionary or developmental mode. The processual-historical tradition has not received as much attention, although Kenneth Bock (1974), Victor Turner (1974), and Sally Falk Moore (1978a) have made a beginning.

5. Substantive data on the Bureau of American Ethnology are derived from the annual reports of its director to the secretary of the Smithsonian Institution, volumes 1 (1879–80) through 19 (1897–98); the records of the 1903 investigation of the affairs of the bureau; and an unpublished manuscript by John Swanton in the National Archives. Valuable secondary sources include Fewkes 1897; Darrah 1951; Meadows 1952; Stegner 1954; Dupree 1957; Judd 1968; Fowler and Fowler 1969, 1971; Darnell 1969, 1971, 1974; Noelke 1974; Hinsley 1976a, 1976b, 1979, 1981; Mark 1980; and Moses 1984.

6. Powell described the Utes and their leaders under political conditions that were not analyzed fully until the 1950s, when the frontier conditions of new economic expansion were studied ethnographically. In such "development decades," far apart as they were historically and geographically, the common phasal element is a rapidly changing economic field and the opportunities it offers for political aggrandizement. This point is developed further in Chapter 5.

Powell called the Native Americans among whom he worked "the Numic-speaking peoples." (This term is now being used again after a half-century in which the Numa lived in the annals of political ethnography as the Plateau Shoshonians. To avoid confusion, Julian Steward's later usage of Shoshoni and Ute will be used here. The Shoshoni have contributed to the discipline's changing perception of its field, and not only in matters political. The relation of a subsistence environment to political organization and processes of acculturation [Powell's term] were two of the many themes addressed through Shoshoni ethnography.)

7. This goal is shared by Morgan (1851:180): "We have met the red man upon the war path and not at the Fireside. We have dealt with him as his oppressor, and not as his friend. His evil traits form the standard of judgement; and when his virtues rise up before us, they create surprise, rather than answer expectation because the standard of estimation is universally unjust." Compare Powell (Fowler and Fowler 1971:37): "The popular idea of the Indian is that he is a savage and that he roams through the forest, across the plains and over the mountains like a wild beast. Nothing is farther from the truth." The manuscript in which this passage appears is called "Indian Life." The Fowlers suggest that it was originally read as a lecture, probably "Indian Life Beyond the Rocky Mountains," given during a month-long lecture tour in the Midwest in 1874.

8. In what follows I am drawing largely on the Powell-Ingalls Report of 1874 and to a lesser extent on the seventy-six unpublished ethnographic manuscripts reproduced in Fowler and Fowler 1971.

9. Information about Kanosh is scattered throughout Powell's manuscripts, e.g., Fowler and Fowler 1971:16, 17, 29–30, 103–104, 106, 111, 207. Further information was gleaned from Alter 1932:158, 162, 163, 173, 174, 175, 199, 227, 392, 398, 413, 414, 424. Corn Creek's proximity to Fillmore, the first capital of the Mormon colony of Deseret (later Utah) and Kanosh's role as a go-between for other Native American groups make him a prominent figure. Announcements of Kanosh's arrival in town often appeared in the *Deseret News* in the 1850s. On June 28, 1875, eighty-five members of Kanosh's band were baptized Mormons, bringing the total to around a hundred (Alter 1932). An even better known Native American broker and entrepreneur was Ely S. Parker, the Seneca Indian who collaborated with Morgan: see Armstrong 1978. A broker who failed was Wovoka of the Utes: see Mooney 1896 and Kehoe 1989.

10. More needs to be known about Ward's position at the bureau, where "he spent much of his time—during office-hours as well as after—writing his *Dynamic Sociology*" (Darrah 1951:212). For similarities between Powell's and Ward's social philosophies, see Darrah 1951:280–281, especially the cryptic note 16.

11. Fortes (1969) traced the sociological tradition in anthropology back to Maine and Morgan but made no reference to Powell and Dorsey's seminal use of the concept of the kinship polity in spite of his own use of the term to head a chapter.

12. See, for example, Walter J. Hoffman's account of the Grand Medicine Society of the Ojibway (1886–87) and John G. Bourke's account of the Apache

medicine men who were "antagonistic to the rapid absorption of new ideas and the adoption of new customs" (1892:451). Bourke recommended that they should be ridiculed and routed, and proposed doing so by enlisting the services of Apache schoolchildren as missionaries of civilization.

13. Colby 1977 and Moses 1984 provide biographies of Mooney. While both are excellent, neither fully treats the exact course of Mooney's fieldwork or his Irish political activities.

14. Kehoe suggests, however, that focusing on religious movements and military defeats "reinforced the myth of the primitive," so that subsequent analyses of the Ghost Dance became a "tradition of misinterpretation" (1989:127, 133).

15. For an account of the political problems that Mooney's report caused the bureau in Washington circles, see Hinsley 1981. In his introduction to that report, Powell attempted to play down Mooney's pan-human characterization of the movement (1896:ix–ixi). See also Colby 1977.

16. Collini's argument is directed against Talcott Parsons's charge that little work that was later to enter the sociological tradition (Weber, Durkheim, Pareto, Marx) came from Britain, an argument accepted by Hughes (1958), Burrow (1966), Abrams (1968), and Anderson (1968), among others. Collini (1978) portrays idealism as the intellectual milieu in which L. T. Hobhouse's sociology developed. This became immediately relevant to political anthropology through Hobhouse's coauthored book *The Material Culture and Social Institutions of the Simpler Peoples* (see below, Chapter 2). Its more diffuse influence on the classicists Gilbert Murray, Jane Harrison, and F. M. Cornford suggests an alternative to the primitivization of anthropology that subsequently occurred. One can only speculate on R. R. Marett's knowledge of the work of D. G. Ritchie at Oxford. His methodological essay on "Economic Laws" in *Darwin and Hegel, With other Philosophical Studies* (1893), for example, or *Darwinism and Politics* (1889) is particularly relevant. As Collini puts it, "where past thinkers had access to the appropriate range of concepts and were interested in the relevant set of problems, then it can be illuminating to consider why their thought did not develop further in a certain direction, if only as a way of focussing on the limits and presuppositions of their actual thinking" (1978:6). A comparison of the 1874 edition of *Notes and Queries*, discussed below, with that of 1912 might reveal the influence of the idealist critique of positivism and the natural sciences. Idealism's "closest links, both intellectually and institutionally, were with the study of law, though here as elsewhere there is something of a mystery about what happened to the legacy of Maine, which in England seems to peter out in the study of 'comparative politics'" (Collini 1978:33).

17. The specifics of this amalgamation are to be found in Van Keuren 1982, Gruber 1967, and Burrow 1966. Differences between ethnology and anthropology are set out in Hallowell 1960, Burrow 1966, and Gruber 1967. Accounts of when and how "ethnology becomes anthropology" are to be found in Gruber 1967. Both attempted a science of man, that is, the application of the analytic technique of classification to human phenomena. The difference lay in the limits of the system within which such a classification was meaningful. In the nineteenth century, ethnology dealt with the reconstruction of nonrecorded histories and the substantiation of those that were recorded only fragmentally, and anthropology dealt with the study of the origin, nature, and history of the

human species, the sciences of mankind. Ethnology deals with man in respect to his varieties, while anthropology deals with man as compared with the lower animals (Gruber 1967:13). In England after 1860, *anthropology* became the inclusive term, *ethnology* the specialized. In the United States, *ethnology* remained the inclusive term. The American Ethnological Society was founded in 1842, and the American Association for the Advancement of Science established an ethnology subsection in 1869. This was changed to an anthropology subsection in 1873, becoming Subsection 4 in 1982. The Bureau of Ethnology was founded, as we have seen, in 1879.

18. Max Muller, a German ethnologist, had actually persuaded the British government to publish a series of colonial records containing trustworthy information on the languages, customs, laws, religions, and monuments of the inhabitants of the colonies. The secretary of state, in agreeing, suggested that funds should be raised by the colonies themselves, but his memorandum apparently was lost (Muller 1891).

19. A member of the English gentry, Augustus Henry Lane-Fox Pitt-Rivers acquired additional names with property inheritance, and additional titles as he advanced through the Grenadier Guards regiment of the British army. Following Chapman 1985 and Stocking 1987, I refer to him as Pitt-Rivers throughout, retaining, however, the hyphen dropped in those works. Prior to 1880 his publications were listed under Lane Fox.

20. For the execution of the evolutionary argument in the physical arrangement of the Oxford museum, see Chapman 1985.

21. It is to be hoped that this state of affairs will change following the publication of R. Brian Ferguson's *The Anthropology of War* (1988), in which Pitt-Rivers's several publications are listed.

22. Echoes of this alternative historical comparative method would later be heard in the debate between Radcliffe-Brown and Isaac Schapera in the late 1930s (Chapter 3) and were resurrected by Evans-Pritchard a short while later (Chapter 4). The mainstream use of the sociological comparative method emerges in Chapter 2, where it figures prominently in the promulgation of scientific methodology.

Maine distinguished his own historical method from the sociological-evolutionary method when he recognized a division of labor between Morgan and himself, with Morgan studying primitive societies and he ancient (Stocking 1987:183, citing the Morgan Papers, Rush Rhees Library, Rochester, New York: Maine to Morgan Oct. 29, 1880).

23. The nature of the village community was central to a debate among Indianists (anthropologists and historians) in the 1950s and 1960s (Chapter 5). In the course of the debate, Louis Dumont reviewed the colonial literature on the subject. He found Sir Thomas Elphistone and Sir Charles Metcalfe to be leading exponents of the "little Republic" ideal type. "These communities contain in miniature all the materials of a State within themselves, and are almost sufficient to protect their members, if all governments are withdrawn" (Dumont 1966:72). Sir Charles Metcalfe wrote: "The Village Communities are little Republics having nearly everything that they want within themselves, and almost independent of any foreign relations" (quoted in Dumont 1966:73). The significance of the village community as a political unit was briefly debated by

Mesoamericanists in the 1930s (Chapter 3) and again in the 1940s.

24. This is true for his research on both the village community and law. Rosen has suggested that "the political implications of Maine's studies are vital to an understanding of his work. . . . [H]is emphasis on corporate group, individual contract, and the role of the progressive elites went a long way toward rescuing law from its perceived role as simply the expression of the power of the sovereign" (1986:xiv). See also Grossi 1981 for Maine's impact on the legal recognition of communal landholding in late-nineteenth-century Italy. Maine's influence on Oliver Wendell Holmes, Roscoe Pound, and legal realism should also be noted.

A sustained analysis of Maine's later writings on India led Bock (1974) to present an alternative assessment of Maine's contribution to that generally provided in anthropology texts. He argued that Maine "far from being even a variant in the evolutionist camp, stood in basic opposition to the essentialist tenets of that school. His outlook, his objectives, and his method differed profoundly from those of the traditional developmentalists. To notice the difference is not just to try to set the historical record straight. Maine's work can be viewed rather as a *distinctive alternative* to the central tendencies of nineteenth century evolutionism" (1974:233, emphasis added). Trautmann (1987), it should be pointed out, does not agree with Bock. This I take to be a result of Trautmann's focus on kinship in his own reading of Maine. Maine's work is overdue for reevaluation in political anthropology, which for the past half-century has accepted Smellie's judgment that "the political ideas of Sir H. Maine are outside the mainstream of English political thought. They are a slight eddy indicating the presence of conflicting currents below the surface" (1928:65). Raymond Cocks's *Sir Henry Maine: A Study in Victorian Jurisprudence* (1988) begins to set the record straight. Most instructively, it also notes the errors of some anthropologists of law that result from their selective use of Maine's publications. For Maine's impact on the anthropology of law, see Redfield 1950, Firth 1963, Gluckman 1965, Moore 1978b, Kuper 1985a, Mackenzie 1982, Rosen 1986, and Starr 1989.

25. Collini, Winch, and Burrow (1984) suggest, however, that a bias toward classification and away from process may well have been built into the use of the comparative method from the start. They quote (1984:234) journalist John Morley's review of Maine's *Popular Government*, in which he extends the historical method, as he calls it, from the study of legal institutions to political institutions. "It is obvious," Morley wrote, "that systems of government, called by the same name, bearing the same superficial marks, founded and maintained on the same nominal principles, framed in the same verbal forms, may yet work with infinite diversity of operation, according to the variety of social circumstances around them." This critique would reappear several times in the course of the development of political anthropology.

26. See Lawrence Krader, *The Ethnological Notebooks of Karl Marx* (1974). Marx commented on Indian society in a series of articles for the *New York Herald Tribune* between 1853 and 1867. In these he studied precolonial Asian society in connection with his analysis of early forms of society based on communal property and the different forces through which this dissolved into secondary class forms of property. Marx's articles were reprinted in collected form

in India itself in the mid 1940s contemporaneously with R. Palme Dutt's analysis (1950) of colonialism in India. His work on India and China begins to enter mainstream anthropology in 1957 with Wittfogel's *Oriental Despotism* and the response it provoked (see Chapter 6). *Critique of Anthropology* ran a special issue on the Asiatic mode of production, signaling the orthodoxy of the left. Teodor Shanin's *Late Marx and the Russian Road* appeared in 1983.

27. For a review of these materials, see Klass 1980. Valuable commentaries on his work appear in Kutsenkov 1986 and Omvedt 1981, 1982.

28. I am grateful to Dorothy Vincent for undertaking the calculations involved.

29. The discussion in this section can take the shape it does because of the archival labors of several scholars who have worked on the Boas papers in the American Philosophical Society archives (Stocking 1965; Gruber 1967; Rohner 1969; Adams 1981; Cannizzo 1983) and in the archives of British Columbia and the federal government of Canada (Fisher 1977; Knight 1978). The exact amount of time Boas spent among the Kwakiutl and the methods he adopted in his inquiries gave rise to a large critical literature as the dominance of the Boasian school in American anthropology came under challenge. Prior to his arrival in British Columbia, Boas had worked with the Inuit (Eskimo) from 1883 to 1884. He then attempted unsuccessfully to raise funds for research into the relationship between groups of western Inuit and Native Americans of the Northwest. He eventually spent three months in 1886 in British Columbia, his field expenses being covered by the sale of ethnological specimens. In January 1888, Hale invited him to join the British Association expedition.

Considerable attention is now being paid to the eye-witness accounts of George Hunt (Codere 1966; Goldman 1975; Cannizzo 1983). Cannizzo has argued (1983:45) that George Hunt's contribution to the ethnology of the Kwakiutl "goes beyond his role as majordomo of the ethnographic tour, for it is to a large extent his descriptions of Kwakiutl life and culture that have been distilled in the massive scholarly literature on these people of the Northwest Coast. George Hunt is one of the most important originators of our current view of 'traditional' Kwakiutl society; he is a primary contributor to the invention of the Kwakiutl as an ethnographic society." Of Boas's more than five thousand pages on the Kwakiutl, Hunt contributed data for more than two-thirds (Rohner 1969).

30. Among the motors of political inequality were secret societies and slavery. The more societies a man belonged to, the higher was his standing. The secret societies were, according to Boas, a form of organization that alternated every winter with clan organization: the clan system was profane; the secret system, sacred. The societies were composed of exclusive groups of men and women and had their origin, he believed, in Kwakiutl methods of warfare (1895). Northwest Coast slavery is discussed in Nieboer's study of slavery as an industrial system (see Chapter 2). Verne Ray pointed out the nature of Boas's bias in 1955, and his discussion may be quoted here both as prolegomenon to the pursuit of the political Kwakiutl and more importantly as an observation applicable to many other political ethnographies as well. Ray wrote that "the ethnographic picture of the Northwest Coast as visualized, taught, and accepted by many anthropologists is that which in fact applies only to the nobility

of the southern Kwakiutl. . . . [T]here are masses of ethnographic data relating to the distinctions between the upper and the lower classes and the cultural disabilities suffered by the latter" (1969:161). The topic was pursued both in a reevaluation of Boas's ethnography and in its own right in Drucker 1939, 1965; Garfield 1966; Drucker and Heizer 1967; Adams 1973; Chun 1980; Donald 1982; Kobrinsky 1975; Rousseau 1979; and Ruyle 1973. A useful review appeared in Adams 1981.

Fisher 1977 is an historian's reevaluation of potlatching in the historical context of the fur trade. Drawing on various archives and early narratives, the historian documents its political importance to emergent leaders—Kwakiutl Kanoshes—who specialized in dealing with European traders. George Hunt himself, it should be pointed out, was not Kwakiutl but the son of a Tlingit mother and a Scottish fur trader (Cannizzo 1983).

31. Both R. E. Dennett, a trader, and E. D. Morel, a severe critic of colonialism in Africa (Chapter 2), owe a great deal to Kingsley's patronage. Her opinion of Dennett's work was not shared by professional reviewers (e.g., Starr 1911). Yet she was led by his writings on the folklore of the Fjort, for example, to suggest that some of the stories in his book are similar to leading cases in Western jurisprudence. Her own work on law appeared in 1897 and 1898.

32. She often compared political development in nineteenth-century West Africa with that in Europe in the thirteenth century, hence her use of the term *early.*

33. A critical anthropological assessment of Mary Kingsley is overdue. It should preferably be done by a West Africanist who is also a feminist or a Marxist. Biographies by Gwynn (1933) and Howard (1957) provide references to her self-deprecating relationship with professional anthropologists, particularly Tylor, her "great ju-ju" (Gwynn 1933:134), and her joyful belligerence toward those she calls "cabinet comparative ethnologists," who view her as a writer and propagandist. Howard is appreciative of her participation in colonial politics—her defense of the liquor trade, opposition to the hut tax, advocacy of a savanna-belt union of British territories uniting Nigeria and Uganda, and above all her attack on the Crown Colony system—and Flint (1964, 1965) begins to place this in context. R. S. Rattray assessed her influence in the field of West African administration and anthropology. Porter 1968 and Rich 1986 place her within the context of liberal political thinking about empire. Rich's chapter on her role in the emergence of cultural relativism is particularly valuable for its references to pioneer Pan-Africanists Joseph Renner Maxwell and Sylvester Williams.

34. This was Audrey Richards, a London anthropologist who, as director of the East African Institute for Social and Economic Research at Makerere College, had the ear of Sir Andrew Cohen, governor of Uganda. A large portrait of Richards hangs in the office of the institute's present director.

CHAPTER 2. THE UNEASY YEARS , 1899–1918

1. On the Edwardian era in Britain, see Hawthorn 1976, MacRae 1961, Abrams 1968, Briggs 1975, P. Thompson 1975, Nowell-Smith 1964, Collini 1978, Raison 1969, Fletcher 1971, Marwick 1965, and Quinton 1975. The autobiographies of Marett (1941) and Westermarck (1929) and biographies of Elliot

Smith (Dawson 1938), and Haddon (Quiggin 1942) are particularly valuable and helpful. On the Progressive age in the United States, see Jaher 1964, Carter 1971, Trani and Wilson 1977, Butler 1939–40, Hofstadter 1955, Elkins and McKitrick 1974, and Feis 1950. For a useful discussion of emerging distinctions between sociology and anthropology on both sides of the Atlantic, see Voget 1975:138–145.

2. The distribution was as follows:

	English	German	French	Other/Unknown
HWG	452	268	131	46
Holsti	307	182	75	40
Nieboer	183	89	64	28

3. Its unsettled nature was due in part to long-drawn-out paradigmatic competition related surely to longevity: Frazer died at the age of 87, Tylor and Haddon at 85, Spencer at 83, Marett and Westermarck at 77.

4. The intellectual dimensions of the Red and the Black cannot be spelled out here. Harvard-trained African-Americans and New York socialists and communists, many of them recent immigrants from Europe, joined to combat not racism alone but also the suppression of labor unions at home and American imperialism abroad. For several Blacks and Reds, this led to enduring marital ties and a family commitment to political engagement. See Willis 1963, 1970; and Bond 1987, 1988.

5. The comparative method had, of course, long been seen as revelatory, but there can have been few messianic utterings as devout as those of Freeman: "On us a new light has come. I do not hesitate for a moment to say that the discovery of the Comparative Method in philology, in mythology—let me add in politics and history and the whole range of human thought—marks a stage in the progress of the human mind at least as great and memorable as the revival of Greek and Latin learning" (quoted in Collini, Winch, and Burrow 1984:207).

6. For a discussion of Nieboer's use of the comparative method, see Evans-Pritchard 1981. Nieboer claimed as his mentors Tylor, Steinmetz, and Westermarck. Nowhere does he refer to Durkheim, whose book *Les regles de la méthode sociologique* was published in 1895.

7. Nieboer's definition of slavery corresponds exactly with that used by the United Nations. Chattel slavery—total ownership of one person by another—is distinguished from, but related to, debt bondage (the pledging of labor for an unspecified time to pay off a debt), serfdom (the condition of agricultural laborers who cannot leave the estate where they live and work), child exploitation, and servile forms of marriage.

8. See, for example, the last chapter of *The Origin of the Family, Private Property and the State* (Engels 1884/1972). For critiques of Nieboer, see Patterson 1977. For a defense of Nieboer, see Engerman 1973. The historian Philip D. Curtin went to some pains to point out that the relationship between land surplus and labor shortage that Nieboer sought to demonstrate was "most commonly discussed . . . in the 1830s and 1840s by the 'Colonial Reformers' headed by E. Gibbon Wakefield and finds especially detailed treatment in Herman Merivale, *Lectures on Colonization and Colonies*. The fact is that Nieboer

repeated the idea without proper credit to its source" (Curtin 1977:67). Nieboer's brief allusion (1900:xix) apparently was not enough. There would appear to be three possible explanations for Nieboer's cursory allusion: (1) that it reflected the widening gulf between the new professionalizing science of man and earlier scholarship in political economy; (2) that Nieboer assumed that the work of the political economists was so familiar to his readers that this brief allusion would trigger a host of references in their minds; and (3) that Nieboer was methodologically removing his ethnological contribution from Wakefield's context of colonial expansion. I consider the last to be the most likely.

9. Nieboer used as his data base the 391 tribal societies listed in tables compiled by S. R. Steinmetz. He did not, however, restrict his own study to ethnological materials. He also sought to explain why serfdom (for him, a mitigated form of slavery) disappeared in western Europe.

10. Westermarck's scholarship possessed a dual emphasis. On the one hand, he stressed first-hand field research, speaking the language of the people, and continuing investigations over several years, and on the other, he emphasized the comparative study of institutions. This is reflected in the work of his students, including those interested in the political aspects of the societies in which they worked. Among the first was Gunnar Landtman, who carried out research among the Kiwai Papuans of British New Guinea between 1910 and 1912. Gerald C. Wheeler and Rudolph Holsti (later to become a member of the Finnish cabinet) attributed part of the success of their work to Westermarck's training, and Raymond Firth suggested in 1981 that perhaps Bronislaw Malinowski acquired more from his Finnish mentor than he acknowledged (1981:123–124).

11. It is difficult today to see the London School of Economics as other than the cradle of Malinowski's anthropology, but an understanding of the range of its ethnographic base and interdisciplinary nature may be gained from a brief review of its officers of instruction between 1904 and 1913. They included Haddon (1904–1909), Wheeler (1909–1910), Seligman (1910–1913), Rivers (1912–1913), and Malinowski (1913). Malinowski gained his doctorate in anthropology there in 1916.

12. On British anthropology's "long affair with Durkheimianism" (Collini 1978:35), see Lukes 1973, Stocking 1984, and Vincent 1986a.

13. The outlines of several London and Cambridge University lecture courses have been published (Stocking 1984; Urry 1985). Topics of a political nature were, over time, given less and less attention.

14. On primitivism, see Lovejoy and Boas 1935; Diamond 1962, 1974; Willio 1969; and particularly Long 1980, where both chronological and cultural primitivism are discussed in relation to the concept of civilization.

15. Leenhardt criticized Malinowski and Van Gennep for turning too quickly to the analysis of action (i.e., magic and ritual) before the phenomenological questions raised had been fully answered.

16. The frisson between Durkheim and Van Gennep is discussed in Lukes 1973 and Zumwalt 1982. The tension between Van Gennep's folklore (European peasant studies) and the sociology of *L'Année Sociologique* is reflected in sociological anthropology in Britain and to a lesser extent in the United States. Symptomatic of Van Gennep's position beyond the pale was the fact that *Les*

Rites de Passage (1909) was not translated into English until 1960.

17. Haddon Papers, Envelope 12040, Museum of Archaeology and Ethnology, Cambridge.

18. No consideration is given here to Rivers's ideas on government and politics as expressed in the posthumous *Social Organization* (1924), edited by W. J. Perry. I have not been able to examine the original manuscript to disentangle Rivers's ideas from those of Perry. Rivers's views on chieftainship, however, may have been born of his Toda as well as Melanesian experience. He observed that

> no other feature of simple society suffers such rapid modification under the external influence of the European, which is now permeating all parts of the world. The European official who visits a new region will at once ask for the chief, by which he means a person with whom he can negotiate, and who will act as an intermediary between the people and himself. Sometimes the real chief steps forward, when he comes to wield powers of which till then he had not dreamed, so that the whole institution of chieftainship, as well as the mode of government, soon suffers great modification. In other cases, in response to the demand of the stranger, the place of the chief is taken by some other man, who is thus vested with an authority wholly foreign to the people. In Melanesia authority may thus fall into the hands of one whose position depends on his having paid a visit to Sydney, and his having acquired some pidgin-English, with the result that the representative of the British Government is one who had little prestige, and conducts his business apart from those whom the people regard with reverence. In Africa European influence seems to have acted in two ways. In some cases it has, as in Melanesia, produced a form of chieftainship with definite authority which was unknown before; while in other cases, where chieftainship had already developed towards the attainment of real authority in relation to justice, there has been the opposite effect, and a once powerful institution of chieftainship has disappeared, leaving only a number of petty headmen. (1924:165–166)

Rivers's constant historicizing of field data is striking. In 1914 he attributed gerontocracy in Melanesia to immigrant influence. Baker (1983), reviewing the leadership of Big Men and elders in the South Pacific, found Rivers's hypothesis anything but farfetched.

19. In "Caste Dominance and Coercion in the Nilgiris" (1963), Fox discusses reciprocal relations among the Todas, herders of buffaloes, and other groups (agriculturalists, artisans, and jungle dwellers). Reevaluating Rivers's data, Fox found that *jajmani* (a "reciprocal service relationship between the village castes") provided a dominant caste with "political empire over the other village groups and coercion" (1963:493–494). The regional focus of Rivers's ethnography denies a focus on Indian village communities as "primitive isolates." Fox's own work is a fine early application of political ecology.

20. For a discussion of the influence of *The Todas* on Indian officials and the Todas themselves, see Mandelbaum 1980:288–289. Leach (1968a:527) reports that for many years it "served British anthropologists as a model for ethnographic monographs."

21. Rivers, in fact, provides a precedent for processual extended case analysis. "I am myself aware," he wrote, "that I have often complicated, perhaps even obscured, the story I am telling by the mass of detail with which it is accompanied" (1914:vi). Compare Turner 1957. "The Case of Kiugi's Buffaloes," which follows, provided a model of political analysis widely adopted in the 1950s, especially by the Manchester School (Chapter 5).

22. Prince Peter's wife worked with the widow of Kuriolv. She discovered that "after having rid himself of rivals and wives alike by the habitual Toda method of indirect poisoning through the agency of the Kurumbas, he was himself murdered in the same way by his wife" (Peter 1963:266). Prince Peter thought Rivers erred in finding no crime among the Todas: "under a peaceful exterior, many serious acts of aggression had taken and were still taking place. Personal feuds of intense hatred and jealousy, especially among the older men, seemed to be the reasons for what were not just empty accusations of witchcraft, but unmistakably crimes, and I gathered so much evidence of this that I have come to think that there are very few influential old Todas who die a natural death. They are more usually done away with by their rivals, through the time honoured method of having them poisoned by the Kurumbas" (1963:266). Prince Peter may have been right; on the other hand, fieldworkers are used to inexplicable deaths being attributed to sorcery. Whether Rivers was wrong cannot, of course, be demonstrated from field data created sixty years later.

23. Rivers wrote in 1913: "A typical piece of intensive fieldwork is one in which the worker lives for a year or more among a community of perhaps four or five hundred people and studies every detail of their life and culture; in which he comes to know every member of the community personally; . . . studies every feature of life and custom in concrete detail and by means of the vernacular language" (1913:7).

24. The new society's concern with the dispossession of the land of indigenous peoples, the role of multinational companies, international funding agencies, and governments bent on "development" at all costs reentered anthropology shortly after its name was changed in 1957 to the Anti-Slavery Society for the Protection of Human Rights. Its policy of directing action toward governments and international bodies predated by two decades the shift within anthropology of the topic of slavery from the subfield of economics to that of politics. For the most part, however, anthropologists have continued to view slavery as an economic or social institution, even as of religious significance, but rarely as a matter of political and central theoretical importance.

25. Correspondence between John Linton Myres and Barbara Freire-Marreco in the Myres Collection at the Bodleian Library suggests how difficult it was for a young woman in Edwardian Britain to obtain a professional post. I am grateful to Col. Frederick Myres for permission to use this archive. From 1909 to 1913 Barbara Freire-Marreco held a Somerville Research Fellowship and worked among the Tewa. Returning to England, she lectured at LSE until 1923, when she married Robert Aitken. She carried out fieldwork on agriculture, linguistics, and folklore in Spain between 1926 and 1932. For photographs and a short text, see Babcock and Parezo 1988.

26. It had long been argued that the study of savage life was "of peculiar importance to England, forming as we do, part of a great empire, with colonies

in every part of the world, and fellow-citizens in many stages of evolution" (Lubbock, quoted in Barnett 1956:1). Anthropology in colonial service took six major forms: ethnological intelligence reports, ethnological sections in government departments or bureaus of native affairs, the appointment of government anthropologists, training schemes for colonial personnel, the establishment of research institutes, and experiments in applied or practical anthropology.

27. Hocart published "A Native Fijian on the Decline of his Race," an early equivalent of "The Peasant Speaks," in 1912. It was reprinted in Bohannan and Plog 1967. As Bohannan put it, "Anthropologists such as Hocart translated the *cri de coeur* of the 'natives'" (Bohannan and Plog 1967:xiv).

28. The following examples are taken from the RAI Archives, Files A, A10:3, A11, A12, A18, A22, A57.34.

29. The assessment that follows is based largely on Colonial Office personnel records (CO 877/1, No. 3781; CO 583, No. 176/1003; and CO 429/29). For a discussion of their contents, see Vincent 1986a:333–334.

30. The title for this section is taken from Colonial Office descriptions of Northcote-Thomas as a sandal-wearing vegetarian and "a rum person" (Lackner 1973:135).

31. The quotation comes from the RAI Archives, File A22.

32. Would Rivers, had he lived, asks Slobodin (1978:2), "while venturing into politics, have pioneered in the anthropology of politics?" The immediate stimulus for Rivers's entry into politics was Bertrand Russell's imprisonment for pacifism. After the war, with Russell he frequented the company of Fabians, Socialists, and Labourites in London, among them Graham Wallas, George Bernard Shaw, H. G. Wells, Hugh Dalton, and Harold Laski. His growing anti-imperialism led him to question the use of anthropology for the benefit of subject peoples. Included in the Labour party platform on which he ran for Parliament were independence for Egypt, self-government for India, the acceptance of the Irish Free State constitution, a graduated levy on fortunes over 5,000 pounds sterling, and the nationalization of mines and railways (Slobodin 1978).

33. My provisional reevaluation of diffusionism is based on the archives of the RAI (A10:3); Langham 1981; Burridge 1965, 1973; Elkin 1974; Dawson 1938; Corris 1973; and Green 1981.

34. The antidiffusionist bias lingers on in the subconscious even of those who are beginning to appreciate the diffusionist vision. Thus Appadurai: "Diffusionism, *whatever its defects and in whatever guise,* has at least the virtue of allowing everyone the possibility of exposure to a world larger than their current locale" (1988b:39, emphasis added). Examples may be given of the pariah treatment accorded to diffusionists. Perry is frequently referred to as a schoolteacher; he was, in fact, Reader in the Department of Anatomy at University College. Reference is rarely made to Daryll Forde's collaboration with Elliot Smith at University College or his diffusionist study *Ancient Mariners: The Story of Ships and Sea Routes* (1926). Fortes chose to describe it as a potboiler (1976:471).

35. Opponents inevitably challenged the diffusionist vision at its most vulnerable point, taking the part for the whole. "The writings of the period on diffusion give the impression that the contemporary critics had not examined thoroughly the theory as Elliot Smith developed and presented it in his books

and articles from 1911 to 1933, or as W. J. Perry presented it in *The Children of the Sun*, 1923, and W. H. Rivers in *The History of Melanesian Society*, Vol. II, 1914, and in his articles in Part III of *Psychology and Ethnology*, 1926. Did the critics see the proposition in its complexity and entirety? Or, when coming to, or lighting at random on, a statement, a suggestion, or an inference which ran counter to their long accepted opinions and theories, did they, as I suspect, reject the concept 'lock, stock and barrel'? They probably read no more, at least not with the 'seeing eye'. This is a 'natural' reaction to the uncongenial, to that which disturbs" (Elkin 1974:147).

36. "Diffusionism appears on the surface as contingent and arbitrary"; Burridge explained, "and the problem of deriving principles of cultural transmission or of peoples' movements and migrations from the empirical facts of diffusion—as distinct from simply generalizing on the facts—remains evasive. Where evolution evokes pattern, diffusionism evokes the random and demands both the worst and the best of imaginations. Consequently, the logic or systematics of cultural transmissions and population movement ... have not since W. H. Rivers' *History of Melanesian Society* (1914) much occupied social or cultural anthropologists" (1973:48). The logic of the system was, perhaps, already less evasive than Burridge appreciated. Cultural transformations and population movements are seen to be functions of global capitalism. Within an analysis of global capitalism in the twentieth century lie both a mode of ordering anthropological data and the energies of a considerable number of political anthropologists. Indeed, in 1965 Burridge himself even had such a vision.

37. G. C. Wheeler, *Mono-Alu Folklore*, 1926. Unpublished Wheeler manuscripts, MS 170822, MS 184245, School of Oriental and African Studies, London. Wheeler was educated at St. Charles College, London, and obtained a B.A. (Philosophy Honours) as an external student at the University of London in 1905. He then studied under Westermarck at the London School of Economics. He had to scratch around for financial support for fieldwork in Oceania in 1908. On his return he collaborated on *The Material Culture and Social Institutions of the Simpler Peoples* (Hobhouse, Wheeler, and Ginsberg 1915). During World War I, Wheeler served in the British Military Mission in Brazil, and for two years after that with the Allied Control Commission in Germany. He then taught an occasional course at the University of London, earned a living from translations, and eventually published his first monograph, *Mono-Alu Folklore*, in 1926. He died in 1943, at age seventy-one, his passing unmarked by an obituary in any professional anthropological journal.

38. We shall return to Wheeler's monograph in Chapter 3, noting its impact on Alexander Lesser. See also Vincent 1988b.

39. It was then attributed to Max Weber. I am not aware whether Wheeler read Weber; he certainly read German.

40. A position that Lord Raglan, for one, continued to argue well into the 1950s against the sanctification of sociological anthropology in the image of Radcliffe-Brown. The Welsh peer was a lifelong friend of Daryll Forde, who at one time taught at the University of Aberystwyth. (See, for example, *Man* 1944:107, in which Lord Raglan argues that Radcliffe-Brown was himself involved in conjectural history; his "Webs of Fantasy" correspondence with Mair, Beattie, and Cranstone on the subject of history in *Man* 1953:152, 229, 281,

304; 1954:19, 42, 74, 98, 124; 1955:59, 60; and Mair's reply in *Man* 1943, along with comments by H. J. Braunholtz, J. H. Hutton, Margaret Read, J. L. Myres— and Lord Raglan. Marett also claimed that he had "always insisted to myself that anthropology was no 'barbarology', but dealt with Man universal—with 'Everyman' so to speak—and not merely the savage" (1941:163).

41. Within the academy, Boas treated the work of American anthropologists lightly, a reflection "of attitudes held by educated Germans of that time when American science, scholarship, and general Kultur were held in low repute" (Altschuler 1967:112). Most of Boas's students at this time (Lowie, Sapir, Goldenweiser, Radin, and Kroeber) were foreign-born or the children of immigrants and all were fluent in German. For the ethnological theory on which Lowie and the others drew, see Heine-Geldern 1964.

42. Starr may be criticized for failing to establish an anthropology department within the University of Chicago, but he was active in seeking posts for his former students. In the Philippines, the Bureau of Non-Christian Tribes was headed by David P. Barrows and Merton L. Miller (Class of 1897), alongside Albert E. Jenks of Wisconsin (Class of 1899). In 1905 Starr sought posts for his graduate students at the Bureau of American Ethnology in Washington. Holmes regretted that the bureau was fully staffed: "few die and none resign in Government service" (Holmes to Starr, May 16, 1905, quoted in Noelke 1974:313). For a fuller analysis of Starr in the political context of his times, see Vincent 1987.

43. Mooney's affinities are with Van Gennep and Leenhardt, not Durkheim. He estimated that he spent two-thirds of his time in the field; testimony of James Mooney, pp. 962–984, unpublished manuscript, National Anthropological Archives, Smithsonian Institution.

44. Aboriginal California communities became a major focus of revisionist interest in the 1980s. Considerable documentation and reevaluation of their ethnology was sparked by their legal claims against the federal government between 1949 and 1954 and again in 1976 (Chapter 4).

45. Business interests fueled America's transcontinental expansion. In the eighteenth century, at the instigation of land speculators from Pennsylvania and Maryland, states possessing western lands were pressured one by one to cede them to the United States. In 1803 Louisiana was purchased from the French; Gulf Florida was acquired from Spain in the same year and the remainder in 1821. Texas and Oregon were acquired as part of the concept of Manifest Destiny, and regions obtained from Mexico in 1848 were absorbed into the United States from the date of cession. After the success of the industrial North in the Civil War, the United States embarked upon a more militant economic imperialism overseas. It purchased its first noncontiguous acquisition, Alaska, from Russia in 1867. American imperialism was, however, significantly different from the older European imperialisms. The United States, with its vast continental resources, did not depend on tropical lands as they did. Rather, it was the overseas consumer markets that attracted American business; the stimulation of Latin America and oriental tastes for things manufactured in America was its main goal (Veblen 1923; Perkins 1962; Lopez 1966; Magdoff 1969).

46. For a discussion of the phenomenon in Africa, see Thornton 1983. Few fieldworkers can have been as explicitly romantic about the relationship of

ethnographer to ethnologist as Barton. To document this point, a long extract from a letter from Barton to Starr (Starr Papers, Regenstein Library) is quoted in Vincent 1984.

47. Barton insisted that his data related only to the Ifugao who lived in the vicinity of Kiangan. Officers at the Bureau of Non-Christian Tribes at the time, and anthropologists later, generalized his materials. The colonial situation thus became ethnicized (Vincent 1987).

48. Comments on Barton's legal ethnography include Lowie 1920, 1927a; Hartland 1924; Radin 1932; Hoebel 1954; Nader, Koch, and Cox 1966; Gulliver 1969; and Jaspan 1970.

49. For Hoebel and others of an evolutionary bent, the existence of the *monkalun* was a sign of "a first step in the development of juridical institutions" (1954:114). More generally, the role of the mediator became critical for the analysis of so-called stateless polities after the publication of Evans-Pritchard's *The Nuer* in 1940.

50. Although the primary source for the account that follows is *Ifugao Law* (1919), use was also made of Barton's *Ifugao Economics* (1922) and *Philippine Pagans* (1938).

51. Barton was apparently unaware of the debate that raged in academic anthropology about the relationship of kinship to locality. Lowie's elaboration of Barton's inadequacies in this respect in his early book on *The Origin of the State* (1927b) in a sense bestowed legitimacy on the work of the amateur ethnographer. Indeed, in response to Lowie's comments and his subsequent entry into the fold of the Berkeley department, Barton shifted ground in the course of his publications between 1919 and 1949. This was not for the better (see Vincent 1987).

52. See Harris 1968. Lowie reached a destructive climax in 1915 when he took it upon himself to review in the *American Anthropologist* Rivers's posthumous *Kinship and Social Organization*, a work reviewed only 150 pages before in the same journal by E. A. Webster. Lowie devoted two whole pages of his review to a disagreement with Rivers's high opinion of Morgan, railing against Morgan's "intolerable diffuseness, the pages and pages of irrelevant data," his "lack of clearness and logical rigor," and his "naive evolutionism" (1915:329–330). He concluded: "He was the typical incarnation of the 'comprehensive and weak mind' (esprit ample et faible) in Duheim's classification of intellects; as soon as research became intensive and rigorous, it was natural that he should become the object of unhistorical contempt" (Lowie 1915:331).

53. This characterization of certain Native Americans as being "without true political organization" lasted for a very long time in textbooks. See, for example, Driver 1961.

CHAPTER 3. PROMISE, DEPRESSION, AND NEW DEALS, 1919–1939

1. The substantive data in this section are drawn from Noggle 1966, Grun 1975, Carter 1971, and Kinder and Hilgemann 1978. Beals described this era in anthropology as an iconoclastic time when anti-theory flourished, attacking "the great systems of the Marxian, Kulturkreis and Heliolithic schools" (1982:4).

2. Throughout the 1920s, Lowie made no reference at all to the work of Durkheim. He first cited him in 1948 in his Huxley Lecture at the Royal Anthropological Institute in London.

3. I have taken the phrase "Law in Action" from Roscoe Pound's "Law in Books and Law in Action" (1910).

4. Malinowski was in good company. In 1921, Justice Cardozo noted: "Life may be lived, conduct may be ordered, it *is* lived and ordered, for unnumbered human beings without bringing them in the field where the law can be misread, unless indeed the misreading be accompanied by conscious abuse of power. Their conduct never touches the borderland, the penumbra where controversy begins. They go from birth to death, their action restrained at every turn by the power of the state, and not once do they appeal to judges to make the boundaries between right and wrong. I am unable to withold the name of law from rules which exercise this compulsion over the fortunes of mankind" (1921:130).

5. And this on the eve, as it were, of his LSE students' embarking on a study of culture contact in sub-Saharan Africa—all building on his insights and sharing his professional values. None, however, paid much attention to the legal structuring of the contact situation, later to be studied as colonial law. Among his administrator-cum-anthropologist students, an Australian, Ian Hogbin, conducted research into sorcery and administration in Polynesia. His monograph *Law and Order in Polynesia* (1934) tends to be overshadowed by the introduction Malinowski wrote for it. Concern with the named individual in society ultimately distinguishes Malinowski's anthropology from the microsociology of Radcliffe-Brown.

6. "The progressive ascent of specialists of different kinds through a series of positions in one or more hierarchical structures, and the concomitant residential mobility through a number of communities at one or more steps in this ascent, forms a characteristic combination of social and spatial mobility which I propose to call spiralism" (Watson 1964:147). The concept is a valuable one for the history of science: within anthropology, the spiralism of, for example, Julian Steward or Clifford Geertz provides outstanding cases. The individualism implicit in it needs to be tempered, perhaps, by the adoption of the concept of opportunity chains (White 1970).

7. As yet, research into Radcliffe-Brown's achievements and influence is extraordinarily fragmentary, apart from Stocking 1984. It consists almost entirely of isolated reevaluations launched on various grounds. Murdock suggested that Radcliffe-Brown had "voiced all his major theoretical and methodological ideas" by 1925. Thereafter, while his contemporaries and students advanced, "he himself stood still. . . . The social anthropology of Radcliffe-Brown becomes increasingly recognised as a synonym for emasculated anthropology" (Murdock 1960:157). Elkin 1956 develops a critique voiced earlier by Lowie (1937) to make the point that, although Radcliffe-Brown was no fieldworker, he disdained the amateurs (such as E. H. Man, M. V. Portman, and R. H. Mathews) on whose work he depended in the Andamans, where he worked in Hindustani and with an interpreter (1956:249–250).

The limitations of Radcliffe-Brown's scientific inquiries are best illustrated by his notes on a manuscript that Daisy Bates, an Australian amateur ethnographer, wrote on aboriginal genealogies sometime around 1920. These show his inclination to impose order on field data. They are reproduced below along with Bates's own reply, made some thirty years later when she was in her eighties.

ARB: There are discrepancies and therefore errors.

DMB: Not errors, discrepancies, the natives' own. [ARB notes that the two genealogies she has transcribed are obviously of the same people but do not tally.]

DMB: I knew but I had to take all and each one from the natives and therefore they are the true genealogies.

ARB: If you had been collecting the genealogies with any pretence at accuracy, you would have gone over these again with the natives in the endeavour to discover the errors, understand how they came to be made and then correct them.

DMB: This is rather caddish of Brown, but he can't help that. How interesting his own pedigree would be. (Quoted in White 1981:207)

For a biography of Daisy Bates, see Salter 1971. It should be noted, perhaps, that Bates's own contribution also remains controversial (Pilling 1976; Howard 1976).

Because it raises issues of amateur and professional status, gender discrimination, class, and as in the case of Mary Kingsley, great public renown (because Bates held public office), the complexity of the discourse needs to be explored not simply as part of political anthropology's history of ideas but also of its practices. Remember that Rivers, Brown's teacher, clearly recognized the political significance of the selectivity that genealogies entail.

8. When discussing the lack of organized government in an Andaman village, Radcliffe-Brown remarked that there were really no men worthy of being called chiefs, simply "big men." His finding, he suggested, "is not quite in agreement" with that of E. H. Man, an officer in the penal settlement at Port Blair whose articles on the islanders were published at the end of the nineteenth century. Radcliffe-Brown did not explore the possibility that changes might have occurred in political organization.

9. These include Evans-Pritchard (1933) and Wilson D. Wallis (1931). That the book appears to have been little read may be attributed in part to the fact that MacLeod was described as a diffusionist. Recently Stocking, noting that MacLeod was one of the most prolific authors represented in the *American Anthropologist* between 1921 and 1945, described him as a "middle-level theorist" (1976:52). Most of MacLeod's writings were on the political economy of Native Americans. Biographical details on MacLeod are hard to come by. He was educated at the University of Pennsylvania and taught at the Wharton School of Business.

10. See Chapter 4. Mishkin (1940:5) draws on MacLeod's account of Spanish missions and nomads; Jablow (1951:25) incorporated MacLeod's contrast of the effect of the Spanish crown's interest in the American continent with those of British and French business enterprises, a contrast developed by Secoy (1953:3–4) in relation to the sale of guns beyond the moving frontier. Leacock (1954) has MacLeod's work in the bibliography of her thesis on the Naskapi but makes no

specific citation. Eric Wolf's magisterial synthesis of this corpus of ethnography in *Europe and the People Without History* (1982:127–194) contains no reference to MacLeod. As Stocking suggested, "MacLeod's institutional and intellectual marginality . . . led to his disappearance from the collective memory of the discipline" (1976:52).

11. A section of MacLeod's *The American Indian Frontier* (chap. 13, pp.152–171) is reprinted in Bohannan and Plog 1967 under the title "Celt and Briton: Britain's Oldest Frontier in Relation to the New."

12. The title of this section is deliberately anachronistic. "African models in the New Guinea highland" (Barnes 1962) were a later manifestation of the same phenomenon, the extension of a model beyond its viable limits. See, for example, Kuper 1982:72. Genealogical reckoning and manipulation appear to have been sparked by Evans-Pritchard's belief that "one of the first systematic field studies of a lineage system was my own study of the Nuer of the Anglo-Egyptian Sudan, which began in 1929. A more prolonged and detailed study was Professor Fortes' investigation of the Tallensi of the Gold Coast, begun in 1934" (1958:10).

Fortes himself offered a different version. In *Kinship and the Social Order* (1969) he constructed a tradition dating back not only to Maine but also to Morgan which was developed by Rivers and Radcliffe-Brown before Evans-Pritchard and he did their field studies. Fortes also offered a microgenealogy that linked Evans-Pritchard's Nuer study directly to Radcliffe-Brown and to the Boasians: "Evans-Pritchard states in his review of my *Dynamics of Clanship* . . . that the suggestion of how to handle the data of Nuer descent groups came from a conversation with Radcliffe-Brown in 1931. . . . I was present on this occasion. Evans-Pritchard was describing his Nuer observations, whereupon Radcliffe-Brown said, as he stood in front of the fireplace: 'My dear Evans-Pritchard, it's perfectly simple, that's a segmentary lineage system, and you'll find a very good account of it by a man called Gifford.'" (Fortes 1979:viii). One wonders whether Radcliffe-Brown considered Gifford a Boasian. But above all, the mind boggles at the former director of education for Tonga (Radcliffe-Brown) so arrogantly dismissing the contribution of the scholar he first met at Berkeley, and at the indirect way in which the scientific recognition is ultimately bestowed (with Radcliffe-Brown's back to the fireplace), as if Fortes cannot make the direct accreditation without legitimizing it through the recollections of the elders. This speaks volumes about the defensive isolation of British social anthropology.

I have chosen in this section to focus on connections and continuities among a group of Berkeley anthropologists because of the group's later significance for the anthropological study of politics, specifically the attention they paid to the environment and ecology. This needs to be complemented by a consideration of such texts as Verne F. Ray's *Cultural Relations in the Plateau of Northwestern America* (1939), one-third of which is devoted to political organization. In this work, culture traits relating to warfare, bases of chieftainship, class, and rank are mapped and clustered along continua (e.g., from strict local autonomy to tribal organization and from strict heredity to achievement). It becomes apparent that these presumed diacritica of levels of complexity do not adhere as closely as some might have expected. Ray then relates his explanations for this—couched in terms of ethnic affiliations, tribal organization, lines of demarcation, and territorial rights—to social stratification (in particular, class, rank, and slavery). He describes warfare and pacifism among Native Americans east of the Rocky Mountains against the touchstone of the cultures of the Pacific Northwest more familiar to anthropologists. Ray thus addresses "important historical problems of an inter-areal character" (1939:4) in a manner resembling past diffusionist techniques and future "controlled comparison" (Eggan 1954).

13. For a recent authoritative statement on the Miwok, see Levy 1984. Levy adopted Kroeber's "tribelets" as the ultimate units of political sovereignty, each tribelet's settlement appearing to have been the "headquarters" of a localized patrilineage. In later articles (1944, 1955) Gifford referred to the lineage of the tribelet's chief as a "royal family," suggesting his eventual Tonga-ization of the Miwok after field research in those islands.

14. Gayton could not concur with Gifford, who had argued the extreme case that lineages (of the Miwok type, with name, individual polity, and private land) underlay the political organization of *all* California tribes (1930a).

15. Forde returned to Britain from Berkeley to take up an appointment at University College, London and then to become a professor of anthropology at the University of Wales in Aberystwyth. He published the classic *Habitat, Economy and Society* in 1934. This became a primary undergraduate text in social anthropology departments, but the academy that adopted it tended to value it more as an illustration of the comparative method (with ecology replacing the genetic explanations of philologists) than as a demonstration of the relationship between environment and institutional function. Not until after his fieldwork in Wales and West Africa, further archaeological work with V. Gordon Childe, and service as a director and later president of the International African Institute was an alternative reading of the text—and, indeed, of anthropology—offered by Forde in 1970. It consisted, as Emyrys Peters put it, of "an insistence on interposing history between man and his environments" (Fortes 1976:463).

Forde's memorialists (Fortes 1976; Gluckman 1974b; Horton 1974) chose to ignore the historical dimension of his contribution to the discipline. Fortes, indeed, wrote, "The functionalism imposed on Forde—as it has been on so many other soi-disant objectors—by the discipline of field research, is, however, best shown in the Yako studies, by which, it is clear, he would most have wished to be remembered" (1976:476)

16. Useful accounts of Childe's contribution may be found in Trigger 1980, especially pp. 172–175, on evolution; pp. 175–182, on causality; pp. 96–103, on functionalism; pp. 128–130, on archaeology as a social science; and pp. 104–110, on *Man Makes Himself*. Sally Green, *Prehistorian: A Biography of V. Gordon Childe* (1981) contains a complete bibliography. Barbara McNairn's *The Method and Theory of V. Gordon Childe* (1980) is particularly valuable in the present context for its discussion of the concept of culture, historical theory, and Childe and Marxism.

17. Among the works Childe translated was Georges Davy's *From Tribe to Empire* (1926), which contained a fine critique of Durkheim by the series editor, Henri Berr.

18. An account of the incident and its repercussions appears in a chapter on academic politics in Caffrey 1989:272–274. Ruth Benedict had to defend departmental practices before the University administration and to attend the trial of the Apache accused of the murder. The Bureau of American Ethnology tightened its requirements for anthropological fieldwork.

19. For an account of Lesser's career and the political milieu in which he wrote, see Vincent 1988b.

20. Mintz 1985 discusses Lesser's acknowledgments to Childe and Maine. Vincent 1988b explores the link with Wheeler.

21. According to Mintz (1979a:30), Steward recalled in 1948 that Leslie Spier, editor of the *American Anthropologist*, rejected "Ecological Aspects" because it was "too radical." There is no definitive biography of Steward. Hanc 1981 is a master's thesis in the Department of Anthropology at the University of Chicago.

22. Steward failed to realize the contingent nature of his own observations among the Shoshoni. Robert Murphy, a student of Steward who, with his wife, later conducted field research among them, stressed the importance of the Depression in shaping the Shoshoni political organization Steward observed. He also suggested that Steward was really less interested in the environment than in "the realm of social action involved in material production, i.e. work. Quite simply, the theory of cultural ecology is concerned with the process of work. . . . And it is from the analysis of activity, rather than of institutions and values, that the theory is derived" (1981:155–156). Wolf similarly suggested (1978) that it was Steward's interest in the social action involved in material production, the labor process, that underlay the basic research strategy formulated for the study of Puerto Rico in the 1950s.

23. Even within the text, the cases brought before the village council of elders (*panchayat*) documented jajman abuse of privilege and power (Wiser 1936:96–98). Justice repeatedly escaped the client/servant. Discussions of the strengthening of the Hindu jajmani system and Brahmanical theories of law (including Maine's *Village Communities of East and West*), contemporary law reports, and newspaper accounts all led Wiser to reiterate the prevailing view that the jajmani system was entrenched in both Hindu and British law. He considered the weakening of the panchayat and the strengthening of "the powerful individual" to be a result of this (1936:111).

24. On the occasion of Charlotte Wiser's publication of *Four Families of Karimpur* (1978), Clive Dewey noted that "at three of the vital turning-points in the evolution of South Asian anthropology [the Wisers] published books which nudged their fellow workers in a new direction" (1980:391).

25. See also Kuper 1972. She returned to the theme of "The Monarchy and the Military in Swaziland" in a 1978 paper in which she noted that Swaziland is one of the few African countries that has experienced neither violence nor despotism since decolonization. She accounts for this historically.

CHAPTER 4. CLASSICAL SIMPLICITY, COMPLEXITY, AND CLASS, 1940–1953

1. Sources for this section include Grun 1975 and Kinder and Hilgemann 1978.

454 Notes to Pages 229–253

2. Non-American and younger readers may find it difficult to accept the importance of McCarthyism in creating an academic milieu in which a specifically political anthropology was unlikely to flourish. See, however, Richard Hofstadter's *Anti-Intellectualism in American Life* (1963); Earl Latham, ed., *The Meaning of McCarthyism* (1966); and Fred J. Cook *The Nightmare Decade: The Life and Times of Senator Joseph R. McCarthy* (1971). The case of Owen Lattimore is discussed in Cook 1971:209–238, 369–379. Born in China, he was in the 1950s a government advisor on U.S. relations in the Far East and in 1938 the director of the Walter Hines Page School of International Relations at Johns Hopkins University. Charged with being a Soviet spy, Lattimore's acquittal was tinged with ambiguous charges, and his career was placed at risk. Seen by some (e.g., Cook 1971:238) as a scapegoat for U.S. trauma over its "loss" of China, Lattimore's academic downfall could only serve as a warning to anthropologists in China studies and Marxists of the narrow bounds of loyal American activity.

3. The reports used in the lawsuit were published as *American Indian Ethnohistory* (Horr 1974). Summaries and evaluations appeared in *Ethnohistory* (1984).

4. Their work later became available in four volumes edited by Ralph L. Beals and Joseph A. Hester (1974).

5. The region of the Great Plains was first treated as an entity by the military writer Colonel Richard I. Dodge in *The Plains of the Great West and Their Inhabitants* (1877). Wolf's *Europe and the People Without History* (1982) draws extensively on the dissertations of his Columbia contemporaries discussed in this section.

6. Moore 1985a contains a review of the "Grand Legal Comparisons in an Evolutionary Mode" in which she discusses the contributions of Diamond (1971), Service (1975), Roberts (1979), and Newman (1983).

7. For Thomas and Znaniecki, "The situation is the set of values and attitudes with which the individual or the group has to deal in a process of activity and with regard to which this activity is planned and its results appreciated. Every concrete activity is the solution of a situation. The situation involves three kinds of data: (1) The objective conditions under which the individual or society has to act, that is, the totality of values—economic, social, religious, intellectual, etc.—which at the given moment affect directly or indirectly the conscious status of the individual or the group. (2) The pre-existing attitudes of the individual or the group which at the given moment have an actual influence upon his behavior. (3) The definition of the situation, that is, the more or less clear conception of the conditions and consciousness of the attitudes" (1927:68).

8. Barton corrected this deficiency in *The Half-Way Sun* (1930a).

9. Gluckman explains the nature of his intellectual historiography: "I have not cited Aristotle, the Leninist writers, and Max Weber in order to confess that, when we anthropologists formulate ideas as original that have in fact been advanced by earlier writers, we are lacking in scholarship. My examples indicate that political scientists and sociologists have been dealing with the same problems; and it is reassuring to find that similar theories are independently advanced to solve these problems. An anthropologist's scholarship has to be assessed in his own discipline, and he can only draw on other subjects to

tackle its problems. Indeed, though immediately it seems that these other disciplines can be helpful to us, we should be alert lest their formulations lead us away from developing our own analyses. Too much scholarship can be sterilizing" (1963:13).

10. See, for example, Fenton 1950. Lord Raglan described it as "a classified scrapbook of extracts relating to savage warfare from ethnological sources . . . purporting to be scientific" (1950:150). The book was reprinted in 1971 with a foreword by political scientist David C. Rapoport. His comment would still be valid today: "Everyone I know who has read this book [except Fenton and Raglan!] considers it a classic. The rub is that I have not met many who have read it. In 1949 academics were not interested in military questions. Anthropologists reviewed the work, and they believed it to be relevant only to those interested in primitive peoples" (1971:v).

11. According to Firth (1960:37), Radcliffe-Brown served "in person as the classical standard of authority" right up to his death in 1954.

12. The crucial word was *how*. In an important critique, Asad discussed the ambivalence of Fortes and Evans-Pritchard on the significance of the economy. On the one hand, they argued that "mere differences in modes of livelihood do not determine differences in political structure" but, on the other hand, that "In a general sense, modes of livelihood . . . determine the dominant values of people and strongly influence . . . their political systems" (1985:25).

13. In Meek's words, "this can only be regarded as the roughest of working definitions since numerous societies, which the editors would class as stateless, display some or many of the features of the so-called primitive states. A single independent village-group or canton of the Ibo of Nigeria, who would obviously be included among the 'stateless' societies, may be possessed of some form of central authority, administrative machinery, and judicial institutions, and among its members there may also be marked distinctions of rank and status, which are assumed to be characteristic of 'state' societies" (Meek 1941:42).

14. Evans-Pritchard's political anthropology took on a new cohesiveness after 1950.

15. Leach certainly remedied this in *Pul Eliya* (1968b), a magnificent analysis of village politics based on kinship and property squabbles in Sri Lanka. This ethnography truly challenged the constitutional paradigm in a way that *Political Systems of Highland Burma* did not. It also began the deconstruction of kinship, joining the path pioneered by Blackstone and Maine and later to be followed by Africanists writing on nepotism and customary law (Chapters 5 and 6).

16. In a 1977 reprint of *Political Systems of Highland Burma*, Leach distinguishes historicists from logical Marxists among his critics and observes how his own position had shifted over the years.

17. After an excellent summary of the ethnography, Cline (1942) suggested that Evans-Pritchard's findings required a more careful presentation than he had made. The material had been gathered, recorded, and published hastily; there were numerous errors and a poor index; a wilderness of detail, conjecture, and ambiguity entangled the reader throughout. The book, he wrote, quite simply needed rewriting.

18. Fortes and Evans-Pritchard 1940:17. A substantive inquiry into the African case was conducted by a student of Marvin Harris (Stevenson 1968). He attached particular importance to the Ibo case, which, as we have seen, was also disquieting to Meek.

19. Fortes wrote an unwittingly revealing obituary of Forde. He was, he noted, "outside the *circle* of 'functionalist' social anthropology associated with Malinowski at the London School of Economics. Indeed he was regarded by *those of us who came from that circle* as a human geographer with ethnological interests rather than as a social anthropologist" (1976:459, emphasis added). And again, "Forde was never, as I noted earlier on, associated with Malinowski or Radcliffe-Brown, and he never explicitly took up a 'functionalist' position. Indeed . . . he would have been regarded as belonging to *the anti-functionalist movements of the twenties and thirties*" (1976:475).

Forde provides an excellent example of the marginalized academic who became a frontiersman in political anthropology. Being neither a woman nor a colonial, Forde, a Londoner and the son of a clergyman, suffered the "disadvantage" of acquiring his education first at a grammar school and then not at Oxbridge but at University College, London. He was reputed to be an excellent teacher.

20. The account that follows is based on Brown 1973, Colson 1977a, Richards 1977, and Wilson 1977. Unlike many critiques of anthropology and colonialism, Brown's work was based on research into Colonial Office archives, newspapers and journals, correspondence, and the Zambia National Archives. Funds to support the RLI were hard to come by, and its name was adopted for fund-raising purposes at the time of the Rhodes jubilee and the Livingstone centenary.

21. Recalling the incident, Colson (1985b:193) noted the parallel between Wilson and James Mooney, who was banned from the Oklahoma reservations after he had testified on behalf of Native Americans practicing the peyote cult.

22. Barnes has been described as "Britain's most formidable critic of Empire in the 1930s" (McAdam 1977:43). His book *Soviet Light on the Colonies* (1944) contrasted Soviet policy toward its non-Russian populations in central Asia with British colonialism in central Africa. Rich (1986) placed Barnes among a developing left-wing cohort, among whom the best known were Sydney Olivier and Norman Leys.

23. E. Munday (provincial commissioner, Eastern Province) wrote: "Research workers should not be allowed to discuss political questions or criticize Government without working in close collaboration with a District Officer. . . . Amateur enthusiasts come out, full of strange ideas, which they disseminate without fear of consequences, and Government has to clear up the mess, possibly with the help of arms, a weapon which the anthropologist is so adverse to. He is, by nature of his training, devoid of civic responsibility and a pacifist. He is quite irresponsible and is not interested in the outcome of his propaganda, except as a scientist and explorer. His mind is generally academic. I can say this with knowledge as my mother's first cousin, Professor H. M. Chadwick, is a foremost anthropologist at Cambridge University and a member of the college at which I spent 3 years, and from my close connection with Dr. Richards. Both are quite irresponsible as to the results of their actions and both can talk in a

language quite unintelligible to the ordinary human" (quoted in Brown 1979:534).

24. Howard Becker's "Ionia and Athens: Studies in Secularization," an unpublished Chicago doctoral dissertation, greatly influenced Redfield. Becker's perception of the folk society fed even more directly into views of immigrant ethnic groups in American cities. Murdock noted that "the reader is irresistibly reminded of Herbert Spencer's all-embracing theory of evolution from undifferentiated homogeneity to differentiated heterogeneity. In theories of this order the present reviewer sees little nourishment" (1943:136). He forecast that *The Folk Culture of Yucatan* would be better remembered for its ethnography than for its theory.

25. Redfield's work was provocative. He stimulated "some very hard thinking about matters with which social science has not really come to grips," wrote Steward. "Even to disagree with Redfield is to be very much in his debt" (1956:565). "I learned much from Robert Redfield," Mintz was later to write. "One reason he was so instructive . . . was because he was so dead wrong, and he was so eloquent in his wrongness that I always found his books immensely stimulating" (1981:165). Both would have agreed with Weber, who said there was more to learn from a major author who was wrong than from a nonentity who was right (Runciman 1972).

26. Lewis discussed theory and method at some length in his important book *Anthropological Essays* (1970). A study of art, science, and politics in the work of Oscar Lewis by political scientist Susan M. Rigdon appeared in 1988. It draws on all Lewis's field materials and professional correspondence. Because of the importance of Lewis's critique of Redfield's Tepoztlán work, Stocking has now published Redfield's side of the correspondence (1989).

27. The units selected for area-study programs, Steward noted, "are determined by a number of considerations which may have little to do with scientific theory; the importance of the area in world affairs, the institution's facilities, availability of funds, and others" (1950:8–9).

28. Ironically, today many anthropologists have tended, for various reasons, to disassociate themselves from multidisciplinary area institutes.

29. The outcome of these changes was revealed most strikingly in social historian William B. Taylor's "Between Global Process and Local Knowledge: An Inquiry into Early Latin American Social History, 1500–1900" (1985).

30. Steward referred to Lattimore 1949.

31. Silverman's view of Steward's role in the Puerto Rico project is based on unpublished correspondence between participants, materials provided by Mintz and Wolf, drafts of theoretical statements, and notes on team meetings (Silverman 1981:66n10).

32. The idea of levels of sociocultural integration was borrowed from the biologist Alex Novikoff, who had himself taken it from Joseph Needham. Wolf noted that "Needham, in 1936, had written an essay on 'Integrative Levels' which rephrased in Marxian terms what had until then been an idealist or vitalist concept, associated with such names as Henri Bergson, Hans Driesch, and A. Whitehead" (1978:21).

33. Roseberry noted the use of Marxist language such as *labor power*, the

invasion of capital, substructure, and *superstructure* but observed that the cultural historical method was itself non-Marxist. "Nowhere does capitalism enter into the analysis as an independent or dependent variable other than by euphemistic reference to 'external influences'" (Roseberry 1978:33).

34. The ethnographic community studies reviewed by Steward included Lynd and Lynd 1929; Parsons 1936; Redfield 1941; West 1945; and Yang 1945. The social relations studies were those of Powdermaker 1939; Davis, Gardner, and Gardner 1941; Warner and Lunt 1941; Drake and Clayton 1945; and Dollard 1937.

35. Embree's study was welcomed in Australia as a sign that social anthropology was growing up. "For decades," A. P. Elkin wrote, "it paid attention almost solely to primitive illiterate peoples. But now it is more sure of its methods and so is studying communities of a higher type" (1949:18). Australian anthropology remained ambivalent, however, in its application of British and American traditions. To this day, American anthropology is much more widely read in Australia than in Britain.

36. This judgment was forcefully reiterated by Robert Nisbet in discussing "The Rise and Fall of Social Class." He criticized community studies for their nonhistorical and noncontextual character. "At its extreme," he wrote, "especially in some of the works of W. Lloyd Warner and his students, the class perspective has the attributes of a Never Never land: observations carefully sterilized of historical considerations, constructed of self-fulfilling interviews and premises, skilfully extrapolated through use of linear scales and multiple correlations; the whole possessing a certain internal consistency, even credibility, but, on overview, possessing about as much relation to national American society as James Branch Cabell's enchanted land of Poictesme does to Times Square" (1968:111).

37. Within political anthropology, the textbook produced by the interactionists Eliot Chapple and Carleton Coon, *Principles of Anthropology* (1940), contained a long chapter on political institutions that has never received mainstream recognition.

38. The effect of Whyte's liberal politics on his analysis of the Italian slum was critically reviewed by Washington (1978).

CHAPTER 5. ROMANTICISM, BOOM, AND BUST, 1954–1973

1. This section is largely derived from Grun 1975 and Kinder and Hilgemann 1978. For the intellectual context of the American science of politics, see Crick 1959.

2. Gough was a Cambridge-trained anthropologist who carried out field research in Kerala, India, in 1947 under the auspices of Fortes, Evans-Pritchard, and Gluckman. Her *Rural Society in Southeast India* (1981) was prefaced by an account of her later work in Tamil Nadu state. She tells how both Leslie White and David Aberle (her husband) introduced her to American anthropology. Since 1957 she has been increasingly influenced by Marxism. "New Proposals for Anthropologists" appeared first in the *Economic and Political Weekly* of Bombay in September 1967 and was then reprinted in the *Monthly Review* in April 1968 and *Current Anthropology* in December 1968. Given events in the United States and Europe, its appearance was timely. In November 1976 Gough

visited Hanoi as a guest of the Women's Union of Vietnam. She published *Ten Times More Beautiful: The Rebuilding of Vietnam* in 1978.

3. *Directory of the American Anthropological Association*, 1969; *Directory of the Association of Social Anthropologists*, 1969.

4. Hoffman (1973) associates the elaboration of general systems theory in political science with the Cold War, noting the role played in its propagation by the Carnegie and Ford foundations. He considers Easton's "theoretical universality . . . nothing more or less than practical mystification" (1973:257). Easton's contemporary critics included Leonard Binder, C. Wright Mills, Leo Strauss, and Barrington Moore, Jr. Within political science, systems thinking gave way to behavioralism (Eulau 1963) even as in anthropology it was supplanted by action theory. It may not be a coincidence that criticism of Easton within British political science emerged from the two universities at the cutting edge of action theory—the universities of Manchester and Sussex (where Bailey taught). A most useful discussion appears in W.J.M. Mackenzie's *Politics and Social Science* (1967). In the preface, the author acknowledges his debt to "Manchester" discussions, mentioning in particular Dorothy Emmet, Ely Devons, and Max Gluckman.

5. General systems theory penetrated the discipline most successfully in the analysis of ecosystems. I have reviewed this trend (Vincent 1986b) from Geertz's pioneering *Agricultural Involution: The Process of Ecological Change in Indonesia* (1963a) to Andrew P. Vayda's "Holism and Individualism in Ecological Anthropology" (1986).

6. A. F. Bentley's *The Process of Government: A Study of Social Pressures* (1908) was reprinted in 1967 with an introduction by Peter H. Odegard. Political anthropologists were not all in favor of using what Easton called "a constructive system" as an analytical device. Some argued that if "the political" is not distinguished by the natives, it cannot and should not be distinguished by the anthropologist.

7. Kuper points out the analytical inadequacy of separating kinship and politics but fails to define "the political." His system is not a black box. It includes the structure of the system and the manipulation of that structure in a given situation. He conveys a sense of constant flux.

8. Colson was also an intellectual granddaughter of Marett, having been educated at the University of Minnesota by Wilson D. Wallis, a Rhodes scholar at Oxford, where he studied under Marett.

9. Thus Aristide Zolberg suggested six "fresh avenues for exploration" to political scientists: the colonial situation, law, the study of ideology, grass-roots politics, the relationship between tradition and modernity, and comparative studies (1966:151). Vincent 1969 suggested that these sounded like well-trodden ground to the anthropologist.

10. Some saw the problem as one of incorporation (Lienhardt 1964; Cohen and Middleton 1967) and simply took on the definition of the problem as experienced by the colonial administration on the eve of independence. Since colonial administrators usually tried to make local government congruent with indigenous political boundaries, anthropology's continuing role in the study of contemporary politics was assured. Thus Fallers suggested: "A primary task for political anthropology in the future is the detailed study of the ways in which the old

societies, which must now be conceptualized as local ethnic units within the new national societies, relate to these new political institutions. Broadly speaking, it would appear that the traditional polities which in the colonial period were made to function . . . as primarily 'administrative units', in the period of independence, are coming to function primarily as 'political units'" (1963b:329). Hence the focus on "tribalism" and "retribalism" in the years that followed, deflecting attention from palace politics in the corridors of power, with their accompanying military coups d'etat and reshufflings of office within the national elite.

11. A further reevaluation of Nuer ethnography is now needed. The historian Douglas Hamilton Johnson, in a two-volume doctoral dissertation (1980) based on previously unused documentary sources, existing ethnography, and oral history, notes that the "innumerable attempts to reassess or revise Evans-Pritchard's innovative and monumental studies of the Nuer" have paid insufficient attention to the accuracy of sources and historical context. Johnson does not consider it his task to provide the necessary critique but suggests that "anthropologists more familiar with the place of Evans-Pritchard's work in the field of anthropology" may wish to push the theoretical implications of his findings further (1980:Pt. 1:11). Certainly this seems a more substantive way ahead for political anthropologists than analyses of Evans-Pritchard's writing style or of his ethnography as text (Geertz 1983, 1988; Marcus and Fischer 1986). Again, the distinction may be noted between those who address problems in the political condition of the peoples studied and those who address problems within the academic discipline of anthropology. This issue is reviewed and discussed further in Chapter 6.

12. The relation between ecological analyses and process theory is discussed in Vincent 1986b.

13. Keesing's grammarlike *rules* were sought as *regularities* by most political anthropologists.

14. Nadel died in Australia in 1956 at the age of fifty-three. He was senior lecturer at LSE in 1946 and in 1948 moved to head the newly created department at Durham. In 1950 he took up the newly established chair of anthropology and sociology at the Australian National University. Freeman 1956 provides a perceptive note on his contribution to processual theory. Firth described Nadel as an "intellectual free-lance" (1960:38), but his work must also be recognized as part of a growing trend in Britain in the 1950s toward reexamining the assumptions and methodologies of the field. Salat 1983 provides a valuable discussion of Nadel's familiarity with Weber's writings, which for him, unlike several of the Americans, was "unfiltered" through Talcott Parsons. He was using the German texts in Libya in the 1940s. Nadel "placed Weber's action theory at the base of all practical and theoretical reflections" (Salat 1983:102).

15. The first phase (1937–1942), remember, developed around the Rhodes-Livingstone Institute in central Africa; the second (1942–1954) at Manchester University; and the third (1954–1975) after Gluckman's retirement from the Manchester chair, in connection with research in Israel. For general discussions of the Manchester School, see Firth 1975a, 1975b; Werbner 1984; and van Binsbergen 1981. The importance of the Manchester department (like that of Oxford) derived in part from its virtual concentration on postgraduate training.

Firth also attached significance to Gluckman's multidisciplinary seminar (1975a).

16. Gluckman was born in 1911. The first generation of his student-colleagues were born between 1918 (Barnes and Mitchell) and 1929 (Frankenberg). Members of a second generation, which included G. K. Garbett, N. E. Long, E. E. Marx, S. Deshen, P. L. Sansom, M. Shokeid, J. Uberoi, R. P. Werbner, J. M. Pettigrew, and M. J. Aronoff, were born between 1934 and 1940.

17. Compare, for example, Radcliffe-Brown: "Science as distinct from history or biography is not concerned with the particular, the unique but only with the general, with kinds, with events which recur. The actual relation of Tom, Dick and Harry, or the behaviour of Jack and Jill may go down in our field notebooks and may provide the illustrations for general description. But what we need for scientific purposes is an account of the form of the structure" (1952:192).

18. Geertz suggested that anthropology "confuses locus of study [the community] with object of study. You can study different things in different places and some things you can study only in confined localities, but that doesn't mean you are studying the place itself" (1972:461–462). And elsewhere: "The bulk of what I have eventually seen (or thought I have seen) in the broad sweep of social history I have seen (or thought I have seen) first in the narrow confines of county towns and peasant villages" (1968:x).

Bailey observed: "At one level we will be discussing specific communities (even specific people in them) at a specific period. But to do this and nothing else is to fail. We want to raise questions (and answer some of them) which far transcend villages in Europe in the middle of the twentieth century, because they are questions which can be asked about change and development in many parts of the world, at all periods in history, and about human assemblages of other kinds besides the peasant village" (1971:27).

19. This section draws on Vincent 1978, developing some of its ideas. I now try to develop more clearly a distinction between action theory and process theory, particularly after perceiving the applications of the two terms in ecological anthropology (Vincent 1986b).

20. Or, indeed, any dialectic. For a discussion, see Robert Murphy's "On Zen Marxism" (1963) and his explicit critique of Leach's *A Runaway World* (1968c) in *The Dialectics of Social Life* (1971).

21. Here I again follow the practice introduced in Chapter 1 of stringing together sentences taken in seriatim from the text (Bailey 1969:1–11) with my own glosses in parentheses. The book is tightly argued and contains illustrative ethnography from several apparently very different political settings.

22. I attempt to begin to come to grips with the processual paradigm in "System and Process" (1986b), drawing particularly on insights offered by R. J. Bernstein, *The Restructuring of Social and Political Theory* (1978), and Virginia Hunter's *Past and Process in Herodotus and Thucydides* (1982). The ethnography of Johannes Fabian (1979, 1980) takes on some of the issues that Turner raised in his last publications.

23. The subtitle of this section is a paraphrase of *Process and Form in Social Life*, the title of volume 1 of Barth's collected essays (1981a, 1981b) suggesting how he himself would like his contribution to theory to be viewed. Note the

sequence of the terms: *process* generates *form*. Euphony suggests *form* and *process* but Barth emphasizes agency.

24. Barth was trained at LSE but followed his mentor, E. R. Leach, when the latter left for a post at Cambridge. In "Models Reconsidered" (1981a) and "Swat Pathans Reconsidered" (1981b), Barth expresses intellectual indebtedness to Bateson, Kroeber, Leach, Mayer, and Nadel.

25. Jarvie reviewed the methodological individualism debate. As a student of Karl Popper at LSE, he began the story in the 1950s. "The task of social theory," wrote Popper, "is to construct and analyse our sociological models carefully in descriptive or nominalist terms, that is to say, in terms of individuals, of their attitudes, expectations, relations, etc.—a postulate which may be called 'methodological individualism'" (1945/1962, 2:91). Jarvie made no reference to Sartre's similar individual, actor-oriented phenomenological and existential approach in *Being and Nothingness* (1943). Sartre then moved toward a philosophical position that placed the individual in relation to the social group, polity, and history while identifying increasingly with Marxism. He criticized both philosophy and the social sciences for nonprocessual thinking and functional interpretation. He also used a "social field" concept (Sartre 1963:76). I owe this comment to Diane Ciecawy.
A most valuable contribution to the debate within political anthropology appeared in 1973. This took the form of J. I. Prattis's "Strategising Man," which adopted a distinction between satisficing and maximizing behavior. Prattis suggested that satisficing and maximizing "can be considered as rational solutions to human choice problems, if we examine rationality in terms of strategising, and not in terms of exclusive maximising, sacrificing, or in unique patterns of reciprocity and redistribution" (1973:46). I am grateful to Estellie Smith for bringing Prattis's article to my attention.

26. Particularly at this time Sylvia Thrupp, Keith Thomas, and Eric Hobsbawm.

27. While Gough and Asad may be recognized as the leading voices in opposition to a restrictive anthropology, many "subterranean" critics of the discipline's analysis of colonialism may also be discerned. Australian scholars were among the first to focus attention on the colonial encounter and on decolonization. Charles W. M. Hart provides an early example. A student under Radcliffe-Brown at Sydney in 1925, at Chicago with Redfield, and at LSE with Malinowski in the 1930s, Hart became a professor at Wisconsin in 1947. His "Colonial Peoples In Transition" (1953) was based on a Wisconsin course, Contemporary Trends in Modern Civilization. Hart questioned the American faith that independence would solve the problems of colonial territories. "As the old style colonial governors move out," he wrote, "the commisars from Moscow and the promoters from New York move in" (1953:207). Hart drew his data from North Korea, Indonesia, and Latin America.

28. The phrase "the judicial process" has to be associated in the mind of any anthropologist with Max Gluckman, but his actual usage was rather narrow: "a process of reasoning" by judges in which they "applied" concepts to cases (1955b:218).

29. Epstein 1958; Moore 1978b; Frankenberg 1982; Werbner 1984. Few of Gluckman's RLI and Manchester colleagues, apart from A. L. Epstein, shared

his interest in law. Closest in empathy to Gluckman's scholarship was, perhaps, Sally Falk Moore, a lawyer by training as well as an anthropologist who appreciated more than most the intellectual heritage on which Gluckman drew (Moore 1969, 1978b). Her commentaries on Gluckman's work were therefore particularly valuable in defining and redefining the field as the period drew to a close.

30. For critiques along these lines and reevaluations of Barotse law, see Moore 1978b and Frankenberg 1979.

31. Gluckman drew heavily on Moore's arguments in his Radcliffe-Brown lecture in social anthropology delivered at the British Academy in June 1974. In this lecture he reiterated his interest in the principles of law shared by all legal systems and went on to suggest similarities between contemporary aspects of certain bodies of African law (contract and treason law, for example) and early European law. He demonstrated, as always, the importance he attached to anthropologists reading the work of jurisprudes and legal historians. Finally, in reevaluating the feud, he entered into the debate between structuralists, whose primary emphasis was on corporate groups and levels (Kuper and Smith), and processualists, who operated with the concept of social fields (Moore and Peters), and true to the Mancunian tradition he did so much to create, he came down on the side of the processualists.

32. The subtitle of this section, "Process and Decision," reflects Gulliver's chapter in *Cross-Examinations: Essays in Memory of Max Gluckman* (1978), and I infer a preference in this later work for association with process theory rather than action theory as I have distinguished them here.

33. Moore is much more sanguine than Smith about comparative studies (1969).

34. Gluckman (1955c) provided a lengthy review of *The Law of Primitive Man: A Study in Comparative Legal Dynamics* (Hoebel 1954) for *Man* that was almost wholly unfavorable, largely because of Hoebel's gutting of ethnography. This was true not only of the Ashanti and Trobrianders, whom Gluckman discussed, but of the Ifugao as well. Gluckman observed: "At the time when Malinowski wrote, books written by modern professional anthropologists were few and we had time and eagerness to read and enjoy the riches of ethnographical and factual detail. Publishing costs were lower and detail could be reproduced. As monographs have multiplied and publishing costs have risen, the emphasis has changed to the shorter book stating only general principles. I believe this tendency may rob anthropology of its strength. Hoebel shows that in time it may well render particular studies useless. For Malinowski himself provided the material (though in other books) by which we can assess the validity of his theory; and it is material which, as here, can be used by others to develop alternative theories" (1955c:94). Hoebel, he pointed out, used ethnographic materials selectively to advance his own analysis of law.

35. With independence in the offing, colonial governments began to undertake the codification of native "customary" law in Africa in the 1950s. In 1964 William Twining reviewed anthropological studies of customary law, the ambiguous nature of which was fully appreciated by Maine. As Maine had observed, the recording and codification of customs "at once altered their character. They are generally collected from the testimony of village elders; but when

these elders are once called upon to give their evidence, they necessarily lose their position. . . . That which they have affirmed to be custom is henceforward to be sought from the decision of the Courts of Justice, or from official documents which those courts received as evidence. Usage, once recorded upon evidence given, immediately becomes written and fixed law" (1861:72).

36. Francis Snyder (1981b) has remarked on the strong links between legal anthropology and elite universities—Yale, Berkeley, Harvard, Columbia, and Wisconsin—in the United States.

37. Gulliver notes references to Gluckman's work in Julius Stone, *Social Dimensions of Law and Justice* (1966), H.L.A. Hart, *The Concept of Law* (1961), and Denis Lloyd, *Introduction to Jurisprudence* (1959). The third edition (1972) of the Lloyd work, "much read in North America" (Gulliver 1978:xvi), has a chapter on "Historical and Anthropological Jurisprudence." I am indebted to Philip Gulliver for the specifics in the institutionalization of the subfield in the account that follows.

38. Anthropologists were also obliged to put their expertise at the service of those other disciplines. In 1957 the Committee on International Anthropology (established within the National Research Council and funded by the Carnegie Corporation) began to issue a series of field guides to familiarize American researchers with the problems they might encounter in the field. Five "significant areas" were chosen: Oceania, western and central Africa, Japan, India, and Brazil.

CHAPTER 6. CRISIS AND CONSOLIDATION, 1974 TO THE PRESENT

1. Between 1974 and 1987 the number of departments listed in the AAA guide increased from 270 to 377. These now included not simply Canadian but several British and Australian departments as well. Museums continued to account for around 60 professional anthropologists, but by 1987, 37 were to be found in research organizations, compared to 4 in 1976. Ten served the federal government. The number of individual anthropologists rose from 3,342 to 4,795 between 1974 and 1987. Meanwhile undergraduate enrollment fell from 21,402 in 1974 to 14,306 in 1987. Graduate enrollment increased from 6,580 in 1974 to 7,086 in 1987. These figures were extrapolated by Anastasia Karakasidou in connection with her critical study of symbolic anthropology. I am grateful to her for permission to use them here.

Scholte distinguished the crisis *in* anthropology from the crisis *of* anthropology. The former "reifies the *texts* of ethno-*logical* systems at the expense of understanding the *contexts* of *ethno*-logical activities" (Scholte 1984:425). Scholte in this cleverly balanced sentence chose not to emphasize *systems* and *activities*.

2. Scholte (1981) noted the religious tone of several of the reviews of *Reinventing Anthropology* and discussed the language Leach used in the *New York Review of Books* under the head "Anthropology Upside Down" (1974). Gluckman's review in the same journal a few issues later was called "Report from the Field" and referred to Scholte and his "fellow believers" in New York, who "work in a welter of anachronistic emotion, without intellect or scholarship" (1974a:44). Similarly, Jarvie in a critique of Johannes Fabian and his "rad-

ical cohorts Diamond, Hymes, Scholte, Wolf et al.," alerted his readers to the danger of a "phenomenological putsch" (1975:261).

3. The decline of community can clearly be seen from the *Annual Review of Anthropology*. Reviews of community studies in Mesoamerica, the Middle East, and Europe appeared between 1977 and 1979. Thereafter reviewers reported on regions—South Africa (1980), the Mediterranean (1982), Eastern Europe (1983), south central Africa (1984), the Andean region (1984), western Africa (1985), Southeast Asia (1986), and Central America (1987). These were accompanied by periodic reviews by indigenous anthropologists of their national anthropologies.

4. My use of the term counter-Marxist rather than non-Marxist is deliberate. Marxist contributions became more numerous after 1978 (O'Laughlin's 1975 essay marking, perhaps, the end of an era of "respectable" academic Marxism in the United States), and counter-Marxist statements flourished after 1984, a resonant year for the literary-inclined.

5. One can only continue to be struck, however, by how little Marxist anthropology enters into mainstream Marxism. Thus, for example, no anthropologists were represented in the publication *Marxism and the Interpretation of Culture* (Nelson and Grossberg 1988) in spite of the obvious affinities suggested by its title.

6. The *Annual Review of Anthropology* covered the following mix of old and new topics: state formation in Africa (Southall 1974), legal processes (Collier 1975), social stratification (Cancian 1976), the origin of the state (Wright 1977), ethnicity (Ronald Cohen 1978), manipulative strategies (Vincent 1978), political symbolism (Abner Cohen 1979), the world capitalist system (Nash 1981), contemporary hunter-gatherers (Barnard 1983), political language (Parkin 1984), divine kingship (Feeley-Harnik 1985), peasant ideologies in the Third World (Kahn 1985), and chiefdoms in archaeological and ethnohistorical perspective (Earle 1987).

7. The work of Norman Long is particularly interesting in this respect. A Manchester-trained anthropologist, he carried out his first field research in Africa, adopting action theory and a social fields approach. Research in Peru (Long 1975) encouraged him to bridge these ideas and world-systems thinking with political brokers. Long's work is also significant in that it marked a growing trend for British anthropologists and historians to work in Latin America, hitherto the preserve of scholars from the United States. Cosmopolitical paradigms were thus carried to class-conscious British anthropology—albeit uneuo cessfully by political ethnography.

8. Anthropological use of archival records varies considerably, of course. There is a clear difference between the ethnohistorians and political ethnographers of Latin America working with Spanish colonial records and those working in much of the rest of the Third World, where reliable archival records go back only to the nineteenth century.

9. These included articles by Friedman (1978), Gough (1978a), Magubane (1979), Mintz (1978b), Price (1985), and Trouillot (1982) that appeared in Wallerstein's own journal, *Review*. As a fellow sociologist once at Columbia University, Wallerstein had clearly taken to heart Mullins's words on the institutional-

ization of theory. Having moved after the events of 1968 to the State University of New York at Binghamton, Wallerstein established there both the Braudel Center for international scholarship in world-systems and its journal, *Review.*

10. Those most frequently identified and read by political anthropologists were Meillassoux, Godelier, Rey, and Terray. Seddon (1978) and Kahn and Llobera (1981) have elaborated on the school. For a discussion of their contribution as a "breakthrough in anthropological theory" that itself inspired the formation of a critical Dutch school, see Van Binsbergen and Geschiere (1985). The Dutch Africanists noted that it was the Manchester School's emphasis on social process and extended case analysis as well as the transactional theories of Bailey, Barth, and Boissevain that led them to the relevance of Marxist insights (Van Binsbergen 1977; Geschiere 1978; Van Binsbergen and Geschiere 1985). Their problem, as they saw it, was to relate micropolitical analyses with issues of state formation, colonization, and decolonization.

11. I owe the crystallization of this concept to Ashraf Ghani, who organized a panel on the subject at the AAA annual meeting in Chicago in 1987. The alliterative phrase has, of course, appeared in several publications but without any cross-referencing among its users.

12. Sir Keith Joseph, *Reversing the Trend* (quoted in Corrigan 1980:xvii). The full quotation from Sir Keith reads: "Unlike some countries in Europe and the New World, e.g. Holland and the U.S., Britain never had a capitalist ruling class or a stable *haute bourgeoisie.* As a result, capitalist or bourgeois values have never shaped thought and institutions as they have in some countries. . . . Britain never really internalized capitalist values, if the truth be known. For four centuries, since wealthy commercial classes with political standing began to be thrown up following the supercession of feudalism and the selling off of monastic property, the rich man's aim was to get away from the background of trade—later industry—in which he had made his wealth and power. Rich and powerful people founded landed-gentry families; the capitalist's son was educated not in capitalist values but against them, in favour of the older values of army, church, upper civil service, professions and landowning. This avoided the class struggles between middle and upper strata familiar from European history—but at what cost?" (Joseph 1976:60–61). Gertrude Himmelfarb's book *The New History and the Old* had just been published when William Safire wrote of his encounter with her on the PanAm shuttle (*New York Times Magazine,* February 21, 1988, p.16).

13. "History from below" was, of course, not a new coinage but one that was emblazoned on the banner of the "new" social history in the 1970s. I am drawing here on ideas expressed earlier in a local conference (Vincent 1973) and an international congress (Vincent 1983).

14. Ethnicity has not proved to be a viable concept in the analysis of politics, although it is still used categorically and descriptively. We can now delineate its short life span and note a return to the use of such terms as *minorities* or *migrants* in its place. In the early 1970s political anthropologists saw ethnicity as essentially a political phenomenon (Cohen 1978) to be studied in terms of individual strategies (Charsley 1974; Deshen 1974; Grillo 1974). Following the paradigms of Leo Despres (1975) and Abner Cohen (1974b), scholars investigated ethnicity mainly as a social and political phenomenon sui generis.

The emergence and popularity of the concept has been related to a backlash in U.S. politics following the achievements of the civil rights movement and African-American political advancement in the 1960s. Since 1980 it appears to have proved a less than useful concept for either a political anthropology "of the whole" or political anthropology "from below." In my own work I have moved from ethnicity as essentially "a mask of confrontation" in certain situations (1971) to the structuring of ethnicity (1974) and the relation of emergent ethnicity to political expansion (1989a). The widespread and penetrating adoption of the terms *ethnic* and *ethnicity* by journalists and laymen has defeated academic efforts to give them concrete and specific meaning. This in itself merits political analysis. Meanwhile, the analysis of inequalities, asymmetrical relations, and subaltern groups has proceeded quite happily without the ethnic vocabulary.

15. For the development of this interest in legal anthropology and semantic anthropology, see Comaroff and Roberts 1981, Parkin 1984, and Werbner 1984. The idea of society as discourse may, for our purposes, most directly be traced to Dan Sperber, *Man Made Language* (1980), William M. O'Barr, *Linguistic Evidence: Language, Power and Strategy in the Courtroom* (1982), and G. Therborn, *The Ideology of Power and the Power of Ideology* (1980). For a current statement, see Parkin 1984.

16. A review of Marxist perspectives in the sociology of law appeared in the *Annual Review of Sociology* (Spitzer 1983) and was listed among articles of interest in other annual reviews by the editors of volume 12 of the *Annual Review of Anthropology* that year. The work of Fitzpatrick alone represents anthropology. The structuralist trinity is composed of Althusser, Balibar, and Poulantzas, with Poulantzas moving away from the others to observe: "Law does not only deceive and conceal . . . nor does it merely repress people by compelling or forbidding them to act. . . . It also organizes and sanctions certain *real rights* of the dominated classes" (1982:190), a position followed, across the boundary, by Thompson.

17. See Levinson, Butler, McGann, and Hamilton 1989. In this book, Marjorie Levinson calls her chapter "The New Historicism: Back to the Future"; Marilyn Butler calls hers "Repossessing the Past: the Case for an Open Literary History"; and Jerome McGann calls his "The Third World of Criticism."

References

ABBREVIATIONS

AA	*American Anthropologist*
AE	*American Ethnologist*
AMNH	American Museum of Natural History
AQ	*Anthropological Quarterly*
ARA	*Annual Review of Anthropology*
ASA	Association of Social Anthropologists
BAAS	British Association for the Advancement of Science
Bijdragen	*Bijdragen Tot de Taal, -Land, -en Volkekunde*
BJS	*British Journal of Sociology*
CA	*Current Anthropology*
CRSA	*Canadian Review of Sociology and Anthropology*
CSSH	*Comparative Studies in Society and History*
DA	*Dialectical Anthropology*
EJS	*European Journal of Sociology*
Hist. Sci.	*History of Science*
IESS	*International Encyclopedia of the Social Sciences*
JPS	*Journal of Peasant Studies*
JRAI	*Journal of the Royal Anthropological Society*
LSR	*Law and Society Review*
NLR	*New Left Review*
RLJ	*Rhodes-Livingstone Journal*
SWJA	*Southwestern Journal of Anthropology*
UCPAAE	*University of California Publications in American Archaeology and Ethnology*

Abel, Richard

1973　A comparative theory of dispute institutions in society. *LSR* 8:217–347.

1979　Western courts in non-Western settings: Patterns of court use in colonial and neo-colonial Africa. In *The Imposition of Law*, edited by Sandra B. Burman and Barbara E. Harrell-Bond. New York: Academic Press.

1981　Conservative conflict and the reproduction of capitalism: The role of informal justice. *International Journal of the Sociology of Law* 9:245–267.

Abrams, Philip
    1968   *The origins of British sociology, 1834–1914: An essay with selected papers.* Chicago: University of Chicago Press.

Adams, John W.
    1973   *The Gitskan potlatch: Population flux, resource ownership and reciprocity.* Toronto: Holt, Rinehart and Winston.
    1981   Recent ethnology of the Northwest Coast. *ARA* 10:361–392.

Adams, Richard N.
    1956   Cultural components of Central America. *AA* 58:881–907.
    1970   *Crucifixion by power: Essays on Guatemalan national structure, 1944–1966.* Austin: University of Texas Press.

Adams, Robert McCormack
    1977   World picture, anthropological frame. *AA* 79:265–279.

Ajisaje, Ajawik
    1924   *Laws and customs of the Yoruba people; With a portrait of the author.* London: Routledge.

Allott, Antony N.
    1966   The codification of the law of civil wrongs in common law African countries. *Sociologus* 16:101–122.

Alter, J. Cecil
    1932   *Utah, the storied domain: A documentary history of Utah's eventful career, comprising the thrilling story of her people from the Indians of yesterday to the individualists of today.* New York: American Historical Society.

Althusser, Louis
    1969   *For Marx.* London: Verso.

Altschuler, Milton
    1967   Review of *The social organization of ethnological theory*, by Leslie White. *AA* 65:112.

Amin, Samir
    1974   *Accumulation on a world scale: A critique of the theory of underdevelopment.* New York: Monthly Review Press.
    1976   *Unequal development: An essay on the social formation of peripheral capitalism.* New York: Monthly Review Press.
    1977   Comment. *Insurgent Sociologist* 7:99–103.
    1978   *The Arab nation.* London: Zed Press.

Anderson, Elin L.
    1937   *We Americans: A study of cleavage in an American city.* New York: Russell and Russell.

Anderson, Perry
    1968   Components of the national culture. *NLR* 62:1–57.

Andrzejewski, Stanislaus
    1954a   Review of *Changing military patterns on the Great Plains*, by Frank Secoy. *Man* 48:173.
    1954b   *Military organization and society.* London: Routledge and Kegan Paul.

Appadurai, Arjun
    1988a   Introduction: Place and voice in anthropological theory. *Cultural Anthropology* 3:16–20.
    1988b   Putting hierarchy in its place. *Cultural Anthropology* 3:36–49.
Apthorpe, Raymond
    1970   Some problems of evaluation. In *Co-operatives and rural development in East Africa*, edited by Carl Gosta Widstrand. New York: Africana.
Ardener, Edwin
    1971   The new anthropology and its critics. *Man* 6:449–468.
Ardener, Edwin, and Shirley Ardener
    1965   A directory study of social anthropologists. *BJS* 16:295–314.
Arensberg, Conrad M.
    1972   Culture as behavior: Structure and emergence. *ARA* 1:1–26.
Armstrong, William H.
    1978   *Warrior in two camps: Ely S. Parker, Union general and Seneca chief.* Syracuse, N.Y.: Syracuse University Press.
Asad, Talal
    1972a   Market model, class structure and consent: A reconsideration of Swat political organization. *Man* 7:74–94.
    1973b   Two European images of non-European rule. *Economy and Society* 2:263–277.
    1979   Anthropology and the analysis of ideology. *Man* 14:607–627.
    1985   Primitive states and the reproduction of productive relations: Some problems in Marxist anthropology. *Critique of Anthropology* 25:21–33.
Asad, Talal, ed.
    1973a   *Anthropology and the colonial encounter.* London: Ithaca Press.
Babcock, Barbara A., and Nancy J. Parezo
    1988   *Daughters of the desert: Women anthropologists and the Native American Southwest, 1880–1980, An illustrated catalogue.* Albuquerque: University of New Mexico Press.
Bacon, Elizabeth
    1941   Review of *Social and economic organization of the Rowanduz Kurds*, by E. R. Leach. *AA* 43:288–290.
Baden-Powell, Baden Henry
    1892   *The land-systems of British India.* 3 vols. Oxford: Clarendon Press.
Bailey, Frederick G.
    1951   Review of *The Cheyenne in Plains Indian trade relations, 1795–1840*, by Joseph Jablow. *AA* 53:172–173.
    1957   *Caste and the economic frontier: A village in highland Orissa.* Manchester: Manchester University Press.
    1960   *Tribe, caste and nation: A study of political activity and political change in highland Orissa.* Manchester: Manchester University Press.
    1963   *Politics and social change: Orissa in 1959.* Berkeley: University of California Press.

1964   Two villages in Orissa (India). In *Closed systems and open minds: The limits of naivety in social anthropology*, edited by Max Gluckman and Ely Devons. Edinburgh: Oliver and Boyd.

1966   Anthropology. In *A guide to the social sciences*, edited by Norman Mackenzie. London: Weidenfeld and Nicolson.

1968   Parapolitical systems. In *Local-level politics: Social and cultural perspectives*, edited by Marc J. Swartz. Chicago: Aldine.

1969   *Stratagems and spoils: A social anthropology of politics.* Oxford: Basil Blackwell.

1972   Conceptual systems in the study of politics. In *Rural politics and social change in the Middle East*, edited by Richard Antoun and Iliya Harik. Bloomington: Indiana University Press.

1977   *Morality and expediency: The folklore of academic politics.* Chicago: Aldine.

1982   Review of *Process and form in social life*, by Fredrik Barth. *AE* 9:584–585.

Bailey, Frederick G., ed.

1971   *Gifts and poison: The politics of reputation.* Oxford: Basil Blackwell.

1973   *Debate and compromise: The politics of innovation.* Totowa, N.J.: Rowman and Littlefield.

Baker, Victoria J.

1983   Elders in the shadow of the Big Man. *Bijdragen* 139:1–17.

Balandier, Georges

1951   La situation coloniale: Approche theoretique. *Cahiers internationaux de sociologie* 11:44–79.

1967   *Anthropologie Politique.* Paris: Presses Universitaires de France.

1970   *Political Anthropology.* Translated by A. M. Sheridan-Smith. London: Allen Lane.

Banaji, Jairus

1970   The crisis of British anthropology. *NLR* 64:71–85.

Bancroft, Hubert Howe

1874   *The native races of the Pacific states of North America.* Vol. 1: *Wild tribes.* San Francisco: A. L. Bancroft.

1882   *The native races of the Pacific states of North America.* Vol. 2: *Civilized nations.* San Francisco: A. L. Bancroft.

Bannister, R. C.

1979   *Social Darwinism: Science and myth in Anglo-American social thought.* Philadelphia: Temple University Press.

Banton, Michael P., ed.

1965   *Political systems and the distribution of power.* ASA Monograph 2. London: Tavistock.

1966   *The social anthropology of complex societies.* ASA Monograph 4. London: Tavistock.

Barber, Bernard B.

1961   Resistance by scientists to scientific discovery. *Science* 134:596–602.

Barker, Francis, et al.

1984   *Confronting the crisis.* Colchester: University of Essex.

Barkun, Michael, ed.
1973   *Law and the social system.* New York: Lieber-Atherton.
Barnard, Alan
1983   Contemporary hunter-gatherers: Current theoretical issues in ecology and social organization. *ARA* 12:193–214.
Barnes, John A.
1951   History in a changing society. *RLJ* 11:1–9.
1954   Class and committee in a Norwegian island parish. *Human Relations* 7:39–58.
1958   Indigenous politics and colonial administration. *CSSH* 2:133–149.
1961   Law as politically active: An anthropological view. In *Studies in the sociology of law,* edited by Geoffrey Sawer. Canberra: Australian National University Press.
1962   African models in the New Guinea highlands. *Man* 62:5–9.
1972   *Social networks.* An Addison-Wesley module in anthropology. Reading, Mass.: Addison-Wesley.
Barnes, Leonard
1944   *Soviet light on the colonies.* London: Gollancz.
Barnett, Homer G.
1938   The nature of the potlatch. *AA* 40:349–357.
1956   *Anthropology in administration.* Evanston, Ill.: Row Peterson.
Barrett, Stanley R.
1984   *The rebirth of anthropological theory.* Toronto: University of Toronto Press.
Barth, Fredrik
1956   Ecologic relationships of ethnic groups in Swat, North Pakistan. *AA* 58:1079–1089.
1959a   *Political leadership among Swat Pathans.* London School of Economics Monograph on Social Anthropology, no. 19.
1959b   Segmentary opposition and the theory of games: A study of Pathan organization. *JRAI* 89:5–21.
1963   *The role of the entrepreneur in social change in northern Norway.* Bergen: Norwegian Universities Press.
1966   *Models of social organization.* Royal Anthropological Institute Occasional Paper 23. London: Royal Anthropological Institute of Great Britain and Ireland.
1981a   *Process and form in social life: Selected essays of Fredrik Barth.* Vol 1. London: Routledge, Chapman and Hale.
1981b   Features of person and society in Swat. *Collected essays on Pathans: Selected essays of Fredrik Barth.* Vol. 2. London: Routledge, Chapman and Hale.
Barth, Fredrik, ed.
1969   *Ethnic groups and boundaries.* Boston: Little, Brown.
Barton, Roy F.
1919   Ifugao law. *UCPAAE* 15:1–186.
1922   Ifugao economics. *UCPAAE* 15:385–446.
1930a   *The half-way sun: Life among the headhunters of the Philippines.* New York: Brewer and Warren.

1930b   Paths of vengeance in Luzon. *Travel* 55:24–29, 53.
1930c   White man's law among Filipino Tribesmen. *Asia* 30:410–416, 445–448.
1938   *Philippine pagans: The autobiographies of three Ifugaos.* London: Routledge.
1949   *The Kalingas: Their institutions and custom law.* Chicago: University of Chicago Press.
1969   *Ifugao law.* Foreword by Fred Eggan. Berkeley and Los Angeles: University of California Press.

Bateson, Gregory
1936   *Naven: A survey of the problems suggested by a composite picture of the culture of a New Guinea tribe drawn from three points of view.* Cambridge: Cambridge University Press.

Beals, Alan R.
1955   Interplay among factors of change in a Mysore village. In *Village India,* edited by McKim Marriott. Chicago: University of Chicago Press.

Beals, Ralph L.
1951   Urbanism, urbanization and acculturation. *AA* 53:1–10.
1982   Fifty Years in Anthropology. *ARA* 11:1–23.

Beardsley, Edward H.
1973   The American scientist as social activist: Franz Boas, Burt G. Wilder, and the cause of racial justice, 1900–1915. *Isis* 64:50–66.

Beattie, John H. M.
1960   *Bunyoro: An African kingdom.* New York: Holt, Rinehart and Winston.
1964   *Other cultures: Aims, methods and achievements in social anthropology.* London: Cohen and West.

Beidelman, Thomas O.
1971   Nuer priests and prophets: Charisma, authority, and power among the Nuer. In *The Translation of Culture: Essays to E. E. Evans-Pritchard,* edited by Thomas O. Beidelman. London: Tavistock.

Bell, Colin, and Howard Newby
1971   *Community studies: An introduction to the sociology of the local community.* New York: Praeger.

Bell, F.L.S.
1935   Warfare among the Tonga, *Oceania* 5:253–279.

Belmont, Nicole
1979   *Arnold van Gennep: The creator of French ethnography.* Translated by Derek Coltman. Chicago: University of Chicago Press.

Bender, G. J.
1967   Political socialization and political change. *Western Political Quarterly* 20:390–407.

Bendix, Reinhard, ed.
1971   The comparative analysis of historical change. In *Scholarship and partisanship: Essays on Max Weber,* edited by Reinhard Bendix and Gunter Roth. Berkeley: University of California Press.

Beneria, Lourdes, ed.
   1982   *Women and development: The sexual division of labor in rural societies*. New York: Praeger.
Benison, Saul
   1953   Railroads, land, and iron: A phase in the career of Lewis Henry Morgan. Ph.D. diss., Columbia University.
Benjamin, Walter
   1969   Theses on the philosophy of history. In *Illuminations*, edited by Hannah Arendt. New York: Schocken.
Bennett, John W.
   1969   Northern plainsmen: Adaptive strategy in agrarian life. Chicago: Aldine.
Bentley, Arthur F.
   1908   *The process of government: A study of social pressures*. Chicago: University of Chicago Press.
   1908/   *The process of government: A study of social pressures*. Introduction
   1967   by Peter H. Odegard. Chicago: University of Chicago Press.
Bernstein, Richard J.
   1978   *The restructuring of social and political theory*. Philadelphia: University of Pennsylvania Press.
Besnard, Philippe, ed.
   1983   *The sociological domain: The Durkheimians and the founding of French sociology*. Cambridge: Cambridge University Press.
Black, Charles L.
   1969   *Structure and relationship in constitutional law*. Baton Rouge: Louisiana State University Press.
Black, Donald
   1984   *Toward a general theory of social control*. 2 vols. Orlando, Fl.: Academic Press.
Blackwood, Beatrice
   1934   *Both sides of the Buka passage: An ethnographic study of the social, sexual, and economic questions in the North-western Solomon Islands*. Oxford: Clarendon Press.
Bloch, Maurice
   1983   *Marxism and anthropology: The history of a relationship*. Oxford: Oxford University Press.
Boas, Franz
   1895/   *The social organization and the secret societies of the Kwakiutl In-*
   1925   *dians*. Washington, D.C: American National Museum.
Bock, Kenneth E.
   1974   Comparison of histories: The contribution of Henry Maine. *CSSH* 16:232–262.
Bodley, John H.
   1988   Idealists versus realists: Anthropology and the politics of genocide. Paper presented at the Eighty-seventh Annual Meeting of the American Anthropological Association, Phoenix, Arizona.

Boeke, Julius H.
1948   *Economics and economic policy of dual societies as exemplified by Indonesia.* New York: International Secretariat, Institute of the Pacific.

Bohannan, Paul J.
1957   *Justice and judgement among the Tiv.* London: Oxford University Press.
1963   *Social anthropology.* New York: Holt, Rinehart and Winston.
1965   The differing realms of the law. In *The ethnography of law,* edited by Laura Nader, Special Publication of *American Anthropologist* 67:33–42.
1967   Introduction. In *Beyond the frontier: Social process and cultural change.* New York: Natural History Press.

Bohannan, Paul J., ed.
1967   *Law and warfare: Studies in the anthropology of conflict.* New York: Natural History Press.

Bohannan, Paul J., and Fred Plog, eds.
1967   *Beyond the frontier: Social process and cultural change.* New York: Natural History Press.

Boissevain, Jeremy
1964   Factions, parties and politics in a Maltese village. *AA* 66:125–187.
1966   Patronage in Sicily. *Man* 1:18–33.
1968   The place of non-groups in the social sciences. *Man* 3:542–556.
1971   Second thoughts on quasi-groups. *Man* 6:468–472.
1974a   Towards a sociology of social anthropology. *Theory and Society* 1:211–230.
1974b   *Friends of friends: Networks, manipulations and coalitions.* Oxford: Basil Blackwell.

Bond, George C.
1987   Anthropologists, organizations and constituencies. *Practicing Anthropology* 9:15–17.
1988   A social portrait of St. Clair Drake: An American anthropologist. *AE* 15:762–781.

Bookman, Ann, and Sandra Morgen, eds.
1988   *Women and the politics of empowerment.* Philadelphia: Temple University Press.

Boserup, Esther
1970   *Women's role in economic development.* London: Allen and Unwin

Boulding, Kenneth E.
1956   General systems theory: The skeleton of science. *General Systems* 1:11–17.
1968   *Beyond economics: Essays on society, religion, and ethics.* Ann Arbor: University of Michigan Press.

Bourdieu, Pierre
1972   *Esquisse d'une theorie de la practique, precede de trois études d'ethnologie Kabyle.* Geneva: Librairie Droz.
1977   *Outline of a theory of practice.* Translated by Richard Nice. Cambridge: Cambridge University Press.

Bourke, John G.
 1892   Apache medicine men. In Bureau of Ethnology, *Ninth Annual Report*. Washington, D.C.: Government Printing Office.
Brabrook, Edward
 1874   Law. In *Notes and queries on anthropology*. London: BAAS.
Brailsford, Henry N.
 1914   *The war of steel and gold: A study of the armed peace*. London: G. Bell and Sons.
Braudel, Fernand
 1972   *The Mediterranean and the Mediterranean world in the age of Philip II*. New York: Harper and Row.
Brenner, Robert
 1977   The origins of capitalist development: A critique of neo-Smithian Marxism. *NLR* 104:25–92.
Briggs, Asa
 1975   The political scene. In *The Edwardians: The remaking of British society*, edited by Paul Thompson. London: Granada.
British Association for the Advancement of Science (BAAS)
 1874   *Notes and queries on anthropology: For the use of travellers and residents in uncivilized lands*. London: BAAS.
 1912   *Notes and queries on anthropology*. 4th ed. London: BAAS.
Brown, Paula, and Georgeda Buchbinder, eds.
 1976   *Man and woman in the New Guinea highlands*. Washington, D.C.: American Anthropological Association.
Brown, Richard
 1973   Anthropology and colonial rule: The case of Godfrey Wilson and the Rhodes-Livingstone Institute, Northern Rhodesia. In *Anthropology and the colonial encounter*, edited by Talal Asad. London: Ithaca Press.
 1979   Passages in the life of a white anthropologist: Max Gluckman in Northern Rhodesia. *Journal of African History* 20:525–541.
Brunton, R.
 1975   Why do the Trobriands have chiefs? *Man* 10:544–558.
Bryce, James
 1888   *The American commonwealth*. 2 vols. 3d ed. New York: Macmillan.
Bullock, Charles
 1928   *The Mashona: The indigenous natives of Southern Rhodesia*. Cape Town: Guta.
Bunzel, Ruth
 1952   *Chichicastenango: A Guatemalan village*. Monograph of the American Ethnological Society 22. New York: J. J. Augustin.
Burawoy, Michael B.
 1977   Marxism and sociology. *Contemporary Sociology* 6:9–17.
Burke, Kenneth
 1957   *The philosophy of literal form: Studies in symbolic action*. New York: Vintage Books.
Burman, Sandra B., and Barbara E. Harrell-Bond, eds.
 1979   *The imposition of law*. New York: Academic Press.

.irridge, Kennelm O. L.

1965   "Culture and personality" and history: A review. *Cahiers d'Histoire Mondiale* 9:15–29.

1973   *Encountering aborigines, a case study: Anthropology and the Australian aboriginal.* New York: Pergamon Press.

Burrow, John W.

1966   *Evolution and society: A study in Victorian social theory.* Cambridge: Cambridge University Press.

1974   "The Village Community" and the uses of history in late nineteenth-century England. In *Historical perspectives: Studies in English thought and society, in honour of G. H. Plumb*, edited by Neil McKendrick. London: Europa.

Burton, John W.

1981   Pastoral Nilotes and British colonialism. *Ethnohistory* 28:125–132.

Butler, Marilyn

1985   Against tradition: The case for a particularized historical method. In *Historical studies and literary criticism*, edited by Jerome McGann. Madison: University of Wisconsin Press.

Butler, Nicholas Murray

1939–   *Across the busy years: Recollections and reflections.* 2 vols. New
40   York: Scribner.

Butt, Audrey J.

1960   The birth of a religion. *JRAI* 90:66–106.

Byres, T. J., and H. Mukhia, eds.

1985   *Feudalism and non-European societies.* London: Frank Cass.

Cady, John F.

1954   Review of *Political systems of highland Burma*, by E. R. Leach. *Annals of the American Academy of Political and Social Science* 294:170.

Caffrey, Margaret M.

1989   *Ruth Benedict: Stranger in this land.* Austin: University of Texas Press.

Cain, Maureen, and Alan Hunt

1979   *Marx and Engels on law.* New York: Academic Press.

Cain, Maureen, and Kalman Kulcsar

1981–   Thinking disputes: An essay on the origins of the dispute industry.
82   *LSR* 16:375–102.

Cairns, Huntington

1931   Law and anthropology. In *The making of man: An outline of anthropology*, edited by Victor Francis Calverton. New York: Modern Library.

Cancian, Frank

1976   Social stratification. *ARA* 5:227–248.

Cannizzo, Jeanne

1983   George Hunt and the invention of Kwakiutl culture. *CRSA* 20:44–58.

Cardoso, Fernando H.

1977   The consumption of dependency theory. *Latin American Research Review* 12:7–24.

Cardozo, Benjamin N.
1921   *The nature of the judicial process.* New Haven: Yale University Press.

Carter, Ian
1975   *Farm life in northeast Scotland, 1840–1914: The poor man's country.* Edinburgh: John Donald.

Carter, Paul A.
1971   *The spiritual crisis of the Gilded Age.* De Kalb: Northern Illinois University Press.

Chanock, Martin
1985   *Law, custom, and social order: The colonial experience in Malawi and Zambia.* Cambridge: Cambridge University Press.

Chapman, Charlotte Gower
1928/   *Milocca: A Sicilian village.* Cambridge, Mass.: Schenkman.
1971

Chapman, William Ryan
1985   Arranging ethnology: A.H.L.F. Pitt-Rivers and the typological tradition. In *Objects and others: Essays on museums and material culture,* edited by George W. Stocking, Jr. *History of Anthropology,* vol. 3. Madison: University of Wisconsin Press.

Chapple, Eliot, and Carlton Coon
1940   *Principles of anthropology.* New York: Holt, Rinehart and Winston.

Charsley, Simon R.
1974   The formation of ethnic groups. In *Urban ethnicity,* edited by Abner Cohen. ASA Monograph 12. London: Tavistock.

Chayanov, Aleksandr V.
1966   *The theory of peasant economy.* Homewood, Ill.: R. D. Irwin.

Childe, V. Gordon
1925   *The dawn of European civilization.* New York: Knopf.
1936   *Man makes himself.* London: Watts.
1941   War in prehistoric societies. *Sociological Review* 33:126–138.
1946   *What happened in history.* London: Penguin Books.

Chirot, Daniel
1976   *Social change in a peripheral society: The creation of a Balkan colony.* New York: Academic Press.

Chodorow, Nancy
1978   *The reproduction of mothering: Psychoanalysis and the sociology of gender.* Berkeley: University of California Press.

Chun, A. J.
1980   Slavery as a mode of exchange among the Kwakiutl Indians of the Northwest Coast. *Chicago Anthropology Exchange* 8:4–29.

Claessen, Henri J. M., and Peter Skalnik, eds.
1978   *The early state.* The Hague: Mouton.
1981   *The study of the state.* The Hague: Mouton.

Clark, Terry N.
1968   Emile Durkheim and the institutionalization of sociology in the French university system. *EJS* 9(1):37–71.

Clifford, James
    1982   *Person and myth: Maurice Leenhardt in the Melanesian world.*
            Berkeley: University of California Press.
Cline, H.
    1952   Mexican community studies. *Hispanic American Historical Review*
            32:212–242.
Cline, W.
    1942   Review of *The political system of the Anuak of the Anglo-Egyptian
            Sudan*, by E. E. Evans-Pritchard. *AA* 44:494–496.
Cobb, Richard C.
    1970   *The police and the people: French popular protest, 1789–1820.* Ox-
            ford: Clarendon Press.
Cocks, Raymond C. J.
    1988   *Sir Henry Maine: A study in Victorian jurisprudence.* Cambridge:
            Cambridge University Press.
Codere, Helen
    1950   *Fighting with property: A study of Kwakiutl potlatching and war-
            fare, 1792–1930.* American Ethnological Society Monograph 18.
            New York: J. J. Augustin.
Codere, Helen, ed.
    1966   *Kwakiutl ethnography: Franz Boas.* Chicago: University of Chicago
            Press.
Cohen, Abner
    1969a   Political anthropology: The analysis of the symbolism of power rela-
            tions. *Man* 4:215–235.
    1969b   *Custom and politics in urban Africa.* London: Routledge and Kegan
            Paul.
    1974a   *Two-dimensional man.* London: Routledge and Kegan Paul.
    1979   Political symbolism. *ARA* 8:87–113.
Cohen, Abner, ed.
    1974b   *Urban ethnicity.* ASA Monograph 12. London: Tavistock.
Cohen, Ronald
    1965   Political anthropology: The future of a pioneer. *AQ* 38:117–131.
    1973   Political anthropology: In *Handbook of social and cultural anthro-
            pology*, edited by John J. Honigmann. Chicago: Rand McNally.
    1978   Ethnicity: Problem and focus in anthropology. *ARA* 7:379–403.
Cohen, Ronald, and John Middleton
    1967   *Comparative political systems.* New York. Natural History Press
Cohn, Bernard S.
    1959   Some notes on law and change in North China. *Economic Develop-
            ment and Cultural Change* 8:79–93.
    1968   Notes on the history of the study of Indian society and culture. In
            Structure and change in Indian society, edited by Milton Singer and
            Bernard S. Cohn. Chicago: Aldine.
    1985   The command of language and the language of command. In *Subal-
            tern Studies*, edited by Ranajit Guha, 4:276–329. Delhi: Oxford Uni-
            versity Press.

Colby, William Munn
  1977   Routes to Rainy Mountain: A biography of James Mooney, ethnolo-
          gist. Ph.D. diss., University of Wisconsin.
Cole, Douglas
  1973   The origins of Canadian anthropology, 1850–1910. *Journal of Cana-
          dian Studies* 8:33–45.
Coleman, James S.
  1965   *Education and political development.* Princeton, N.J.: Princeton
          University Press.
Collier, Jane F.
  1970   Review of *Law without precedent*, by Lloyd A. Fallers. *American
          Ethnologist* 74:854–858.
  1973   *Law and social change in Zinacantan.* Stanford, Calif.: Stanford
          University Press.
  1975   Legal processes. *ARA* 4:121–144.
Collini, Stefan
  1978   Sociology and idealism in Britain, 1880–1920. *EJS* 19:3–50.
Collini, Stefan, Donald Winch, and John Burrow
  1984   *That noble science of politics: A study in nineteenth-century intel-
          lectual history.* Cambridge: Cambridge University Press.
Colson, Elizabeth.
  1948   Modern political organization of the Plateau Tonga. *African Studies*
          7:85–98.
  1953   Social control and vengeance in Plateau Tonga society. *Africa*
          23:199–211.
  1958   The role of Bantu bureaucratic norms in African political structure.
          In *Systems of political control and bureaucracy in human societies,*
          edited by Verne F. Ray. Proceedings of the Annual Spring Meeting of
          the American Ethnological Society. Seattle: University of Washing-
          ton Press.
  1966   The alien diviner and local politics among the Tonga of Zambia. In
          Political anthropology, edited by Marc Swartz et al. Chicago: Aldine.
  1968   Political anthropology: The field. *IESS* 12:189–193.
  1971   *The social consequence of resettlement: The impact of the Kariba
          resettlement upon the Gwembe-Tonga.* Manchester: Manchester
          University Press.
  1974   *Tradition and contract: The problem of order.* Chicago: Aldine.
  1976   Culture and progress. *AA* 78:261–271.
  1977a   From Livingstone to Lusaka, 1948–51. *African Social Research*
          24:297–307.
  1977b   A continuing dialogue: Prophets and local shrines among the Tonga
          of Zambia. In *Regional cults,* edited by Richard Werbner. ASA
          Monograph 16. New York: Academic Press.
  1985a   Defining American Ethnology. In *Social contexts of American
          ethnology, 1840–1984,* edited by June Helm. 1984 Proceedings of
          the American Ethnological Society. Washington, D.C.: American An-
          thropological Association.

1985b   Using anthropology in a world on the move. *Human Organization* 44:191–196.

1985c   Political organization in tribal societies: A cross-cultural comparison. Paper presented at the D'Arcy McNickle Center, Newberry Library, February 14, 1985.

Comaroff, John L.

1982   Dialectical systems, history and anthropology: Units of study and questions of theory. *Journal of Southern African Studies* 8:143–172.

Comaroff, John, and Simon Roberts

1981   *Rules and processes: The cultural logic of dispute in an African context.* Chicago: University of Chicago Press.

Conklin, Harold C.

1960   Research proposal: Ethnoecological study of agriculture in the Philippines. Mimeographed. New York.

Cook, Fred J.

1971   *The nightmare decade: The life and times of Senator Joseph R. McCarthy.* New York: Random House.

Copans, Jean

1974   *Critiques et politiques de l'anthropologie.* Paris: Maspero.

Coquery-Vidrovich, Catherine

1975   Research on an African mode of production. *Critique of Anthropology* 4–5:38–71.

Corrigan, Philip, ed.

1980   *Capitalism, state formation and Marxist theory.* London: Quartet Books.

Corris, Peter

1973   *Passage, port and plantation: A history of Solomon Islands labour migration, 1870–1914.* Carlton, Australia: Melbourne University Press.

Crane, Diana

1972   *Invisible colleges: Diffusion of knowledge in scientific communities.* Chicago: University of Chicago Press.

Crick, Bernard

1959   *The American science of politics: Its origins and conditions.* London: Routledge and Kegan Paul.

Cunnison, Ian

1951   *History of the Luapula.* Rhodes-Livingstone Papers, no. 21. Manchester: Manchester University Press.

1957a   Review of *Alur society*, by Aidan Southall. *RLJ* 22:70–72.

1957b   History and genealogies in a conquest state. *AA* 59:20–31.

Curtin, Philip D.

1977   Slavery and empire. In *Slavery in Africa: Historical and anthropological perspectives*, edited by Susan Miers and I. Kopytoff. Madison: University of Wisconsin Press.

Dalton, George

1974   How exactly are peasants "exploited"? *AA* 76:553–561.

Danquah, Joseph B.
1928   *Gold Coast: Akan laws and customs and the Akim Abuakwa con-stitution.* London: Routledge.
Darnell, Regna
1969   The development of anthropology, 1879–1920: From the Bureau of American Ethnology to Franz Boas. Ph.D. diss., University of Pennsylvania.
1971   The professionalization of American anthropology: A case study in the sociology of knowledge. *Social Science Information* 10:83–103.
1974   *Readings in the history of anthropology.* New York: Harper and Row.
Darrah, William Culp
1951   *Powell of the Colorado.* Princeton, N.J.: Princeton University Press.
Darwin, Charles
1871   *The descent of man and selection in relation to sex.* London: G. Murray.
Davis, Allison, Burleigh B. Gardner, and Mary Gardner
1941   *Deep South: A social anthropological study of caste and class.* Chicago: University of Chicago Press.
Davy, Georges
1924   *Elements de sociologie appliqué à la morale et à l'education.* Vol. 1: *Sociologie politique.* Paris: Delagrave.
1926   *From tribe to empire: Social organization among the primitives and in the Ancient East.* London: K. Paul, Trench, Trubner and Company.
Dawson, Warren R., ed.
1938   *Sir Grafton Elliot Smith: A biographical record by his colleagues.* London: Jonathan Cape.
De Man, Paul
1982   Introduction to *Toward an aesthetic of reception,* by Hans Robert Jauss. Minneapolis: University of Minnesota Press.
Deshen, Shlomo A.
1974   Political ethnicity and cultural ethnicity in Israel during the 1960s. In *Urban ethnicity,* edited by Abner Cohen. ASA Monograph 12. London: Tavistock.
Despres, Leo, ed.
1975   *Ethnicity and resource competition in plural societies.* The Hague: Mouton.
De Tocqueville, Alexis
1862   *Democracy in America.* Cambridge, Mass.: Sever and Francis.
Dewey, Clive
1972   Images of the village community: A study in Anglo-Indian ideology. *Modern Asian Studies* 6:291–328.
1980   Review of *Four families of Karimpur,* by Charlotte Wiser. *Journal of Asian Studies* 39:391.
Diamond, A. S.
1971   *Primitive law: Past and present.* London: Methuen.
Diamond, Stanley
1962   *The tangled bank.* New York: Atheneum.

1970   Un ethnocide. *Les Temps Moderne* 238:1194–1206.

1974   *In search of the primitive.* New Brunswick, N.J.: Transaction-Dutton.

Disraeli, Benjamin

1881   *Sybil; or, The two nations.* London: Oxford University Press.

Divale, William F.

1971   *Warfare in primitive societies: A selected bibliography.* Los Angeles: California State College, Center for the Study of Armament and Disarmament.

Dixon, R. B.

1905   The Northern Maidu. AMNH *Bulletin* 17:119–346.

Dodge, Richard I.

1877   *The Plains of the Great West and their inhabitants, Being a description of the Plains, game, Indians, etc., of the Great North American Desert.* New York: Putnam.

Dolby, R.G.A.

1977   The transmission of science. *History of Science* 15:1–43.

Dolgin, Janette, D. Kemnitzer, and David Schneider, eds.

1977   *Symbolic anthropology: A reader in the study of symbols and meanings.* New York: Columbia University Press.

Dollard, John

1937   *Caste and class in a southern town.* New Haven: Yale University Press.

Domar, E. D.

1970   The course of slavery or serfdom. *Journal of Economic History* 30:18–32.

Domhoff, G. William

1969   Who made American foreign policy, 1945–1963? In *Corporations and the cold war,* edited by David Horowitz. New York: Monthly Review Press.

Donald, L. H.

1982   Was Nuu-cha-nulth-akt society based on slave labour? In *The development of political organization in native North America,* edited by Elizabeth Tooker. 1979 Proceedings of the American Ethnological Society. Washington, D.C.: American Ethnological Society.

Dorsey, James Owen

1883   *Omaha Sociology,* Smithsonian Institution, Bureau of Ethnology, *Third Annual Report.* Washington, D.C.: Government Printing Office.

Douglas, Mary

1975   *Implicit Meanings.* London: Routledge and Kegan Paul.

Drake, St. Clair, with E. Clayton

1945   *Black metropolis: A study of Negro life in a northern city.* New York: Harcourt, Brace and World.

Driberg, Jack H.

1928   Primitive law in East Africa. *Africa* 1:63–72.

Driver, Harold E.

1961   *Indians of North America.* Chicago: University of Chicago Press.

Drucker, Philip
1939   Rank, wealth and kinship in Northwest Coast society. *AA* 41:55–64.
1965   *Cultures of the North Pacific Coast.* San Francisco: Chandler.
Drucker, Philip, and R. F. Heizer
1967   *To make my name good: A re-examination of the Southern Kwakiutl potlatch.* Berkeley: University of California Press.
Du Bois, Cora
1950   Review of *The Kalingas,* by Roy F. Barton. *AA* 52:81–82.
1980   Some anthropological hindsights. *ARA* 9:1–13.
Duley, Margot I., and Mary I. Edwards, eds.
1986   *The cross-cultural study of women: A comprehensive guide.* New York: Feminist Press.
Dumia, Mariano A.
1979   *The Ifugao world.* Quezon City, Philippines: New Day Publishers.
Dumont, Louis
1966   The "village community" from Munro to Maine. *Contributions to Indian Sociology* 9:67–89.
1977   *From Mandeville to Marx: The genesis and triumph of economic ideology.* Chicago: University of Chicago Press.
Dundas, Charles
1921   Native laws of some Bantu tribes of East Africa. *JRAI* 51:217–278.
Dupree, A. Hunter
1957   *Science in the federal government: A history of policies and activities to 1940.* Cambridge, Mass.: Harvard University Press.
Durham, Mary E.
1928   *Some tribal origins, laws, and customs of the Balkans.* London: Allen and Unwin.
Durkheim, Emile
1893   *Division of labour.* Paris: Alcan.
1895   *Les regles de la methode sociologique* (The rules of sociological method). Paris: Alcan.
Dutt, Rajani Palme
1950   *Britain's crisis of empire.* London: Lawrence and Wishart.
Dyson-Hudson, Neville
1972   The study of nomads. In *Perspectives on nomadism,* edited by William Irons and Neville Dyson-Hudson. Leiden: E. J. Brill.
Earle, Timothy K.
1987   Chiefdoms in archaeological and ethnohistorical perspective. *ARA* 16:271–308.
Easton, David
1953   *The political system.* New York: Knopf.
1959   Political anthropology. In *Biennial Review of Anthropology, 1959,* edited by Bernard J. Siegel, 210–262.
1965a *A framework for political analysis.* New York: Prentice-Hall.
1965b *A systems analysis of political life.* New York: Wiley.
Ebihara, May
1985   American ethnology in the 1930s: Contexts and currents. In *Social contexts of American ethnology, 1840–1984,* edited by June Helm.

1984 Proceedings of the American Ethnological Society. Washington, D.C.: American Anthropological Association.

Eddy, E. M., and W. L. Partridge
1978   *Applied anthropology in America*. New York: Columbia University Press.

Edmonson, Munro S.
1972   Review of *Crucifixion by power*, by Richard Adams. *AA* 74:77–79.

Eggan, F.
1954   Social anthropology and the method of controlled comparison. *AA* 56:743–763.
1965   *The social anthropology of North American tribes*. Chicago: University of Chicago Press.
1969   Foreword to *Ifugao law*, by Roy F. Barton. Berkeley: University of California Press. Originally published 1919.
1972   Lewis Henry Morgan's systems: A re-evaluation. In *Kinship studies in the Morgan centennial year*, edited by Priscilla Reining. Washington, D.C.: Anthropological Society of Washington.

Eisenstadt, S. N.
1959   Primitive political systems: A preliminary comparative analysis. *AA* 61:200–222.

Elias, Norbert, Herminio Martins, and Richard Whitley
1982   Scientific establishments and hierarchies. In *Sociology of the Sciences 6*, edited by N. Elias, H. Martins, and R. Whitley. Dordrecht: Reidel.

Elkin, A. P.
1949   Man and his cultural heritage. *Oceania* 20:1–18.
1956   A. R. Radcliffe-Brown, 1880–1955. *Oceania* 26:239–251.
1974   Elliot Smith and the diffusion of culture. In *Grafton Elliot Smith: The man and his work*, edited by A. P. Elkin and N.W.G. Macintosh. Sydney, Australia: Sydney University Press.

Elkins, Stanley, and Eric McKitrick, eds.
1974   *The Hofstadter aegis: A memorial*. New York: Knopf.

Ellis, F.
1951   Patterns of aggression and the war cult in southwestern Pueblos. *SWJA* 7:177–201.

Embree, John F.
1939   *Suye Mura: A Japanese village*. Chicago: University of Chicago Press.

Engels, Frederick
1884/   *The origin of the family, private property and the state, in the light*
1972   *of the researches of Lewis H. Morgan*. Edited by Eleanor Burke Leacock. New York: International Publishers.

Engerman, Stanley L.
1973   Some considerations relating to property rights in man. *Journal of Economic History* 33:43–65.

Epstein, A. L.
1958   *Politics in an urban African community*. Manchester: Manchester University Press.

1967   The case method in the field of law. In *The craft of social anthropology*, edited by A. L. Epstein. London: Tavistock.

Etienne, Mona, and Eleanor Leacock, eds.

1980   *Women and colonialization: Anthropological perspectives.* New York: Bergin and Garvey/Praeger.

Eulau, Heinz

1964   *Behavioral persuasion in politics.* New York: Random House.

Evans, Grant

1987   Sources of peasant consciousness in South-east Asia: A survey. *Social History* 12:193–211.

Evans, Michael

1970   Notes on D. Easton's model of the political system. *Journal of Commonwealth Political Studies* 8:117–133.

Evans, P.

1986   State, capital and the transformation of dependence: The Brazilian computer case. *World Development* 14:791–808.

Evans-Pritchard, E. E.

1933   Review of *The origin and history of politics*, by William Christie MacLeod. *Man* 33:74.

1937   *Witchcraft, oracles and magic among the Azande.* Oxford: Clarendon Press.

1940a   *The political system of the Anuak of the Anglo-Egyptian Sudan.* London: Percy Lund, Humphries.

1940b   *The Nuer: A description of the modes of livelihood and political institutions of a Nilotic people.* Oxford: Clarendon Press.

1949   *The Sanusi of Cyrenaica.* Oxford: Clarendon Press.

1951   *Kinship and marriage among the Nuer.* Oxford: Clarendon Press.

1957a   Zande warfare. *Anthropos* 52:239–262.

1957b   Zande border raids. *Africa* 27:217–231.

1958   Preface to *Tribes without rulers: Studies in African segmentary systems*, edited by John Middleton and David Tait. London: Routledge and Kegan Paul.

1971   *The Azande: History and political institutions.* Oxford: Oxford University Press.

1981   *History of anthropological thought*, edited by André Singer. London: Faber.

Evens, T.M.S.

1977   The predication of the individual in anthropological interactionism. *AA* 79:579–597.

Ewers, John C.

1955   *The horse in Blackfoot Indian culture: With comparative material from other western tribes.* Washington, D.C.: Government Printing Office.

Fabian, Johannes

1979   The anthropology of religious movements: From explanation to interpretation. *Social Research* 46:4–25.

1980   *Time and the other: How anthropology makes its object.* New York: Columbia University Press.

Fairgreaves, James
    1915   *Geography and world power: A textbook of matriculation standard,
            illustrating the geographic control of history.* London: London Uni-
            versity Press.
Fallers, Lloyd A.
    1955   The predicament of the modern African chief: An instance from
            Uganda. *AA* 57:290–305.
    1963a   Equality, modernity and democracy in the new states. In *Old
            societies and new states: The quest for modernity in Asia and Af-
            rica,* edited by Clifford Geertz. New York: Free Press.
    1963b   Political sociology and the anthropological study of African politics.
            EJS 4(2): 311–329.
    1969   *Law without precedent: Legal ideas in action in the courts of colo-
            nial Busoga.* Chicago: Aldine.
    1974   *The social anthropology of the nation-state.* Chicago: Aldine.
Faris, Robert E. L.
    1967   *Chicago sociology, 1920–1932.* Chicago: University of Chicago
            Press.
Faron, Louis C.
    1954   The acculturation of the Araucanian Picunche during the first
            century of Spanish colonization in Chile. Ph.D. diss., Columbia
            University.
Fathauer, G. H.
    1954   The structure and causation of Mohave warfare. *SWJA* 10:97–118.
Favre, Pierre
    1983   The absence of political sociology in the Durkheimian classifica-
            tions of the social sciences. In *The sociological domain: The Durk-
            heimians and the founding of French sociology,* edited by Philippe
            Besnard. Cambridge: Cambridge University Press.
Feaver, George
    1969   *From status to contract: A biography of Sir Henry Maine, 1822–
            1888.* London: Longmans.
Feeley-Harnick, Gillian
    1985   Issues in divine kingship. *ARA* 14:273–313.
Feis, Herbert
    1950   *The diplomacy of the dollar: First era, 1919–32.* Baltimore: Johns
            Hopkins Press.
Felstiner, W.L.F.
    1974   Influences of social organization on dispute processing. *LSR* 9:63–
            94.
Fenton, William N.
    1950   Review of *Primitive war,* by H. H. Turney-High. *AA* 52:246–247.
Ferguson, Adam
    1767/   *An essay on the history of civil society.* Edited by Duncan Forbes.
    1966   Edinburgh: Edinburgh University Press.
Ferguson, R. Brian, with Leslie E. Farraghar
    1988   *The anthropology of war: A bibliography.* Occasional Papers of the
            Henry Frank Guggenheim Foundation, no. 1.

Ferguson, W. S.
1918   The Zulus and the Spartans: A comparison of their military systems. *Harvard African Studies* 2:197–234.
Fewkes, Jesse W.
1897   Anthropology. In *The Smithsonian Institution, 1846–1896*, edited by George Brown Goode. Washington, D.C.: Smithsonian Institution.
Firth, Raymond
1936   *We the Tikopia: A sociological study of kinship in primitive Polynesia.* London: G. Allen and Unwin.
1944   The future of social anthropology. *Man* 44:19–24.
1951a   *Elements of social organization.* London: Watts.
1951b   Contemporary British social anthropology. *AA* 53:474–489.
1954a   Foreword. In *Political systems of highland Burma*, by Edmund R. Leach. London: Bell.
1955   Social organization and social change. *JRAI* 85:1–18.
1956   Alfred Reginald Radcliffe-Brown, 1881–1955. *Proceedings of the British Academy* 42:286–302.
1960   Recent trends in British social anthropology. In *Men and cultures*, edited by Anthony F.C. Wallace. Selected Papers of the Fifth International Congress of Anthropological and Ethnological Sciences. Philadelphia: University of Pennsylvania Press.
1962   Introduction. In *Human nature and the study of society: The papers of Robert Redfield.* Vol. 1. Edited by Margaret Park Redfield. Chicago: University of Chicago Press.
1963   Preface to the Beacon Paperback edition of *Ancient Law*, by Sir Henry Sumner Maine. Boston: Beacon Press.
1964   *Essays on social organization and values.* London School of Economics Monographs on Social Anthropology, no. 28. London: Athlone Press.
1975a   Max Gluckman, 1911–1975. *Proceedings of the British Academy* 61:479–496.
1975b   An appraisal of modern social anthropology. *ARA* 4:1–26.
1981   Bronislaw Malinowski. In *Totems and teachers: Perspectives on the history of anthropology*, edited by Sydel Silverman. New York: Columbia University Press.
1986   The founding and early history of the A.S.A. *Annals of the Association of Social Anthropologists of the Commonwealth* 7:4–10.
Fisher, Robin A.
1977   *Contact and conflict: Indian-European relations in British Columbia, 1774–1890.* Vancouver: University of British Columbia Press.
Fitzpatrick, Peter
1980   *Law and state in Papua New Guinea.* New York: Academic Press.
Flack, J. Kirkpatrick
1975   *Desideratum in Washington: The intellectual community in the capital city, 1870–1900.* Cambridge, Mass.: Schenckman.
Fletcher, Ronald
1971   *The making of sociology: A study of sociological theory.* London: Joseph.

Flint, John E.

1964   Introduction. In *West African Studies*, edited by Mary Kingsley. 3d ed. London: F. Cass.

1965   Introduction to *Travels in West Africa, Congo Francais, Corisco and Cameroons*, edited by Mary Kingsley. 3d ed. London: F. Cass.

Forde, C. Daryll

1926   *Ancient mariners: The story of ships and sea routes*. London: Howe Press.

1931   Ethnography of the Yuma Indians. *UCPAAE* 28:83–278.

1934   *Habitat, economy and society*. London: Methuen.

1938   Fission and accretion in the patrilineal clans of a semi-Bantu community in southern Nigeria. *JRAI* 68:311–368.

1939   Kinship in Umor: Double unilateral organization in a semi-Bantu society. *AA* 41:523–553.

1948   The integration of anthropological studies. *JRAI* 78:1–10.

Forde, C. Daryll, and Phyllis Kaberry, eds.

1967   *West African kingdoms in the nineteenth century*. London: Oxford University Press.

Fortes, Meyer

1936   Culture contact as a dynamic process. An investigation in the northern territories of the Gold Coast. *Africa* 9:24–55.

1949   *The web of kinship among the Tallensi*. London: Oxford University Press.

1953   The structure of unilineal descent groups. *AA* 55:17–41.

1958   Introduction. In *The developmental cycle in domestic groups*, edited by Jack Goody. Cambridge: Cambridge University Press.

1969   *Kinship and the social order: The legacy of Lewis Henry Morgan*. Chicago: Aldine.

1976   Cyril Daryll Forde, 1902–1973. *Proceedings of the British Academy* 62:458–483.

1979   Preface to *Segmentary lineage systems reconsidered*, edited by L. Holy. Belfast: Queen's University, Department of Anthropology.

Fortes, Meyer, and E. E. Evans-Pritchard, eds.

1940   *African political systems*. London: Oxford University Press.

Fortune, Reo F.

1939   Arapesh warfare. *AA* 41:22–41.

1947   The rules of relationship behaviour in one variety of primitive warfare. *Man* 47:108–110.

Foster, George M.

1952   Review of *Life in a Mexican village*, by Oscar Lewis. *AA* 54:239–240.

1953   What is folk culture? *AA* 55:159–173.

Foster-Carter, A.

1974   Neo-Marxist approaches to development and under-development. In *Sociology and development*, edited by Emmanuel de Kadt and Gavin Williams. London: Tavistock.

Foucault, Michel

1977   *The archaeology of knowledge*. New York: Pantheon.

1980   *Knowledge and power.* New York: Pantheon.
Fowler, Don D., and Catherine S. Fowler
1969   John Wesley Powell, anthropologist. *Utah Historical Quarterly* 37:158–164.
1971   *Anthropology of the Numa: John Wesley Powell's manuscripts on the Numic peoples of western North America, 1868–1880.* Smithsonian Contributions to Anthropology, no. 14. Washington, D.C.: Smithsonian Institution Press.
Fox, Richard G.
1963   Caste dominance and coercion in the Nilgiris. *Papers of the Michigan Academy of Science, Arts and Letters* 48:493–512.
Frank, Andre Gunder
1967   Sociology of development and the underdevelopment of sociology. *Catalyst* 3:20–73.
1969a   *Capitalism and underdevelopment in Latin America: Historical studies of Chile and Brazil.* New York: Monthly Review Press.
1969b   *Latin America: Underdevelopment or revolution.* New York: Monthly Review Press.
1972   *Lumpenbourgeoisie: Lumpendevelopment; Dependence, class, and politics in Latin America.* New York: Monthly Review Press.
1974   Dependence is dead, long live dependence and the class struggle: A reply to critics. *Latin American Perspectives* 1:87–106.
1975   Development and underdevelopment in the New World: Smith and Marx vs. the Weberians. *Theory and Society* 2:431–466.
Frank, Jerome
1930   *Law and the modern mind.* New York: Coward-McCann.
Frankel, Barbara
1987   Comment on "Anthropology as interpretive quest," by Roger Keesing. *CA* 28:169–170.
Frankenberg, Ronald
1957   *Village on the border: A social study of religion, politics and football in a North Wales community.* London: Cohen and West.
1979   Economic anthropology or political economy: The Barotse social formation, a case study. In *The new economic anthropology*, edited by John Clammer. New York: St. Martin's Press.
1982   *Custom and conflict in British society.* Manchester: Manchester University Press.
Freedman, Maurice
1954   Review of *Political systems of highland Burma*, by Edmund R. Leach. *New Statesman and Nation* 47:334–335.
1960   The growth of a plural society in Malaysia. *Pacific Affairs* 33:158–168.
Freeman, J. D.
1956   Siegfried Frederick Nadel, 1903–1956. *Oceania* 27:1–11.
Freire-Marreco, Barbara
1912   Government and politics. In *Notes and queries on anthropology.* London: BAAS.

Fried, Morton H.

1957   The classification of corporate unilineal descent groups. *JRAI* 87:1–29.

1960   On the evolution of social stratification and the state. In *Culture in history*, edited by Stanley Diamond. New York: Columbia University Press.

1964   Anthropology and the study of politics. In *Horizons of anthropology*, edited by Sol Tax. Chicago: University of Chicago Press.

1966   Some political aspects of clanship in a modern Chinese city. In *Political anthropology*, edited by Marc Swartz, Victor Turner, and Arthur Tuden. Chicago: Aldine.

1967   *The evolution of political society: An essay in political anthropology.* New York: Random House.

1968   The state. *IESS* 16:143–150.

Fried, Morton H., Marvin Harris, and Robert Murphy, eds.

1968   *War: The anthropology of armed conflict and aggression.* Garden City, N.Y.: Natural History Press.

Friedl, Ernestine

1950   An attempt at directed culture change: Leadership among the Chippewa, 1640–1948. Ph.D. diss., Columbia University.

1975   *Women and men: An anthropologist's view.* New York: Holt, Rinehart and Winston.

Friedman, Jonathan

1978   Crisis in theory and transformations of the world economy. *Review* 2:131–146.

1987   An interview with Eric Wolf. *CA* 28:107–118.

Fuentes, Annette, and Barbara Ehrenreich

1983   *Women in the global factory.* Boston: South End Press.

Furner, Mary O.

1975   *Advocacy and objectivity: A crisis in the professionalization of American social science, 1865–1905.* Lexington: University Press of Kentucky.

Furnivall, J. S.

1948   *Colonial policy and practice: A comparative study of Burma and Netherlands India.* Cambridge: Cambridge University Press.

Furtado, Celso

1970   *Obstacles to development in Latin America.* Garden City, N.Y.: Anchor.

Gadamer, Hans-Georg

1976   *Philosophical hermeneutics.* Berkeley: University of California Press.

Gailey, Christine W.

1980   Putting down sisters and wives: Tongan women and colonialization. In *Women and colonialization*, edited by Mona Etienne and Eleanor Leacock. New York: Bergin and Garvey/Praeger.

1983   Categories without culture: Structuralism, ethnohistory and ethnocide. *DA* 8:241–250.

1985   The state of the state in anthropology. *DA* 9:65–89.

1986   *Hard choices: The context of women's involvement in small-scale enterprises.* Women and International Development Working Paper, no. 16. Harvard/MIT Group.

1987   *Kinship to kingship: Gender hierarchy and state formation in the Tongan Islands.* Austin: University of Texas Press.

Garbett, G. K.

1967   Prestige, status and power in a modern valley: Korekore chiefdom, Rhodesia. *Africa* 77:307–326.

Gardner, Lloyd C., ed.

1966   *Different frontier: Selected readings in the foundations of American economic expansion.* Chicago: Quadrangle Books.

Garfield, Viola E.

1966   The Tsimshian and their neighbours. In *The Tsimshian and their arts,* edited by Viola E. Garfield and Paul S. Wingert. Seattle: University of Washington Press.

Garson, G. David

1978   *Group theories of politics.* New York: Sage.

Gayton, Anna H.

1930a   Yokuts-Mono chiefs and shamans. *UCPAAE* 24:361–420.

1931   The Ghost Dance of 1870 in south-central California. *UCPAAE* 28:57–82.

1945   Yokuts and Western Mono social organization. *AA* 47:409–426.

1946   Culture-environment integration: External references in Yokuts life. *SWJA* 2:252–268.

Gayton, Anna H., and Stanley S. Newman

1940   Yokuts and Western Mono myths. *University of California Anthropological Records* 5:1–110.

Geertz, Clifford J.

1963a   *Agricultural involution: The process of ecological change in Indonesia.* Berkeley: University of California Press.

1967   Politics past, politics present: Some notes on the uses of anthropology in understanding the new states. *EJS* 8:1–14.

1968   *Islam observed: Religious development in Morocco and Indonesia.* New Haven: Yale University Press.

1972   Summary comments. In *Rural politics and social change in the Middle East,* edited by Richard Antoun and Ilya Harik. Bloomington: Indiana University Press.

1973   *The interpretation of cultures: Selected essays.* New York: Basic Books.

1977   Centers, kings, and charisma: Reflections on the symbolics of power. In *Culture and its creators: Essays in honor of Edward Shils,* edited by Joseph Ben-David and Terry Nicholas Clark. Chicago: University of Chicago Press.

1983   *Local knowledge: Further essays in interpretive anthropology.* New York: Basic Books.

1988   *Works and lives: The anthropologist as author.* Stanford, Calif.: Stanford University Press.

Geertz, Clifford J., ed.
    1963b   *Old societies and new states: The quest for modernity in Asia and Africa.* New York: Free Press.
Geison, Gerald L.
    1981   Scientific change, emerging specialities and research schools. *History of Science* 19:20–40.
Gellner, Ernest
    1988   The stakes in anthropology. *American Scholar* 57 (1): 17–30.
Genovese, Eugene D.
    1974   *Roll, Jordan, roll: The world the slaves made.* New York: Vintage Books.
Geschiere, Peter
    1978   The articulation of different modes of production: Old and new inequalities in Maka villages (southeast Cameroon). In *Social stratification and class formation: African perspectives 1978/2*, edited by R. Buijtenhuijs and Peter Geschiere. Leiden: African Studies Centre.
Gibbs, James, Jr.
    1963   The Kpelle moot: A therapeutic model for the informal settlement of disputes. *Africa* 33:1–11.
Giddens, Anthony
    1979   *Central problems in social theory: Action, structure and contradiction in social analysis.* Berkeley and Los Angeles: University of California Press.
Gifford, Edward Winslow
    1924   Euro-American acculturation in Tonga. *Journal of the Polynesian Society* 33:281–292.
    1926   Miwok lineages and the political unit in aboriginal California. *AA* 28:389–401.
    1944   Miwok lineages. *AA* 46:376–381.
    1955   Central Miwok ceremonies. *University of California Anthropological Records* 14:261–318.
Gilmore, David D.
    1982   Anthropology of the Mediterranean area. *ARA* 11:175–205.
Gilmore, Grant
    1961   Legal realism: Its causes and cure. *Yale Law Journal* 70:1037–1047.
Gilsenan, Michel
    1982   *Recognizing Islam: Religion and society in the modern world.* London: Croom Helm.
Ginsberg, Morris
    1934   *Sociology.* London: Methuen.
    1965   Introduction to *The Material culture and social institutions of the simpler peoples: An essay in correlation,* by Leonard T. Hobhouse, Gerald C. Wheeler, and Morris Ginsberg. 2d ed. London: Routledge and Kegan Paul.
Glickman, Maurice
    1972   The Nuer and the Dinka: A further note. *Man* 7:586–594.
    1974   The Dinka and the Nuer. *Man* 9:141–142.

Gluckman, Max
1940   Analysis of a social situation in modern Zululand. *Bantu Studies* 14:147–174.
1941   *Economy of the Central Barotse Plain.* Rhodes-Livingstone Paper 7. Livingstone, Northern Rhodesia: Rhodes-Livingstone Institute.
1947a   Malinowski's contribution to social anthropology. *African Studies* 6:57–76.
1947b   Malinowski: Fieldworker and theorist. *Africa* 17:103–121.
1949a   *Malinowski's sociological theories.* Rhodes-Livingstone Paper 16. Livingstone, Northern Rhodesia: Rhodes-Livingstone Institute.
1949b   The village headman in British Central Africa. *Africa* 19:89–101.
1955a   *Custom and conflict in Africa.* Oxford: Basil Blackwell.
1955b   *The judicial process among the Barotse of Northern Rhodesia.* Manchester: Manchester University Press.
1955c   Review of *The law of primitive man*, by E. Adamson Hoebel. *Man* 55:93–95.
1956   Political institutions. In *The institutions of primitive society: A series of broadcast talks*, edited by E. E. Evans-Pritchard. Oxford: Basil Blackwell.
1958   *Analysis of a social situation in modern Zululand.* Rhodes-Livingstone Paper 28. Manchester: Manchester University Press.
1960   The rise of a Zulu empire. *Scientific American* 202:157–168.
1962   The crisis in the folk societies. In *The ethic of power: The interplay of religion, philosophy, and politics*, edited by Harold D. Lasswell and H. Cleveland. New York: Harper.
1963   *Order and rebellion in tribal Africa.* London: Cohen and West.
1965   *Politics, law and ritual in tribal society.* Oxford: Basil Blackwell.
1967   *The judicial process among the Barotse of Northern Rhodesia.* 2d ed. Manchester: Manchester University Press.
1968   Inter-hierarchical roles: Professional and party ethics in tribal areas in south and central Africa. In *Local-level politics: Social and cultural perspectives*, edited by Marc J. Swartz. Chicago: Aldine.
1972   Preface. *The ideas in Barotse jurisprudence.* 2d ed. New Haven: Yale University Press.
1974a   Report from the field. *New York Review of Books*, November 28, pp. 43–44.
1974b   Daryll Forde, 1902–1973. *Africa* 44:1–5.
1975   African traditional law in historical perspective. *Proceedings of the British Academy, 1974* 60:295–337.
Gluckman, Max, ed.
1969   *Ideas and procedures in African customary law.* London: Oxford University Press.
Gluckman, Max, and Ely Devons, eds.
1964   *Closed systems and open minds: The limits of naivety in social anthropology.* Edinburgh: Oliver and Boyd.
Gluckman, Max, and Fred Eggan
1965   Introduction. *Political systems and the distribution of power*, edited

by Michael Banton. ASA Monograph 2. London: Tavistock.

Goddard, P. E.
1903   Life and culture of the Hupa. *UCPAAE* 1:1–88.

Godelier, Maurice
1973a   *Horizon, trajets marxistes en anthropologie.* Paris: Maspero.
1977   *Perspectives in Marxist anthropology.* Cambridge: Cambridge University Press.

Godelier, Maurice, ed.
1973b   *Sur les societes precapitalistes: Textes choisis de Marx, Engels, Lenine.* Paris: Editions Sociales.

Godoy, Ricardo
1978   The background and context of Redfield's Tepoztlán. *Steward Anthropological Society Journal* 10:47–79.

Goetzmann, William H.
1966   *Exploration and empire: The explorer and the scientist in the winning of the American West.* New York: Knopf.

Goldenweiser, Alexander
1924   Review of *Primitive Law*, by E. Sidney Hartland. *AA* 26:445.

Goldman, Irving
1937   The Ifugao of the Philippine Islands. In *Cooperation and competition among primitive peoples*, edited by Margaret Mead. New York: McGraw-Hill.
1975   *The mouth of heaven.* New York: Wiley.

Goldschmidt, Walter
1946   *Small business and the community: A study in central valley of California on effects of sale of farm operations.* Washington, D.C.: Government Printing Office.
1947   *As you sow: Three studies in the social consequences of agribusiness.* New York: Harcourt, Brace.
1950   Social class in America: A critical review. *AA* 52:483–498.
1976   Anthropology as context. *AA* 78:519–520.
1985   The cultural paradigm in the post-war world. In *Social Contexts of American Ethnology, 1840–1984*, edited by June Helm. 1984 Proceedings of the American Ethnological Society. Washington, D.C.: American Anthropological Association.

Goodale, Jane C.
1971   *Tiwi wives: A study of the women of Melville Island, North Australia.* Seattle: University of Washington Press.

Goody, Jack
1962   *Death, property and the ancestors: A study of mortuary customs of the Lodogaa of West Africa.* London: Tavistock.
1966a   The prospects for social anthropology. *New Society* 60:574–576.
1973   British functionalism. In *Main currents in cultural anthropology*, edited by Raoul Naroll and Freda Naroll. New York: Appleton-Century-Crofts.

Goody, Jack, ed.
1966b   *Succession to high office.* Cambridge: Cambridge University Press.

Gough, Kathleen

1968   New proposals for anthropologists. In Social responsibilities symposium. *CA* 9:403–407.

1968–   Peasant resistance and revolt in South India. *Pacific Affairs* 41:526–
69   544.

1971   Nuer kinship: A reexamination. In *The translation of culture: Essays to E. E. Evans-Pritchard*, edited by Thomas O. Beidelman. London: Tavistock.

1975   The origin of the family. In *Toward an anthropology of women*, edited by Rayna Reiter. New York: Monthly Review Press.

1978a   Agrarian relations in Southeast India, 1750–1976. *Review* 2:25–53.

1978b   *Ten times more beautiful: The rebuilding of Vietnam.* New York: Monthly Review Press.

1981   *Rural society in southeast India.* Cambridge: Cambridge University Press.

Gouldner, Alvin W.

1970   *The coming crisis of Western sociology.* New York: Basic Books.

Gramsci, Antonio

1971   *Selections from the prison notebooks of Antonio Gramsci.* Edited and translated by Quinton Hoare and Geoffrey Nowell Smith. New York: International Publishers.

Green, Margaret Joan

1947   *Ibo village affairs: Chiefly with reference to the village of Umueke Agbaja.* London: Sidgwick and Jackson.

Green, Sally

1981   *Prehistorian: A biography of V. Gordon Childe.* Bradford-on-Avon: Moonraker Press.

Greenhouse, Carol

1986   *Praying for justice.* Ithaca, N.Y.: Cornell University Press.

Greuel, Pierre J.

1971   The leopard-skin chief: An examination of political power among the Nuer. *AA* 73:1115–1120.

Grillo, Ralph D.

1974   Ethnic identity and social stratification on a Kampala housing estate. In *Urban ethnicity*, edited by Abner Cohen. ASA Monograph 12. London: Tavistock.

Grinnell, George B.

1910   Coup and scalp among the Plains Indians. *AA* 12:296–310.

1915   *The fighting Cheyenne.* Norman: University of Oklahoma Press.

Grossi, Paolo

1981   *An alternative to private property.* Translated by Lydia G. Cochrane. Chicago: University of Chicago Press.

Gruber, Jacob W.

1966   In search of experience. In *Pioneers of American anthropology*, edited by June Helm. American Ethnological Society, monograph 43. Seattle: University of Washington Press.

1967   Horatio Hale and the development of American anthropology. *Pro-*

ceedings of the American Philosophical Society 3:5–35.

Gruber, Jacob W., and Walter Goldschmidt, eds.

1959   *The anthropology of Franz Boas.* American Anthropological Association, memoir 89. Washington, D.C.

Grun, Bernard

1975   *The timetables of history: A horizontal linkage of people and events.* New York: Simon and Schuster.

Gulliver, Philip H.

1963   *Social control in an African society: A study of the Arusha, agricultural Masai of northern Tanganyika.* London: Routledge and Kegan Paul.

1969   Case studies of law in non-Western societies. In *Law in culture and society,* edited by Laura Nader. Chicago: Aldine.

Gulliver, Philip H., ed.

1978   *Cross examinations: Essays in memory of Max Gluckman.* Leiden: Brill.

1979   *Disputes and negotiations.* New York: Academic Press.

Gutkind, Peter C. W., ed.

1970   *The passing of tribal man in Africa.* Leiden: Brill.

Gutmann, Bruno

1926   *Chagga Law.* Translated by A. M. Nagler. Human Relations Area Files. New Haven: Yale University Press.

Gwynn, Stephen

1933   *Life of Mary Kingsley.* London: Macmillan.

Hagstrom, Warren O.

1965   *The scientific community.* New York: Basic Books.

Haight, B.

1972   A note on the leopard-skin chief. *AA* 74:1313–1317.

Hall, Stuart

1978   Marxism and culture. *Radical History Review* 18:5–14.

Hall, Stuart, C. Critcher, T. Jefferson, J. Clarke, and B. Roberts

1978   *Policing the crisis: Mugging, the state, and law and order.* London: Macmillan.

Hallowell, A. I.

1960   The beginnings of anthropology in America. In *Selected papers from the* American Anthropologist, *1888–1920,* edited by Frederica de Laguna. Washington, D.C.: American Anthropological Association.

Halpern, J. M., and D. A. Kideckel

1983   Anthropology in Eastern Europe. *ARA* 12:337–402.

Hamnett, Ian, ed.

1977   *Social anthropology and law.* ASA Monograph 14. New York: Academic Press.

Hanc, Joseph Robert

1981   Influences, events and innovations in the anthropology of Julian Steward: A revisionist view of multilinear evolution. Master's thesis, University of Chicago.

Hannerz, Ulf

1987   Anthropology's other press: Training ground, playground, underground. *CA* 28:214–219.

Harries, C. L.

1929   *The laws and customs of the Bapedi and cognate tribes of the Transvaal.* Johannesburg: Hortors.

Harris, Marvin

1959   The economy has no surplus? *AA* 61:185–199.

1968   *The rise of anthropological theory: A history of theories of culture.* New York: Crowell.

Harris O., and K. Young

1981   Engendered structures: Some problems in the analysis of reproduction. In *The anthropology of pre-capitalist societies*, edited by Joel S. Kahn and J. R. Llobera. London: Macmillan.

Harriss, John

1982   *Capitalism and peasant farming: Agrarian structure and ideology in northern Tamil Nadu.* New York: Oxford University Press.

Hart, Charles W. M.

1953   Colonial peoples in transition. In *The challenge of our times*, edited by F. Daniels and T. M. Smith. Madison: University of Wisconsin Press.

Hart, Herbert L. A.

1961   *The concept of law.* Oxford: Clarendon Press.

Hartland, E. Sidney

1924   *Primitive law.* London: Methuen.

Haskell, Thomas L.

1977   *The emergence of professional social science: The American Social Science Association and the nineteenth century crisis of authority.* Urbana: University of Illinois Press.

Hatch, Elvin

1973   *Theories of man and culture.* New York: Columbia University Press.

Hawthorn, Geoffrey

1976   *Enlightenment and despair: A history of social theory.* New York: Cambridge University Press.

Hay, Douglas, ed.

1975   *Albion's fatal tree: Crime and society in eighteenth-century England.* London: Allen Lane.

Hayakawa, T.

1964   Karl Llewellyn as a law man from Japan sees him. *Rutgers Law Review* 18 /17–737.

Heffernan, William C.

1983   Two stages in Karl Llewellyn's thought. *International Journal of the Sociology of Law* 11:134–166.

Heine-Geldern, R.

1964   One hundred years of ethnological theory in the German-speaking countries: Some milestones. *CA* 5:407–416.

Heizer, Robert F.

1978   Introduction to *Handbook of North American Indians*, William C. Sturtevant, General Editor. Vol. 8: *California*, edited by Robert F. Heizer. Washington, D.C.: Smithsonian Institution.

Hellman, E., and Q. Whyte
    1955   Introduction, dedicated to Dr. A. W. Hoernle. *Race Relations Journal* 22:1–5.
Helm, June, ed.
    1968   Essays on the problem of the tribe. *Proceedings of the American Ethnological Society*. Washington, D.C.
Herskovits, Melville J.
    1938a   *Acculturation: The study of culture contact.* Locust Valley, N.Y.: Augustin.
    1938b   *Dahomey: An ancient West African kingdom.* 2 vols. New York: Augustin.
    1941   Review of *African political systems*, edited by Meyer Fortes and E. E. Evans-Pritchard. *AA* 43:465–468.
    1944   Review of *The Nuer*, by E. E. Evans-Pritchard. *AA* 46:396–400.
    1948   *Man and his works.* New York: Knopf.
    1965   A genealogy of ethnological theory. In *Context and meaning in cultural anthropology*, edited by Melford Spiro. New York: Free Press.
Hewitt, John N. B.
    1907   Confederation. In *Handbook of American Indians North of Mexico*, edited by Frederick W. Hodge. Bureau of American Ethnology, Smithsonian Institution, Bulletin, no. 30. Washington, D.C.
Hexter, J. H.
    1972   The sown and the waste, or the second record. In *The history primer*, by J. H. Hexter. London: Allen Press.
Himmelfarb, Gertrude
    1987   *The new history and the old.* Cambridge, Mass.: Belknap Press of Harvard University Press.
Hinsley, Curtis M., Jr.
    1976a   The development of a profession: Anthropology in Washington, D.C., 1846–1903. Ph.D. diss., University of Wisconsin.
    1976b   Amateurs and professionals in Washington anthropology, 1879 to 1903. In *American anthropology: The early years*, edited by John Murra. 1974 Proceedings of the American Ethnological Society. Washington, D.C.: American Anthropological Association.
    1979   Anthropology as science and politics: The dilemma of the Bureau of American Ethnology, 1879 to 1904. In *The uses of anthropology*, edited by Walter Goldschmidt. Washington, D.C.: American Anthropological Association.
    1981   *Savages and scientists: The Smithsonian Institution and the development of American anthropology, 1846–1910.* Washington, D.C.: Smithsonian Institution Press.
    1985   Hemispheric hegemony in early American anthropology, 1841–1851: Reflections on John Lloyd Stephens and Lewis Henry Morgan. In *Social Contexts of American Ethnology, 1840–1984*, edited by June Helm. 1984 Proceedings of the American Ethnological Society. Washington, D.C.: American Anthropological Association.
Hirst, Paul
    1979   *On law and ideology.* Atlantic Highlands, N.J.: Humanities Press.

Hobhouse, Leonard Trelawny
  1906   *Morals in evolution.* New York: Holt.
Hobhouse, Leonard Trelawny, Gerald C. Wheeler, and Morris Ginsberg
  1915   *The material culture and social institutions of the simpler peoples: An essay in correlation.* London: Chapman-Hall.
Hobsbawm, Eric J.
  1964   *Pre-capitalist economic formations: Karl Marx.* New York: International Publishers.
  1972   Peasants and politics. *Journal of Peasant Studies* 1:3–22.
Hobsbawm, Eric J., and Terence Ranger
  1983   *The invention of tradition.* Cambridge: Cambridge University Press.
Hobsbawm, Eric J., and George Rudé
  1968   *Captain Swing: A social history of the great English agricultural uprising of 1830.* London: Lawrence and Wishart.
Hobson, John A.
  1902   *Imperialism: A study.* London: Nisbet.
Hocart, Arthur M.
  1913   Fijian heralds and envoys. *JRAI* 43:109–118.
  1931   Warfare in Eddystone of the Solomon Islands. *JRAI* 61:301–324.
  1912/ A native Fijian on the decline of his race. In *Beyond the frontier:*
  1967   *Social process and culture change,* edited by Paul Bohannan and Fred Plog. New York: Natural History Press.
Hodge, Frederick Webb, ed.
  1907   *Handbook of American Indians North of Mexico.* Bureau of American Ethnology, Smithsonian Institution, Bulletin, no. 30. Washington, D.C.
Hodgen, Margaret
  1964   *Early anthropology in the sixteenth and seventeenth centuries.* Philadelphia: University of Pennsylvania Press.
Hoebel, E. Adamson
  1940   *The political organization and law-ways of the Comanche Indians.* American Anthropological Association, Memoir 54. Washington, D.C.
  1941   Review of *Law and status among the Kiowa Indians,* by Jane Richardson. *AA* 43:645–647.
  1949   Introduction to *The Kalingas,* by Roy F. Barton. Chicago: University of Chicago Press.
  1954   *The law of primitive man: A study in comparative legal dynamics.* Cambridge, Mass.: Harvard University Press.
  1961a Three studies in African law. *Stanford University Law Review* 13:418–422.
  1961b Karl Llewellyn: Anthropological Jurisprude. *Rutgers Law Review* 18:735–744.
  1972   Feud: Concept, reality and method in the study of primitive law. In *Essays on modernization of underdeveloped societies,* edited by A. R. Desai. New York: Humanities Press.

Hoffman, John
    1973   David Easton and the paradox of politics. Ph.D. diss., University of
            Sussex.
Hoffman, Walter J.
    1886–   The Grand Medicine Society of the Ojibway. *Annual Report of the*
    87   *Bureau of American Ethnology,* 7:143–300.
Hofstadter, Richard
    1948   *The American political tradition and the men who made it.* New
            York: Knopf.
    1955   *The Age of Reform: From Bryan to F.D.R.* New York: Vintage.
    1963   *Anti-intellectualism in American Life.* New York: Random House.
Hogbin, H. Ian
    1934   *Law and order in Polynesia: A study of primitive legal institutions.*
            New York: Harcourt Brace.
    1935   Sorcery and administration. *Oceania* 6:1–32.
Holder, Preston
    1951   The role of Caddoan horticulturalists in culture history on the Great
            Plains. Ph.D. diss., Columbia University.
    1970   *The hoe and the horse on the Plains: A study of cultural develop-*
            ment among North American Indians. Lincoln: University of Ne-
            braska Press.
Hollingshead, A. de Belmont
    1949   *Elmtown's youth: The impact of social classes on adolescents.* New
            York: Wiley.
Holmes, Oliver Wendell, Jr.
    1899   Law in science and science in law. *Harvard Law Review* 12:443–463.
Holsti, Rudolph
    1914   *The relation of war to the origin of the state.* Annales Academic
            Scientarium Fennicae XIII. Helsingfors, Finland.
Hooker, M. B.
    1975   *Legal pluralism.* Oxford: Clarendon Press.
Horr, David Agee, comp.
    1974   *California Indians,* vols. 1–6. American Indian ethnohistory series.
            New York: Garland.
Horton, Robin
    1974   Daryll Forde, 1902–1973. *Africa* 44:8–10.
Howard, Cecil
    1957   *Mary Kingsley.* London: Hutchinson.
Howard, Michael C.
    1976   Comment on Pilling's review. *AA* 78:356–357.
Howe, M. de Wolf
    1953   *Holmes-Laski letters: The correspondence of Mr. Justice Holmes*
            and Harold J. Laski, 1916–1935. Cambridge, Mass.: Harvard Univer-
            sity Press.
Hughes, H. Stuart
    1958   *Consciousness and society: The reorientation of European social*
            thought, 1890–1930. New York: Random House.

Huizer, Gerrit, and Bruce Mannheim, eds.
1979   *The politics of anthropology: From colonialism and sexism toward a view from below.* The Hague: Mouton.
Humphreys, Sally
1985   Law as discourse. *History and Anthropology* 1:241–264.
Hunt, Alan
1978   *The sociological movement in law.* Philadelphia: Temple University Press.
1981   Marxism and the analysis of law. In *Marxism and law*, edited by Piers Beirne and R. Quinney. New York: Wiley.
Hunt, George T.
1940   *The wars of the Iroquois: A study in intertribal trade relations.* Madison: University of Wisconsin Press.
Hunter, Monica
1936   *Reaction to conquest: Effects of contact with Europeans on the Pondo of South Africa.* London: Oxford University Press.
Hunter, Virginia
1982   *Past and process in Herodotus and Thucydides.* Princeton, N.J.: Princeton University Press.
Hyden, Goren
1980   *Beyond Ujamaa in Tanzania: Underdevelopment and an uncaptured peasantry.* Berkeley: University of California Press.
Hymes, Dell, ed.
1969   *Reinventing anthropology.* New York: Pantheon.
Ibbetson, Denzil
1892   Appendix 3. In *The tribes and castes of Bengal*, edited by H. H. Risley. Vol. 2. Calcutta: Bengal Secretariat Press.
Idris-Soven, Ahmed, Elizabeth Idris-Soven, and Mary K. Vaughan, eds.
1973   *The world as a company town.* The Hague: Mouton.
Irvin, T. T.
1977   The Northwest Coast potlatch since Boas, 1897–1972. *Anthropology* 1:65–77.
Jablow, Joseph
1951   *The Cheyenne in Plains Indian trade relations, 1795–1840.* American Ethnological Society Monograph 19. New York: J. J. Augustin.
Jaher, Frederic Cople
1964   *Doubters and dissenters: Cataclysmic thought in America, 1885–1918.* London: Free Press of Glencoe.
James, Wendy
1973   The anthropologist as reluctant imperialist. In *Anthropology and the colonial encounter*, edited by Talal Asad. London: Ithaca Press.
Jameson, Frederic
1981   *The political unconscious: Narrative as a socially symbolic act.* Ithaca, N.Y.: Cornell University Press.
Jarvie, Ian C.
1964   *The revolution in anthropology.* London: Routledge and Kegan Paul.
1972a   *Concept and society.* London: Routledge and Kegan Paul.

1972b   *Functionalism.* Minneapolis: Burgess.
1974   Review of *Anthropologists and anthropology*, by Adam Kuper. *Philosophy of the Social Sciences* 4:302–305.
1975   Epistle to the anthropologists. *AA* 77:253–266.
Jaspan, M. A.
1970   Review of 1969 edition of *Ifugao law*, by Roy F. Barton. *Man* 5:554–555.
Jayawardena, Chandra
1960   Review of *Political leadership among Swat Pathans*, by Fredrik Barth. *AA* 62:612.
Johnson, Douglas Hamilton
1980   History and prophecy among the Nuer of the southern Sudan. Ph.D. diss., University of California, Los Angeles.
Joseph, Sir Keith
1976   *Reversing the trend.* London: Rose Books.
Judd, Neil M.
1968   *The Bureau of American Ethnology: A partial history.* Norman: University of Oklahoma Press.
Kaberry, Phyllis
1939   *Aboriginal woman: Sacred and profane.* London: Routledge.
Kadushin, C.
1968   Power, influence and social circles: A new methodology for studying opinion makers. *American Sociological Review* 33:686–699.
Kahl, Joseph A.
1976   *Modernization, exploitation and dependency in Latin America: Germani, Gonzalez Casanova, and Cardoso.* New Brunswick, N.J.: Transaction Books.
Kahn, Joel S.
1981   Mercantilism and the emergence of servile labour in colonial Indonesia. In *The anthropology of pre-capitalist societies*, edited by Joel S. Kahn and J. R. Llobera. London: Macmillan.
1985   Peasant ideologies in the Third World. *ARA* 14:49–75.
Kahn, Joel S., and J. R. Llobera, eds.
1981   *The anthropology of pre-capitalist societies.* London: Macmillan.
Kamenka, Eugene, and Alice Ehr-Soon Tay
1980   *Law and social control.* Melbourne, Australia: Edward Arnold.
Kay, C.
1974   Comparative development of the European manorial system and the Latin American hacienda system. *JPS* 2(1): 69–98.
Kay, George
1975   *Development and underdevelopment: A Marxist analysis.* London: Macmillan.
Keane, A. H.
1896   *Ethnology.* Cambridge: Cambridge University Press.
Keesing, Felix M.
1934   *Taming Philippine headhunters: A study of cultural change in northern Luzon.* London: Allen and Unwin.
1937   *The Philippines: A nation in the making.* Shanghai: Kelly.

Keesing, Roger M.
1970   Shrines, ancestors, and cognatic descent: The Kwaio and Tallensi. *AA* 72:755–775.
1972   Simple models of complexity: The lure of kinship. In *Kinship studies in the Morgan centennial year,* edited by Priscilla Reining. Washington, D.C.: American Anthropological Association.
1981   *Cultural anthropology: A contemporary perspective.* New York: Holt, Rinehart and Winston.
1985   Kwaio women speak: The micropolitics of autobiography in a Solomon Island society. *AA* 87:27–39.
1987   Anthropology as interpretive quest. *CA* 28:161–169, 174–176.
Kehoe, Alice Beck
1989   *The Ghost Dance: Ethnohistory and revitalization.* New York: Holt, Rinehart and Winston.
Kelly, Lawrence C.
1985   Why applied anthropology developed when it did: A commentary on people, money, and changing times, 1930–1945. In *Social contexts of American ethnology, 1840–1984,* edited by June Helm. 1984 Proceedings of the American Ethnological Society. Washington, D.C.: American Anthropological Association.
Kennett, Austin
1925   *Bedouin justice: Laws and customs among the Egyptian Bedouin.* Cambridge: Cambridge University Press.
Kinder, Hermann, and Werner Hilgemann
1978   *The Penguin atlas of world history.* Vol. 2: *From the French Revolution to the present.* Translated by Ernest A. Menze. Harmondsworth, Eng.: Penguin Books.
King, Anthony
1969   Review of *Stratagems and Spoils,* by F. G. Bailey. *New Society* 13:883.
Kingsley, Mary H.
1897/ *Travels in West Africa, Congo Français, Corisco and Cameroons.*
1965   London: Macmillan.
1898   Introduction to *Notes on the Folklore of the Fjort (French Congo),* by R. E. Dennett. London: David Nutt.
Kirchhoff, Paul
1959   The principles of clanship in human society. In *Readings in Anthropology,* edited by Morton H. Fried. New York: Crowell.
Klass, Morton
1980   *Caste: The emergence of the South Asian social system.* Philadelphia: Institute for the Study of Human Issues.
Knight, Rolf
1978   *Indians at work: An informal history of native Indian labour in British Columbia, 1858–1930.* Vancouver: New Star Books.
Kobrinsky, V. H.
1975   Dynamics of the Fort Rupert class struggle: Fighting with property vertically revisited. In *Papers in honor of Henry Hawthorn,* edited by V. Serle and H. C. Taylor. Bellingham: West Washington State College.

Krader, Lawrence

1961   Review of *Political leadership among Swat Pathans*, by Fredrik Barth. *AA* 63:1122.

1974   *The ethnological notebooks of Karl Marx*. Assen, Netherlands: Van Gorcum.

1975   *The Asiatic mode of production: Sources, development and critique in the writings of Karl Marx*. Assen, Netherlands: Van Gorcum.

Kroeber, Alfred L.

1904   Types of Indian culture in California. *UCPAAE* 2:81–103.

1920   Review of *Primitive society*, by Robert H. Lowie. *AA* 22:380.

1925   *Handbook of the Indians of California*. Bureau of American Ethnology Bulletin 78. Washington, D.C.: USGPO.

1928   Law of the Yurok Indians. *Proceedings of the 22nd International Congress of Americanists*. Rome: Riccardo Garroni.

1949   Roy Franklin Barton, 1883–1947. *AA* 51:91–95.

1953   *Anthropology today: An encyclopedic inventory*. Chicago: University of Chicago Press.

1957   *Style and civilizations*. Ithaca, N.Y.: Cornell University Press.

1959   A history of the personality of anthropology. *AA* 61:398–404.

1962   The nature of land-holding groups in aboriginal California. In *Two papers on the aboriginal ethnography of California*, edited by D. H. Hymes and Robert F. Heizer. University of California Archaeological Survey Report 56. Berkeley.

Kuhn, Thomas S.

1961   *The structure of scientific revolutions*. Chicago: University of Chicago Press.

1977   *The essential tension: Selected studies in scientific tradition and change*. Chicago: University of Chicago Press.

Kuper, Adam

1970a   *Kalahari village politics: An African democracy*. Cambridge: Cambridge University Press.

1970b   Gluckman's village headman. *AA* 72:355–358.

1973   *Anthropologists and anthropology: The British school, 1922–1972*. London: Allen Lane.

1982   Lineage theory: A critical retrospect. *ARA* 11:71–95.

1985a   Ancestors: Henry Maine and the constitution of primitive society. *History and Anthropology* 1:265–286.

1985b   Review of *Functionalism historicized*, edited by George W. Stocking, Jr. *AE* 12:523.

Kuper, Hilda Beemer

1937   The development of the military organization in Swaziland. *Africa* 10:55–74, 176–205.

1947   *An African aristocracy: Rank among the Swazi of Bechuanaland*. London: Oxford University Press.

1972   A royal ritual in a changing political context. *Cahiers d'Etudes Africaines* 12:593–615.

1978   The monarchy and the military in Swaziland. In *Social system and tradition in southern Africa,* edited by John Argyle and Eleanor Preston-White. Oxford: Oxford University Press.

1984   Function, history, biography: Reflections on fifty years in the British anthropological tradition. In *History of anthropology,* vol. 2: *Functionalism historicised,* edited by George W. Stocking, Jr. Madison: University of Wisconsin Press.

Kuper, Hilda, and Leo Kuper

1965   *African law: Adaptation and development.* Berkeley: University of California Press.

Kuper, Leo, and Michael G. Smith, eds.

1969   *Pluralism in Africa.* Berkeley: University of California Press.

Kutsenkov, A.

1986   The origin of caste and the caste system. *Soviet Anthropology and Archaeology* 24:3–25.

La Capra, Dominick

1985   *Rethinking intellectual history: Texts, contexts, language.* Ithaca, N.Y.: Cornell University Press.

Lackner, Helen

1973   Colonial administration and social anthropology: Eastern Nigeria, 1920–1940. In *Anthropology and the colonial encounter,* edited by Talal Asad. London: Ithaca Press.

Laclau, Ernest

1971   Feudalism and capitalism in Latin America. *NLR* 67:19–38.

Lamphere, Louise

1987   *From working daughters to working mothers: Immigrant women in a New England industrial community.* Ithaca, N.Y.: Cornell University Press.

Lan, David

1985   *Guns and rain: Guerillas and spirit mediums in Zimbabwe.* Berkeley: University of California Press.

Langham, Ian G.

1981   *The building of British social anthropology: W.H.R. Rivers and his Cambridge disciples in the development of kinship studies, 1898–1931.* Dordrecht, Netherlands: D. Reidel.

Lanternari, Vittorio

1963   *The religion of the oppressed: A study of modern messianic cults.* New York: Knopf.

Latham, Earl, ed.

1966   *The meaning of McCarthyism.* Boston: D. C. Heath.

Lattimore, Owen

1949   *Inner Asian frontiers of China.* New York: American Geographic Society.

1962   *Studies in frontier history: Collected papers, 1928–1958.* London: Oxford University Press.

Lawrence, Peter

1967   *Don Juan in Melanesia.* Brisbane: University of Queensland Press.

1975   The ethnographic revolution. *Oceania* 45:253–271.

Leach, Edmund R.

1940   *Social and economic organization of the Rowanduz Kurds.* Monographs on Social Anthropology 3. London: Percy/Lund, Humphries.

1950   Review of *The web of kinship among the Tallensi,* by Meyer Fortes. *Man* 52:21–22.

1954   *Political systems of highland Burma: A study of Kachin social structure.* London: Bell and Sons.

1960   The frontiers of Burma. *CSSH* 3:49–68.

1961   *Rethinking anthropology.* London: Athlone Press.

1963   Law as a condition of freedom. In *The concept of freedom in anthropology,* edited by David Bidney. The Hague: Mouton.

1964   Introductory note to *Political systems of highland Burma: A study of Kachin social structure.* Boston: Beacon Press.

1968a   W.H.R. Rivers. *IESS* 13:526–528.

1968b   *Pul Eliya: A village in Ceylon; A study of land tenure and kinship.* Cambridge: Cambridge University Press.

1968c   *A runaway world?* Oxford: Oxford University Press.

1968d   Social structure. *IESS* 14:482–489.

1974   Anthropology upside down. *New York Review of Books.* February 5, pp. 33–35.

1977   Supplementary note to 1977 edition. In *Political systems of highland Burma: A study of Kachin social structure.* Atlantic Highlands, N.J.: Humanities Press.

Leach, Edmund, S. N. Mukherjee, and John Ward, eds.

1985   *Feudalism: Comparative studies.* Sydney: Sydney Association for Studies in Society and Culture.

Leacock, Eleanor

1952   The Montagnais-Naskapi "hunting territory" and the fur trade. Ph.D. diss., Columbia University.

1954   *The Montagnais "hunting territory" and the fur trade.* American Anthropological Association Memoir 78. Menasha, Wis.: American Anthropological Association.

1972   Introduction to *The origin of the family, private property and the state, in light of the researches of Lewis H. Morgan,* by Frederick Engels. New York: International Publishers.

1977   Women in egalitarian society. In *Becoming visible: Women in European history,* edited by R. Bridenthal and C. Koonz. Boston: Houghton Mifflin.

1981   *Myths of male dominance.* New York: Monthly Review Press.

1982   Marxism and anthropology. In *The Left academy,* edited by Bernard Ollman and E. Vernoff. New York: McGraw-Hill.

Lesser, Alexander

1933   *The Pawnee Ghost Dance hand game: A study of cultural change.* Columbia University Contributions to Anthropology 16. New York: Columbia University Press.

1935   Functionalism in social anthropology. *AA* 37:386–393.

1939   Problems versus subject matter as directives of research. *AA* 41:574–582.

1961   Social fields and the evolution of society. *SWJA* 17:40–48.

Levinson, Marjorie, Marilyn Butler, Jerome McGann, and Paul Hamilton
1989   *Rethinking historicism: Critical readings in Romantic history.* Oxford: Basil Blackwell.

Levy, Richard
1984   Eastern Miwok. In *Handbook of North American Indians,* vol. 8: *California,* edited by Robert F. Heizer. Washington: Smithsonian Institution.

Lewellen, Ted
1983   *Political anthropology: An introduction.* South Hadley, Mass.: Bergin and Garvey.

Lewin, Julius
1940   Review of *African political systems,* edited by Meyer Fortes and E. E. Evans-Pritchard. *Bantu Studies* 14:455–456.

Lewin, Kurt
1951   *Field theory in social science: Selected theoretical papers.* New York: Harper.

Lewis, Oscar
1942   *The effects of white contact upon Blackfoot culture, with special reference to the role of the fur trade.* Monographs of the American Ethnological Society 6. New York: J. J. Augustin.
1951   *Life in a Mexican village: Tepoztlán restudied.* Urbana: University of Illinois Press.
1958   Foreword to *The Hindu Jajman system,* edited by W. Henricks Wiser. Lucknow, India: Lucknow Publishing House.
1964   *Pedro Martinez: A Mexican peasant and his family.* New York: Random House.
1970   *Anthropological essays.* New York: Random House.

Leys, Colin
1974   *Underdevelopment in Kenya: The political economy of neo-colonialism, 1964–1971.* Berkeley: University of California Press.

Lienhardt, Ronald Godfrey
1964   *Social anthropology.* London: Oxford University Press.

Lindenbaum, Shirley
1976   A wife is the hand of man. In *Man and woman in the New Guinea highlands,* edited by Paula Brown and Georgeda Buchbinder. Washington, D.C.: American Anthropological Association.

Linton, Ralph
1936   *The study of man.* New York: Appleton-Century.
1944   Nomad raids and fortified pueblos. *American Antiquity* 10:28–32.

Linton, Ralph, ed.
1940   *Acculturation in seven American tribes.* New York: Appleton.

Lipset, Seymour Martin
1963   *The first new nation: The United States in historical and comparative perspective.* New York: Basic Books.

Llewellyn, Karl N.
1930a   *The bramble bush: Lectures on law and its study.* Tentative printing

for the use of students at Columbia University School of Law, New York.

1930b   *Cases and materials on the law of sales.* Chicago: Callaghan.

1931   Some realism about realism. *Harvard Law Review* 44:1222–1264.

1941   The theory of "legal science." *North Carolina Law Review* 20:1–23.

1951   *The bramble bush: Lectures on law and its study.* 2d ed. Dobbs Ferry, N.Y.: Oceana Publications.

1960   *The common law tradition: Deciding appeals.* Boston: Little, Brown.

Llewellyn, Karl N., and E. Adamson Hoebel

1941   *The Cheyenne way: Conflict and case law in primitive jurisprudence.* Norman: University of Oklahoma Press.

Lloyd, Denis

1959   *Introduction to jurisprudence, with selected texts.* London: Stevens.

Lloyd, Peter C.

1962   *Yoruba land law.* London: Oxford University Press, for the Nigerian Institute of Social and Economic Research.

1965   The political structure of an African kingdom. In *Political systems and the distribution of power,* edited by Michael P. Banton. ASA Monograph 2. London: Tavistock.

1966a   Traditional rulers. In *Political parties and national integration in tropical Africa,* edited by James Coleman and Carl Rosberg. Berkeley: University of California Press.

Lloyd, Peter C., ed.

1966b   *The new elites of tropical Africa.* Studies presented and discussed at the sixth international African seminar at the University of Ibadan, Nigeria, July 1964. Oxford: Oxford University Press.

Locke, Alain, and Bernhard J. Stern, eds.

1942   *When peoples meet: A study in race and culture contact.* New York: Committee on Workshops, Progressive Education Association.

Long, C. H.

1980   Primitive/civilized: The locus of a problem. *History of Religions* 20:43–61.

Long, Norman

1968   *Social change and the individual: A study of social and religious responses to innovation in a Zambian rural community.* Manchester: Manchester University Press.

1975   Structural dependency, modes of production and economic brokerage in rural Peru. In *Beyond the sociology of development,* edited by Ivan Oxaal et al. London: Routledge and Kegan Paul.

1977   *An introduction to the sociology of rural development.* London: Tavistock.

Lopez, Salvador P.

1966   The colonial relationship. In *Philippine-American relations,* edited by Frank H. Golay. New York: Solidaridad.

Lovejoy, Arthur O., and George Boas

1935   *A documentary history of primitivism and related ideas.* Baltimore: Johns Hopkins University Press.

Lowie, Robert H.
1915   Review of *Kinship and social organization*, by W.H.R. Rivers. *AA* 17:329–331.
1920   *Primitive society*. New York: Boni and Liveright.
1927a   Anthropology and law. In *The social sciences*, edited by William F. Ogburn and Alexander Goldenweiser. New York: Houghton Mifflin.
1927b   *The origin of the state*. New York: Russell and Russell.
1936a   Lewis Henry Morgan in historical perspective. In *Essays in anthropology: Presented to A. L. Kroeber*, edited by Robert H. Lowie. Berkeley: University of California Press.
1936b   Introduction to *A black civilization: A social study of an Australian tribe*, by W. Lloyd Warner. New York: Harper and Row.
1937   *The history of ethnological theory*. New York: Holt, Rinehart and Winston.
1948a   Some aspects of political organization among the American aborigines. *JRAI* 78:11–24.
1948b   *Social organization*. New York: Rinehart.
1959   *Robert H. Lowie, ethnologist*. Berkeley: University of California Press.
Lubbock, Sir John
1870   *The origin of civilization and the primitive condition of man: Mental and social conditions of savages*. London: Longmans, Green.
Lukes, Stephen
1973   *Emile Durkheim: His life and work, a historical and critical study*. London: Allen Lane / Penguin Press.
Lutkehaus, Nancy
1982   Ambivalence, ambiguity and the reproduction of gender hierarchy in Manam society, 1933–79. *Social Analysis* 12:36–51.
Lynd, Robert S., and Helen M. Lynd
1929   *Middletown: A study in American culture*. New York: Harcourt, Brace.
1937   *Middletown in transition: A study in cultural conflicts*. New York: Harcourt, Brace.
McAdam, Anthony
1977   Leonard Barnes and South Africa. *Social dynamics* 3:41–53.
MacCurdy, G. G.
1902   Twenty years of Section H anthropology. *Science* 15:512–534.
MacDermott, B. H.
1972   The Nuer are not Dinka. *Man* 7:480.
McElroy, James Logan
1984   Social reform in the Burned-Over District: Rochester, New York, as a test case, 1830–1854. Ph.D. diss., State University of New York at Binghamton.
McGann, Jerome J.
1985   *Historical studies and literary criticism*. Madison: University of Wisconsin Press.
McGee, William J.
1898   Piratical acculturation. *AA* 11:243–249.

1906   Recent progess in American Anthropology: A review of the activities of institutions and individuals from 1902 to 1906. *AA* 8:466–467.

MacKenzie, William J. M.

1967   *Politics and social science.* Harmondsworth, Eng.: Penguin Books.

1982   The knights of the textbooks. In *Custom and conflict in British society,* edited by Ronald Frankenberg. Manchester: Manchester University Press.

MacLeod, William Christie

1928a   *The American Indian frontier.* New York: Knopf.

1928b   Economic aspects of indigenous American slavery. *AA* 30:632–650.

McNairn, Barbara

1980   *The method and theory of V. Gordon Childe.* New York: Columbia University Press.

MacRae, Donald G.

1961   *Ideology and society: Papers in sociology and politics.* London: Heinemann.

Magdoff, Harry

1969   *The age of imperialism: The economics of U.S. foreign policy.* New York: Monthly Review Press.

Magubane, Bernard

1979   Theoretical implications: A roundtable discussion. *Review* 3:340–345.

Maine, Henry Sumner

1861   *Ancient law.* London: John Murray.

1871   *Village-communities in the East and West.* London: John Murray.

1875a   *Lectures on the early history of institutions (A sequel to* Ancient law*).* London: John Murray.

1875b   *The effects of observation of India on modern European thought: Rede lecture.* Reprinted in *Village-communities in the East and West,* 3d ed. London: John Murray.

1876   *Village-communities in the East and West.* 3d ed. London: John Murray.

1883   *Dissertations on early law and custom.* London: John Murray.

1885   *Popular government.* London: John Murray.

Mair, Lucy P.

1943   Communication. *Man* 43:62–63.

1955   Webo of fantasy *Man* 38:70.

1962   *Primitive government.* Harmondsworth, Eng.: Penguin Books.

1963   *New nations.* Chicago: University of Chicago Press.

1965a   *An introduction to social anthropology.* New York: Holt, Rinehart and Winston.

1965b   How small-scale societies change. In *Penguin survey of the social sciences,* edited by Julian Gould. Harmondsworth, Eng.: Penguin.

1967   *The new Africa.* London: Watts.

1969   *Anthropology and social change.* London: Athlone Press.

1975   How far have we got in the study of politics? In *Studies in African social anthropology,* edited by Meyer Fortes and Sheila Patterson. New York: Academic Press.

Malinowski, Bronislaw
　1911　Review of *The tribe and intertribal relations in Australia*, by Gerald C. Wheeler. *Man* 11:25–28.
　1913　*The family among the Australian aborigines: A sociological study.* London: University of London Press.
　1920　War and weapons among the natives of the Trobriand Islands. *Man* 20:10–12.
　1922　*Argonauts of the western Pacific: An account of native enterprise and adventure in the archipelagoes of Melanesian New Guinea.* Studies in Economics and Political Science, no. 65. London: Routledge.
　1925　Review of *Primitive law*, by E. Sidney Hartland. *Nature* 116:230–235.
　1926a　*Crime and custom in savage society.* London: Kegan Paul, Trench and Trubner.
　1926b　Primitive law and order. *Nature* 117:9–16.
　1934　Introduction to *Law and order in Polynesia: A study of primitive legal institutions*, by H. Ian Hogbin. New York: Harcourt, Brace.
　1935　*Coral gardens and their magic: A study of the methods of tilling the soil and of agricultural rites in the Trobriand Islands.* 2 vols. London: Allen and Unwin.
　1936　The deadly issue. *Atlantic Monthly* 158:659–669.
　1942　A new instrument for the interpretation of law—especially primitive. *Yale Law Journal* 51:1237–1254.
Mandelbaum, David G.
　1963　Introduction to *Behind mud walls*, by William and Charlotte Wiser. Berkeley: University of California Press.
　1980　The Todas in time perspective. *Reviews in Anthropology* 7:278–302.
Manghezi, Alpheus
　1976　*Class, elite and community in African development.* Uppsala: Scandinavian Institute of African Studies.
Marcus, George, and D. Cushman
　1982　Ethnographies as texts. *ARA* 11:25–69.
Marcus, George E., and Michael M. J. Fischer
　1986　*Anthropology as cultural critique: An experimental moment in the human sciences.* Chicago: University of Chicago Press.
Marett, Robert R.
　1912　*Anthropology.* New York: Holt.
　1927　E. B. Tylor. *Dictionary of national bibliography, 1912–1921.*
　1941　*A Jerseyman at Oxford.* London: Oxford University Press.
Mark, Joan
　1980　*Four anthropologists: An American science in its early years.* New York: Science History Publications.
Marwick, Arthur
　1965　*The deluge: British society and the First World War.* London: Bodley Head.
Marwick, M. G.
　1965　*Sorcery in its social setting: A study of the Northern Rhodesian Cewa.* Manchester: Manchester University Press.

Marx, Karl
   1973   *Grundrisse: Foundations of the critique of political economy.* Trans-
           lated and with a foreword by Martin Nicolaus. Harmondsworth,
           Eng.: Penguin Books. Originally published 1939.
Masterman, Charles F. G.
   1902   *The heart of the empire: Discussions of problems of modern city
           life in England.* London: Unwin.
Mayer, Adrian C.
   1966   The significance of quasi-groups in the study of complex societies.
           In *The social anthropology of complex societies,* edited by Michael
           P. Banton. ASA Monograph 4. London: Tavistock.
Mead, Margaret
   1932   *The changing culture of an Indian tribe.* New York: Columbia Uni-
           versity Press.
   1973   Changing styles of anthropological fieldwork. *ARA* 2:1–26.
Meadows, Paul
   1952   *John Wesley Powell: Frontiersman of science.* University of Ne-
           braska Studies, no. 10. Lincoln: University of Nebraska Press.
Meek, C. K.
   1941   Review of *African political systems,* edited by Meyer Fortes and
           E. E. Evans-Pritchard. *Man* 41:41–42.
Meek, Ronald L.
   1976   *Social science and the ignoble savage.* New York: Cambridge Univer-
           sity Press.
Meillassoux, Claude
   1975   *Femmes, greniers et capitaux.* Paris: Libraire Francois Maspero.
   1981   *Maidens, meal and money: Capitalism and the domestic economy.*
           Cambridge: Cambridge University Press.
Mencher, Joan P.
   1978   *Agriculture and social structure in Tamil Nadu: Past origins and
           present transformations, and future prospects.* Delhi: Allied
           Publishers.
Mencher, Joan P., ed.
   1983   *The social anthropology of peasantry.* Bombay: Somaiya Publica-
           tions; Atlantic Highlands, N.J.: Humanities Press.
Mendelson, E. M.
   1960   Review of *Sons of the shaking earth,* by Eric R. Wolf. *Man* 55:246.
Merivale, Herman
   1928   *Lectures on colonization and colonies.* London: Oxford University
           Press.
Merry, Sally
   1989   Interpreting American litigiousness. In *History and power in the
           study of law,* edited by June Starr and Jane F. Collier. Ithaca, N.Y.:
           Cornell University Press.
Middleton, John, and David Tait, eds.
   1958   *Tribes without rulers: Studies in African segmentary systems.* Lon-
           don: Routledge and Kegan Paul.

Mills, C. Wright
　1948　Edward Westermarck and the application of ethnographic methods to marriage and morals. In *Introduction to the history of sociology*, edited by Harry Elmer Barnes. Chicago: University of Chicago Press.
Miner, Horace
　1952　The folk-urban continuum. *American Sociological Review* 17:529–537.
Mintz, Sydney W.
　1951　Cañamelar: The contemporary culture of a rural Puerto Rican proletariat. Ph.D. diss., Columbia University.
　1953a　The folk-urban continuum and the rural proletarian community. *American Journal of Sociology* 59:136–143.
　1953b　The culture history of a Puerto Rican sugar-cane plantation, 1876–1949. *Hispanic American Historical Review* 33:224–251.
　1956　Cañamelar: The subculture of a rural sugar plantation proletariat. In *The people of Puerto Rico: A study in social anthropology*, edited by Julian Steward. Urbana: University of Illinois Press.
　1960　*Worker in the cane: A Puerto Rican life history*. New Haven: Yale University Press.
　1974a　The rural proletariat and the problem of rural proletarian consciousness. *JPS* 1:291–325.
　1974b　*Caribbean transformations*. Chicago: Aldine.
　1976　On the concept of the Third World. *DA* 1:377–382.
　1977　The so-called world system: Local initiative and local response. *DA* 2:253–270.
　1978a　The role of Puerto Rico in modern social science. *Revista Interamericana* 8:5–16.
　1978b　Was the plantation slave a proletarian? *Review* 2:81–98.
　1979a　The role of water in Steward's cultural ecology. *Steward Anthropological Society Journal* 11:17–32.
　1979b　Slavery and the rise of peasantries. *Historical Reflections* 6:213–242.
　1981　Discussion. In *Totems and teachers: Perspectives on the history of anthropology*, edited by Sydel Silverman, 165. New York: Columbia University Press.
　1982　Descrying the peasantry. *Review* 6:209–225.
Mintz, Sidney W., ed.
　1985　*History, evolution and the concept of culture: Selected papers by Alexander Lesser*. Cambridge: Cambridge University Press.
Mishkin, Bernard
　1940　*Rank and warfare in Plains Indian culture*. Monographs of the American Ethnological Society 3. New York: J. J. Augustin.
Mitchell, J. Clyde
　1956　*The Yao village: A study in the social structure of a Nyasaland tribe*. Manchester: Manchester University Press.
　1966　Theoretical orientations in African urban studies. In *The social anthropology of complex societies*, edited by Michael Banton. ASA Monograph 4. London: Tavistock.

Moerman, Michael
  1965   Ethnic identification in a complex civilization: Who are the Lue?
          AA 67:1215–1230.
Moise, E.
  1982   The moral economy dispute. *Bulletin of Concerned Asian Scholars*
          14:72–76.
Mooney, James
  1889   Folklore of the Carolina mountains. *Journal of American Folklore*
          2:95–104.
  1894   *The Siouan tribes of the East*. Bureau of Ethnology Bulletin 22.
          Washington, D.C.: Government Printing Office.
  1896   The Ghost Dance and the Sioux outbreak of 1890. In *Fourteenth
          Annual Report of the Bureau of Ethnology*, pt. 2. Washington, D.C.:
          Government Printing Office.
  1907   The Ghost-Dance. In *Handbook of American Indians North of
          Mexico*, Bulletin no. 30, edited by F. W. Hodge. Washington, D.C.:
          Smithsonian Institution.
  1965   *The Ghost-Dance religion and the Sioux outbreak of 1890*. Edited
          by Anthony F. C. Wallace. Chicago: University of Chicago Press.
Moore, Sally Falk
  1958   *Power and property in Inca Peru*. New York: Columbia University
          Press.
  1965   Comment on Cohen's "Establishment of identity in a social nexus."
          AA 67:748–751.
  1969   Law and anthropology. *Biennial Review of Anthropology, 1969*. Stan-
          ford, Calif.: Stanford University Press.
  1970   Review of *Law without precedent*, by Lloyd A. Fallers. *AA* 72:1482–
          1484.
  1972   Legal liability and evolutionary interpretation: Some aspects of
          strict liability, self-help, and collective responsibility. In *The alloca-
          tion of responsibility*, edited by Max Gluckman. Manchester: Man-
          chester University Press.
  1973   Law and social change: The semi-autonomous social field as an ap-
          propriate subject of study. *LSR* 7:719–746.
  1978a   *Law as process: An anthropological approach*. London: Routledge
          and Kegan Paul.
  1978b   Archaic law and modern times on the Zambezi. In *Cross examina-
          tions*, edited by Philip H. Gulliver. Leiden: Brill.
  1985a   Legal systems of the world: An introductory guide to classifications,
          typological interpretations and bibliographical sources. In *Law and
          the social sciences*, edited by Leon Lipson and Stanton Wheeler.
          New York: Russell Sage Foundation.
  1985b   Dividing the pot of gold: Social and symbolic elements in an instru-
          mental negotiation. *Negotiation Journal* 1:29–43.
  1986   *Social facts and fabrications: "Customary law" on Kilimanjaro,
          1880–1980*. Cambridge: Cambridge University Press.
Morel, Edmund D.
  1905   *Red rubber!* Liverpool: G. Richardson and Sons.

Morgan, Lewis H.

1851   *League of the Ho-de-no-sau-nee, or Iroquois.* Rochester, N.Y.: Sage and Broa.

1877   *Ancient society; or, Researches in the lines of human progress from savagery through barbarism to civilization.* New York: World Publishing.

Moses, L. G.

1984   *The Indian man: A biography of James Mooney.* Urbana: University of Illinois Press.

Moss, C. R.

1920   Nakaloi law and ritual. *UCPAAE* 15:207–342.

Mosse, George Lackmann

1961   *The culture of western Europe: The nineteenth and twentieth centuries.* Chicago: Rand McNally.

Mudimbe, V. Y.

1973   *L'autre face du royaume: Une introduction a la critique des langages en folie.* Lusanne: Editions L'age d'homme.

Mukhia, H.

1981   Was there feudalism in Indian history? *JPS* 8:273–310.

Muller, Max

1891   On the work of Major J. W. Powell, director of the U.S. Ethnological Bureau. Report of Section H. *61st Meeting of the British Association for the Advancement of Science,* Cardiff, August 1891.

Mullins, Nicholas C., with J. Carolyn Mullins

1973   *Theories and theory groups in contemporary American sociology.* New York: Harper and Row.

Murdock, George P.

1943   Review of *Folk culture of Yucatan,* by Robert Redfield. *AA* 45:133–136.

1951   British social anthropology. *AA* 53:465–473.

1960   Review of *Method in social anthropology: Selected essays,* by A. R. Radcliffe-Brown, edited by M. N. Srinivas. *AA* 62:156–157.

Murphy, Robert F.

1963   On Zen Marxism: Filiation and alliance. *Man* 63:17–19.

1971   *The dialectics of social life: Alarms and excursions in anthropological theory.* New York: Basic Books.

1977   Introduction: The anthropological theories of Julian H. Steward. In *Evolution and ecology. Essays on social transformation by Julian H. Steward,* edited by Jane C. Steward and Robert F. Murphy. Urbana: University of Illinois Press.

1981   Julian Steward. In *Totems and teachers: Perspectives on the history of anthropology,* edited by Sydel Silverman. New York: Columbia University Press.

Myres, John Linton

1916   The influence of anthropology on the course of political science. *University of California Publications in History* 4:1–81.

Nadel, Siegfried F.

1940   The Kede: A riverain state in northern Nigeria. In *African political systems*, edited by Meyer Fortes and E. E. Evans-Pritchard. Oxford: Oxford University Press.

1951   *The foundations of social anthropology.* London: Cohen and West.
1956   Understanding primitive peoples. *Oceania* 26:159–173.
1957   *The theory of social structure.* London: Cohen and West.

Nader, Laura
1965   Choices in legal procedure: Shia Moslem and Mexican Zapotec. *AA* 67:394–399.

Nader, Laura, ed.
1969   *Law in culture and society.* Chicago: Aldine.

Nader, Laura, and D. Metzger
1963   Conflict resolution in two Mexican communities. *AA* 65:584–592.

Nader, Laura, and Barbara Yngvesson
1973   On studying the ethnography of law and its consequences. In *Handbook of social and cultural anthropology*, edited by John Honigman. Chicago: Rand McNally.

Nader, Laura, Klaus F. Koch, and B. Cox
1966   The ethnography of law: A bibliographic survey. *CA* 7:267–294.

Nader, Laura, and Harry F. Todd, Jr., eds.
1978   *The disputing process: Law in ten societies.* New York: Columbia University Press.

Nash, June
1975   Nationalism and fieldwork. *ARA* 4:225–246.
1981   Ethnographic aspects of the world capitalist system. *ARA* 10:393–423.

Nash, June, and Maria Patricia Fernandez-Kelly, eds.
1983   *Women, men, and the international division of labor.* Albany: State University of New York Press.

Nash, June, and Helen Safa, eds.
1986   *Women and change in Latin America: New directions in sex and class.* New York: Praeger.

Needham, Rodney
1974   *Remarks and inventions: Skeptical essays about kinship.* London: Tavistock.

Nelson, Cary, and Lawrence Grossberg
1983   *Marxism and the interpretation of culture.* Urbana: University of Illinois Press.

Nettl, J. Peter
1967   *Political mobilization: A sociological analysis of methods and concepts.* London: Faber.

Newcombe, W. W., Jr.
1950   A re-examination of the causes of Plains warfare. *AA* 52:317–330.

Newcomer, P. J.
1972   The Nuer are Dinka: An essay on origins and environmental determinism. *Man* 7:5–11.

Newman, Katherine S.
1983   *Law and economic organization.* Cambridge: Cambridge University Press.

Nieboer, Hermann J.
1900   *Slavery as an industrial system: Ethnological researches.* The
        Hague: Martinus Nijhoff.
Nisbet, Robert
1968   The rise and fall of social class. In *Tradition and revolt: Historical
        and sociological essays,* by Robert Nisbet. New York: Random
        House.
Noelke, V. Hull McKinnon
1974   The origin and early history of the Bureau of American Ethnology,
        1879–1910. Ph.D. diss., University of Texas, Austin.
Noggle, B.
1966   The twenties: A new historiographical frontier. *Journal of American
        History* 53:299–314.
Nowell-Smith, Simon Harcourt, ed.
1964   *Edwardian England, 1901–1914.* London: Oxford University Press.
Nugent, David
1982   Closed systems and contradiction: The Kachin in and out of history.
        Man 17:508–527.
O'Barr, Jean F., ed.
1982   *Perspectives on power: Women in Africa, Asia and Latin America.*
        Durham, N.C.: Duke University, Center for International Studies.
O'Barr, William M.
1982   *Linguistic evidence: Language, power and strategy in the court-
        room.* New York: Academic Press.
Oberg, Kalervo
1940   The kingdom of Ankole. In *African political systems,* edited by
        Meyer Fortes and E. E. Evans-Pritchard. Oxford: Oxford University
        Press.
O'Brien, Denise, and Sharon Tiffany, eds.
1984   *Rethinking women's roles: Perspectives from the Pacific.* Berkeley:
        University of California Press.
O'Laughlin, Bridget
1975   Marxist approaches in anthropology. *ARA* 4:341–370.
Ollman, Bernard, and E. Vernoff
1982   *The left academy: Marxist scholarship on American campuses.*
        New York: McGraw-Hill.
Omvedt, Gail
1981   Caste and class. *Book Review* 5:11–18.
1982   Review essay: Caste. *Bulletin of Concerned Asian Scholars* 14:62–
        66.
Ong, Aihwa
1987   *Spirits of resistance and capitalist discipline: Factory women in
        Malaysia.* Albany: State University of New York Press.
Ortner, Sherry
1974   Is female to male as nature is to culture? In *Woman, culture and
        society,* edited by Michelle Zimbalist Rosaldo and Louise Lamphere.
        Stanford, Calif.: Stanford University Press.

Ortner, Sherry, and Harriet Whitehead, eds.
1981   *Sexual meanings: The cultural construction of gender and sexuality.* Cambridge: Cambridge University Press.
Otterbein, Keith F.
1973   The anthropology of war. In *Handbook of social and cultural anthropology,* edited by John J. Honigman. Chicago: Rand McNally.
Owusu, Maxwell
1975   Policy studies, development and political anthropology. *Journal of Modern African Studies* 13:367–381.
Owusu, Maxwell, ed.
1975   *Colonialism and change: Essays presented to Lucy Mair.* The Hague: Mouton.
Oxaal, Ivan, T. Barnett, and D. Booth, eds.
1975   *Beyond the sociology of development: Economy and society in Latin America and Africa.* London: Routledge and Kegan Paul.
Paine, Robert
1971   A theory of patronage and brokerage. In *Patrons and brokers in the east Arctic,* edited by Robert Paine. St. John's, Newfoundland: Memorial University.
1974   *Second thoughts about Barth's models.* Royal Anthropological Institute, Occasional Paper 32. London: Royal Anthropological Institute.
Parker, A. C.
1919   *The life of General Ely S. Parker.* Buffalo: Buffalo Historical Society.
Parkin, David
1984   Political language. *ARA* 13:345–365.
Parsons, Elsie Clews
1936   *Mitla: Town of souls and other Zapoteco-speaking pueblos of Oaxaca, Mexico.* Chicago: University of Chicago Press.
Patterson, Orlando
1977   Slavery. *Annual Review of Sociology* 3:407–449.
Pepper, Stephen C.
1942   *World hypotheses: A study in evidence.* Berkeley: University of California Press.
Perelman, Michael
1984   *Classical political economy: Primitive accumulation and the social division of labor.* London: F. Pinter.
Perkins, Whitney T.
1962   *Denial of empire: The United States and its dependencies.* Leiden: A. W. Sythoff.
Perry, William J.
1923a   *The children of the sun: A study in the early history of civilization.* London: Methuen.
1923b   Pugnacity. *Monist* 33:116–138.
Peter, Prince
1963   *A study of polyandry.* The Hague: Mouton.
Peters, Emrys L.
1967   Some structural aspects of the feud among camel-herding Bedouin of Cyrenaica. *Africa* 37:261–282.

Phear, Sir John Budd
1880   *The Aryan village in India and Ceylon.* London: Macmillan.
Piddocke, Stuart
1965   The potlatch system of the southern Kwakiutl: A new perspective. *SWJA* 21:244–264.
Pilling, A. R.
1976   Howard's comments on Daisy Bates and Radcliffe-Brown. *AA* 78:357–358.
Pitt-Rivers, Augustus Lane-Fox
1874   War. In *Notes and queries on anthropology: For the use of travellers and residents in uncivilized lands.* London: BAAS.
1906   *The evolution of culture and other essays,* edited by John L. Myres. Oxford: Clarendon Press.
Pitt-Rivers, George Henry Lane-Fox
1927   *The clash of culture and the contact of races: An anthropological and psychological study of the laws of racial adaptability, with special reference to the depopulation of the Pacific and the government of subject races.* London: Routledge.
Pletsch, C. E.
1981   The three worlds, or the division of social scientific labor, circa 1950–1975. *CSSH* 23:565–590.
Polanyi, Karl
1968   *Primitive, archaic and modern economies,* edited by George Dalton. Boston: Beacon.
Polanyi, Karl, Conrad Arensberg, and Harold Pearson, eds.
1957   *Trade and market in the early empires.* New York: Glencoe.
Popkin, Samuel L.
1979   *The rational peasant: The political economy of rural society in Vietnam.* Berkeley: University of California Press.
Popper, Karl
1945/ The open society and its enemies. 2 vols. London: Routledge.
1962
Porter, Bernard
1968   *Critics of empire: British radical attitudes to colonialism in Africa, 1895–1914.* London: Macmillan.
Posner, R.
1980   A theory of primitive society with special reference to primitive law. *Law and Economics* 13:1–53.
Pospisil, Leopold
1958a   *Kapauka Papuans and their law.* New Haven: Yale University, Department of Anthropology.
1958b   Social change and primitive law: Consequences of a Papuan legal case. *AA* 60:832–837.
1959   Multiplicity of legal systems in primitive societies. *Bulletin of the Philadelphia Anthropological Society* 12:1–4.
1965   A formal analysis of substantive law: Kapauka Papuan laws of inheritance. *AA* 67:166–185.

1971   *Anthropology of law: A comparative theory.* New York: Harper and Row.

1979   Legally induced cultural change in New Guinea. In *The imposition of law,* edited by Sandra B. Burman and Barbara E. Harrell-Bond. New York: Academic Press.

Post, Ken

1973   Peasantisation and rural political movements in western Africa. *EJS* 13:223–254.

Post, Louis Freeland

1923   *The deportation delirium of nineteen-twenty: A personal narrative of an historic official experience.* Chicago: C. H. Kerr.

Poulantzas, N.

1982   Law. In *Marxism and law,* edited by P. Beirne and R. Quinney. New York: Wiley.

Pound, Roscoe

1908   Mechanical jurisprudence. *Columbia Law Review* 8:605–623.

1910   Law in books and law in action. *American Law Review* 44:35–36.

Powdermaker, Hortense

1939   *After freedom: A cultural study of the Deep South.* New York: Viking Press.

Powell, John Wesley

1880   Sketch of Lewis H. Morgan, president of the American Association for the Advancement of Science. *Popular Science Monthly* 18:114–121.

1881   Wyandotte government: A short study of tribal society. *First annual report of the Bureau of Ethnology,* 59–69. Washington, D.C.: Government Printing Office.

1881–   On kinship and the tribe. *Third annual report of the Bureau of*
82   *Ethnology,* xliv–lxix. Washington, D.C.: Government Printing Office.

1882   Annual address of the president. *Transactions of the Anthropological Society of Washington* 1:106–129.

1884   Director's report. Smithsonian Institution Bureau of Ethnology. *Fifth Annual Report, 1883–84.* Washington, D.C.

Powell, John Wesley, and George W. Ingalls

1874   Report on the condition of the Ute Indians of Utah; the Pai-Utes of Utah, northern Arizona, southern Nevada, and southeastern California; the Go-Si Utes of Utah and Nevada; the Northwestern Shoshones of Idaho and Utah; and the Western Shoshones of Nevada. In *Anthropology of the Numa,* edited by Don D. Fowler and Catherine S. Fowler. Smithsonian Contributions to Anthropology, no. 14. Washington, D.C.: Smithsonian Institution Press.

Prattis, J. I.

1973   Strategizing man. *Man* 8:46–58.

Price, Derek Jack de Solla

1963   *Little science, big science.* New York: Columbia University Press.

1965   Networks of scientific papers. *Science* 149:510–515.

Price, Richard
  1985   The dark complete world of a Caribbean store: A note on the world system. *Review* 9:215–219.
Provinse, John
  1937   The underlying sanctions of Plains Indian culture. In *Social anthropology of North American tribes*, edited by Fred Eggan. Chicago: University of Chicago Press.
Pyenson, Lewis
  1982   Cultural imperialism and the exact sciences: German expansion overseas, 1900–1930. *History of Science* 20:1–43.
Quiggin, Alison Hingston
  1942   *Haddon, the head hunter: A short sketch of the life of A. C. Haddon.* Cambridge: Cambridge University Press.
Quinn, Naomi
  1977   Anthropological studies in women's status. *ARA* 6:181–226.
Quinton, A.
  1975   Thought. In *The Edwardians: The remaking of British society*, edited by Paul Thompson. London: Granada.
Radcliffe-Brown, Alfred Reginald
  1922   *The Andaman Islanders.* Cambridge: Cambridge University Press.
  1933a   Primitive law. *IESS* 9:202–206.
  1933b   Social sanctions. *IESS* 8:531–534.
  1935   Patrilineal and matrilineal succession. *Iowa Law Review* 20:286–303.
  1939   Preface to *Suye Mura: A Japanese village*, by John Embree. Chicago: University of Chicago Press.
  1940   Preface to *African political systems*, edited by Meyer Fortes and E. E. Evans-Pritchard. Oxford: Oxford University Press.
  1952   *Structure and function in primitive society.* Glencoe, Ill.: Free Press.
  1954   Introduction to *Military organization and society*, by Stanislaus Andrzejewski. London: Routledge and Kegan Paul.
Radin, Paul
  1932   *Social anthropology.* New York: McGraw-Hill.
Raglan, Lord
  1942   Summary of a communication by the Rt. Honourable Lord Raglan to the Royal Anthropological Institute, 27 October. *Man* 36:58–61.
  1944   Communication. *Man* 38:104–107.
  1950   Review of *Primitive war*, by H. H. Turney-High. *Man* 33:150.
  1953   Communication. *Man* 47:152, 229, 281, 304.
  1954   Communication. *Man* 48:19, 42, 74, 98, 124.
  1955   Communication. *Man* 49:59, 60.
Raison, Timothy, ed.
  1969   *The founding fathers of social science.* London: Penguin Books.
Ranger, Terence O.
  1978   Growing from the roots: Reflections on peasant research in central and southern Africa. *Journal of Southern African Studies* 5:99–133.
  1982   Tradition and travesty: Chiefs and administration in the Makoni

district, Zimbabwe, 1960–1980. *Africa* 52:20–41.

Rapp, Rayna [see also Reiter]

1977   Gender and class: An archeology of knowledge concerning the origin of the state. *DA* 2:309–316.

1978   Family and class in contemporary America: Notes towards an understanding of ideology. *Science and Society* 42:278–300.

1979   Review essay: Anthropology. *Signs* 4:492–513.

Rapoport, David C.

1971   Foreword to *Primitive war: Its practice and concepts,* by H. H. Turney-High. 2d ed. Columbia: University of South Carolina Press.

Rattray, R. A.

1929   *Ashanti law and constitution.* Oxford: Clarendon Press.

Ray, Verne F.

1939   *Cultural relations in the plateau of northwestern America.* Publication of the F. W. Hodge Anniversary Publication Fund, no. 3. Los Angeles: Southwest Museum.

Ray, Verne F., ed.

1969   Cultural stability and cultural change. *Proceedings of the 1957 Annual Spring Meeting of the American Ethnological Society.* Seattle: University of Washington Press.

Redfield, Margaret Park, ed.

1962   *Human nature and the study of society: The papers of Robert Redfield.* Chicago: University of Chicago Press.

Redfield, Robert

1928   My adventures as a Mexican. *University of Chicago Magazine* 20:242–247.

1930   *Tepoztlán: A Mexican village.* Chicago: University of Chicago Press.

1934a   *Chan Kom: A Maya village.* With Alfonso Villa Rojas. Washington, D.C.: Carnegie Institution of Washington.

1934b   Culture changes in Yucatan. *AA* 36:57–69.

1941   *The folk culture of Yucatan.* Chicago: University of Chicago Press.

1947   The folk society. *AJS* 53:293–308.

1950   'Maine's *Ancient law. Western Political Quarterly* 3:574–589.

1953   Relations of anthropology to the social sciences and to the humanities. In *Anthropology today: An encyclopedic inventory,* edited by A. L. Kroeber. Chicago: University of Chicago Press.

1955   *The little community: Viewpoints for the study of a human whole.* Chicago: University of Chicago Press.

1956   *Peasant society and culture.* Chicago: Phoenix Books/University of Chicago Press.

1960   *The little community and peasant society and culture.* Chicago: University of Chicago Press.

Redfield, Robert, Melville Herskovits, and Ralph Linton

1936   Memorandum on the study of acculturation. *AA* 38:149–152.

Reiter, Rayna [see also Rapp]

1977   The search for origins: Unraveling the threads of gender hierarchy. *Critique of Anthropology* 3:5–24.

Reiter, Rayna, ed.
  1975   *Toward an anthropology of women.* New York: Monthly Review
         Press.
Resek, Carl
  1960   *Lewis Henry Morgan: American scholar.* Chicago: University of
         Chicago Press.
Rey, Pierre Phillipe
  1971   *Colonialisme, neo-capitalisme et transition au capitalisme: Exam-
         ple du 'comilog'au Congo-Brazzaville.* Paris: Maspero.
  1975   The lineage mode of production. *Critique of Anthropology* 3:27–79.
  1976   *Capitalisme Negrier: La marche des paysans vers le proletariat.*
         Paris: Maspero.
Rex, John
  1969   Max Weber. In *The founding fathers of social science,* edited by
         Timothy Raison. London: Penguin Books.
Rich, P. B.
  1986   *Race and empire in British politics.* Cambridge: Cambridge Univer-
         sity Press.
Richards, Audrey I.
  1940   The political system of the Bemba of north-eastern Rhodesia. In *Afri-
         can political systems,* edited by Meyer Fortes and E. E. Evans-Pritch-
         ard. Oxford: Oxford University Press.
  1960   *East African chiefs.* Cambridge: Cambridge University Press.
  1961   Anthropology on the scrap-heap? *Journal of African Administration*
         13:3–10.
  1977   The Colonial Office and the organization of social research. *Anthro-
         pological Forum* 4:32–51.
Richardson, Jane
  1940   *Law and status among the Kiowa Indians.* New York: Augustin.
Rigdon, Susan M.
  1988   *The culture facade: Art, science, and politics in the work of Oscar
         Lewis.* Urbana: University of Illinois Press.
Risley, Herbert H.
  1890– The study of ethnology in India. *Journal of the Anthropological Insti-
  91   tute* 20:235–248.
  1892   *The tribes and castes of Bengal.* 2 vols. Calcutta: Bengal Secretariat
         Press.
  1908   *The people of India.* Calcutta. Thacker, Spink.
Ritchie, David G.
  1889   *Darwinism and politics.* London: S. Sonnenschein.
  1893   *Darwin and Hegel, with other philosophical studies.* London: S.
         Sonnenschein.
Rivers, William Halse Rivers
  1900   A genealogical method of collecting social and vital statistics. *JRAI*
         30:74–82.
  1906   *The Todas.* London: Macmillan.
  1910   The genealogical method of anthropological inquiry. *Sociological
         Review* 3:1–12.

1912   Social organization. *Notes and queries on anthropology.* 4th ed. London: BAAS.

1913   Anthropological research outside America. In *Reports on the present conditions and future needs of the science of anthropology.* Carnegie Institution Publication, no. 200. Washington, D.C.

1914   *The history of Melanesian society.* 2 vols. Cambridge: Cambridge University Press.

1917   The government of subject peoples. In *Science and the nation,* edited by A. C. Seward. Cambridge: Cambridge University Press.

1924   *Social organization.* Edited by W. J. Perry. London: Kegan Paul, Trench and Trubner.

1926   *Psychology and ethnology.* Edited by G. Elliot Smith. London: Kegan Paul, Trench and Trubner.

Rivers, William H. Rivers, ed.

1922   *Essays on the depopulation of Melanesia.* Cambridge: Cambridge University Press.

Roberts, Simon

1979   *Order and dispute: An introduction to legal anthropology.* Harmondsworth, Eng.: Penguin Books.

Rohner, R. P., ed.

1969   *The ethnography of Franz Boas: Letters and diaries of Franz Boas written on the Northwest Coast from 1886–1931.* Chicago: University of Chicago Press.

Rooksby, R. L.

1971   W.H.R. Rivers and the Todas. *South Asia* 1:109–121.

Rosaldo, Michelle Zimbalist, and Louise Lamphere, eds.

1974   *Woman, culture and society.* Stanford, Calif.: Stanford University Press.

Roseberry, William

1978   Historical materialism and the people of Puerto Rico. *Revista/Review Interamericana* 8:26–36.

Rosen, Lawrence

1984   *Bargaining for reality.* Chicago: University of Chicago Press.

1986   Introduction to *Ancient law,* by Sir Henry Sumner Maine. Tucson: University of Arizona Press.

Ross, Edward Alsworth

1901   *Social control: A survey of the foundation of order.* New York: Macmillan.

Rousseau, J.

1979   Stratification and chiefship: A comparison of Kwakiutl and Kayan. In *Challenging anthropology,* edited by D. Turner and G. Smith. Toronto: McGraw-Hill Ryerson.

Rowbotham, Sheila

1972   *Women, resistance and revolution: A history of women and revolution in the modern world.* New York: Pantheon Books.

Royal Anthropological Institute Archives.

1910   Report of the Anthropological Survey of Mr. Northcote W. Thomas. Box A22.

Royce, Charles C.

1884   The Cherokee nation of Indians: A narrative of their official relations with the colonial and federal governments. Smithsonian Institution, Bureau of Ethnology, *Fifth Annual Report, 1883–84*. Washington, D.C.: Government Printing Office.

1897   Indian land cessions in the United States. Introduction by Cyrus Thomas. Smithsonian Institution, Bureau of Ethnology, *Seventh Annual Report, 1896–1897*. Washington, D.C.: Government Printing Office.

Runciman, Walter G.

1970   *Sociology in its place and other essays*. Cambridge: Cambridge University Press.

1972   *A critique of Max Weber's philosophy of social science*. Cambridge: Cambridge University Press.

Ruyle, R.

1973   Slavery, surplus and incipient stratification on the Northwest Coast: The ethnoenergetics of an incipient stratification system. *CA* 14:603–617.

Sacks, Karen

1975   Engels revisited: Women, the reorganization of production and private property. In *Toward an anthropology of women*, edited by Rayna Rapp. New York: Monthly Review Press.

1976   State bias and women's status. *AA* 75:1682–1700.

1982   *Sisters and wives: The past and future of sexual equality*. Urbana: University of Illinois Press.

Safa, Helen

1981   Runaway shops and female employment: The search for cheap labor. *Signs* 7:418–433.

Safire, William

1988   On language. *New York Times Magazine*. February 28, p.16.

Sahlins, Marshall

1961   The segmentary lineage: An organization of predatory expansion. *AA* 63:322–345.

1968   *Tribesmen*. New York: Prentice-Hall.

1972   *Stone age economics*. Chicago: Aldine-Atherton.

Sahlins, Marshall D., and Elman R. Service, eds.

1960   *Evolution and culture*. Ann Arbor: University of Michigan Press.

Said, Edward

1978   *Orientalism*. New York: Pantheon.

Salat, Jana

1983   *Reasoning as enterprise: The anthropology of S. F. Nadel*. Göttingen: Edition Herodot.

Salter, Elizabeth

1971   *Daisy Bates: The great white queen of the never never*. Sydney: Angus and Robertson.

Sartre, Jean-Paul

1943   *L'être et le neant, essai d'ontologie phénoménologique* (Being and nothingness). Paris: Gallimard.

1963   *Search for a method.* New York: Knopf.

Sawer, Geoffrey, ed.
1961   *Studies in the sociology of law.* Canberra: Australian National University Press.

Schapera, Isaac
1937   *Handbook of Tswana law and custom.* London: Oxford University Press.
1940   The political organization of the Ngwato of Bechuanaland Protectorate. In *African political systems,* edited by Meyer Fortes and E. E. Evans-Pritchard. Oxford: Oxford University Press.
1953   Some comments on comparative method in social anthropology. *AA* 55:353–362.
1956   *Government and politics in tribal societies.* London: Watts.
1957   Malinowski's theories of law. In *Man and culture: An evaluation of the work of Bronislaw Malinowski,* edited by Raymond Firth. London: Routledge and Kegan Paul.

Scheele, Raymond
1950   Warfare of the Iroquois and their northern neighbors. Ph.D. diss., Columbia University.

Schiller, Arthur
1965   Law. In *The African world: A survey of social research,* edited by Robert A. Lystad. New York: Praeger.

Schneider, Jane
1977   Was there a pre-capitalist world-system? *Peasant Studies* 6:20–29.

Scholte, Bob
1981   Critical anthropology since its reinvention. In *The anthropology of pre-capitalist societies,* edited by Joel S. Kahn and J. R. Llobera. London: Macmillan.
1983   Cultural anthropology and the paradigm concept: A brief history of their recent convergence. In *Functions and uses of disciplinary histories* 7, edited by Loren Graham, Wolf Lopenies, and Peter Weingart. Dordrecht: D. Reidel.
1984   Comment on "The thick and the thin: On the interpretive theoretical paradigm of Clifford Geertz," by P. Shanckman. *CA* 25:261–270.

Schurtz, Heinrich
1902   *Alterklassen und Männerbünde.* Berlin: Reimer.

Scott, James C.
1976   *The moral economy of the peasant: Rebellion and resistance in Southeast Asia.* New Haven: Yale University Press.
1977   Peasant revolution: A dismal science. *Comparative Politics* 9:231–248.
1985   *Weapons of the weak: Everyday forms of peasant resistance.* New Haven: Yale University Press.
1986   Introduction: Everyday forms of peasant resistance. *JPS* 13:1–35.

Scott, Joan Wallach
1986   Gender: A useful category of historical analysis. *American Historical Review* 91:1053–1075.

1988   *Gender and the politics of history.* New York: Columbia University Press.
Scudder, Thayer, and Elizabeth Colson
1980   *Secondary education in the formation of an elite: The impact of education on Gwembe district, Zambia.* New York: Academic Press.
Seaton, S. Lee, and Henri Claessen, eds.
1979   *Political anthropology: The state of the art.* The Hague: Mouton.
Secoy, Frank R.
1951   A functionalist-historical view of Plains Indian warfare: The processes of change from the 17th to the early 19th century. Ph.D. diss., Columbia University.
1953   *Changing military patterns on the Great Plains (17th century through early 19th century).* American Ethnological Society Monograph 21. New York: J. J. Augustin.
Seddon, David, ed.
1978   *Relations of production: Marxist approaches to economic anthropology.* London: Frank Cass.
Seidman, Robert B.
1978   *The state, law and development.* New York: St Martin's Press.
Seligman, C. G., and Brenda Z. Seligman
1918   The Kababish, a Sudan Arab tribe. *Harvard African Studies* 2:105–186.
Service, Elman R.
1950   Spanish-Guarani acculturation in early colonial Paraguay: The encomienda from 1537 to 1620. Ph.D. diss., Columbia University.
1962   *Primitive social organization.* New York: Random House.
1975   *Origins of the state and civilization.* New York: Norton.
Shanin, Teodor
1983   *Late Marx and the Russian road: Marx and "the peripheries of capitalism."* London: Routledge and Kegan Paul.
Shanin, Teodor, ed.
1987   *Peasants and peasant societies: Selected readings.* 2d ed. Oxford: Basil Blackwell.
Sider, Gerald
1976   Lumbee Indian cultural nationalism and ethnogenesis. *DA* 1:161–172.
1980   The ties that bind: Culture and agriculture, property and propriety in the Newfoundland village fishery. *Social History* 5:1–39.
1986   *Culture and class in anthropology and history: A Newfoundland illustration.* Cambridge: Cambridge University Press.
Sidgwick, Henry
1904   *Miscellaneous essays and addresses.* New York: Macmillan.
Siegel, Bernard J., Alan F. Beals, and Stephen A. Tyler
1987   Preface. *ARA* 16:v–vi.
Silva, Edward T., and Sheila A. Slaughter
1984   *Serving power: The making of the academic social science expert.* Westport, Conn.: Greenwood Press.

Silverman, Sydel
  1974   Bailey's politics. *JPS* 2:111–120.
  1983   The concept of peasant and the concept of culture. In *The social anthropology of peasantry*, edited by Joan P. Mencher. Atlantic Highlands, N.J.: Humanities Press.
Silverman, Sydel, ed.
  1981   *Totems and teachers: Perspectives on the history of anthropology.* New York: Columbia University Press.
Sjoberg, Gideon
  1952   Folk and feudal societies. *American Journal of Sociology* 58:231–239.
Skinner, Quentin
  1969   Meaning and understanding in the history of ideas. *History and Theory* 8:3–53.
Slobodin, Richard
  1978   *W.H.R. Rivers.* New York: Columbia University Press.
Smellie, K. B.
  1928   Sir Henry Maine. *Economica* 8:64–74.
Smith, Adam
  1784/   *An inquiry into the nature and causes of the wealth of nations.*
  1976   Dunwoody, Ga.: N. S. Berg.
Smith, Carol
  1984   Local history in global context. *CSSH* 26:193–228.
Smith, Carol, ed.
  1976   *Regional analysis.* 2 vols. New York: Academic Press.
Smith, Carol A., and J. Boyer
  1987   Central America since 1979. Pt. 1. *ARA* 16:197–221.
Smith, Grafton Elliot
  1911   *The ancient Egyptians and the origin of civilization.* London: Harper.
Smith, Marion W.
  1937   The war complex of the Plains Indians. *Proceedings of the American Philosophical Society* 78(3): 425–464.
Smith, Michael G.
  1956   On segmentary lineage systems. *JRAI* 86:39–81.
  1960   *Government in Zazzau, 1800–1950.* London: Oxford University Press.
  1965a   *The plural society in the British West Indies.* Berkeley: University of California Press.
  1965b   The sociological framework of law. In *African law: Development and adaptation*, edited by Hilda Kuper and Leo Kuper. Berkeley: University of California Press.
  1966a   Pre-industrial stratification systems. In *Social structure and mobility in economic development*, edited by Neli Smelser and Seymour Martin Lipset. Chicago: Aldine.
  1966b   A structural approach to comparative politics. In *Varieties of political theory*, edited by David Easton. Englewood Cliffs, N.J.: Prentice-Hall.
  1974   *Corporations and society: The social anthropology of collective action.* Chicago: Aldine.

Smith, R. J., ed.
1974   Social organization and the applications of anthropology: Essays in honor of Lauriston Sharp. Ithaca, N.Y.: Cornell University Press.
Smith, William Robertson
1894   Lectures on the religion of the Semites. London: A. and C. Black.
Snyder, Francis G.
1981a   Capitalism and legal change: An African transformation. New York: Academic Press.
1981b   Anthropology, dispute processes and law: A critical introduction. British Journal of Law and Society 8:141–180.
Snyderman, George
1948   Behind the tree of peace: A sociological analysis of Iroquois warfare. Pennsylvania Archaeologist 18:3–4.
Social Science Research Council (SSRC)
1968   Research in social anthropology: An SSRC review of current research. London: Social Science Research Council.
Southall, Aidan W.
1965   A critique of the typology of states and political systems. In Political systems and the distribution of power, edited by Michael Banton. ASA Monograph 2. London: Tavistock.
1966   The concept of elites and their formation in Uganda. In The new elites of tropical Africa, edited by Peter C. Lloyd. London: Oxford University Press.
1968   Orientations in political anthropology. Canadian Journal of African Studies 6:42–52.
1970   The illusion of tribe. In The passing of tribal man in Africa, edited by Peter C. W. Gutkind. Leiden: Brill.
1974   State formation in Africa. ARA 3:153–165.
1976a   Ethnicity, political development and modernization in Africa. ARA 3:636–642.
1976b   Nuer and Dinka are people: Ecology, ethnicity and logical possibility. Man 11:463–491.
1988a   The segmentary state in Africa and Asia. CSSH 30:52–82.
1988b   On mode of production theory: The foraging mode of production and the kinship mode of production. DA 12:165–192.
Southwold, Martin
1964   Leadership, authority and the village community. In The King's men: Leadership and status in Buganda on the eve of independence, edited by Lloyd A. Fallers. London: Oxford University Press.
Spencer, Herbert
1896   Principles of sociology. New York: Appleton. Originally published 1876.
Sperber, Dan
1980   Man made language. London: Routledge and Kegan Paul.
Spieth, Jacob van
1911   Die religion der Eweer in Sud-Todo. Göttingen: Vandehoeck and Ruprecht.

Spitzer, S.
    1983   Marxist perspectives in the sociology of law. *Annual Review of Sociology* 9:103–124.
Spivak, Gayatri Chakravorty
    1985   Subaltern studies: Deconstructing historiography. In *Subaltern studies IV: Writings on South Asian history and society*, edited by R. Guha. Oxford: Oxford University Press.
Spradley, James P., and David W. McCurdy
    1971   *Conformity and conflict: Readings in cultural anthropology.* Boston: Little, Brown.
Stanner, W.E.H.
    1959   Continuity and schism in an African tribe: A review. *Oceania* 29:208–217.
Starr, Frederick
    1892   *Some first steps in human progress.* Chicago: University of Chicago Press.
    1911   Review of *Nigerian studies*, by E. Dennett. *AA* 13:481–483.
Starr, June
    1958   Leadership and cognatic residence groups in Ifugao, Bantok and Kalinga. Master's thesis, Columbia University.
    1978   *Dispute and settlement in rural Turkey: An ethnography of law.* Leiden: Brill.
    1989   The "invention" of early legal ideas: Sir Henry Maine and the perpetual tutelage of women. In *History and power in the study of law*, edited by June Starr and Jane F. Collier. Ithaca, N.Y.: Cornell University Press.
Stavenhagen, Rodolfo
    1975   *Social classes in agrarian societies.* Garden City, N.Y.: Anchor Press / Doubleday.
Stegner, Wallace
    1954   *Beyond the hundredth meridian: John Wesley Powell and the second opening of the West.* Boston: Houghton Mifflin.
Stein, Peter
    1980   *Legal evolution: The story of an idea.* Cambridge: Cambridge University Press.
Stern, Bernhard J.
    1931   *Lewis Henry Morgan: Social evolutionist.* Chicago: University of Chicago Press.
Stern, G., and P. Bohannan
    1970   *American Anthropologist*: The first eighty years. *Newsletter of the American Anthropological Association* 11:6–12.
Stevenson, Robert F.
    1968   *Population and political systems in tropical Africa.* New York: Columbia University Press.
Steward, Julian H.
    1933   Ethnography of the Owens Valley Paiute. *UCPAAE* 33:233–350.
    1936   The economic basis of primitive bands. In *Essays in anthropology*

presented to A. L. Kroeber, edited by Robert H. Lowie. Berkeley: University of California Press.

1937a   Ecological aspects of southwestern society. *Anthropos* 32:87–104.

1937b   Linguistic distributions and political groups of the Great Basin Shoshoneans. *AA* 39:625–634.

1938   *Basin-Plateau aboriginal sociopolitical groups*. Bureau of American Ethnology Bulletin, no. 120. Washington, D.C.

1949   Cultural causality and law: A trial formulation of the development of early civilization. *AA* 51:1–27.

1950   *Area research: Theory and practice.* New York: Social Science Research Council.

1955   *Theory of culture change.* Urbana: University of Illinois Press.

1956a   Review of *The little community*, by Robert Redfield. *AA* 58:564–565.

Steward, Julian H., ed.

1956   *The people of Puerto Rico: A study in social anthropology.* Urbana: University of Illinois Press.

Stinchcombe, Arthur

1965   Hacienda and plantation in Yucatan. *America Indigena* 25:35–63.

Stocking, George W., Jr.

1965   From physics to ethnology: Boas' arctic expedition as a problem in the historiography of the behavioral sciences. *Journal of the History of the Behavioral Sciences* 1:53–66.

1968   *Race, culture, and evolution: Essays in the history of anthropology.* Chicago: University of Chicago Press.

1974   *The shaping of American anthropology, 1883–1911: A Franz Boas reader.* Washington, D.C.: American Anthropological Association.

1976   Ideas and institutions in American anthropology: Thoughts toward a history of the interwar years. In *Selected papers from the* American Anthropologist, *1921–1945*, edited by George W. Stocking. Washington, D.C.: American Anthropological Association.

1979a   *Anthropology at Chicago: Tradition, discipline, department.* Chicago: University of Chicago Press.

1979b   Anthropology as Kulturkampf: Science and politics in the career of Franz Boas. In *The uses of anthropology*, edited by W. Goldschmidt. Washington, D.C.: American Anthropological Association.

1984   Radcliffe-Brown and British Social Anthropology. In *History of Anthropology, vol. 2: Functionalism historicized: Essays on British social anthropology*, edited by George W. Stocking, Jr. Madison: University of Wisconsin Press.

1985   Yours affectionately, Rex: Radcliffe-Brown during and after WWII. *History of Anthropology Newsletter* 12:3–11.

1987   *Victorian anthropology.* New York: Free Press.

1989   Ideal types and aging glands: Robert Redfield's response to Oscar Lewis's critique of Tepoztlán. *History of Anthropology Newsletter* 16:3–10.

Stocking, G. W., Jr., ed.

1983   *History of Anthropology*, Vol. 1: *Observers observed: Essays on ethnographic fieldwork*. Washington, D.C.: American Anthropological Association.

Stoler, Ann L.
1977   Class structure and female autonomy in rural Jara. *Signs* 3:77–89.
1985   *Capitalism and confrontation in Sumatra's plantation belt, 1870–1979*. Princeton, N.J.: Princeton University Press.
1986   Plantation politics and protest on Sumatra's coast. *JPS* 13:124–143.

Stone, Julius
1966   *Social dimensions of law and justice*. Stanford, Calif.: Stanford University Press.

Strathern, Andrew
1971   *The rope of Moka: Big men and ceremonial exchange in Moot Hagen*. Cambridge: Cambridge University Press.

Strathern, Marilyn
1972   *Women in between: Female roles in a male world*. New York: Seminar Press.

Strong, W. Duncan
1935   *Introduction to Nebraska archaeology*. Washington, D.C.: Smithsonian Institution.
1936   Anthropological theory and archaeological fact. In *Essays in anthropology presented to A. L. Kroeber*, edited by Robert Lowie. Berkeley: University of California Press.

Sturtevant, William
1983   Tribe and state in the sixteenth and twentieth centuries. In *The development of political organization in native North America*, edited by Elizabeth Tooker. 1979 Proceedings of the American Ethnological Society. Washington: American Ethnological Society.

Sugarman, D., ed.
1983   *Legality, ideology and the state*. London: Academic Press.

Sumner, Charles
1979   *Reading ideologies: An investigation into the Marxist theory of ideology and law*. London: Academic Press.

Sumner, William Graham
1907   *Folkways: A study of the sociological importance of usages, manners, customs, mores, and morals*. Boston: Ginn.

Susser, Ida S.
1982   *Norman Street: Poverty and politics in an urban neighborhood*. New York: Oxford University Press.
1986   Political action among working-class women in a U.S. city. *AE* 13:108–117.

Swadesh, Morris
1948   Motivations in Nootka warfare. *SWJA* 4:76–93.

Swanton, John R.
n.d   Papers. MS. no. 4651. Washington, D.C.: Smithsonian Institution, National Museum of Natural History, National Anthropological Archives.
1907   Ethnological position of the Natchez Indians. *AA* 9:513–528.

1911   *Indian tribes of the Lower Mississippi Valley.* Bureau of American Ethnology Bulletin 43. Washington, D.C.: Government Printing Office.

1917   The social significance of the great confederacy. *Proceedings of the 19th International Congress of Americanists, 1915.* Washington, D.C.

1931   The Caddo social organization and its possible historical significance. *Journal of the Washington Academy of Science* 21:203–206.

Swartz, Marc J., ed.

1967   *Local-level politics: Social and cultural perspectives.* Chicago: Aldine.

Swartz, Marc J., Victor W. Turner, and Arthur Tuden, eds.

1966   *Political anthropology.* Chicago: Aldine.

Tax, Sol

1941   World view and social relations in Guatemala. *AA* 43:27–42.

Tax, Sol, ed.

1949   *Heritage of conquest: The ethnology of Middle America.* Viking Fund Seminar on Mid-American Ethnology, New York City, August 28–September 3, 1949. Glencoe, Ill.: Free Press.

Taylor, William B.

1985   Between global process and local knowledge: An inquiry into early Latin American social history, 1500–1900. In *Reliving the past: The worlds of social history,* edited by Oliver Zunz. Chapel Hill: University of North Carolina Press.

Teggart, Frederick J.

1916   Prologomena to history: The relation of history to literature, philosophy and science. *University of California Publications in History* 4:155–292.

Terray, Emmanuel

1969   *Le marxisme devant les sociétés "primitives": Deux études.* Paris: Maspero.

Thackray, Arnold, and J. Morrell

1981   *Gentlemen of science: Early years of the British Association for the Advancement of Science.* Oxford: Clarendon Press.

Therborn, G.

1980   *The ideology of power and the power of ideology.* London: New Left Books.

Thomas, Northcote Whitridge

1906   *Natives of Australia.* The native races of the British Empire. London: A. Constable.

1910   *Anthropological report on the Edo-speaking peoples of Nigeria.* 2 vols. London: Harrison and Sons.

1913–
14   *Anthropological report on the Ibo-speaking peoples of Nigeria.* 6 vols. London: Harrison and Sons.

1916   *Anthropological report on Sierra Leone.* London: Harrison.

Thomas, William Isaac, and Florian Znaniecki

1918   *The Polish peasant in Europe and America: Monograph of an immigrant group.* Boston: P. G. Badger.

Thompson, Edward P.
  1971   The moral economy of the English crowd in the eighteenth century. *Past and Present* 50:76–136.
  1975   *Whigs and hunters: The origin of the Black Act.* London: Allen Lane.
  1978   Eighteenth-century English society: Class struggle without class. *Social History* 3:133–161.
Thompson, Paul Richard, ed.
  1975   *The Edwardians: The remaking of British society.* London: Granada.
Thoreson, T.H.H.
  1975   Paying the piper and calling the tune: The beginnings of academic anthropology in California. *Journal of the History of the Behavioral Sciences* 11:257–275.
Thornton, Robert J.
  1983   Narrative ethnography in Africa, 1850–1920: The creation and capture of an appropriate domain for anthropology. *Man* 18:502–520.
Thurnwald, Richard
  1932   The psychology of acculturation. *AA* 34:557–569.
Tilly, Charles
  1978   *From mobilization to revolution.* Reading, Mass.: Addison-Wesley.
Tompkins, Jane
  1985   *Sensational designs: The cultural work of American fiction, 1790–1860.* New York: Oxford University Press.
Tooker, Elizabeth
  1978   The League of the Iroquois: Its history, politics and ritual. In *Handbook of North American Indians*, vol. 15: *Northeast*, edited by Bruce G. Trigger. Washington, D.C.: Smithsonian Institution.
  1983a   The structure of the Iroquois League: Lewis H. Morgan's research and observations. *Ethnohistory* 30:141–154.
  1983b   Introduction to *The development of political organization in native North America*, edited by Elizabeth Tooker. 1979 Proceedings of the American Ethnological Society. Washington, D.C.: American Ethnological Society.
Toulmin, Stephen
  1972   *Human Understanding: General introduction and part I.* Vol. 1. Oxford: Clarendon Press.
Trani, Eugene, and David L. Wilson
  1977   *The presidency of Warren G. Harding.* Lawrence. Regents Press of Kansas.
Trautmann, Thomas R.
  1987   *Lewis Henry Morgan and the invention of kinship.* Berkeley: University of California Press.
Trigger, Bruce G.
  1980   *Gordon Childe: Revolutions in archaeology.* New York: Columbia University Press.
Trouillot, Michel-Rolph
  1982   Motion in the system: Coffee, color and slavery in eighteenth century Saint-Domingue. *Review* 5:331–388.

Tschopik, Harry, Jr.
   1947   *Highland communities of central Peru: A regional survey.* Washington, D.C.: Government Printing Office.

Turner, Brian S.
   1979   *Marx and the end of orientalism.* London: Allen and Unwin.

Turner, Victor W.
   1957   *Schism and continuity in an African society.* Manchester: Manchester University Press.
   1964   Witchcraft and sorcery: Taxonomy versus dynamics. *Africa* 34:314–324.
   1969   *The ritual process: Structure and anti-structure.* London: Routledge and Kegan Paul.
   1974   *Dramas, fields and metaphors: Symbolic action in human society.* Ithaca, N.Y.: Cornell University Press.

Turney-High, H. H.
   1940   Review of *Basin-Plateau aboriginal sociopolitical groups*, by Julian H. Steward. *AA* 42:136.
   1949   *Primitive war: Its practice and concepts.* Columbia: University of South Carolina Press.
   1981   *The military: The theory of land warfare as behavioral science.* West Hanover, Mass.: Cristopher Publishing House.

Turton, Andrew
   1986   Patrolling the middle ground: Methodological perspectives on everyday peasant resistance. *JPS* 13:36–48.

Twining, William
   1964   *The place of customary law in the national legal systems of East Africa.* Chicago: University of Chicago Law School.
   1967   *Karl Llewellyn and the realist movement.* London: Weidenfeld and Nicolson.

Tylor, Edward
   1871   *Primitive culture.* London: John Murray.
   1881   *Anthropology: An introduction to the study of man and civilization.* London: John Murray.
   1884   How the problems of American anthropology present themselves to the English mind. *Transactions of the Anthropological Society of Washington* 3:81–95.
   1889   On a method of investigating the development of institutions: Applied to laws of marriage and descent. *JRAI* 18:245–269.
   1891– Anniversary address. *Journal of the Anthropological Institute* 21:1–
   92   17.

Urry, James
   1973   *Notes and queries on anthropology* and the development of field methods in British anthropology, 1870–1920. *Proceedings of the Royal Anthropological Institute for 1972*, 45–57.
   1985   W. E. Armstrong and social anthropology at Cambridge, 1922–26. *Man* 20:412–433.

Useem, John, Ruth Useem, and P. Tangent
  1942   Stratification in a prairie town. *American Sociological Review* 7:331–342.
Van Allen, J.
  1972   "Sitting on a man": Colonialism and the lost political institutions of Igbo women. *Canadian Journal of African Studies* 6:169–182.
Van Binsbergen, Wim M.
  1977   Occam, Francis Bacon and the transformation of Zambian society. *Cultures et développement* 9:489–520.
  1981   The unit of study and the interpretation of ethnicity. *Journal of South African Studies* 8:51–81.
Van Binsbergen, Wim M., and Pierre Geschiere, eds.
  1985   *Old modes of production and capitalist encroachment: Anthropological explorations in Africa.* London: Routledge and Kegan Paul.
Van Gennep, Arnold
  1909   *Les rites de passage* (The rites of passage). Paris: Nourry.
  1960   *The rites of passage.* Translated by Monika B. Vizedom and Gabrielle L. Caffee. Introduction by Solon T. Kimball. Chicago: University of Chicago Press.
Van Keuren, David Keith
  1982   Human science in Victorian Britain: Anthropology in institutional and disciplinary formation, 1863–1908. Ph.D. diss., University of Pennsylvania.
Van Velsen, Jaap
  1964   *The politics of kinship: A study in social manipulation among the Lakeside Tonga of Nyasaland.* Manchester: Manchester University Press.
  1967   The extended case method and situational analysis. In *The craft of social anthropology,* edited by A. L. Epstein. London: Tavistock.
Vayda, Andrew P.
  1986   Holism and individualism in ecological anthropology. *Reviews in Anthropology* 13:295–313.
Veblen, Thorstein
  1923   *Absentee ownership and business enterprise in recent times: The case of America.* New York: B. W. Huebsch.
Verdery, Katherine
  1983   *Transylvanian villagers: Three centuries of political, economic and ethnic change, 1700–1980.* Berkeley: University of California Press.
Vincent, Joan
  1969   Anthropology and political development. In *Politics and change in developing countries,* edited by Colin Leys. Cambridge: Cambridge University Press.
  1971   *African elite: The Big Men of a small town.* New York: Columbia University Press.
  1973   *History from the bottom up: Third world societies.* Newton, Pa.: Bucks County Community College, Department of Humanistic Studies.

1974   The structuring of ethnicity. *Human Organization* 33:375–379.
1978   Political anthropology: Manipulative strategies. *ARA* 7:175–194.
1982   *Teso in transformation: The political economy of peasant and class in eastern Africa.* Berkeley: University of California Press.
1983   Political consciousness and struggle among an African peasantry. In *The Social anthropology of peasantry*, edited by Joan P. Mencher. Atlantic Highlands, N.J.: Humanities Press.
1984   Primitivization in the Philippines: The intellectual and social context of Barton's *Ifugao law* (1919). Tenth Annual Meeting, American Ethnological Society, Asilomar, California.
1985   Anthropology and Marxism. *AE* 12:137–147.
1986a   Functionalism revisited: An unsettled science. *Reviews in Anthropology* 13:331–339.
1986b   System and process, 1974–1985. *ARA* 15:99–119.
1987   Meta-ethnography: Romance and realism in Barton's *Ifugao law*. Paper delivered at the 86th annual meeting of the American Anthropological Association, Chicago, November 18–22.
1988a   Sovereignty, legitimacy and power: Prolegomena to the study of the colonial state. In *Political anthropology*, vol. 6: *State formation and political legitimacy*, edited by Ronald Cohen and Judith D. Toland. Myron J. Aronoff, Series Editor. New Brunswick, N.J.: Transaction Books.
1988b   Ahead of his time: Production and reproduction in the work of Alexander Lesser. *AE* 15:743–751.
1988c   Local knowledge and global processes in two border villages: Political violence in County Fermanagh. In *Ireland from below: Social change and local community*, edited by Chris Curtin and Thomas Wilson. Galway: University of Galway Press.
1988d   Trading places: Cultural and legal pluralism in colonial Uganda. Paper presented at the IUAES Symposium on Legal Pluralism in Industrialized Societies, Zagreb, Yugoslavia.
1989a   In the shadow of the armory: Structures of production and the production of ethnic culture. Paper delivered at the Annual Meeting of the Society for Economic Anthropology, Mount Pleasant, Michigan.
1989b   Beyond ethnography: Palimpsest for the 1990s. Paper delivered at the Advanced Seminar on Meta-Ethnography, School of American Research, Santa Fe, New Mexico, June 4–10, 1989.
Vinnikov, I.
1935   *Materials from the archives of Lewis Henry Morgan.* Moscow: Academy of Sciences.
Voget, Fred W.
1975   *A history of ethnology.* New York: Holt, Rinehart and Winston.
Vogt, W. P.
1976   The uses of studying primitives: A note on the Durkheimians, 1890–1914. *History and Theory* 15:33–44.
Von Bertalanffy, L.
1956   General systems theory. *General Systems* 1:1–10.

Wagley, Charles, and Marvin Harris
1955   A typology of Latin American subcultures. *AA* 57:428–451.
Wallace, Anthony F. C.
1956   Revitalization movements. *AA* 58:264–281.
1965   Introduction to *The Ghost-Dance religion and the Sioux outbreak of 1890*, by James Mooney. Chicago: University of Chicago Press.
Wallerstein, Immanuel
1974a   Trends in world capitalism. *Monthly Review* 26:12–18.
1974b   *The modern world-system: Capitalist agriculture and the origins of the European world economy in the sixteenth century.* New York: Academic Press.
1979   *The capitalist world-economy: Essays.* New York: Cambridge University Press.
Wallis, Wilson D.
1923   Some phases of Armenian social life. *AA* 25:582–584.
1931   Review of *The American Indian frontier*, by William Christie Mac-Leod. *AA* 33:631.
1957   Anthropology in England early in the present century. *AA* 59:781–790.
Walters, R. G.
1980   Signs of the times: Clifford Geertz and the historians. *Social Review* 47:537–556.
Warner, William Lloyd
1931   Murngin warfare. *Oceania* 1:457–483.
1936   *A black civilization: A social study of an Australian tribe.* New York: Harper and Row.
1949   *Democracy in Jonesville: A study in quality and inequality.* New York: Harper.
Warner, W. Lloyd, ed.
1963   *Yankee City.* Abridged ed. New Haven, Conn.: Yale University Press.
Warner, W. Lloyd, and Paul S. Lunt
1941   *The social life of a modern community.* Yankee City Series, vol. 1. New Haven: Yale University Press.
Warner, W. Lloyd, Marchia Meeker, and Kenneth Eells
1949   *Social class in America: A manual of procedure for the measurement of social status.* Chicago: Science Research Associates.
Washington, Robert E.
1978   An urban slum revisited. *Reviews in Anthropology* 5:149–164.
Watson, Alan
1974   *Legal transplants: An approach to comparative law.* Edinburgh: Scottish Academic Press.
1977   *Society and legal change.* Edinburgh: Scottish Academic Press.
Watson, Graham
1984   The social construction of boundaries between social and cultural anthropology in Britain and North America. *Journal of Anthropological Research* 40:351–366.
Watson, William
1964   Social mobility and social class in industrial communities. In

Closed systems and open minds: The limits of naivety in social anthropology, edited by Max Gluckman and Ely Devons. Edinburgh: Oliver and Boyd.

Wax, Murray
    1956   The limitations of Boas' anthropology. *AA* 58:63–74.
Webb, Beatrice
    1926   *My apprenticeship.* New York: Longmans, Green.
Weber, Gay
    1974   Science and society in nineteenth century anthropology. *History of Science* 12:260–283.
Weber, Max
    1902/   *The Protestant ethic and the spirit of capitalism.* Translated by Tal-
    76   cott Parsons. Introduction by Anthony Giddens. New York: Scribner.
    1925   *Wirtschaft und Gesellschaft* (Economy and society). Tübingen: J.C.B. Mohr.
    1947   *The theory of social and economic organization,* edited by Talcott Parsons. New York: Free Press.
Webster, Hutton
    1908   *Primitive secret societies: A study in early politics and religion.* New York: Macmillan.
Wedgwood, Camilla H.
    1930a   Some aspects of warfare in Melanesia. *Oceania* 1:5–33.
    1930b   The nature and functions of secret societies. *Oceania* 1:129–145.
    1936   Women in Manam. *Oceania* 7:401–429, 8:170–193.
Weimann, Robert
    1969   *Structure and society in literary history: Studies in the history and theory of historical criticism.* Charlottesville: University Press of Virginia.
Weiner, Annette
    1976   *Women of value, men of renown: New perspectives on Trobriand exchange.* Austin: University of Texas Press.
Weingrod, Alex
    1967   Political sociology, social anthropology and the study of new nations. *BJS* 18:121–134.
Wells, Herbert George
    1903   *Mankind in the making.* London: Chapman and Hall.
Werbner, Richard P.
    1969   Constitutional ambiguities and the British administration of royal careers among the Bemba of Zambia. In *Law in culture and society,* edited by Laura Nader. Chicago: Aldine.
    1977   *Regional cults.* ASA Monograph 16. New York: Academic Press.
    1984   The Manchester School in south-central Africa. *ARA* 13:157–185.
Wessman, James W.
    1981   *Anthropology and Marxism.* Cambridge, Mass.: Schenkman.
West, James [pseudonym of C. Withers]
    1945   *Plainville, U.S.A.* New York: Columbia University Press.
Westermarck, Edward A.
    1929   *Memories of my life.* New York: Macaulay.

1936   Methods in social anthropology. Huxley Memorial Lecture. *JRAI* 64:223–248.

Wheeler, Gerald Camden

1910   *The tribe and intertribal relations in Australia.* London: John Murray.

1926   *Mono-Alu folklore, Bougainville Strait, western Solomon Islands.* London: Routledge.

White, Harrison C.

1970   *Chains of opportunity: System models of mobility in organizations.* Cambridge, Mass.: Harvard University Press.

White, Isabella

1981   Mrs. Bates and Mr. Brown: An examination of Rodney Needham's allegations. *Oceania* 51:193–210.

White, Leslie A.

1940   *Pioneers in American anthropology: The Bandelier-Morgan letters, 1873–1883.* 2 vols. Albuquerque: University of New Mexico Press.

1959   *The evolution of culture.* New York: McGraw-Hill.

1963   *The ethnology and ethnography of Franz Boas.* Bulletin of the Texas Memorial Museum, 6. Austin.

1966   The social organization of ethnological theory. *Rice University Studies* 52:1–66.

Whitten, Norman E., Jr.

1970   Network analysis in Ecuador and Nova Scotia: Some critical remarks. *CRSA* 7:269–280.

Whitten, Norman E., Jr., ed.

1981   *Cultural transformations and ethnicity in modern Ecuador.* Urbana: University of Illinois Press.

Whyte, William Foote

1943a   *Street corner society: The social structure of an Italian slum.* Chicago: University of Chicago Press.

1943b   A challenge to political scientists. *American Political Science Review* 37:692–697.

Wike, Joyce A.

1951   The effect of the maritime fur trade on Northwest Coast Indian society. Ph.D. diss., Columbia University.

Willis, William S., Jr.

1955   Colonial conflict and the Cherokee Indians, 1710–1760. Ph.D. diss., Columbia University.

1963   Divide and rule: Red, white and black in the Southeast. *Journal of Negro History* 48:157–176.

1969   Skeletons in the anthropological closet. In *Reinventing anthropology*, edited by Dell Hymes. New York: Pantheon.

1970   Anthropology and Negroes on the southern colonial frontier. In *The black experience in America*, edited by James P. Curtis and Lewis L. Gould. Austin: University of Texas Press.

Wilson, Godfrey

1940   Anthropology as a public service. *Africa* 10:43–61.

1941   *An essay on the economics of detribalization in Northern Rhodesia.*
        Livingstone, Northern Rhodesia: Rhodes-Livingstone Institute.
Wilson, Monica
1977   The first three years, 1938–41. *African Social Research* 24:275–284.
Winkler, E. A.
1969   Political anthropology. In *Biennial Review of Anthropology*, edited
        by Bernard J. Siegel. Stanford, Calif.: Stanford University Press.
Wiser, Charlotte Viall
1978   *Four families of Karimpur.* Syracuse, N.Y.: Syracuse University,
        Maxwell School of Citizenship and Public Affairs.
Wiser, William Henricks
1936   *The Hindu Jajmani system: A socio-economic system of interrelat-
        ing members of a Hindu village community in services.* Lucknow,
        India: Lucknow Publishing House.
1958   *The Hindu Jajmani system: A socio-economic system of interrelat-
        ing members of a Hindu village community in services.* 2d ed.
        Foreword by Oscar Lewis. Lucknow, India: Lucknow Publishing
        House.
Wiser, William Henricks, and Charlotte Viall Wiser
1930   *Behind mud walls.* New York: Richard R. Smith.
1963   *Behind mud walls.* Rev. ed. Foreword by David Mandelbaum. Berke-
        ley: University of California Press.
Wittfogel, Karl A.
1957   *Oriental despotism: A comparative study of social power.* New
        Haven: Yale University Press.
Wolf, Eric R.
1950   San José: Subculture of a "traditional" coffee municipality. Ph.D.
        diss., Columbia University.
1953   La formación de la nación: Un ensayo de formulación. *Ciencias
        Sociales* 4:50–62, 98–111, 146–171.
1955   Types of Latin American peasantry: A preliminary discussion. *AA*
        57:452–471.
1956a   San José: Subcultures of a "traditional" coffee municipality. In *The
        people of Puerto Rico: A study in social anthropology*, edited by
        Julian H. Steward. Urbana: University of Illinois Press.
1956b   Aspects of group relations in complex society. *AA* 58:1065–1078.
1958   The Virgin of Guadalupe: A Mexican national symbol. *Journal of
        American Folklore* 71:34–39.
1959   *Sons of the shaking earth.* Chicago: University of Chicago Press.
1964   *Anthropology: Humanistic scholarship in America.* The Princeton
        Studies. Englewood Cliffs, N.J.: Prentice-Hall.
1965   Review of *Rassen, Ethnien, Kulturen*, by Wilhelm E. Muhlmann. *AA*
        67:1026–1029.
1966a   Kinship, friendship and patron-client relations in complex societies.
        In *The social anthropology of complex societies*, edited by Michael
        Banton. ASA Monograph 4. London: Tavistock.
1966b   *Peasants.* Englewood Cliffs, N.J.: Prentice-Hall.

1969   *Peasant wars of the twentieth century.* New York: Harper and Row.
1978   Remarks on *The people of Puerto Rico. Revista/Review Interameri-cana* 8:18–25.
1981   The mills of inequality: A Marxian approach. In *Social inequality,* edited by Gerald D. Berreman. New York: Academic Press.
1982   *Europe and the people without history.* Berkeley: University of California Press.

Wolf, Eric R., and Edward C. Hansen
1972   *The human condition in Latin America.* New York: Oxford University Press.

Wolf, Eric R., and Sydney W. Mintz
1957   Haciendas and plantations in Middle America and the Antilles. *Social and Economic Studies* 6:380–411.

Wolfe, Alvin W.
1970   On structural comparisons of networks. *CRSA* 7:226–244.

Wolin, Sheldon
1960   *Politics and vision: Continuity and innovation in Western political thought.* Boston: Little, Brown.

Wolpe, H.
1975   The theory of internal colonialism: The South African case. In *Beyond the sociology of development: Economy and society in Latin America and Africa,* edited by Ivar Oxaal, T. Barnett, and D. Booth. London: Routledge and Kegan Paul.

Worsley, Peter M.
1956   The kinship system of the Tallensi: A reevaluation. *JRAI* 86:37–75.
1957   *The trumpet shall sound: A study of "cargo" cults in Melanesia.* London: MacGibbon and Keo.
1961   The analysis of rebellion and revolution in modern British social anthropology. *Science and Society* 21:26–37.
1964   *The third world.* London: Weidenfeld and Nicolson.
1968   Review of *Political anthropology,* edited by Marc Swartz, Victor W. Turner, and Arthur Tuden. *BJS* 19:100–103.
1974   The state of theory and the status of theory. *Sociology* 8:1–17.

Wright, Henry T.
1977   Recent research on the origin of the state. *ARA* 6:379–397.

Yang, Martin C.
1945   *A Chinese village: Taitou, Shantung province.* New York: Columbia University Press.

Young, Kate, Carol Wolkowitz, and Roslyn McCullagh
1984   *Of marriage and the market: Women's subordination internationally and its lessons.* 2d ed. London: Routledge and Kegan Paul.

Zavella, Patricia
1987   *Women's work and Chicano families: Cannery workers of the Santa Clara valley.* Ithaca, N.Y.: Cornell University Press.

Zolberg, Aristide R.
1966   *Creating political order: The party-states of West Africa.* Chicago: Rand McNally.

1968   The structure of political conflict in the new states of tropical Africa. *American Political Science Review* 62:70–87.

Zumwalt, Rosemary
1982   Arnold van Gennep: The hermit of Bourg-la-Reine. *AA* 84:299–313.

Zunz, Oliver, ed.
1985   *Reliving the past: The worlds of social history.* Chapel Hill: University of North Carolina Press.

Index

311, 312, 317, 337, 340, 351, 362, 392; criticism of, 347–48; on political action, 349–50; on political economy, 238–39; works by, 238, 334, 338, 342, 345–48
Balandier, Georges, 9, 12, 231
Bancroft, Hubert Howe, 96, 131–32
Bands, 330; political organization of, 194–97
Barnes, John A., 337, 339, 340, 351, 366
Barnes, Leonard, 281; work by, 278, 456n.22
Barnett, Homer G., 242
Barotseland, 376–77
Barrows, David Prescott, 203
Barth, Fredrik, 311, 321, 351, 392, 462n.24; on political organization, 357–62; work by, 365
Barton, Roy Franklin, 137, 159, 307, 352, 424, 447–48nn.47, 48, 51; works by, 138–46, 151, 249
Barzun, Jacques, 200
Basin-Plateau Aboriginal Sociopolitical Groups (Steward), 194, 196, 197
Batson, Gregory: work by, 268
Baudin, Anatole, 33
Baudin, Nicholas, 14
Beals, Ralph, 228, 232
Beard, Charles, 174
Beattie, John H. M., 227
Beemer, Hilda, 202. *See also* Kuper, Hilda Beemer
Behavioralism, 305
Behind Mud Walls (Wiser and Wiser), 209, 212
Bemba, 227, 259–60, 263
Benedict, Ruth, 200, 233, 245, 289
Benjamin, Walter, 27
Bentley, A. F., 316; work by, 248
Besnard, Philippe, 102–3
Beveridge, William, 201
Biennial Review of Anthropology, 384
Black, Charles L., Jr.: work by, 378
Black Byzantium (Nadel), 284
Black Civilization, A (Warner), 217

Blackfeet, 234; political economy of, 235–37
Bloch, Maurice: work by, 425
Boas, Franz, 8, 19, 56, 59, 67, 83, 84, 85, 87, 96, 147, 171, 245, 447n.41; at Columbia University, 11, 135; on culture contact, 200, 201; on Kwakiutal culture, 71–73, 77; on racial segregation, 125–26; work by, 72
Body politic, 47–48
Boer War, 8, 79
Bohannan, Paul, 24, 227; on law, 159–60, 312, 375, 376, 384; work by, 379
Boissevain, Jeremy: on nongroups, 351–53; work by, 352
Boserup, Ester, 410
Bourdieu, Pierre: work by, 421
Brabrook, Edward, 58; scientific guidelines, 59–60
Brailsford, Henry N.: work by, 116–17
Bramble Bush, The (Llewellyn), 248
Braudel, Fernand: work by, 389
Braunholtz, H. J., 257
Bridge, The. See *An Analysis of a Social Situation in Modern Zululand*
British Association for the Advancement of Science, 33, 57, 86; anthropological studies by, 58–59, 71, 108
British East Africa, 117
British Empire, 8, 60, 116–17, 153, 218; indirect rule by, 152, 154
Brown, Arthur Reginald. See Radcliffe-Brown, Arthur Reginald
Bryce, James, 304
Bullock, Charles, 157
Bunzel, Ruth, 412
Bureau of American Ethnology (BAE), 15, 38, 78, 150, 428; foreign studies by, 134–35; politics of, 39–42; Powell's direction of, 44–47; on warfare, 52–53, 56; works of, 127–29
Bureau of Ethnology of the Philippines, 203

About the Author

Joan Vincent was born in England but has lived most of her life in Africa and the United States. She received an honors degree in social anthropology from the London School of Economics, an M.A. in political science from the University of Chicago, and a doctorate in anthropology from Columbia University. Her first book, *African Elite: The Big Men of a Small Town*, was the product of her field research in Uganda in 1966 and 1967, and her second book, *Teso in Transformation: The Political Economy of Peasant and Class in Eastern Africa*, won the Wheeler-Voegelin Prize of the American Society for Ethnohistory. Professor Vincent's current study is an historical anthropological account of the politics and culture of the Irish famine. She holds the position of Professor of Anthropology at Barnard College and is a member of the graduate faculties of Columbia University.